The Complete Reference™

Star Schema

About the Author

Christopher Adamson is an expert in star schema design and an experienced data warehousing practitioner. He speaks and teaches worldwide, writes about data warehousing, and provides data warehousing services through Oakton Software LLC.

As a consultant, Chris works with customers in all industries to develop data warehousing strategies, identify and prioritize projects, design and modify solutions, and manage implementations. His customers have included Fortune 500 companies, government agencies, and data warehousing software vendors.

Chris has taught dimensional design to thousands of students worldwide. He is a faculty member at The Data Warehousing Institute (TDWI), teaches at conference events, and provides onsite education.

Chris has penned many articles and books about data warehousing. He is author of *Mastering Data Warehouse Aggregates* (Wiley 2006) and co-author of *Data Warehouse Design Solutions* (Wiley 1998). He blogs about data warehousing and answers questions from readers at www.StarSchemaCentral.com.

Chris is the founder of Oakton Software LLC, and can be contacted through his web site at www.ChrisAdamson.net.

The Complete Reference™

Star Schema

Christopher Adamson

New York Chicago San Francisco
Lisbon London Madrid Mexico City
Milan New Delhi San Juan
Seoul Singapore Sydney Toronto

The McGraw·Hill Companies

Cataloging-in-Publication Data is on file with the Library of Congress

Star Schema: The Complete Reference™

5 6 7 8 9 0 DOC DOC 1 0 9 8 7 6 5 4 3

ISBN 978-0-07-174432-4
MHID 0-07-174432-0

Sponsoring Editor
Lisa McClain

Editorial Supervisor
Jody McKenzie

Project Manager
Vipra Fauzdar, Glyph International

Acquisitions Coordinator
Meghan Riley

Technical Editor
Jim Hadley

Copy Editor
Mike McGee

Proofreader
Andy Saff

Indexer
Jack Lewis

Production Supervisor
Jim Kussow

Composition
Glyph International

Illustration
Glyph International

Cover Designer
Jeff Weeks

To Gladys, Justin, and Carter. You are the source of unending happiness, you lift me up when I need it, and I will always be proud of you.

Contents at a Glance

Contents

Part III Dimension Design

Part IV Fact Table Design

Part V Performance

Part VI Tools and Documentation

Acknowledgments

This book would not have been possible without the help of many people. That list starts with *people like you*—people who have read my books, attended my classes, e-mailed me questions, and visited my blog. Over the years, your comments and questions have helped me shape this reference to dimensional design. I hope you will find it relevant, practical, and useful. Thanks for your feedback, and keep it coming.

This book was also made possible by my customers, past and present. Thank you for always providing new challenges. Meeting them together never fails to be a fulfilling experience.

Lisa McClain of McGraw-Hill made this book a reality. My thanks to her for championing the project, and to everyone who has worked on this book's development, production, marketing, and distribution.

Several people have given me opportunities over the years, without which you would not be reading these words today. Thanks to Cameron Hendershot and Marilyn Feldman, Joe Warren, Argee Mahecha, Matt Comstock, Mike Venerable, and David Wells. Many colleagues have also influenced my trajectory, some unknowingly so. Thanks to Jesse Baldwin, Jim Hadley, Mike Lynott (who taught me about "unboiling frogs"), Greg Jones, and Randall Porter. I am also grateful to Chris Date and Laura Reeves, who have given me useful advice.

Special thanks to Ralph Kimball, whose generous advice, support, and encouragement have been greatly valued, and whose contributions to this field are of immeasurable value to us all.

I love teaching and want to thank everyone at The Data Warehousing Institute who makes it possible. Wayne Eckerson, Paul Kautza, Yvonne Baho, Sandra Prescott, Brenda Woodbridge, Jennifer Noland, Nancy Hanlon, and Heather Flynn are a few of the people at TDWI to whom I am indebted. My gratitude also goes out to all others not named here who organize TDWI events with professionalism and attention to detail.

To my friends and family: your friendship and love are what is most valuable to me. I cannot name all of you here, but you know who you are. Special thanks and love to Mom, Sis, Jason, Aya, Papa, Magal, Shell, Eli, and Sofie. My love also to Dad who, though no longer here, continues to be an important part of who I am.

Introduction

Dimensional design is a pillar of every modern-day data warehouse architecture. Based on a disarmingly simple approach to process measurement, dimensional design enables extraordinarily powerful analytics. The products of dimensional design—the star schema, the snowflake, and the cube—can be found in virtually every data warehouse implementation.

Despite this popularity, relatively little is written about dimensional design. Although some outstanding works are available, most assume a particular architecture or philosophy—my own prior work included. Additionally, these treatments are organized around vertical industries or major business functions, making them difficult to refer to when faced with a specific design challenge.

This book is a complete reference to dimensional design—the first intended for *any* reader. The best practices presented in this volume cut across *all* architectures, including those espoused by W.H. Inmon and Ralph Kimball. Organized around the key concepts of dimensional design, this book provides full, in-depth treatment of each topic, sequenced in a logical progression from fundamentals through advanced techniques.

This book is designed for both beginners and experts in dimensional design. If you are a beginner, it is the ideal place to start. Each chapter provides you with best practices and their underlying rationale, detailed examples, and the criteria you need to make design decisions. If you are an expert, you will be able to use this guide as a reference. Whenever you face a particular design challenge, you will find a chapter or section dedicated to the topic.

Dimensional design enables profoundly powerful business analysis. A solid understanding of the underlying principles is essential, whether you are directly involved in design activities, work with dimensional data structures, manage projects, or fund implementations. Mastery of the techniques and best practices in this book will help you unleash the full potential of your data warehouse, regardless of architecture, implementation scope, or software tools.

About This Book

This book has been designed as a complete, in-depth reference for *anyone* who works with dimensional data—the star, the snowflake, or the cube.

- The content is organized into chapters and sections dedicated to the core concepts of dimensional design so you can find everything you need to know about a particular topic in one place.
- Each topic is treated comprehensively. Full explanations for best practices allow you to make informed design decisions based on operational realities.

- No assumptions are made about your data warehouse environment. The best practices here apply in *all* architectures, including those espoused by W.H. Inmon and Ralph Kimball.
- Specific software products are not referenced, but the ways in which your tools may influence design decisions are fully explored.

The result is a treatment that is comprehensive and useful, regardless of your level of experience, data warehouse architecture, or available tools.

Organized Around Core Concepts

This book is organized around the core concepts of dimensional modeling, rather than a series of business scenarios by vertical industry. Focusing on these concepts allows a complete treatment of each topic, without forcing you to flip back and forth between various business cases. Each topic is explored in depth, rather than spread across multiple chapters.

This comprehensive treatment of each concept allows *Star Schema: The Complete Reference* to serve as a useful resource. Experienced modelers will find what they need with a quick scan through the Table of Contents. Need to brush up on the implications of a snapshot design? Everything you need can be found in Chapter 11. Thinking about implementing a bridge table? It's all there in Chapter 9. Need to implement a hybrid slow change? A complete discussion can be found in Chapter 8. Each chapter concludes with references to external treatments of the topic, should you wish to search for more examples.

For those new to dimensional design, the material has been sequenced so the book can be read cover to cover. The first three chapters explore fundamentals, and subsequent sections delve deeply into various aspects of dimensional design. Help on choosing where to start is provided at the end of this introduction.

Comprehensive and Practical, Not Dogmatic

While this book highlights a series of best practices, the underlying motivation is always fully explored. You will learn the *reasons* for these guidelines, and develop the ability to make informed decisions on how to apply them. The result is a practical approach to data warehouse design—one that is responsive to organizational and operational context, rather than independent of it.

Dimensional designers, for example, are often trained to record information at the lowest level of detail possible. The reasons for this guideline are fully explained in Chapter 3, along with situations where these reasons might not apply. Similarly, designers are always taught that different business processes deserve their own models, or stars. Chapter 4 explains why this is the case, and fully explores what happens when this guideline is relaxed.

Even when you stick to the best practices, there is no single "right way" to model a particular business process. You will learn how each design option strikes a balance among business value, the required effort to construct reports, the complexity of the load process, and cost. Flattening a recursive hierarchy, for example, simplifies reporting and reduces development cost, but limits the power of the final solution; the alternatives are fully explored in Chapter 10. Derived schemas can make reporting easier and improve performance, but provide significant additional work to load data into the data warehouse, as described in Chapter 14.

Architecture-Neutral

This book makes no assumptions about your data warehouse architecture. The best practices outlined in these pages apply whether you follow W.H. Inmon's Corporate Information Factory approach or Ralph Kimball's dimensional data warehouse "bus" approach, or simply build subject-area data marts. In each of these paradigms, there is a place for dimensional data. No matter how you put dimensional design to work, this book will allow you to make the most of it.

If you don't know anything about these thought leaders or their recommended architectures, you will learn something about them in Chapter 2. There, you will find a high-level overview of various approaches, and information on how dimensional design fits into each. What you *won't* find is an argument in favor of one approach over another. This book's coverage of dimensional design is disentangled from such considerations. Anyone can use it.

Common Vocabulary

This book is designed to service any data warehouse architecture, but it is necessary to establish a common vocabulary. When it comes to dimensional design, that vocabulary comes from Ralph Kimball. By providing a way to talk about dimensional design, he has made a valuable contribution to the world of data warehousing, giving us terms like *grain*, *conformance*, and *slowly changing dimensions*. These and other terms can be found in his seminal work on dimensional design: *The Data Warehouse Toolkit, Second Edition*, by Ralph Kimball and Margy Ross (Wiley, 2002).

Wherever possible, this book makes use of terminology established by Kimball and Ross. Each term will be fully explained. However, it is not presumed that the reader adheres to Kimball's approach to data warehousing. His approach is one of several architectures that make use of dimensional design. These architectures are discussed in Chapter 2; the principles in this book can be employed in any of these situations.

Product-Independent

This book makes no assumptions about specific hardware or software products in your data warehouse architecture. The dimensional techniques described are largely universal, and can be implemented using tools and technologies from a variety of vendors.

This is *not* to say that the software products used by your organization will not influence your dimensional design. To the contrary, they *can*, *will*, and *should* bear such influence. Although specific software products will not be discussed, the influence of various kinds of tools will be explored. These include database management systems (DBMSs), reporting or business intelligence (BI) software, and data integration or extract transform load (ETL) tools.

The capabilities of your RDBMS and reporting tools, for example, may drive the decision to produce a "snowflake" design, rather than a star, as you will learn in Chapter 7. The capabilities of a business intelligence tool, or the sophistication of its users, may shape your approach to schema design issues outlined in Chapter 16. Development of the ETL process is complex, and may benefit from some design considerations discussed in Chapter 17.

Snowflakes and Cubes

Most of the examples in this book feature the star schema. The principles of dimensional modeling can also be used to design snowflakes and cubes. The best practices are largely the same, with a few exceptions that are highlighted and explored. The snowflake is featured in Chapter 7; the influence of business intelligence tools on this design option are discussed in Chapter 16. The cube is introduced in Chapter 3; many useful ways to pair stars with cubes are explored in Chapters 14, 15, and 16.

Who Should Read This Book

This book is written for you, the data warehouse practitioner. If your work in any way involves stars, snowflakes, or cubes, then this is your guide to all things dimensional. No assumptions are made regarding your skill level, role, or preferred architecture.

You may design dimensional models, work with dimensional data, manage activities, or pay the bills. Your role may fall into a variety of categories, including:

- Business Analysis
- Data Architecture / Star Schema Design
- Business Intelligence and Reporting
- Data Integration or ETL
- Database Administration
- Quality Assurance
- Data Administration
- Project Management
- Executive Leadership / IT Management
- Power User

It will be assumed that you have a basic familiarity with relational database concepts like tables, columns, and joins. There will be occasional examples of SQL code; these will be fully explained for the benefit of novice readers.

No assumptions are made about your level of experience. If you are new to dimensional design, you will probably want to read this book from cover to cover. Experienced practitioners may prefer to skip directly to areas of particular interest. The next section provides advice on how to proceed.

Using This Book

This book is designed to be used in two ways. You can read it cover to cover, or consult it as a reference. The book is divided into six parts, with chapters organized in a logical progression. When looking for a particular topic, you can scan the chapter and section headings to find what you need. Key features of each chapter help highlight important concepts and aid your understanding of them.

Key Features of Each Chapter

Each chapter in this book provides in-depth treatment of a core topic in dimensional design. Design techniques are evaluated, best practices are identified, and alternatives are fully explored. When you finish a chapter, you will understand the design principles, the reasons behind best practices, and how to evaluate possible design alternatives.

Some special elements are used to help highlight important information.

Tips

"Tips" are used to highlight best practices:

TIP *Whether reading the book cover to cover, or skipping around to pertinent passages, tips will be there to highlight the key lessons of each section.*

These tips are like conclusions; they result from a full exploration of design alternatives. Reading the body of the chapter will bring to light the reasons behind these guidelines, along with situations in which you may wish to deviate.

Examples

Detailed examples are used to illustrate every design technique. Most examples are accompanied with schema designs, as well as instance diagrams that illustrate the content of important tables. These diagrams will help you understand design techniques; the text will refer to them, call out important features, highlight the sample data, and show how the technique works to solve the design challenge.

Notes

Some examples may feature design elements that are not central to the focus of the topic or section. Interesting but off-topic considerations are highlighted in "Notes," which may also direct you to other chapters where the topic is fully explored.

NOTE *Notes are used to alert you to additional considerations dealt with elsewhere in the book, or to touch on topics not central to dimensional design.*

Further Reading

Each chapter ends with a section on "Further Reading." Here you can get information on where to find more examples of the techniques presented in the chapter. Some of these references highlight refinements or alternatives to the techniques presented; others provide examples drawn from different business cases or industries. The majority of books cited focus on the Kimball approach to data warehouse design, but can be employed in other architectures as well.

Contents of This Book

Star Schema: The Complete Reference is divided into six parts, each of which focuses on a major category of dimensional design techniques. A summary of each section follows. For additional details, you may wish to scan the Table of Contents.

Part I: Fundamentals

Part I focuses on the fundamentals of dimensional design. It includes chapters that focus on process measurement, data warehouse architecture, and star schema design.

Chapter 1: Analytic Databases and Dimensional Design The fundamentals of process measurement are introduced in this chapter, including facts, dimensions, and the star schema.

Chapter 2: Data Warehouse Architectures Three very different architectures make use of the star schema, including those advocated by W.H. Inmon and Ralph Kimball. This chapter sorts through each architecture's use of the star, and highlights how the same terms take on different meanings in each paradigm.

Chapter 3: Stars and Cubes In this chapter, you will learn the fundamentals of star schema design and slowly changing dimensions, and explore the different ways cubes may be incorporated into a data warehouse architecture.

Part II: Multiple Stars

Part II takes the first steps out of the neat and perfect world of the simple example and ventures into the real world of complex designs. It deals with a fundamental challenge that novice designers must learn to tackle: modeling different business processes as different stars.

Chapter 4: A Fact Table for Each Process This chapter teaches you how to identify discrete processes and provide separate stars for each. It also looks at how to produce analysis that crosses process boundaries.

Chapter 5: Conformed Dimensions The concept of conformed dimensions allows you to support and compare a variety of business processes, ensuring compatibility even if implementations make use of different technologies. Dimensional conformance is often considered to be of strategic importance, and can serve as the basis of a roadmap for incremental implementation.

Part III: Dimension Design

Part III dives deeply into advanced techniques that surround the dimensions of a dimensional design. It is divided into five chapters.

Chapter 6: More on Dimension Tables In this chapter, you will learn how to determine what dimensions to place in the same table, how to stem unmanageable growth in dimension tables, and how to handle information that is optional or unavailable.

Chapter 7: Hierarchies and Snowflakes This chapter explores the technique known as snowflaking, and explains how modeling attribute hierarchies may facilitate the implementation of reporting tools.

Chapter 8: More Slow Change Techniques This chapter goes beyond the basic type 1 and type 2 slow changes presented in Chapter 3, covering type 3 slow changes, time-stamping techniques, and hybrid slow change responses.

Chapter 9: Multi-Valued Dimensions and Bridges Sometimes, a dimension can take on multiple values with respect to a single fact, such as multiple salespeople collaborating on a single order. This chapter explores techniques for dealing with these situations, from simple flattening to the use of bridge tables.

Chapter10: Recursive Hierarchies and Bridges Dimensions often embody recursive hierarchies, such as departments that report to other departments. This chapter shows how to flatten these hierarchies for a simple solution, and how to make use of a hierarchy bridge for powerful and flexible analysis.

Part IV: Fact Table Design

Part IV provides in-depth treatment of advanced features that center on fact tables. It is composed of three chapters.

Chapter 11: Transactions, Snapshots, and Accumulating Snapshots This chapter covers situations in which a standard transaction-based fact table falls short, and shows how periodic snapshots and accumulating snapshots can be put to use.

Chapter 12: Factless Fact Tables Sometimes fact tables contain no facts. In this chapter, you will learn about transaction-based factless fact tables, as well as factless fact tables that capture coverage or conditions.

Chapter13: Type-Specific Stars This chapter looks at situations where subsets of data have different facts and dimensions, and shows how to make use of core and custom stars for a single process.

Part V: Performance

Any dimensional schema can be supplemented with additional structures that are intended to improve performance or simplify the reporting process. Part V looks at two kinds of supplemental data structures that support high performance.

Chapter 14: Derived Schemas This chapter teaches you to use derived schemas to provide enhanced performance, simplify report development, or address specific departmental needs.

Chapter 15: Aggregates This chapter shows how summary tables, or aggregates, can provide powerful performance boosts when implemented wisely.

Part VI: Tools and Documentation

The last part of this book looks at additional topics of interest for the developers of dimensional models.

Chapter 16: Design and Business Intelligence This chapter explores the influence of business intelligence (BI) tools on your dimensional design. It explores some common dimensional features that often strain BI tools, as well as techniques to mitigate any shortcomings.

Chapter 17: Design and ETL This chapter provides an overview of the process of loading the dimensional schema, and highlights numerous model features that can assist ETL developers in optimizing the process.

Chapter 18: How to Design and Document a Dimensional Model This provides standard tasks and deliverables that can be worked into your data warehouse life cycle, regardless of architecture.

Where to Start

As mentioned earlier, you can read this book from cover to cover, or skip directly to sections that deal with a topic of interest. How you make use of it will largely depend on your current skill level.

Beginners Those new to dimensional design should start by reading Part I: Fundamentals. Once you've finished that section, you can read the rest in sequence, or skip to any section of particular interest. If you are getting ready to start a project, you may wish to turn to the last chapter: "How to Design and Document a Dimensional Model."

Novices If you have some dimensional design experience, you may wish to skip the fundamentals in Part I. However, you are encouraged to review the data warehouse terms described at the end of Chapter 2. Terms like "data warehouse," "data mart," and "source system" can take on very different meanings in different architectures; Chapter 2 explains how these terms will be used in this book. If you've done most of your learning "on the job," you may also want to review Chapter 3 for standard dimensional terminology used in this book—terms such as "grain," "natural key," and "slowly changing dimension" are all defined there.

Experts Experienced dimensional modelers can use this book as a reference, consulting it for detailed information on design issues as they arise. A quick scan through the Table of Contents will help you find any dimensional design topic of interest. You may also wish to read the book cover to cover, enhancing your mastery of dimensional design.

Regardless of how you approach the material in these pages, it will enable you to master the principles of dimensional design, unlocking the full potential of your data warehouse.

PART I Fundamentals

CHAPTER

1 Analytic Databases and Dimensional Design

This book describes a set of powerful and effective techniques for the design of analytic databases. These techniques unleash business analytics in a very simple way: *they model the measurement of business processes.*

The dimensional model of a business process is made up of two components: measurements and their context. Known as facts and dimensions, these components are organized into a database design that facilitates a wide variety of analytic usage. Implemented in a relational database, the dimensional model is called a star schema. Implemented in a multidimensional database, it is known as a cube. If any part of your data warehouse includes a star schema or a cube, it leverages dimensional design.

This chapter introduces the basic concepts of dimensional design, which arose in response to the unique requirements of analytic systems. The concept of measurement is defined in terms of facts and dimensions, and translated into a database design, or star schema. This chapter shows how basic interaction with a star schema can support a wide variety of measurement scenarios, and defines two simple guiding principles for the development of dimensional solutions.

Dimensional Design

Information systems fall into two major categories: those that support the execution of business processes and those that support the analysis of business processes. The principles of dimensional design have evolved as a direct response to the unique requirements of analytic systems. The core of every dimensional model is a set of business metrics that captures how a process is evaluated, and a description of the context of every measurement.

Purpose

Analytic systems and operational systems serve fundamentally different purposes. An operational system supports the *execution* of a business process, while an analytic system supports the *evaluation* of the process. Their distinct purposes are reflected in contrasting usage profiles, which in turn suggest that different principles will guide their design.

Operational Systems

An operational system directly supports the execution of a business process. By capturing details about significant events or transactions, it constructs a record of activities. A sales system, for example, captures information about orders, shipments, and returns; a human resources system captures information about the hiring and promotion of employees; an accounting system captures information about the management of the financial assets and liabilities of the business. The activities recorded by these systems are sometimes known as *transactions.* The systems themselves are sometimes called *online transaction processing (OLTP) systems,* or *transaction systems* for short.

To facilitate the execution of a business process, operational systems must enable several types of database interaction, including inserts, updates, and deletes. The focus of these interactions is almost always atomic: a specific order, a shipment, a refund. These interactions will be highly predictable in nature. For example, an order entry system must provide for the management of lists of products, customers, and salespeople; the entering of orders; the printing of order summaries, invoices, and packing lists; and the tracking order status.

Because it is focused on process execution, the operational system is likely to update data as things change, and purge or archive data once its operational usefulness has ended. When a customer moves, for example, his or her old address is no longer useful for shipping products or sending invoices, so it is simply overwritten.

Implemented in a relational database, the optimal schema design for an operational system is widely accepted to be one that is in *third normal form.* The design may be depicted as an *entity-relationship model,* or ER model. Coupled with appropriate database technology, this design supports high-performance inserting, updating, and deleting of atomic transactions in a consistent and predictable manner. Developers refer to the characteristics of transaction processing as the ACID properties—atomic, consistent, isolated, and durable.

Analytic Systems

While the focus of the operational system is the execution of a business process, the analytic system supports the *evaluation* of the process. How are orders trending this month versus last? Where does this put us in comparison to our sales goals for the quarter? Is a particular marketing promotion having an impact on sales? Who are our best customers? These questions deal with the measurement of the overall orders process, rather than asking about individual orders.

Interaction with an analytic system takes place exclusively through queries that *retrieve* data about business processes; information is not created or modified. These queries can involve large numbers of transactions, in contrast to the operational system's typical focus on individual transactions. Specific questions asked are less predictable, and more likely to change over time. Historic data will remain important to the analytic system long after its operational use has passed. The differences between operational systems and analytic systems are highlighted in Figure 1-1.

The principles of dimensional modeling address the unique requirements of analytic systems. A dimensional design is optimized for queries that may access large volumes of

	Operational System	Analytic System
Purpose	Execution of a business process	Measurement of a business process
Primary Interaction Style	Insert, Update, Query, Delete	Query
Scope of Interaction	Individual transaction	Aggregated transactions
Query Patterns	Predictable and stable	Unpredictable and changing
Temporal Focus	Current	Current and historic
Design Optimization	Update concurrency	High-performance query
Design Principle	Entity-relationship (ER) design in third normal form (3NF)	Dimensional design (Star Schema or Cube)
Also Known As	Transaction System On Line Transaction Processing (OLTP) System Source System	Data Warehouse System Data Mart

Figure 1-1 Operational systems vs. analytic systems

transactions, not just individual transactions. It is not burdened with supporting concurrent, high-performance updates. It supports the maintenance of historic data, even as the operational systems change or delete information.

Measurement and Context

The founding principle of dimensional design is disarmingly simple. Dimensional design supports analysis of a business process *by modeling how it is measured.*

Measurement is easy to discern, whether by listening to people talk or reading a report or chart. Consider the following business questions:

- What are gross margins by product category for January?
- What is the average account balance by education level?
- How many sick days were taken by marketing employees last year?
- What are the outstanding payables by vendor?
- What is the return rate by supplier?

Each of these questions centers on a business process: sales, account management, attendance, payables, return processing. These process-centric questions do not focus on individual activities or transactions. To answer them, it is necessary to look at a group of transactions.

Most importantly, each of these questions reveals something about how its respective business process is *measured.* The study of sales involves the measurement of *gross margin.* Financial institutions measure *account balance.* In human resources, they measure *number of absences.* The finance department measures *payables.* Purchasing managers watch the *return quantities.*

Without some kind of context, a measurement is meaningless. If you are told "sales were $10,000," there is not much you can do with this information. Is that sales of a single product, or many products? Does it represent a single transaction, or the company's total sales from conception to date? Without some context, the measurement is useless.

As with the measurements themselves, context is revealed in business questions or reports. In the preceding questions, for example, gross margin is viewed in the context of *product categories* and *time* (the month of January). Sick days are viewed in the context of a *department* (marketing) and *time* (last year). Payables are viewed in the context of their *status* (outstanding) and *vendor.*

These two simple concepts, measurement and context, are the foundation of dimensional design. Every dimensional solution describes a process by capturing what is measured and the context in which the measurements are evaluated.

Facts and Dimensions

In a dimensional design, measurements are called *facts,* and context descriptors are called *dimensions.* Every dimensional design sorts information requirements into these categories. They may be identified within statements or questions, or found within report specifications. Sorting them into categories for facts and dimensions is easy, once you know what to look for.

Facts and Dimensions in Speech

In a spoken or written statement, the word "by" is almost always followed by a dimension. Consider the question "What are order dollars *by* product category for January?" Clearly, the person asking this question wants a separate measurement for each product category, as indicated by the words "by product category." Product category is a dimension.

Similarly, the word "for" is also a good indicator of the presence of a dimension. In this case, the next word is likely to be an instance value of a dimension. For example, "What are order dollars by product category *for January*?" Here, "for" is followed by "January." January is a value or instance of a dimension. The dimension is not named, but we can infer that it is month.

Facts tend to be numeric in value, and people want to see them at various levels of detail. You can identify facts by looking for things that people want to "roll up" or "break out." Again, look at the question "What are order dollars by product category for January?" Here, order dollars will presumably be numeric, and they can be rolled up by categories.

Not everything that is numeric is a fact. Sometimes, a numeric data element is really a dimension. The key is to determine how it is being used. Is it something that can be specified at varying levels of detail? If so, it is a fact. Is it providing context? If so, it is a dimension. "Show me margin dollars by order number," contains two numeric elements. Margin dollars can be specified at various levels of detail, and the speaker is asking that it be rolled up by order number. Clearly, "margin dollars" is a fact. What about order number? It too is numeric, but the speaker is not asking that order numbers be added together. Instead, order number is being used to specify the context for margin dollars. Order number is a dimension.

Other examples of numeric data elements behaving as dimensions include size, ages, phone numbers, document numbers, and unit amounts such as unit cost or unit price. The clue that these elements are dimensions lies in their use. The numbers themselves are not rolled up or down according to the question. Instead, they specify the context by which something else may be rolled up or down.

Facts and Dimensions in Reports

Facts and dimensions can also be recognized by considering how they would be used if they were stored in a database and shown on a report. Dimensions serve as "filters," or "query predicates." The report page shown in Figure 1-2, for example, is filtering detailed data for the western region and January 2009. These filters imply several dimensions: region, month, and year.

Order Report Western Region
January 2009 (cont'd)

Category	Product	SKU	Quantity Sold	Cost	Order Dollars
Packaging	Box - Large	011-4822	700	$ 950.53	$ 1,100.00
	Box - Medium	011-4899	1,250	$ 1,001.84	$ 1,380.00
	Box - Small	011-5744	1,200	$ 1,200.72	$ 1,330.00
	Clasp Letter	011-1729	400	$ 352.82	$ 356.00
	Envelope #10	021-0011	2,000	$ 2,017.46	$ 2,080.00
	Envelope Bubble	021-0012	1,200	$ 866.51	$ 1,212.00
	All Packaging			*$ 6,389.88*	*$ 7,458.00*
Pens	Gel Pen Black	017-1999	5000	$ 116.39	$ 120.00
	Gel Pen Blue	017-2444	2990	$ 600.88	$ 624.91
	Silver Pen	017-3001	50	$ 128.46	$ 130.00
	All Pens			*$ 845.73*	*$ 874.91*
Grand Total				***$207,229.42***	***$214,896.91***

Page 10 of 10

Figure 1-2 Sample page from an orders report

In a report, dimensions also serve to specify groupings or "break levels," or to identify levels of subtotals. This can be seen in the orders report, where *category* is used to break up the report into sections; individual categories are also used to label rows containing subtotals. These features are clues that *category* is a dimension.

Dimensions can also be identified by their use in controlling the aggregation of measurements. In the orders report, several measurements are specified for each product name and SKU. (SKU is a retail term that identifies an individual product, or "stock keeping unit.") Product and SKU are dimensions. Notice, too, that dimension values may be used to sort data.

Facts can also be spotted based on their use in queries or reports. Elements that are aggregated, summarized, or subtotaled are facts. Clearly, the report in Figure 1-2 contains the facts cost and order dollars. These numbers are being specified at various levels, including products, categories, and a grand total. Look again, and you may notice another fact: quantity ordered. Although it is not being subtotaled, this number is presumably being aggregated. In this case, it looks like quantity ordered by product is being aggregated from individual orders.

The style of the report in Figure 1-2 is sometimes referred to as tabular. Other reports may cross-reference facts and dimensions in matrix format, or even display facts graphically. The values being plotted are facts; axis values, bar labels, and qualifications are dimensions.

In some cases, it can be hard to tell whether a data element is a fact or a dimension. Sometimes, a single data element can be used in both ways. Chapter 6, "More on Dimension Tables," discusses behavioral attributes, which are dimensions that have been derived from facts. Later, Chapter 11, "Transactions, Snapshots, and Accumulating Snapshots," looks at techniques used to construct facts out of dimension values. It is also possible to find a process where there does not appear to be a clear measurement. Chapter 12, "Factless Fact Tables," describes how the factless fact table can be used to deal with this kind of situation. You also may find that some important business metrics are not so easily "rolled up." Chapter 3, "Stars and Cubes," considers nonadditive facts, while Chapter 11 discusses the curious case of semi-additive facts.

Grouping Dimensions and Facts

A dimensional design organizes facts and dimensions for storage in a database. It is common for a set of dimensions to share relationships to one another, independent of facts. These are grouped together in a single table to reflect their natural clustering. Similarly, facts that are available at the same level of detail are grouped together.

For example, suppose a study of the orders process reveals the facts and dimensions shown in Figure 1-3. In this example, products are being sold by a distributor to retail stores, so the customers are companies. Each of the facts listed in the column on the left may be rolled up according to the dimension values in the right-hand column.

Notice natural affinities exist among the dimension values. Some of them clearly belong together. For example, product and product description both seem to be associated with SKU. Salesperson name is determined by salesperson ID. Other dimensions are more distantly associated. Products, for example, have brands. Salespeople work in regions. Figure 1-4 shows how the facts and dimensions for the orders process might be grouped together.

Facts	Dimensions
Order Dollars	Product
Cost Dollars	Product Description
Quantity Ordered	SKU
	Brand Code
	Brand
	Brand Manager
	Category Code
	Category
	Order Date
	Month of Order
	Quarter of Order
	Fiscal Period of Order
	Year of Order
	Salesperson
	Salesperson ID
	Territory
	Territory Code
	Territory Manager
	Region
	Region Code
	Region VP
	Customer
	Customer ID
	Headquarters State of Customer
	Billing Address
	Billing City
	Billing State
	Billing Zip
	SIC Code of Customer
	Industry Name of Customer

Figure 1-3 Facts and dimensions for the orders process

The diagram in Figure 1-4 depicts measurement of the orders process. It identifies the important measurements for the process and shows the dimensional context in which those measurements are evaluated. The facts and dimensions in this diagram can be combined in a number of ways, answering a wide array of business questions. Take any fact (or facts), add the word "by," and then any combination of dimensions. The diagram can be easily understood by a businessperson. "Things I measure" go in the middle; "the ways I look at them" go in the surrounding boxes, loosely grouped or categorized.

The dimensional framework for the orders process in Figure 1-4 can easily be translated into a database design, or more specifically a *dimensional design*. A dimensional design organizes facts and dimensions for storage in a database management system. In a relational database management system (RDBMS), the design is referred to as a *star schema*. In a multidimensional database (MDB), the design is referred to as a *cube*. This chapter introduces the star schema; we will return to cubes in Chapter 3.

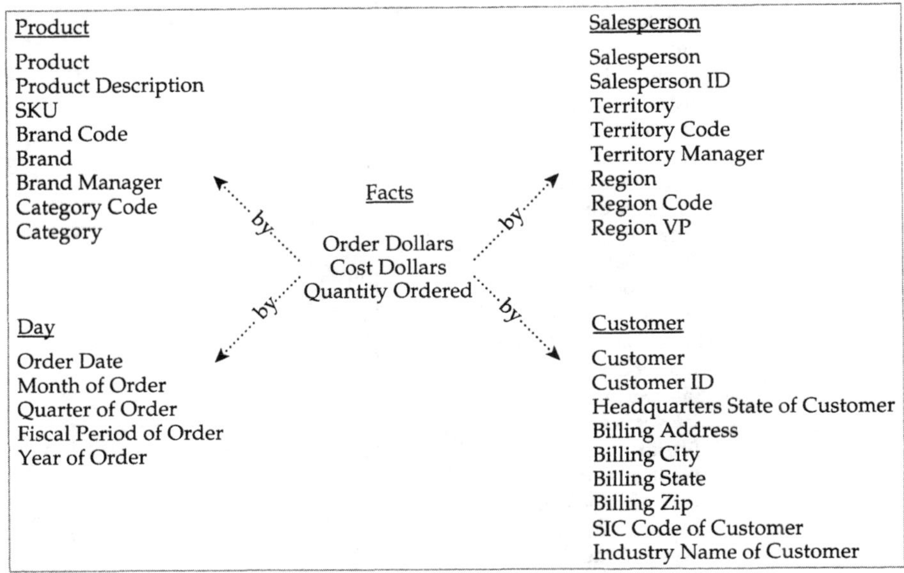

Figure 1-4 Sorting out facts and dimensions for the orders process

The Star Schema

A dimensional design for a relational database is called a star schema. Related dimensions are grouped as columns in dimension tables, and the facts are stored as columns in a fact table. The star schema gets its name from its appearance: when drawn with the fact table in the center, it looks like a star or asterisk. Figure 1-5 shows a simple star schema, based on the facts and dimensions for the orders process.

Dimension Tables

In a star schema, a dimension table contains columns representing dimensions. As discussed, these columns will provide context for facts. Sometimes, "dimension table" is simply shortened to "dimension." This may give rise to confusion, since that word can also describe the individual columns. For example, when describing the schema shown in Figure 1-5, one might refer to the columns product, product_description, and SKU as dimensions, but it is also common practice to refer to the table itself as the product dimension.

Generally, you can tell from the context whether the word "dimension" refers to a table or column. When it would not otherwise be clear, this book will use the terms *dimension attribute* and *dimension table* to make the distinction.

The dimension tables serve to provide the rich context needed for the study of facts. In queries and reports, the dimensions will be used to specify how facts will be rolled up—their level of aggregation. Dimension values may be used to filter reports. They will be used to provide context for each measurement, usually in the form of textual labels that precede facts on each row of a report. They may also be used to drive master-detail relationships, subtotaling, cross-tabulation, or sorts.

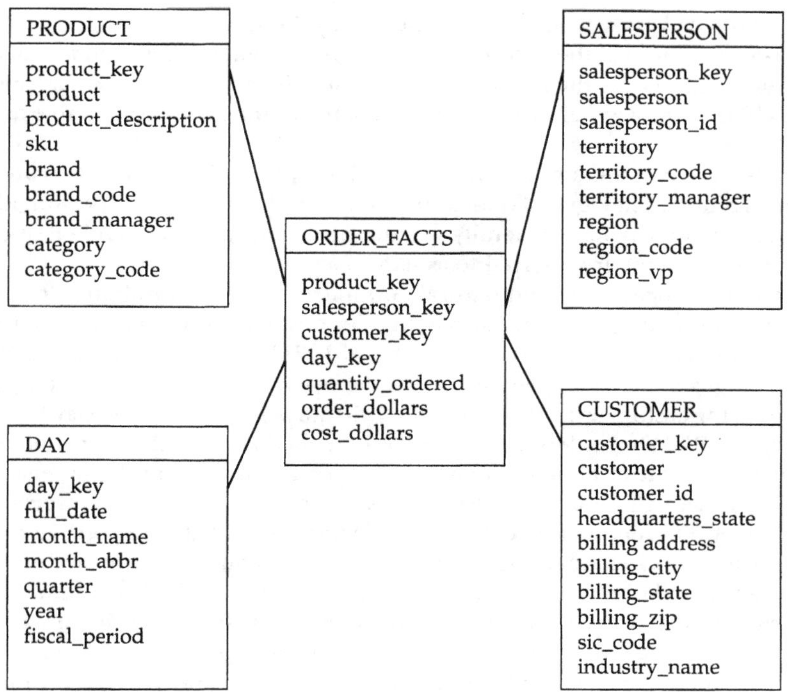

Figure 1-5 A simple star schema for the orders process

Readers with experience designing operational systems will notice that the dimension tables are not in third normal form. At first, many developers find this disconcerting. For example, there may be a strong desire to move brand, brand_code, and brand_manager into a separate table called brand, Remember, though, that a dimensional model serves a different purpose from an ER model. It is not necessary to isolate repeating values in an environment that does not support transaction processing. Designers do occasionally perform additional normalization within dimensions, although they usually avoid doing so. In such cases, the schema is referred to as a *snowflake.* The additional tables that result are sometimes called *outriggers.* Situations in which snowflaking may be useful are discussed in Chapter 7, "Hierarchies and Snowflakes."

Because the dimensions in a dimension table are often loosely related, it can sometimes be difficult to decide how to group things. For example, should sales region be part of the salesperson dimension, or does it belong as a separate geographical dimension? Issues like this are tackled in Chapter 6.

Keys and History

In a star schema, each dimension table is given a surrogate key. This column is a unique identifier, created exclusively for the data warehouse. Surrogate keys are assigned and maintained as part of the process that loads the star schema. The surrogate key has no intrinsic meaning; it is typically an integer. Surrogate keys are sometimes referred to as *warehouse keys.* The surrogate key is the primary key of the dimension table.

In this book, surrogate keys will be easily identifiable by the suffix "_key" in the column name. In Figure 1-5, for example, the surrogate key for the customer dimension is called *customer_key*, the surrogate key for the salesperson dimension is called *salesperson_key*, and so forth. Illustrations in this book will always list the surrogate key for a dimension table as its first attribute.

Dimension tables also contain key columns that uniquely identify something in an operational system. Examples in Figure 1-5 include customer_id, sku, and salesperson_id. In the operational systems, these columns identify specific customers, products, and salespeople, respectively. These key columns are referred to as *natural keys*.

The separation of surrogate keys and natural keys allows the data warehouse to track changes, even if the originating operational system does not. For example, suppose that customer ABC Wholesalers is identified by customer_id 10711 in an operational system. If the customer changes its headquarters location, the operational system may simply overwrite the address for customer_id 10711. For analytic purposes, however, it may be useful to track the history of ABC Wholesalers. Since the star schema does not rely on customer_id to identify a unique row in the customer dimension, it is possible to store multiple versions of ABC Wholesalers, even though both have the same customer_id—10711. The two versions can be distinguished by different surrogate key values. While it would also be possible to support change tracking by supplementing a natural key with a sequence number, the surrogate key allows fact and dimension tables to be joined based on a single column.

The term *slowly changing dimension* refers to the manner in which a dimensional schema responds to changes in a source system. Detailed examples will be explored in Chapter 3, "Stars and Cubes." Advanced techniques are explored in Chapter 8, "More Slow Change Techniques."

Fact Tables

At the core of a star schema is the fact table. In addition to presenting the facts, the fact table includes surrogate keys that refer to each of the associated dimension tables. The simple orders star in Figure 1-5, for example, includes the facts quantity_ordered, cost_dollars, and order_dollars. It also includes surrogate keys that refer to products, salespeople, customers, and order dates.

Together, the foreign keys in a fact table are sometimes considered to identify a unique row in the fact table. This is certainly true in Figure 1-5, where each fact table row represents orders of a product sold by a salesperson to a customer on a given day. In other cases, however, the foreign keys in a fact table are not sufficient to identify a unique row. As we will see in Chapter 3, sometimes a fact table row can be uniquely identified by a *subset* of its foreign keys, or even by using some nonkey attributes.

Each row in the fact table stores facts at a specific level of detail. This level of detail is known as the fact table's *grain*, a term that will be explored in Chapter 3. The information held in fact tables may be consumed at a variety of *different* levels, however, by aggregating the facts. In some data warehouse architectures, it is critical that the star schema capture information at the lowest level of detail possible. In other architectures, this is less important because a separate part of the data warehouse architecture is reserved for atomic data. These variations in data warehouse architecture are explored in Chapter 2, "Data Warehouse Architectures."

Using a Star Schema

There is still much to be said about the fundamentals of dimensional design, a discussion that continues in Chapter 3, but enough background has now been provided to look at an important feature of the star schema: *how it is actually used.* Understanding the basic usage pattern of the star schema allows the dimensional designer to make intelligent choices.

Querying Facts

Most queries against a star schema follow a consistent pattern. One or more facts are requested, along with the dimensional attributes that provide the desired context. The facts will be summarized in accordance with the dimensions present in the query. Dimension values are also used to limit the scope of the query, serving as the basis for filters or constraints on the data to be fetched and aggregated.

A properly configured relational database is well equipped to respond to such a query, which is issued using Structured Query Language (SQL). Suppose that someone has asked to see a report showing order dollars by product category and product name during the month of January 2009. The orders star schema from Figure 1-5 can provide this information, even though order dollars is stored at a lower level of detail. The SQL query in Figure 1-6 produces the required results, summarizing tens of thousands of fact table rows.

The `SELECT` clause of the query indicates the dimensions that should appear in the query results (category and product), the fact that is requested (order dollars), and the manner in which it will be aggregated (through the SQL `SUM()` operation). The `FROM` clause specifies the star schema tables that are involved in the query.

The `WHERE` clause serves two purposes. First, it filters the query results based on the values of specific dimension columns (month and year). It also specifies the join relationships between tables in the query. In terms of processing time, joins are among the most expensive operations the database must perform; notice that in the case of a star schema, dimension attributes are always a maximum of one join away from facts. The `GROUP BY` clause specifies the context to which the fact will be aggregated by the relational database; the `ORDER BY` clause uses dimensions to specify how the results will be sorted.

For readers new to dimensional design, there are two key insights to take away. First, the star schema can be used in this manner with any combination of facts and dimensions. This permits the star to answer questions that may not have been posed during the design process. Although facts are stored at a specific level of detail, they can be rolled up or summarized at various levels of detail. The reporting possibilities increase dramatically as the richness of the dimension tables is increased.

Second, note that the ability to report facts is primarily limited by the level of detail at which they are stored. While it is possible to aggregate the detailed fact table rows in accordance with any set of dimensions, it is not possible to produce a *lower* level of detail. If a fact table stores daily totals, for example, it cannot be used to look at an individual order. The importance of this limitation depends in part on your data warehouse architecture, as you will see in the next chapter.

Of course, star schema queries can get much more complex than this example. Queries may build on this template in a number of ways. A very important type of report requires that we merge query results sets from more than one star. These *drill-across reports* will be discussed in Chapter 4, "A Fact Table for Each Process." Some reports add subqueries to the mix, enhancing the selection of relevant facts, as discussed in Chapter 16, "Design and Business Intelligence." Another type of report necessitates the performance of set operations with the results of more than one query, as discussed in Chapter 12. It is also possible that facts may be aggregated in other ways, perhaps by averaging them or simply counting them.

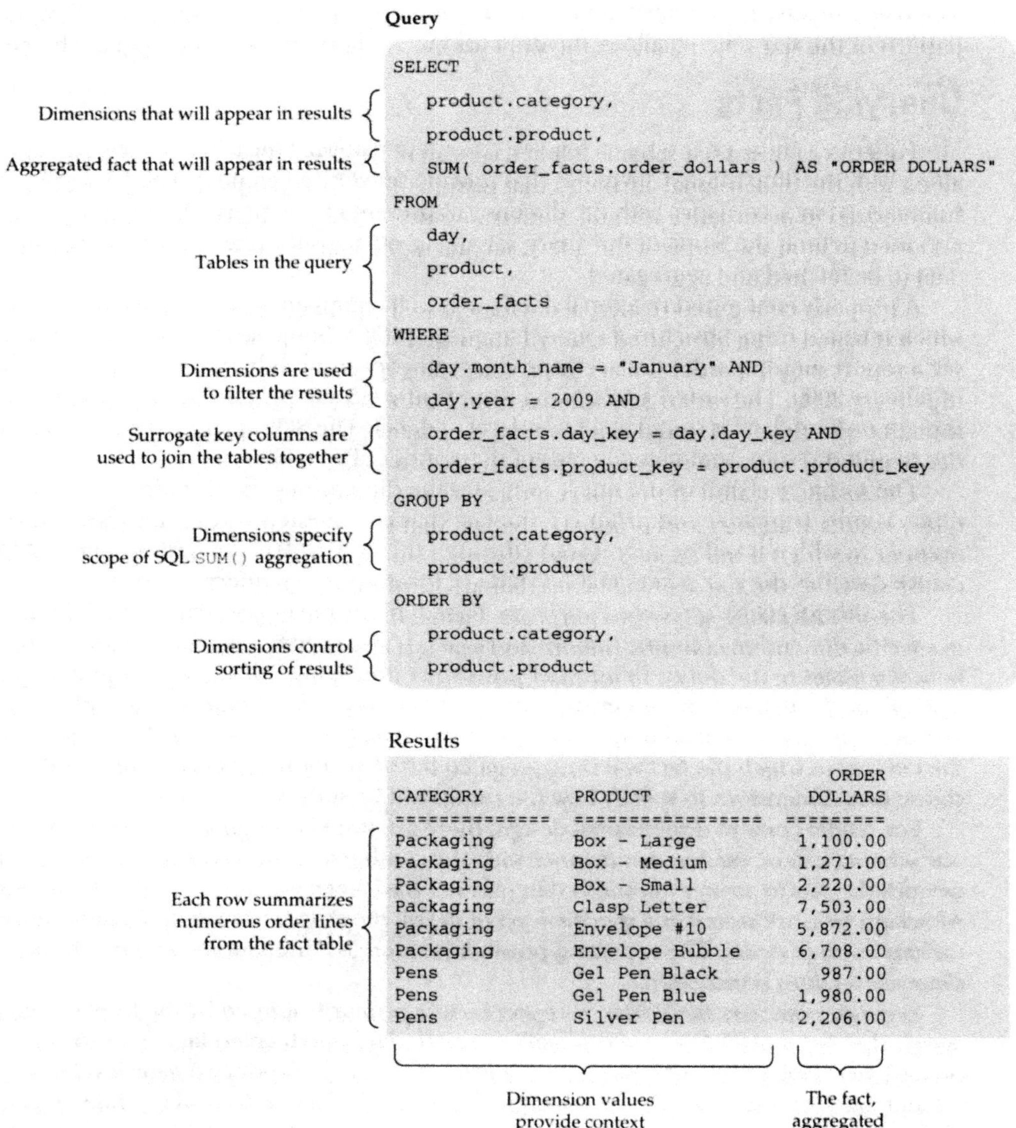

Figure 1-6 Querying the star schema

Browsing Dimensions

An often overlooked, but equally important, form of interaction with a dimensional schema is the *browse* query. Browsing is the act of exploring the data within a dimension. The results of browse queries appear as reference data, and may make useful reports. A browse activity may also be an exploratory precursor to a larger query against the fact table.

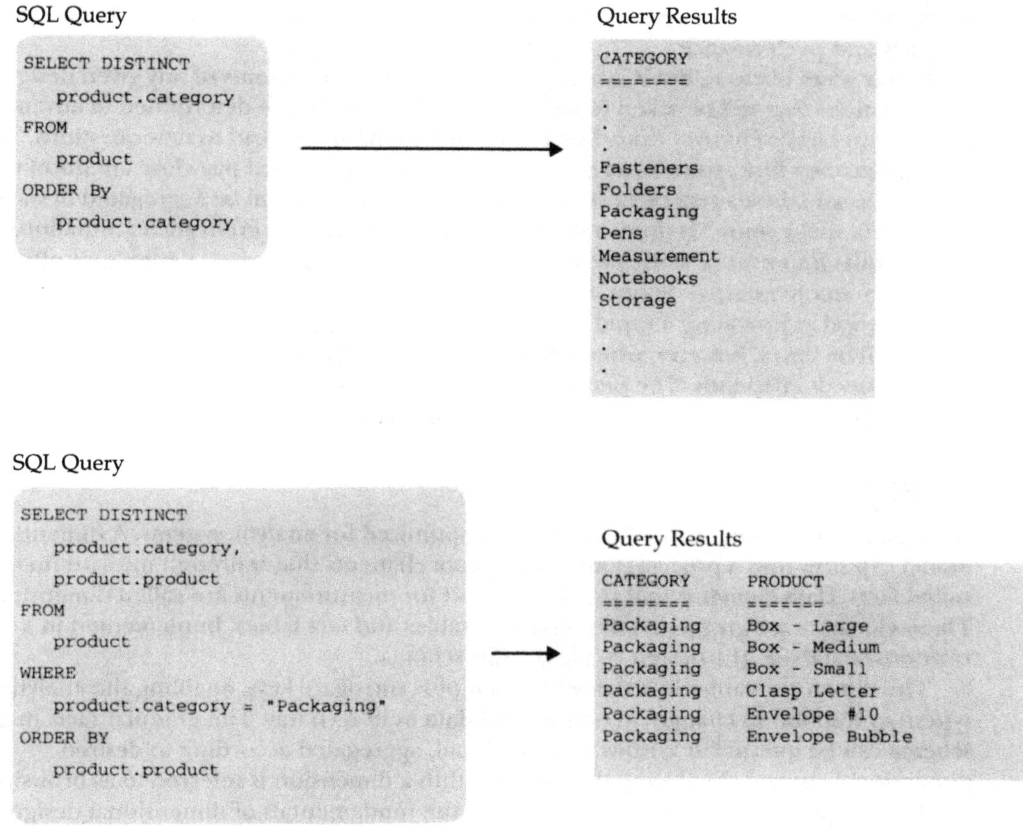

SQL Query
SELECT DISTINCT
product.category
FROM
product
ORDER BY
product.category
Query Results
CATEGORY
========
.
.
.
Fasteners
Folders
Packaging
Pens
Measurement
Notebooks
Storage
.
.
.
SQL Query
SELECT DISTINCT
product.category,
product.product
FROM
product
WHERE
product.category = "Packaging"
ORDER BY
product.product
Query Results
CATEGORY PRODUCT
======== =======
Packaging Box - Large
Packaging Box - Medium
Packaging Box - Small
Packaging Clasp Letter
Packaging Envelope #10
Packaging Envelope Bubble

Figure 1-7 Browse queries and their results

Like a query against a fact table, a browse query is not limited to studying information at the level of detail stored in the database. Instead, queries may browse for distinct combinations of attribute values. Figure 1-7 shows some queries that browse the product dimension.

The first browse in Figure 1-7 simply fetches a list of product categories. The second browse seeks the list of products within a specific category. Browse queries may return many attributes from within a dimension; some tools support browsing in a grid-like interface.

The browse query is important in several respects. It may serve as the basis for the selection of query predicates, or filters, for a query that involves a fact table. A browse query may also allow users to explore the relationship between dimension values. This kind of browsing may be considered when making decisions about how to group attributes into dimensions, as discussed in Chapter 6.

Guiding Principles

The remainder of this book covers a wealth of dimensional design techniques which you can use to describe any business process. Sometimes it will be useful to understand the reason some of these techniques have been developed. Other times, it may be necessary for you to choose from some design options. Two simple guiding principles drive these decisions: accuracy and performance.

It may seem obvious, but it is important to consider the *accuracy* of any given design. The questions that will be asked of an operational system can be determined in advance, and remain consistent over time, but analytic questions always lead to new questions. They will change over time, sometimes dramatically so. Designers must pay close attention to how a dimensional schema represents facts. Is it possible that they will be aggregated in ways that do not make sense? Is there a design alternative that can prevent such a situation?

Of equal importance is the *performance* of the schema. An analytic design may offer little value over an operational design if it cannot produce timely results. Dimensional designs are very good at providing a rapid response to a wide range of unanticipated questions. There will be times, however, when a basic design may not be able to serve important business needs efficiently. The performance profile of a solution may drive the decision to provide information in more than one format, as will be seen throughout this book.

Summary

Dimensional modeling is a design approach optimized for analytic systems. A dimensional model captures how a process is measured. Data elements that represent measurements are called facts. Data elements that provide context for measurements are called dimensions. These elements are grouped into dimension tables and fact tables. Implemented in a relational database, the design is called a star schema.

The dimension tables in a star schema employ surrogate keys, enabling the analytic system to respond to changes in operational data in its own way. The granular facts in a star schema can be queried at various levels of detail, aggregated according to desired dimensional context. Exploring the details within a dimension is referred to as browsing.

This chapter has only begun to introduce the fundamentals of dimensional design. After a discussion of architectures in Chapter 2, Chapter 3 will return to the basics of dimensional design.

Further Reading

For more information on the design of operational systems, there is no finer reference than Chris Date's *An Introduction to Database Systems, Eighth Edition* (Addison Wesley, 2003). This book fully explains the principles of normalization used to support transaction processing in a relational database management system.

A wealth of information is available on the differences between operational and analytic systems. Two good places to start are Chapter 1 of Ralph Kimball and Margy Ross's *The Data Warehouse Toolkit, Second Edition* (Wiley, 2002) and Inmon, Imhoff, and Sousa's discussion in *The Corporate Information Factory, Second Edition* (Wiley, 2000).

For more information on separating facts from dimensions, you can consult any book on dimensional design. *Data Warehouse Design Solutions* (Adamson and Venerable; Wiley, 1995) and *Mastering Data Warehouse Aggregates* (Adamson; Wiley, 2006) both cover the topic in their opening chapters, as does Kimball and Ross's *The Data Warehouse Toolkit*. These books also cover the prototypical query pattern for a star schema; the browse query is discussed in *The Data Warehouse Toolkit*.

CHAPTER

2 Data Warehouse Architectures

There is a wide range of opinion regarding the optimal data warehouse architecture. Opinions are sometimes so strongly held that a colleague of mine often refers to a "religious war" in data warehousing. That may overstate things, but everyone will agree to this: data warehouse architectures vary widely.

One of the ways in which data warehouse architectures diverge is in their use of dimensional design. Some architectures place a heavier emphasis on the star schema, while others use it in a limited capacity. The principles of dimensional design are the same, wherever they are put to use. This book is concerned with these principles.

With a diversity of architectures, however, comes confusion. The same terms are used to describe different things. Different terms are used to describe the same thing. Characteristics of one approach are misinterpreted to apply in other situations. In order to understand dimensional design, it is important to clear up this confusion. To do so requires a brief look at data warehouse architecture.

This chapter groups data warehouse architecture into three categories. The first two are often called *enterprise data warehouse* architectures, and are closely associated with W. H. Inmon and Ralph Kimball, respectively. The third does not have a well-known figurehead but is equally common.

While these architectures differ in fundamental ways, there is a place for the star schema in each of them. By understanding these approaches, we can avoid misunderstandings in terminology and develop a clear understanding of the capability of the star schema.

If you are looking for an answer to the question, "What is the best data warehouse architecture?" you will not find it here. There is no discussion of pros and cons. Nor will you find comprehensive specifications for each architecture.

Instead, the objectives for this chapter are simple:

1. To understand each approach at a high level
2. To understand the place of the star schema in each
3. To eliminate some common misconceptions

If you have a data warehouse or analytic application in production, don't expect a direct match with one of these archetypes. Each real-world implementation is different. Yours may contain elements from one or more of these architectures. You should make an effort to understand the alternatives, however. This will give you a better grasp of what is and what is not true about dimensional design.

Inmon's Corporate Information Factory

In May of 2000, a well-known thought leader in data warehousing had this to say about dimensional design:

> *...if I had to design a data mart tomorrow, I would not consider using any other approach.*

No, it wasn't Ralph Kimball. Those words were written by W.H. Inmon, in an article that appeared in *DM Review* magazine. Although it is not a surprise to people who follow Inmon's approach to data warehousing, these words never cease to astound adherents of other approaches. I am not sure how we reached this state of affairs, although I suspect that the trade press's desire to contrast Inmon with Kimball is partly to blame. So I will begin by shining some light on Inmon's approach.

Bill Inmon is a prolific writer and contributor to the data warehousing community. Through hundreds of articles and dozens of books, he has developed and shared an approach to data warehousing that he calls the *Corporate Information Factory*. This hub-and-spoke architecture is common, even in IT shops that do not attribute their architecture to Inmon.

A highly simplified depiction of the Corporate Information Factory appears in Figure 2-1. Some liberties have been taken, removing numerous components that are not relevant to this discussion and using some generic terminology. For the purpose of understanding the underlying data architecture, and the place of the star schema in it, this diagram is true to Inmon's approach.

To understand this architecture, start by looking at the left side of the diagram. There, you will find the operational systems, or transaction systems, that support the business. The data stores associated with these systems may take a number of different forms, including hierarchical data, relational data, and even simple spreadsheets. For the sake of simplicity, only four operational systems are depicted. In the real world, any organization's portfolio of operational systems is sure to be significantly larger.

These systems feed a process labeled ETL for "extract, transform, load." This process consolidates information from the various operational systems, integrates it, and loads it into a single repository called the *enterprise data warehouse*. This processing step is nontrivial. It may require accessing information in a variety of different formats, resolving differing representations of similar things, and significant restructuring of data. Some organizations refer to this process as data integration. It may be a batch process that runs periodically or a transaction-based process that occurs in near real time. The final result is the same: the enterprise data warehouse.

The enterprise data warehouse is the hub of the corporate information factory. It is an *integrated repository* of *atomic data*. *Integrated* from the various operational systems, it contains a definitive and consistent representation of business activities in a single place. *Atomic* in nature, the data in this repository is captured at the lowest level of detail possible.

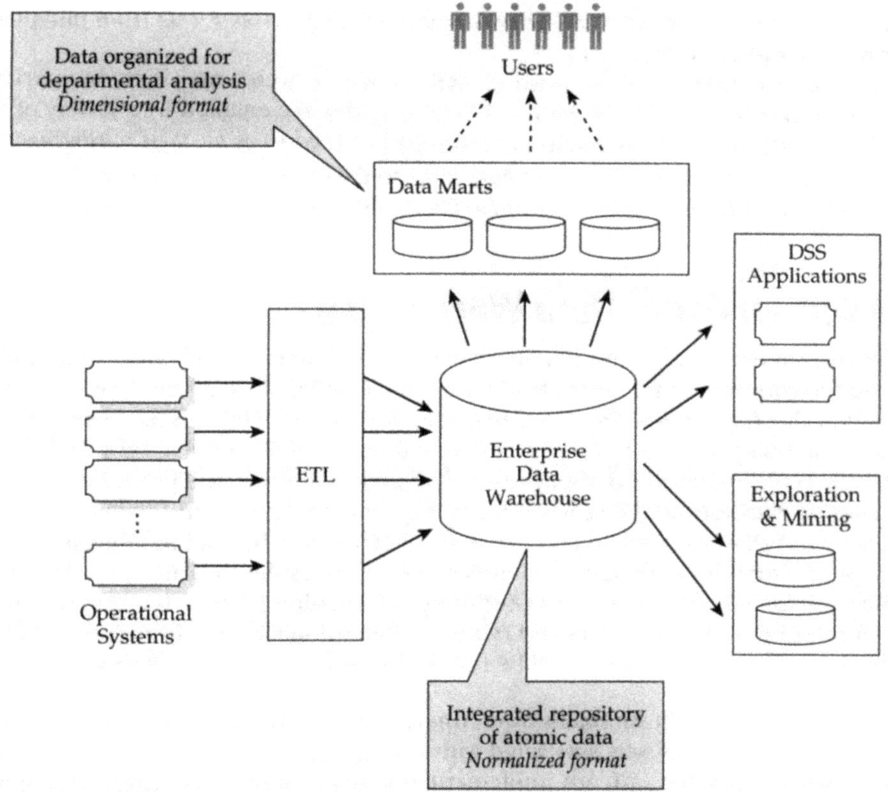

Figure 2-1 A simplified view of W.H. Inmon's architecture: the Corporate Information Factory

In the Corporate Information Factory architecture, the enterprise data warehouse is not intended to be queried directly by analytic applications, business intelligence tools, or the like. Instead, its purpose is to feed additional data stores dedicated to a variety of analytic systems. The enterprise data warehouse is usually stored in a relational database management system, and Inmon advocates the use of third normal form database design.

Surrounding the enterprise data warehouse are numerous other components. Of interest here are the data marts, which appear along the top of the diagram. These are databases that support a departmental view of information. With a subject area focus, each data mart takes information from the enterprise data warehouse and readies it for analysis. As the earlier quotation suggests, Inmon advocates the use of dimensional design for these data marts. The data marts may aggregate data from the atomic representation in the enterprise data warehouse.

Note that Inmon reserves the term ETL for the movement of data from the operational systems into the enterprise data warehouse. He describes the movement of information from the enterprise data warehouse into data marts as "data delivery." This book will use the term ETL more generically, to describe any process that extracts data from one place and stores it somewhere else.

The data marts serve as the focus for analytic activities, which may include queries, reports, and a number of other activities. These activities are enabled by a variety of different tools, including some that are commonly referred to as *business intelligence tools* and *reporting tools.* This book will collectively refer to these tools as *business intelligence tools.* Note, though, that Inmon reserves this term for a particular application in the Corporate Information Factory.

Kimball's Dimensional Data Warehouse

Ralph Kimball has made numerous important contributions to the world of data warehousing, and his top two contributions both relate to dimensional design. First, in the 1990s, he was largely responsible for popularizing star schema design. Through his writings, Kimball synthesized and systematized a series of techniques that had been in use as early as the 1960s. He explained how dimensional design provided an understandable and powerful way to develop analytic databases, and he gave us the terminology that is used throughout this book.

Second, Kimball developed an enterprise architecture for the data warehouse, built on the concept of dimensional design. Sometimes referred to as the "bus architecture," it shares many characteristics of Inmon's Corporate Information Factory. It allows for an integrated repository of atomic data and relies on dimensional design to support analytics. In this book, Kimball's architecture will be referred to as the *dimensional data warehouse* architecture.

To those unfamiliar with Kimball's work, this second contribution often comes as a surprise. Because he is so closely associated with the star schema, he is often assigned blame for shortcomings associated with any implementation that utilizes a star, regardless of its architecture. Other times, the star schema itself is assigned blame. In order to sort things out, it is necessary to take a brief look at Kimball's architecture, which is depicted in Figure 2-2. Again, the diagram is somewhat simplified. In this case, it has been laid out to highlight similarities to Inmon's architecture.

Though the diagram in Figure 2-2 appears quite different from that in Figure 2-1, the two architectures actually share many characteristics in common. Like the Corporate Information Factory, this architecture begins by assuming a separation of the operational and analytic systems. As before, operational systems appear on the far left of the diagram. Again, these may incorporate data stores that are relational and nonrelational, and are likely to be numerous.

Moving to the right, an ETL process consolidates information from the various operational systems, integrates it, and loads it into a single repository. If that sounds familiar, it should. The Corporate Information Factory has an analogous process.

The dimensional data warehouse in the center of Figure 2-2 is the end result of the ETL process. It is an integrated repository for atomic data. Again, that should sound familiar. The same definition was given for Inmon's enterprise data warehouse. It contains a single view of business activities, as drawn from throughout the enterprise. It stores that information in a highly granular, or atomic, format.

The dimensional data warehouse differs from the enterprise data warehouse in two important ways. First, it is designed according to the principles of dimensional modeling. It consists of a series of star schemas or cubes, which capture information at the lowest level of

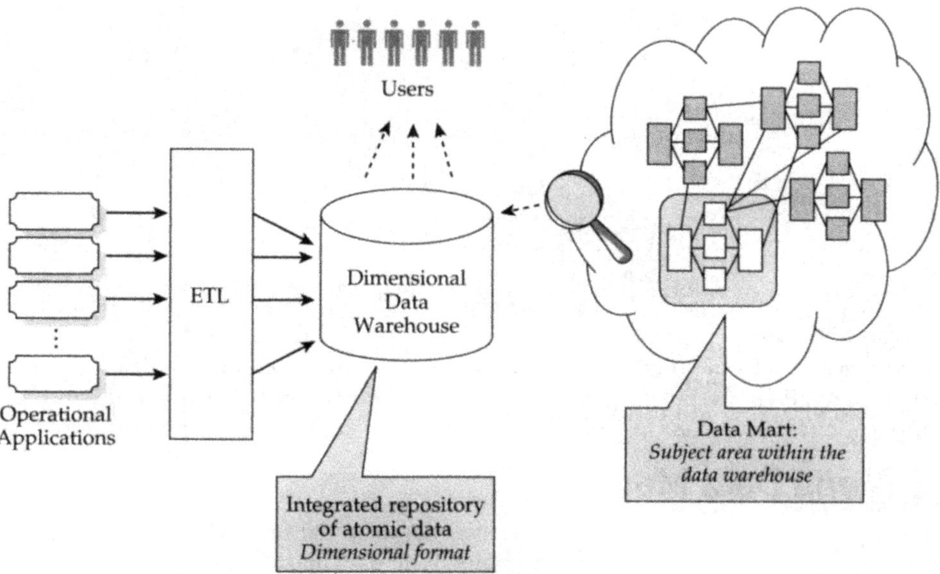

Figure 2-2 Ralph Kimball's data warehouse architecture: the dimensional data warehouse

detail possible. This contrasts with the Inmon approach, where the enterprise data warehouse is designed using the principles of ER modeling.

Second, the dimensional data warehouse may be accessed directly by analytic systems. Although it is not required, this is explicitly permitted by the architecture. The concept of a data mart becomes a logical distinction; the data mart is a subject area within the data warehouse. In Figure 2-2, this is represented by the box that highlights a subset of the tables in the dimensional data warehouse.

These two key differences are often tempered by accepted variations in the architecture. The construction of a dimensional design from a variety of operational data sources can be challenging, and ETL developers often find it useful to design a multi-step process. Sometimes, a set of tables in third normal form is an intermediate step in this process. Kimball considers this an acceptable feature of a dimensional data warehouse, provided that these staging tables are not accessed directly by any processes other than the ETL process. When such a set of tables is in place, the dimensional data warehouse comes to resemble the Corporate Information Factory more closely. Both contain a normalized repository of data not accessed by applications, and dimensional representations that are accessed by applications.

In another accepted variation in the architecture, architects choose to insulate the dimensional data warehouse from direct access by analytic applications. In such cases, new data marts may be constructed by extracting data from the dimensional data warehouse. These data marts may aggregate the dimensional data, or even reorganize it into new dimensional structures. Again, this variation increases the resemblance to the Corporate Information Factory, where data marts are seen as separate entities from the integrated repository of atomic data.

The dimensional data warehouse is not necessarily centralized in a single database, though that may be implied by Figure 2-2. In fact, the dimensional data warehouse may be a single logical repository, distributed among numerous physical databases. The concept of conformance is used to ensure enterprise capability, as discussed in Chapter 5, "Conformed Dimensions." This concept governs the consistent use of key enterprise dimensions across subject areas, ensuring that this information can be brought together when distributed across physical databases, even from different vendors. As you will learn in Chapter 5, this concept does not benefit the Kimball architecture exclusively. In the case of the dimensional data warehouse, it is a central principle.

As previously mentioned, this book will use the term dimensional data warehouse to refer to this architecture. The term ETL will be used in the broad sense, referring to any activity that moves data from one database to another. Likewise, tools and applications that access analytic data, including packaged business intelligence tools, reporting tools, and analytic applications, will be lumped together under the term business intelligence tools.

Stand-Alone Data Marts

The final architecture to be discussed in this chapter is the stand-alone data mart. Unlike the architectures described previously, stand-alone data marts are not closely associated with any well-known advocate. There is good reason for this. While stand-alone data marts may achieve rapid and inexpensive results in the short term, they can give rise to long-term costs and inefficiencies. These shortcomings are not always reason enough to eschew the stand-alone data mart, but they have contributed to confusion over the capabilities of the star schema.

The stand-alone data mart is an analytic data store that has not been designed in an enterprise context. It is focused exclusively on a subject area. One or more operational systems feed a database called a data mart. The data mart may employ dimensional design, an entity-relationship model, or some other form of design. Analytic tools or applications query it directly, bringing information to end users. This simple architecture is illustrated in Figure 2-3.

Development of a stand-alone data mart is often the most expedient path to visible results. Because it does not require cross-functional analysis, the data mart can be put into production quickly. No time must be spent constructing a consolidated view of product or customer, for example. No time must be spent comparing data from the sales system with

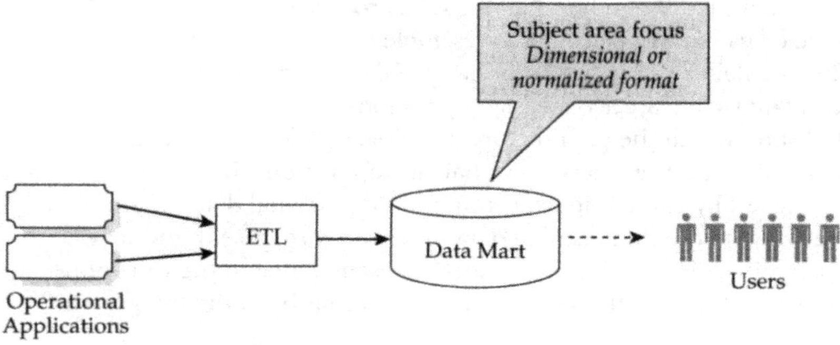

Figure 2-3 A stand-alone data mart

what is tracked in the accounting system. Instead, the implementation takes a direct route from subject area requirements to implementation.

Because results are rapid and less expensive, stand-alone data marts find their way into many organizations. They are not always built from scratch. A stand-alone data mart may become part of the application portfolio when purchased as a packaged application, which provides a prebuilt solution in a subject area. Packaged data marts may also be available as add-ons to packaged operational applications. Prebuilt solutions like these can further increase the savings in time and cost.

Even in organizations committed to an enterprise data warehouse architecture, stand-alone data marts can be found. Sometimes, they are present as legacy systems, in place before the commitment to the enterprise architecture. In other cases, they may be built within user organizations, entirely outside the domain of the IT department. Mergers and acquisitions can bring with them new analytic data stores that have not been integrated into the preexisting architecture.

For all these reasons, the stand-alone data mart is a reality for many businesses and organizations. Yet it is almost universally maligned. While often considered a short-term success, the stand-alone data mart frequently becomes a long-term headache. To understand why, it helps to look at what happens when more than one subject area is supported via stand-alone data marts. Figure 2-4 depicts the proliferation of stand-alone data marts across multiple subject areas.

While a single stand-alone data mart may appear to be the most efficient path to results, the presence of multiple data marts exposes inefficiencies. In Figure 2-4, multiple ETL processes are loading data from the same source systems. The data marts themselves may be based on different technologies, and the user audiences may be relying on separate query and reporting infrastructures. These characteristics often earn stand-alone data marts the label "stovepipe," meant to connote a lack of compatibility. They compound the cost of the total solution, requiring the maintenance of redundant technologies, processes, and skill sets.

Even when these technical inefficiencies are minimized, a more serious deficiency may be lurking in the data itself. If each data mart is built to address a narrow set of needs, what happens when these needs expand? Lacking a repository for granular data, a data mart may fail to answer a future question that requires more detail than originally anticipated. Similarly, consider what happens when someone wants to compare information from two

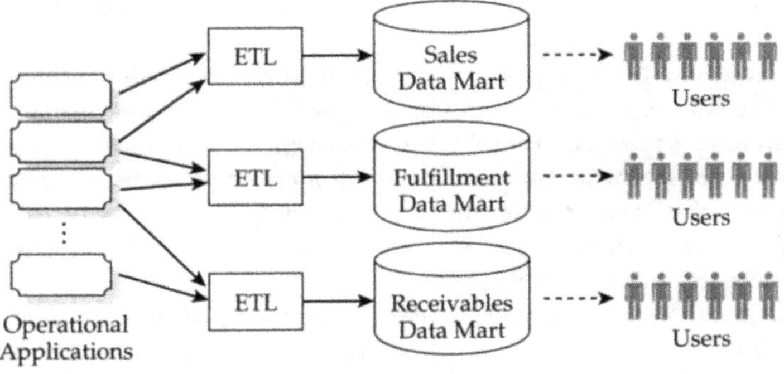

Figure 2-4 Multiple stand-alone data marts

or more data marts. If these subject areas do not share consistent definitions of common entities (such as products, departments, or customers), then it may be impossible to compare the information. Worst of all, redundant load processes may apply different rules to source data, leading to systems that provide contradictory results.

These issues cause stand-alone data marts to become islands of information. Developed to satisfy a narrow set of needs, they fail to support cross-functional analysis. Extensive rework may be required to adapt them to a deeper or wider set of demands. Short-term savings give way to long-term costs.

These deficiencies should not necessarily preclude the implementation of a stand-alone data mart. As long as there is a shared understanding of the potential future cost, a subject area focus may make sense. It keeps costs low and minimizes activities that precede the delivery of some initial capability. Too often, though, the easy route is taken without buy-in from all parts of the business.

Stand-alone data marts often employ dimensional design. This is so common, in fact, that the shortcomings of stand-alone data marts are sometimes blamed on the star schema. It has become a common misconception that the star schema is for aggregated data, or that the use of the star schema leads to stovepipes.

By now it should be clear that these failures are not the result of the use of dimensional design. Stand-alone data marts may contain aggregated data, and they are likely to exhibit incompatibilities with one another, but this is not a failure of the star schema. Rather, it is a shortcoming of the narrow scope of the stand-alone data mart.

Architecture and Dimensional Design

All of these architectures are successfully put to use by businesses and organizations throughout the world. Your data warehouse architecture may closely match one of these paradigms, or you may find it incorporates elements of each. A high-level comparison of these approaches allows you to cut through the noise and confusion that surround the star schema. The three architectural paradigms discussed in this chapter are summarized in Figure 2-5.

Contrasting the Approaches

Inmon's Corporate Information Factory and Kimball's dimensional data warehouse have an *enterprise focus.* They aim to support analytic needs across a business or organization. This approach permits them to address the requirements within a subject area, as well as questions that span subject areas.

An enterprise focus requires a project approach that deals with data requirements from multiple organizations. The data warehouse cannot be designed by listening to one set of needs at a time. The team must explore and resolve disparate representations of common data elements with significance that varies by audience. Customers or products, for example, may be relevant in manufacturing, sales, marketing, and accounting. There may be numerous systems that have diverging views of these same data elements. The data warehouse design must accommodate all these views in a unified manner.

The stand-alone data mart, in contrast, lacks an enterprise focus. Its development considers requirements from one group or department. Because of this narrow focus, its development is not hampered by the need to explore the use of common data elements across the business; it can focus on the specific systems in a particular subject area.

Architecture	Advocate	Also Known As	Description	Role of Dimensional Design
Corporate Information Factory	Bill Inmon	• Atomic data warehouse • Enterprise data warehouse	• *Enterprise data warehouse* component is an integrated repository of atomic data • It is *not* accessed directly • *Data marts* reorganize data for departmental use/analysis	Dimensional design used for data marts only
Dimensional Data Warehouse	Ralph Kimball	• Enterprise data warehouse • Bus architecture • Architected data marts • Virtual data marts	• *Dimensional data warehouse* is an integrated repository of atomic data • It may be accessed directly • Subject areas within the dimensional data warehouse sometimes called *data marts* • Data marts not required to be separate databases	All data is organized dimensionally
Stand-Alone Data Marts	No takers, yet common	• Data mart • Silo • Stovepipe • Island	• Subject area implementation without an enterprise context	May employ dimensional design

Figure 2-5 Three data warehouse architectures

As a result of their common scope, the two enterprise architectures share an architectural characteristic in common: *each has a single integrated repository of atomic data.* In the Corporate Information Factory, this repository is called the enterprise data warehouse. In the dimensional data warehouse, this repository is called...the dimensional data warehouse. The *integrated nature* of the central repository is consistent with an enterprise focus. It brings together various vantage points on common entities, such as customer or product. Likewise, its atomic focus addresses enterprise objectives. Data is not collected at the level of detail required by a particular group or subject area. Instead, it is collected at the lowest level of detail available, allowing it to satisfy any analytic requirement.

Stand-alone data marts, in contrast, are not necessarily integrated or atomic. Focused on a subject area, each stand-alone data mart addresses the specific needs of a particular group. It does not aim to integrate varying views of key entities such as customer, product, or department. Because it is crafted to meet the needs of one particular point of view, the stand-alone data mart may summarize operational data.

The components of each architecture are contrasted in Figure 2-6. For each architecture in the diagram, the first three columns describe enterprise characteristics. Lacking an enterprise focus, the stand-alone data mart does not feature an integrated repository. While the two enterprise architectures both incorporate an integrated repository of atomic data, they differ in how it is designed and used. Kimball advocates the use of dimensional design, Inmon does not. This is represented in the second column of Figure 2-6. The next column shows how this repository is used. Kimball allows the repository to be queried directly, Inmon does not.

Moving from the enterprise implications of each architecture to each architecture's treatment of the subject area, again there are similarities and differences. All three architectures feature the concept of a data mart, which describes the support of a particular

	Enterprise Level			Subject Area Level		
	Integrated Repository of Atomic Data	Format	Direct Access	Data Marts	Format	Direct Access
Corporate Information Factory	✓	3NF	No	Physical	Dimensional*	Yes
Dimensional Data Warehouse	✓	Dimensional	Yes*	Logical*	Dimensional	Yes
Stand-Alone Data Marts	✕	*n/a*	*n/a*	Physical	Dimensional*	Yes

* Optional

Figure 2-6 Characteristics of each architecture

department or business process. Their profiles and capabilities differ significantly. These are summarized under the subject area heading in Figure 2-6.

For Inmon, the data mart is a separate physical set of tables built for departmental use. It may aggregate detailed data and be built to suit the specific viewpoint of a department or group. In these respects, it bears some similarities to the stand-alone data mart; however, the data mart in a Corporate Information Factory draws its information from the enterprise repository. Its content is, therefore, consistent with an enterprise view of information. The same cannot be guaranteed for the stand-alone data mart.

For Kimball, the data mart is not required to be a separate physical data store. Instead, it can be a logical construct—a subset of the warehouse tables. Optionally, separate data mart tables may be built. When this is done, they will draw from the integrated repository. The data marts are consistent with an enterprise view of information, either because they embody that view or because they draw from it.

The Common Element

Although they have significant differences, each of these architectures has a place for dimensional design. Kimball's dimensional data warehouse emphasizes it most strongly, relying on dimensional data structures to serve both enterprise and departmental needs. Inmon relies on the dimensional model to provide a departmental solution in the context of an enterprise solution. The stand-alone data mart uses dimensional design without any enterprise context.

Regardless of how dimensional design is used, the techniques are the same. The concepts described in this book apply in each of these architectures. You can use them to build a full-blown dimensional data warehouse, in keeping with Ralph Kimball's approach. You can use them to design data marts that serve as departmental spokes surrounding a central data warehouse, as in Bill Inmon's architecture, or you can put them to use in support of a single subject area, as a stand-alone data mart.

This is not to say that architecture does not influence dimensional design. While the techniques are universal, some best practices will vary based on architectural context. This will be most evident in Chapter 3, where you will learn that in a dimensional data warehouse, fact table grain must be set at the lowest possible level of detail. This guideline can benefit the other architectures as well but is not required.

Similarly, Chapter 5 will highlight the strategic emphasis on dimensional conformance in a dimensional data warehouse. Conformance is the central feature in this architecture, enabling the compatibility of information across subject areas. Conformance benefits the other architectures as well but is not the key to providing an integrated view of enterprise data.

Having looked at the different ways dimensional design is used, it should now be clear that the following common misconceptions are false:

- Inmon is anti–star schema.
- Kimball does not think an enterprise focus is necessary.
- Data marts are islands of information.
- Dimensional design is for aggregated data.
- Star schemas are stovepipes.

Some of these misconceptions result from superficial or sensationalized treatment of Inmon vs. Kimball. Others stem from the failure to separate dimensional design, or the concept of a data mart, from a particular approach.

Terms Used in This Book

These three architectures use the same terms to describe different things. While this book does not make any assumptions about your architecture, it is not possible to avoid using terms like "data warehouse" or "data mart." When you encounter these terms in this book, here is what they mean:

Data warehouse will describe any solution that contains an analytic database, including stand-alone data marts. This term will *not* be meant to imply a central or integrated repository.

Enterprise data warehouse will be used to refer to the central repository of the Corporate Information Factory. Use of this term is not meant to imply that other data warehouse architectures lack an enterprise focus.

Data mart will refer to a subject area in *any* architecture. Use of this term is not meant to imply departmental focus or the lack of an enterprise context.

ETL will refer to any activity that moves information between structured data stores. The use of this term in the generic sense is not intended as a slight to the Corporate Information Factory, where it has a more specific definition.

Source system will refer to the computer system(s) from which a star schema gets its data. In the case of a data mart in a Corporate Information Factory, the source system is the enterprise data warehouse. In the case of a star schema in a dimensional data warehouse or stand-alone data mart, the source system is an operational system.

Business Intelligence will be used to describe any software product used to create reports and other information products for end users. It is not meant to imply a separate analytic data store, nor the use of any particular form of packaged software.

Using these generic definitions, it will be possible to address dimensional design techniques in a manner befitting any data warehouse architecture, including yours.

Summary

Dimensional design figures into data warehouse architectures in very different ways. Inmon's Corporate Information Factory consolidates information from throughout the enterprise into a central repository called an enterprise data warehouse. It is characterized by a third normal form design, and it is not queried directly by warehouse applications. Outward from this hub radiate data marts, each tailored to the needs and viewpoint of a particular business group. These data marts sport a dimensional design and are queried by data warehouse applications.

Kimball's dimensional data warehouse also has an enterprise focus. It brings together data from throughout the enterprise into a central repository called the dimensional data warehouse. This repository is characterized by a dimensional design and may be queried directly. A data mart is a logical construct, or subset of the tables. Optionally, separate dimensional structures may be built to support departmental needs.

The stand-alone data mart addresses the needs within a subject area, without an enterprise context. It may leverage dimensional design, or it may follow other techniques. The limitations of this approach may be accepted by an organization in a trade-off for rapid access to results and reduced costs. However, they should not be interpreted as indicating shortcomings of data marts or dimensional design.

Each of these architectures has a place for the star schema. Generalized definitions for key terms like "data warehouse" and "data mart" allow this book to deal with dimensional design in a manner that is applicable to all architectures.

Further Reading

The quotation from Bill Inmon comes from his article "The Problem with Dimensional Modeling," *DM Review*, May 2000.

Much has been written on Inmon's Corporate Information Factory architecture. The most comprehensive coverage is provided in the book *The Corporate Information Factory, Second Edition* by W. H. Inmon, Claudia Imhoff, and Ryan Sousa (Wiley, 2000).

Ralph Kimball's dimensional data warehouse architecture is described in Chapter 1 of *The Data Warehouse Toolkit, Second Edition*, by Ralph Kimball and Margy Ross (Wiley, 2002). It also discusses some of the myths about star schema covered in this chapter, as well as others. Although Kimball does not dedicate an entire book to his architecture, the basic philosophy permeates *The Toolkit.* Additional information can be found in *The Data Warehouse Lifecycle Toolkit, Second Edition*, by Ralph Kimball, Margy Ross, Warren Thornthwaite, Joy Mundy, and Bob Becker (Wiley, 2008).

Because it is not a formal architecture, there is no book to describe the stand-alone data mart. Any discussion of implementation in a single subject area can be considered data-mart-centric. Individual subject areas from *The Data Warehouse Toolkit*, implemented in the absence of an enterprise context, would fit the bill. Similarly, *Data Warehouse Design Solutions* by Chris Adamson and Mike Venerable (Wiley, 1998) provides dimensional designs for various warehouse subject areas.

CHAPTER 3

Stars and Cubes

Now that you have the basic concepts of measurement under your belt and have reviewed the various ways dimensional design can be employed, you are ready to learn the fundamentals of dimensional design. This chapter covers basics in four categories: dimension table features, fact table features, slowly changing dimensions, and cubes.

As you learned in Chapter 1, "Analytic Databases and Dimensional Design," surrogate keys are employed to identify rows in dimension tables. This chapter explores the reasons for this practice. You have also learned that, as the providers of measurement context, dimension tables play an important role in the star schema. This chapter provides techniques to enrich the assortment of dimensions available and examines why you should not shy away from redundancy.

Next, this chapter examines the fact table. As a representation of a business process, it is crucial that all relevant measurements be represented, even where some appear redundant. Many important business indicators, however, don't take kindly to being aggregated. This chapter will look at how to handle these nonadditive facts. You will also learn how to set the grain of a fact table, why we call it sparse, and when to use the amusingly named degenerate dimensions.

The power of data warehousing stems in part from its ability to provide access to historic data. The data warehouse must be able to respond to changes to information in a way that does not disrupt the ability to study history. Dimensional designs deal with this issue through a series of techniques collectively known as "slowly changing dimensions." This chapter will explore the three primary ways to handle change and when it is appropriate to use each.

Last, this chapter describes the implementation of a dimensional design in a multidimensional database, where it is known as a cube. Stars and cubes will be contrasted, and you will learn the different ways the cube can be incorporated into a dimensional architecture.

Dimension Table Features

A well-developed set of dimension tables provides powerful and diverse analytic capabilities. As you saw in Chapter 1, the dimensions provide contextual information, without which reports would be meaningless. Successful dimension design hinges on the proper use of keys, the development of a richly detailed set of dimension columns, and a rejection of the urge to save space.

Surrogate Keys and Natural Keys

In a star schema, each dimension table is assigned a surrogate key. As discussed in Chapter 1, this key is not a carryover from an operational system. It is created especially for the data warehouse or data mart. Surrogate keys are usually integers, generated and managed as part of the extract, transform, load (ETL) process that loads the star schema. The key values have no intrinsic meaning and are not of interest to users of the data warehouse. In each row of the dimension table, the surrogate has a unique value. In the star schema in Figure 3-1, surrogate keys for each dimension table are labeled "SK." In this book, surrogate keys will easily be identified by the suffix "_key" in their column name.

Separate and distinct from surrogate keys, one or more natural keys will also be present in most dimension tables. The natural keys are identifiers carried over from source systems. They may not uniquely identify a row in the data warehouse, but they do identify a corresponding entity in the source system. In Figure 3-1, natural key columns are designated "NK."

Unlike surrogate key values, the values in natural key columns may have meaning to users of the data warehouse. Even when they do not carry significant meaning, their presence is necessary for the ETL routines that load fact tables, as discussed in Chapter 17, "Design and ETL."

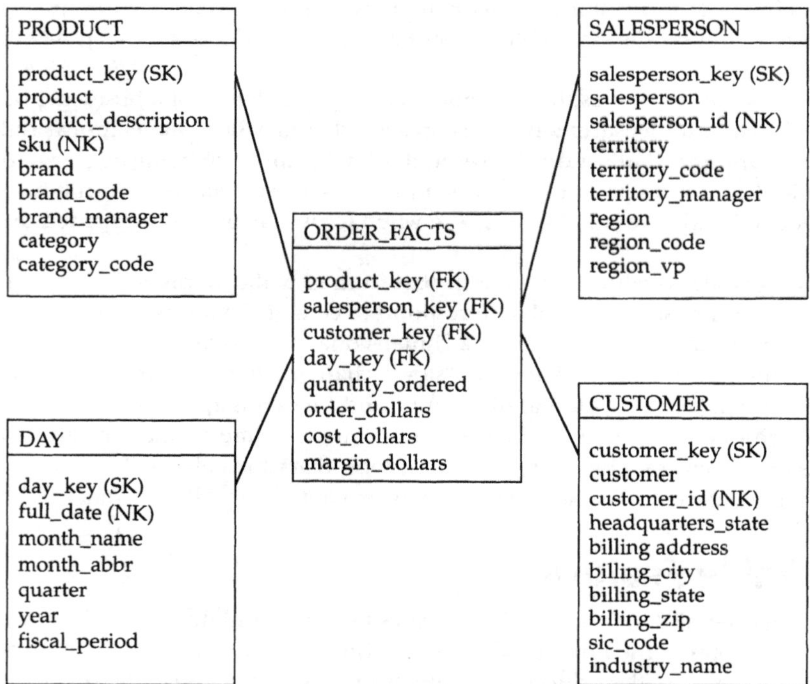

Figure 3-1 Surrogate keys (SKs) and natural keys (NKs)

Sometimes, the natural key for a dimension table consists of more than one column. This occurs when the source system uses a multi-part key to identify the entity. For example, a purchasing contract may be identified by a type code and sequence number. When more than one system can be the source for a dimension, the natural key may be composed of the identifier from the source system and an additional identifier that indicates which source it came from. For example, a bank may have more than one system for deposit accounts after acquiring another bank. The natural key for a customer dimension might, therefore, consist of an identifier used in a source system, in conjunction with a column that indicates the system from which the identifier came.

The use of surrogate keys as unique identifiers allows the data warehouse to respond to changes in source data in whatever manner best fits analytic requirements. Because the dimension table does not rely on the natural key to identify unique rows, it can maintain history even if the source system does not. For example, an order entry system might contain a record for customer_id 404777, which includes the customer's address. If the system overwrites the address when a customer moves, it is not tracking history. Were the customer dimension table to use the same customer_id to identify unique rows, it would be able to store only one row for customer_id 404777. It would be unable to maintain the history of the address. By using a surrogate key, it becomes possible to maintain two versions of customer_id 404777. This technique is known as a type 2 slow change, and will be fully discussed later in this chapter.

TIP Assign each dimension table a surrogate key. This single column will be used to uniquely identify each row in the table.

A possible alternative to the use of a surrogate key is to supplement the natural key with a sequence number. For example, the primary key of the customer dimension table might consist of the customer_id and a version_number column that contains a sequence number. Like the use of surrogate keys, this technique permits the data warehouse to track history independently of the source system, allowing the table to store multiple versions of a customer. This approach provides no value in simplifying the schema design or load process, however, which must still identify and maintain version history. More importantly, this technique requires multi-part foreign keys to be maintained in the fact table. If customers are identified by customer_id and sequence_no, this pair of columns must be present in order_facts as well. This multi-column foreign key complicates the join process, makes SQL more difficult to read, and in some cases may befuddle efforts to optimize the RDBMS for star join query execution.

Another theoretical alternative to the use of a surrogate key is to supplement a natural key with time stamps. While time stamps may be useful, a multi-part foreign key would still be required in fact tables, potentially leading to the same difficulties as the sequence number. In addition, a designer may be tempted to eliminate multi-column joins by storing only the natural key in the fact table; however, this severely complicates queries and risks error. For example, assume that customer_id 404777 has moved, and therefore has two rows in the dimension table. Each fact table row contains only the natural key 404777. To identify which version of the customer corresponds to each fact table row, it is necessary to compare order date with the time stamps in the dimension table. This process can be onerous, particularly if one is constructing a report that aggregates a large number of orders. It also becomes difficult for database administrators to tune the system, preventing them, for example, from declaring a foreign key in the fact table and potentially leading to poor query optimization. Worse, if the date qualification is omitted, facts associated with customer_id 404777 will be double-counted.

It is not common practice to use version numbers or time stamps as part of a unique identifier. Surrogate keys simplify the schema design and allow for clean, single-column joins. Time stamps are frequently included in dimension tables, but not as part of the unique identifier. In Chapter 8, "More Slow Change Techniques," you will see how time stamps can be used to enable point-in-time analysis of dimension data, to sequence a version history of dimension values, and to streamline the ETL process.

Rich Set of Dimensions

Dimensions provide context for facts. Without context, facts are impossible to interpret. For example, I might tell you, "Order dollars are $40,000." This statement is of no use to you. It presents a fact (order dollars) without any explanation. Is this orders for one product or all products? Is it one day's worth of orders or one year's? To understand what "$40,000" means, you need more information. "Order dollars were $40,000 for electronic products in January 2009." By adding dimensional context—a product category, a month, and a year—the fact has been made useful.

As you saw in Chapter 1, dimensions and their values add meaning in many ways:

- They are used to filter queries or reports.
- They are used to control the scope of aggregation for facts.
- They are used to order or sort information.
- They accompany facts to provide context on reports.
- They are used to define master–detail organization, grouping, subtotaling, and summarization.

Put to these uses, dimensions unlock the value of facts. Dimensions can be added to queries in different combinations to answer a wide variety of questions. The larger the set of dimension attributes, the more ways that facts can be analyzed.

TIP Provide a rich and comprehensive set of dimension attributes. Each new attribute dramatically increases the number of analytic possibilities.

Dimension tables with a large number of attributes maximize analytic value. They can be thought of as *wide*. If you listed their contents, each row would be quite long. In addition to storing common attributes, dimension tables store commonly used combinations of attributes. Codes may be supplemented with corresponding description values. Flags are translated from Boolean values into descriptive text, and multi-part fields are both preserved and broken down into constituent pieces. It is also important not to overlook numeric attributes that can serve as dimensions.

Common Combinations

In operational systems, it is common practice to break data elements down to constituent parts whenever possible. From these components, it is possible to construct any combinations that may be needed. For example, customer name may be broken down and stored as a first name, middle initial, and last name. These attributes can be combined to produce a full name, if needed.

These components have analytic value and, of course, will be included in a dimensional design. Unlike the operational schema, however, the dimensional schema should also include dimensions that represent common combinations of these elements. For example, if a large number of reports group information by full name, or in a last-name-first format, then these common usages should also appear as discrete dimension columns. This principle can be seen at work in Figure 3-2.

The customer dimension in Figure 3-2 shows how the three components of a customer name, such as John P. Smith, may be used to construct five attributes in the customer dimension table. Because each of these attributes is made available in the dimensional

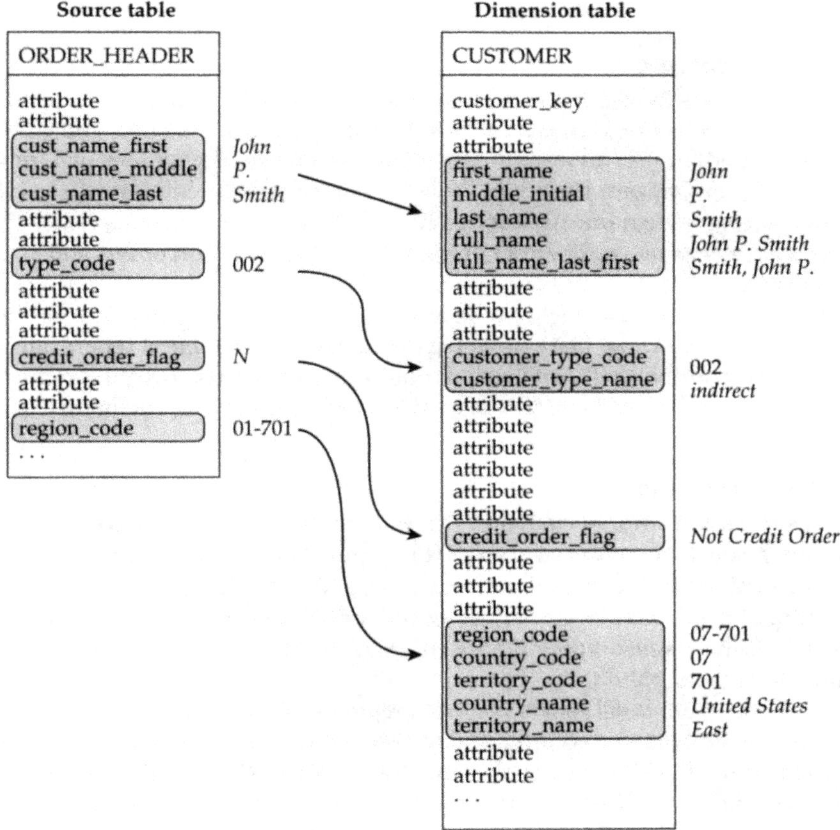

Figure 3-2 Constructing a rich set of dimension attributes

design, it is easy to use them to organize data, sort reports, order data, and so forth. Since they are not calculated in queries, it is possible for database administrators to index these columns, providing for efficient query performance.

Codes and Descriptions

In operational systems, it is common for the list of appropriate values in a domain to be described using codes. Elsewhere, a separate table is used to provide the corresponding descriptions. Often called reference values or lookup values, these descriptions may be more useful than the codes themselves. For example, a source table that stores order information might capture the type of customer. Rather than store various values, such as "Direct," "Indirect," or "Other," the table only stores codes such as 001, 002, or 003. A separate reference table maps these codes to the description values. This facilitates maintenance of the appropriate list of values and streamlines storage.

From an analytic perspective, both the code and description are useful dimensions. For example, Figure 3-2 shows a type_code of 002 transformed into a pair of attributes in the dimensional design: one for the code and one for the description. Because the dimension table carries both, users are able to filter, access, and organize information in whatever way they see fit.

Flags and Their Values

Columns whose values are Boolean in nature are usually referred to as flags. In an operational system, these values may be stored in several ways. One method uses a column with a Boolean data type. Another method uses an integer, which will contain only the values 0 or 1, or a character, which will contain only the values "Y" or "N." Some systems employ a special case of a code with two possible values: one indicating "True" and the other indicating "False." In Figure 3-2, the source column credit_order_flag contains a "Y" for credit orders and an "N" for noncredit orders.

In a dimensional design, these flags may be used to filter queries or group facts. By storing a descriptive value for the flag, we make using the flag easier. For example, a report can break up orders into "Credit Order" and "Not Credit Order" categories. These descriptors are far more useful than 0/1 or Y/N, and can also be used less ambiguously when defining a query predicate or filter.

Multiple-Part Columns

Operational systems often contain attributes that have multiple parts, each part bearing some sort of significance. Account codes are a common example, made up of parts such as a company identifier, account code, subaccount code, and so forth. In a dimensional design, the entire attribute may be stored, along with additional attributes that isolate its constituent parts. If these subcomponents are codes, they may also be accompanied by corresponding description values.

In Figure 3-2, the operational system records a region code in the format *XX-YYY*. The first part of this code designates a country, and the second part designates a territory within that country. The value 07-701, for example, contains country code 07 and territory code 701, which correspond to the United States and East, respectively. The dimensional design contains the full code, as well as the constituent codes and their corresponding descriptions.

Dimensions with Numeric Values

While the majority of dimensions contain data that is textual, sometimes dimensions contain numeric data. Given that facts tend to be numeric, this can occasionally lead to confusion. Application of the tests described in Chapter 1 will allow you to sort out dimensions from facts.

You have already seen examples of dimensions that contain numeric data. In Figure 3-2, for example, numeric content may be found in customer_type_code, country_code, and territory_code. Other common examples of numeric data elements are sizes, telephone numbers, and Zip codes. All of these examples are clearly dimensions. They will be used to provide context for facts, to order data, to control aggregation, or to filter query results.

Some numeric attributes are less easy to identify as dimensions. For example, the unit price associated with an order is numeric. If 100 widgets are sold at $10 apiece, is the $10 unit price a fact or a dimension? Recall from Chapter 1 that if an attribute is commonly aggregated or summarized, it is a fact. If it is used to drive aggregations or summarizations, however, it is a dimension. In the case of a unit price, it is not useful to sum unit prices across multiple orders. On the other hand, it is useful to group orders by unit price, perhaps to answer the question, "How many did I sell at $10 each versus $12 each?" The unit price is, therefore, behaving as a dimension.

TIP It is not always clear whether a numeric data element is a fact or a dimension. When in doubt, pay close attention to how it will be used. If the element values are used to filter queries, order data, control aggregation, or drive master-detail relationships, it is most likely a dimension.

While unit amounts are dimensions, extended amounts are facts. As you will see later in this chapter, multiplying a unit amount by the transaction quantity produces a value that can be aggregated or summarized. The unit amount is a useful dimension, and the extended amount is a useful fact. Both have their place in the dimensional design.

Behavioral Dimensions and Hybrid Attributes

A very powerful analytic technique uses behavior patterns to analyze facts. Consider this question: "Are customers who generate over $1 million in sales receiving better discounts than those who generate $500,000 or less?" Orders are tracked by a fact. To answer this question, we must group the customers based on their past order activity. The groupings are then used as a dimension, and they are used to study discounts.

A dimension that is computed based on facts is called a *behavioral dimension.* If the frequency with which we update behavioral groupings is relatively infrequent, this technique can add very powerful capability. If the groupings need to be up to date each time they are used, it may be more sensible—but also more time-consuming—to compute them when reports are executed. These considerations are discussed in Chapter 6, "More on Dimension Tables."

Last, it is important to recognize that there are situations where a single attribute may behave both as a dimension and as a fact. This often happens when employing *time-stamped* dimensions, which are discussed in Chapter 8.

Grouping Dimensions into Dimension Tables

Dimension attributes are grouped into tables that represent major categories of reference information. Junk dimensions collect miscellaneous attributes that do not share a natural affinity.

When principles of normalization are applied to a dimension table, the result is called a *snowflake.* Though not the norm, snowflakes may be useful in the presence of specific software tools. Unlike entity-relationship design, dimensional design fully embraces redundant storage of information.

Grouping Dimensions Based on Affinity

The dimension tables in a star schema are groupings of dimensional attributes that represent major categories of reference information. These categories usually have strong business significance. In Figure 3-1, the dimension tables represent time, products, customers, and salespeople. Each has major significance across various parts of the business. The attributes within a dimension table may bear various relationships to one another, but the design does not attempt to model these relationships. Products, brands, and categories are grouped in a single product table; salespeople, territories, and regions are grouped in a single salesrep table.

Schema designers sometimes find it challenging to determine the best way to group dimension attributes into tables. The appropriate categories may not be self-evident. In other cases, overlapping attributes may lead to confusion. What should be done, for example, if both salesreps and customers have addresses? Advice for sorting dimension attributes into tables is provided in Chapter 6.

Junk Dimensions Have No Affinity

In some cases, it can be useful to create a table that contains dimensions that do not have any real relationship to one another. The orders schema shown in Figure 3-1, for example, might benefit from the addition of several attributes to describe the type of order being placed, whether it was a credit order, whether it was solicited, and whether it represents a reorder. While these various indicators do not relate directly to one another, they can be combined into a single table for convenience. The result is a *junk dimension,* as depicted in Figure 3-3.

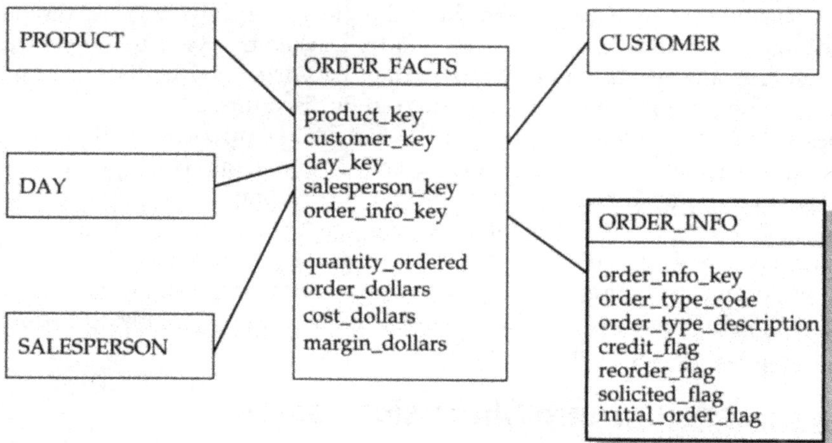

Figure 3-3 A junk dimension table collects unrelated dimensions for convenience

A junk dimension like the order_info table in Figure 3-3 has no natural key. It can be built by populating it with each possible combination of column values (a Cartesian product). When facts are loaded, they are associated with the row in this table that corresponds to the appropriate values of the various columns.

A similar technique proves useful in situations where it is necessary to control growth of a dimension table that is undergoing rapid changes. Discussed in Chapter 6, a *mini-dimension* relocates a set of attributes that would otherwise be stored in one of the other dimensions.

Snowflakes and Outriggers

You may have noticed that dimension tables contain a lot of redundancy. For example, the product table in Figure 3-1 contains several brand attributes. Presumably, there are far fewer brands than there are products. Storing brand attributes in the product table requires brand values to be repeated for many products.

Entity-relationship modelers use principles of normalization to drive this kind of redundancy out of relational designs. Brand attributes, for example, would be removed from the product table and stored in a separate table. In their place, a foreign key reference to the new brand table is added. In a dimensional design, the result is a variation on the star schema called a *snowflake schema*. The brand table is referred to as an *outrigger*.

This technique provides numerous benefits for operational systems, which must support a wide variety of transaction types concurrently. Analytic systems are used differently, and do not usually benefit from this kind of design. Snowflakes may be useful, however, if your RDBMS or business intelligence software is specifically optimized for snowflakes. There are also some situations where limited use of outriggers provides analytic benefit. These issues are fully explored in Chapter 7, "Hierarchies and Snowflakes."

TIP Do not use the principles of normalization to guide dimension table design. Analytic databases do not benefit from these techniques. Situations that call for snowflakes and outriggers are the exception rather than the rule.

Benefits of Redundancy

Even those not steeped in the practice of entity-relationship modeling may be put off by some of the techniques described in this chapter. Newcomers to dimensional design are often repulsed by redundant storage of multiple part codes and their components, storage of common combinations of elements such as names, or the expansion of flag values from Boolean indicators into descriptive text. These techniques can seem wasteful. Why not simply perform these computations "on the fly" at query time? The precomputation and storage of these redundant data elements have three advantages in an analytic environment: performance, usability, and consistency.

Recall that dimensions are used to specify query predicates, define the scope of aggregation, govern the ordering of data, and establish master–detail structure in reports. If these elements must be computed at query time, performance will be significantly impacted. Precomputing and storing these columns reduces the burden on the DBMS at query time, allows the database administrator to optimize performance through the use of indexes and other techniques, and opens the door to more efficient query execution.

Second, this level of redundancy makes it much easier for users to interact with the analytic database. It is far easier for the end user to select data where the country is "United States" rather than look for records where the first two digits of region_code are 07. If a report calls for customer names to appear in a last-name-first format, it is much easier to select that in a single column than it is to concatenate multiple fields together, omitting the space after first name if there is no middle initial, and so forth. If a user wants to break out credit orders, it is much easier to have a flag that reads "Credit Approved" or "Credit Not Approved" than it is to translate a Boolean value. A business intelligence tool may provide some of this functionality but does not offer the simultaneous performance benefits.

Last, explicit storage of all dimensions guarantees that they are consistent, regardless of the application being used. A business intelligence tool can be used to make it easier to provide full names, isolate substrings, or decode flags, but these shortcuts are only available to users who are interacting with the analytic database through that tool. If there are other tools in use, or if report developers are writing their own SQL, there is the danger that these dimensions are not being constructed consistently.

TIP Embrace redundancy in the dimensional model. Explicit storage of each dimension attribute maximizes performance, aids usability, and guarantees consistency across applications. The rules of normalization are best suited to the needs of operational systems, not analytic systems.

None of this should be interpreted as an argument against the use of business intelligence tools. In fact, these tools are extremely valuable components of the data warehouse architecture. Using these tools in an effort to save space, however, is misguided. Storing dimensions explicitly ensures performance, usability, and consistency. Computing dimensions on the fly saves a few dollars worth of disk space.

Fact Table Features

Every fact table represents a business process by capturing measurements that describe it. It is crucial that all relevant measurements be represented, even when some appear redundant. Some facts, however, cannot be aggregated. These *nonadditive* facts are usually broken down into other facts that can.

The level of detail at which the fact table records information is referred to as its *grain.* It is important to identify the grain of each fact table clearly and avoid situations of mixed grain. Fact tables do not contain rows for every combination of dimension values. Instead, they exhibit a characteristic called *sparsity.* On occasion, the fact table may host one or more *degenerate dimensions.* As you will see, these columns may participate in the grain of the fact table.

Fact Tables and Processes

The fact table is the engine for business process measurement. It is the locus for storage of the detailed measurements that describe the process. The facts are accompanied by foreign keys that provide dimensional context for each measurement. In some cases, the fact table may also contain dimensions, as discussed shortly.

If dimension tables are wide, fact tables are *deep.* A fact table usually accumulates rows more quickly than the associated dimension tables, often coming to overshadow the dimension tables

product_key	day_key	salesperson_key	customer_key	quantity_ ordered	order_ dollars	cost_ dollars
102291	3831	2991	240123	882	8822.29	8028.28
194482	2931	1992	572339	249	2499.29	2274.35
183882	2983	2933	937759	3394	33940.29	30885.66
102291	3831	2991	240123	882	8822.29	8028.28

Table 3-1 Sample Rows from a Fact Table

when it comes to row count. Fortunately, the rows of fact tables tend to be nice and compact. The foreign keys are usually integers, and the facts are usually integers or floating point decimal numbers. An example is shown in Table 3-1.

The compact nature of fact table rows enables the table to accumulate a large number of rows without generating inordinate storage requirements. A list of sample rows from a dimension table would be significantly wider. Not only do dimension tables have more columns but many of those columns contain textual data. In fact, each row would probably be so wide it would be hard to print in this book, even in landscape format. Compared to fact tables, however, dimension tables contain relatively few rows.

Capturing Facts

As the locus for process measurement, the fact table should contain every fact relevant to the process it describes, even if some of the facts can be derived from others. Facts are stored at a specific level of detail but can be rolled up to various levels of dimensionality. This aggregation is made possible by a characteristic called *additivity*. Some measurements stubbornly refuse to exhibit this trait, but usually they can be broken down into components that do.

Capture All Measurements

In a dimensional design, each fact table describes a business process. It should provide a comprehensive set of relevant measurements, even if some are redundant. The explicit storage of each fact ensures consistent measurement regardless of the tools used to develop queries and reports. Because most facts are numeric, the incremental cost to store an additional column is minimized.

An example is evident in the orders star shown in Figure 3-3. The fact table in this star contains the following facts:

- quantity_ordered
- order_dollars
- cost_dollars
- margin_dollars

Notice that margin dollars can be computed by subtracting cost dollars from order dollars. Some designers may be tempted to eliminate the margin dollars, allowing it to be computed within reports, within a view, or through the semantic layer provided by a business intelligence product. Storage of the fact in the fact table, however, allows margin dollars to be computed as part of the ETL process. This guarantees consistent computation of margin dollars and consistent representation regardless of the tools being used. Its computation is also preferable to the use of a view, which can hamper efforts to tune the DBMS for optimized query execution.

Another common error is to store unit amounts in the fact table rather than extended amounts. As seen earlier, unit amounts can be useful dimensions. They can also be used to compute extended amounts, which are useful facts. For example, the order_facts table in Figure 3-3 contains quantity_ordered and order_dollars. Each of these facts is fully additive, providing full analytic flexibility. If the table had stored unit_price in lieu of order dollars, it would be necessary to compute order_dollars within queries. Explicit storage of the relevant fact enables performance and consistency.

NOTE Don't interpret this explanation as a reason to exclude unit amounts from schema designs. In many situations, unit amounts are valuable dimensions for analysis. If there is not a clear dimension table where they can be stored, they may be placed in the fact table as degenerate dimensions, as described later in this chapter.

Nonadditive Facts

Although a fact table stores facts at a specific level of detail, the facts themselves can be expressed at various levels of summarization. This principle enables facts to be combined with various dimensions to answer an array of business questions. The sample query shown in Figure 1-6, for example, took order_dollars, which was stored by day, product, customer, and salesperson, and aggregated it to the product level.

The ability to summarize individual facts by adding them together is referred to as *additivity*. Figure 3-3 depicts four facts: quantity_ordered, order_dollars, cost_dollars, and margin_dollars. Each of these facts is fully additive; they may be summed up across any and all of the dimensions in the schema, producing a meaningful result.

Unfortunately, not every measurement exhibits additivity. Many key business metrics are expressed as rates or percentages. This type of measurement is never additive. For example, Table 3-2 shows the margin rate on each of the orders for "Gel Pen Red" on January 1.

Day	Salesperson	Product	Customer	Margin Rate
1/1/2009	Jones	Gel Pen Red	Balter Inc.	3.02%
1/1/2009	Jones	Gel Pen Red	Raytech	3.02%
1/1/2009	Baldwin	Gel Pen Red	Venerable Holdings	3.02%
1/1/2009	Baldwin	Gel Pen Red	eMart LLC	3.02%
1/1/2009	Baldwin	Gel Pen Red	Shatter & Lose	3.02%
1/1/2009	Sebenik	Gel Pen Red	Comstock Realty	3.02%
1/1/2009	Sebenik	Gel Pen Red	RizSpace	3.02%
1/1/2009	Sebenik	Gel Pen Red	StarComp	3.02%
1/1/2009	Sgamma	Gel Pen Red	Implosion Town	3.02%
			Sum:	**27.18%**

Table 3-2 Margin Rates Cannot Be Added Together

The margin rate is the percentage of the sale that represents profit, and it is closely monitored by management. In this table, each individual transaction has a margin rate of 3.02 percent. It is not possible to summarize the margin rate for these transactions by adding them together. This would produce a margin rate of over 27 percent, which is clearly incorrect.

Luckily, there is a solution. Ratios can be broken down into underlying components that are additive. In this case, the margin rate is the ratio of the margin dollars to order dollars. These components are fully additive. They can be stored in a fact table and safely aggregated to any level of detail within a query or report. An example report is shown in Figure 3-4. The nonadditive fact margin_rate is not stored in the fact table; it is computed as the ratio of the sums of margin dollars and order dollars. This computation may be done in a query or by additional processing logic in the reporting tool. Care must be taken with subtotals and grand totals in the report; the margin rate in these rows must be computed as the ratio of the subtotals for margin dollars and order dollars.

While nonadditive facts are not stored in fact tables, it is important not to lose track of them. For many processes, ratios are critical measurements without which a solution would leave much to be desired. Nonadditive facts should be documented as part of the schema design, as described in Chapter 18, "How to Design and Document a Dimensional Model."

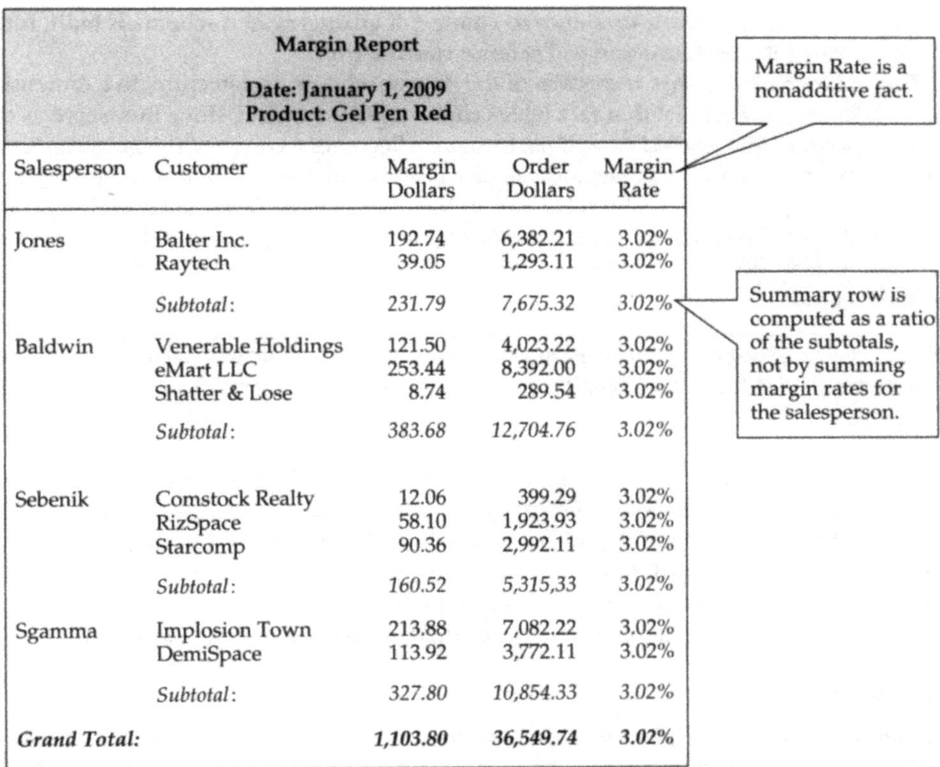

Margin Report

Date: January 1, 2009
Product: Gel Pen Red

Salesperson	Customer	Margin Dollars	Order Dollars	Margin Rate
Jones	Balter Inc.	192.74	6,382.21	3.02%
	Raytech	39.05	1,293.11	3.02%
	Subtotal:	*231.79*	*7,675.32*	*3.02%*
Baldwin	Venerable Holdings	121.50	4,023.22	3.02%
	eMart LLC	253.44	8,392.00	3.02%
	Shatter & Lose	8.74	289.54	3.02%
	Subtotal:	*383.68*	*12,704.76*	*3.02%*
Sebenik	Comstock Realty	12.06	399.29	3.02%
	RizSpace	58.10	1,923.93	3.02%
	Starcomp	90.36	2,992.11	3.02%
	Subtotal:	*160.52*	*5,315,33*	*3.02%*
Sgamma	Implosion Town	213.88	7,082.22	3.02%
	DemiSpace	113.92	3,772.11	3.02%
	Subtotal:	*327.80*	*10,854.33*	*3.02%*
Grand Total:		***1,103.80***	***36,549.74***	***3.02%***

Margin Rate is a nonadditive fact.
Summary row is computed as a ratio of the subtotals, not by summing margin rates for the salesperson.

Figure 3-4 Nonadditive facts are computed as the ratio of additive facts

NOTE This is not the end of the story on additivity. In addition to additive and nonadditive facts, you may also encounter facts that are semi-additive. Semi-additivity is discussed in Chapter 11, "Transactions, Snapshots, and Accumulating Snapshots."

Grain

The level of detail represented by a fact table row is referred to as its *grain*. Declaring the grain of a fact table is an important part of the schema design process. It ensures there is no confusion about the meaning of a fact table row, and guarantees all facts will be recorded at the same level of detail.

Grain may be described in a number of ways. Many schema designers describe grain simply by enumerating the associated dimensions. For example, the grain of order_facts in Figure 3-1 can be described as "Orders by Day, Salesperson, Product, and Customer."

While this may sound like stating the obvious, it reveals important information about the star. In this case, the statement of grain has the following implication: on a given day, if a customer places multiple orders for the same product with the same salesperson, these orders will be combined into a *single* row. This aggregation potentially discards useful information.

In most situations, schema designers try to avoid aggregating data before loading it into a fact table. By keeping the most granular data possible, the star is able to address a wider variety of analytic needs. Initial business requirements may not call for detailed data, but analytic requirements have a tendency to change. If an aggregated schema is built, future requests for detailed information will require starting over.

This guideline holds true regardless of the data warehouse architecture. In a dimensional data warehouse, it is crucial that fact tables capture granular data, since they serve as the central repository for detailed data. If performance becomes a concern, the granular fact table may be supplemented with aggregates, as discussed in Chapter 15. The guideline may be relaxed in a Corporate Information Factory architecture, where a separate repository contains granular data. In this scenario, a data mart fact table may aggregate data without fear of losing information. Nevertheless, a future request to study granular data will require redevelopment of the data mart.

TIP Set the fact table grain at the lowest level of detail possible. This guideline helps ensure maximum analytic flexibility. It can be relaxed if there is a separate repository for granular data, but may limit future utility.

In many cases, a clear statement of grain can be made without reference to the dimension tables in a schema. This form of grain statement is usually preferable, because it ties grain to a business term or an artifact of the business processes. For the orders process, grain might be defined as "orders at the order line level of detail." This clearly speaks to the business process and leaves no doubt about the meaning of a fact table row. The design in Figure 3-3 does not meet this definition of grain, but it can be adjusted to do so, as you will see shortly.

Sparsity

Rows are recorded in fact tables to represent the occurrence of business activities. This means that fact tables do not contain a row for every possible combination of dimension values. The number of combinations that appear in the fact table is relatively small in comparison to the number of possible combinations. This characteristic of fact tables is called *sparsity*.

Consider the orders process again. The order_facts table only records rows for orders that have taken place. If a particular customer does not order a particular product from a particular salesperson on a particular day, no row is recorded. This is a good thing. If every combination of dimension values were represented in the fact table, it would quickly accumulate a huge number of rows.

NOTE Some fact tables are denser than others. Some examples will be provided as part of Chapter 11's discussion of snapshot models.

Degenerate Dimensions

Sometimes, it is not possible to sort all the dimensions associated with a business into a neat set of tables. In situations like this, it may be appropriate to store one or more dimensions in the fact table. When this is done, the dimension column is called a *degenerate dimension.*

Although stored in the fact table, the column is still considered a dimension. Like the dimension columns in other tables, its values can be used to filter queries, control the level of aggregation, order data, define master–detail relationships, and so forth. Degenerate dimensions should be used cautiously. Because the fact table accumulates rows at a rapid pace, the inclusion of degenerate dimensions can lead to an excessive consumption of space, particularly for textual elements. In most cases, candidates for degenerate dimensions are better placed in junk dimensions. Transaction identifiers are exceptions to this guideline.

TIP Avoid overusing degenerate dimensions. If an attribute is not a transaction identifier, consider placing it in a junk dimension instead.

Transaction identifiers are commonly stored as degenerate dimensions. They may also serve as a unique identifier for fact table rows, and define fact table grain. The orders star in Figure 3-3 was criticized for not storing granular data. It can be redesigned to store information at the order line level of detail by adding degenerate dimensions that identify the order and order line. The result is shown in Figure 3-5.

The grain of the fact table in Figure 3-5 can be stated as "orders at the order line level of detail." This has been achieved by adding transaction identifiers from the source system to identify discrete order lines: the order_id and order_line. Together, these two attributes can serve as a unique identifier for fact table rows.

NOTE Although transaction identifiers are commonly stored as degenerate dimensions, this is not a hard-and-fast rule. In some cases, the storage of transaction identifiers in fact tables can be a problem for business intelligence tools. These products sometimes have difficulty generating queries if the same data element is present in more than one table. This situation will be discussed in Chapter 16, "Design and Business Intelligence."

As an alternative to this design, it is possible to construct a dimension *table* to represent the order line. This dimension table would contain the order number and order line number. It could also contain the attributes shown in the order_info dimension of Figure 3-5. This alternative keeps the degenerates out of the fact table. That may seem useful, but notice that it would not save any space. Because each fact table row represents exactly one order line, the dimension and fact table would contain the same number of rows.

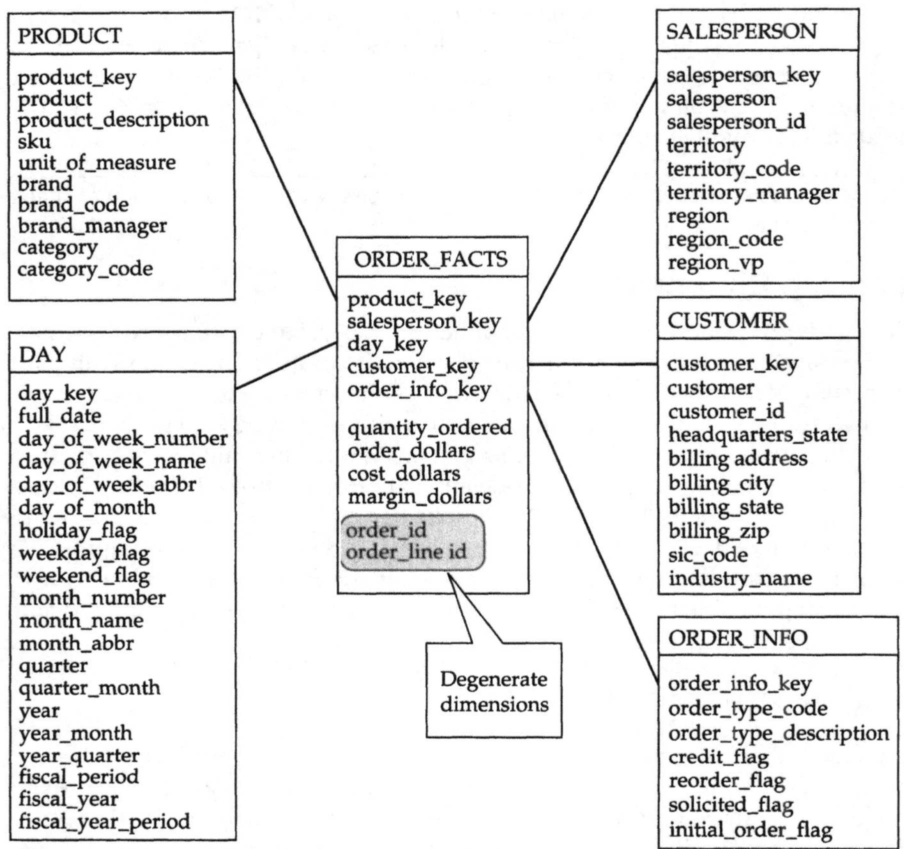

Figure 3-5 Degenerate dimensions define the grain of this fact table

Slowly Changing Dimensions

The data in dimension tables originates in operational systems. In a dimensional data warehouse or stand-alone data mart, it comes directly from the operational system. In a Corporate Information Factory, it is first moved to the enterprise data warehouse, and then to a dimensional data mart. Once information makes its way into a dimension table, it may change in the operational source. For example, a customer's date of birth is updated to correct an error, or a customer's address is updated when they move.

Because the downstream star schema uses a surrogate key as the primary key of each dimension table, it does not have to handle changes the same way the source does. The operational system may track the change history of each data element, or it may simply overwrite with the changed values. Regardless, the star schema can respond to each change in whatever manner makes most sense for measuring the overall business process.

In every dimensional design, it is crucial to identify how changes in source data will be represented in dimension tables. This phenomenon is referred to as *slowly changing dimensions*. This term gets its name from the relatively slow rate at which dimensions accumulate changes, at least when compared with fact tables, which accumulate rows at a rapid pace. A variety of responses to changed data elements are possible. In some cases, there may be no analytic value in preserving history. In other cases, it may be critical that historic data be maintained.

Figure 3-6 shows a customer record in an order entry system at three different points in time. The record in question is that of customer_id 9900011, which happens to be someone named Sue Johnson. Notice that on January 1, 2007, her date of birth is indicated as March 2, 1961, and she lives in the state of Arizona (AZ). Later, her date of birth has been changed from a date in 1961 to 1971. Still later, this same customer has moved; her state of residence is now California (CA). This operational system has handled both changes in the same way: by overwriting the record for customer_id 9900011.

Suppose that this operational system feeds a dimension table in a star schema that tracks orders. Analytic requirements may call for the changes to be treated differently. In the case of Sue's date of birth, the business may consider the change history to be insignificant. As in

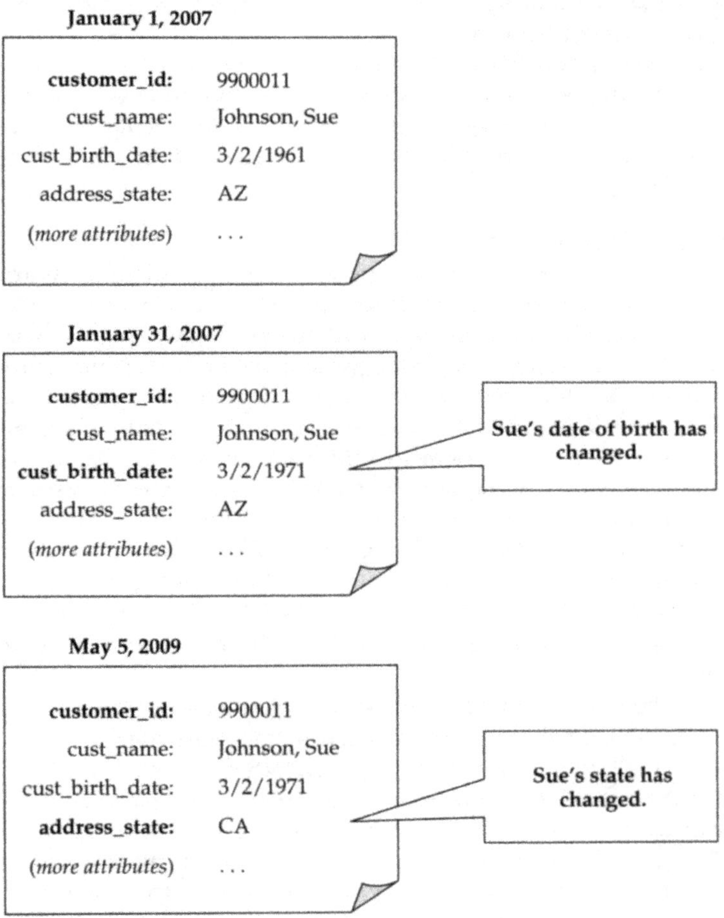

Figure 3-6 Changes in operational data

the operational system, it may be best simply to update the record for Sue in a customer dimension table. Sue's address change, on the other hand, may have more significance. She may have placed some orders while living in Arizona and some more orders while living in California. If someone is studying order history by state, it is important that each of Sue's orders be associated with the correct state.

These two changes to customer 9900011 can be used to illustrate the most common types of slow change response in a star schema: the type 1 slow change and the type 2 slow change. These responses overwrite transaction history and preserve it, respectively. There is also a less common type 3 response. It is used in situations that do not require historic context but do call for use of both the before and after values of the changed data element.

Type 1 Change

When the source of a dimension value changes, and it is not necessary to preserve its history in the star schema, a type 1 response is employed. The dimension is simply overwritten with the new value. This technique is commonly employed in situations where a source data element is being changed to correct an error.

By overwriting the corresponding dimension in the star schema, the type 1 change obliterates the history of the data element. The star carries no hint that the column ever contained a different value. While this is generally the desired effect, it can also lead to confusion. If there were any associated *facts* before the change occurred, their historic context is retroactively altered.

Overwriting the Dimension Value

Recall, for example, the change in date of birth for Sue Johnson. According to Figure 3-6, Sue Johnson was initially recorded as having a birth date in 1961. Later, her date of birth was updated to show she was born in 1971. People's birth dates do not change, so when this information was updated in the source system, it was presumably the correction of an error.

Assume that a star schema has been developed to track the orders process, with a dimension table called *customer*. This table carries the customer_id as a natural key, and also has columns for the customer's name, date of birth, and state of residence. The top portion of Figure 3-7 shows the state of affairs in the star schema before any changes have occurred. In the customer dimension table, there is a row for Sue, which is highlighted. You can see that this row contains the customer_id 990001. This is a natural key column; it identifies the record for Sue in the source system. There is also a surrogate key called customer_key, which contains the value 1499. Sue's date of birth is shown as 3/2/1961, and her state is shown as AZ. Presumably, there are numerous other columns in the customer table that are not shown in the picture.

Just below this table, still in the top half of Figure 3-7, a row from a fact table is shown. The customer_key in this row is 1499, which refers to Sue's record in the customer dimension table. You can interpret this row as follows: on the date represented by day_key 2322, Sue bought five units of whatever product is represented by product_key 10119. One would not ordinarily be studying key values, but the corresponding tables have been omitted to keep the diagram simple.

The bottom half of Figure 3-7 shows what the star schema looks like after a type 1 change to Sue's date of birth occurs. The row in the customer dimension table for customer_id 9900011 has been updated; Sue's date of birth is now shown as 3/2/1971. This row is still represented by the surrogate key 1499.

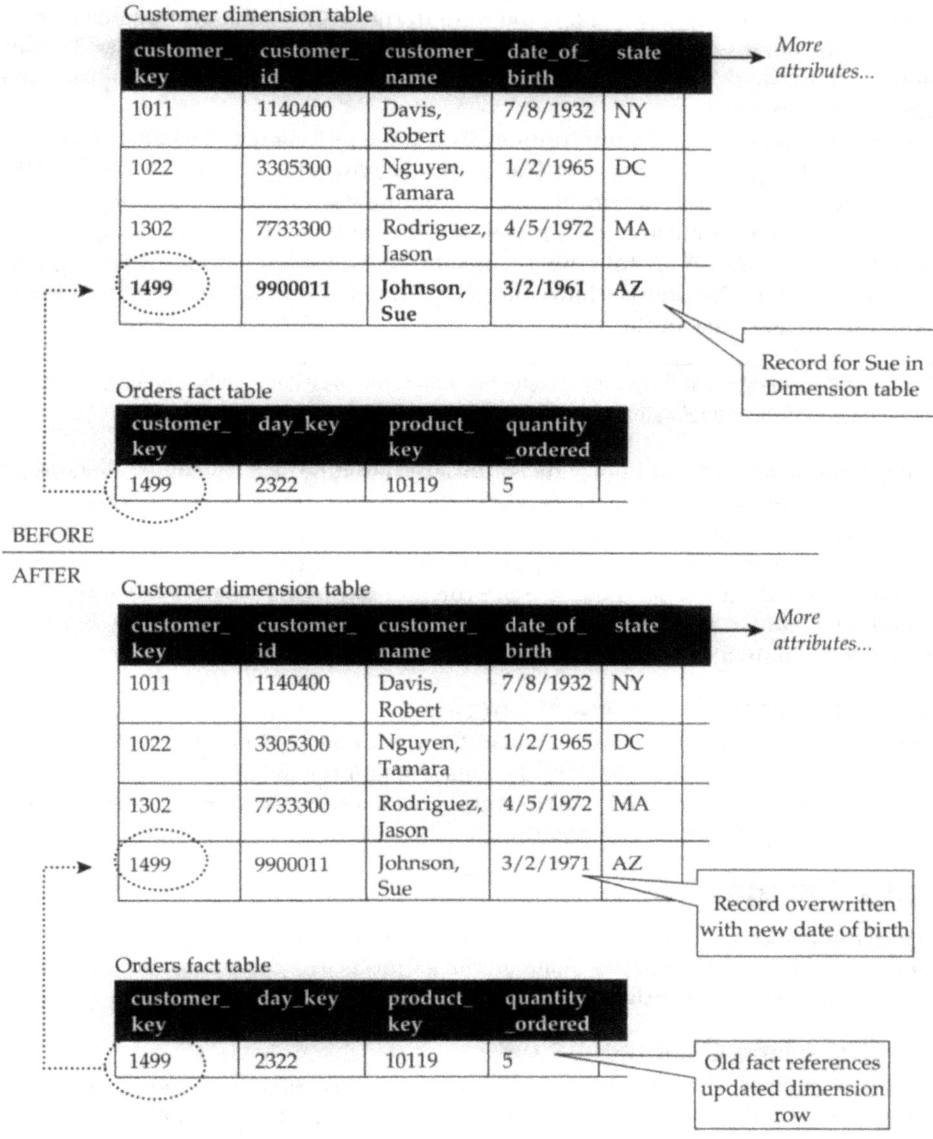

Figure 3-7 A type 1 change: before and after

Preexisting Facts Have a New Context

A type 1 change has an important effect on facts, one that is often overlooked. When a record is updated in a dimension table, the context for existing facts is restated. This effect can give rise to confusion.

An example is provided by the change in Sue's date of birth. The "before" picture in the top half of Figure 3-7 shows an order in the fact table for Sue. It was placed on whatever day is represented by day_key 2322. If you were to run a query that grouped orders for that day by the customer's date of birth, Sue's order would be grouped together with other customers born on 3/2/1961. Suppose that someone created a report to do just that and printed out the results.

Now, move forward to a point in time after the type 1 change has taken place. The bottom half of Figure 3-7 shows that Sue is now listed with a date of birth of 3/2/1971. You run the same report—taking all orders from the day represented by day_key 2322 and grouping them by customers' birth dates. Your report will count Sue's past order with people born on 3/2/1971, while the one printed previously will count it among people born on 3/2/1961. The reports have different figures, even though they both describe activity for the same day in the past.

TIP Use type 1 changes carefully. They restate the context for associated facts. Confusion can be minimized by educating systems analysts and business users.

Steps can be taken to minimize the confusion caused by type 1 changes. Systems analysts responsible for supporting the data warehouse users must be aware of this phenomenon so they are prepared to address confusion. Developers of reports can place the query execution date within the report footer or cover page, signaling to readers the date as of which the report was current. Any reports that are pre-run and stored for users can be automatically updated on a regular basis so users do not unintentionally access "stale" data. For many organizations, though, the preferred approach is to avoid the type 1 change.

History of Dimension Is Not Maintained

In addition to restating the context of facts, the type 1 change fails to track the history of the dimension itself. No change history of the data element is maintained in the star schema. In a Corporate Information Factory architecture, the data warehouse may maintain this history in the enterprise data warehouse repository.

Type 2 Change

Most operational changes are dealt with in a star schema as type 2 changes. The type 2 change preserves the history of facts. Facts that describe events before the change are associated with the old value; facts that describe events after the change are associated with the new value.

Inserting a New Dimension Row

The second method for responding to a change in source data is to insert a new record into the dimension table. Any previously existing records are unchanged. This type 2 response preserves context for facts that were associated with the old value, while allowing new facts to be associated with the new value.

Sue Johnson's change of address provides an example where a type 2 change can be useful. Recall from Figure 3-6 that over the years, Sue has lived in Arizona, and later in California. She may have placed some orders while living in Arizona and other orders while living in California. A type 1 response to Sue's change in address would have the undesirable side effect of restating the context for orders that Sue placed before she moved. They would become associated with California, even though Sue lived in Arizona at the time.

Figure 3-8 illustrates a type 2 response to Sue's change of address. In the "before" section of this diagram, there is a record in the dimension table that shows customer_id 9900011 (Sue) as residing in the state of Arizona (AZ). This row has a surrogate key value of 1499. A row in the fact table contains this key value, indicating that Sue has placed an order.

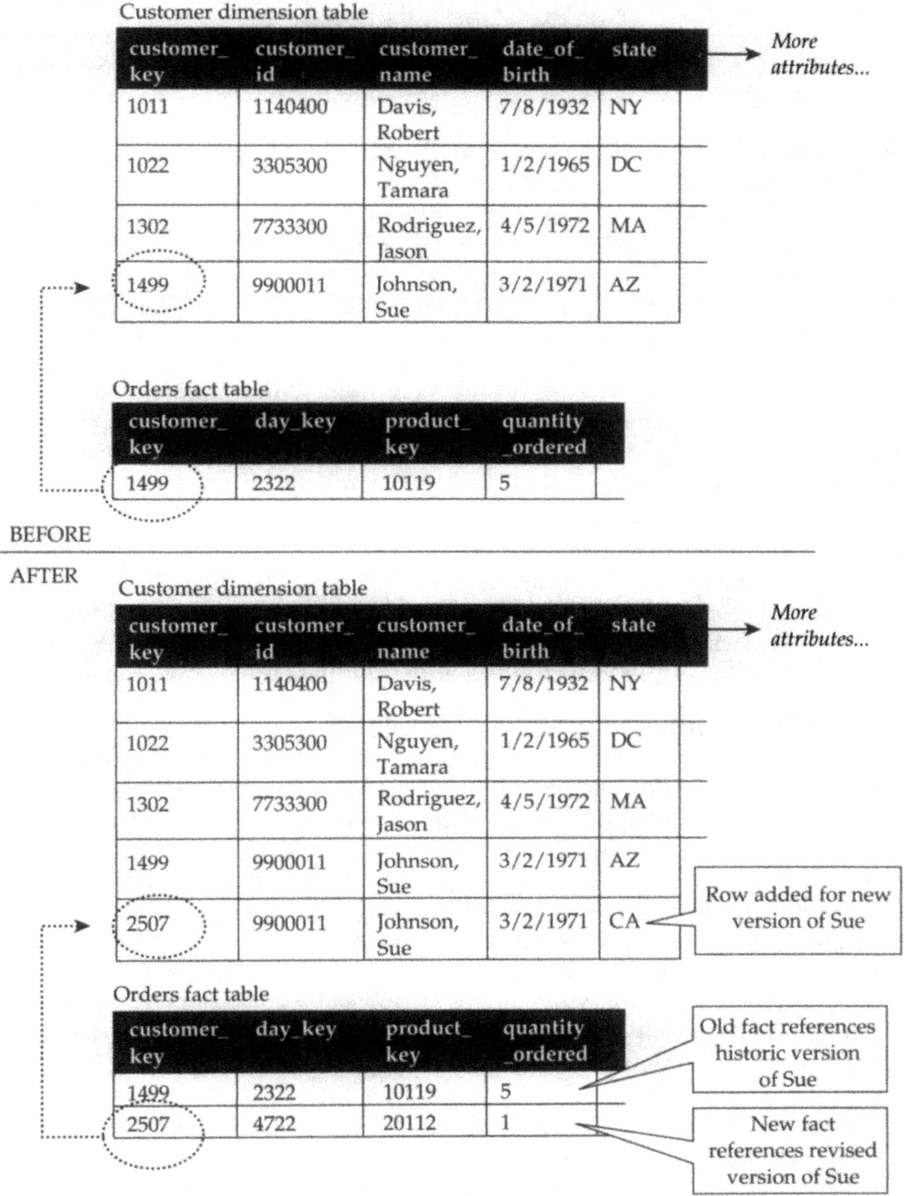

BEFORE

Customer dimension table

customer_key	customer_id	customer_name	date_of_birth	state
1011	1140400	Davis, Robert	7/8/1932	NY
1022	3305300	Nguyen, Tamara	1/2/1965	DC
1302	7733300	Rodriguez, Jason	4/5/1972	MA
1499	9900011	Johnson, Sue	3/2/1971	AZ

Orders fact table

customer_key	day_key	product_key	quantity_ordered
1499	2322	10119	5

AFTER

Customer dimension table

customer_key	customer_id	customer_name	date_of_birth	state
1011	1140400	Davis, Robert	7/8/1932	NY
1022	3305300	Nguyen, Tamara	1/2/1965	DC
1302	7733300	Rodriguez, Jason	4/5/1972	MA
1499	9900011	Johnson, Sue	3/2/1971	AZ
2507	9900011	Johnson, Sue	3/2/1971	CA

Orders fact table

customer_key	day_key	product_key	quantity_ordered
1499	2322	10119	5
2507	4722	20112	1

Figure 3-8 A type 2 change: before and after

The lower half of Figure 3-8 shows what happens when Sue's address changes. In the dimension table, the preexisting row for Sue is left untouched. It still shows Sue as residing in Arizona. A new record has been added for Sue. This record carries surrogate key 2507. This new row indicates that customer 9900011 is Sue Johnson and that she lives in the state of California (CA).

This type 2 response has the effect of creating "versions" of Sue in the dimension table. Where there was previously one row representing Sue, there are now two. This "versioning" is made possible because the dimension table does not rely on the natural key, customer_id, as its unique identifier.

Historic Context of Facts Is Preserved

By creating multiple versions of the dimension, a type 2 response avoids restating the context of previously existing facts. Old facts can remain associated with the old row; new facts can be associated with the new row. This has the desired effect of preserving past history, while allowing new activity to be associated with the new value.

To understand how the type 2 change preserves history, look at the fact table in the lower half of Figure 3-8. After the type 2 change has occurred, the order placed before Sue moved remains associated with the "old" version of Sue. You can use the foreign key value in the fact table to verify this. Tracing customer_key 1499 to the customer table leads to a row that identifies customer 9900011 as Sue Johnson, living in Arizona. The fact table now contains a new row, this one for an order placed *after* the move. The new row carries the surrogate key 2507, which refers to the "new" version of Sue, living in California. Any reports that group orders by state will continue to group Sue's old order with "AZ," while her new order will be grouped with "CA."

When a type 2 change occurs, not all dimension values will be altered. For example, after Sue moved, her date of birth remained the same: 3/2/1971. Any query that groups orders by date of birth will associate all of Sue's orders with that date. If someone wants to look at all orders associated with Sue, they can group all orders for her customer_id, which is 9900011.

History of Dimension Is Partially Maintained

A type 2 change results in multiple dimension rows for a given natural key. While this serves to preserve the historic context of facts, it can trigger new forms of confusion. Users may be confused by the presence of duplicate values in the dimension tables. Designers may be lulled by a false sense that they are preserving dimensional history.

Type 2 changes can confuse end users because they cause duplicate values to appear in dimension tables. For example, after Sue Johnson's change of address, there are two rows in the dimension table for her customer_id. If someone were to query the dimension table to get the name associated with customer_id 9900011, both rows would be returned. This side effect can be avoided by issuing browse queries that select *distinct* values. A flag may also be added to indicate the current row for a given natural key value. Examples of such flags are provided in Chapters 8, "More Slow Change Techniques," and 17, "Design and ETL."

TIP Type 2 changes preserve the dimensional detail surrounding facts. They may confuse users, however, by appearing to duplicate information in dimension tables. Avoid this confusion by issuing browse queries that select distinct values, and by offering a flag to indicate whether each row represents the current version for its natural key value.

Although the type 2 change preserves the historic context of *facts*, it does not preserve history in the *dimension*. It is easy to see that a given natural key has taken on multiple representations in the dimension, but we do not know *when* each of these representations was correct. This information is only provided by way of a fact.

For example, after the change to Sue's address has occurred, the dimension table in Figure 3-8 shows that there have been two versions of Sue, but it cannot tell us what Sue looked like on any given date. Where was she living on January 1, 2008? The dimension table does not carry this information. If there is an order for January 1, 2008, we are in luck, because the orders fact table will refer to the version of Sue that was correct at the time of the order. If there is not an order on that date, we are unable to determine what Sue looked like at that point in time.

It may be clear to you that this problem is easily rectified by adding a date stamp to each version of Sue. This technique allows the dimension to preserve both the history of facts and the history of dimensions. Another possibility is to build an additional fact table that associates versions of Sue with various dates. These techniques will be explored in Chapter 8.

Choosing and Implementing Response Types

An important part of star schema design is identification of slow change processing rules for dimensions. For a given source change, the correct response is dictated by analytic requirements. A single dimension may exhibit type 1 responses to some changes and type 2 responses to other changes. The ETL developer will be responsible for applying these rules during the loading process.

Designing Response Types

Although slow changes are triggered by the source data, we tend to talk about them with respect to the dimension table. In the case of Sue Johnson, for example, we refer to the dimension table's date_of_birth column as a type 1 attribute, and the state column as a type 2 attribute. These designations are shorthand for the following two statements:

> "For any given customer_id in the dimension table, if the source of the date_of_birth value changes, overwrite existing dimension rows with the new value."

> "For any given customer_id in the dimension table, if the source of the state value changes, insert a new row into the dimension table."

As you can see, it is much easier to say that date_of_birth is a type 1 attribute, and state is a type 2 attribute. Figure 3-9 shows what this might look like in a diagram.

The differences between type 1 and type 2 slow change responses are summarized in Figure 3-10. Most of the time, a type 2 response is the most appropriate. It does not restate previously existing facts, nor does it destroy the dimension table's ability to maintain history. Unfortunately, novice design teams often choose the opposite route, handling all changes as type 1. This invariably leads to problems that cannot be corrected without reloading the original source data. Type 1 changes can also introduce additional complexity, as discussed in the sidebar "Type 1 Complications."

There are situations in which the change of a source element may result in *either* type of response. Many operational systems log the change history for significant entities. Sometimes, these systems record the reason for a change, which in turn may dictate how the star schema

CUSTOMER	
customer_key	SK
customer_id	NK
first_name	2
middle_initial	2
last_name	2
full_name	2
full_name_last_first	2
gender	1
data_of_birth	1
address	2
city	2
state	2
zip_code	2
marital_status	2
daytime_phone	2
evening_phone	2
. . .	

Legend:

SK Surrogate Key

NK Natural Key

1 Type 1

2 Type 2

Figure 3-9 Documenting the slow change rules for a dimension table

should respond. For example, a change to a customer's marital status may be treated as a type 1 change if the operational system records it as "error correction" or a type 2 change if the change is logged as a result of an actual change in marital status.

TIP For each dimension attribute, choose and document the appropriate slow change response. If you are uncertain, the type 2 response is safest. When a source system captures the reason for a change, a single attribute may drive either type of response.

In addition to the type 1 and type 2 techniques introduced in this chapter, additional responses to source data changes are possible. Options include the type 3 response, hybrid responses, and time-stamped variations. Though less common, these techniques meet additional analytic challenges that will be discussed in Chapter 8.

	Action	Effect on Facts
Type 1	Update Dimension	Restates History
Type 2	Insert New Row in Dimension Table	Preserves History

Figure 3-10 Summary of slowly changing dimension techniques

Type 1 Complications

In addition to changing the history of facts, type 1 changes introduce other complications. If a dimension attribute is designated as type 1, and it is not fully dependent on the table's natural key, the update response must be carefully evaluated. For example, a product table may include a brand code (type 2) and brand name (type 1). A change to a product's brand name may result in an update, if the name associated with the brand code was changed, or may result in a new row, if the product is to be associated with a different brand altogether. This situation will require documentation that is more detailed than what is shown in Figure 3-9.

Additionally, *any* type 1 attribute may introduce problems for the maintenance of aggregate tables or cubes that draw data from the star. This phenomenon will be explored in Chapter 15.

Implementation of Slow Change Processing

When a dimension table exhibits multiple response types, as in Figure 3-9, ETL developers must factor in a variety of possible situations. For example, a type 1 change may require updating *multiple* rows in the dimension table. If Sue Johnson's date of birth had been corrected *after* she had moved, for example, the type 1 change to her birth date would apply to multiple rows. Otherwise, some versions of Sue would indicate one date of birth, while others indicate another. The ETL developer must also consider the possibility that type 1 and type 2 changes occur at the same time. For example, it may be that Sue moves (type 2) and has her date of birth corrected (type 1) on the same day. A *single* source record for Sue will contain the seeds for *both* type 1 *and* type 2 responses.

It is important to acknowledge the fact that slow change processing makes the lives of ETL developers very difficult. Slow change requirements impact every part of the loading process, both in terms of complexity and in terms of processing time. ETL developers may face the additional challenge of determining whether changes have taken place at all. These activities are discussed in Chapter 17, along with some common design tweaks that can help streamline the process.

Cubes

Dimensional models are not always implemented in relational databases. A multidimensional database, or MDB, stores dimensional information in a format called a *cube*. The basic concept behind a cube is to precompute the various combinations of dimension values and fact values so they can be studied interactively.

Multidimensional Storage vs. Relational Storage

The primary advantage of the multidimensional database is speed. A cube allows users to change their perspective on the data interactively, adding or removing attributes to or from their view and receiving instantaneous feedback. This process is often referred to as Online

Analytical Processing, or OLAP. OLAP interaction with a cube is highly responsive; there is instantaneous feedback as you slice and dice, drill up and drill down. In contrast, a star schema is interacted with through a query-and-response paradigm. Each change in the information detail on display requires the issuance of a new query.

Another advantage of the multidimensional database is that it is not hampered by the limitations of SQL. Because it specializes in the storage of facts and dimensions, it can offer interfaces to ask for information that SQL does not traditionally handle well. MDBs were providing running totals, rankings and other statistical operations long before these capabilities were added to SQL. Multidimensional databases may also offer specialized support for recursive hierarchies, which may be ragged, something that requires a bridge table in the star schema world. (More on this in Chapter 10, "Recursive Hierarchies and Bridges.")

Of course, all this capability comes with a cost. As the number of dimensions and their values increase, the number of possible combinations that must be precomputed explodes. This limits the ability of the cube to scale with large volumes of data. Typical measures to stem this limitation invariably reduce some of the benefits offered by the cube.

Data in an MDB is accessed through an interface, which is often proprietary, although MDX has gained wide acceptance as a standard. Still, the ability to write queries in this environment is a skill that is not as widely available. In contrast, there is a large pool of information technology professionals who understand SQL, and a wider variety of reporting tools that support it. To some, this is another disadvantage of the MDB. Figure 3-11 summarizes the differences in these technologies.

Variations on the MDB Theme

The marketplace encapsulates the functionality of the multidimensional database in a variety of ways. Some implementations are positioned as a full-blown database management system, where a cube is managed on an MDB server. Other implementations utilize the cube to enable a specific front-end application; these tools may be categorized as OLAP products.

	Data Structure	Access Language	Style of Interaction	Advantages
Relational Database	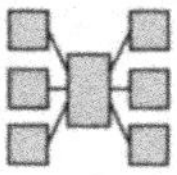 Star Schema	Structured Query Language (SQL)	Query and response	Scalable Widely understood access language
Multi-dimensional Database	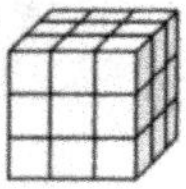 Cube	Proprietary API or MDX	Interactive (OLAP)	Fast Expressive access language

These distinctions are beginning to fade

Figure 3-11 Alternative storage technologies for dimensional data

Still other tools assemble cubes from the results of queries against a relational database. This enables them to offer limited slicing and dicing in the context of a business intelligence tool. These are sometimes referred to as ROLAP products.

The distinctions between multidimensional and relational technology are beginning to fade. Many tools that we used to think of as relational database management systems (RDBMS) now incorporate multidimensional storage capabilities, often as a way to provide increased performance for relational data. These database products are now better described by the more general term database management system (DBMS). Additional innovations include SQL extensions for interaction with dimensional structures, the automated generation of cubes from tables, and the rewrite of queries from the SQL access language to MDX or vice versa. Vendors in these hybrid environments are also boosting the scalability of the cube, by allowing the database administrator to control the amount of precalculated intersections that are stored.

Cubes and the Data Warehouse

Each of the three data warehouse architectures from Chapter 2, "Data Warehouse Architectures," can be adapted to incorporate the use of cubes. Used as a primary data store, the cube replaces a star schema to store dimensional data; as a derived data store, it supplements a star.

When cubes are used as the primary storage for dimensional data, the solution may be limited by the scalability of the cube. A smaller number of dimensional attributes may be practical, and the grain of the cube may be limited. This may be a concern in a stand-alone data mart, or in a dimensional data warehouse architecture, where the dimensional data store is loaded directly from operational data. Any aggregation performed during this step represents analytic detail lost. The benefits may include the more expedient delivery of a solution and a high-performance analytic environment. This trade-off has lesser significance in a Corporate Information Factory, where a separate repository of atomic data is always maintained.

Typically, the cube will replace relational storage as the primary data store in specific subject areas where the data sets are smaller. These subject areas are often supported by packaged solutions that provide a very tight analytic experience within this limited domain. A common example is budgeting, where vendors offer prebuilt analytics based on dimensional storage.

Instead of displacing relational storage, the cube can also be used to supplement it. This practice allows the cube to participate in any of the architectures described in Chapter 2 as an additional layer. By supplementing relational storage with one or more cubes, developers can ensure comprehensive storage of detailed dimensional data in stars, while taking advantage of the performance and expressive capability of the cube.

TIP Stars and cubes work well together. If you build a star, you can take advantage of the scalability of the relational database to store very granular and detailed information. From this detail, you can build cubes to support an interactive query experience.

This coexistence of stars and cubes can take on two variations. In one configuration, a star schema may serve as the integrated repository of atomic data, while the cube serves as a data mart. In another configuration, the star schema may serve as a data warehouse or mart, with cubes used as an additional layer for high-performance reporting. In either configuration, the cube serves the same purposes as derived schemas and aggregates, which are discussed in Chapters 14 and 15, respectively.

The Database of the Future

If the previous 15 years are any indication, the next 15 years should bring dramatic changes. The marketplace is on pace to render the storage format of dimensional data irrelevant. A single database management architecture will eventually store the dimensional model in whatever format makes the most sense, whether that is relational tables, a cube, or something entirely different. Users and applications will interact with it in their choice of language, be it SQL or a multidimensional API. Their queries will be rewritten and redirected in real time to suit the underlying storage technique in use. By the time we get there, you may be designing star schemas that are actually stored as cubes, accessing them via SQL, and receiving responses at OLAP speed.

Summary

This chapter covered the basic features of the star schema. This long list of topics can be grouped into four categories.

Dimension tables

- Dimension tables contain natural keys and surrogate keys. This allows the analytic schema to track history independently of the source.
- Dimension tables should be wide. A rich set of dimensional attributes enables a powerful analytic environment. Columns should be provided for codes and their associated descriptions, concatenated fields as well as their parts, common combinations of values, and descriptive representation of flags.
- Some dimensions are numeric; they can be distinguished from facts based on how they are used.
- Dimension tables are not placed in third normal form.
- Junk dimensions accumulate unrelated dimension attributes.
- Behavioral dimensions are derived from facts to produce powerful analytic options.

Fact tables

- Fact tables contain compact rows composed of foreign key references to dimensions, and facts.
- Fact tables should contain all facts relevant to a process, even if some can be computed from others.
- Nonadditive facts such as ratios should be decomposed into fully additive components, and computed at report creation time.
- Fact tables are sparse; they record rows only when something happens.

- It is crucial that the grain of a fact table can be stated, either in dimensional terms or with respect to a business term.
- A dimension stored in a fact table is called a degenerate dimension. This technique is usually reserved for transaction identifiers that exhibit high cardinality.

Slow changes

- The warehouse responds to changes in source data through a process known as slowly changing dimensions.
- A type 1 slow change overwrites a dimension attribute when its corresponding source changes. The dimension table does not reflect history, and the historic context of existing facts is altered.
- A type 2 slow change creates a new version of the dimension row when the source value for one of its attributes changes. The dimension table maintains a version history, although it is not tied to time. The historic context of historic facts is preserved.

Cubes

- A dimensional model can also be implemented in a multidimensional database, where it is known as a cube.
- Cubes enable a fast and powerful form of interaction known as OLAP.
- The languages that support interaction with cubes support some types of analysis that are hard to express using SQL.
- Storage requirements increase as dimension attributes are added or the number of transactions increases.
- Cubes can serve as primary dimensional data stores but have limited scalability.
- Cubes can serve as a powerful supplement to a star schema, enabling focused and interactive analysis.

Further Reading

The fundamentals of star schema design presented in this chapter are covered in every book that deals with dimensional design. Briefer treatment of the basics can be found in the author's previous work: *Data Warehouse Design Solutions* (Adamson and Venerable, Wiley, 1995), and *Mastering Data Warehouse Aggregates* (Adamson, Wiley, 2006). Both introduce the basics of fact tables and dimension tables in their opening chapters.

The concepts of dimension tables, surrogate keys, fact tables, grain, sparsity, and slowly changing dimensions are universally accepted features of dimensional design. They were first codified by Ralph Kimball in magazine articles and later in the first edition of *The Data Warehouse Toolkit.* Now in its second edition, Ralph Kimball and Margy Ross's *The Data Warehouse Toolkit, Second Edition* (Wiley, 2002) covers the fundamentals of fact tables and dimension tables in Chapter 1. Slow changes are described in Chapter 4.

An alternative perspective on facts and dimensions can be found in *Mastering Data Warehouse Design* by Claudia Imhoff, Nicholas Galemmo, and Jonathan Geiger (Wiley, 2003). This book introduces facts and dimensions in Chapter 5, and provides examples of data delivery processes that move data from the enterprise data warehouse into a dimensional data mart.

All of the books mentioned here provide brief descriptions of OLAP and cubes. For in-depth coverage of the multidimensional database, the cube, and online analytical processing, see *OLAP Solutions, Second Edition* by Erik Thomsen (Wiley, 2002).

PART

II

Multiple Stars

CHAPTER

4 A Fact Table for Each Process

It is rare to find a subject area that can be fully described by a single fact table. It is impossible to find an enterprise that can be covered by a single fact table. In almost every practical application, multiple fact tables will be necessary.

As a general rule of thumb, dimensional designs include a single fact table for each process to be studied. This allows each process to be analyzed individually, without undue complications that result from designs where a single fact table covers multiple processes. This chapter presents techniques you can use to determine when you are dealing with multiple processes, and explains the implications of not describing them in separate fact tables.

While analysis of individual processes is useful, some of the most powerful analytics cross process boundaries. In a dimensional environment, this will require combining information from more than one fact table. This chapter looks at what happens when this is done incorrectly, and provides a two-step process to ensure accurate results. This process is called *drilling across.* You will learn that there are multiple ways in which query and reporting tools handle this process, each with its own advantages and disadvantages. Finally, you will learn what to do when the available tools cannot drill across.

Fact Tables and Business Processes

Dimensional models describe how people measure their world. As previous chapters have emphasized, each star schema contains a fact table that is home to measurements describing a particular process. The measurements, or facts, are given context by their related dimensions. The grain of the fact table describes the level of detail at which the facts are recorded.

A simple rule of thumb governs the distribution of facts across fact tables:

TIP To be studied individually, each process should have its own fact table.

When designers follow this guideline, users are able to study each individual process without undue complication. In a few moments, we will begin looking at what some of those complications might be. First, it is necessary to address the ambiguity of the word *process.*

Some readers may be struggling with the guideline just given. What exactly is a process? Those steeped in the world of information engineering may be familiar with the concept of process modeling, a lesser-known companion to entity-relationship modeling. While the entity-relationship model is used to describe information, the process model is used to describe business activity. Just as the entity-relationship guides the database design of an operational system, the process model guides design of the functional components.

Here's the rub: process models involve functional decomposition. That is to say: one process can be broken down into several subprocesses. For example, the sales process may be broken down into subprocesses for order entry, shipment, invoicing, and returns management. If we try to apply the guideline stated earlier, we run into a complication: sales seems to be a process, but it also seems to be made up of other processes. Does the study of sales require multiple fact tables, or just one?

Rather than use the concepts of process modeling to drive star schema development, two simple tests can be used to separate measurements into multiple fact tables.

TIP For a given pair of facts, ask these questions:

1. Do these facts occur simultaneously?
2. Are these facts available at the same level of detail (or grain)?

If the answer to either of these questions is "no," the facts represent different processes.

When two facts do not describe events at the same point in time, or are not specified at the same grain, they describe different processes. For example, consider measurements such as quantity ordered and quantity shipped. Orders and shipments do not necessarily occur simultaneously. When an order is placed, information about shipments has yet to be determined. Shipment information is finalized later. Quantity ordered and quantity shipped also fail to share the same level of detail or grain. Shipment quantities are associated with specific shippers, while order quantities are not.

In this case, quantity ordered and quantity shipped failed both tests. Orders and shipments are two separate processes. If there will be people who want to analyze either process on its own, it will necessitate multiple fact tables. To understand why, we will look at these examples in more detail.

NOTE While it *is* important that each process that will be studied individually has its own fact table, it is *not* the case that every fact table should correspond to one process.

Multiple-process fact tables can be useful when *comparing* processes. They are derived from other fact tables, and may contain aggregated data. For example, sales analysis may be supported by creating a star that summarizes multiple stars: proposals, orders, shipments, and returns. Examples will be explored in Chapter 14, "Derived Schemas."

If there is no desire to study the processes individually, fact tables for the individual processes may be omitted. This may lead to difficulty if a user decides to focus on one fact, as you are about to learn.

Facts that Have Different Timing

When two or more facts describe events that do not take place at the same time, they describe different processes. If they are placed in a single fact table, analysis of the individual processes will be hampered. Placing them in separate fact tables allows each process to be studied more easily.

To understand how this happens, it is useful to study an example. Presume that business requirements for the sales department have been identified and are expressed as follows:

- Analyze **Quantity Ordered** by ***Date***, ***Customer***, and ***Product***
- Analyze **Quantity Shipped** by ***Date***, ***Customer***, and ***Product***

These statements identify measurements (facts) in bold text, and context (dimensions) in bold italic text. Each expresses the lowest level of detail at which the measurement will be studied.

Although they share the same dimensionality, the two measurements do not occur at the same time. For example, on days when a customer orders a product, there may not be shipments. Quantity Ordered and Quantity Shipped do not describe the same process.

A Single Fact Table Causes Difficulties

The star schema at the top of Figure 4-1 attempts to address the requirements using a single fact table: sales_facts. It contains the facts quantity_ordered and quantity_shipped. Attributes of the associated dimension tables have been omitted from the illustration. The grain of this fact table requires that orders, shipments, or both be recorded by day, product, and customer. This might also be stated as "shipments and/or orders." The presence of "and/or" in a statement of grain is usually a sign of problems to come, as you will see shortly.

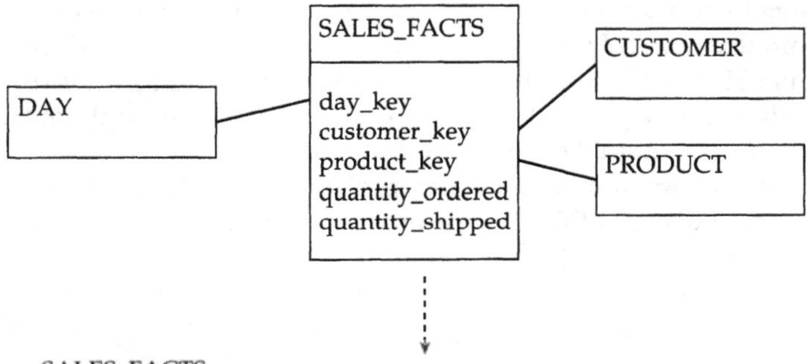

SALES_FACTS

day_key	customer_key	product_key	quantity_ordered	quantity_shipped
123	777	111	100	0
123	777	222	200	0
123	777	333	50	0
456	777	111	0	100
456	777	222	0	75
789	777	222	0	125

These zeros will cause trouble

Figure 4-1 Facts with different timing in a single table

To determine how well this star supports analysis of orders and shipments, it is necessary to look inside the fact table. The lower half of Figure 4-1 shows several rows of data from sales_ facts. The first three columns are foreign keys that refer to the dimension tables. Although these keys carry no intrinsic meaning, values have been chosen for this example to make them easy to distinguish from one another.

All six of the sample rows are for the same customer, identified by customer_key 777. For the purposes of this discussion, the customer will be called "customer 777." In reality, surrogate keys do not have any intrinsic meaning, but this will make the example easier to follow. The first three rows identify orders that took place on the same day, as identified by day_key 123. We will call this day "day 123." On that day, customer 777 ordered three different products, which we will refer to as product 111, product 222, and product 333.

These three rows of orders provide a dilemma. What values should be placed in the quantity_shipped column? There were no shipments on day 123. Two possibilities are to record NULL values, or to record values of 0. For the time being, assume that a zero is recorded for quantity_shipped when there is an order but no shipment on a particular day.

Continuing down the table of sample rows, notice that the next two rows describe activity for the same customer on day 456. On that day, shipments occurred for products 111 and 222. On this day, the converse situation exists: there are shipments of products to customer 777 but no orders. In this case, the value 0 is recorded for quantity_ordered. Similarly, the final row of sample data shows that on day 789, another shipment occurred for product 222.

Now suppose that someone is interested in studying shipments to customer 777, and that they generate a report from this fact table. They might run a simple query to produce a report like the one shown in Figure 4-2, showing quantity shipped by product. This report summarizes the fact table data from Figure 4-1. Again, it is not customary to study key values; normally you would expect to see natural keys or product names.

When a single fact table tracks two or more processes, problems occur when someone is interested in studying only one process. In this case, the process being examined is shipments, and the problem is evident in the final row of the report. Although product 333 has not shipped during the reporting period, it appears on the report, with a quantity_shipped of 0. A typical report might be much larger, containing numerous zeros scattered throughout. This can

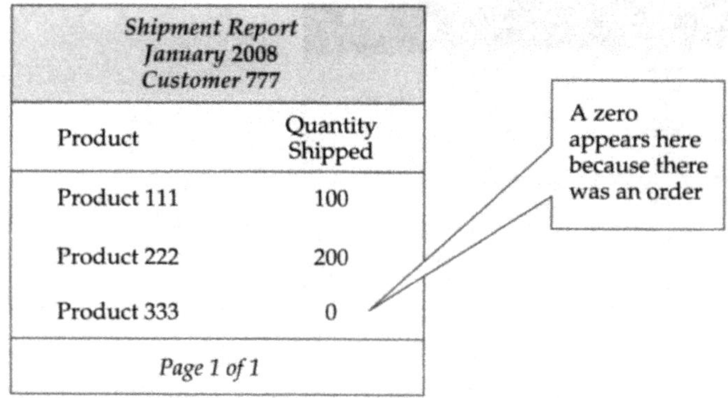

Shipment Report
January 2008
Customer 777
Product
Quantity Shipped
Product 111
100
Product 222
200
Product 333
0
Page 1 of 1
A zero appears here because there was an order

Figure 4-2 A report that focuses on shipping has extraneous data

be very confusing to end users, who will rightly ask, "Why is product 333 showing up on this report? We did not ship product 444 either, and I don't see that one on the report. What gives?"

The appearance of product 333 on this report is easily explained: it is there because the customer ordered it during the time period in question. The order caused a row to be recorded in the fact table. Since there was no shipment of that product to that customer on the same day, the quantity_shipped was recorded as 0. This explanation is little consolation to business users trying to analyze shipment data. They are not interested in the fact that orders occurred. To them, these zero-valued facts are a perplexing annoyance.

The phenomenon of zero-valued facts showing up on reports is common when multiple processes are modeled in a single fact table. If people want to study only one of the processes, they will encounter what appear to be extraneous rows. This is attributable to a lapse in sparsity. In the case of quantity_shipped, its pairing with quantity_ordered required a row to be recorded when an exclusive focus on shipments would not. Notice that the use of NULL values would not have solved the problem. Product 333 would still appear on the report, only this time with a blank instead of a zero.

TIP When two or more facts do not occur simultaneously, they represent different processes. Placing them in a single fact table will hamper analysis of the individual processes.

One might be tempted to try addressing the zero-valued result problem at query time rather than schema design time. For example, the query to produce the report in Figure 4-2 might be adjusted to contain a `HAVING` clause:

```
SELECT product_key, SUM(quantity_shipped) FROM sales_facts
GROUP BY product_key
HAVING SUM(quantity_shipped) > 0
```

In order to work around a shortcoming of the design, the reporting process has been made more complicated. This adjustment to the SQL must be tacked onto *every query* that studies shipments; a similar clause must be added to every query that focuses on orders. If there is more than one fact associated with each process, it will be necessary to keep track of which clauses to add in each situation.

This workaround is an example of something an old friend of mine used to call "boiling the frog." You may have heard this story before. If you place a frog into a pot of water on the stove, and turn up the temperature a degree, he will not notice the change. If you continue to increase the temperature by one degree at a time, each change is so small that he will continue not to perceive any changes. Eventually, he will boil to death. In reality, of course, the frog will jump out of the pot at some point. The story, however, illustrates the effect of poor schema design. Report developers are like the frog in the story. Every "workaround" that they must employ is like a one-degree change in temperature. Each workaround seems small, but their cumulative effect can be unbearable. When studying one process, it will always be necessary to insert the `HAVING` clause. Other types of queries will be impacted as well—counts, averages, subqueries, and correlated subqueries will all be rendered more complicated. Worse, it will also be important to remember that when studying the two processes together, the `HAVING` clause must be removed. Schema design time, as my friend used to say, is your chance to "un-boil" the frog.

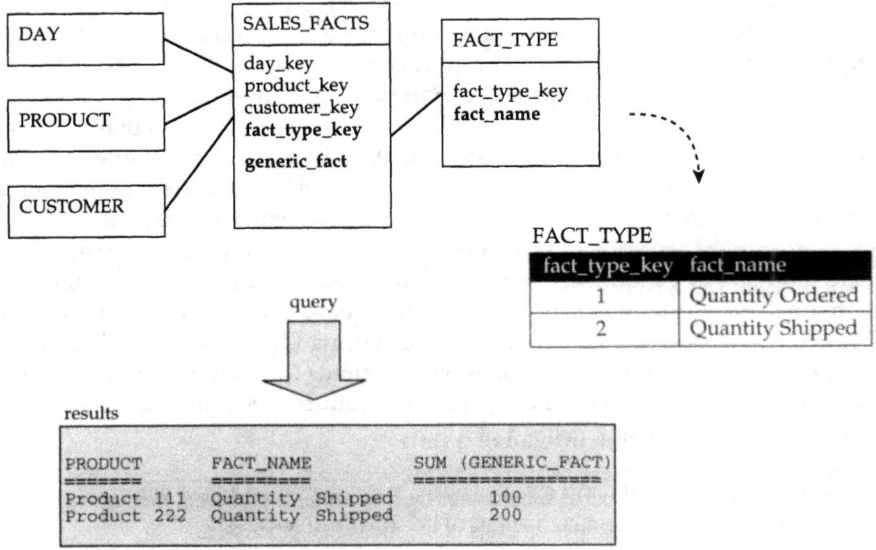

Figure 4-3 Modeling a generic fact complicates cross-process analysis

A variation on the single fact table solution is to record only one generic fact. A new dimension will determine whether it represents an order or a shipment. An example of this technique is shown in Figure 4-3. This approach solves the zero-valued row problem, because each row is either an order or a shipment. Notice that queries must still qualify on the type of fact to be studied. In addition, the query results will show up in an unusual format that will require additional formatting inside reports. This format becomes even more problematic for queries that compare both processes. Information desired in a columnar format will be returned in different rows. Once again, design shortcomings will cause suffering among report developers.

Modeling in Separate Fact Tables

Rather than come up with other ways to boil the frog, the preferred solution is to model each process in its own fact table. In the case of orders and shipments, an example is provided in Figure 4-4. Notice that each fact table shares the common dimensions day, product, and customer. Each stores only the appropriate facts; there is no need to record extraneous zeros.

Set up in this manner, it is now possible to study the individual process without additional bother. Those seeking information about orders can use order_facts; those seeking information about shipments can use shipment_facts. If either of these processes has additional facts, they can be added to the appropriate fact table.

There is another matter to be considered: now that the facts are recorded in separate fact tables, how does one study them together? Before we get to that question, let's take a look at the other clue that two facts describe different processes.

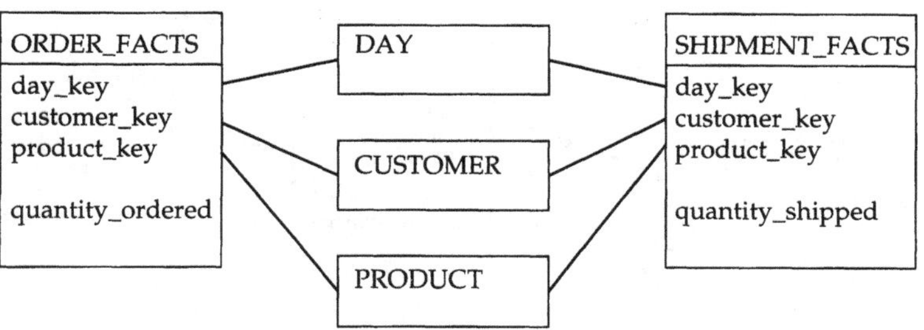

ORDER_FACTS

day_key	customer_key	product_key	quantity_ordered
123	777	111	100
123	777	222	200
123	777	333	50

SHIPMENT_FACTS

day_key	customer_key	product_key	quantity_shipped
456	777	111	100
456	777	222	75
789	777	222	125

Figure 4-4 Separating the two processes into separate fact tables with shared dimensions

Facts that Have Different Grain

When two or more facts describe events with differing grain, they describe different processes. As with facts of differing timing, if they are placed in a single fact table, analysis of the individual processes can be hampered. Placing them in separate fact tables allows each process to be studied more easily.

To understand how this happens, the orders and shipments example will be extended. Presume that business requirements for the sales department have been identified and are expressed as follows:

- Analyze **Quantity Ordered** by ***Date***, ***Customer***, and ***Product***
- Analyze **Quantity Shipped** by ***Date***, ***Customer***, ***Product***, and ***Shipper***

These requirements differ from the previous example in one critical aspect: quantity_shipped comes with an additional dimensional detail: the shipper. This information only applies to shipments, not to orders.

A Single Fact Table Causes Difficulties

The star schema at the top of Figure 4-5 attempts to address the requirements using a single fact table: sales_facts. It contains the facts quantity_ordered and quantity_shipped. The grain of this fact table requires that orders, shipments, or both be recorded by day, product, customer, and optionally shipper. As you have already seen, the presence of "or" in a statement of grain is a sign of problems to come. This time, other complications exist as well.

This star differs from the one shown in Figure 4-1 in that it includes a shipper dimension. In order to deal with situations where a day, product, and customer combination has orders but no shipments, this design adds a special row to the shipper dimension. This row, as

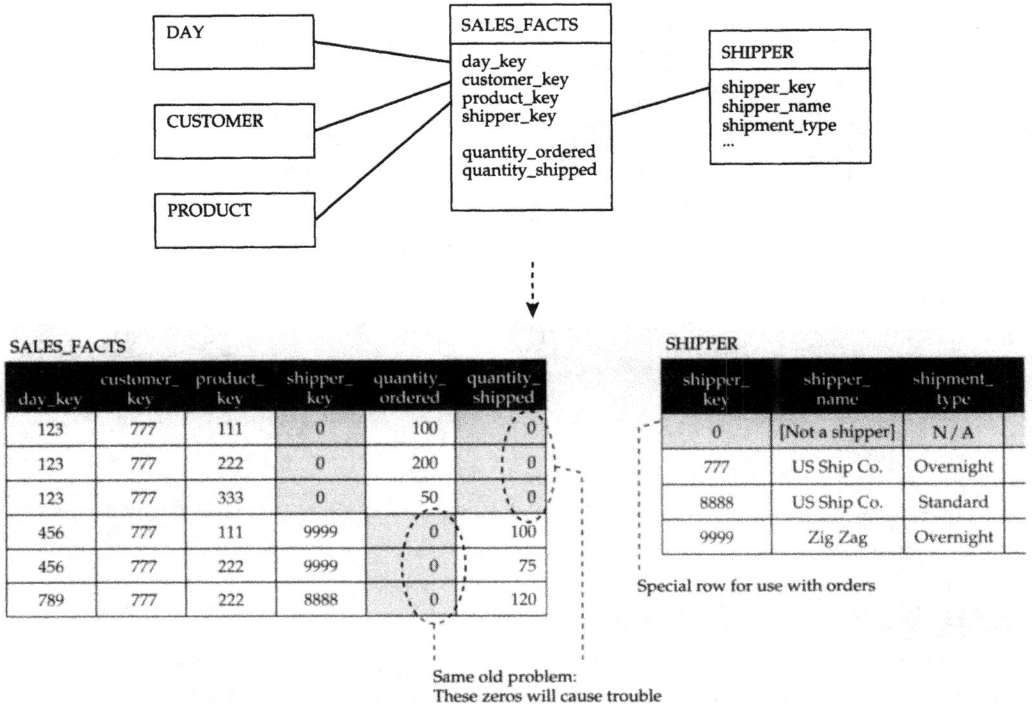

SALES_FACTS

day_key	customer_key	product_key	shipper_key	quantity_ordered	quantity_shipped
123	777	111	0	100	0
123	777	222	0	200	0
123	777	333	0	50	0
456	777	111	9999	0	100
456	777	222	9999	0	75
789	777	222	8888	0	120

SHIPPER

shipper_key	shipper_name	shipment_type
0	[Not a shipper]	N / A
777	US Ship Co.	Overnight
8888	US Ship Co.	Standard
9999	Zig Zag	Overnight

Figure 4-5 Facts with different grain in a single table

highlighted in the diagram, happens to have the surrogate key value 0. This key value is used in the first three rows of the fact table, for situations where there is an order but no shipment.

Now consider how this multi-process fact table behaves when a user analyzes a single-process: shipments. The sample report in Figure 4-6 shows quantity shipped by product and shipper for customer 777. Again, it is not customary to study key values; normally you would expect to see natural keys or product names.

As in the previous example, this report has a confusing preponderance of rows with the value 0. In addition, these rows contain the cryptic shipper name "[not a shipper]." As before, the presence of these rows may be confusing to business users, who note that other products which did not ship do not appear on the report. This situation can be dealt with using the same techniques described previously: adding a `HAVING` clause, or generalizing the facts. As before, the result is undue complication for the reporting effort when a single process is being studied.

NOTE The situation in this example becomes exacerbated when orders and shipments occur on the same day for the same product and customer. In this case, it becomes necessary to store two rows. One corresponds to the orders, which have no attendant shipper data, and the other is for the shipments, which have no order data. In fact, orders and shipments will never be recorded in the same fact table row!

Shipment Report by Shipper January 2008 Customer 777		
Product	Shipper Name	Quantity Shipped
Product 111	[not a shipper]	0
Product 111	Zig-Zag Inc.	100
Product 222	[not a shipper]	0
Product 222	Zig-Zag Inc.	75
Product 222	US Ship Co.	125
Product 333	[not a shipper]	0
Page 1 of 1		

Figure 4-6 A report that focuses on shipping has confusing data

An alternative single-fact table design allows NULL keys for fact table rows with no shipper. Unfortunately, this approach further complicates the reporting challenges. The use of NULL keys does cause the extraneous rows to disappear from the shipper report, as shown in the first report in Figure 4-7. This works because the shipper dimension has been included in the report. Unfortunately, the second report in the figure shows that, when the shipper table is *not* involved in the query, zero-valued facts return. This occurs because there is no join from the fact table to the shipper dimension.

TIP When two or more facts have different grain, they represent different processes. Placing them together in a single fact table will hamper analysis of the individual processes.

Further complicating matters, allowing NULL values for the shipper_key in the fact table requires a *different* join configuration when studying orders and shipments together. In such a case, it would be necessary to perform an outer join, so as not to omit the rows with orders and no facts. This outer join, in turn, would make it difficult to qualify for a particular shipper type.

NOTE Do not generalize this example to assume that optional relationships are the problem. In this example, problems occur because the facts have different grain. One fact involves shipper, the other does not.

There *are* cases when a single fact has an optional relationship to a dimension. For example, some orders may have supervisory approval, while others do not. This supervisory involvement does not affect the grain of the fact. Strategies for dealing with optional relationships are discussed in Chapter 6, "More on Dimension Tables."

Part II

SALES_FACTS

day_key	customer_key	product_key	shipper_key	quantity_ordered	quantity_shipped
123	777	111	(NULL)	100	0
123	777	222	(NULL)	200	0
123	777	333	(NULL)	50	0
456	777	111	9999	0	100
456	777	222	9999	0	75
789	777	222	8888	0	125

SHIPPER

shipper_key	shipper_name	shipment_type
7777	US Ship Co.	Overnight
8888	US Ship Co.	Standard
9999	Zig Zag	Overnight

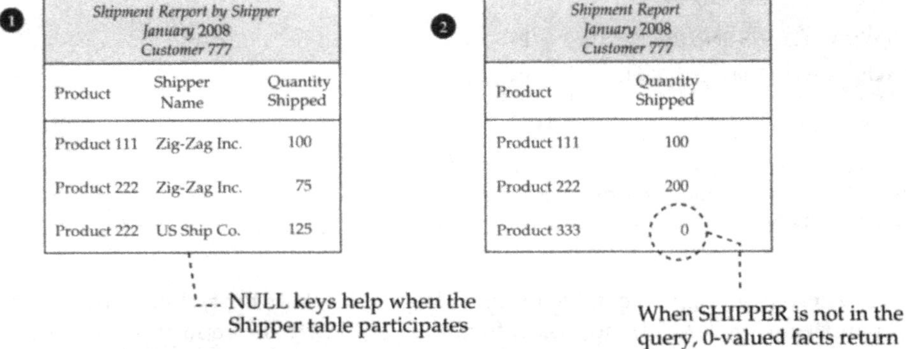

1 *Shipment Rerport by Shipper*
January 2008
Customer 777

Product	Shipper Name	Quantity Shipped
Product 111	Zig-Zag Inc.	100
Product 222	Zig-Zag Inc.	75
Product 222	US Ship Co.	125

2 *Shipment Report*
January 2008
Customer 777

Product	Quantity Shipped
Product 111	100
Product 222	200
Product 333	0

Figure 4-7 Allowing NULL foreign key values does not solve the problem

Modeling in Separate Fact Tables

When two facts exhibit different grain, they represent different processes. As seen earlier, placing them in a single fact table will generate trouble when someone focuses on one of the processes. Rather than complicating the analysis process for these users, the facts are placed in different fact tables. Figure 4-8 shows an example.

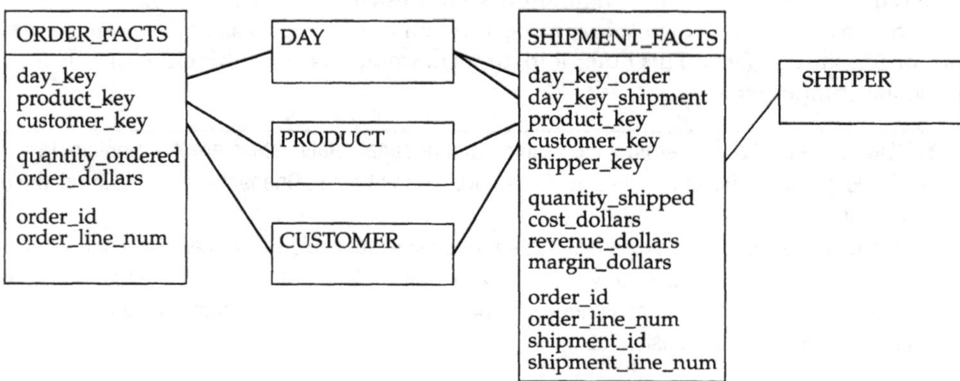

Figure 4-8 Separating the two processes into separate fact tables

Additional detail has been added to the pair of stars in Figure 4-8, to fill out the example and follow some best practices you have already learned. More facts have been added to each fact table, even where some seem redundant. The orders process generates order dollars; the shipping process generates product cost and revenue. Think about how these additional facts may have complicated the "generic fact" alternative. To capture orders at the lowest level of detail, degenerate dimensions have been added to capture the order_id and order_line. In this example, a shipment can be tied to an order, so these degenerate dimensions appear in shipment_facts as well. The shipment fact table also includes degenerate dimensions to identify the shipment_id and shipment_line. Notice that shipments have two relationships to day: one that represents the date of the order, the second representing the date of the shipment. This design technique will be described in more detail in Chapter 6.

In most situations, you will find that facts from different processes exhibit *both* the characteristics described in this chapter: they do not occur simultaneously, *and* they are available at different levels of dimensionality. These differences usually become clear when you look beyond the requirements to identify the lowest level of detail at which each fact is available. In some situations, facts occur simultaneously but have different grain. Measurements that apply only to the order header, and not to individual order lines, for example, might belong in a separate fact table.

Analyzing Facts from More than One Fact Table

While analysis of individual processes is useful, the ability to compare them is equally important. Some of the most powerful analytics work across process boundaries. Examples include the comparison of forecasts to actuals, production to orders, orders to shipments, and so forth. A properly constructed dimensional design achieves this important synergy.

As this chapter has shown, when there is more than one business process, and each process will be studied individually, it is important to provide one fact table per process. Otherwise, single-process analysis is seriously hampered. Now it is necessary to consider what happens when someone wants to compare the processes.

When comparing facts from different fact tables, it is important not to collect them in the same SQL `SELECT` clause. Doing so risks double counting, or worse. Instead, the information must be gathered in a two-step process called *drilling across*. This process has nothing to do with drilling up or down into data; it describes the steps involved in crossing from one star to another.

The process of drilling across, and the consequences of doing so incorrectly, will be explained by returning to the simplified orders and shipments example. Figure 4-9 illustrates a pair of stars, one representing orders and one representing shipments. Beneath them, a simple report compares orders to shipments during a period of time. This simple report will be used to illustrate the wrong way and the right way to query multiple fact tables.

After establishing guidelines that describe *what* needs to happen when drilling across, we will look at *how* it is commonly done. A drill-across report can be constructed using three primary methods. For situations where the toolset does not support any of these approaches, there is a schema design solution as well.

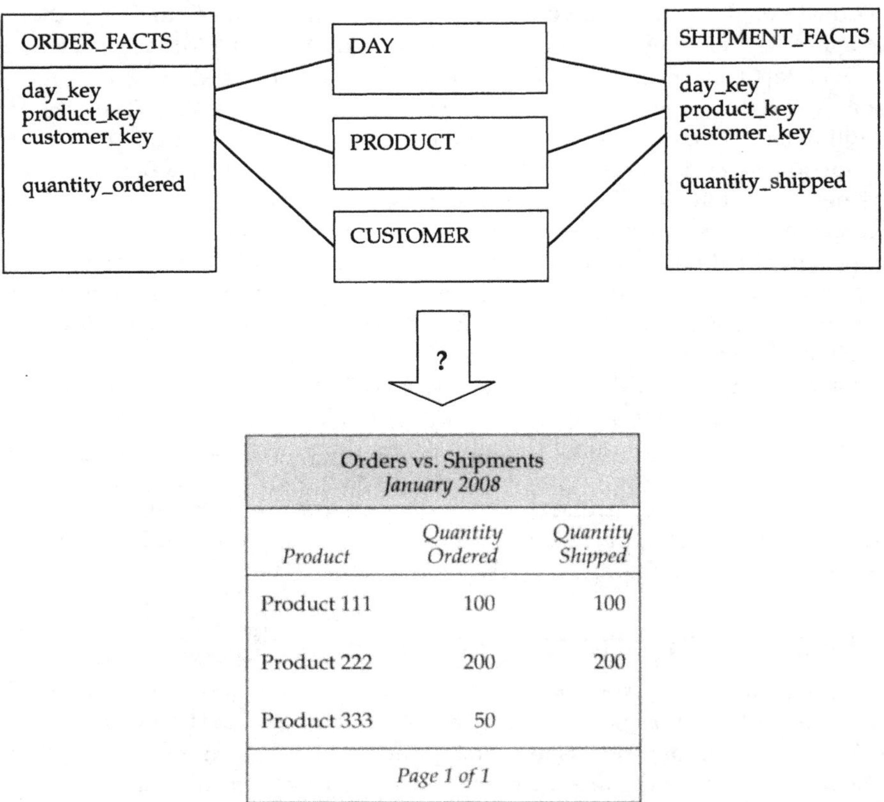

Orders vs. Shipments
January 2008

Product	*Quantity Ordered*	*Quantity Shipped*
Product 111	100	100
Product 222	200	200
Product 333	50	

Page 1 of 1

Figure 4-9 A report involving multiple fact tables

The Peril of Joining Fact Tables

A dimension table can be thought of as the parent in a parent–child relationship with a fact table. If the dimension is related to other fact tables, child rows in each of the fact tables can be thought of as siblings; they share a common parent. For example, a given product may have multiple corresponding rows, or "children," in an order_facts table. The same product may also have one or more child rows in shipment_facts. The fact tables at the top of Figure 4-10 illustrate this phenomenon. The product designated by product_key 222 has one corresponding row in order_facts, and two corresponding rows in shipment_facts. The order for product 222 is a sibling of each of the two shipments.

When a SQL query attempts to join siblings together, either directly or through a common parent, the RDBMS will match each child from one table with each of its siblings in the other. The result is known as a Cartesian product. This occurs when two fact tables are joined directly together or through a common dimension. In a query summarizing orders and shipments by product, for example, the single order for product 222 will be paired with each of the two shipments for product 222. This has the unfortunate effect of double counting the order. If there were three shipments, it would be tripling the count. The same would happen to a shipment if there were multiple corresponding orders.

ORDER_FACTS

day_key	customer_key	product_key	quantity_key
123	777	111	100
123	777	222	200
123	777	333	50

SHIPMENT_FACTS

day_key	customer_key	product_key	quantity_shipped
456	777	111	100
456	777	222	75
789	777	222	125

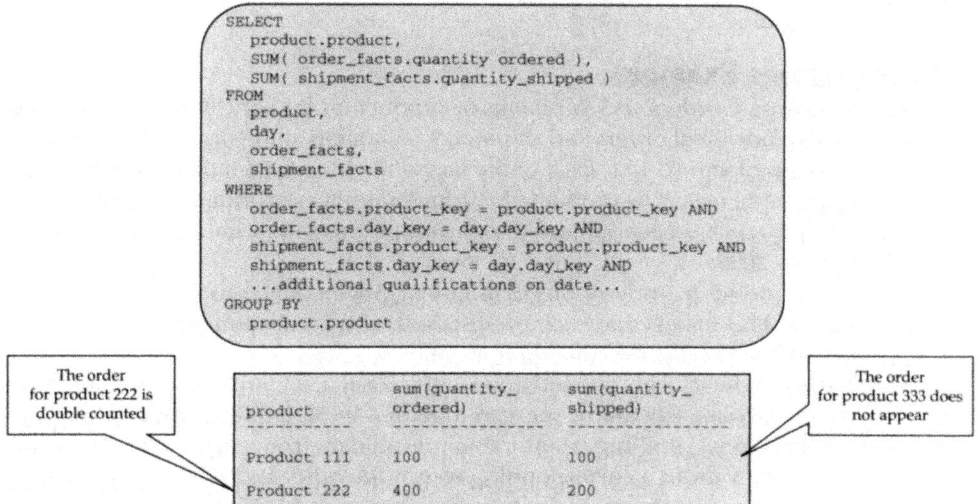

SELECT
product.product,
SUM(order_facts.quantity ordered),
SUM(shipment_facts.quantity_shipped)
FROM
product,
day,
order_facts,
shipment_facts
WHERE
order_facts.product_key = product.product_key AND
order_facts.day_key = day.day_key AND
shipment_facts.product_key = product.product_key AND
shipment_facts.day_key = day.day_key AND
...additional qualifications on date...
GROUP BY
product.product
The order for product 222 is double counted
product sum(quantity_ ordered) sum(quantity_ shipped)
Product 111 100 100
Product 222 400 200
The order for product 333 does not appear

Figure 4-10 Joining two fact tables leads to trouble

TIP Never attempt to join to two fact tables, either directly or through a common dimension. This can produce inaccurate results.

The result of this Cartesian effect is evident in the report at the bottom portion of Figure 4-10. The query attempts to select total orders and total shipments and group them by product. Since product 222 has one order and two shipments within the scope of aggregation, the order is double counted. The resulting report incorrectly shows 400 units ordered.

Also notice that product 333 does not show up in the report at all. Although it was ordered, there were no corresponding shipments. The RDBMS was therefore not able to join the order to corresponding shipments. The SQL-literate reader may suggest substituting outer joins to the dimension tables; however, this will not solve the problem as the query has been qualified within the day dimension.

Drilling Across

The proper way to compare two processes is called *drilling across.* This term has a tendency to cause confusion. Although the word "drill" is used, this process is unrelated to the drill-up, drill-down, or drill-through capabilities of many query and reporting tools. Instead, the term is meant to describe crossing multiple processes. While it is common to speak of a drill-across operation as a drill-across query, the operation is often carried out through more than one query.

Drilling across is successfully completed by decomposing the collection of data into discrete steps. The first step summarizes facts from each star at a common level of detail; the second step combines them. The technique can be used on two or more stars, across multiple databases, and even on data stored in RDBMSs from different vendors. You can also use drill-across techniques to query a single star more than once, producing useful comparison reports.

A Drill-Across Example

In order to compare orders and shipments by product for January 2008, it is first necessary to summarize the individual orders and shipments separately, at the desired level of dimensional detail. At the top of Figure 4-11, each of the fact tables is queried individually. The orders query provides total orders by product; the shipments query provides total shipments by product. Each query has been subjected to the same constraints, in order to return results only for January 2008.

These two queries provide results that have aggregated facts to exactly the same level of dimensionality. This means that each product will have at most one row in each result set. Each result set has exactly the same dimensionality.

Once the facts have been queried and summarized at a common level of dimensionality, the intermediate result sets can be merged together. In SQL terms, a full outer join is required. That is to say, it is important to include all data from each result set, even if there is a row in one set without a corresponding row in the other set. This merge operation provides the final results shown in the bottom of Figure 4-11. During this merge operation, it is possible to produce comparisons of the various metrics. In the illustration, the ratio of orders to shipments during the period has been added.

By separating the process into two phases, the drill-across solution has avoided double counting the order for product 222, and has not lost track of the order for product 333. This simple example can be extrapolated into a two-phase procedure for drilling across.

Drill-Across Procedure

Every drill-across operation has two phases, as summarized in Figure 4-12. Phase 1 retrieves facts from each fact table, applying appropriate filters, and outputting the result at the desired level of dimensional detail. Phase 2 merges the intermediate result sets together. During the merge process, it is possible to add comparisons of the facts from different processes.

This process is not limited to two fact tables. It can be expanded to work with three, four, or any number *n* of fact tables. In the first phase, each of the *n* fact tables is queried. This generates *n* intermediate result sets, all at the same level of dimensional detail. Each of the *n* sets is then combined a pair at a time. Any sequence is acceptable, as all result sets share the same level of dimensional detail. Any ratios can be constructed as a last step.

The diagram in Figure 4-13 illustrates a report that drills across four fact tables. The first contains information about sales calls, the second tracks sales proposals, the third tracks orders, and the fourth tracks shipment revenue. The report at the bottom of the page rolls up key measurements from each of these tables by period and sales region, and indicates the ratio of sales calls to orders.

ORDER_FACTS

day_key	customer_key	product_key	quantity_ordered
123	777	111	100
123	777	222	200
123	777	333	50

SHIPMENT_FACTS

day_key	customer_key	product_key	quantity_shipped
456	777	111	100
456	777	222	75
789	777	222	125

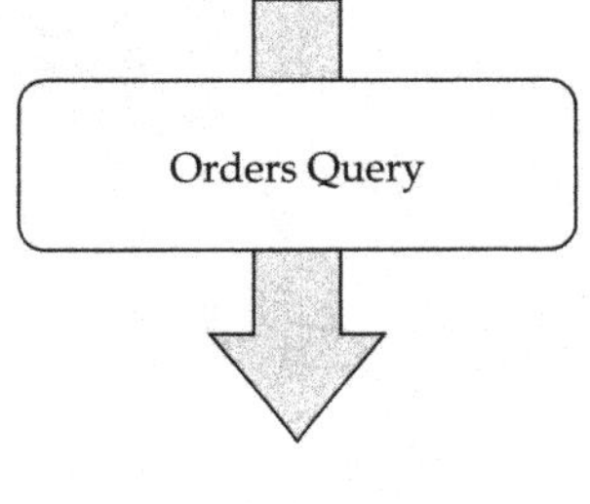

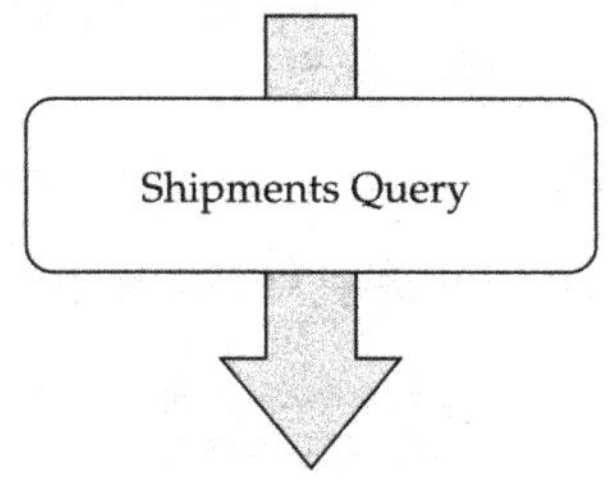


```
product          quantity ordered
===========      ================
Product 111      100
Product 222      200
Product 333      50
```

```
product          quantity shipped
===========      ================
Product 111      100
Product 222      200
```

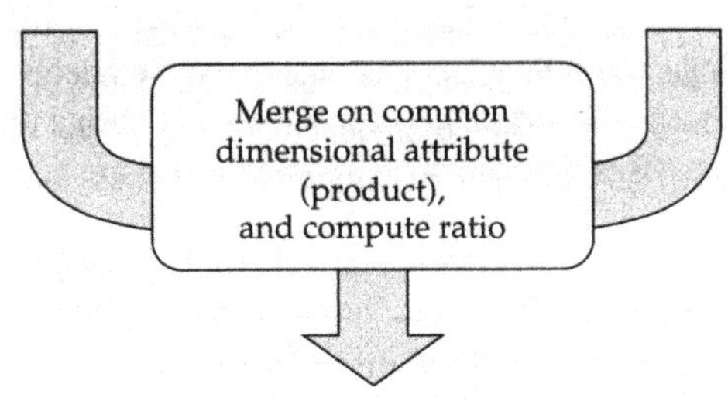


```
product       quantity ordered   quantity shipped   ratio
===========   ================   ================   ======
Product 111         100                100            100%
Product 222         200                200            100%
Product 333          50                                 0%
```

Figure 4-11 Drilling across orders and shipments

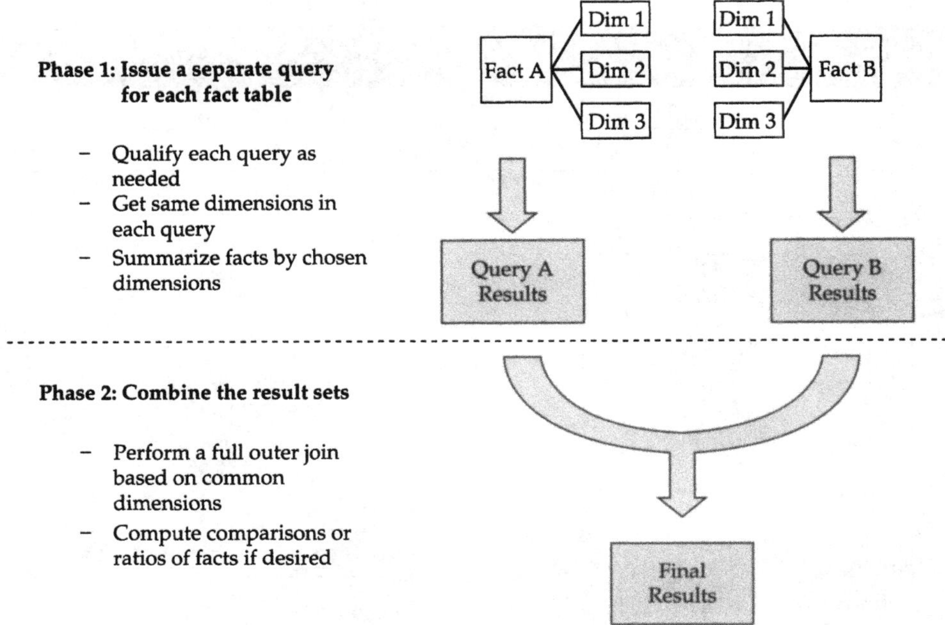

Figure 4-12 Drilling across

TIP Cross-process ratios are powerful measurements. Because they do not correspond to a single column, or even a single table, they are often lost in the metadata collected by design tools and reporting software. These ratios should be documented at design time, highlighting the interaction between business processes that can be supported by the star schemas.

In principle, there is no reason that each of the fact tables participating in a drill-across report must reside in the same database. The queries in Phase 1 can take place on different database instances, or even databases from different vendors. In Figure 4-13, each of the four stars resides in a different database, from a different vendor. The intermediate result sets are then combined to produce the final report.

For all of this to work, it is important that the common dimensions be the *same* in each database, both in terms of *structure* and *content*. In terms of structure, their presence in each star allows the common dimensions to be retrieved by each phase 1 query. In terms of content, the identical representation of dimension values enables merging of the intermediate results during Phase 2.

For example, in Figure 4-13, the period and region dimensions are present in all stars. This allows each Phase 1 query to aggregate information by period and region. The content of these dimensions is represented identically as well. In all databases, periods are specified as “Q1” through “Q4” and regions as “North,” “South,” and so forth. Because the content values are identical, they can be used to join the result sets together in Phase 2. If one or more of the databases had different region designations, or specified periods as “First Quarter” through “Fourth Quarter,” it would not be possible to complete the merge.

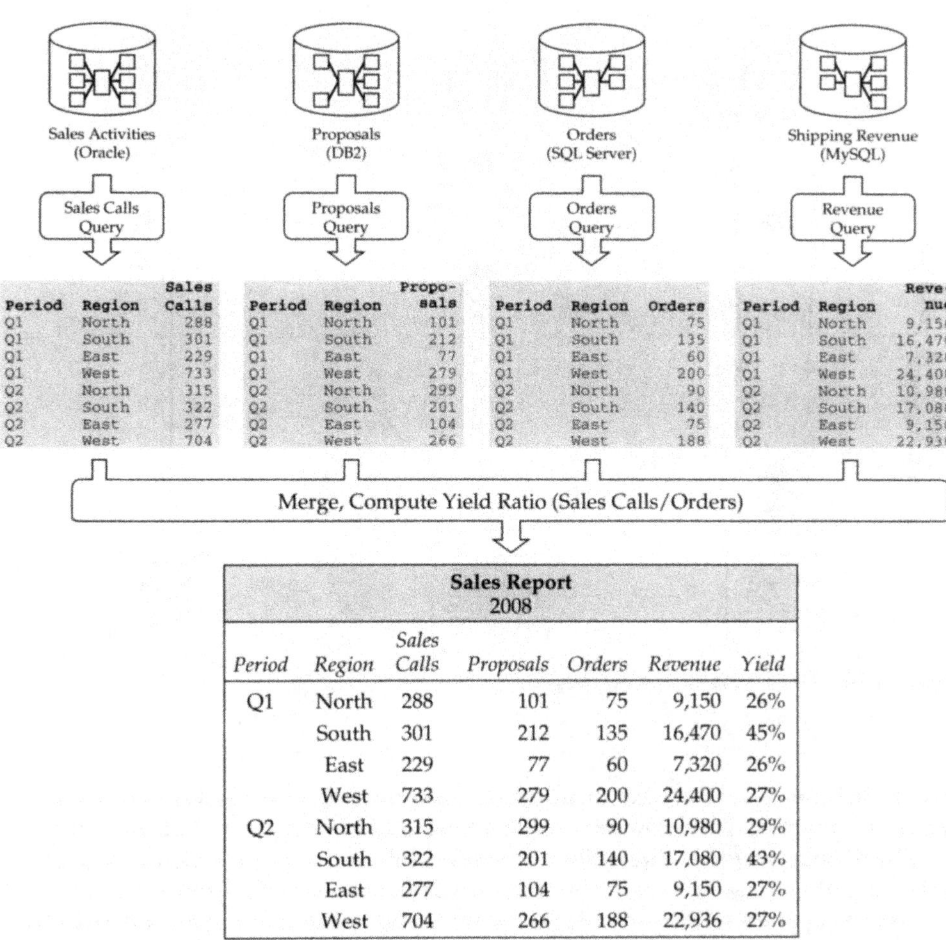

Period	Region	Sales Calls
Q1	North	288
Q1	South	301
Q1	East	229
Q1	West	733
Q2	North	315
Q2	South	322
Q2	East	277
Q2	West	704

Period	Region	Propo-sals
Q1	North	101
Q1	South	212
Q1	East	77
Q1	West	279
Q2	North	299
Q2	South	201
Q2	East	104
Q2	West	266

Period	Region	Orders
Q1	North	75
Q1	South	135
Q1	East	60
Q1	West	200
Q2	North	90
Q2	South	140
Q2	East	75
Q2	West	188

Period	Region	Reve-nue
Q1	North	9,150
Q1	South	16,470
Q1	East	7,320
Q1	West	24,400
Q2	North	10,980
Q2	South	17,080
Q2	East	9,150
Q2	West	22,936

Sales Report
2008

Period	*Region*	*Sales Calls*	*Proposals*	*Orders*	*Revenue*	*Yield*
Q1	North	288	101	75	9,150	26%
	South	301	212	135	16,470	45%
	East	229	77	60	7,320	26%
	West	733	279	200	24,400	27%
Q2	North	315	299	90	10,980	29%
	South	322	201	140	17,080	43%
	East	277	104	75	9,150	27%
	West	704	266	188	22,936	27%

Figure 4-13 Drilling across four fact tables

Clearly, this "sameness" of dimensions is crucial for drilling across. It will be formalized and extended in Chapter 5, as the principle of *conformed dimensions.* Conformed dimensions are the key to ensuring that analysis can cross multiple stars or even multiple subject areas.

Finally, notice that the drill-across process can be applied to a single star to produce useful comparisons. For example, a "this year versus last" report might show orders by region for the current period and the same period last year, with a ratio showing the percent increase. This report can be constructed by querying orders by region for this year, and again for last year. The two sets of results can then be joined on region values for a "current year versus last" comparison.

Drill-Across Implementations

The guidelines in Figure 4-12 specify *what* needs to happen when drilling across. *How* these steps are carried out is another matter. A number of ways will meet the challenge, whether

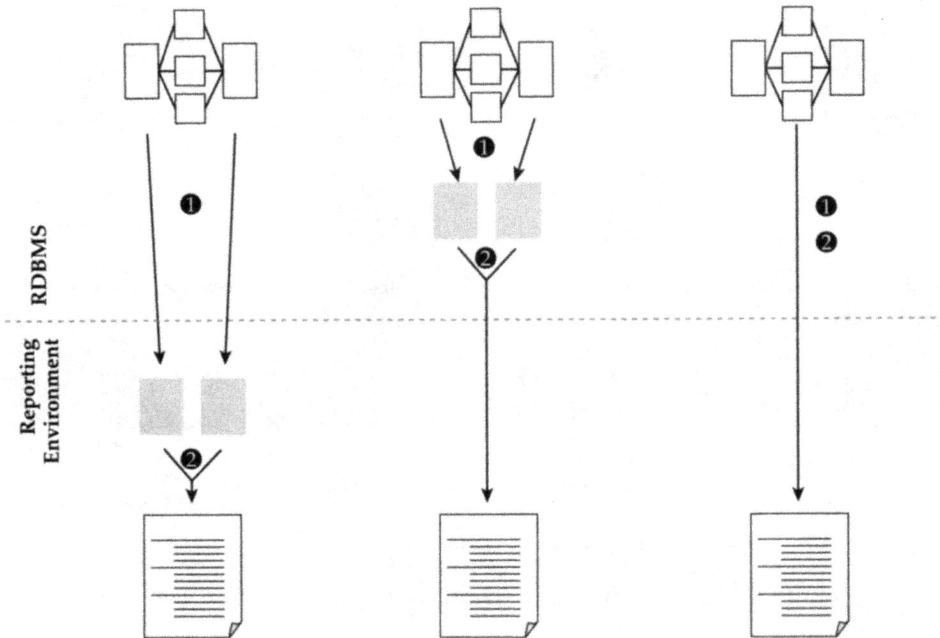

Figure 4-14 Three ways to drill across

you are writing code by hand, or using a business intelligence tool that automatically generates queries. Three common implementations are depicted in Figure 4-14.

The diagram depicts three different ways to drill across. Each begins with a pair of stars at the top of the page and ends with a report at the bottom of the page. The phases of the drill-across operations are indicated by the numerals 1 and 2; intermediate result sets are depicted as gray boxes. It may be helpful to think in terms of the orders and shipments example. Phase 1 involves separate queries for orders and shipments, each grouping results by product. Phase 2 merges these intermediate result sets and produces a ratio for the final report.

The diagram also segregates activities based on where they take place: on the database versus within a reporting environment. The database may be a single RDBMS instance or a distributed implementation; the reporting environment may be a simple desktop client or a combination of application servers, web servers, and browsers.

Splitting the Processing

The first implementation approach, on the left side of Figure 4-14, splits the processing between the RDBMS environment and the reporting environment. In the top half of the diagram, two queries are executed: one for each of the stars. Each of these queries retrieves the same dimensions, and aggregates the respective facts to that level.

The results of these queries are sent to the reporting environment, where Phase 2 will be performed. Whether on a desktop tool or application server, this phase is not performed by the RDBMS. The reporting application merges the result sets in this environment to produce the final report.

This approach may be implemented using procedural logic, supported by your reporting tool, or automatically invoked by a business intelligence product (see the sidebar). In each case, it effectively avoids the hazard of joining two fact tables, providing accurate and consistent results.

The execution of Phase 2 outside the realm of the database is often criticized as inefficient. Detractors point out that information is moved across the network to an application server to be joined, despite the fact that the RDBMS is specifically designed to join data sets. Notice, however, that the join process in Phase 2 is a full outer join. This process requires each data set to be sorted consistently, and then merged together. If the DBMS is asked to sort the data before it is forwarded to the application server, all that remains is the merge, which is relatively simple. In fact, performance *gains* may be realized by performing this merge without the overhead of the RDBMS.

Business Intelligence Tools and Automation of Drill-Across Reports

Reporting tools allow users to build queries and lay out the results in a variety of ways. Business intelligence tools take this concept one step further, allowing queries to be built without requiring any specific knowledge of the database.

These tools achieve this result by mapping together two views of information: a business view and a physical view. The business view is a representation of "things available to report on," and is the only view made available to users. Behind the scenes, the business view of information is mapped to the physical database schema. This mapping of the two views is configured by a technical developer.

When users drag data elements onto a report canvas, the tool uses information it understands about the business view and how it maps to a physical view to generate the necessary queries. The concept of a business view that is mapped to physical structures is called a *semantic layer*. It has been patented by Business Objects (now a part of SAP) and is employed by numerous vendors.

Each of the three paradigms for drilling across presented in this chapter has been employed by at least one commercially available business intelligence tool. In theory, this allows the tool to identify requests that involve more than one fact table, and to respond by generating the appropriate processing. The catch here is that the tool may require very specific configuration to support automated drill-across. Complicating the situation, some tools can drill across only in limited situations. Unfortunately, most vendors do not refer to this process as drilling across, instead using their own name for the process, and leaving it to the technical staff to figure out how it should be configured. These topics are discussed in Chapter 16, "Design and Business Intelligence."

Using Temporary Tables

The second approach is similar to the first, but relies on the RDBMS to perform both phases of processing. Shown in the center of Figure 4-14, the process begins the same way. Phase 1 executes queries for each star. This time, however, the results are not forwarded to the reporting environment. Instead, they are spooled to temporary tables on the RDBMS.

In Phase 2, an additional query is sent to the RDBMS. This query joins the two temporary tables, and optionally computes any ratios. The results of this final query are forwarded to the reporting environment.

This implementation has the advantage of keeping data on the RDBMS. Information is not moved to the reporting environment until the final step. Less processing resources may be required in the reporting environment, but more overhead is potentially required in the RDBMS environment. In fact, database administrators (DBAs) often cringe when this implementation scenario is presented. They will need to be sure that sufficient temporary space is available, that joins on the temporary tables do not consume excessive processing resources, that log files will not balloon, and that the application remembers to clean up the temporary tables when done. On the other hand, this approach fully leverages the power of the database.

Leveraging SQL

The third implementation scenario keeps processing on the database, but eliminates the need to explicitly manage temporary tables. This feat is achieved through the use of relatively new extensions to the SQL standard. As shown on the right side of Figure 4-14, a single SQL statement performs all phases of the process.

The query that achieves this drill-across operation contains two sub-queries, the results of which are joined by the main query. The `COALESCE` operator is used to consolidate dimension values from the subordinate queries; an `NVL()` function might be used in its stead. Such a query might look like the following:

```
SELECT
    COALESCE ( orders_query.product, shipments_query.product),
    orders_query.quantity_ordered,
    shipments_query.quantity_shipped,
    orders_query.quantity_ordered / shipments_query.quantity_shipped as "Ratio"
FROM
    (
    SELECT
        product.product,
        SUM (order_facts.quantity_ordered) as quantity_ordered
    FROM
        day,
        product,
        order_facts
    WHERE
  ... joins and constraints on date ...
```

```
    ) orders_query
FULL OUTER JOIN
    (
    SELECT
        product.product,
        SUM (shipment_facts.quantity_shipped) as quantity_shipped
    FROM
        day,
        product,
        shipment_facts
    WHERE
  ... joins and constraints on date ...
    ) shipments_query
ON
    orders_query.product = shipments_query.product
```

This query looks complicated because it *is* complicated. It has two nested queries, which have been aliased orders_query and shipments_query. These two queries correspond to Phase 1 of the drill-across operation. They are subordinate to the main query, which joins them together based on the common dimension attribute, which is product. The main query corresponds to Phase 2 of the operation.

Use of this form of SQL removes some of the DBA objections incurred by the use of temporary tables, but does not eliminate the DBMS overhead necessary to compute the results. While temporary tables are not explicitly created, joined, and dropped, the DBMS is doing the same work. The primary difference is that the application is not managing the various stages.

When Your Tool Cannot Drill Across

You may be using a reporting tool or business intelligence tool that does not support any of the drill-across methods described earlier. This is particularly likely if your reporting tool is cube-based; many OLAP tools permit interaction with a single cube at a time.

Regardless of the reasons that prevent drilling across at report creation time, there is a solution: the drill-across operation can be performed in advance, with the results stored in a new fact table or cube. This single fact table is used for queries and reports that compare processes. The original fact tables are used when studying individual processes.

You have already seen an example of a drill-across fact table. Figure 4-5 showed a single fact table storing facts from the orders and shipments processes. While this fact table hampered single-process analysis, where extraneous 0s had a nasty tendency to get in the way, it nicely supports cross-process analysis.

TIP When available tools cannot drill across, or when drill-across reports suffer from poor performance, design and build a merged fact table that summarizes the processes at a common level of detail. This derived table performs the drill-across operation when the warehouse tables are loaded, instead of performing it at query time.

Part II

The drill-across fact table, or merged fact table, can be implemented as a supplement to the process-specific fact tables. While this requires additional work during the load process, it pays dividends at query time. Even if your tools are capable of drilling across, this approach may improve performance.

The merged fact table can be built using the process-specific fact tables as a source, rather than returning to the original data source. In this sense, it is a form of summary table, or *derived table.* It can also be implemented as a cube, rather than a star schema. The merged fact table, and other forms of derived tables, will be studied in more detail in Chapter 14, "Derived Schemas."

Summary

This chapter has taken the first major step away from the simplicity of a basic star toward the more complicated solutions demanded by the real world. You have learned how and why separate processes should be modeled in separate fact tables, and how to construct queries that perform cross-process analysis.

- When dealing with multiple processes, separate fact tables permit unhampered analysis of the individual processes.
- When you are unsure whether two facts describe different processes, check to see whether they occur at different times or exhibit different grain. If so, they represent different processes.
- When multiple processes are described in a single fact table, analysis of a single process is hampered.
- When combining information from multiple fact tables in a single report, joining two fact tables directly or through common dimensions can result in the over-counting of some facts, and a failure to count other facts.
- The proper way to combine information is to drill across in two phases. The first phase collects information from each star and aggregates it to a common level of detail. The second phase merges these result sets together.
- There are several ways to drill across. If none is supported by the toolset, or if performance is poor, a merged fact table or cube can be built that precomputes the results of a drill-across operation.

As noted in this chapter, the ability to support both single-process analysis and cross-process analysis is a powerful characteristic of a good dimensional design. This synergy relies heavily on consistent representation of dimensions and their values. The next chapter develops the concept of *conformed dimensions,* a crucial feature of every dimensional model. Organized properly, conformed dimensions allow analysis to cross processes and even subject areas, with powerful results.

This chapter does not close the book on the topic of multiple fact tables. In addition to developing a separate fact table for each process, there are times when a single process may benefit from multiple fact tables.

- Different fact tables can provide unique perspectives on the same process. Chapter 8, "More Slow Change Techniques," introduces three ways to describe a single process: transaction, snapshot, and accumulating snapshot variants.

- Some fact tables do not describe processes so much as conditions. These fact tables often contain no facts, and are discussed in Chapter 12, "Factless Fact Tables." They provide additional insight into the analysis of process-focused stars.
- In some cases, a single process exhibits variation in the facts and dimensions collected; this can be addressed with the core and custom versions of a fact table, as presented in Chapter 13, "Type-Specific Stars."
- *Derived fact tables* reorganize data from existing fact tables to reduce the complexity of creating reports or improve performance. In addition to the merged fact table introduced in this chapter, derived fact tables can pivot, slice, and reorganize data, as discussed in Chapter 14.
- A fact table that describes a process may also be supplemented by summary tables, or *aggregates*, which are discussed in Chapter 15, "Aggregates."

Further Reading

The exploration of how to identify processes and why they require different fact tables builds on an introduction to the topic that originally appeared in Chapter 1 of *Data Warehouse Design Solutions*, by Chris Adamson and Mike Venerable (Wiley, 1998).

Another perspective on the phenomenon of zero-valued facts in reports is presented in Chapter 6 of the same book, where the possibility of violating sparsity to support calculation of averages is explored and rejected in the context of an inventory schema.

Drill-across capability is an essential feature of the dimensional data warehouse architecture. The concept is described by Kimball and Ross in Chapter 3 of *The Data Warehouse Toolkit, Second Edition* (Wiley, 2002), in the context of value chain integration. They also define drilling across in the book's glossary as "separate queries that are merged together in a separate pass by matching row headers." Unlike the previous edition of the book, these are the only two mentions of the term "drill across." Their desire to back away from the term is understandable since people tend to associate the word "drill" with the features of OLAP tools. In the absence of a better substitute, however, I have chosen to feature the term prominently.

Examples of drill-across operations can be found in both of the books mentioned here. *Data Warehouse Design Solutions* includes examples for sales and returns, and sales and warranty costs in Chapter 4, production overhead, material usage, and labor usage in Chapter 5, production versus defects in Chapter 7, budgets versus spending in Chapter 8, revenues versus expenses and other finance applications in Chapter 9, and profitability analysis in Chapter 10.

In the *Data Warehouse Toolkit*, you can find examples of separate fact tables for individual processes such as sales and inventory (Chapter 3), headers and line items (Chapter 5), solicitation and response (Chapter 6), trips and segments (Chapter 11), and registration and attendance (Chapter 12).

I describe the construction of a merged fact table that precomputes drill-across processing in Chapter 9 of *Mastering Data Warehouse Aggregates* (Wiley, 2006). The example used compares sales activity to planning numbers.

CHAPTER 5

Conformed Dimensions

Analytics that cross process boundaries are extremely powerful. This holds true within a subject area and across the enterprise. As the previous chapter showed, *process-focused* analytics require separate fact tables, and *cross-process* analytics require bringing this information together. This is accomplished by *drilling across*, and its success or failure hinges on dimensions.

This chapter focuses on insuring cross-process capability through *conformed dimensions*. With the right dimension design and content, it is possible to compare facts from different fact tables, both within a subject area and across the enterprise. Many powerful metrics can only be provided in this manner. Incompatible dimensions, on the other hand, prevent drilling across. The resulting stovepipes can be frustrating.

The requirements for conformed dimensions are spelled out as a series of rules. It is possible to memorize these rules and follow them blindly, but students of dimensional design are better off understanding *why* they are important. Before enumerating the conditions for conformance, this chapter takes a closer look at how dimensions make or break a successful drill-across.

Conformance, it turns out, can take many forms. This chapter will look at several ways that dimensions can conform and offer practical advice to keep your designs out of trouble.

Conformed dimensions can do more than enable drilling across. They can serve as the focus for planning enterprise analytic capability. This chapter closes with practical considerations surrounding conformance in each of the major data warehouse architectures—the Corporate Information Factory, the dimensional data warehouse "bus" architecture, and the stand-alone data mart.

The Synergy of Multiple Stars

Dimensional designs are usually implemented in parts. Regardless of architecture style, it is impractical to organize a single project that will encompass the entire enterprise. Realistic project scope is achieved by subdividing the enterprise into subject areas and subject areas into projects.

Over time, as each new star is brought online, the organization receives two kinds of analytic benefits. First, and most obviously, it becomes possible to analyze the business process measured by the star. The value of this benefit alone is usually significant. People gain valuable insight into business activity, whether they are directly involved in the process, responsible for it, or simply interested parties. Some processes, such as sales, may gain attention from all levels of the enterprise.

With each new star comes a second kind of benefit, often expected but sometimes unanticipated. Not only does the star afford insight into a new business process, but it also allows the process to be studied in conjunction with others. Again, this kind of analysis may be of interest to people who are involved in a particular process area, but it is equally likely to interest higher levels of corporate management.

A powerful example of cross-process analysis appeared in Chapter 4, "A Fact Table for Each Process." The report in Figure 4-13 compared information from numerous processes: sales call activity, delivery of sales proposals, orders, and shipments. Looking across these processes to form a consolidated picture of business activity is highly useful for sales management, company executives, directors, and investors.

The report in Figure 4-13 also contained a measurement called *yield*, which represented the ratio of sales calls made to orders taken. This single metric may be one of the most important indicators tracked by interested parties, and it can only be constructed by crossing process boundaries. As Chapter 4 advised, schema designers need to be alert to the existence of business measurements that cross process boundaries. Because these measurements do not exist as a column in a table somewhere, they may be easily lost in the shuffle if not documented and targeted for delivery.

Every business has chains of linked processes, often beginning with product development or acquisition, extending through customer acquisition, and culminating in the collection of revenues. These chains can be found at micro- and macro-levels. Within a subject area such as sales, for example, there may be a series of linked processes like those in Figure 4-13. Sales are also a participant in a macro-level chain, connecting product manufacturing, sales, marketing, customer support, and finance.

The stars that represent each process connect to one another through common dimensions. This can be envisioned graphically, as depicted in Figure 5-1. Orders, shipments, and a variety of other stars relate to one another through a set of dimensions. These dimensions, which appear in the center column of the diagram, serve as a framework, across which process comparisons are supported. Any two fact tables that link to the same dimension can theoretically be compared using the drill-across technique described in Chapter 4.

At a logical level, when a series of stars share a set of common dimensions, the dimensions are referred to as *conformed dimensions*. As suggested in the previous chapter, two fact tables do *not* have to share the same *physical* dimension table to support comparison. If the separate dimension tables *conform*, it will be possible to drill across them.

When dimensions do not conform, short-term victories give way to long-term defeat. Orders and shipments stars, for example, might be implemented one at a time. As each is brought online, new insights are afforded to various groups of interested parties. In this respect, each successful implementation reflects well on the data warehouse team that brought it to fruition. If these individual stars do not share a common view of what a customer is, or what a product is, that goodwill may eventually give way to indifference or disdain. While it is possible to study orders or shipments, it is not possible to compare them.

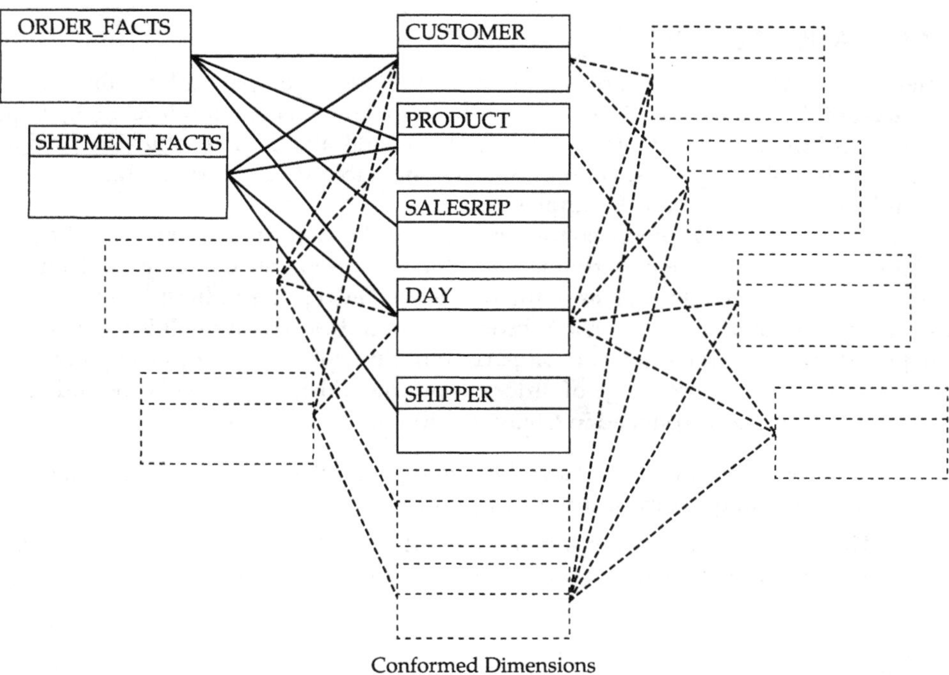

Figure 5-1 Multiple stars

At best, the response is frustration over a missed opportunity. At worst, a general distrust of the analytic infrastructure develops.

As you will see later in this chapter, dimensions can conform in a variety of ways. While conformance may be conveyed by a diagram like the one in Figure 5-1, such pictures quickly become difficult to lay out and understand. The crucial concept of conformance is often better depicted through alternate means.

As the key to long-term success, conforming dimensions are crucial in any data warehouse architecture that includes a dimensional component. Before spelling out the requirements for conformance and their implications, let's take a closer look at how they support, or fail to support, drilling across. Understanding how and why this process breaks down sheds important light on the concept of dimensional conformance.

Dimensions and Drilling Across

Dimensions are the key enablers of the drill-across activity that brings together information from different processes. Drill-across failure occurs when dimensions differ in their structure or content, extinguishing the possibility of cross-process synergy. Dimension tables need not be identical to support drilling across. When the attributes of one are a subset of another, drilling across may also be possible.

Part II

What Causes Failure?

Dimensions and their content are central to the process of comparing fact tables. In the first phase of drilling across, dimensions are used to define a common level of aggregation for the facts from each fact table queried. In the second phase, their values are used to merge results of these queries. Dimensional incompatibilities can disrupt this process. The stars in Figure 5-2 are rife with examples.

The stars in Figure 5-2 describe two processes: orders and returns. Each has been implemented by a separate department and resides in a separate database. Individually, these stars permit valuable analysis of the processes they represent. Both include dimension tables representing day, customer, and product. Given these commonalities, it is reasonable to expect these stars should permit comparison of these processes. For example, one might ask to see returns as a percentage of orders by product during a particular period. The two drill-across phases, as introduced in Chapter 4, would unfold as follows:

1. A query is issued for each fact table, aggregating the respective facts (quantity ordered and quantity returned) by product.
2. These intermediate result sets are merged based on the common product names, and the ratio of quantity ordered to the quantity returned is computed.

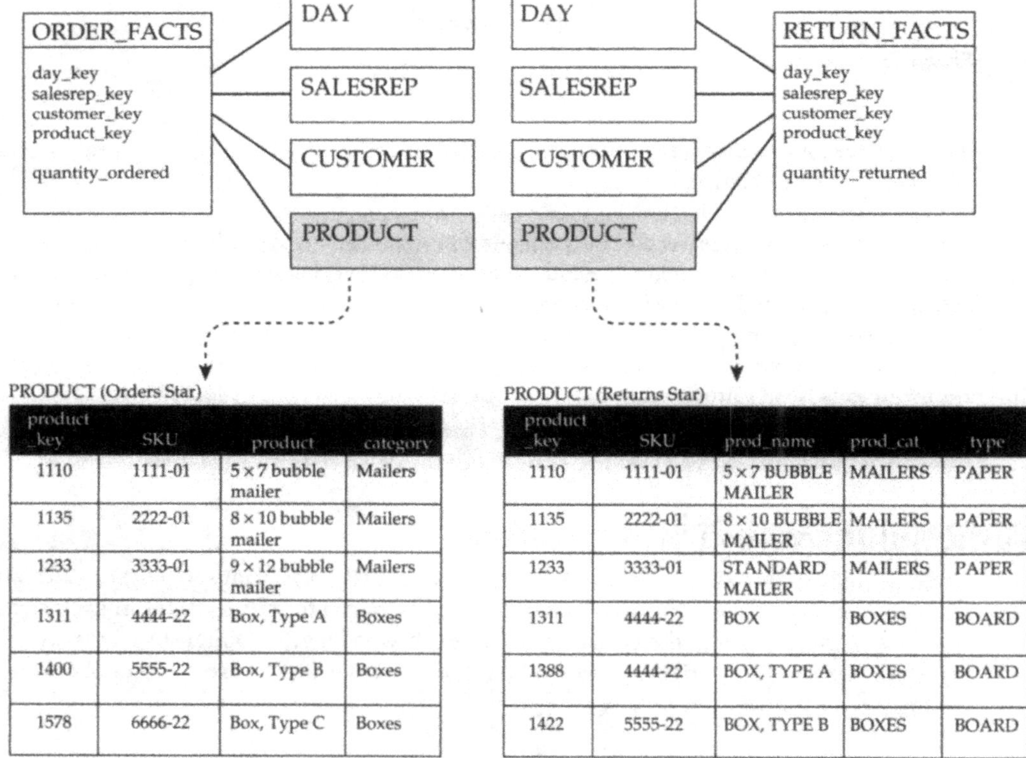

PRODUCT (Orders Star)

product_key	SKU	product	category
1110	1111-01	5 x 7 bubble mailer	Mailers
1135	2222-01	8 x 10 bubble mailer	Mailers
1233	3333-01	9 x 12 bubble mailer	Mailers
1311	4444-22	Box, Type A	Boxes
1400	5555-22	Box, Type B	Boxes
1578	6666-22	Box, Type C	Boxes

PRODUCT (Returns Star)

product_key	SKU	prod_name	prod_cat	type
1110	1111-01	5 x 7 BUBBLE MAILER	MAILERS	PAPER
1135	2222-01	8 x 10 BUBBLE MAILER	MAILERS	PAPER
1233	3333-01	STANDARD MAILER	MAILERS	PAPER
1311	4444-22	BOX	BOXES	BOARD
1388	4444-22	BOX, TYPE A	BOXES	BOARD
1422	5555-22	BOX, TYPE B	BOXES	BOARD

Figure 5-2 Product dimensions that do not conform

A similar process might be followed to drill across various other dimension attributes such as product type or category, or across dimension attributes from the day, customer, or salesperson tables.

Unfortunately, several factors prevent these stars from supporting this activity, at least when it comes to products. The problems lie in the respective product tables. Differences in their structure and content get in the way of comparing orders and returns.

Differences in Dimension Structure

The two product dimension tables have many differences, any one of which can foil an attempt to drill across. First, consider differences in the *structure* of the dimension tables.

- The product dimension table in the orders star contains a type dimension; the one in the returns star does not. It may be difficult or impossible to compare orders to returns based on product type depending on other characteristics of the tables.
- Columns that appear to be the same thing are named differently in the two stars. For example, the column that contains the name of the product is called *product* in the orders star, and *prod_name* in the returns star. A similar situation exists for the columns that contain category descriptions. These differences may stand in the way of drill-across operations as well.

It can be tempting to dismiss these differences since a skilled developer might be able to work around them. Although product type is not present in the orders star, a developer might be able to match each product from the orders star to a product type in the returns star. The SKU, which is the natural key, might be used to support this lookup process. After these equivalences are identified, orders could be aggregated by type and compared to returns.

Similarly, a developer could work around the differences in column names to compare orders and returns by category. Applying his or her knowledge of column equivalencies, the developer groups orders by category, and groups returns by prod_cat. When joining these intermediate result sets, the developer would match the category from the orders query with prod_cat from the returns query.

These workarounds are further examples of what Chapter 4 referred to as "boiling the frog." They range from simple to complex, but each compensates for design-level shortcomings by complicating the reporting process. These kinds of workarounds have many drawbacks:

- Specific knowledge is required to drill across.
- It may not be possible for anyone but the most skilled developers to use workarounds to compare the processes.
- Workarounds risk inconsistent and inaccurate results when applied incorrectly.
- Workarounds stand in the way of the automated generation of drill-across reports for ad hoc reporting tools.

Not every structural incompatibility can be overcome by a workaround. If the two stars have different definitions of a product, there may be deeper difficulties. This might occur if one star takes into account packaging differences, while the other does not. Timing may also get in the way. If one star collects data on a monthly basis, while the other does so on a weekly basis, there would be virtually no way to compare this data. Weeks and months cannot be rolled up to any common level of summarization.

Last, reliance on these workarounds depends on some consistency in the content of the two versions of the dimension. If there are also content differences, it may become impossible to overcome structural differences.

Differences in Dimension Content

In the case of the stars in Figure 5-2, further difficulties are evident when you examine the *content* of the product dimension tables:

- Product names and categories are formatted differently. The orders star uses mixed case and punctuation; the returns star formats data in all caps without punctuation. These differences will get in the way during the merge phase of drilling across since these values are the basis of the merge.
- Names are not consistent. SKU 3333-01 is called "9 × 12 bubble mailer" in the orders star, and "STANDARD MAILER" in the returns star. It may be that a change in product name was handled as a type 1 change for orders and was ignored for returns. The inconsistent names will impede the merging of intermediate result sets for queries that involve the product name.
- The product with the natural key 4444-22 has one row in the orders star but two rows in the returns star. It appears that this product underwent a change in category that was treated as a type 1 change in the orders star, and a type 2 change in the returns star. It is possible to compare orders and returns by category, but the orders will skew toward the more recent value.
- The product with SKU 6666-22 is present in the orders star but not in the returns star. This will not impede drilling across, but is an indicator that inconsistencies exist between the tables.
- The product with SKU 5555-22 is assigned different surrogate key values in the two stars. Care must be taken when joining tables.

Again, it may be possible to work around some of these limitations, but the impact on the reporting process would be severe, and not all the issues can be overcome. For example, developers might try to address the first limitation by converting all text to uppercase and stripping punctuation before joining two intermediate result sets together. This will have a negative impact on query performance, since the product name for each granular fact must be adjusted and sorted prior to aggregation. This will not help in situations where product names are recorded differently, as is the case with product 3333-01.

Some of the limitations might be dealt with by only referring to SKUs when querying each star, then using a single dimension table to determine the associated dimension values. The facts from each star could then be aggregated before merging intermediate result sets. Again, this additional processing will severely hamper performance. It will require that each report be constructed by a skilled developer and thus eliminate any chance that a business intelligence tool could generate a drill-across report. Furthermore, it will not work in situations where one table omits a particular product, or where a product has multiple rows in one of the dimension tables.

None of these considerations takes into account the confusion that users may experience when trying to interpret the results. How does one compare orders and returns for a product if each star specifies the product differently? Which product name should be placed on the report? What if this report is compared to one that uses the other name? The last two incompatibilities on the list may not directly hamper a drill-across operation but can lead to situations where analysts working with data sets from the two stars produce erroneous results by linking a dimension table to a fact table from the other star.

Preliminary Requirements for Conformance

To support successful drill-across comparisons, designers must avoid incompatibilities like those in Figure 5-2. The issues that rendered the two product dimension tables incompatible can be addressed by requiring that the two tables be the same. As noted in Chapter 4, there are two crucial parts to this sameness: the tables must be the same in *structure* and in *content.*

Same Structure Structurally, the tables should have the same set of dimension columns. This avoids the need to piece together missing information such as the product_type column. Corresponding dimension columns should have the same names so there is no ambiguity in where their equivalencies lie. They should also have the same data type definitions since their content will be identical.

These structural equivalences support the first phase of a drill-across operation. The dimension columns can be relied upon to define a consistent scope of aggregation for each fact table. In the first phase of drilling across, each fact table can be queried using the same dimensional groupings, without the need for a special processing workaround. Additionally, the structural compatibility supports a successful merge in the second phase, although content will also play a crucial role.

Same Content In terms of content, the values found in dimension columns must be expressed identically. If the name of product 3333-01 is "9 × 12 bubble mailer" in the orders star, it should be "9 × 12 bubble mailer" in the returns star. This common value will allow intermediate results from each star to be joined during the second phase of a drill-across operation. Use of consistent value instances avoids the need to clean up or convert corresponding column values so that they match, and guarantees that values will support the merge of intermediate results.

Corresponding dimension tables should provide consistent results when substituted for one another. In terms of content, this requires that they contain the same set of rows, that corresponding rows share the same surrogate key values, and that slow change processing rules have been applied consistently. These requirements, however, do not apply in cases where the corresponding dimension tables describe different levels of summarization.

Identical Tables Not Required

In the case of orders versus returns, the problems from Figure 5-2 can be remedied by requiring product dimension tables that are identical in structure and content. Dimension tables can also offer a degree of compatibility when they are not identical. This occurs when the dimension tables describe things at different levels of detail.

Suppose that the same company tracking orders also has sales goals, which are recorded in a sales plan. The sales goals are specified by month and sales territory, and there are various versions of the plan. Stars for orders and goals are depicted in Figure 5-3. Unlike the orders and returns, these fact tables have different grains and share no common dimension tables.

Despite these differences, these stars do share some common dimension *attributes.* These common dimensions are highlighted in Figure 5-3. For example, each goal has an associated month, as recorded in the month table. Each order also has an associated month, as recorded in the day table. It should be possible to aggregate facts from both stars by month and then compare the results.

In fact, every dimension attribute in the month table is present in the day table. Any of these common dimensions can be used to aggregate orders and goals (drill-across Phase 1) and then join the result sets together (drill-across Phase 2). Similarly, all the dimension attributes in the territory table are also present in the salesrep table. Any of these common dimensions can be used as the basis for drilling across. Figure 5-4 provides an example.

The report at the bottom of Figure 5-4 compares orders and goals by month and territory. It is assembled via the same two-phase drill-across process with which you should now be familiar. In Phase 1, separate queries extract facts from each star, aggregating them to a common level of dimensional detail: month and territory. In Phase 2, these intermediate results sets are merged, and the ratio of the two facts is constructed. This process works, even though the two stars do not share a single dimension table.

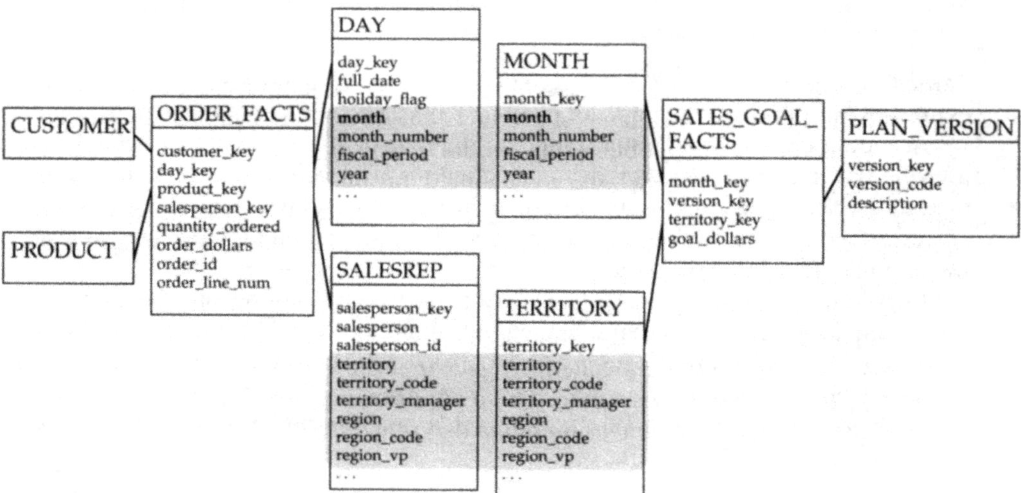

Figure 5-3 These stars do not share common dimension tables but do share common dimension attributes

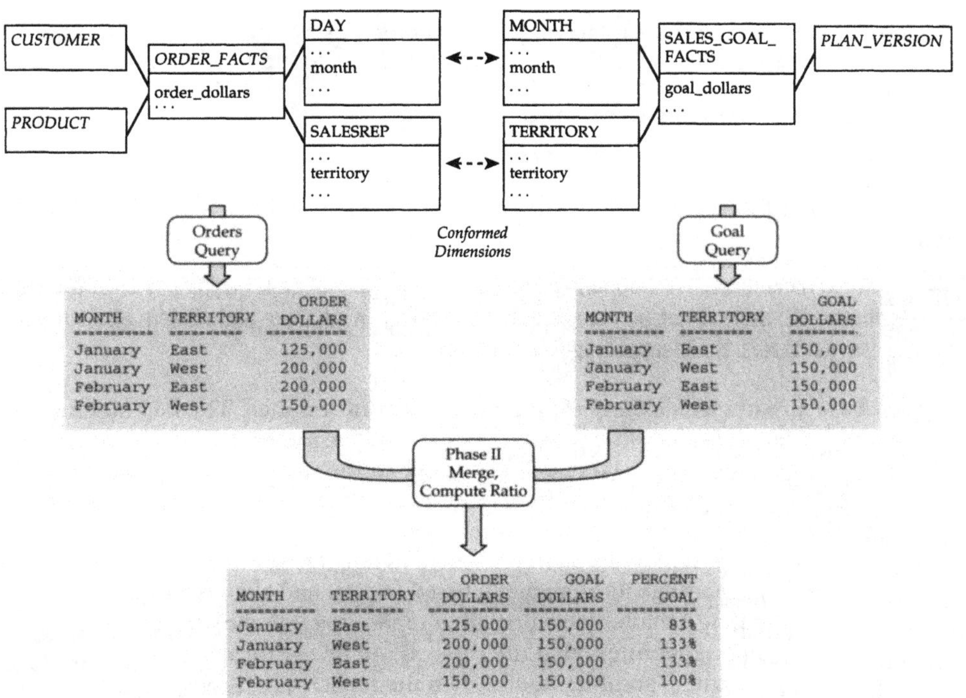

Figure 5-4 Drilling across order_facts and sales_goal_facts

Conformed Dimensions

When dimension tables exhibit the compatibility necessary to support drilling across, they are *conformed dimensions.* Identical dimensions ensure conformance, but conformance can take several other forms as well. Fact tables and conformed dimensions can be planned and documented in a matrix format and serve as the blueprint for incremental implementation.

Types of Dimensional Conformance

Having explored the ways in which dimensions enable or prevent drilling across, the rules of conformance can now be spelled out. As you may have surmised, dimension tables can conform in several ways. You have already encountered the two most common ways dimensions can conform: shared dimensions and conformed rollups. Degenerate dimensions can also conform. A fourth style of conformance is less commonly accepted; it allows for *overlapping dimensions.*

Shared Dimension Tables

The most obvious form of dimensional conformance occurs when two stars share the same logical dimension table. This shared dimension may be the same physical table, or it may consist of two or more identical tables. If implemented as two or more identical tables, shared dimensions must exhibit the characteristics discussed in this chapter:

- The tables share the same structure.
- The tables share the same content.

When two or more dimension tables meet these requirements, the tables are said to conform.

TIP A shared dimension table supports drilling across related fact tables using any of its dimension attributes. Separate dimension tables that are identical in structure and content also support drilling across fact tables; the identical replicas conform.

You have already seen examples of this type of conformance. The fact tables for orders and shipments in Figure 4-8 shared day, product, and customer dimension tables. As has already been observed, these stars need not reside in the same physical database, or even in databases from the same vendor. As long as they are identical in structure and content, they can support comparison of orders and shipments.

When a conformed dimension is implemented as separate physical tables, a single ETL process should be responsible for updating it based on new and changed source data. This may be achieved by updating a master table first, then replicating it to the separate physical locations. This practice guarantees that the replicas will be identical, cuts down on duplicative processing, and guarantees accurate results when the replicas are used for analysis. For larger tables, replication may not be practical. In this case, a single ETL process should identify new and changed rows, perform key management once, and apply the changes to each replica.

TIP When there is more than one copy of a shared dimension, a single ETL process should be responsible for processing new and changed data.

When replicas are built separately, it is difficult to guarantee that two versions of a dimension will be identical. Each must follow identical rules to construct dimension attributes from the source data, follow the same slow change processing rules, and produce the same set of rows. Use of the same key values is also important, guaranteeing interchangeability of the dimension tables. As observed earlier in this chapter, a divergence on any of these fronts will result in incompatibilities.

Separate load processes can tempt developers to relax some of these requirements, allowing one version to contain rows not present in another, or dropping the requirement that they share the same key values. This approach risks problems during analysis. Use of the incorrect replica with a given fact table will yield incorrect results. If the data warehouse produces wrong results, it will not be used.

NOTE A variation of the shared dimension allows a replica to contain a subset of rows of the base dimension, usually corresponding to a subtype of the entity represented. This subset may be embellished with additional attributes unique to the particular subtype. This variation is explored in Chapter 13, "Type-Specific Stars."

Conformed Rollups

Dimension tables do not need to be identical to conform. Dimension tables that are not identical can still support drilling across if they meet the following conditions:

- The dimension attributes of one table are a subset of the dimension attributes of the other.
- The common dimension attributes share the same structure and content.

When these requirements are met, the dimension tables conform. Related fact tables can be compared by drilling across on any of the common dimension attributes. The smaller of the two dimensions is called a *conformed rollup*; the larger is called the *base dimension*.

In the orders-versus-goals example from Figure 5-3, the month and territory tables are conformed rollups of day and salesrep, respectively. Shared attributes are highlighted in the diagram. Every dimension attribute from month is present in day; every dimension attribute in territory is present in salesrep. Note that each conformed rollup has one column not present in the base dimension: its surrogate key.

Part II

TIP When the dimension attributes from one table are a *subset* of those from another, and the common attributes share the same structure and content, the table containing the subset is called a conformed rollup. Related fact tables can be compared by drilling across on any of the common dimension attributes.

The requirement that the shared dimension columns contain the same content requires some additional scrutiny. Clearly, it is important that instance values be recorded in the same way. Construction of the report from Figure 5-4, for example, requires that value instances of the attribute month, as found in the day and month tables, be expressed consistently as "January," "February," and so forth. It also requires that value instances of the attribute territory, as found in the salesrep and territory tables, be expressed consistently as "North," "South," and so forth. These identical instance values make it possible to join the intermediate result sets together in Phase 2 of the drill-across operation.

It is also important that each distinct combination of instance values of the shared attributes be present in both tables. If the day table, for example, contains any rows that represent the month of January and the year 2009, the month table should also contain that combination of instance values. Otherwise, the two tables will produce different results for the same browse query. Figure 5-5 illustrates these equivalences.

The best way to guarantee that the instance values of the conformed rollup match those of the base dimension is to designate the base dimension as its source. This ensures consistent computation of value instances based on the source data. Developers may choose to process the base dimension first, then review the new and changed rows to process the rollup. Alternatively, they may choose to build a single routine that processes source data and applies new and changed rows to the base and rollup simultaneously. Some developers prefer to handle the situation by using a staging area to normalize the structures, processing, and looking for changes at an atomic level, then applying them to the base and rollup tables.

ETL developers often discover a bizarre side effect of the conformed rollup. Application of a type 1 change can sometimes require the merging of two rows in the rollup dimension.

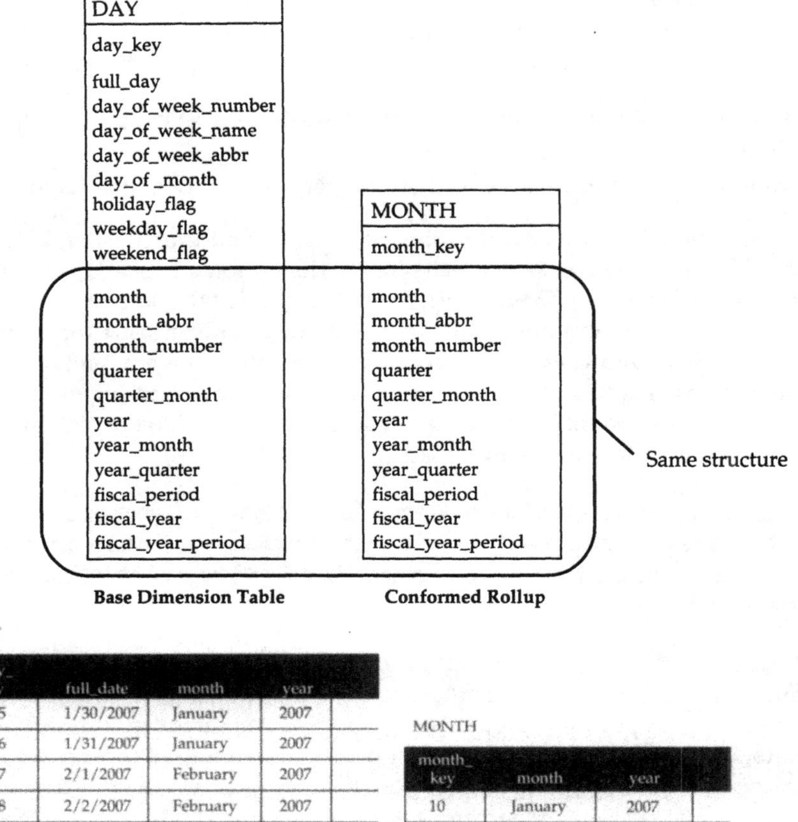

Figure 5-5 Month is a conformed rollup of day

The problem here is that the surrogate keys of rows being merged may already be referenced by existing fact table rows; merging them would require updating some foreign keys in the fact table. To avoid this additional processing, rollup dimensions are sometimes permitted to contain rows that, besides their surrogate key, are identical.

Conforming Degenerate Dimensions

Recall from Chapter 3, "Stars and Cubes," that degenerate dimensions are dimension attributes stored in the fact table. This technique is commonly reserved for transaction identifiers or document identifiers. In Figure 3-5, the order_facts table contained degenerate dimensions that identified the specific order and order line.

The same degenerate dimensions may appear in more than one fact table. For example, when a portion of an order ships, a shipments fact table may record the original order number and order line. This occurred in Figure 4-8. The degenerate dimensions order_id and order_line_num were present in both order_facts and shipment_facts.

It is possible to drill across on degenerate dimensions. Success depends on the same requirements that have been repeated throughout this chapter: the common dimension attributes must have the same structure and the same content. This allows them to specify the same scope of aggregation when querying each fact table in Phase 1, and allows them to be joined on during Phase 2.

With identical tables and conformed rollups, care is taken to ensure that the same combination of values is present in each table. This enables browse queries to provide the same results. You should be able to select distinct month and year values from either table in Figure 5-5 and get the same answer. In the case of degenerate dimensions, this requirement is relaxed. Enforcement of the requirement would lead to sparsity violations and complicate reporting efforts. For example, if we required the same distinct set of order_id values to appear in the order_facts and shipment_facts tables from Figure 4-8, it would be necessary to place a row into shipment_facts every time a new order occurred. This would generate unwanted rows in shipment_facts, with fact values of zero. These zero-valued facts would clutter shipment reports in much the same way encountered in the previous chapter, with multi-process fact tables. (See Figures 4-1 and 4-2 to refresh your memory.)

Overlapping Dimensions

In rare cases, non-identical dimension tables may conform through a set of overlapping attributes. Although valid, these situations often beg for the creation of a third dimension. If it is not crucial to cross-browse the attributes in question, a third dimension will better provide for consistent content. If their relationships at any point in time are important, additional fact tables can track this information. The additional fact tables may be avoided by making use of a limited form of snowflaking.

Intersecting Attributes When two tables share a set of common attributes, but one is not a perfect subset of the other, neither table can be described as a conformed rollup. A common example involves geography, as depicted in Figure 5-6. At the top of this diagram, dimension tables are shown that describe customers and salespeople. Both dimension tables contain information about regions. In the case of salespeople, these attributes identify the regions to which they are assigned. In the case of customers, these attributes identify the regions in which they exist. Neither of these tables is a conformed rollup of the other; each has a set of dimension attributes not shared by the other. This is illustrated by the Venn diagram in the center of Figure 5-6.

It may be useful to drill across the overlapping attributes. For example, profitability analysis may factor in customer support calls and salesperson compensation, each rolled up by region. For this to work, the common dimension attributes must share the same structure and content.

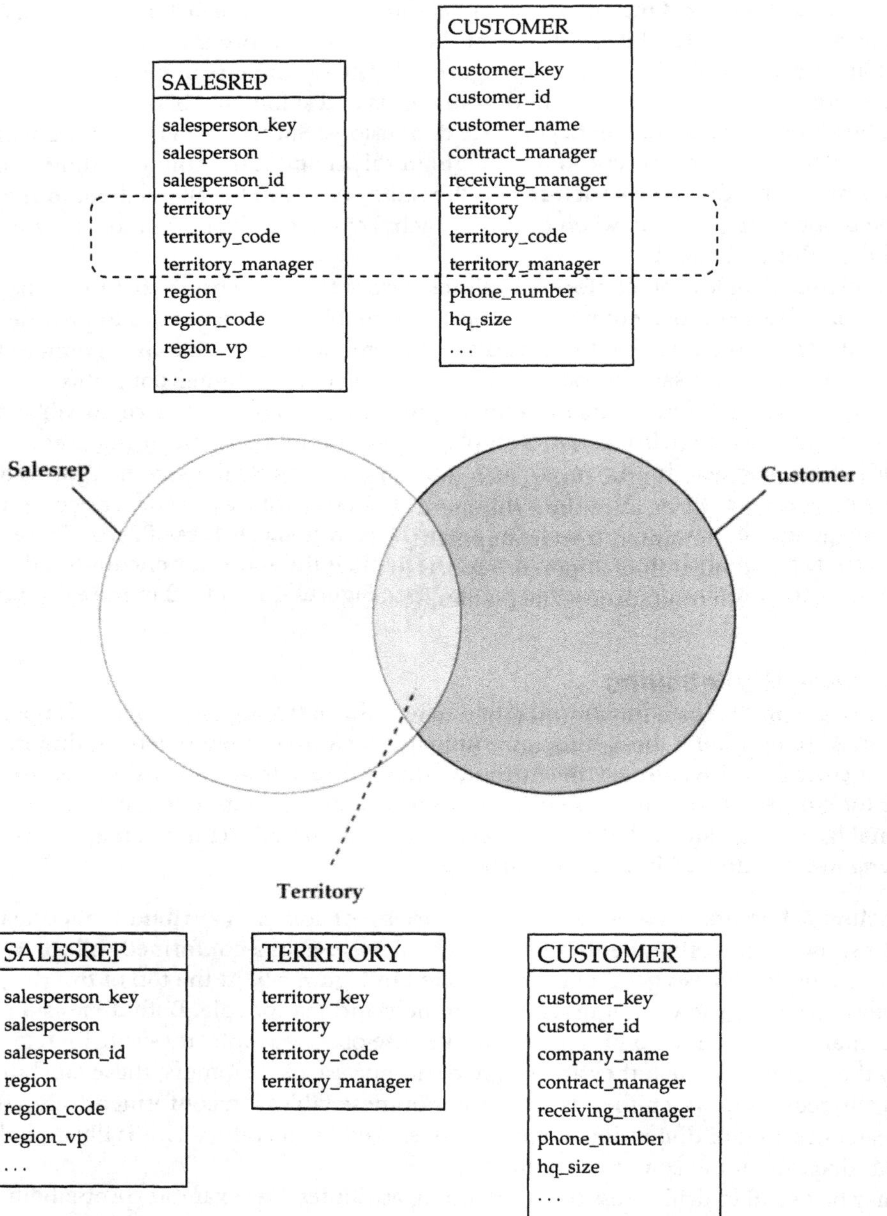

Figure 5-6 Common attributes of overlapping dimensions may conform or may be isolated as a third dimension

TIP When two dimensions overlap, they can conform across their common attributes. The common attributes must share the same content and structure.

Overlapping dimension tables are usually maintained by separate ETL processes. This means that there is a risk, however small, that they will be loaded with inconsistent values. The routines that load customer, for example, may interpret regions differently from the routines that load salesrep. Any slip in consistency will foil attempts to drill across. Overlapping dimensions may also foil the automated drill-across capabilities of business intelligence software. These tools frequently expect conformed dimensions of the rollup variety.

For these reasons, designers generally try to avoid overlapping dimensions. At least three alternatives exist that allow the overlapping attributes to be removed to a separate table.

Creating a Third Table to Avoid Overlap An alternative in this situation is to remove the common attributes from both tables and place them in a third dimension. This alternative is illustrated at the bottom of Figure 5-6. Territory information is relocated into a single table, ensuring consistency for drill-across operations. This approach may have an undesirable consequence: it is no longer possible to browse territories with customers or salesreps.

The choice between overlapping dimensions and the creation of a third dimension may be driven by analytic requirements. Is it important for the users to browse the overlapping attributes in conjunction with the other attributes from each dimension? If not, the overlapping attributes can be moved to a third table.

Creating a Third Table and Tracking Relationships If the relationships between the dimensions in question and their overlapping attributes change over time, and it is important to be able to get a picture of how they were related at a particular point in time, creation of a third dimension can be supplemented by additional fact tables to track relationships.

In the case of the territory data, this solution would entail creating a territory table, as depicted in the bottom of Figure 5-6. Additional fact tables can be built to track the relationship of customers to territories over time, and the relationship of salesreps to territories over time. These are likely to be *factless fact tables,* a topic that is discussed in Chapter 12, "Factless Fact Tables."

Creating a Third Table as an Outrigger The last option for avoiding overlapping dimension tables is to create a third dimension table that is related directly to the original two tables. This approach results in a form of *snowflaking*. The table created to avoid the overlap is known as an *outrigger*.

For the territory information, this approach would entail creating a separate territory table, as was done at the bottom of Figure 5-6, and adding territory_key to the salesrep and customer tables. This technique allows salesrep or customer to be joined directly to territory, allowing salesrep or customer data to be browsed with territory attributes. This approach, however, may also defeat the star-join optimization capability of many RDBMSs. Outriggers are discussed in Chapter 7, "Hierarchies and Snowflakes."

TIP When dimensions overlap, there is a risk that common attributes will not be maintained consistently. If this is a concern, consider the alternatives. Will placing the overlapping attributes in a third table harm the analytic capability of the solution? If not, split the dimensions in three. If so, consider supplementing a third dimension with additional fact tables, or treating it as an outrigger.

Planning Conformance

Conformed dimensions are the linchpins of the dimensional model. Without conformance, the data warehouse fails to support cross-process analysis, misses out on possible synergies, and is characterized by islands of information. Conformance is, therefore, a central feature of the dimensional design, often documented in a matrix format. With a carefully planned infrastructure of conformed dimensions, it is possible to implement one star at a time without risking the incompatibilities that stand in the way of comparing processes.

Conformance Design

Earlier in this chapter, Figure 5-1 captured the notion of conformed dimensions through a table diagram. The key dimensions of the enterprise appeared as a column in the center of the diagram; they related to fact tables that appeared on either side. This diagram illustrates the central role played by the conformed dimensions in bringing together information from the various fact tables.

While this kind of diagram is familiar to any developer of database applications, it is not particularly well suited to the task of documenting conformance. Even as presented, the diagram is difficult to read. Add column level detail, and it becomes impossible to fit on a page. Most implementations will involve a larger number of dimensions, and a much larger set of fact tables. The enterprise-level dimensional diagram quickly becomes a bewildering web of relationship lines. And this diagram fails to convey conformance relationships based on non-identical tables, such as the one between a base dimension and a conformed rollup.

A better way to illustrate conformed dimensions is to use a matrix diagram. With columns representing the core conforming dimensions, and rows representing various processes or fact tables, conformance can be illustrated by placing checkmarks in the appropriate intersections. An example appears in Figure 5-7.

A conformance matrix can convey the levels of conformance within a dimension by grouping the base dimension with conformed rollups. Figure 5-7 contains several examples. Columns for product and category, for example, are grouped together under the common

	day			*product*		*salesrep*					
	day	*month*	*quarter*	*product*	*category*	*salesrep*	*territory*	*region*	*customer*	*warehouse*	*order_line*
order_facts	✓	✓	✓	✓	✓	✓	✓	✓	✓		✓
shipment_facts	✓	✓	✓	✓	✓	✓	✓	✓	✓	✓	✓
return_facts	✓	✓	✓	✓	✓	✓	✓	✓	✓	✓	✓
inventory_facts	✓	✓	✓	✓	✓					✓	
receivables_facts	✓	✓	✓						✓		✓
sales_goal_facts		✓	✓				✓	✓			
demand_forecast_facts			✓		✓			✓			

Figure 5-7 A conformance matrix

heading *product*. Similarly, day, month, and quarter are grouped under *day*; salesrep, territory, and region are grouped under *salesrep*. These shaded vertical bands represent sets of conformed dimensions; the locus of intersection with facts is indicated by checkmarks. Any two fact tables can be compared where checkmarks appear in the same column. All of the processes can be studied at the quarterly level, for example. All but demand forecast can be studied at the monthly level. Only the first five can be studied at the daily level.

TIP Document dimensional conformance across fact tables or subject areas using matrix diagrams.

Degenerate dimensions that will serve as the basis for drilling across should also appear on a conformance matrix. While they are not separate tables, these dimensions are a critical link between processes and are characterized by the same importance when it comes to support of cross-process analysis. An example appears in Figure 5-7, where order_line appears as a degenerate dimension. It can be used with orders, shipments, returns, and receivables.

A conformance matrix of this sort need not include every dimension that is part of the data warehouse. Instead, it may depict only those that are crucial in linking together different processes or subject areas. The diagram in Figure 5-7, for example, does not include dimensions like shipper, return_reason, or account, which are presumably localized to individual fact tables.

In larger implementations, a high-level conformance matrix may illustrate one set of dimensions, as just described. This high-level conformance matrix can be supplemented with additional subject area matrices, each of which includes a wider range of dimension tables. This combination of matrices represents the macro- and micro-levels of process relationships discussed at the beginning of this chapter.

Of course, mapping out a set of conformed dimensions on a matrix does not guarantee it will be possible to implement them. Designing conformed dimensions requires a deep look at every process involved, a careful review of available source data, and a written set of requirements that describes how these dimensions map back to available source data. Development and documentation of the dimensional model will be discussed in detail in Chapter 18, "How to Design and Document a Dimensional Model."

Incremental Implementation

The conformance matrix serves as a blueprint for implementation. It shows where all the fact tables connect to one another. This allows each fact table to be implemented individually, with the confidence that, as each is brought online, it will work together with those that came before it. With a dimensional framework in place, incremental implementation can proceed without fear of incompatibilities. Figure 5-8 illustrates a series of implementation projects, which together represent numerous enterprise processes.

If these projects are implemented without a dimensional framework, the milestones labeled T2 and T3 will probably fail to deliver cross-process capability. Incompatible dimensions will get in the way of drilling across. Equally undesirable, there may be redundant processes loading similar dimensions in each subject area. The final result will be disappointing in terms of capability, while consuming undue amounts of IT resources.

If, on the other hand, this incremental implementation is preceded by the development of a set of conformed dimensions, this framework will avoid the pitfalls of nonconformance.

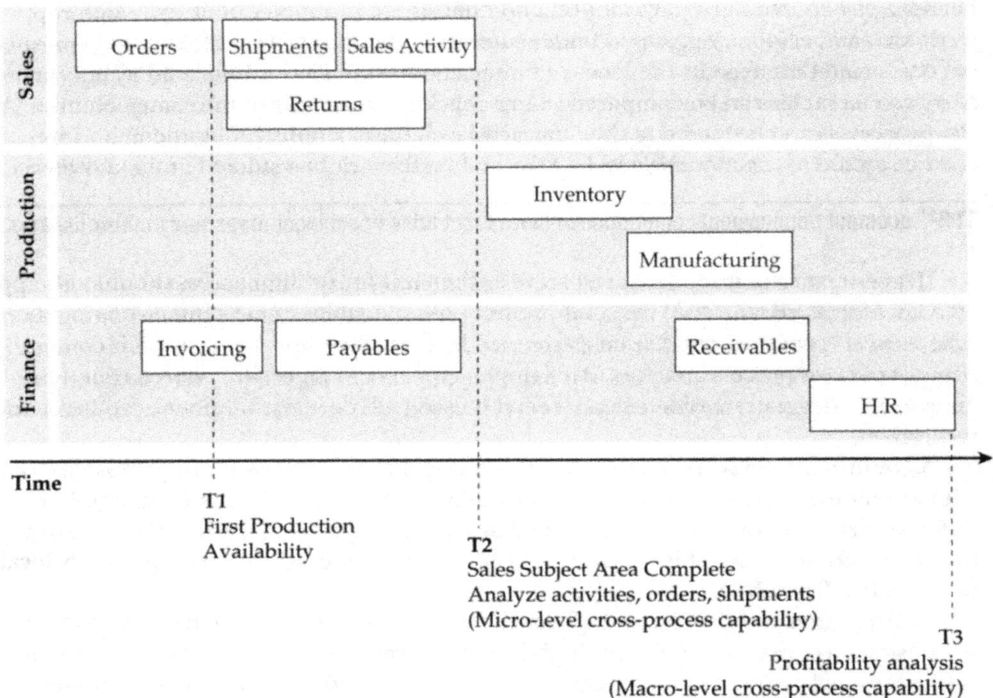

Figure 5-8 Incremental implementation

In addition to achieving analytic synergies at T2 and T3, the infrastructure may be streamlined. The day dimension, for example, need only be developed once, during the first project. In fact, the later projects may require the construction of far fewer dimension tables than the earlier projects. Of course, this requires some upfront analysis, a luxury that is not always afforded.

Architecture and Conformance

The relative emphasis on conformance varies with the data warehouse architecture. Because it is founded on the dimensional model, conformance is a central feature of Kimball's dimensional data warehouse. Inmon's Corporate Information Factory does not rely on the dimensional model to integrate enterprise data and therefore places a reduced emphasis on conformance. The stand-alone data mart does not have an enterprise context by definition. While it may include dimensions that conform internally, it is likely to exhibit incompatibilities with other data marts. This section sorts out these various approaches to dimensional conformance.

Dimensional Data Warehouse

The dimensional data warehouse architecture, as described in Chapter 2, "Data Warehouse Architectures," relies on the star schema as an integrated repository of atomic data, drawn from all parts of the enterprise. Data marts are either subsets of this dimensional repository, dimensional structures derived from it, or some combination of the two. Conformed dimensions are the key to enterprise scope, serving as the infrastructure that integrates subject areas. This means that the dimensional design, including a conformance plan, must be conducted as a strategic, upfront process.

Strategic Planning Includes Conformance Design

In a dimensional data warehouse, dimensional design is a strategic activity, rather than a design-stage activity. It is conducted upfront, before any implementation projects begin. The dimensional design may be developed as a stand-alone project, or it may be incorporated into a strategy project, which also includes activities to establish technical architecture, select tools, and set implementation priorities.

The conformance framework of the dimensional model is a top-level focus of dimensional data warehouse design. Kimball and Ross refer to the conformance framework as the *conformance bus*. It allows the model to meet the needs of each individual subject area, while also preserving the ability to compare subject areas. This makes it the key to supporting enterprise scope, allowing process comparison at the micro- and macro-level.

The development and documentation of the dimensional design are fully explored in Chapter 18. Documentation will include enterprise-level conformance matrices that map the key conformed dimensions to individual subject areas and to individual fact tables. An example of the latter appears in Figure 5-7. Base dimensions and their derived rollups are also clearly highlighted, using illustrations similar to the one in Figure 5-5.

Because the dimensional model will serve as an integrated repository for atomic data, the design process must also include tasks that identify the source system and processing rules for each conformed dimension. This ensures that integration of data from disparate source systems is feasible. Without this step, the dimensional design is likely to represent wishful thinking; implementation projects will discover that the model does not mesh with how information is gathered and that the actual data stores cannot support the dimensions as designed. During upfront design, all available data sources for each conformed dimension must be identified. Processing rules must be developed for the consolidation of this information into the set of attributes that make up the dimensional model. This nontrivial task is one of the largest of the design process, as it must reconcile conflicting views of key entities and take into account the quality of source data. The identification of source data is discussed further in Chapter 18.

TIP In a dimensional data warehouse, dimensional design is a strategic activity. Conformed dimensions are a central feature of the design, providing enterprise capability.

Once the dimensional design and conformance framework are complete, implementation projects can begin in earnest. Each implementation project builds around the conformance framework established during the upfront planning process. As each subject area is brought online, it will interlock with previously implemented components through the conformed dimensions. Implementations may also take place in parallel, as shown in Figure 5-8.

This approach allows the dimensional data warehouse to deliver on the synergies described at the start of this chapter. Each successive implementation empowers insight into a new business process and also allows that process to be compared with those that came before it. Compatibility is ensured through the upfront planning of conformed dimensions; stovepipes are avoided.

In addition to providing enterprise compatibility across subject areas, the dimensional model serves other strategic functions in this architecture. It is used as the focal point for project prioritization, communicates functional scope to business users, and communicates technical scope to IT management. These topics are discussed in Chapter 18.

Pressures of Reality

Even for organizations committed to dimensional data warehousing, this ideal vision may be tempered by reality. The existing portfolio of analytic systems may include legacy solutions that are not integrated or are incompatible. Mergers and acquisitions bring additional systems into the fold. In these cases, data warehouse managers often choose to develop a conformance model, and adapt legacy systems to that model over time. See the discussion of stand-alone data marts that follows for tactics used in bringing legacy systems into conformance.

A variety of forces within the business may also limit the organizational willingness to invest in upfront analysis. The strategic planning process is a difficult one for many organizations to invest in, as its deliverables do not include an operational system. Although a midsized organization may be able to develop a dimensional model and conformance matrix over the course of 8 to 12 weeks, resources may not be available. Packaged solutions may beckon, and new systems may be brought into the data warehouse through mergers and acquisitions.

As a result of these pressures, it is not uncommon for subject area implementations to proceed without initial investment in the development of a dimensional model complete with a conformance plan. This may lead to a swifter return on investment, but it risks incompatibility with future requirements. The risks may be mitigated by performing a cross-enterprise analysis of the dimensions present in the subject area. This does not completely eliminate risks, however, so it is important that everyone understand what they are getting into. Key decision makers must be well informed on the pros and cons of the approach, and agree together on the path taken. These decision makers should include IT management, decision makers from each business area, and executive management. Acceptance from all these stakeholders ensures that finger pointing and recrimination will not ensue when future incompatibilities are encountered. Decisions like these remain open to second guessing, however, and IT managers should do their best to drive toward the ideal of upfront planning.

Corporate Information Factory

The Corporate Information Factory architecture, as described in Chapter 2, includes an integrated repository of atomic data, drawn from all parts of the enterprise. This repository is not dimensional. Data marts are derived from this repository and may incorporate dimensional design. In this architecture, conformance of dimensions within a data mart remains an imperative. While not required, organizations may find value in conformance across data marts as well.

Conformance within Data Marts

In a Corporate Information Factory, information is extracted from the enterprise data warehouse and organized for departmental use in data marts. As this and the previous chapter have noted, the activity within a particular department is likely to be composed of multiple processes. Studied individually, they require separate fact tables. Studied together, they require drilling across. Drilling across (as this chapter has stated repeatedly) requires conformed dimensions.

Because the data marts of the Corporate Information Factory draw their information from an integrated repository, the challenges of maintaining conformance are reduced, at least from the perspective of the dimensional modelers. The burden of bringing together disparate sources is still present, but it falls to the designers of the enterprise data warehouse. It is there that the disparate and sometimes conflicting views of key business entities must be resolved. Designers of the dimensional data marts need only concern themselves with a single view of information: that provided by the enterprise data warehouse.

Although the pressure is reduced, it still behooves data mart designers to plan and document conformance. A single department may partake in numerous business processes, and conformed dimensions are required to compare them. Implementation may be planned in phases; as each phase is brought online, it should interoperate with those before it. A conformance matrix similar to that in Figure 5-7 should be a central feature of the data mart design; documentation of conformed rollups as depicted in Figure 5-5 should also be included.

Conformance across Data Marts

In Chapter 3, it was noted that the existence of an enterprise data warehouse for the storage of atomic data allows dimensional designers to loosen the requirement that fact table grain be set at the lowest level possible. That chapter also noted that when a data mart summarizes the base data, the organization may one day regret the decision. When a departmental user asks a question that is not answered by summary data, new fact tables will be required.

Similar considerations apply to the concept of conformance across data marts. Because the data mart is defined as a database that organizes analytic data for departmental use, the requirement to conform across data marts may be relaxed. Each department can maintain its own view of information. If these views become incompatible, however, the veracity of data warehouse information may be called into question. This danger is mitigated by the fact that all data marts are derived from the same source: the enterprise data warehouse.

The development of incompatible views of data will necessitate development of a new data mart if it becomes necessary to compare the processes. For example, if inventory and sales data marts are built for warehouse managers and sales managers, respectively, these data marts may not support the comparison of inventory levels to sales activity. This may occur if inventory is sampled weekly and sales is sampled monthly. This incompatibility may drive the development of a third data mart, strictly for comparison of these processes.

In order to avoid these unpleasant consequences, the Corporate Information Factory can benefit from the same kind of dimensional conformance planning that serves the dimensional data warehouse. Dimensions of interest across the enterprise can be planned once and mapped to the enterprise data warehouse. This process is significantly simpler, since the integration of disparate data sources has been performed during the design of the enterprise data warehouse itself.

TIP In a Corporate Information Factory, conformed dimensions are crucial within data marts. Planning conformance across data marts is not required, although it can eliminate the need for additional development to support cross-functional analysis.

Practitioners of the Corporate Information Factory and dimensional data warehouse alike often establish a single function responsible for the construction of dimension tables. This function provides a master set of dimension tables that are consumed by additional functions dedicated to their propagation across subject areas, and the population of fact tables that refer to them.

Stand-Alone Data Marts

By definition, the stand-alone data mart lacks an enterprise context. Its information is pulled directly from operational systems and does not incorporate an integrated repository of enterprise data. While the stand-alone data mart may exhibit conformance internally, it is likely to be incompatible with other data marts. Although widely criticized for the inefficiencies and incompatibilities that result, the stand-alone data mart is an almost universal phenomenon, appearing as a result of departmental investment, mergers, and acquisitions, or the purchase of packaged applications.

Organizations facing pressure to develop a solution rapidly for a particular subject area, or saddled with legacy stand-alone data marts, typically follow one of three strategies to cope with the attendant problems. They learn to live with it, plan to conform dimensions as they go, or work to retrofit incompatible dimensions into a conformed model.

Living with Incompatibilities

It is often the case that business objectives require expedience, that funding is not available to develop an enterprise-level conformance strategy, or that politics cannot sustain a strategy phase. In these cases, IT organizations may be pressured to build or buy a solution for a specific subject area.

It is important to recognize that the decision being made to choose this path is not merely a technical one. In fact, it is a *business decision* that has *technical implications*. The expertise of an IT professional may be an input into such a decision, but it is not the only factor. As described earlier, the choice to develop a data mart without first planning an infrastructure of conformed dimensions should be an informed decision, in which numerous stakeholders participate. These decision makers should include IT management, decision makers from each business area, and executive management. These parties must be fully apprised of the pitfalls of this approach.

The potential pitfalls can be expressed in nontechnical language, by describing the impacts on the business. Exclusive focus on a single process may result in a solution that cannot be compared with other processes down the line. Facilitating such comparison may require redevelopment, resulting in a higher long-term total cost of ownership. Redundant operations will make inefficient use of IT resources that are required to maintain them. Business disputes may arise from competing representations of data. IT professionals can present this information, provide business examples, and even quantify some of the implications. Done professionally, this form of input is unemotional and not dogmatic. It supports a business decision that takes non-IT factors into account.

Conforming Along the Way

Businesses often delude themselves into thinking they can conform as they go. "We can build a data mart for Sales," the theory goes, "and then adjust it as needed when we get around to inventory." This approach underestimates the level of effort required to adjust dimensions once they are in production. In addition to the redevelopment, retesting, and redeployment of the ETL routines that maintain the dimension, there are also existing queries, reports, dashboards, and other processes that will be impacted by changes to dimension design.

Whether well informed or misguided, the risks inherent in the choice to push forward with a subject area solution can be mitigated, although not eliminated. While the organization may not tolerate the development of a dimensional model of enterprise scope, it may be possible to take some time to focus on key dimensions. This is accomplished by adjusting project scope to spend extra time looking at enterprise needs with respect to the chosen dimensions. This requires that developers have the insight to recognize what portions of the model may impact other subject areas.

If the team can identify dimensions that may have enterprise implications, these dimensions can be fully developed with respect to the business requirements they satisfy and the operational sources that feed them. Rather than limit their design to what is required by the solution under development, they can be fleshed out in recognition of the needs of other areas. Rather than limit their sources to the operational systems that are a part of the subject area in question, all operational sources for the dimension are considered.

This approach strikes a delicate balance between the development of a complete enterprise dimensional model with a conformance framework, and the rigid focus on a single subject area. Although it does not guarantee an easy ride when future subject areas are considered, it mitigates *some* of the risk that incompatibilities will be discovered. While it does not entail dedication of resources to an intensive strategy product, it does expand project scope to consider business needs and operational sources from other parts of the organization.

As with the other techniques for coping with stand-alone data marts, the choice of this route should be an informed decision that is made jointly by key stakeholders from IT, business units, and executive management.

Retrofitting Dimensions

Stand-alone data marts can be brought into conformance with the remaining data warehouse infrastructure by retrofitting dimensions. This option is appealing when a bulwark of conformed dimensions is in place, and one or more legacy applications do not conform. When it becomes necessary to enhance one of the legacy stand-alone data marts, its dimensions can be retrofitted for conformance.

This process sounds easier than it turns out to be. Successful retrofitting of an existing data mart may require a complex system of views and other tricks, used to minimize the impact of changes on other parts of the system as the retrofitting takes place. The process is akin to reconstructing a bridge while traffic is driving over it; the challenges can be monumental.

With respect to the schema design, the task may seem disarmingly simple:

- Map each row in the nonconforming dimension to one in the corresponding table from the enterprise dimensional model.
- Add any additional attributes that are missing from the enterprise dimensional model.
- In the stand-alone data mart, use the mappings to reassign fact table foreign keys so they refer to the conforming dimension.

Though reasonable on the surface, this short list fails to take into account deep incompatibilities in the data, and completely ignores the impact on the front-end applications that query the stand-alone data mart.

On the data side, it may not be possible to establish a one-to-one match between the rows of two nonconforming dimension tables. This may result from inconsistent definitions of what the dimension represents but can also be more insidious. If the two dimensions handle slow change processing differently, for example, it may not be possible to consolidate them without referring back to the original source data to mediate differences. Simple mappings are not sufficient, and fact table keys must be adjusted based on natural keys and dates associated with each row.

Equally serious is the impact on the front-end reports and applications. While it may be possible to bring a dimension into conformance through a retrofitting process, each dependent front-end information product will be impacted—queries, reports, dashboards, and so on. Each will require redevelopment based on the new information structure. Changes in content will also have an impact; filters or query predicates may need to be changed to be consistent with newer representations of the information.

Summary

Conformed dimensions are a crucial component of the successful dimensional design. Conformed dimensions allow users to ask questions that cross process boundaries, within a single subject area or across the enterprise. Answers to these questions can be very powerful. The key performance indicators of many businesses include metrics that can only be evaluated in this way.

This chapter has provided you with the knowledge necessary to develop conformed dimensions of many types. It explored the process of drilling across, providing you with insight into how dimension design can make or break this process.

- Drilling across fails when two or more fact tables do not share dimensions with the same structure and content. Having identical dimensions avoids this failure, but dimensions can also conform when one summarizes another.

Using this insight, requirements for conformance were developed. Four kinds of conformance were developed.

- Tables that are identical in structure and content conform. Shortcomings in these areas can sometimes be worked around, but the cost is increased complexity in developing reports, poor performance, and a risk of inaccurate results.
- Tables can conform when the dimension attributes of one are a subset of another. The tables are known as a *rollup dimension* and a *base dimension*. They will not share a common surrogate key, but the common attributes must possess the same structure and content.
- Degenerate dimensions can serve as the basis for conformance. Again, the corresponding columns should be consistent in structure and content, but it is not required that every fact table share the same set of instance combinations, as to do so would force violations of sparsity.

- Overlapping dimensions can also conform. Some designers prefer to avoid this situation, since it requires that multiple processes load equivalent dimension columns in the same way.

Conformed dimensions are a crucial part of every data warehouse that incorporates the star schema, regardless of architecture. This chapter provided practical advice for use across all implementations, and considerations for each of the major architectures described in Chapter 2.

- Conforming dimensions are best illustrated through matrices, since the number of criss-crossing relationships can easily clutter a table diagram. Matrices can describe conformance within a data mart or across data marts.
- Conformed dimensions are a central feature of the dimensional data warehouse architecture, produced as part of a strategic design effort. This initial work allows individual implementations to proceed individually, ensuring they will fit together as each comes online.
- In a Corporate Information Factory, the importance of planning conformance is lessened because of the presence of the enterprise data warehouse. Conformance is still a necessity within data marts, and conformance across data marts can help avoid the need for additional data marts to cross subject areas.
- Stand-alone data marts do not conform. The associated risks can be partially mitigated by planning for conformance of a few key dimensions with known importance across the enterprise. Stand-alone data marts may be retrofitted to work with existing conformed dimensions, but this process is not trivial.

Further Reading

This chapter observed that dimensional models often develop chains of stars that represent interrelated business processes. Other examples are worth reading about:

- Ralph Kimball and Margy Ross discuss the concept of a value chain in a retail context in Chapter 3 of *The Data Warehouse Toolkit, Second Edition* (Wiley, 2002).
- Mike Venerable and I describe the chain of relationships between budgets, commitments, and spending in Chapter 8 of *Data Warehouse Design Solutions* (Wiley, 1997).

Discussion of conformed dimensions can be found in any book that deals with dimensional design. Of particular note are the following treatments:

- Kimball and Ross present conformed dimensions as the key to *bus architecture* in Chapter 3 of *The Data Warehouse Toolkit.*
- Conformed rollups can be considered a form of aggregation since they summarize a base dimension. In Chapter 3 of *Mastering Data Warehouse Aggregates* (Wiley, 2006), I provide tips for aggregate dimension design and ETL requirements.

The last part of this chapter touched on the process of planning data warehouse implementation projects around conformed dimensions. More detailed coverage can be found elsewhere. Depending on your architecture, you might want to consult one of these books:

- For the dimensional data warehouse, a more detailed discussion is provided in *The Data Warehouse Lifecycle Toolkit, Second Edition* (Ralph Kimball, Margy Ross, Warren Thornthwaite, Joy Mundy, and Bob Becker; Wiley, 2008.) This book deals with the entire data warehouse life cycle. Conformance is specifically addressed in Chapter 7.
- A process tuned to the Corporate Information Factory architecture is spelled out in *Mastering Data Warehouse Design* (Claudia Imhoff, Nicholas Galemmo, and Jonathan Geiger; Wiley, 2003). Here, conformed dimensions in data marts are a natural extension of the major pillars of each subject area in the atomic data warehouse, which is developed from operational sources through an eight-step process described in Chapter 4 of that book.

Tools for planning implementations around conformed dimensions and designing and documenting conformance are provided in Chapter 18, "How to Design and Document a Dimensional Model."

PART III

Dimension Design

CHAPTER

6 More on Dimension Tables

Dimension tables are the foundation of powerful analytics. You have already learned much about them in previous chapters. These fundamentals, however, do not address a variety of real-world concerns that you are likely to encounter. The next several chapters move beyond the basics, covering a progression of advanced dimension design topics. Mastery of these topics will prepare you to confront real-world complexity and respond to it with simple and powerful solutions.

If you are not reading this book from cover to cover, you may be drawn to this chapter because you have a question involving dimensions. Some of what you are looking for may have appeared in prior chapters. Here is a quick recap of what has already been covered:

- **Chapter 1 introduced the dimension** as a fundamental part of the dimensional model, providing a context for facts and enabling rich and powerful reporting. Techniques were provided to identify dimensions in reports and the spoken word, and the star schema was introduced.
- **Chapter 3 described the dimension table** in detail, from its rich set of attributes to its use of surrogate keys to the ways in which type 1 and type 2 slowly changing dimensions represent history.
- **Chapter 5 explained conformed dimensions**, which enable cross-process analysis through a procedure called drilling across. The key to scaling across subject areas, conformed dimensions allow fact tables to work together to produce powerful reports.

This chapter builds on these fundamentals to address a handful of the more complicated issues surrounding dimension design. It is divided into five sections, covering the following topics:

- **"Grouping Dimensions into Tables"** describes how to identify when dimensions belong in the same table and when they should be placed in separate tables.

- **"Breaking Up Large Dimensions"** explains what to do, and what not to do, when dimension tables would be too large to maintain effectively. Several alternatives are explored, including the mini-dimension, which has the unique ability to stem growth without sacrificing detail.
- **"Dimension Roles and Aliasing"** covers what happens when a fact table has multiple relationships to a single dimension table. These relationships are called roles, and they do not require making copies of the dimension table. Multiple roles can be addressed in a single query through SQL aliasing.
- **"Avoiding the NULL"** describes the analytic headaches caused by NULL values, and how to avoid them. NULL foreign keys in fact tables are also avoidable through "special-case rows." These are used when a fact table has an optional relationship to a dimension, when the dimensional context for a fact is invalid, and when facts arrive at the data warehouse before the dimensional detail is available.
- **"Behavioral Dimensions"** describes how facts can be turned into additional dimensions, enabling past history to provide context for facts in very powerful reports.

This collection of topics is just the beginning of your tour of advanced dimension techniques. Future chapters will explore hierarchies, snowflakes, and outriggers, provide more techniques for slowly changing dimensions, solve the problem of multi-valued attributes, and look at recursive hierarchies.

Grouping Dimensions into Tables

Experienced designers don't usually have difficulty in determining how to group dimension attributes into tables. Most dimension tables correspond to categories of analysis that hold deep significance to the business and are evident on a *prima facie* basis. There are times, however, when you will be uncertain as to the best way to organize dimensions into tables.

Some of this uncertainty can be attributed to the nature of dimensional modeling. Unlike an entity-relationship (ER) model, a dimensional model does not expose every relationship between attributes as a join. Recognizing this difference is the first step toward sorting out a confusing situation. Relationships that are contextual tend to pass through fact tables, while natural affinities are represented by co-locating attributes in the same dimension table. If consideration of these characteristics does not help, you can make the decision by considering the implications for the usability of the schema.

Two Ways of Relating Dimension Attributes

In a star schema, the relationship between a given pair of dimension attributes may be expressed explicitly or implicitly. Dimensional modelers do not think about dimensions in these terms, but those with a background in entity-relationship modeling may be confused until this distinction is brought to light.

Relationships of the explicit variety are the most familiar. They take the form of joins that intersect in a fact table, which provides an important context for the relationship. The dimensions may be related in other contexts as well, as represented by other fact tables. Explicit relationships between dimension rows may be numerous and volatile.

Less familiar are implicit relationships, which occur when two attributes are located in the same table. Implicit relationships imply a natural affinity between attributes, rather than a relationship that can take many contexts. These relationships tend to be more consistent, and they are browsable.

Explicit Relationships Describe Context

As you have already learned, every fact table bears foreign key references to dimension tables. These references provide the dimensional context for the facts. These joins can also be thought of as providing information about relationships between the dimension tables. The business process measured by the fact table is the context for this relationship.

Once again, we will turn to the orders process for an example. Figure 6-1 reprises the orders star that was introduced in Chapter 1 and embellished in Chapter 3. The grain of the fact table is the individual order line. Dimension tables represent the day of an order,

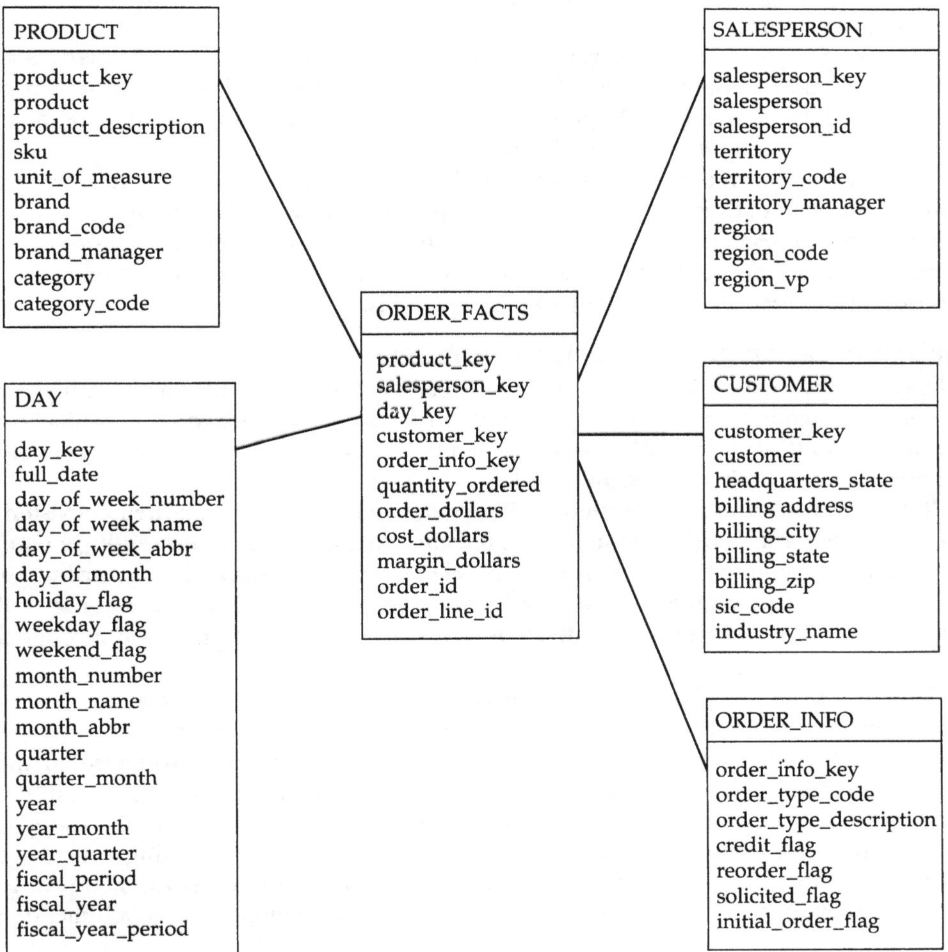

Figure 6-1 A fact table explicitly relates dimension tables

Part III

the product being ordered, the customer who placed the order, and the salesperson who took the order. Degenerate dimensions identify the particular order line, and the junk dimension order_info specifies miscellaneous characteristics of the order.

Each row in this fact table refers to a specific day, product, customer, salesperson, and order. For example, a fact table row may record the fact that on January 1, 2008 (a day), Hal Smith (a salesperson) took an order for 100 black ballpoint pens (a product) from ABC Stationery Emporium (a customer) as part of order number 299113. The fact table row records a relationship among these instances of day, salesperson, product, customer, and order. They are related to one another *in the context* of this particular order.

Each of these dimension instances—ABC Stationery, Hal Smith, January 1, black ballpoint pens—may be related in other ways as well. ABC Stationery Emporium may have ordered other things from Hal Smith, perhaps on the same order or perhaps on completely different days. All of these relationships are made explicit by recording additional rows in the fact table, using the appropriate foreign keys. Each of these is a separate relationship in the context of an order.

These dimensions can also be related in other contexts. A customer and salesperson, for example, may also become related when a proposal is presented, a product is returned, and so forth. If customer and salesperson can be related in different contexts, they belong in separate dimension tables. Fact tables will provide the different contexts.

Those familiar with entity-relationship modeling are doubtless familiar with this type of explicit relationship. Every fact table is an example of what ER modelers refer to as an intersect table. It resolves a potential many-to-many relationship between each of the associated tables. Another type of relationship is implied in dimensional models, one that does not involve primary key / foreign key associations.

Implicit Relationships Describe Affinities

Unlike an entity-relationship model, a dimensional model also includes relationships that are not made explicit through joins. Although dimensional modelers do not think about their models in these terms, this distinction can be a source of confusion for ER modelers who are new to star schema design.

Relationships between dimension attributes can be implied through their coexistence in a table. These relationships tend to exist only in a single context, representing a natural affinity rather than one based on process activities. The relationships among attributes in a dimension table may change over time but tend to be less volatile than those of the explicit variety. When implicit relationships do change, their history can be preserved through a type 2 slow change response.

The orders star from Figure 6-1 contains many examples of implicit relationships. Within the product table, for example, are dimension attributes called *product* and *brand*. Since more than one product may share the same brand, an ER model would isolate these attributes in separate tables, relating them via a primary key / foreign key relationship. This approach makes sense in the context of an operational system, which must often support a high volume of concurrent transactions inserting, updating, and deleting data. As you learned in Chapter 1, dimensional models are not intended for an operational profile. Instead, they are optimized to support queries that potentially aggregate large volumes of data.

In this context, there is no need to separate brand from product. To do so would potentially impact the performance of queries involving large volumes of data by requiring additional join processing.

NOTE In some situations, dimensional modelers use primary key / foreign key associations to make this kind of relationship explicit. This typically results in a variant of the star schema known as a *snowflake*, which will be discussed in Chapter 7, "Hierarchies and Snowflakes."

Unlike the relationship between a customer and salesperson, the relationship between a product and brand does not take on multiple contexts. Products and brands are related in only one way: membership in a brand. It is a natural affinity that does not depend on the execution of business activities. At a given point in time, a particular product has one associated brand. This relationship does not depend on a sale, the manufacturing process, or other significant processes tracked by the business.

The relationship is not necessarily constant. It may change over time, and when it does, the change history can be tracked. If the brand designation of a particular product changes, for example, history can be preserved through a type 2 slow change. A new row is added to the dimension table for the product, and this new row contains the new brand designation.

NOTE Perhaps a small audience is interested in tracking a business process that assigns brands to products. While this analytic requirement may suggest a fact table, the relatively small amount of activity argues for a different approach. Chapter 8, "More Slow Change Techniques," provides a potential solution in the *time-stamped dimension*.

When Struggling with Dimension Groupings

Those new to the dimensional approach may face situations where they are not sure whether two dimensions belong in the same dimension table. If salespeople are assigned to customers, why separate customer and salesperson into different tables, as is done in Figure 6-1? Why not place them together? How about making brand a dimension table and including its surrogate key in the fact table?

Rather than attempt to resolve these questions using the language of ER modeling, it is best to look at the ways in which the attributes relate and the ways in which they are used. For a given pair of attributes, consider the context of the relationship. Do they share a natural affinity, or can they be related in different contexts? Those that tend to share a stable affinity may be stored together; those that tend to be related only in the context of events, transactions, or conditions belong in separate fact tables. When in doubt, you can consider the browsability of alternative designs.

Grouping Dimensions Based on Affinity

In a dimensional model, dimensions are grouped into tables based on natural affinity. Products and brands, for example, are related to one another prior to an order being placed. A transaction is not required to establish a relationship between these elements. In fact, a product has a brand even if there are no orders for it. More importantly, these attributes can only be related in one way, or one context.

On the other hand, some elements are only related based on transactions or activities. Salespeople and customers, for example, are brought together *only* when transactions, such as orders, occur. These attributes, therefore, belong in separate tables; their relationships will be captured in the fact table. This allows customers and salespeople to have numerous interactions, perhaps even in different pairings. The relationships are defined by the transactions.

TIP When two dimension attributes share a natural affinity, and are only related in one context, they belong in the same dimension table. When their relationships are determined by transactions or activities, and they can occur in multiple contexts, they should be placed in separate dimension tables.

Looking deeper, you may also realize that salespeople and customers may be related in multiple contexts. For example, salespeople may be assigned to customers, they may take calls from customers, and they may visit customers. Each of these relationships flows from a different process and can be thought of as an activity or transaction: an assignment of a salesperson to a customer, a phone call being made, or a visit to a customer site. These various associations can be captured through a series of fact tables, each representing a different process. As described in Chapter 5, these relationship chains may offer rich analytic possibilities when used individually or compared.

The Browsability Test

If you are not sure whether two attributes belong together in a dimension table, consider how they will be used. Recall from Chapter 1 that a query focused on the values within a dimension is called a browse query. Natural affinities like product and brand can be separated from transactional relationships like customers and salespeople by evaluating browsability. Would someone want to browse the values of these attributes together? Placing them in separate dimensions would prevent this.

The separation of product and brand, as shown in Figure 6-2, destroys the browsability of these attributes. In this configuration, it is only possible to study the intersection of products and brands in the context of orders. If there is no order for a particular product, it will not be possible to identify its brand. It makes more sense to place these attributes in a single table. Salespeople and customers, on the other hand, have a relationship only when transactions occur. This relationship may also be more volatile. A given customer may speak with a different salesperson each time an order is placed. In this case, the transaction defines the relationship and is embodied in the fact table.

The astute reader may observe that in a situation where a business assigns salespeople to specific customers, it may be possible to merge their attributes. This would allow users to browse the list of customers assigned to a particular salesperson; however, salespeople and customers may engage in other activities with various contexts, as noted earlier. Salespeople take calls from customers, process returns, and so forth. Clearly, the business considers salespeople and customers to be two separate things. If it is necessary to track the assignment of customers to salespeople, a factless fact table may be called for. This technique will be discussed in Chapter 12, "Factless Fact Tables."

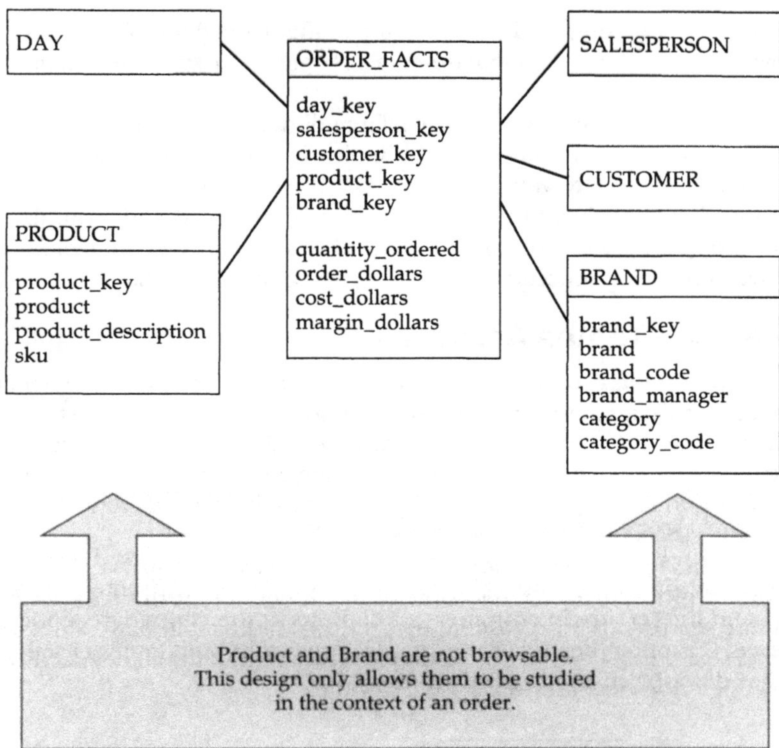

Figure 6-2 Separation of product and brand destroys browsability

Breaking Up Large Dimensions

A large set of dimension attributes enables the rich analytic capability that makes the data warehouse valuable. Chapter 3 provided advice on how to fill out dimension tables with useful attributes, which contribute to the formulation of powerful queries and the development of useful reports. It is not uncommon for dimension tables to contain well over 100 attributes. Not every dimension is this wide, but every business tends to have two or three major dimensions for which a great deal of information is collected. Wide dimensions usually center on some variation of products and customers. Examples include companies, people, documents, accounts, contracts, students, laws, regulations, locations, and so forth.

Sometimes, a dimension table becomes so wide that database administrators become concerned about its effect on the database. Such a concern may be purely technical but is completely valid. Very wide rows, for example, may impact the way that the database administrator allocates space or designates block size.

Large dimensions can also become a concern for ETL (extract, transform, load) developers. When a table has scores of type 2 attributes, incremental updates to the dimension can become a tremendous processing bottleneck. On top of this, large dimension tables may involve so many slow-changing dimensions that developers begin to question the meaning of the word "slow."

The first instinct of many designers is to divide a large dimension in half, with the two resulting tables sharing the same surrogate key. This limits row size but does have some drawbacks. While it may deal directly with width, it does not necessarily address processing bottlenecks or uncontrolled growth, and may require establishing some workarounds. Numerous options avoid splitting a dimension arbitrarily. One technique, the mini-dimension, is particularly effective in reducing processing bottlenecks and limiting growth.

Splitting Dimension Tables Arbitrarily

When the length of a dimension row pushes the database administrator over the edge, it is time to rethink dimension design. One common solution to the overly long dimension row is a simple separation of attributes into two tables. These two tables use the same surrogate key values, and they share a one-to-one relationship with one another. The excessive row length is split across the two tables, bringing row size back into the comfort zone of the database administrators. An example is shown in Figure 6-3.

The customer table in Figure 6-3 is divided into two parts: customer_part1 and customer_part2. For any given surrogate key, some of the dimension attributes are stored in customer_part1 and the rest are in customer_part2. Rows in the tables have a one-to-one correspondence. Customer_key 102, for example, appears in both tables exactly once. Together, these rows describe customer A501: Halfway, Inc.

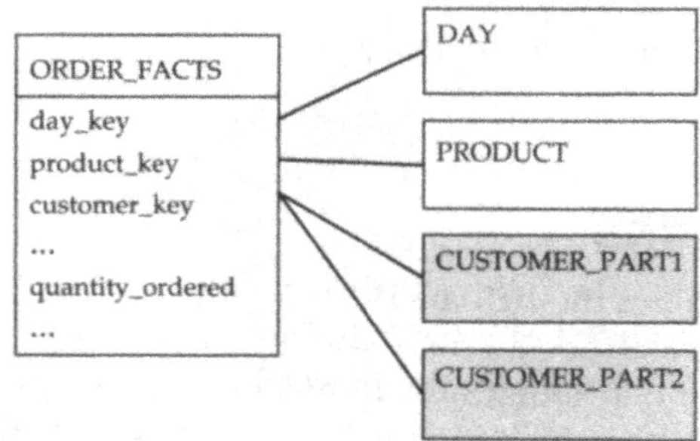

CUSTOMER_PART1

customer_key	customer_id	customer_name	address_line1
102	A501	Halfway Inc.	192 Elm St.
281	A472	Wooly Links LTD	4710 Maple Ave.
966	A472	Wooly Links LTD	4710 Maple Ave.
1407	A593	ABC Paper	4022 Davis Highway

CUSTOMER_PART2

customer_key	customer_id	hq_location	annual_revenue
102	A501	Grayville, MT	500,000_1,000,000
281	A472	Springfield, NH	Greater than 1,000,000
966	A472	Lawson, NH	Greater than 1,000,000
1407	A593	North Palte, IA	Less than 500,000

Figure 6-3 Arbitrary separation of customer attributes

Drawbacks to Arbitrary Separation

While this approach addresses issues raised by database administrators, it replaces them with a series of new challenges. More importantly, it may not address any issues raised by the ETL developers.

Join Options By splitting the customer table into two halves that share the same surrogate key, there are now multiple ways to join the tables in the star. In and of itself, this is not an issue—however, it may lead to confusion, and may pose problems for business intelligence tools that automatically generate queries.

Figure 6-3 depicts each of the customer_keys joining back to customer_key in the fact table. This join configuration is the logical way to combine customer attributes when querying the fact table. It fits the basic query pattern introduced in Chapter 1 and allows the DBMS to perform a star join. When someone wants to *browse* all attributes of customer as a single logical dimension, however, the appropriate configuration may be to join customer_part1 and customer_part2, using the customer_key.

While this seems a simple distinction, when there are large teams or turnover among developers, inconsistent or improper usage may result. For example, someone might include all three joins in a query, linking each part of "customer" to the fact table as well as to one another. Another possibility is that a developer will join the fact table to customer_part1, and then join customer_part1 to customer_part2. This configuration sounds reasonable, but the extra join may lead to sub-optimal performance. This potential issue is discussed in Chapter 7.

Business intelligence tools that automatically generate SQL queries can be thrown off when multiple ways exist to join tables. This situation may force a choice between browsability and star join optimization so that the tables are joined in a single determinate way. (This and similar issues are further explained in Chapter 16, "Design and Business Intelligence.")

Fact Table Foreign Key Declarations The preceding issues notwithstanding, representing each dimension row in two parts may present a purely technical issue. The two dimension tables share the same surrogate key, providing for a complete representation of the dimension. Although we understand that the foreign key in the fact table references each of these tables, a relational database management system (RDBMS) cannot be configured for this double-reference. Each foreign key can refer to only one table. If primary key / foreign key relationships are enabled in the database, the DBA must specify which table is referred to by customer_key in the fact table.

It is possible to work around this limitation by storing two copies of customer_key in the fact table. In the example, the customer_key in order_facts might be replaced by customer_key_part1 and customer_key_part2. This is unappealing because both columns will contain the same value, but it allows the database administrator to define foreign key relationships to customer_part1 and customer_part2.

ETL Processing For ETL developers, splitting a table into two parts poses a unique challenge. While there are two physical tables, the developers must treat them as one logical table. This complicates ETL processing and means that splitting the dimension table does not mitigate any processing issues surrounding the large dimension.

The ETL developers must treat the split dimension table as a single logical table in order to process new and changed source data correctly. The two halves of each row must remain synchronized as slow changes take place. This means that ETL developers must work with long rows, even if they are to be stored across two tables. As a side effect of the arbitrary division, one or the other table may contain rows that are identical, other than their surrogate key.

In Figure 6-3, you will notice that customer ID A472 has two rows in customer_part1 and customer_part2. These multiple versions of the customer resulted when a type 2 slow change to the customer's headquarters location occurred. This change is visible in customer_part2; headquarters moved from the city of Springfield to the city of Lawson. As with any type 2 change, a new row was created for the same natural key. Surrogate key 281 identifies the original version of the customer, and surrogate key 966 identifies the new one. In customer_part1, these two rows look identical; other than their surrogate keys, there are no differences.

Since the ETL developer must consider these two parts of the split table when processing new data, the ETL process does not see any benefit from the division of the table into two parts. If there are a large number of type 2 attributes, an ETL bottleneck may remain. Each time a source row changes, the ETL process must scrutinize all the type 2 columns to determine whether a type 2 change has occurred, regardless of whether the attributes are all in one customer table or divided across two.

Alternatives to Split Dimensions

Splitting rows across two tables presents practical problems and does not always resolve ETL issues. Faced with exceedingly large dimension tables, schema designers may wish to look for alternatives. These may include dividing the dimension into two dimensions, relocating some free-form text fields, or looking for opportunities to construct a mini-dimension.

Two Dimensions

When a dimension has an overwhelmingly large number of attributes, this is often a sign that there are two distinct dimensions. If so, the dimension can be redesigned as two tables, each with its own surrogate key. These two dimensions will then participate in explicit relationships via a fact table. Like the salesperson/customer distinction discussed earlier in this chapter, this also allows the attributes to relate in other contexts. Use the tests provided earlier in this chapter to evaluate this possibility. If there is potential for two dimensions, are the relationships volatile? Do they relate in other contexts? If so, separate dimensions are the way to go.

Relocating Free-Form Text Fields to an Outrigger

Excessive row length is often a result of the inclusion of several free-form text fields in the dimension table. Carried over from an operational system, these fields may contain unstructured data that is occasionally used to filter reports. When the number or size of these fields is large, they can be relocated to a separate table and replaced with a foreign key reference. This is an example of the *outrigger* technique, which is discussed in Chapter 7. Use of an outrigger may impede some DBMS optimizers, but when a free-form text field is used to constrain a query, performance will already be impacted. Relocating such fields to separate tables can help maintain a reasonable row size.

Looking for Subtypes

In many cases, a dimension will contain large groups of attributes that each apply to only one subset of its rows. In an operational system, this is referred to as *subtyping*. For example, the attributes of a dimension representing a product may vary significantly, depending on what type of product it is. Books, magazines and compact discs share some common attributes, such as name and SKU, but each subtype also has its own set of attributes.

In situations that involve subtype-specific attributes, dimension row size can be controlled by building a core dimension with only the shared attributes, and separate custom dimensions for each subtype. The core dimension is used when analyzing all subtypes, such as products, and the custom dimensions are used when studying only one particular subtype, such as books, subscriptions, or compact discs. Core and custom dimensions are further explored in Chapter 13, "Type-Specific Stars."

Considering Mini-Dimensions

Last, it may be possible to isolate a subset of the dimension's attributes and use them as the basis for a new dimension called a mini-dimension. Like a junk dimension, this table's attributes do not represent a single analytic concept. This new dimension table can alleviate size problems at the expense of limited browsability. As the next section reveals, the mini-dimension can have an unexpected impact on table growth.

Mini-Dimensions Alleviate ETL Bottlenecks and Excessive Growth

When a dimension table with a large number of rows undergoes a large number of type 2 changes, it can become too large. Constant improvements in DBMS technology may alleviate any concern about table size; 1 million rows may have seemed large a decade ago but is hardly a concern today. Even as advances in storage technology keep pace with a rapidly growing dimension table, it remains necessary to load the table. When an ETL process detects changed source data, it must determine whether it is necessary to apply a type 1 or type 2 change to existing dimension rows. If there are a large number of type 2 attributes, the process of determining how to deal with a change may quickly become a bottleneck.

Consider the example of a health insurance company that has over a million outstanding policies. The company tracks, among other processes that relate to policies, premium payments made by its customers. Figure 6-4 shows a payments fact table, which records information each time a customer makes a payment. The dimensions include the date of the payment, the invoice information, the customer making the payment, the insurance product, and the policy.

Certain aspects of the policies are relatively consistent, while others change more frequently. The bottom portion of Figure 6-4 illustrates what this means for one particular policy, held by Hal Smith. Over the years, a core set of attributes has remained unchanged—his policy number, name, and address—but slow changes to another set of attributes have generated numerous new rows. Hal married, altered coverage based on changes in his wife's employment, adjusted his deductible, added coverage for children, and removed it when they reached adulthood. All these changes in coverage details are significant from an analytic perspective and were handled as type 2 changes. This means that each change generated a new row in the dimension.

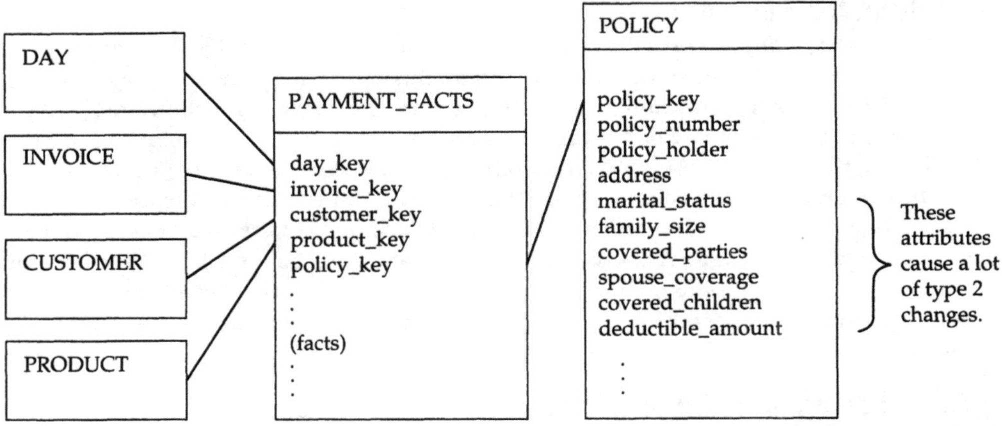

POLICY

policy_key	policy_number	policy_holder	address	marital_status	family_size	covered_parties	covered_children	deductible_amount
12882	40111	Smith, Hal	113 Random Rd.	Single	1	1	0	250
12911	40111	Smith, Hal	113 Random Rd.	Married	2	1	0	250
13400	40111	Smith, Hal	113 Random Rd.	Married	2	2	0	250
14779	40111	Smith, Hal	113 Random Rd.	Married	3	3	1	250
14922	40111	Smith, Hal	113 Random Rd.	Married	3	3	1	500
18911	40111	Smith, Hal	113 Random Rd.	Married	2	2	0	500

Figure 6-4 Growth in the policy dimension

If there are over 1 million policies, and most policies undergo at least one change in their coverage each year, this dimension table may quickly go from being manageable to being a nuisance. With a large number of type 2 attributes, each change to a policy may also require extensive evaluation to determine whether a new row must be generated for the dimension table.

These problems can be solved by removing some attributes from the dimension table and placing them in an entirely new dimension, called a mini-dimension. This separation of elements can have the miraculous effect of eliminating growth and also reduces the impact on the ETL process.

The Mini-Dimension

When a dimension table is projected to grow at an inordinate rate or necessitates ETL processing that is overly time-consuming, a mini-dimension can help. A mini-dimension is created by removing a number of the more volatile attributes from the dimension in question and placing them in a new table with its own surrogate key. These attributes share no direct relationship to one another, and there is no natural key. A one-time-only process can populate this table with data by creating a row for each combination of values.

In the case of the policy dimension, a mini-dimension can be created to isolate the attributes that change more often. These attributes include policy holder demographics, such as marital status and family size, and the policy coverage characteristics, such as the number of covered family members and the deductible amount. In Figure 6-5, these attributes have been removed from the policy table and placed into a mini-dimension called policy_coverage.

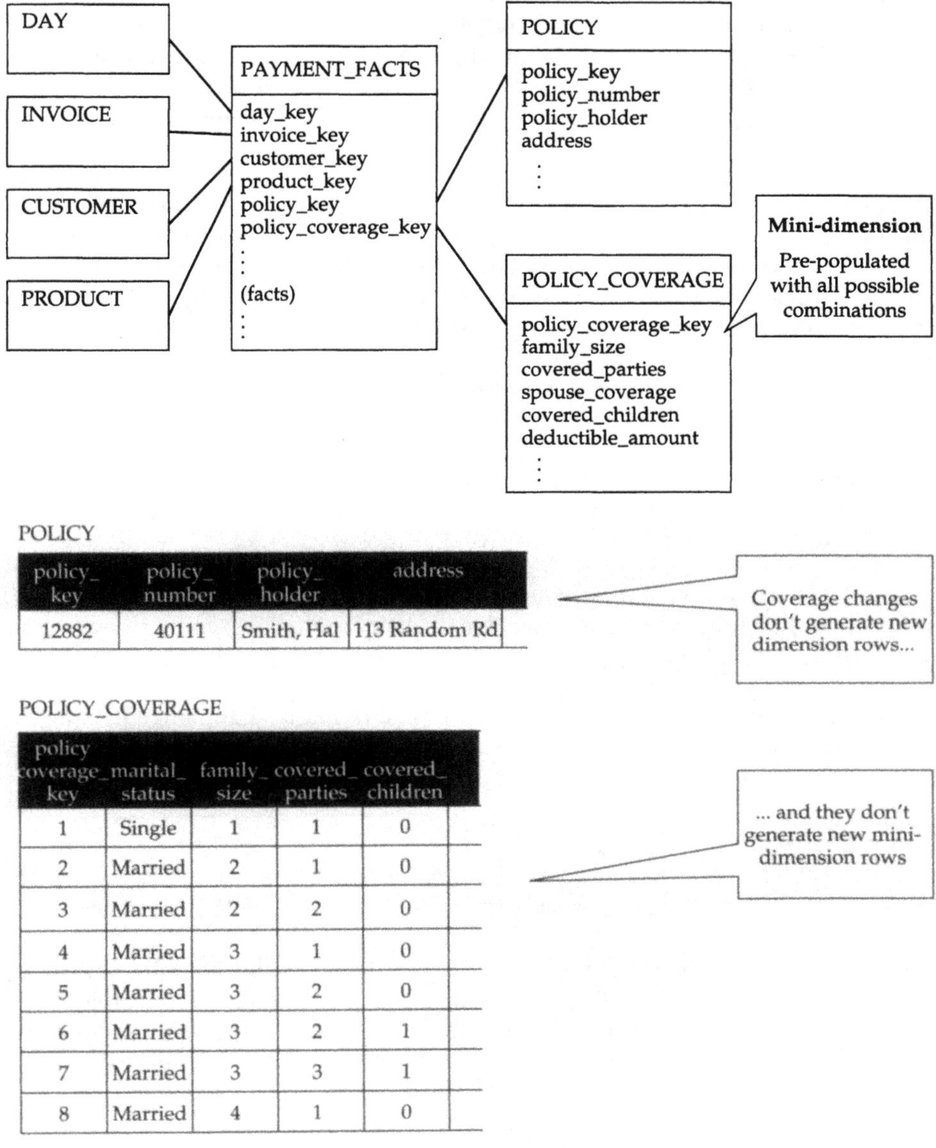

POLICY

policy_key	policy_number	policy_holder	address
12882	40111	Smith, Hal	113 Random Rd.

POLICY_COVERAGE

policy coverage_key	marital_status	family_size	covered_parties	covered_children
1	Single	1	1	0
2	Married	2	1	0
3	Married	2	2	0
4	Married	3	1	0
5	Married	3	2	0
6	Married	3	2	1
7	Married	3	3	1
8	Married	4	1	0

Figure 6-5 A mini-dimension relocates volatile attributes

The policy_coverage table does not have a natural key. Its attributes bear no direct relation to one another, or to any identifier present in the table. In these respects, a mini-dimension is similar to a junk dimension, as described in Chapter 3. Like any other dimension table, the mini-dimension is assigned a surrogate key. Rather than have an ETL process update this table on a regular basis, as is the case for other dimensions, it can be populated once, up front, with all possible value combinations.

It is important to distinguish the mini-dimension from the arbitrarily split dimension table in the previous section. Unlike the split dimension, the mini-dimension does not share surrogate keys with the original dimension table. There is not a one-to-one relationship between the original dimension and the mini-dimension. Fact tables will carry separate foreign keys which refer to the original dimension table and to the mini-dimension.

Growth Is Controlled

Separation of volatile attributes into a separate table can have an astounding effect, all but eliminating table growth, even as changes occur in the source. This surprising effect can be understood by studying the bottom of Figure 6-5. The policy table contains a single row for Hal Smith, whereas it previously required several. Changes in his demographics and coverage do not impact this table, because those attributes are not present. Since the policy_coverage table has been populated in advance with all possible combinations, changes to Hal's policy don't result in any changes here, either. Hal's coverage can change over and over again, but *neither table changes!*

There is a significant benefit to ETL processing as well. Each time the coverage details of a policy change, it is not necessary to scan through the policy dimension table to determine whether a type 2 change is needed. The ETL process for the main dimension is unaffected.

It *is* necessary for ETL developers to know the current coverage characteristics for each policy. This information is required when loading fact table rows. In Figure 6-5, for example, each payment transaction must be associated with the correct policy_coverage row. ETL developers can keep this process manageable by maintaining a mapping of policy to its current policy_coverage_key. Whenever a fact is loaded, this mapping can be consulted to determine the correct policy_coverage_key. This mapping need only be revisited when coverage changes, which is usually only once per year. It may be maintained in a staging area available only to the ETL process, but as you will see shortly, there may be others who can benefit from this mapping.

TIP When tables either (1) grow too quickly or (2) have so many type 2 attributes that change processing becomes a bottleneck, one or more mini-dimensions may help. Move the more volatile attributes into mini-dimension tables and populate them with all possible value combinations.

Since a mini-dimension is pre-populated with all possible value combinations, it is necessary to consider the cardinality of each attribute. If the number of possible combinations will result in a mini-dimension that is excessively large, two or more can be created. In the case of the policy example, this might entail building a coverage mini-dimension and a demographics mini-dimension.

Mini-Dimensions and Browsability

Mini-dimensions do have a potential drawback: they disrupt browsability. The dimension table and the mini-dimension are only related via facts. In the policy example from Figure 6-5, it is not possible to create a browse query that shows the list of policies where the policy holder is married. Policies and marital status come from separate tables, related through payment_facts. If there have been no payments, there will be no fact table rows to link these tables.

In situations that call for mini-dimensions, this limitation is frequently not a concern. It is rare that users wish to construct browse queries that reach down to the most detailed level of a large dimension. The policy coverage attributes, for example, are used to apply filters to queries, drive subtotals, and so forth. Rarely does a user want to browse through this data to the individual policy level.

It is possible to provide limited browsability between a dimension and mini-dimension. This can be achieved by adding a foreign key to the dimension table that refers to the mini-dimension. This reference represents the current corresponding mini-dimension row. In the case of policy, for example, the record for Hal Smith can be supplemented with a foreign key to the policy_coverage table, representing the current coverage characteristics for Hal. In Figure 6-6, this is done by adding pol_coverage_key_current to the policy table. This foreign key just happens to be the same mapping that ETL developers need in order to load facts properly, as discussed earlier.

The cross-browsability enabled by keeping a mini-dimension key in the dimension is limited. For each dimension row, it is only possible to look at the *current* information in the mini-dimension. History is not maintained. For example, it is only possible to see the current policy coverage data for Hal Smith's policy; if his coverage details change, the foreign key is updated in the policy table. In this respect, the foreign key is treated like a type 1 attribute. Tracking the change history or treating the foreign key reference as a type 2 attribute would require a new row to be inserted into the policy table each time Hal Smith's coverage changed. That would defeat the original purpose of the mini-dimension, which was to stem the growth of the policy table.

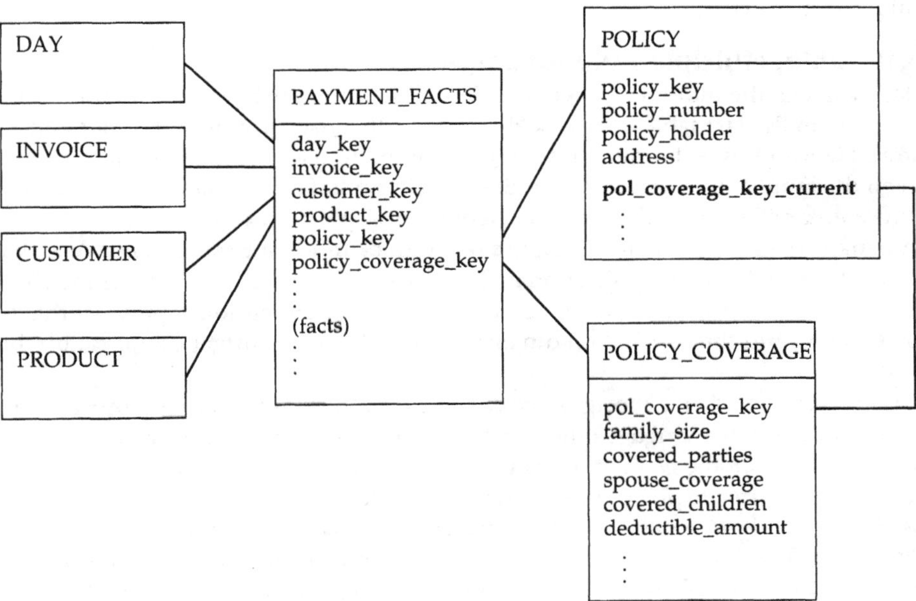

Figure 6-6 A foreign key links policy to the policy_coverage mini-dimension

Part III

TIP A dimension can carry a foreign key reference to a mini-dimension. This reference will help ETL developers when populating fact table rows, and allow users to cross-browse the dimension and mini-dimension. It should not be charged with carrying history, as this would defeat the purpose of the mini-dimension.

As was observed with the split dimension table, this foreign key reference may pose a technical obstacle in the configuration of business intelligence tools that automatically generate queries. When users browse the dimension and mini-dimension, the tables should be joined using the direct relationship between the tables. When users query the fact tables, however, the mini-dimension should be joined to the fact table, not the dimension table. The dimension table's foreign key reference to the mini-dimension should never be used in the join to the fact table, although it may appear to a developer that this is appropriate.

If needed, the full history of the relationships between a dimension and a mini-dimension can be preserved by designing an additional fact table. Each row will identify a row in the dimension, a row in the mini-dimension, and the time frame during which they were associated. It is quite possible that there will be no facts in this table (*factless fact tables* will be discussed in Chapter 12).

Dimension Roles and Aliasing

Measurement of a business process can involve more than one instance of a dimension. When an auto dealer sells a car, for example, two employees are associated with the transaction: the salesperson who sold the car and the manager who approved the sale. These two relationships are called *roles*. In a fact table, they are represented by multiple foreign key references to the same dimension table. At query time, each role can be isolated by using a technique called aliasing.

Single Table, Multiple Relationships

In a star schema, the multiple roles played by a dimension are represented by multiple foreign keys in the fact table. Database designers with a background in ER modeling are comfortable with this technique. It is not uncommon to have more than one relationship between the same pair of tables; ER models usually go so far as to name every relationship. For those unfamiliar with this technique, a brief example is warranted.

A bank uses the star schema in Figure 6-7 to track mortgage settlements. A settlement is an event at which a loan application is signed and becomes a binding contract. The grain of the fact table is one row per settlement. The day dimension represents the date of the settlement, and the application dimension describes the mortgage application that goes into effect.

In this example, when a mortgage goes into effect, there are three employees of the bank who are involved. The mortgage officer is the person who interacts directly with the customer, providing counsel on the types of mortgages available and helping the customer choose the right one. The mortgage processor's job is to gather documents from the applicant that will be used to assess his or her ability to repay a loan, such as bank statements, tax returns, and credit reports. The person who evaluates the application and approves it is known as the underwriter. In Figure 6-7, each of these employees is represented by a foreign key in the fact table: employee_key_officer, employee_key_processor, and employee_key_underwriter.

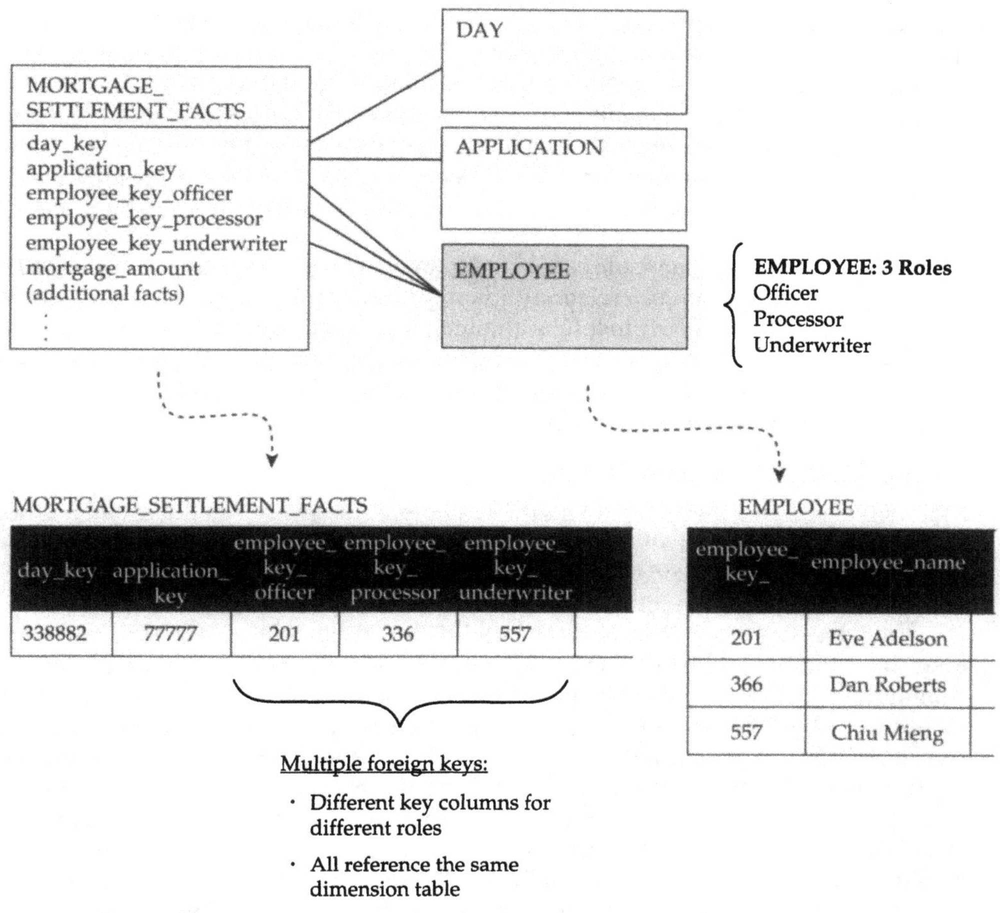

MORTGAGE_SETTLEMENT_FACTS

day_key	application_key	employee_key_officer	employee_key_processor	employee_key_underwriter
338882	77777	201	336	557

EMPLOYEE

employee_key_	employee_name
201	Eve Adelson
366	Dan Roberts
557	Chiu Mieng

Figure 6-7 Employee plays multiple roles in this fact table

Each of these three foreign keys refers to a row in the employee dimension as designated by an employee_key. An example of a row in the fact table is depicted in the bottom of the figure. In this sample row, the application represented by application_key 77777 contains employee_key_officer = 201. In the employee dimension table, employee 201 is someone named Eve Adelson. Similarly, the employee_key_processor refers to Dan Roberts, and the employee_key_underwriter refers to Chiu Mieng.

It is possible that multiple roles are played by the same dimension instance. When this occurs, the fact table foreign keys for the roles will contain the same values. If Eve Adelson had been the mortgage officer and processor, for example, then employee_key_officer and employee_key_processor would each contain the value 201.

TIP A dimension table can participate in more than one relationship with a fact table. Each relationship is known as a role.

When a fact table refers to a dimension table, the foreign key column normally bears the same name as the corresponding primary key column. This is not possible when there are two or more roles. Instead, the foreign key columns should be given names that connote each role. The designation of a standard can help here. In Figure 6-7, for example, the three foreign key references to employee append role descriptors to the key name from the employee table: employee_key_**officer**, employee_key_**processor**, and employee_key_**underwriter**. This makes each role readily identifiable when examining column names in the fact table.

Every time a dimension table is referred to by a fact table, the relationship represents a role. Even if there are not two relationships, it can be useful to name the role designated by each join. This is particularly helpful with time dimensions, which play a different role in each star. In Figure 6-7, for example, the role of the day dimension is "day of settlement." Identifying this context provides useful documentation of the star and may be particularly handy when building drill-across reports.

Using Aliases to Access Roles

Although a fact table may bear multiple foreign key references to a dimension, it is not necessary to build more than one replica of the dimension. In a query, the desired role can be accessed by using the correct join. If more than one role is to be accessed, multiple views or aliases can be used to refer to each role.

Using database views, a separate view of the dimension table is created to represent each role. Queries join the fact table to each view using the appropriate foreign key columns. Each view behaves as a separate instance of the table, allowing them to be treated as separate tables. In the case of the mortgage closings, three views of the employee table can be established: one for the officer, one for the processor, and one for the underwriter.

Creating views is not necessary, because the SQL standard includes the concept of aliasing. Aliases allow a query to refer to more than one logical copy of a single physical table. The top of Figure 6-8, for example, illustrates a query that identifies the three employees associated with application 77777. The SQL statement creates three aliases for the employee table called officer, processor, and employee. Each is joined to the fact table by way of the foreign key appropriate for its role.

In the SQL statement, the `FROM` clause contains three references to the employee table. Each one is followed by the word `ALIAS` and a name designating its role. This tells the database that the query will involve three instances of employee, each with its own name. In the `SELECT` clause, you can see each of these aliases referred to as if it were a table name; the employee names are also being aliased so they can be told apart. In the `WHERE` clause, each alias is connected to the fact table by using the appropriate foreign key. Employee_key_officer is used to join to the officer alias, employee_key_processor is used to join to the processor alias, and employee_key_underwriter is used to join to the underwriter alias. The diagram at the top of the figure illustrates the logical schema created by this use of aliasing. Although there is only one employee table, the DBMS will execute the query as if there were three.

TIP When a fact table and dimension table have multiple relationships, it is not necessary to build multiple copies of the dimension. Each role can be accessed by joining views or aliases of the dimension to the appropriate foreign keys in the fact table.

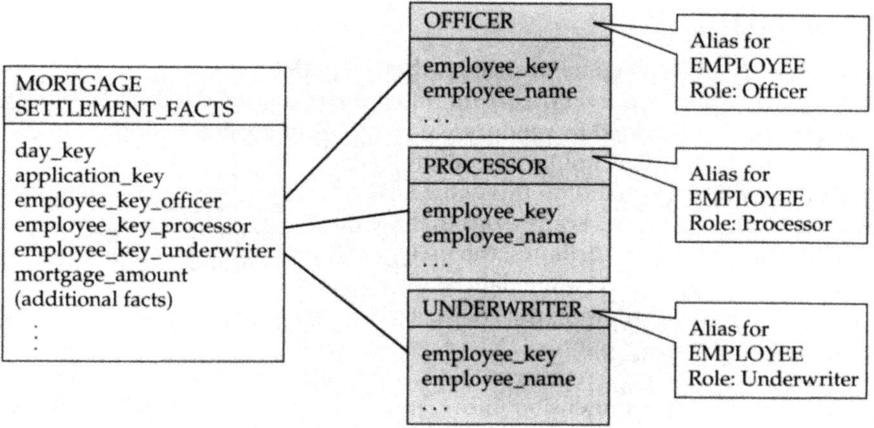

SQL Query

```
SELECT
   officer.employee_name AS officer_name,
   processor.employee_name AS processor_name,
   underwriter.employee_name AS underwriter_name
FROM
   -- Alias the employee table 3 times:
   --
   employee ALIAS officer,
   employee ALIAS processor,
   employee ALIAS underwriter,
   --
   --
   mortgage_closing_facts
WHERE
   --
   -- join to each alias using correct key:
   --
   mortgage_closing_facts.employee_key_officer = officer.employee_key AND
   mortgage_closing_facts.employee_key_processor = processor.employee_key AND
   mortgage_closing_facts.employee_key_underwriter = underwriter.employee_key AND
   --
   --
   mortgage_closing_facts.application_key = 77777
```

Query Results

```
officer_name      processor_name    underwriter_name
===============   ===============   ================
Eve Adelson       Dan Roberts       Chiu Mieng
```

Figure 6-8 Using aliases in a query to access the multiple roles of employee

Many business intelligence and reporting tools have their own forms of aliasing. Typically, such tools will allow a table to be brought into a graphical diagram of the query multiple times, much the way employee appears three times at the top of Figure 6-8.

Avoiding the NULL

In the world of database management systems, there is perhaps nothing more controversial than the NULL. Not part of the set theory on which the relational database is founded, the concept of the NULL was added by vendors as a way to distinguish the absence of data from blank or zero. This may or may not be a good thing, depending on whom you ask.

Regardless of where you stand on this debate, NULL values cause untold complications when using the data warehouse. For reasons that are purely pragmatic, it is best to avoid the use of NULLs. For dimension attributes, the inelegant but practical solution is to store a specific value such as 0 or "N/A" when data is not available.

It is also useful to avoid allowing the NULL as a foreign key value in a fact table. If a relationship to a dimension is optional, NULL values can be avoided by establishing a special row in the dimension to represent "N/A." This same technique can be used when there are facts for which the dimension information has not yet been supplied, for which the operational system has recorded invalid information, or for which the dimension represents something that has not yet occurred.

Problems Caused by NULL

Although the concept of NULL is not part of the relational model, virtually every relational database product supports the use of the NULL "value." NULL is a special data element that can be stored in a database column. A NULL has no meaning, apparently distinguishing it from a blank, empty string, or zero value. This extension to SQL has been widely criticized on a number of grounds, most notably for the fact that it appears to confuse data with metadata and for the twisted logical system it implies.

While this book is not intended to argue over such matters, the use of NULLs in the data warehouse causes significant difficulties when it comes to data analysis. These difficulties are evident in two situations: the use of NULL as a dimension value and the use of NULL as a foreign key column. Practical solutions can avoid some of these problems, although they exhibit some of the same issues to which theoreticians object.

Dimension Columns and NULL

In most relational database management systems, the use of NULLs is allowed by default. Unless the database administrator explicitly specifies that a column must not contain NULL, it is possible to insert one. NULLs need not be explicitly inserted; when a row is added to a table, if a value is not specified for a particular column, it will default to NULL.

Data warehouse practitioners often learn of the pitfalls of these NULL values the hard way. In developing reports, NULLs cause myriad problems that can make the calmest of analysts start pulling their hair out. The problems they encounter all stem from the special status of the NULL: it is not a value and has no meaning. This sounds innocent enough, until you look at what it means in terms of actually using the data.

Understanding the headaches caused by NULLs does not require delving into the academic or philosophical underpinnings of the relational model. One need look no further than the impact of NULL on the process of writing queries. Because a NULL does not represent anything, it cannot be considered equal to anything else—not even another NULL. At the same time, a NULL cannot be considered *not* equal to anything else.

Any traditional comparison will fail if a NULL is involved. Database vendors have, therefore, added special features to SQL that permit testing for NULLs.

Suppose, for example, that a customer table contains a column indicating whether a customer has tax exempt status. In keeping with Chapter 3's advice to spell out flag values, assume that this column does not contain Boolean true/false values but instead contains the values "Tax Exempt" and "Not Tax Exempt." Let us further assume that, for whatever reason, this value is not recorded for a particular customer, Hal Smith. In his case, the column contains a NULL. If you want to generate a report for all customers who do not have a tax exempt status, you probably want Hal Smith to be counted. Unschooled in the dangers of the NULL, you might try to use the *not equal* comparison operator:

```
WHERE tax_exampt_status <> "Tax Exempt"
```

Unfortunately, this constraint will not pick up Hal Smith. His tax exempt status is NULL, which is neither equal nor unequal to the string "Tax Exempt."

The "correct" way to deal with NULLs in SQL comparisons is to use IS NULL or IS NOT NULL comparisons. To find people who do not have a tax exempt status, this might look like:

```
WHERE tax_exampt_status <> "Tax Exempt"
   OR tax_exempt_status IS NULL
```

Combining this with additional comparisons now creates an exercise in the balancing of parentheses. Similar issues are faced when searching strings to ensure they do not contain a particular value, using greater than or less than comparison operators, and so forth. The problems extend into aggregation as well; if you count customers with and without tax exempt status, the total will match the number of customers.

When NULLs are stored in the database, analysts need to jump through a lot of hoops to create accurate reports. Needless to say, the potential for error is strong, and business users can certainly not be expected to construct reports properly, even when using a business intelligence tool. The presence of NULLs therefore increases the report creation burden shouldered by the data warehouse team.

Even when trained analysts are responsible for producing all reports, it can be confusing just explaining what a report means when NULLs are allowed. NULLs also make for unusual conversations between developers and users. Imagine having to ask the question "Do you want customers with a tax_exempt status of 'Not Tax Exempt,' or would you prefer to include customers who do not have a tax exempt status?" This question will be rewarded with a blank stare.

The largest problem created by NULLs cannot be avoided by entrusting all database interaction to developers. While a well-trained analyst can deal with NULLs, there is nothing to stop businesspeople from looking at two reports and misinterpreting the results. If one report shows January sales for tax exempt customers and another shows January sales for customers who are not tax exempt, a reasonable assumption would be that the two figures together represent all of January sales. Unfortunately, this is not the case.

TIP Do not allow the storage of NULLs in dimension columns. Instead, choose a value that will be used whenever data is not available.

Rather than store NULLs in a dimension, star schema designers choose specific values that will be used when a data value is not available. For text columns, the value "N/A" is a trusted standby. For numeric columns, the value 0 is usually chosen, and dates are often defaulted to an arbitrary date in the very far future (more on dates in a moment). Sometimes, a series of different values is used.

In some cases, developers choose to use multiple values that describe why source data is unavailable, such as "Unknown" and "Invalid." Note that while these values lift away the complications of testing for NULLs, they are still objectionable from a theoretical standpoint. Technically speaking, these are not values, but information describing the reason for a lack of a value. In cases where questionable or missing data is expected in a specific column, designers may introduce an additional column to describe the status of the column. For example, our tax_exempt_status column may be supplemented by one that indicates valid_tax_exempt_status, taking on the values "Valid" and "Invalid."

NULL Foreign Keys in Fact Tables

Sometimes, it is not possible to associate a fact with a row in a dimension table. This occurs when the dimension value is unknown or invalid, or the relationship is optional. In an ER model, the traditional solution is to store a NULL value in the foreign key column. Unfortunately, the presence of NULL foreign keys in a fact table leads to more analytic complications. Entire fact table rows disappear from query result sets, unless one makes use of outer joins. Employing an outer join causes query results to contain NULLs, even if dimension tables do not.

An example of an optional relationship occurs in retail sales. You may have noticed that in some stores the cashier will note when a salesperson has helped you. This information may be used to evaluate salespeople or to compute their compensation. Whatever the reason, some sales have an associated salesperson, while some do not. The star schema in Figure 6-9 accommodates this optionality by allowing the salesrep_key to be NULL. Like the NULL value in a dimension column, this approach will lead to problems when formulating queries. The workaround tactics explored for NULL values in dimension columns will not suffice. Additional workarounds will be required.

Notice that there are types of salesreps and that some are managers. Managers may have special flexibility when it comes to pricing, so perhaps someone has asked for a report covering sales in which managers were not involved. A well-meaning developer might mistakenly write a query like this:

```
SELECT
  store.store_name,
  sum(sales_facts.quantity_sold)
FROM
  store,
  salesrep,
  sales_facts
```

```
WHERE
  salesrep.salesrep_type <> 'Manager' AND
  salesrep.salesrep_key = sales_facts.salesrep_key AND
  store.store_key = sales_facts.store_key
GROUP BY
   store.store_name
```

Unfortunately, this SQL query will not pick up all sales where a manager was not involved. For fact table rows where there is no salesperson, the join to the salesrep dimension fails altogether; such facts will not be included in the query results. This occurs because the NULL foreign key cannot be matched to a row in the dimension table.

The only way to produce the desired results is to employ an *outer join*. An outer join instructs the DBMS to include rows from one table, even if it is being joined to another table that does *not* include a corresponding row. If a corresponding row is not found, the database will generate NULL values for its columns in the result set. So, for example, when the fact table in Figure 6-9 is outer-joined to salesrep, the fact table row with a NULL salesrep_key is given a salesrep_name and salesrep_type of NULL. This means that the previously discussed tactics for

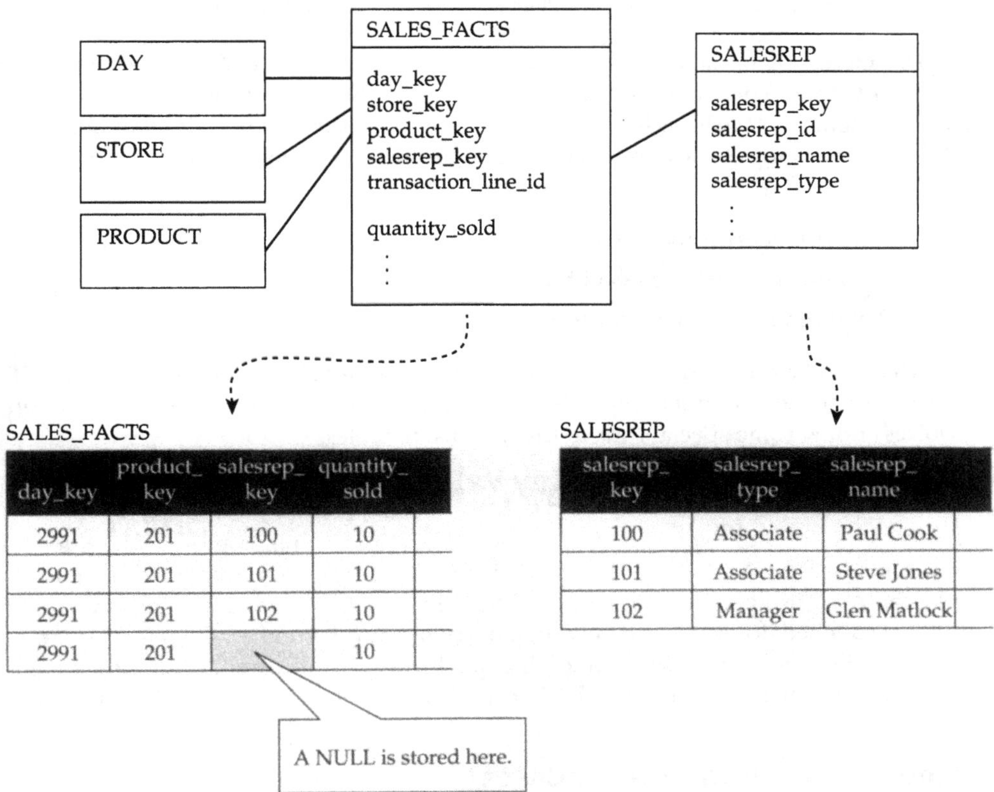

day_key	product_key	salesrep_key	quantity_sold
2991	201	100	10
2991	201	101	10
2991	201	102	10
2991	201		10

salesrep_key	salesrep_type	salesrep_name
100	Associate	Paul Cook
101	Associate	Steve Jones
102	Manager	Glen Matlock

Figure 6-9 A retail sales star allowing NULL keys causes analytic difficulty

dealing with NULLs also come into play. Even if NULL is not stored in the dimension, it will be necessary to test for it:

```
SELECT
    store.store_name,
    sum(sales_facts.quantity_sold)
FROM sales_facts LEFT OUTER JOIN salesrep
    ON sales_facts.salesrep_key = salesrep.salesrep_key
...
WHERE
    (
      salesrep.salesrep_type <> 'Manager' OR
      salesrep.salesrep_type IS NULL
     ) AND ...
GROUP BY
    store.store_name
```

TIP Avoid allowing NULL values in foreign key columns. They require alternative join syntax and create NULL instance values for dimension columns even when NULLs are not stored.

This increasing group of workarounds leans heavily on a cadre of experienced developers to get work done. These developers become similar to the frog of Chapter 4, upon which the water temperature has slowly been increased. Eventually, the frog finds itself in boiling water. While the well-being of the developers is an important consideration, there are other impacts as well:

- The risk of error increases.
- End users cannot create ad hoc reports.
- Valid reports may be misinterpreted.

What is to be done when a particular dimension is not always required by a fact? If NULL foreign keys are not acceptable, what is recorded in the fact table? The solution involves adding some special rows to the dimension tables.

Avoiding NULL Foreign Key Values

Despite the various problems of NULL-valued dimensions columns and NULL-valued foreign keys, sometimes a valid fact cannot be associated with a dimension row. In addition to the optional relationship, there may be transactions for which the dimension information has not yet been supplied, for which the operational system has recorded invalid information, or for which the dimension represents something that has not yet occurred. In all these situations, the technical issues surrounding NULLs can be avoided by creating special rows in the dimension table.

Dimension Rows for Special Cases

When the relationship between a fact table and a dimension table is optional, the problems that come along with NULL values can be avoided by creating a special row in the dimension table.

SALESREP

salesrep_key	row_type	salesrep_type	salesrep_name
0	No Salesrep	n/a	n/a
100	Salesrep	Associate	Paul Cook
101	Salesrep	Associate	Steve Jones
102	Salesrep	Manager	Glen Matlock

Special-case row

SALES_FACTS

day_key	product_key	salesrep_key	quantity_sold
2991	201	100	10
2991	201	101	10
2991	201	102	10
2991	201	0	10

A reference to the special row

Figure 6-10 A special row in the salesrep table helps avoid NULL keys

This row will be referred to by fact table rows that do not have corresponding dimension detail. Although inelegant from an academic standpoint, this technique simplifies reporting and reduces risk.

In the sales_facts star, sales without salesreps are accommodated by adding a special row to the salesrep table. This row will be referred to by fact table rows when there is not a salesrep. The special row in the salesrep table will also carry a non-NULL value for each column, so as to also avoid the problems that come with NULLs. Figure 6-10 shows how this might look.

An extra row has been inserted into the salesrep table in Figure 6-10, with a surrogate key value of 0. When sales are recorded that do not involve salesreps, the fact table row will use this key value, avoiding the need for NULL-valued foreign keys. The special row in the dimension table carries the value "n/a" in each of its columns, avoiding the issues of NULL-valued dimension columns.

Impact on Browsability

The special case row avoids some of the negative impacts associated with NULL values but remains an imperfect solution. The information stored in this row is semantically inconsistent with the definition of the table. In this respect, the underlying concepts of the relational model are still being violated. The salesrep table and its columns are intended to describe salespeople. There is no salesperson called "n/a."

From a pragmatic perspective, one may be willing to live with this compromise, but it also has implications on usability that may be undesirable. Users browsing the dimension table will encounter the special row. "What is this 'n/a' all about?" they may ask. To help stem some of these problems, you can add a column to the dimension table indicating the row type. Each row is either a standard row or a special row. The type indicator can take on values such as "standard" and "special," or be more specific, as in "Salesrep" and "No Salesrep" as in Figure 6-10. This indicator can be used to filter the special rows out of browse queries. A simple constraint is added to the browse query:

```
WHERE
    salesrep.row_type = "Salesrep"
```

It is important to remember to remove this constraint when querying the fact table.

Uses for Special-Case Rows

In addition to the optional relationship, special-case rows can help when a transaction arrives with invalid data, when transactions are loaded before dimensions are processed, and when a time dimension represents something that has not yet occurred.

Optional Relationships

The optional relationship between fact table and dimension table is not common, but it does occur. An optional dimension is acceptable when it is not part of the grain of the fact table. This is the case in the sales example, where the grain of the fact table can be stated as "one row per order line." When a statement of grain includes an optional dimension, as in the orders and shipments design from Figure 4-5, it is a sign of confusion, and analysis will be hampered.

Invalid Data

When a row is loaded into a fact table, the ETL process must identify the correct dimension row to associate with the fact. As described in Chapter 17, "Design and ETL," the raw transactions are typically obtained from the source system with natural keys, which are used to determine dimensional context. A sales transaction, for example, comes from the source system with a date, product code, and customer ID. When the source system contains invalid data, it may not be possible to match the transaction to a dimension row.

This situation may occur, for example, when an order entry system does not validate order inputs against a master product list. In this case, the order entry system may provide transactions with product codes that are not present in the dimension table. Although the product code provided with the transaction is invalid, the transaction itself represents an actual sale. Failure to include it in the fact table will result in an understatement of sales activity.

In this situation, a special row can be added to the product dimension for use when the product associated with a transaction is invalid. Figure 6-11 provides an example. The row with surrogate key 0 indicates an invalid product code. This allows a fact to be loaded for the transaction in question, rather than excluding it from the fact table or using a NULL foreign key.

PRODUCT

product_key	row_type	product_code	product_name
0	Invalid	n/a	n/a
1	Unknown	n/a	n/a
101	Product	B57330-1	Cardboard Box
102	Product	B47770-2	Bubble Envelope

Used when a fact is supplied with an invalid product_code

Used when a fact arrives prior to dimensional context

Figure 6-11 Special-case rows for invalid and unknown products

When this situation is permitted, designers and ETL developers must take care to provide a mechanism for the correction of the data. The best approach is to include transaction identifiers as degenerate dimensions in the fact table. This allows a cleanup process to select the transaction identifiers for all facts recorded with invalid products so that someone can research and correct them. For example:

```
SELECT
  transaction_number
FROM
  order_facts,
  product
WHERE
  product.row_type = "Invalid" AND
  order_facts.product_key = product.product_key
```

This query provides a list of transactions that have invalid facts. An analyst can use this list to research these transactions and provide corrected product codes.

Late-Arriving Data

Sometimes, the data warehouse receives transactions before it receives the relevant dimensional detail. This situation occurs in data warehouses that load data at frequent intervals or in real time. A new product code, for example, may appear in a transaction before information on the product is reflected in the product dimension. As with the invalid data problem, the fact cannot be loaded if there is no row for the product in the dimension table, but excluding the transaction from the fact table understates sales.

Again, the special-case row offers a solution. Rather than hold the transaction until dimensional detail is available, the fact will be associated with a special row in the dimension table indicating an unknown product. An example of such a row appears in the product table from Figure 6-11, bearing a surrogate key value of 1. When a transaction arrives for a product that is not known to the data warehouse, the transaction can be associated with this row. As in the case of the invalid data, a transaction identifier should be stored in the fact table. This will allow the row to be updated with the correct surrogate key once the dimension value is received.

TIP Special-case rows can be added to dimensions to deal with incorrect or missing information. This avoids the need to exclude facts from the warehouse. The star should record sufficient transaction identifiers to allow the anomalous record to be identified and corrected in the future.

Future Events

The last use for special-case rows involves time. When a fact table row represents something that may expire, it is useful to record a pair of dates: the date it became effective and the date it expired. Some examples of this will be encountered when we look at accumulating snapshots in Chapter 11, "Transactions, Snapshots, and Accumulating Snapshots," and coverage tables in Chapter 12, "Factless Fact Tables." Data that is current has an effective date but no expiration date. In this case, a special row in the day dimension can be used to avoid the use of NULLs for the expiration_day_key. When associated with a fact, this row signals that the expiration has not occurred. An example appears in Figure 6-12.

This fact table records the assignment of employees as department managers within an organization. Each row represents an individual's tenure managing a department. The fact table has two day_keys: one for the day the individual became the manager of the department and another for the day the managerial role expired. The pair of dates can be used to

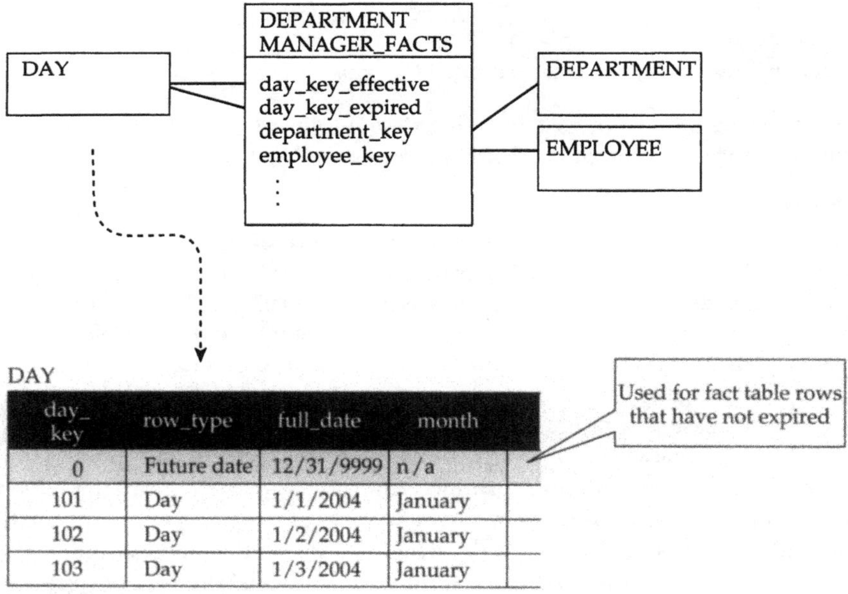

day_key	row_type	full_date	month
0	Future date	12/31/9999	n/a
101	Day	1/1/2004	January
102	Day	1/2/2004	January
103	Day	1/3/2004	January

Figure 6-12 Tracking effective and expiration dates

determine who the manager was at any given point in time. For example, to see who managed each department on July 1, 2007, you might issue this query:

```
SELECT
  department.department_name,
  employee.employee_name
FROM
  department_manager_facts,
  department,
  employee,
  day ALIAS effective_day,
  day ALIAS expiration_day
WHERE
  effective_day.full_date <= 7/1/2007 AND
  expiration_day.full_date >= 7/1/2007 AND
...(additional joins)...
```

This query retrieves fact records that were in effect on 7/1/2007 by aliasing the day dimension and applying the pair of constraints shown in bold type. The first constraint limits the result rows to those where the effective date of the tenure was on or before the date in question; the second limits the results to those where the expiration is on or after the date in question. Together, they select only records that were active on the date in question.

An active department head does not have an expiration date. If the day key in the fact table is recorded as a NULL, the preceding query will fail to identify any manager who was active on 7/1/2007 but has not yet left his or her post. Even using an outer join, the comparison on expiration date will fail. The solution is to use a special-case row in the day dimension, as shown at the bottom of Figure 6-12. The row in the day dimension with the surrogate key value of 0 is used for fact table records that have not expired. An arbitrary future date is used in the day dimension for this row, so that comparisons like the preceding ones do not fail.

There is a caveat, of course. Besides the fact that this special date creates a modern version of the famous "Y2K problem," this date will complicate attempts to construct queries that measure tenure by comparing the effective and expiration dates. Such queries must take care to use the current date for any unexpired rows.

Behavioral Dimensions

A very powerful analytic technique uses past behavior patterns to make sense of current behavior. Consider this question: "Are customers who generate over $1 million in orders receiving better discounts than those who generate $500,000 or less?" This question uses a fact, order dollars, as a dimension, providing a context for the study of discount dollars. Answering this kind of question requires advanced query development and intense processing.

A *behavioral question* is one that groups or filters facts based on the past behavior of members of a dimension. Behavioral dimensions transform facts into dimensions, enabling powerful analytics without complex queries or intensive processing.

Converting Facts to Dimensions at Query Time

Answering a question that groups or filters facts based on past behavior goes beyond the capabilities of the basic `SELECT/GROUP BY` query introduced in Chapter 1. To answer these questions, two major steps are required:

1. Identify past behavior for each member of the dimension in question.
2. Use this information as part of a query studying current behavior.

For the preceding question regarding discounts, the first step requires identifying the past order behavior for each customer, classifying them based on order volume. The second step uses this new information about customers in a query that aggregates the fact discount dollars. These steps may be put together programmatically, perhaps within the environs of a reporting tool. They can also be combined through the construction of a correlated subquery, in which case the first step is subordinated to the second.

Because of the processing required, queries of this nature do not perform well. To cope, behavioral reports are often scheduled to run during batch windows, so that the report is cached and ready for viewing when the user requests it. This interrupts the normal cycle of question, followed by answer, followed by new question. If each new question requires execution of a behavioral query during a batch window, the cycle may stretch out over days.

It should also be noted that an end user cannot be expected to put together a behavioral report. Whether this is done using procedural processing or by using a correlated subquery, the necessary technical skills go beyond even those of junior systems analysts. As a result, requests for these powerful reports often populate the IT backlog, and the data warehouse does not live up to its fullest potential.

TIP Using past behavior to study facts requires the construction of new dimensions from old facts. If done at report time, this process is slow and requires the expertise of a developer.

The solution to this problem extends existing dimension tables to include behavioral data. The additional ETL processing required pays significant dividends.

Designing and Using Behavioral Dimensions

The ability to use past behavior as the context for facts can be supported without a negative impact on query performance. This is achieved by adding columns to dimension tables that track past behavior. These *behavioral dimensions* shift the processing burden away from query and report development, and move it to the ETL process.

Past behavior can be incorporated into a dimension table in three ways, all of which reduce the processing required to answer a behavioral question. A behavioral dimension may capture a past association with another dimension, a fact, or a categorization of a fact.

Past Association with Another Dimension

A behavioral attribute can be used to capture the historic association of a dimension row with information that would normally be stored in another table. Without the behavioral dimension, this past association would only be available by querying a fact table. Most often, the related dimension is a date, and it is added to the dimension table to signify a past event of importance.

For example, analysts in the marketing group may want to be able to use the date of a customer's most recent order to filter queries. Storing this date in the customer table eliminates the necessity to query an orders fact table to find the dates on which each customer last placed an order. Figure 6-13 contains two examples of this technique: first_order_date and last_order_date.

Without these behavioral dimensions, the date of each customer's last order would only be obtainable by querying the order_facts table. Using this information to study current orders would require programmatic logic or a correlated subquery, well out of reach of the average user. By placing this information in the customer table, the query is dramatically simplified. The last_order_date can be used to filter the query in the same way that any other attribute would, without any additional processing.

Historic Fact

A behavioral attribute can also capture a fact of historic significance for storage in the dimension table. This fact is usually qualified in some way, as reflected in the attribute's name. Because this information is stored in the dimension table, the historic fact can be used to filter, group, or order query results without the need for a subquery or procedural logic.

Figure 6-13 contains an example of a historic fact stored in a dimension: annual_sales. This attribute aggregates a year's worth of transaction history and stores the result in the dimension table. There, it serves as an easy source of query constraints. If one wants to look at discount dollars to customers who had over $1,000,000 in annual sales, a simple constraint does the trick:

```
WHERE customer.annual_sales >= 1000000
```

Without this behavioral attribute, a correlated subquery or equivalent would be required, aggregating a year's worth of sales_dollars from the order_facts table for *each* customer.

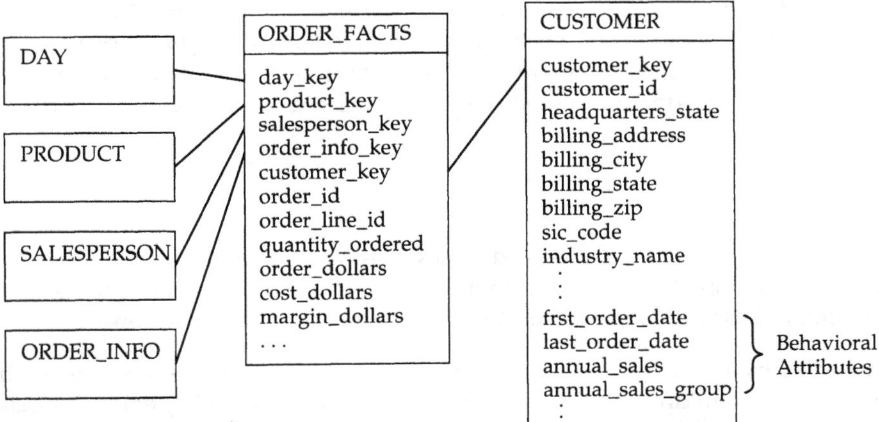

Figure 6-13 Behavioral dimensions in the customer table

Part III

Categorizing Facts

While a historic fact may be useful in qualifying a query, it may be less helpful if the desire is to use it to drive groupings. For example, we might wish to group facts into three categories: those associated with customers of low annual sales, medium annual sales, and high annual sales. Each customer can be placed in one of those buckets, based on historic sales.

In Figure 6-13, this is done through the behavioral attribute annual_sales_group. Whereas annual_sales contains a dollar value, the annual_sales_group attribute identifies three ranges, or "buckets," into which past history is sorted. The values this column takes on might be:

Annual Sales under $500,000
Annual Sales of $500,000 to $1,000,000
Annual Sales over $1,000,000

These buckets work nicely to group query results, while the annual_sales attribute works nicely to filter or sequence results.

Design Considerations for Behavioral Dimensions

In designing behavioral dimensions, you must carefully consider the implications on maintenance. Their slow change characteristics can cause undesirable growth in table size, and their frequency of updating can place undue stress on the ETL process.

For example, if the date_of_last_order was to be designated as a type 2 attribute, its maintenance would require generating a new row in the customer each time an order is placed. This undesirable growth can be prevented by designating the column as a type 1 attribute. Each time it changes, customer rows are simply overwritten. In the rare case that a historic version of the attribute is needed, it can be computed by querying order_facts. For example, if people want to know what each customer's last order date was as of February of last year, they can query the fact table.

The frequency of updating for behavioral attributes can overtax the ETL process. It might not be desirable, for example, to recompute the last year's worth of sales for every customer on a nightly basis. Rather than recomputing this information every day, the column can be defined as sales for the prior four quarters, allowing it to be updated once every three months. This aspect of the column's definition should be properly recorded in user documentation, so that the content is not misinterpreted. Once again, in the rare case that more up-to-date information is required, the report can be produced by querying the fact table.

Summary

This chapter has covered several advanced topics surrounding dimension tables, ranging from the determination of when two attributes belong in the same dimension table to the transformation of facts into dimensions. A quick recap of the primary lessons:

- Two dimensions belong in separate tables if they participate in a relationship that is volatile or in multiple relationships with different contexts. They belong in a single dimension table if they have a less volatile affinity and are related in a single context.

- When dimensions have a very large number of attributes, the table can be broken into two, but some technical complications may arise. Instead, you can look to see whether the table actually represents two dimensions, has free-form comment fields that can be removed to an outrigger, or is subject to the form of subtyping that will be discussed in Chapter 13.
- When a dimension table will grow too rapidly, or will necessitate a maintenance process that will become a processing bottleneck, offload volatile attributes into mini-dimensions. This technique all but eliminates the new rows necessitated by source changes and streamlines the ETL process.
- A fact table can have more than one relationship to a given dimension. These relationships are called roles. They do not require multiple copies of the dimension table; SQL aliasing allows each role to be accessed in a single query.
- The presence of a NULL in a dimension column can provide undue complication when trying to build reports and should be avoided.
- When it is not possible to relate a fact table row to one of the associated dimensions, do not use a NULL foreign key. Instead, add a row to the dimension table for the situation, and link to that row.
- Questions that use past behavior to interpret facts require SQL that is complex and performs poorly. Instead, add behavioral dimensions that will capture information about past behavior. These are easy to use and provide for powerful analytics.

There is still a lot more to say about dimensions. The next chapter explores the implied relationships among attributes within a dimension table, with a look at hierarchies, snowflaking, and the use of outriggers. Slowly changing dimensions are revisited in Chapter 8, which provides some advanced alternatives to type 1 and type 2 slow changes. Chapter 9 looks at what to do when a dimension or attribute repeats an indeterminate number of times, and Chapter 10 deals with recursive hierarchies.

Further Reading

When you are facing issues surrounding advanced topics like the ones in this chapter, it is always valuable to have additional examples to study. Most sources do not go into the same depth as this book, but here are some places where you can find other designs that address these topics.

Mini-Dimensions

- Kimball and Ross provide a detailed example of the mini-dimension technique in Chapter 6 of *The Data Warehouse Toolkit, Second Edition* (Wiley, 2002). They show how removing demographic attributes from a customer table can stem growth. They also use range groupings for the mini-dimension's demographic characteristics, in much the same way that this chapter did with behavioral attributes.
- In Chapter 3 of *Data Warehouse Design Solutions* (Wiley, 1998), Mike Venerable and I provide a demographic mini-dimension in a banking scenario. This example offloads dimensional attributes from a household dimension, and it works out well because many banks get demographic data from an external source at a less frequent time interval.

Roles and Aliasing

- An example of multiple date roles in an orders fact table is provided by Kimball and Ross in Chapter 5 of *The Data Warehouse Toolkit, Second Edition.* They describe the creation of views to isolate each role.
- Several examples of roles can be found in *Data Warehouse Design Solutions.* Chapter 11 provides an inspection fact table that notes the date a defect was detected and the date the defective item was received. Chapter 4 includes a warranty cost fact table that captures the date of warranty service, as well as the date the warranty was purchased.
- As you will learn later in this book, bridge tables allow dimensions to be connected to a star schema in a variety of different ways. In each configuration, the dimension plays a different role. Several examples are provided in Chapter 8 of *Mastering Data Warehouse Aggregates* (Wiley, 2006), by Chris Adamson, and you will encounter more in Chapters 9 and 10 of this book.

The NULL and Special-Case Rows

- As this chapter suggested, the NULL is probably the single largest source of controversy in the world of the relational database. For a full treatment of the topic, I recommend reading Chapter 19 of Chris Date's *An Introduction to Database Systems, Eighth Edition* (Addison-Wesley, 2003). This discussion does not involve the star schema, but it can help you understand the problems associated with the NULL.

Behavioral Dimensions

- Kimball and Ross discuss the use of aggregated facts as attributes in Chapter 6 of *The Data Warehouse Toolkit, Second Edition.* This brief conversation describes the creation of a behavioral dimension that captures the past history of a fact. They also apply the concept of categorization to the mini-dimension's demographic characteristics, in much the same way that this chapter did with annual sales. They refer to this technique as "banding."
- Mike Venerable and I describe transforming facts into dimensions in *Data Warehouse Design Solutions.* Chapter 10 develops a profitability dimension that segments customers based on the cost of doing business with them. Similarly, a status dimension in Chapter 3 transforms customer activities into statuses that indicate what products they own.

CHAPTER 7

Hierarchies and Snowflakes

It is possible to describe a dimension table as a series of parent-child relationships among groups of attributes. Days make up months, months fall into quarters, and quarters fall into years, for example. This chapter explores these attribute hierarchies and their implications for the design and use of dimensional databases.

The chapter begins by developing a basic concept of what it means to drill into data. The attribute hierarchy is then introduced, and its use as a path for drilling up and down is explored. Drilling within an attribute hierarchy turns out to be one out of many ways to drill into data; several other ways to drill are described in detail.

Although a hierarchical view of drilling limits analytic possibilities, many software tools tie their drilling features to the concept of hierarchies. When such a product is being used, it is useful to understand the attribute hierarchies in each dimension. This information may also be helpful in planning conformed dimensions, designing cubes or aggregate tables, or configuring software products that generate them. As with drilling, however, be advised that hierarchies are only one way to summarize information; alternative possibilities exist.

When an attribute hierarchy is instantiated as a series of physical tables, rather than as a single dimension table, the result is a variation of the star schema known as a *snowflake*. You may be particularly tempted to follow this design approach if you have a background in entity-relationship (ER) modeling. Developed for use in an operational setting, this approach offers benefits that do not apply in an analytic setting. Unless a specific software product in your architecture is optimized for the snowflake, it will offer no advantages.

On rare occasions, a limited form of snowflaking is employed to help resolve unmanageable row length or to ensure consistent representation of repeating attributes. Attributes are removed from a dimension table and relocated to a table called an outrigger. The outrigger and dimension tables share a parent–child or master–detail relationship. Because of the potential drawbacks to snowflaking, it is prudent to consider all other options before taking this step.

Drilling

We often talk about analysis as the process of "drilling into data." When you look at a report, for example, you might decide you want to know more. You choose to "drill down." A summarized view is replaced with a more detailed view. You may choose to drill deeper or to go back up and look at things a different way. This interactive exploration of facts characterizes much of the interaction users have with the data warehouse or data mart.

The Concept of Drilling

The word *drill* connotes digging deeper into something. In a dimensional context, that something is a fact. A generic concept of drilling is expressed simply as *the addition of dimensional detail.* Figure 7-1 illustrates this concept. A basic report on the left-hand side of the figure shows a fact, order dollars, broken out by the dimension attribute called category. The dimension attribute month is added to this view, resulting in the report on the right, where order dollars for each category are broken down by month.

In this example, drilling could also have been achieved by replacing month with any other dimension deemed useful. Order dollars by category might be broken down by salesperson, product, customer, or industry. Each provides a different way to further understand order_dollars by category, providing a more detailed picture of the fact.

This basic concept of drilling is sometimes referred to as *drilling down,* in order to distinguish it from the converse activity *drilling up,* wherein dimensional detail is removed from a report. Removal of month from the report on the right side of Figure 7-1, for example, would be an example of drilling up. The term is an oxymoron, since drilling up in a report is the opposite of moving deeper into something. A detailed view of a fact is replaced with one that is more summarized. Perhaps the word "undrill" would be a better choice, but drill up sounds better.

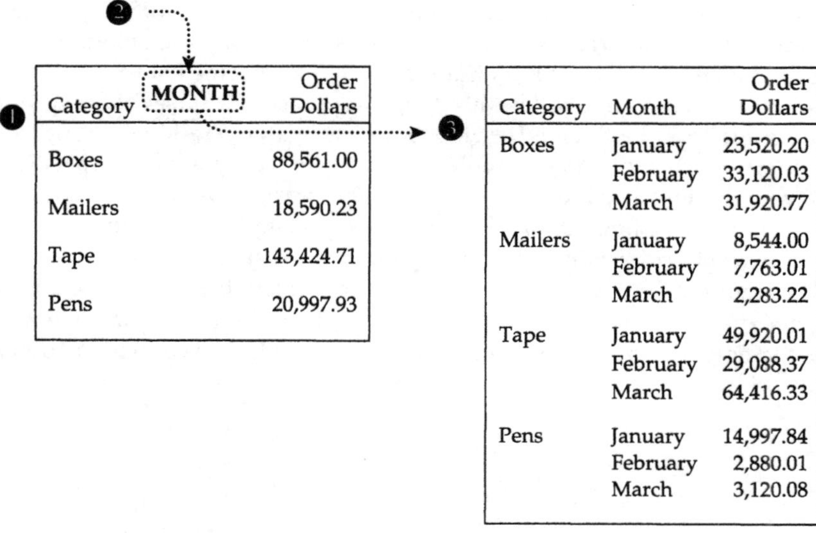

Figure 7-1 Adding dimensional detail

The Reality of Drilling

If you have a different notion of what drilling is, chances are it has been influenced by software products you have used. Developers of query and reporting tools describe a variety of different activities with the term "drill," often embellishing it with various prefixes and suffixes, for example, "drill-up," "drill-down," "drill-though," and "skip-drill." You may be familiar with others as well.

The drill feature of a given software product is usually a special case of the concept just defined. Some tools reserve the term for activities that will have an instantaneous response. If moving from "order dollars by category" to "order dollars by category and month" requires a new SQL query, these products would not describe the activity as drilling. Other tools incorporate the notion of focusing on an instance value. For example, breaking out the specific category "boxes" by month, rather than all categories, might be referred to as "drilling into boxes." Still other tools require that a "drill path" be defined in advance of drilling. Finally, for many tools, the concept of drilling is intertwined with another concept, that of attribute hierarchies. For these products, we drill from years to quarters to months to days or from categories to brands to products.

There is nothing wrong with any of these variations on the theme. Each technique represents a valid form of analysis. Keep in mind that features like these should not serve as the sole roadmap for the exploration of data. If users can only follow an established hierarchy, the results will be frustratingly limited.

Attribute Hierarchies and Drilling

Attribute hierarchies offer a natural way to organize facts at successively deeper levels of detail. Users understand them intuitively, and drilling through a hierarchy may closely match the way many users prefer to break down key business measurements. Other ways exist to make sense of information, however. Some cross attribute hierarchies, some don't involve hierarchies at all, and some involve hierarchies of a very different sort. Still, many business intelligence tools require the definition of attribute hierarchies to support their drill-down feature. If yours does, it will be important to document the attribute hierarchies in each dimension table. This information may also prove useful when planning conformance, or designing and building cubes or aggregates.

The Attribute Hierarchy

Many dimensions can be understood as a hierarchy of attributes, participating in successive master–detail relationships. The bottom of such a hierarchy represents the lowest level of detail described by the dimension table, while the top represents the highest level of summarization. Each level may have a set of attributes and participates in a parent–child relationship with the level beneath it.

The attributes in a product dimension table, for example, may form a simple hierarchy. Products fall within brands, and brands fall within categories. Each of these levels has a set of associated attributes, and they can be organized as a set of successive master–detail relationships, as illustrated in Figure 7-2. Attributes of the product table are grouped into levels, moving from the most highly summarized view of product at the top, down through

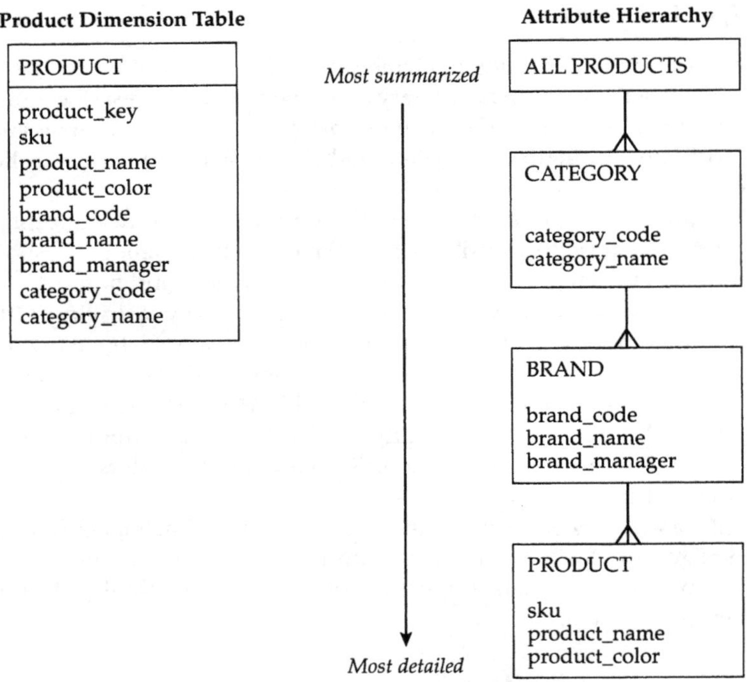

Figure 7-2 An attribute hierarchy in the product table

successive levels of detail. Crows-feet are used to indicate the "many" ends of each one-to-many relationship. At the very top of the hierarchy is the level called "all products." This level contains no attributes; it is added for convenience and represents a complete summarization of the product dimension. At the very bottom of the hierarchy is the level called "product." It represents the most detailed level in the hierarchy.

The product hierarchy can be represented in nondiagrammatic format using the following shorthand:

All Products (1) → Categories (25) → Brands (650) → Products (8000)

Numbers have been added to represent the cardinality, or number of instances, at each level in the hierarchy. The highest level of summarization, all products, is again added for convenience. It represents a complete summarization of the product dimension; studying a fact by all products results in a single row of data. There are 25 categories, 650 brands, and 8000 total products. Don't fall into the trap of assuming each category has 26 brands. The actual values may exhibit an uneven distribution or *skew*; one category, for example, may contain a much larger percentage of the brands than any of the others.

Drilling Within an Attribute Hierarchy

Some software tools link the concept of drilling to the concept of an attribute hierarchy. These tools use the hierarchy as a predefined drill path. When viewing a fact, drilling down is accomplished by adding a dimension attribute from the next level down the hierarchy. This may be a useful way to understand the information in a fact table—providing successively more detailed views of the facts. In this paradigm, drilling up is achieved by removing attributes that belong to the current level of the hierarchy.

For example, suppose the product dimension table described previously is linked to a fact table containing order_dollars. The product hierarchy can be used to provide successive levels of detail for this fact. You begin by studying order dollars across all products, which gives you one row of data. This represents the very top of the product hierarchy; the query would not even touch the product dimension table. Moving down this hierarchy, you add category to the picture. There are 25 categories; order dollars is now being viewed with slightly more detail. Now you add brand. There are 650 brands, so the information is far more granular. Last, you add product to the view of order dollars, taking you to the bottom of the product hierarchy.

In this book, this form of drilling is referred to as *drilling within an attribute hierarchy*. This process adds successive levels of dimensional detail to the report, fitting the definition of drilling defined earlier. It is a special case, however, that limits drill-down options to what is next in the hierarchy. Drilling within a hierarchy is intuitive, and often easily understood by users, but there are other ways that detail can be added to a report.

Other Ways to Drill

It is possible to drill deeper into a fact without sticking to the well-worn path of an attribute hierarchy. Taking other routes to detail may be equally rewarding. The possibilities include following an alternative hierarchy within the dimension, following hierarchies in more than one dimension, drilling without any form of hierarchy, and drilling through instance hierarchies. Some products may not refer to these activities as drilling, but each represents a valid form of analysis.

Multiple Hierarchies in a Dimension

It is often possible to identify multiple attribute hierarchies within a dimension. Each hierarchy includes all the attributes of the dimension but organizes them in a different way. These hierarchies often represent completely different ways in which people view and understand the same information. No one hierarchy has any more validity than the others; each represents a valid way to break down the information in the dimension.

TIP There may be more than one way to organize the attributes of a dimension into a hierarchy. Each represents a valid way to drill down.

The product hierarchy involving categories, brands, and products, for example, provides a view of how a company manages and markets various product lines. The planners responsible for production of these products may find it useful to break product down differently. Their interest lies in how the product is manufactured. Products are understood in terms of business lines, of which there are three, the facility where they are made, of which there are 75, and products. This competing product hierarchy might look like this:

All Products (1) → Business Line (3) → Manufacturing Location (75) → Product (8000)

For these users, there is little interest in brands or categories. This hierarchy is a separate but equally valid way of breaking down the attributes of the product dimension. A fact like order dollars can be understood by adding successive levels of detail from this hierarchy, just as well as any other hierarchy.

Crossing Between Dimensions

In other cases, the preferred drill path may lead from one dimension table to another. You've already seen an example of this process. Figure 7-1 showed order dollars by category, and then built additional detail by adding month. In that case, the drill path followed was:

Categories → Months

This path ignores the product attribute hierarchy, instead adding detail from a different dimension—the day dimension.

Some products reconcile this activity with the hierarchical notion of drilling by observing that there is a hierarchy in each dimension. In addition to the product hierarchy, for example, there is a hierarchy in the day dimension. The day hierarchy for five years of data might look like this:

All Days (1) → Years (5) → Quarters (20) → Months (60) → Days (1826)

The user's initial view of order_dollars in Figure 7-1, then, can be defined in terms of two hierarchies. The report shows orders at the category level in the hierarchy, and for all days in the day hierarchy. When date is added to this view, the user is drilling within the day hierarchy. Notice that moving from all days to month has skipped over two levels in the day hierarchy—years and quarters.

Eschewing Hierarchies Altogether

It is possible to add dimensional detail without the aid of an attribute hierarchy at all. Two characteristics of information make this possible. First, the cardinality of an attribute, or the number of instance values it takes on, is not necessarily determined by where it lies in a hierarchy. Second, some instance values may be found under multiple parents.

For example, the attribute product_color in Figure 7-2 is associated with the lowest level of detail in the product hierarchy. It is quite possible the products are only available in a dozen colors. When viewing order dollars by color, the data is highly summarized, even though product color is at the bottom of the attribute hierarchy. Adding brand_name to this view results in a large increase in detail, despite the fact that brand appears at a higher level of the product hierarchy.

This phenomenon can be explained by expanding the simple attribute hierarchy of Figure 7-1 to represent the relative cardinality of *all* attributes within the product table, rather than grouping them into one set of levels. This perspective acknowledges the presence of a separate hierarchy that moves from color to product. Adding brand to a view of products by color, however, does not involve any of these hierarchies.

Instance Hierarchies

Attribute hierarchies describe relationships among dimension *attributes*. Products fall within brands; brands fall within categories. We can express these rules without referring to actual data. Another form of hierarchy may exist among *instances* of dimensions. For example, employees report to other employees. This kind of hierarchy can only be expressed by referring to specific employees. The relationship is recursive; there may be any number of levels in the hierarchy. At each level of the hierarchy, the attributes of the employee are the same. Other examples of instance hierarchies include departments falling within departments, companies owning other companies, and parts being composed of other parts.

Like an attribute hierarchy, an instance hierarchy may be useful in studying facts. Suppose, for example, that products are sold to corporate customers. Companies may own other companies, which in turn own other companies. It may be useful to roll up all transactions to top-level parent companies. We can then explore the data by drilling down through multiple levels of ownership.

This process does not involve adding or removing attributes to our view of a fact; companies at each level share the same basic dimensional data: names, types, locations. Instead, drilling within an instance hierarchy requires tracing through the ownership relationships between companies. This kind of hierarchy can be accommodated in a dimensional model and is fully discussed in Chapter 10, "Recursive Hierarchies and Bridges."

Documenting Attribute Hierarchies

Although using an attribute hierarchy is not *the only way* to drill into data, it is *a way* to drill into data. If you are using a business intelligence tool that defines drilling in this way, it will be important for you to understand the attribute hierarchies in your dimensions. Graphical depictions of attribute hierarchies are easily understood by developers, who can refer to them when configuring business intelligence tools, planning conformed dimensions, and designing and building cubes or aggregates.

Configuring an Attribute-based Drill Feature

The attribute hierarchy is the primary focus of many business intelligence tools. By defining hierarchies within dimensions, these tools are able to anticipate what users might do and prepare for it. If the user double-clicks a category, for example, the hierarchy is used to determine that brand should be brought into the report. Some tools even use this information to pre-fetch information so it is ready if and when the user requests it.

To leverage the drill capabilities of this kind of tool, it is necessary for a developer to configure it with information about the attribute hierarchies within each dimension. Configuration typically involves defining each level of the hierarchy and providing information about the attributes at each level. Some attributes, such as category_name, brand_name, and product_name, may be the primary attributes for their levels. Other attributes are associated with these levels—for example, product_color is associated with the product level, and brand_manager is associated with brand level.

Many tools will only allow the declaration of a single hierarchy within a dimension. If you have more than one hierarchy, it may be necessary to configure two different environments for drilling down. Refer to Chapter 16, "Design and Business Intelligence," for some advice when faced with this constraint.

A drilling paradigm based on attribute hierarchies should not be viewed as a shortcoming of a business intelligence tool. These products tend to support other ways of studying the data; they're just not referred to as "drilling." The path from color to category, for example, may not be accomplished via a simple double-click but may be done by modifying the query or report layout.

Information to Gather

Attribute hierarchies are best documented graphically. The format introduced in Figure 7-2 is a good starting point. It includes important information about the product attribute hierarchies, such as names for each level of the attribute hierarchy, attributes present at each level, and the one-to-many relationships between instances of each level. One key piece of information is missing: what attribute should be shown when someone drills into a new level in the hierarchy? For example, when users drill from category to brand, should they see brand codes or brand names? This information may be important if the hierarchy will be used to configure a drilling tool. A target attribute for each level in an attribute hierarchy can be indicated using bold text.

The diagram in Figure 7-3 illustrates attribute hierarchies in several dimensions. Boxes denote the levels of each hierarchy. They are arranged along a vertical axis from most highly summarized to most detailed. Crows-feet are used to indicate the one-to-many relationships between levels. The box for each level has a name and includes a list of attributes for the level. The target attribute for drilling is shown in bold.

Notice this diagram incorporates multiple hierarchies within the day dimension; both hierarchies begin and end with days and years but have differing levels in between. It is also possible to diagram each alternative hierarchy separately. This may be necessary if the same attribute appears at different levels in different hierarchies.

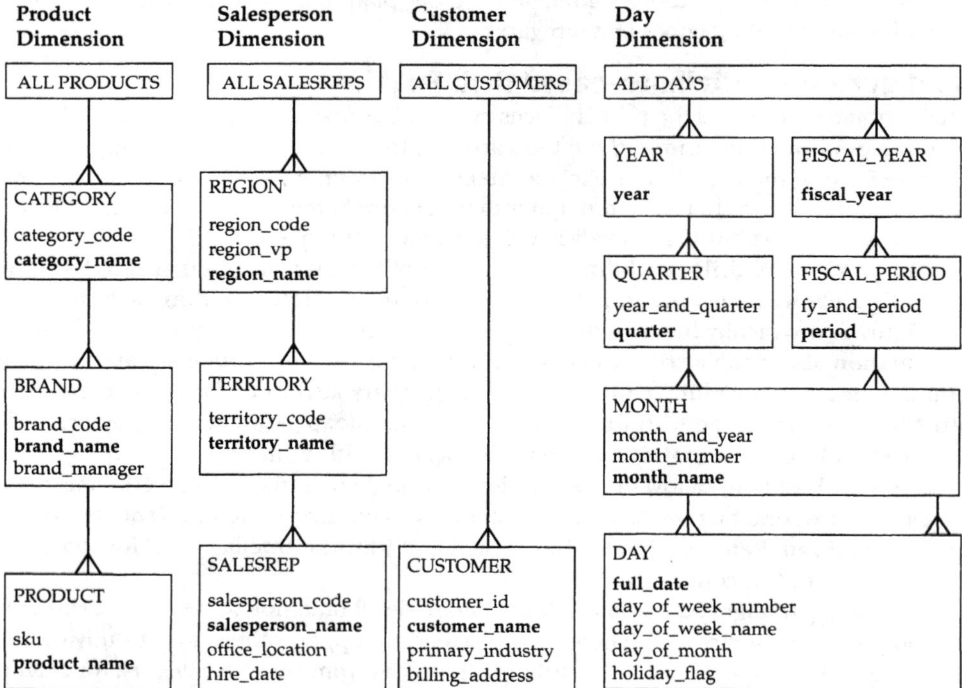

Figure 7-3 Documenting attribute hierarchies

Other Benefits of Documenting Attribute Hierarchies

Understanding hierarchical relationships among attributes in a dimension table may be useful for other reasons. In addition to helping you configure the drilling feature of business intelligence software, information on attribute hierarchies helps with the design of conformed dimensions, cubes, and aggregate tables.

Identifying Conformed Dimensions The many virtues of conformed dimensions were discussed in Chapter 5. Conformed dimensions are the key to powerful cross-process analytics, enabling the drill-across process that brings together data from different stars. Conformed dimensions also serve as the planning blueprint for a network of stars that can be implemented piecemeal, without the risk of stovepipes.

As Chapter 5 showed, two dimension tables need not be identical to conform. Dimensions also conform when the attributes of one are a subset of the other. Figure 5-3 illustrated day and month tables that conform at the monthly level, as well as salesperson and territory tables that conform at the territory level. When dimension tables conform in this manner, the smaller table is known as a conformed rollup.

The relationship between a base dimension and conformed rollup is an example of an attribute hierarchy. Exploration of attribute hierarchies may trigger insights into ways in which information from different processes may be compared. For example, an attribute hierarchy like the one in Figure 7-2 suggests several possible conformed rollups of the product dimension. A brand dimension would include all attributes at or above the brand level. This conformed rollup may be useful if planning or budgeting takes place at the brand level. Documentation of attribute hierarchies can highlight potentialities like this, particularly when a set of conformed dimensions has not been planned in advance.

Cube Design and Management The data warehouse architecture may incorporate cubes and Online Analytical Processing (OLAP) in different ways, as described in Chapter 3. One popular approach stores granular data in a star schema and uses cubes to provide high-performance analysis on subsets of the data. An understanding of the attribute hierarchies within a dimension table can help developers design appropriate cubes.

The attribute hierarchy provides a shorthand vocabulary to define the grain of each cube. For example, a cube may be defined to hold "order dollars at the *brand* (product) and *quarter* (day) levels." In this statement, the dimensions are listed in parentheses, and the levels that define the cube are italicized. It can also be useful to line up all the hierarchies for a given star on a single diagram, and draw a horizontal line to define the aggregation level represented by a cube, as in Figure 7-4.

Some commercially available tools are able to use hierarchy information to generate or maintain the cube. These applications are configured with information, or metadata, about the hierarchies within dimension tables. A developer designing a cube can then specify the desired level to be carried within each dimension. The tool uses the hierarchy information to determine what attributes are available at or above the selected level, and generates the cube accordingly. It may even be able to maintain the cube for you as the base star changes.

NOTE Incremental maintenance of a cube or aggregate table may be prevented if it includes any type 1 dimension attributes. The reasons for this are explored in Chapter 15, "Aggregates," along with advice on how to avoid the problem.

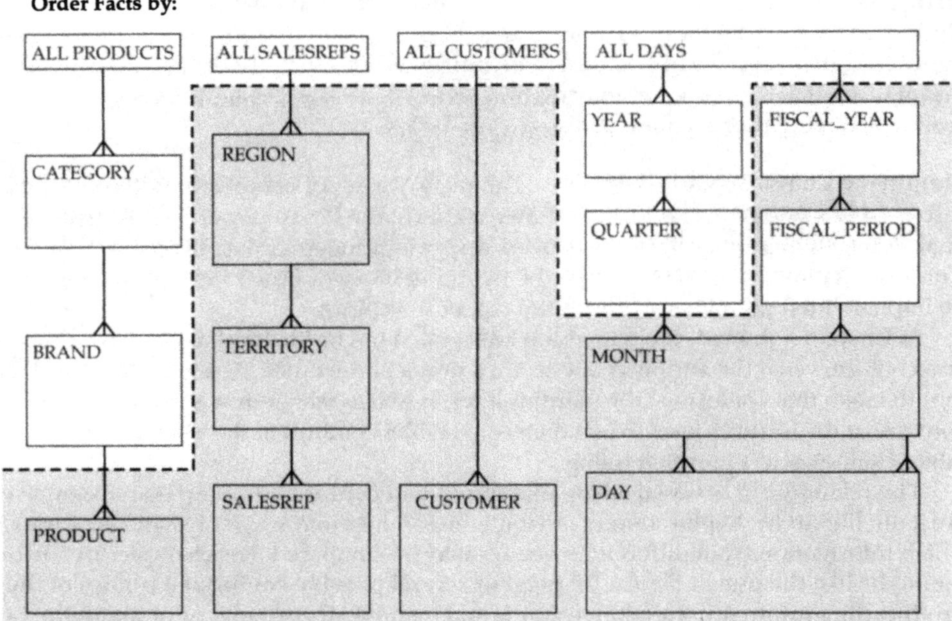

Figure 7-4 Using a hierarchy diagram to design a cube or aggregate

Aggregate Design and Management Documentation of hierarchies among dimension attributes can also help with the design of aggregate stars. Discussed in Chapter 15, "Aggregates," aggregates summarize information in a base star in order to improve query performance. For example, a base star may contain orders by order line, with dimensions for day, product, salesperson, and customer. An aggregate of this star may summarize orders by brand and month. When the business question does not require order-line-level detail, the aggregate star may be used to answer the question. Since it has significantly less data, it will provide a faster answer.

An aggregate star can be planned by identifying the level of summarization it will provide in each dimension. This definition can be documented by graphically indicating the level of summarization along hierarchies in each dimension. This is similar to planning a cube and can also be accomplished using a diagram like the one in Figure 7-4.

Some database products are able to generate and maintain aggregate structures automatically, in much the same way cubes are generated by some multidimensional database tools. Dimensional hierarchies are defined as part of the table definitions, or metadata. This information is then referred to in the definition of aggregate structures and leveraged by the tool to generate and maintain them.

Caveat When Documenting Hierarchies

If you choose to document attribute hierarchies, remember that they represent some, but not all, possibilities for drilling, conformance, cube design, and aggregate design. You have already seen that it is possible to drill without a hierarchy. The same holds true for other forms of summarization. Any attribute may serve as a useful aggregation of data, regardless of its presence at any particular hierarchy level.

TIP Attribute hierarchies are useful, but they are not the only way to drill or summarize data. Don't let an attribute hierarchy constrain the analytic capabilities of your users or limit the design possibilities for cubes and aggregates.

It is possible to define a cube, for example, without leveraging an explicit attribute hierarchy. For the star in Figure 7-4, possibilities include cubes that summarize order data by brand_manager or by product_color. In each of these cases, a hierarchy level is not used to define the summarization, but the cube will carry significantly less detail than the base star. In the same way, an aggregate table might be defined that deviates from the standard attribute hierarchy.

Snowflakes

Until now, each star schema you have seen in this book has consisted of a fact table and a group of dimension tables, with each dimension table joined directly to the fact table. As you learned in Chapter 6, a dimensional design does not expose all the relationships between attributes as joins. Attributes that share natural affinities or nonvolatile relationships, such as product and brand, are placed in a single dimension table; their relationships are implicit.

If you are new to dimensional design, this approach may seem amiss. You may feel a strong urge to model the relationships between dimension attributes, particularly if you have previous experience with ER modeling. The product table from Figure 7-2, for example, includes brand_name and brand_manager, which are fully determined by the brand_code. You could make this relationship explicit by storing brand information in a separate table, linking it to product via a foreign key relationship.

When the relationships between dimension attributes are made explicit in a dimensional design, the result is known as a snowflake. The snowflake gets its name from the appearance it takes when drawn with the fact table in the center. Dimension tables emanate from this center like the branches of a snowflake, as shown in the example in Figure 7-5.

The snowflake in Figure 7-5 was created by instantiating the hierarchies from Figure 7-3 in separate physical tables. This required the addition of surrogate keys to each hierarchy level. Category_key and brand_key, for example, were added to category and brand. Instantiation of the hierarchy also required the addition of foreign keys that identify the parent of each level. Each product, for example, includes a brand_key, which identifies the appropriate brand. It is easy to imagine this snowflake becoming more intricate. Many product attributes, for example, may have codes and descriptions. Each of these code/description pairings may become the basis for additional tables in the snowflake schema.

You may find a snowflake configuration appealing because it exposes a natural taxonomy in the data. For those trained in ER modeling, the snowflake reflects some best practices learned in the service of operational systems; however, it is of little utility for an analytic database, aside from saving some space.

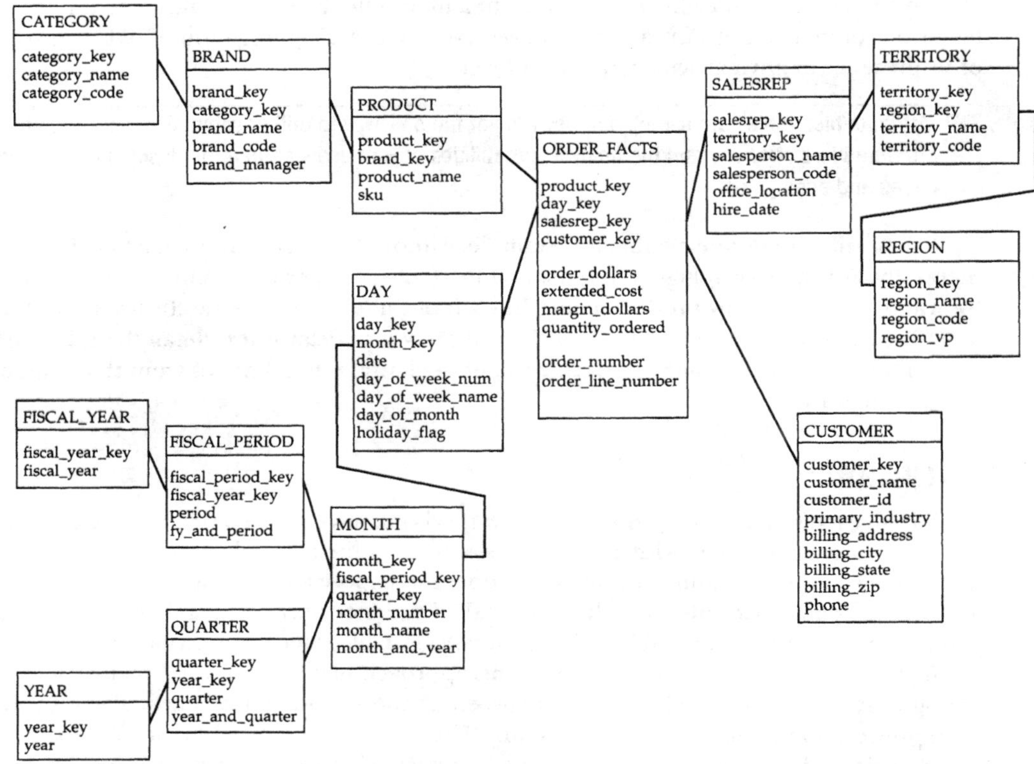

Figure 7-5 A snowflake schema

Avoiding the Snowflake

Snowflaking a dimension is similar to a process called *normalization*, which guides the design of operational systems. This technique was developed to ensure referential integrity of data in operational systems, which support a wide variety of simultaneous transactions that are highly granular. An analytic database does not share this usage pattern, and referential integrity can be enforced by the ETL process. Normalization is therefore not necessary. In fact, modeling the relationships between dimension attributes detracts from usability, complicates ETL, and may even disrupt performance. That said, there are some good reasons you may wish to model a snowflake, as you will see later in this chapter.

Normalization Is Useful in an Operational Setting

Entity-relationship (ER) modeling is often used to design databases that support operational systems, or OLTP (online transaction processing) systems. This form of modeling places a heavy emphasis on capturing the relationships between attributes in much the same way a snowflake does. Through the process of normalization, redundancy is systematically driven out of the data model. Repeating groups are moved to their own tables, and designers ensure

Normalized or Denormalized?

You may have noticed that this chapter avoids referring to a star schema as "denormalized" and a snowflake as "normalized." That's because these terms do not clearly map to the dimensional world. Even in the world of operational systems, they are vague. There are actually several normal forms, known as first normal form, second normal form, and so forth. Each form results from the removal of a specific type of redundancy, such as repeating groups or partially dependent attributes. In an ER model, designers strive to achieve a level known as third normal form (or 3NF), but there are further possible normal forms.

While it may be useful to describe one dimensional design as more normalized than another, labeling a star schema as "denormalized" and a snowflake as "normalized" oversimplifies matters. In a star, for example, dimension attributes do not repeat in fact tables. Instead, they are represented by foreign keys. This represents a degree of normalization, although most stars do not map cleanly to one of the standard forms. Moreover, the use of "denormalized" when describing a star implies that the design started out as normalized. Most designs are not produced in such a manner. "Not normalized" would be a better description.

Similarly, it is also imprecise to refer to a snowflake as normalized. The snowflake in Figure 7-5, for example, might not meet the standards of third normal form. Address information would probably need to be removed from the customer table; fiscal periods would need to be separated from years.

For more information on the mechanics of normalization, consult the "Further Reading" section at the end of this chapter.

that each attribute is fully dependent on its table's unique identifier. Relationships between attributes are made explicit, exposed as primary key/foreign key relationships, or joins.

In an operational setting, the principles of normalization are applied for very practical reasons. As described in Chapter 1, "Analytic Databases and Dimensional Design" operational systems support the full range of transaction types—insert, update, delete, query. Each transaction tends to be focused on individual records, rather than a large group. A large number of these transactions may take place simultaneously. In servicing these transactions, the database must satisfy a set of principles often known as *ACID principles* (atomic, consistent, isolated, and durable). At the same time, there must be a minimal impact on performance.

The principles of normalization help the RDBMS achieve these objectives, maintaining data integrity with maximum efficiency. An update to the name of a brand, for example, need only adjust a single row in a brand table. Extensive resources are not required to support the ability to roll back a transaction before it is completed; only a single row is impacted. More importantly, while this transaction is taking place, the RDBMS need not lock every row of the product table that shares the brand in question. Other users are free to access and update individual products, even while information about the brand is being changed. Data integrity is guarded, since each data element resides in a single place. An incidental benefit also accrues: storing each brand once saves some space.

TIP In operational settings, data sets are normalized to preserve data integrity in the face numerous, simultaneous transactions that insert, update, or delete data. The space saved is a fringe benefit of normalization, not its purpose.

These benefits are made possible by modeling the relationship between attributes describing products and attributes describing brands. What is useful in a data model for an operational system, however, is not necessarily useful for a data model in an analytic system.

Normalization Is Not Useful in an Analytic Setting

The principles of normalization are well suited to the usage profile of an operational system, which supports a wide variety of simultaneous transactions that can modify data. An analytic database does not share this usage pattern and does not call for this level of normalization. The added complexity is not necessary to guarantee data integrity. Instead, it detracts from usability, complicates ETL, and may negatively impact performance.

As you saw in Chapter 1, the usage profile of analytic systems is very different from that of operational systems. Most transactions are queries and tend to focus on large quantities of data rather than atomic transactions. Inserts, updates, and deletes are all generated by the ETL process, rather than by a large number of individual users. Since the ETL process itself can be leveraged to ensure data integrity, normalization is not necessary. In fact, redundancy in the data set offers some advantages.

One advantage is understandability. A business user can easily grasp the meaning of a star schema. Measurements are in the middle, surrounded by options for filtering them or breaking them out. Many queries can be constructed following a simple template, as described in Chapter 1, and this process may even be automated. The simplicity of the star also benefits analysts, who do not have to deal with the intricacies of the data model to ensure accurate results. Instead, they can focus on the development of information products like reports and dashboards. Snowflaking detracts from these advantages.

Redundancy in the data set also simplifies the ETL process. Snowflake designs add complexity. Each additional table created requires its own surrogate key. Primary key / foreign key relationships between dimension tables must be managed, and these dependencies must be factored into the load process. Slow change processing is also more complicated in a snowflake environment, as discussed later in this chapter. (See "Outriggers and Slow Change Processing.")

Avoiding the snowflake may also offer performance benefits. In a star, all facts and dimensions are separated by a maximum of one join. Snowflakes increase the number of joins, giving the RDBMS more work when responding to a query. The simple snowflake in Figure 7-5 contains 13 relationships and might be expanded to include many more. A corresponding star, on the other hand, would include only four. The developers of RDBMS products have come up with innovations to optimize the performance of a star schema. The traditional pair-wise join processing employed in an operational setting is often avoided in favor of a process that saves access to the fact table, which is usually much larger than the rest, for last. Instead, a Cartesian product of all relevant dimension rows is constructed, based on the predicates included in the query. This Cartesian product is then used to identify which rows from the very large fact table need to be accessed. Variations on this approach invert the process, but the result is similar.

TIP There's no real reason to snowflake in an analytic setting. It merely introduces complexity and may detract from performance. A star configuration is easier to understand and maintain, and is likely to perform better.

To be sure, the RDBMS has also evolved to support high-performance query processing for more complex schema designs. Your RDBMS may be able to process queries against snowflakes as efficiently as queries against a star. This does not justify adding complexity to the data model, however. The analytic database does not share the transaction processing requirements that are so well served by a normalized schema. Complexity for complexity's sake benefits no one.

Embracing the Snowflake

Many situations exist in which it may be appropriate to relax the guideline against snowflaking. These situations can be broken down into two major categories. The first category is technology-driven: some products in your architecture may function best with a snowflake design. If that's the case, sticking to stars may limit functionality. Second, some specific modeling challenges cannot be met without decomposing a dimension into more than one table.

Snowflakes and Product Considerations

One of the best reasons to design a snowflake schema is that your database or business intelligence tool requires it. Although this is not the case for the majority of tools, some function better under the more normalized conditions of a snowflake design.

You are most likely to encounter these circumstances with business intelligence software. As noted in Chapter 2, this book employs the term business intelligence to describe any software product used to provide user-consumable information products, such as reports, charts, dashboards, or interactive analysis products. For some of these front-end tools, full functionality can only be achieved if a snowflake design is used. For example, some tools require the use of a snowflake to support aggregates, a topic to be discussed in Chapter 15. Others may require snowflakes in order to automate the drill-across process described in Chapter 5. In both cases, a dogged refusal to snowflake is counterproductive.

While most RDBMS products are optimized for the star schema, some function better with a snowflake design. If this is true of your RDBMS, your vendor will let you know. Whatever the reason, some form of snowflake may be optimal.

These situations are the exception, rather than the rule. Therefore, it is prudent to evaluate the options thoroughly. Tuning your design to the requirements of a specific product may provide the optimum solution today, allowing the fullest set of capabilities or maximum performance. This path also limits options in the future, however. Changing databases or adding new business intelligence tools may introduce products that do not require a snowflake, but you will already have a significant infrastructure built around it. The decision to tailor design to the needs of a particular product is not one you should make in a vacuum. It is a strategic choice and should benefit from multiple points of view. Chapter 18, "How to Design and Document a Dimensional Model," addresses the various parties that may be interested in design decisions.

TIP If your architecture incorporates tools that work better with a snowflake, that is a good reason to snowflake. Since such tools are in the minority, this is as much a strategic decision as it is a design decision. Be sure the appropriate people are involved in making it.

Faulting a tool for working better with a snowflake than a star is perhaps unfair. Snowflake optimization is a disadvantage in a software product mainly because tools that require it are in the minority. If more products provided their best performance in this manner, the equation might be different. It remains true, however, that maintaining a snowflake requires extra work by ETL developers. It is necessary to maintain additional surrogate keys, and slow change processing is also complicated.

Snowflakes and Modeling Challenges

Some modeling challenges cannot be met with a pure star schema. To fully meet analytic requirements in these situations, it will be necessary to introduce some relationships between dimension tables. This occurs when an attribute takes on more than a single value with respect to a fact, as well as in situations that require rolling data up or down through a set of recursive relationships.

Multi-Valued Attributes In most cases, a particular fact will correspond to a single instance value for each dimension attribute. For example, an order is placed for a specific product, from a specific salesperson. The fact table can carry foreign keys that identify the specific order and the specific salesperson. If two products are ordered, the order is broken down into two order lines. Each refers to a single product. This relationship between dimension table and fact table is given a variety of different labels, including parent–child, master–detail, and independent–dependent.

Sometimes, events of significance do not fit this paradigm. Suppose, for example, some situations exist in which two salespeople collaborate to bring in an order. Aliasing can be used to designate primary and secondary salesreps, but what happens when an order comes along that involves three? Similarly, we may wish to record the industry in which each customer operates, only to discover that some customers participate in two, three, or any number of industries.

In cases like these, the standard one-to-many relationship between dimension table and fact table breaks down. The dimension attributes are *multi-valued*, meaning that for a particular fact, it may have more than one instance value. This dilemma can be resolved by using a bridge table, as described in Chapter 9, "Multi-Valued Attributes and Bridges." The result is a form of snowflaking. It also introduces a new wrinkle into the dimensional design: the need to take special steps to avoid double counting.

Recursive Instance Hierarchies As indicated earlier in this chapter, some hierarchies cannot be defined as relationships among attributes. This happens, for example, when one company is made up of other companies. Each of those companies, in turn, may be made up of still more companies. A recursive relationship like this represents an *n*-level hierarchy among instance rows of the dimension. Other examples include employee reporting structures, departmental relationships, and part breakdown structures.

The recursive instance hierarchy becomes an issue when coupled with the requirement to roll facts up or down to different levels in the hierarchy. Attempts to "flatten" the hierarchy often meet with limited success. Chapter 10, "Recursive Hierarchies and Bridges," demonstrates how a hierarchy bridge table can be used to support analysis along an instance hierarchy. Like the solutions for multi-valued attributes, this solution is a limited form of snowflake, and it will introduce the possibility of double counting if used incorrectly.

Repeating Groups Last, designers sometimes choose to allow a limited form of snowflaking when a group of attributes appears more than once in a dimension table. If customers have a billing address and a shipping address, for example, a series of attributes representing address repeats in the dimension table. Although not undesirable in and of itself, this situation may become a matter of concern if the set of repeating attributes is very large or if it appears in a large number of additional places. In these situations, a limited form of snowflaking may be considered: the use of outriggers.

Outriggers

On rare occasions, a repeating set of attributes may lead to concerns over inconsistent representation, particularly if the attributes repeat in multiple tables. If the set of attributes is large, concerns of secondary importance may arise over the attributes' impact on the length of rows. In these situations, developers may consider relaxing the restrictions against snowflaking. The repeating attributes are placed in a new table, linked to the dimension via a primary key / foreign key relationship. Called an outrigger, this table guarantees a single ETL process and consistent representation, but it can have an impact on usability and performance.

Repeating Groups

A common challenge in dimension table design involves repeating groups of attributes. When a dimension table contains a group of attributes that appears multiple times, or which appears in multiple dimension tables, concerns may arise regarding row length or consistency. If other mechanisms to resolve these issues are not effective, outriggers offer a solution of last resort.

The salesrep table in Figure 7-6 contains multiple examples of repeating attributes. Each row in this dimension table represents a salesperson. For any given salesperson, there are two physical office locations of interest to the business. The office where the person works is known as the work location; the office to which the position reports is known as the reporting location. Capturing both these locations requires repeating the ten attributes that describe an office location. A second set of repeating attributes represents significant dates associated with the salesrep. One set represents the date of hire, while a second set reflects the date of the last performance review. Nineteen attributes are associated with a date, and each of these attributes must be repeated twice.

While this dimension table does not have an excessive number of attributes, it is easy to envision it incorporating far more. Dates and locations, for example, may actually have more attributes than pictured, and each addition will be repeated. As the number of attributes grows, the table diagram in Figure 7-6 grows longer, and row length becomes wider.

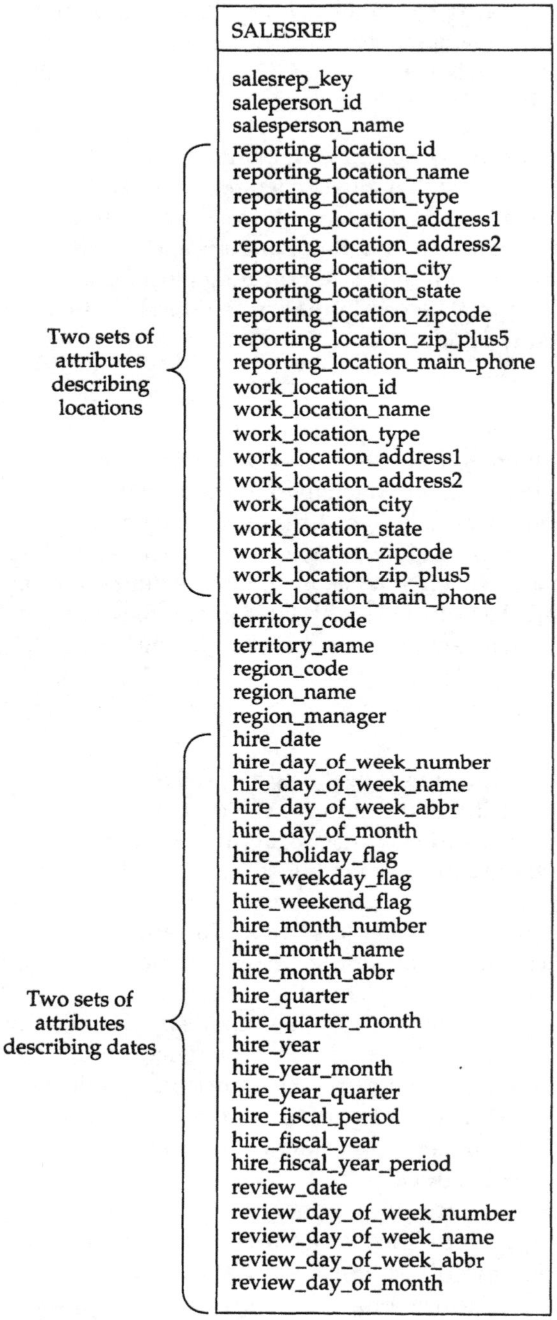

SALESREP
salesrep_key saleperson_id salesperson_name reporting_location_id reporting_location_name reporting_location_type reporting_location_address1 reporting_location_address2 reporting_location_city reporting_location_state reporting_location_zipcode reporting_location_zip_plus5 reporting_location_main_phone work_location_id work_location_name work_location_type work_location_address1 work_location_address2 work_location_city work_location_state work_location_zipcode work_location_zip_plus5 work_location_main_phone territory_code territory_name region_code region_name region_manager hire_date hire_day_of_week_number hire_day_of_week_name hire_day_of_week_abbr hire_day_of_month hire_holiday_flag hire_weekday_flag hire_weekend_flag hire_month_number hire_month_name hire_month_abbr hire_quarter hire_quarter_month hire_year hire_year_month hire_year_quarter hire_fiscal_period hire_fiscal_year hire_fiscal_year_period review_date review_day_of_week_number review_day_of_week_name review_day_of_week_abbr review_day_of_month

Two sets of attributes describing locations

Two sets of attributes describing dates

Figure 7-6 Repeating location and date attributes in a dimension table

Row length should not be a concern simply because a dimension table spans more than one page in a schema diagram. Dimension tables in a star schema can have many attributes, as discussed in Chapter 3. This may be unusual in an ER model but not in a dimensional model. If row size becomes a legitimate technical concern, it may be possible to employ some of the techniques offered in Chapter 6. Sometimes, however, these techniques cannot address the issue. Repeating groups may be a primary contributor to excessive row size, and the solution may be to eliminate them.

A large set of attributes that repeats may also lead to concerns regarding the ETL process. Will the contents of these repeating columns be populated in a consistent manner? Will the exact same codes be transformed into the same description values? What if different ETL programs are populating different instances of the repeating attributes? For example, columns such as reporting_location_type and work_location_type contain the same kind of information. If these location types are derived during the ETL process through a set of rules, storing them as separate attributes risks the possibility that these rules will not be applied consistently. Similarly, if the name of a location changes, this change must be applied consistently to work_location_name and reporting_location_name.

Concerns over redundant ETL processing may grow if the attributes in question appear in other dimension tables as well. There may be another table that also incorporates location information, for example. This may be a concern even if there are relatively few attributes in question or if they do not repeat in a given table. The risk can be mitigated by carefully documenting the process that loads these columns. Developers may also be able to incorporate reusable code or function calls to guarantee consistent maintenance of the columns in question.

Eliminating Repeating Groups with Outriggers

If concerns about row length or ETL consistency cannot be addressed by other means, the solution may be to add an outrigger table. The repeating attributes are placed in a separate table, the outrigger, which is given its own surrogate key. In the original dimension table, the relocated attributes are replaced with one or more foreign key references to the outrigger.

TIP Outriggers may be considered when a set of attributes repeats within a single dimension table or appears in more than one dimension table.

Two outriggers can be constructed for the salesrep dimension that appeared in Figure 7-6. The ten location attributes that appear once for the salesperson's work site and once for the office to which the salesperson reports are moved into a separate location table, depicted in Figure 7-7. This outrigger contains a surrogate key called location_key.

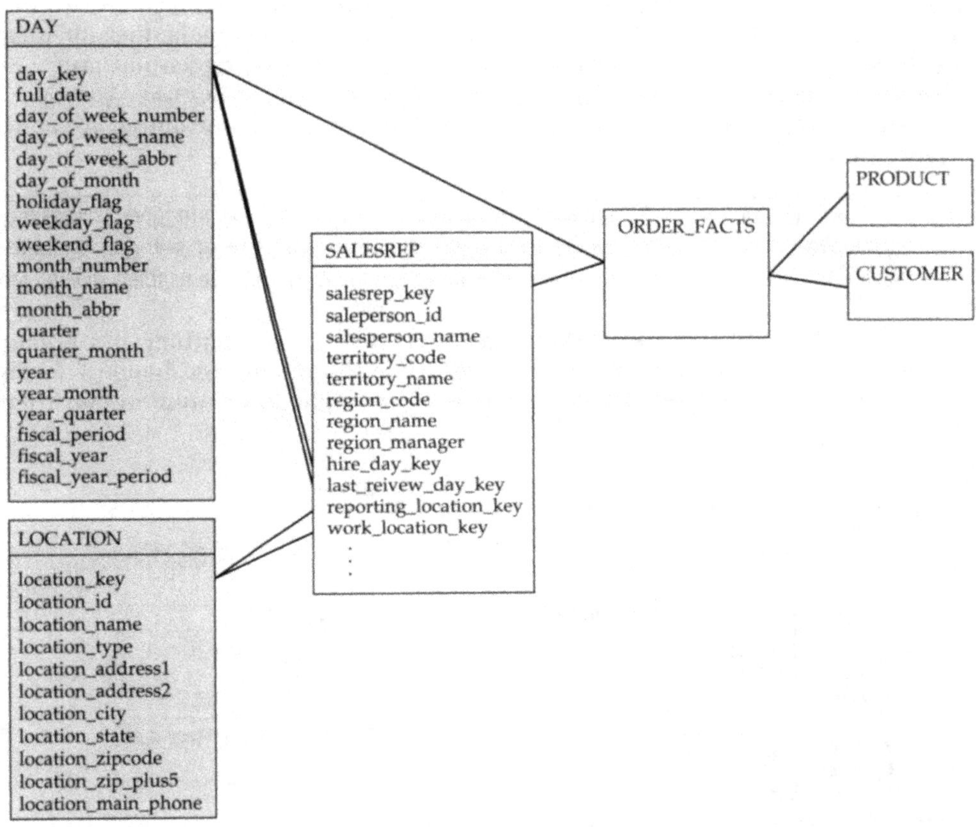

Figure 7-7 Two outriggers for the salesrep dimension

Instead of 20 location attributes, the salesperson dimension includes two foreign key references to the location table: one for the work location and one for the reporting location. Similarly, the two sets of date attributes are replaced by a pair of day_keys: one for the date of hire and one for the date of the salesperson's last review.

To query a schema that includes outriggers in multiple roles, you must use the aliasing techniques described in Chapter 6. An alias is created for each role played by an outrigger, through either SQL, the use of a view, or the capabilities of the reporting tool. Each alias is joined to the appropriate foreign key in the base dimension table, as determined by its role. To query the schema in Figure 7-7, it may be necessary to alias location twice—once for the work site and once for the reporting location. The date table may be aliased three times. Two of these aliases are outriggers for salesrep: the date of hire and the date of last review. The other alias for date is the date of the order, which joins directly to order facts. The set of aliases that can be used when querying this star is depicted in Figure 7-8.

As Figure 7-8 illustrates, the presence of outriggers increases the number of joins that may be involved in querying the star. This translates into an increase in complexity, and potentially a decrease in performance. Additional complexity is unnecessary from a user's point of view, but it is possible to hide the outrigger by replacing the dimension and outriggers with a view. A negative impact on query performance may be more serious. Even if outriggers do not confuse the database's ability to perform a star join, they still increase the number of joins that must be processed. The presence of outriggers in Figure 7-8 *doubles* the number of potential joins to process when querying order facts. Without outriggers, this star would require a maximum of four joins; with the outriggers, it includes eight joins.

TIP Outriggers may be used to streamline ETL or reduce row length, but they introduce complexity and may have an impact on query performance. If you are considering using an outrigger, evaluate the impact it will have on the performance of your database optimizer and the usability of your schema.

Given the potential drawbacks, outriggers should be used sparingly. If row length is a legitimate technical concern for a very wide dimension, refer to Chapter 6 for other techniques to try first. You may be able to define multiple dimensions or construct

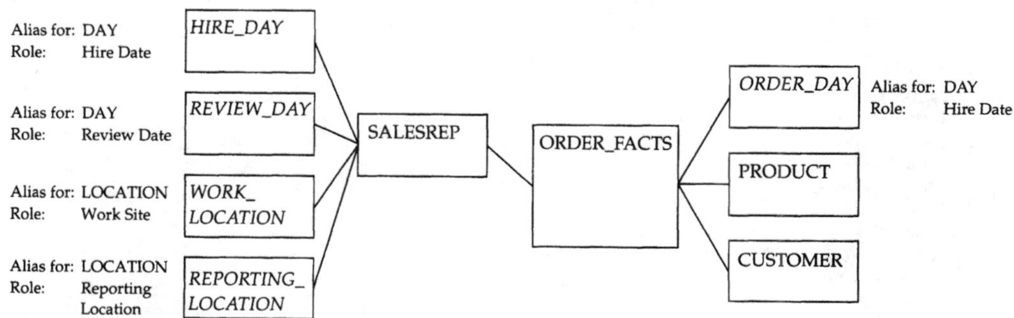

Figure 7-8 Querying a star with outriggers

a mini-dimension to avoid the problem. If not, repeating groups can be replaced by an outrigger. An outrigger may also be used to relocate a small number of very wide columns, such as free-form text fields.

Likewise, the ETL risks associated with repeating attributes can be minimized through other methods. Careful design documentation can drive ETL development and the quality assurance processes. The development of reusable functions as part of the ETL process may also be possible. If the repeating attributes appear in more than one dimension table, or sometimes appear as a dimension on their own, the outrigger may be acceptable. In the example, the attributes of day appear in the salesrep dimension and also serve to capture the order date for order_facts. This is likely to be the case with the location as well; a shipping star, for example, may use the location table to indicate the warehouse from which a package was shipped.

Outriggers and Slow Change Processing

The use of outriggers requires careful attention to slow change processing rules. With an outrigger in place, it may be necessary to apply a type 2 change to a dimension row, even if none of its attributes have changed. The change is precipitated by a type 2 change in the outrigger.

Suppose, for example, that the location outrigger contains an attribute called location_name. Business rules dictate that changes in location names are significant, so if the name of a location changes, a type 2 response is called for. Now suppose that the location with location_id B664 is being renamed from "Operations East" to "Morris Center." In keeping with the requirements of a type 2 response, a new row is added to the location table for location B664 with a new surrogate key and the new location name. This is illustrated in Figure 7-9.

The change in name from "Operations East" to "Morris Center" is not complete when the type 2 response has been processed in the location outrigger table. The salesrep dimension refers to locations, and there are several employees who report to work at location B664. For the type 2 change to be fully reflected, it is also necessary to add a new row to the salesrep table for each of these employees; each new row also receives a new surrogate key. This creates a new version of each employee who works at the location, reflecting the updated location name. Without these new employee rows, the employees would remain associated with the old location name, as would any new facts that link to them.

TIP A type 2 change in an outrigger has a ripple effect, requiring type 2 changes to all related rows in any associated dimension tables.

One might be tempted to simply update the foreign key in the dimension table to reference the new row in the changed outrigger. This, however, approximates a type 1 response, at least with respect to the dimension. For example, it is inappropriate to update an employee's work_location_key to refer to the new record for the Morris Center, because that would have the effect of associating previously recorded facts with the new name, defeating the intended type 2 response.

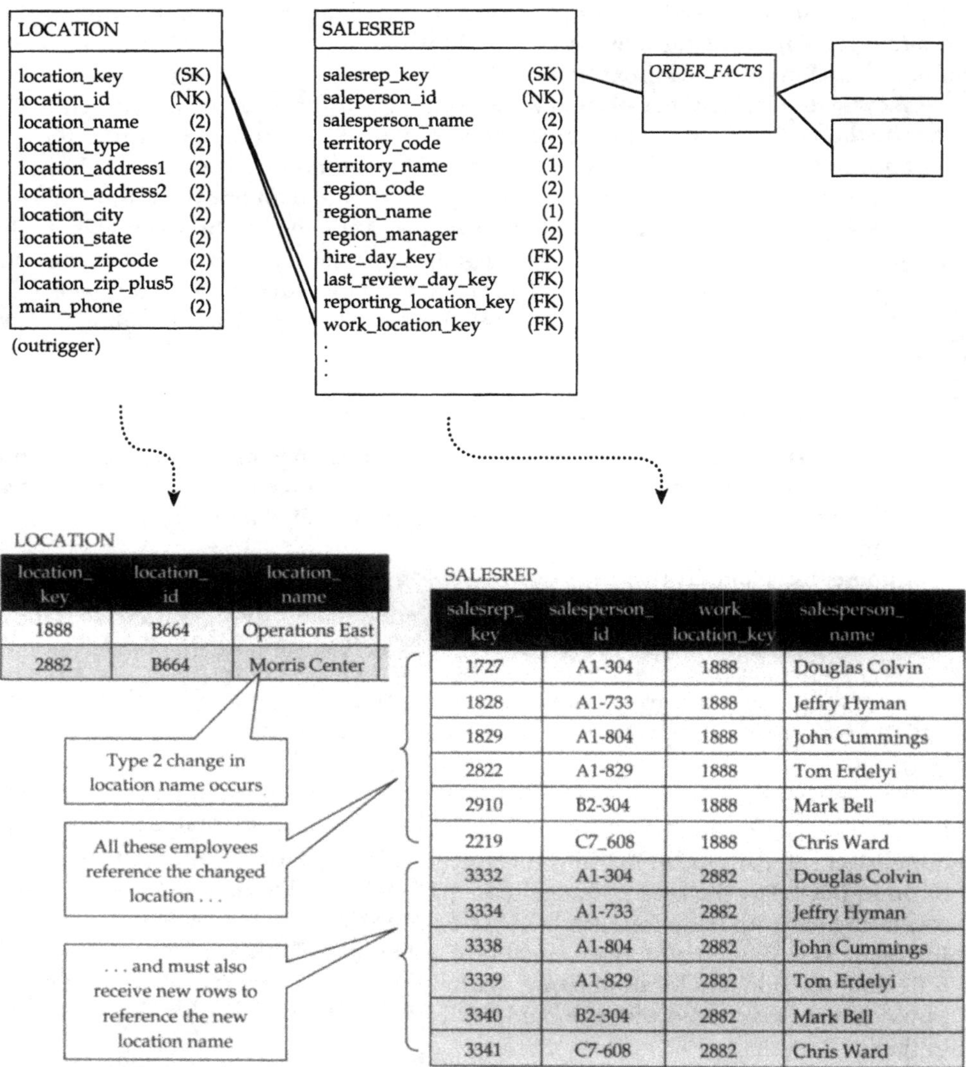

Figure 7-9 Outrigger and cascading slow change

Summary

This chapter explored some of the intricacies that hide within dimension tables. Many tools link the concept of attribute hierarchies with drilling, so you may be forced to document them. Usually it is unnecessary to instantiate attribute relationships in physical tables, unless you have a tool that requires it. On rare occasions, it may be useful to design an outrigger, which takes advantage of these relationships to ensure consistency. Key takeaways from this chapter include:

- Drilling is the activity of adding dimensional detail to a fact. It does not require the presence of a hierarchy, although many software tools do.
- An attribute hierarchy describes parent–child relationships between groups of attributes within a dimension.
- Although some reporting tools define drilling as moving up and down a hierarchy, there are other ways to add and remove detail from a report. Some of these methods may add detail even as they move up a hierarchy.
- If you are working with a business intelligence tool that links drilling to hierarchies, it may be useful to document attribute hierarchies. This may also help with the planning of conformed dimensions, cubes, and aggregates.
- When relationships between attributes in a dimension are expressed explicitly, the result is called a snowflake schema.
- Snowflaking makes sense only if it maximizes the capabilities of your reporting tool or DBMS. Altering your design for a specific tool, however, limits your ability to use other tools in the future.
- Outriggers can be used sparingly when attributes repeat within a table or appear in multiple tables. This limited form of snowflaking guarantees a single consistent ETL process.
- Outriggers may also be helpful if dimension row length is causing technical issues, and other options have been exhausted.

As mentioned in this chapter, there is still more to be said about situations in which a single dimension table is replaced by two or more tables. Chapter 9 describes how bridge tables resolve situations in which dimension tables or attributes must repeat an indeterminate number of times. Chapter 10 discusses how bridge tables can be leveraged to summarize facts across a recursive hierarchy.

Further Reading

Perhaps because the reality of drilling is so tool-specific, not a lot is written about what it means to drill in a dimensional model. You will also not find a lot written about *attribute* hierarchies in texts on dimensional modeling since they are limited ways to view drilling or summarization, and because they are not a physical feature of the database schema. A lot of what you will find written about hierarchies deals with what I call *instance* hierarchies, which will be covered in Chapter 10.

Drilling

- Kimball and Ross define drilling down as the process of adding "row headers" to a report, regardless of what attribute was used to provide them. They don't spend a lot of time on this topic, which makes sense given how many ways the term can be used, but you can read their description in Chapter 2 of Kimball and Ross's *The Data Warehouse Toolkit, Second Edition* (Wiley, 2002).

Attribute Hierarchies

- This chapter touched on the notion that attribute hierarchies may be of use to tools that automate the creation and maintenance of cubes or aggregate tables. You can read more about different ways tools do this in Chapter 4 of *Mastering Data Warehouse Aggregates* (Wiley, 2006), where I provide examples of the automatic generation of brand-level aggregates in a product dimension.
- Figure 7-3 provided an example of a dimension that included more than one hierarchy, and this chapter mentioned that these two hierarchies can also be diagrammed separately. This is not hard to envision, but, if necessary, you can find an illustration of such an alternative in Chapter 3 of *Mastering Data Warehouse Aggregates.*
- For an alternative way to graphically depict multiple hierarchies within a dimension, see Chapter 7 of *A Manager's Guide to Data Warehousing* by Laura Reeves (Wiley, 2009). Reeves defines hierarchies as relative cardinalities among attributes, and provides a mechanism for diagramming them.

Snowflakes

- This chapter advised against the normalization of dimension tables unless your software products require it. For many people, the desire to do so can be quite strong. If you are still tempted to snowflake or are interested in a more detailed argument against the practice, Kimball and Ross provide a list of five reasons not to snowflake in Chapter 2 of *The Data Warehouse Toolkit, Second Edition.*
- Saving storage space is often advanced as an argument in favor of snowflaking. This argument is discussed in Chapter 6 of *The Data Warehouse Lifecycle Toolkit, Second Edition* (Wiley, 2008) by Kimball, Ross, Thornthwaite, Mundy, and Becker. Using a specific example, the authors compute the space saved and show it is a very small fraction (measured in thousandths of a percent) of the overall space consumed by a star. Separately, Kimball and Ross acknowledge that space savings can be more significant in limited situations (see next).

Outriggers

- When a dimension has more than one relationship to the same outrigger, as in Figure 7-7, even the most careful developer can easily make a mistake. The result might be using the location_name where someone reports, rather than the location_name where they work. In *The Data Warehouse Toolkit,* Kimball and Ross recommend creating views for each role and renaming the attributes to be specific to the role. You can read their example, which involves a date outrigger on a store dimension, in Chapter 2 of *The Data Warehouse Toolkit.*
- This book has pointed out several times that space savings in a dimension usually saves very little in cost, while adding a lot in terms of complexity. Kimball and Ross point out that the benefits may be greater for very low cardinality attributes. You can read their example in Chapter 6 of *The Data Warehouse Toolkit.*

Normalization

- For detailed information on the principles of normalization, see Part III of *An Introduction to Database Systems, Eighth Edition* (Addison-Wesley, 2003) by Chris Date.

CHAPTER

8 More Slow Change Techniques

A crucial part of star schema design is determining how changes to source data will be reflected in dimension tables. The change response pattern for each dimension attribute in the star schema must be carefully matched to business requirements. Most requirements can be satisfied by employing the techniques introduced in Chapter 3:

- **Type 1** is used when the history of the data element is not significant. When a source data element changes, the corresponding dimension attribute is overwritten. This causes previously recorded facts to become associated with the changed value. No trace of the old value is left behind.
- **Type 2** is used when it is important to preserve the historic context of facts with respect to the changing data element. When the source data element changes, a new row is added to the dimension table, leaving the previous version unchanged. Previously recorded facts remain associated with the old version; any new facts are associated with the changed version.

This chapter describes situations where these options do not suffice. It is divided into sections for three additional techniques:

- **Time-stamped dimensions** are used when it is necessary to support point-in-time analysis of dimension values, irrespective of associated facts.
- **Type 3 changes** are employed when users want to study all the facts—recorded both before and after the data element changes—using *either* the new value *or* the old value.
- **Hybrid techniques** are employed when requirements conflict, calling for more than one kind of response.

People developing queries and reports will need to know how to exploit these solutions effectively. These techniques also place increased demands on the ETL process. It is, therefore, important to choose wisely, and that requires a thorough understanding of each option.

Time-Stamped Dimensions

The most common response to changes in source data is the type 2 slowly changing dimension. If there is any uncertainty about requirements for historic data, Chapter 3 advised designers to choose a type 2 response. It is the safe choice because it preserves the association of historic dimension values with facts that have been recorded in fact tables. No information is discarded.

The type 2 response has one glaring shortcoming: it cannot tell you what the dimension looked like at any point in time. This is a particular concern if you have a dimensional data warehouse architecture or stand-alone data mart. In these architectures, the dimensional model doubles as the integrated repository of granular data. In a Corporate Information Factory, maintaining a full history in the dimensional data mart is a lesser concern since there is also an enterprise data warehouse repository to hold it. Although not configured for direct access, at least the information is not thrown away.

An additional fact table can come to the rescue and be used to track the history of changes to the dimension. This fact table has the odd characteristic of having exactly the same number of rows as the dimension table, but it does the job. Many designers instinctively gravitate to a more flexible alternative: supplementing the type 2 response with time stamps.

The time-stamped dimension permits three forms of point-in-time analysis within the dimension table itself:

- Easily order a chronological history of changes
- Quickly select dimension rows that were in effect for a particular date
- Easily identify the dimension rows currently in effect

The time-stamped dimension has an unusual property. Joined to a fact table, it behaves like any other dimension table. Used on its own, it also exhibits some of the characteristics of a fact table. The time-stamped approach can also be tremendously useful to ETL developers charged with loading data into fact tables.

Point-in-Time Status of a Dimension

Often, one or more dimension tables in the data warehouse represent closely watched entities. The history of attribute values is significant and is often monitored irrespective of any associated transactions. Documents, contracts, customers, and even employees may be subjected to this deep scrutiny. When it is necessary to support point-in-time analysis within a dimension table, type 2 changes alone will not do the job.

Type 2 Not Sufficient

A type 2 slowly changing dimension preserves the history of values of an attribute and allows each fact to be associated with the correct version. Although this preserves the history of facts, it is not sufficient to provide for point-in-time analysis. What version was current on a particular date? Unless a fact exists for the date in question, it is impossible to know. This is best understood via an example.

The star in Figure 8-1 has a policy dimension similar to the one seen in Chapter 6. The table includes numerous attributes describing significant characteristics of a health insurance policy.

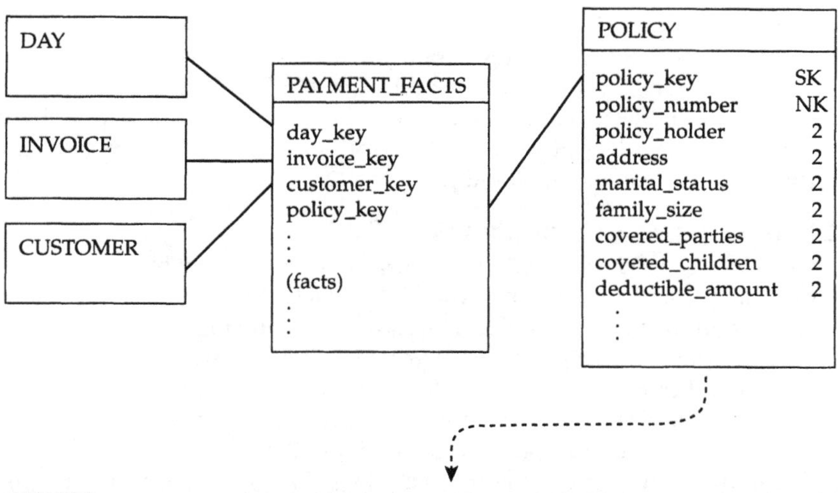

POLICY

policy_key	policy_number	policy_holder	address	marital_status	family_size	covered_parties	covered_children	deductible_amount
12882	40111	Smith, Hal	113 Random Rd.	Single	1	1	0	250
12911	40111	Smith, Hal	113 Random Rd.	Married	2	1	0	250
13400	40111	Smith, Hal	113 Random Rd.	Married	2	2	0	250
14779	40111	Smith, Hal	113 Random Rd.	Married	3	3	1	250
14922	40111	Smith, Hal	113 Random Rd.	Married	4	4	2	500

Figure 8-1 Type 2 changes in a policy dimension

The history of these attributes is carefully followed by the business, so they are designated as type 2. The policy dimension table is associated with a fact table that tracks policy payments that have been made by the policy holder.

The slow changes that accumulate for one particular policy are illustrated in the lower part of the figure. Policy number 40111 is held by someone named Hal Smith and apparently has been active for quite some time. You can see that the policy has undergone several changes. Initially, Hal was single and his policy covered himself alone. Later, he married, but coverage was not added for his spouse. Subsequently, his spouse did become covered, and still later coverage was added for a child. When coverage was added for a second child, you can see that Hal also increased his deductible.

The insurance company needs to be able to understand what each policy looked like at any given point in time. For example, users might want to know how many policy holders were married versus how many were single on a particular date, or what the total number of covered parties was at the close of a fiscal period. Policy payments are completely irrelevant to this analysis.

Unfortunately, the design in Figure 8-1 is not able to answer these questions. Although the dimension table records all the changes to policies, it does not associate them with specific time periods. Was Hal married on November 1, 2005? The dimension table tells us that at different times he has been single and married, but *not* when. Unless there happens to be a row recorded for the policy in payment_facts for November 1, 2005, there is no way to know what the policy looked like on that date.

Tracking Change History Through a Fact Table

Point-in-time analysis of a closely watched dimension can be supported by creating a fact table expressly for the purpose. A row is recorded in the fact table each time the dimension changes. Each row in this fact table contains a foreign key identifying the new row in the dimension table, and one identifying the date it became effective. An additional foreign key can be maintained to indicate the date on which the row expired, which will help produce point-in-time analysis. If each change occurs for a particular reason, this may be captured via an additional dimension. An example appears in Figure 8-2.

The fact table in the figure, policy_change_facts, logs changes to the policy dimension. Its grain is one row for each policy change. Each row contains a policy_key representing the changed policy. A transaction type dimension contains reference information indicating the reason for the change—a new policy, a policy change, or policy cancellation. Two keys refer to the day dimension. Day_key_effective indicates the day on which the policy change went into effect. Day_key_expired will be used to indicate when it was superseded by a new version.

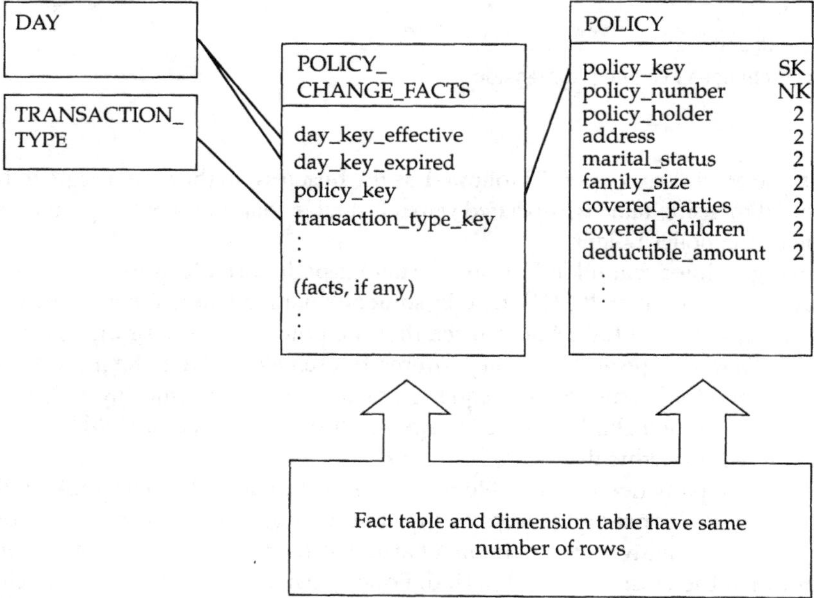

Figure 8-2 A fact table records the change history of the policy dimension

You may notice that this fact table does not contain any facts. That is okay; it is still useful. For example, it can be used to count the number of policies in effect on a particular date with married versus single policy holders. Fact tables like this are known as factless fact tables, and Chapter 12 discusses them in detail.

The dates associated with each row merit some additional scrutiny. As noted, the fact table includes a day_key_effective, indicating when the change went into effect, as well as a day_key_expired, indicating when the change was superseded by a new version. It is useful to avoid overlapping dates, in order to avoid any confusion when building queries. For each row in the fact table, the effective and expiration dates are inclusive. If a policy changes today, today's date is the effective date for the new version of the policy. Yesterday's date is the expiration date for the previous version. The pair of dates can be used to determine the policy's status at any point in time. Add one filter looking for an effective date that is before or equal to the date in question, and another for an expiration date that is greater than or equal to the date in question.

The current version of a policy has not expired, and it has no expiration date. Instead of recording a NULL key, it refers to a special row in the day dimension. This row typically contains the largest date value supported by the relational database management system (RDBMS), such as 12/31/9999. Described in Chapter 6, this technique avoids the need to test for null values when building queries. When the row does expire, the date will be replaced with the actual expiration date.

It is also necessary to look a bit more closely at the grain of the fact table, described earlier as "one row for each policy change." It is important to document what exactly a "policy change" is. If Hal Smith's family size and number of children change on the same day, is that one change or two? In the case of policy changes, it is likely to represent a set of changes that are logged in a source system as part of a single transaction. In other cases, it may be necessary to log each change individually. This may require the ability to store multiple changes for a single day. To support this, you can add a time dimension and a pair of time_keys to supplement the day_keys. The time_keys refer to the time of day the record became effective (time_key_effective) and the time of day it expired (time_key_expired.)

The policy_change_facts star effectively captures the history of changes to the policy dimension, so that people can identify what policies looked like at any particular point in time. This information can now be accessed, even for days when there are no payments.

You may have noticed something peculiar about this fact table. Since it contains a row for each change to a policy, it has the same number of rows as the policy dimension itself. This is not necessarily a bad thing, but it suggests that there may be a more effective way to gather the same information.

The Time-Stamped Solution

A *time-stamped dimension* is one that tracks the history of changes in the dimension table itself, rather than through a separate fact table. The solution captures the same information as a tracking star like the one in Figure 8-2. The dimension is outfitted with additional columns to capture the effective and expiration dates for the row. Optionally, an additional column may track the transaction type or reason for the change. A flag is added, which can be used easily to select the current row in the table for any given natural key.

A Time-Stamped Dimension in Action

A time-stamped version of the policy dimension table is illustrated in Figure 8-3. The first block of attributes contains the usual dimension columns: a surrogate key, the natural key, and a set of dimension attributes. Four additional columns have been added: transaction_type, effective_date, expiration_date, and most_recent_version.

To the right of the table diagram, a grid illustrates the rows recorded in this table for policy 40111, which belongs to our old friend Hal Smith. The first row shows that Hal's policy went into effect on February 14, 2005. At the time, he was single. The policy remained in this state through February 11, 2006. On the next day, February 12, a policy change caused the next row to become effective. This row updated the policy to show that Hal married, with his family size increasing from one family member to two. The row shows that there was only one covered party, which means that Hal's spouse was not covered by the policy. Additional changes to the policy are reflected in the subsequent rows. Study the table closely, and you will see that the effective_date and expiration_date for each changed row line up closely; there are no gaps.

The last row in the illustration shows the current status of Hal Smith's policy. Since it has not expired, the expiration_date is set to 12/31/9999. This date has been specifically designated for use when the policy has not expired. When we are querying the table, this value allows us to avoid the additional SQL syntax that would be necessitated if a NULL had been used.

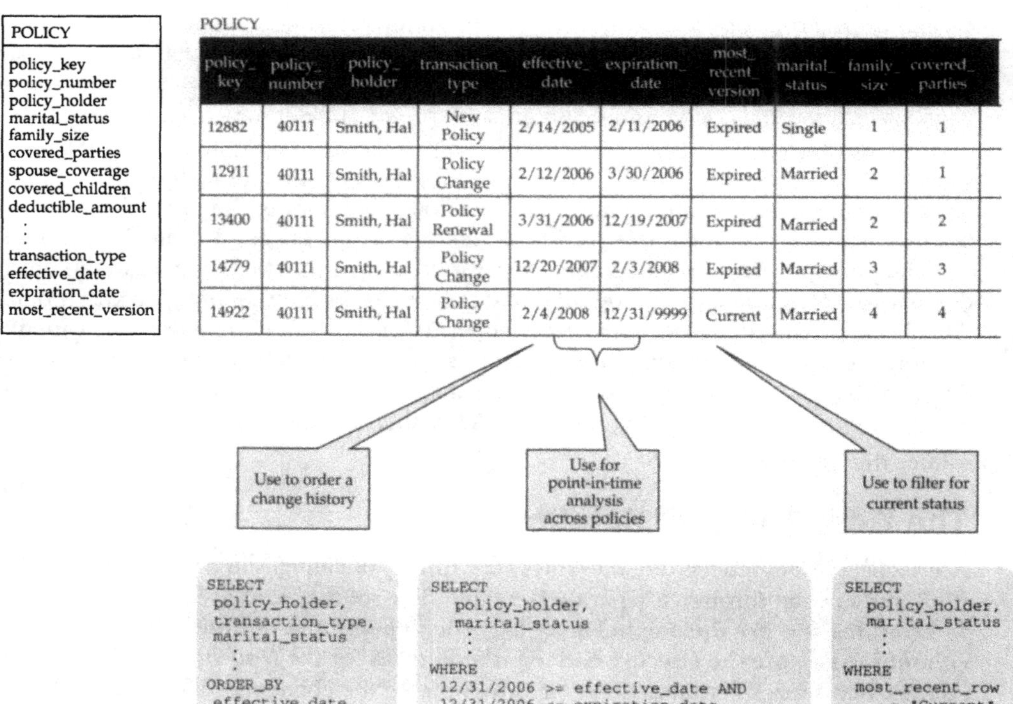

policy_key	policy_number	policy_holder	transaction_type	effective_date	expiration_date	most_recent_version	marital_status	family_size	covered_parties
12882	40111	Smith, Hal	New Policy	2/14/2005	2/11/2006	Expired	Single	1	1
12911	40111	Smith, Hal	Policy Change	2/12/2006	3/30/2006	Expired	Married	2	1
13400	40111	Smith, Hal	Policy Renewal	3/31/2006	12/19/2007	Expired	Married	2	2
14779	40111	Smith, Hal	Policy Change	12/20/2007	2/3/2008	Expired	Married	3	3
14922	40111	Smith, Hal	Policy Change	2/4/2008	12/31/9999	Current	Married	4	4

Figure 8-3 A fact table records the change history of the policy dimension

To filter a query for policy versions that were in effect on 12/31/2006, for example, we only need to add the following to the query predicate:

```
WHERE
   12/31/2006 >= effective_date AND
   12/31/2006 <= expiration_date
```

The most_recent_version flag is added as a convenience, allowing browse queries to filter a dimension table for current records only. In keeping with guidelines from Chapter 3, this column contains descriptive text rather than Boolean values or "Y" and "N." To filter the dimension for the current policy versions, a simple constraint is added:

```
WHERE most_recent_version = "Current"
```

It is also quite simple to single out a single policy and produce an ordered list of changes:

```
WHERE policy_number = 40111
ORDER_BY effective_date
```

TIP A time-stamped dimension adds non-overlapping effective and expiration dates for each row, allowing each type 2 change to be localized to a particular point in time. The effective date can be used to order a transaction history; the effective and expiration dates allow filtering for a specific point in time; a most_recent_version column can simplify filtering for current status.

Part III

This technique can be elaborated upon for situations where multiple discrete changes must be captured during a single day. While it represents additional work to maintain a time-stamped dimension, it pays dividends when it comes to maintaining associated fact tables.

NOTE It might be more precise to refer to this example as a "date-stamped dimension," since time of day is not being recorded. As you will see, this technique *can* be expanded to capture time of day. The term *time stamp* is a popular shorthand for describing any temporal designation, regardless of specificity. Some designers prefer to refer to this technique as *effective dating*. Kimball and Ross refer to dimension tables that track effective and expiration dates as *transaction tracking dimensions*.

Multiple Changes on a Single Day

The policy example only allows for one version of a policy on a given day. If it is necessary to track changes at a finer grain, this can be achieved by adding columns to capture the time of day at which the record became effective and expired: effective_time and expiration_time. Depending on the business case, these columns may represent hours (24 possible values), minutes (1,440 values), or seconds (8,640 possible values). Together with the effective_date and expiration_date, they allow for multiple versions within a given day.

As with the day columns in the prior example, the time columns must allow for no overlap and leave no gaps. For policy changes recorded at the minute level, for example, if one row becomes effective at 12:48 PM, the prior row must expire at 12:47 PM.

With the time columns in place, it is possible to have multiple versions of a policy on a given day. This means that qualifying a query for a particular date may pick up multiple versions of the same policy. This is not desirable if, for example, you are counting the number of covered parties across all policies on a particular date. You must now supplement the date qualifications with time qualifications, as in:

```
WHERE
   12/31/2006 >= effective_date AND
   12/31/2006 <= expiration_date AND
   24:00 >= effective_time AND
   24:00 <= expiration_time
```

You can add a last_change_of_day flag to simplify this kind of query. It will be set to "Final" for the last change to a given policy on a day. End-of-day status for a particular date can now be captured by using this SQL:

```
WHERE
   12/31/2006 >= effective_date AND
   12/31/2006 <= expiration_date AND
   last_change_of_day = "Final"
```

Time-Stamped Dimensions and the ETL Process

Construction of a time-stamped dimension places an extra burden on the developers of the process that loads and maintains the dimension table. When a type 2 change occurs, it will be necessary to identify the prior row to update its expiration_date and most_recent_version columns. Extract, transform, load (ETL) developers may also be charged with grouping a set of changes that occur on a single day into a single time-stamped dimension record. This additional work is not trivial, but ETL developers will find benefits in other areas.

When loading transactions into a fact table, such as Figure 8-1's policy_payment_facts, the ETL process must determine what foreign key to use for each dimension. If a payment is recorded for policy 40111, for example, which policy_key is used in the fact table? Without time stamps, it would be necessary to compare the policy characteristics in the source system with the type 2 attributes in the dimension table. If a payment comes in for policy 40111, with a family size of four and a deductible amount of 500, for example, then surrogate key 14922 should be used. This lookup process is explored in greater detail in Chapter 17, "Design and ETL."

When dimension rows are time-stamped, this work is greatly simplified. To choose the correct surrogate key value, the ETL process need only know the natural key and the date of the transaction. This date can be compared to the effective_date and expiration_date columns in the dimension table to identify the correct key value for use in the fact table.

This characteristic of a time-stamped dimension is particularly valuable when fact tables are implemented incrementally. Suppose, for example, that a year after the policy payment star is implemented, another star is added to track claims against policies. Like the policy payments star, policy_claim_facts will involve the policy dimension table. If each row in the policy dimension has been time-stamped, it will be easy to load the last year's worth of claims into the new fact table. For each historic claim, the date of the transaction is used to single out the appropriate row in the policy table. Without these time stamps, it would be necessary for the source system to supply not only the date of each claim but also a complete picture of the policy, including the policy_number and each of the type 2 attributes. This set of values would be used to identify the associated row in the policy table.

TIP For dimension tables that represent closely watched entities, supplement type 2 changes tracking with date stamps. This will allow for streamlined ETL processing, and will greatly simplify the load process if an additional fact table is added in the future.

It is not necessary to time-stamp every dimension. The additional work may not be necessary if point-in-time analysis is not required. Dimensions that contain reference data, such as the transaction_type table in Figure 8-2, do not require time stamps. For core dimensions that conform across multiple subject areas, however, time-stamping is a useful enhancement.

Dimension and Fact

As with any other dimension table, the time-stamped dimension can be joined to a fact table to analyze facts. The time-stamped policy table from Figure 8-3, for example, can be joined to a policy_payment_facts table to study payments in the usual way. Need to know what were the total January payments on policies covering two or more people? Join the policy dimension to the fact table and constrain on covered_parties. Want to compare the payment habits of single versus married policy holders? Group the query results by marital_status.

When analyzing the dimension table without a fact table, something interesting happens. Some of the dimension attributes take on the characteristics of facts, exhibiting the property of additivity. For example, the following query captures the number of covered parties by state on December 31, 2006:

```
SELECT
   state,
   sum(covered_parties)
FROM
   policy
WHERE
   12/31/2006 >= effective_date AND
   12/31/2006 <= expiration_date
GROUP BY
   state
```

In this query, the dimension column covered_parties is behaving as a fact. Some people like to call it a *hybrid attribute* since it can be used either as a dimension or as a fact. This is a common phenomenon in time-stamped dimensions.

Type 3 Changes

In most dimensional schemas, the bulk of changes to source data generate type 1 and type 2 changes. Occasionally, neither technique satisfies. A third type of change response is called into play when there is a need to analyze all facts, those recorded before and after the change, with *either* the old value *or* the new value. Neither type 1 nor type 2 does the job here.

Solving this problem by storing natural keys in the fact table renders queries difficult to write and opens the door to serious double-counting issues. The preferred approach is to include two attributes for the changed data element, one to carry the current value and one to carry the prior value. Both are updated when a change occurs. Known as a type 3 solution, this allows either to be used to study the entire history.

Study All Facts with Old or New Dimension Values

During the course of planning the appropriate slow change response for each column in a dimension table, you will occasionally identify an attribute with two seemingly contradictory requirements:

- The ability to analyze all facts, recorded before and after the change occurred, using the *new* value.
- The ability to analyze all facts, before and after the change occurred, using the *old* value.

In this situation, neither a type 1 nor a type 2 response is sufficient to keep everyone satisfied. This is best understood in the context of an example.

Suppose that a business measures orders by customer, along with time and several other dimensions. When senior management studies orders, they usually do not dive right into customer detail. Instead, they use some standard regional groupings. They also use these regional groupings to report data externally, to investors or stockholders, and to compare each year's performance to the previous year's. The customer dimension table will need to capture each customer's region.

In identifying the slow change requirements for the region attribute, you learn that regional groupings have changed in the past and that it is likely they will change again in the future. Early in the company's history, for example, there were just two regions: East and West. As the company grew, these groupings became insufficient. What began as the East region was broken down into two regions: Northeast and Southeast.

When changes like this occur, management begins using the new designations immediately. Management also needs to hang onto the old designations, at least for a little while, in order to compare this year's performance to what was reported for the previous year. The requirements for managing changes to a customer's region are enumerated as follows:

- The ability to use the new regions to analyze all facts, whether recorded before or after the changeover
- The ability to use the old regions to analyze all facts, whether recorded before or after the changeover

The first requirement allows managers to move forward with the new groupings immediately. All order history can be grouped into the new Northeast and Southeast categories. The managers can do "this year versus last" comparisons as if the new groupings had always been in place. The second requirement allows the company to move forward using the old groupings. All orders can be grouped under the old value (East) as if *it* had never changed. This permits the results for the current year to be reported externally in a format consistent with the way in which forecasts were provided.

Previous Techniques Not Suitable

Neither a type 1 nor a type 2 response is able to address both these requirements. On its own, the first requirement can be satisfied with a type 1 change, overwriting the old value with the new value. A customer in the region "East," for example, is updated to show "Northeast." The new region value is, therefore, associated with all facts in any associated fact table—both those recorded before the changeover and after the changeover.

Unfortunately, the type 1 response does not meet the second requirement, which calls for the old value to be available. A type 1 change wipes away the previous value of the attribute, as if it never existed. There is no record that the customer whose region has been updated to "Northeast" was ever classified as being in the region "East."

A type 2 response fares worse; it is not able to meet *either* requirement. A type 2 response associates each fact with the version that was current at the time it was recorded. Hence, the old region value (East) is associated with facts recorded prior to the change, and the new values (Northeast, Southeast) are associated with facts recorded after the change. These new values cannot be used to analyze past history, conflicting with the first requirement. The old values cannot be applied to facts recorded after the change, conflicting with the second requirement.

An Ill-Advised Kludge

Faced with this situation for the first time, designers may come up with a solution that works on paper but introduces serious consequences. They design a type 2 solution, which allows the dimension to capture old and new versions of the changed attributes. In the fact table, the dimension's natural key is included in place of its surrogate key.

This approach theoretically allows any version of the change history in the dimension to be used in the analysis of facts. Unfortunately, it renders reporting exceedingly difficult. Worse, it introduces the possibility of inaccurate results if the dimension is not carefully qualified. If you have ever considered doing this, read on. If not, there is no reason to confuse yourself; skip ahead to "The Type 3 Solution."

In this scenario, a row in the fact table may refer to more than one row in the dimension table. There must be a mechanism to allow users to choose the appropriate version of the dimension values when building a query, in order to avoid double counting. This might be achieved by time-stamping the dimension, as discussed earlier in this chapter. Whenever customer is joined to the fact table, it will be necessary to use the time stamps to select the desired version of each customer. Querying the fact table will now require analysts to think as follows:

> I want to see sales by region for the third quarter of last year, using the regional groupings for customers that were current on January 31st of this year.

Each query requires multiple dates or date ranges: one to control the scope of the facts ("the third quarter of last year") and one to control the dimension ("current on January 31st of this year"). This logic is quite tortured; the design approach is yet another example of "boiling the frog." (See Chapter 4 for more on boiling frogs.) It may be possible to train analysts to query the star properly, but there is no hope that end users will be able to build their own queries.

The consequences for improper query construction are dire. As the regions change, multiple versions of customers accumulate in the dimension table. Since each row in the fact table contains the natural key for customers, it is associated with *multiple* rows in the dimension table—one for each version of the customer. Failure to qualify the dimension properly can result in the fact being counted redundantly—once for each version of customer. The result is a serious misstatement of order dollars.

TIP Use of a natural key as a foreign key in the fact table requires the associated dimension table to be carefully qualified every time it participates in a query. Failure to do so can result in double-counting or worse.

The Type 3 Solution

When requirements call for using the old or new values of a changed attribute to study all facts, a type 3 response is used. A pair of attributes is modeled, one attribute for the current value and one for the previous value. When a change occurs, both columns are updated; no rows are added. Users can employ either column in their analysis as desired. The process is repeatable, and the solution can be extended if multiple versions of the changed attribute are required.

A Pair of Attributes, Both to Be Updated

When a dimension attribute is singled out for type 3 treatment, it is modeled as a pair of columns. One column is designated to hold the current value; the other is designated to hold the old value. In the case of customer regions, they might be called region_current and region_previous, as depicted in Figure 8-4.

When a change to the source value occurs, both attributes are updated. The new value is placed in the column representing the current value; this is a standard type 1 response. The old value is moved to the column representing the previous value. No additional rows are created. Since each fact is linked to a single dimension row containing both values, it is possible to create reports that use either value to group all data.

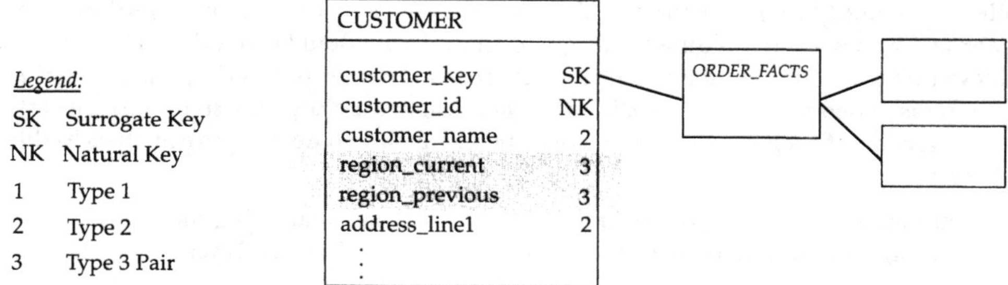

Figure 8-4 A type 3 attribute in the customer dimension

The Type 3 Change in Action

The mechanics of a type 3 change are illustrated in Figure 8-5. In this example, customers in the region called "East" are redesignated as belonging to regions called "Northeast" or "Southeast." The top half of the diagram shows the state of affairs before the change. Several rows from the customer dimension table are shown. Notice that region_current

Customer dimension table

customer_key	customer_ID	customer_name	region_current	region_previous
1011	1140400	Davis, Robert	East	East
1022	3305300	Nguyen, Tamara	East	East
1302	7733300	Rodriguez, Jason	West	West
1499	9900011	Johnson, Sue	West	West

Orders fact table

customer_key	day_key	order_dollars
1011	2322	2000
1011	3422	1000

BEFORE

AFTER

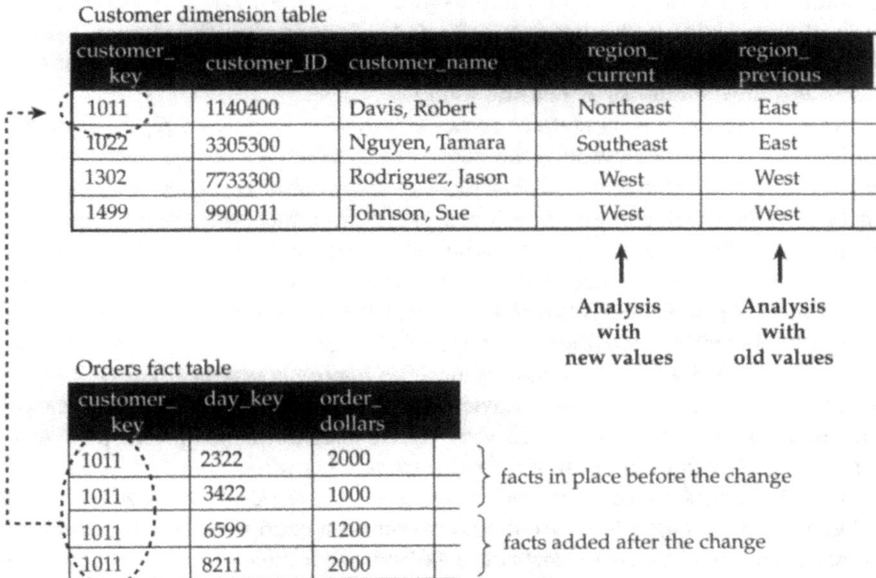

Customer dimension table

customer_key	customer_ID	customer_name	region_current	region_previous
1011	1140400	Davis, Robert	Northeast	East
1022	3305300	Nguyen, Tamara	Southeast	East
1302	7733300	Rodriguez, Jason	West	West
1499	9900011	Johnson, Sue	West	West

Orders fact table

customer_key	day_key	order_dollars
1011	2322	2000
1011	3422	1000
1011	6599	1200
1011	8211	2000

Figure 8-5 A type 3 change in action

contains each customer's region—"East" or "West." There have been no changes yet, so the region_previous is initialized to contain the same values. In the fact table, two rows have been recorded for the customer identified by customer_key 1011. Tracing this back to the customer dimension, you can see that these orders were placed by Robert Davis, who is in the region "East."

Now suppose that the business decides to change the regional groupings. The region that was formerly known as East will be subdivided into Northeast and Southeast. For each customer who was in the East region, a type 3 change occurs. The region_current is updated with the new values. The result can be seen in the lower half of Figure 8-5. Robert Davis now has a region_current of "Northeast." The two orders that Robert Davis placed before the change are still in the fact table. In addition, Robert has placed two additional orders since the change occurred. All four rows are associated with the same row in the dimension table, identified by surrogate key 1011.

This solution allows you to employ either version of the region categorization in queries or reports, simply by using the appropriate column. When you want to study orders using the new scheme, you group order_dollars by region_current. This causes all the orders from Robert Davis to be rolled up under the designation of "Northeast," whether they were recorded before or after the change. When you want to study orders using the old scheme, you group order_dollars by region_previous. Robert's orders now appear under the grouping for "East," regardless of when they occurred.

TIP A type 3 response associates the old and new values of the changed attribute with all transactions. Two dimension attributes are required. One will hold the current value; the other will hold the previous value. When the source changes, both are updated.

In exchange for some additional ETL complexity, the type 3 design buys enough flexibility to meet the dual requirements outlined earlier. The new value can be used to study all transactions, whether they occurred before or after the change, and so can the old value. All that remains is to educate the users or report developers on what each column means and how to choose which one to use.

Notice that the region_current attribute provides a standard type 1 response to the changed data. It always contains the most recent value; it is always overwritten when the value changes. For this reason, the region_current column can be designated as a type 1 attribute in design documentation if you prefer. You may even prefer to think of the change as a type 1/3 change to region. Designating the attributes that produce a type 3 response as a pair, however, may be more useful in communicating to ETL developers how changes should be processed. This is how the region attributes are documented in Figure 8-4.

It is important to recognize that a type 3 change does not preserve the historic context of facts. Each time a type 3 change occurs, the history is restated. There is no way to know, for example, what region Robert Davis was a part of when a particular order was placed. This requires a type 2 approach. As you will see later in this chapter, type 2 and type 3 responses can be combined, in a hybrid response known as type 1/2/3.

Type 3 changes are comparatively rare, but they are occasionally warranted. Redistricting and geographic realignments are the most common examples. Finance and accounting groups often designate new names or classifications for accounts on an annual basis. Such cases have the lucky distinction of occurring at predictable intervals, although this is not always the case.

Repeatable Process

A type 3 change is not a one-time-only process. It can be repeated once, twice, or as many times as needed. Robert Davis's region, for example, may subsequently be changed again. Perhaps as a result of redrawing the region boundaries, he is redesignated as being in the Southeast. When this occurs, what was formerly in region_current (Northeast) is moved to region_previous. The new value (Southeast) is placed in region_current.

A type 3 change preserves only *one* old version of the changed attribute. Once a second change occurs, the fact that Robert Davis was once in the East region is lost. In some cases, it may be useful to maintain multiple values. This can be done by designating three, four, or however many versions of the region column are required. Each time a change occurs, the values are all shifted among these columns.

With multiple versions, the columns can be difficult to name. If the changes occur on a predictable basis, they might be named region_2009, region_2008, region_2007, and so forth. This approach has two distinct disadvantages. First, it requires the DBA to periodically change the names of columns. For example, if requirements call for the current version and the two previous versions, it is necessary at the end of 2009 year to drop the 2007 column and add one for 2010. Second, encoding the year into the column names means new queries and reports will need to be designed each year to refer to the new column names. An alternative that avoids these drawbacks is to name the columns region_current, region_last_year, and region_two_years_ago.

Special Scheduling Not Necessary

The type 3 change is often misunderstood as requiring special advanced scheduling. Although developers may take advantage of the predictability of a type 3 change and handle it with a special process, this is not strictly required. As with any other slow change processing, it is possible to design an ETL process that looks for changes to the attribute in question and applies them if and when they are detected. All that is necessary is to anticipate the *possibility* of the type 3 change and engineer the ETL process accordingly.

There may be good reasons to handle a type 3 change via a special process.

- In most cases, type 3 changes occur *en masse.* A change to the region designations, for example, may affect every customer in the dimension table.
- The information that drives a type 3 change may come from a separate source or involve special rules. Region designations, for example, may be driven by a spreadsheet that maps to Zip codes.
- A type 3 change with multiple versions may involve renaming database columns and developing new reports. Its implementation must be coordinated with these activities.
- The change may occur on a predicable basis, in which case it is not necessary to monitor for it as part of standard processing.

For any of these reasons, it may be useful to handle the type 3 change through a separate scheduled process. This is not mandatory, but it may be convenient for processing purposes.

Documenting the Type 3 Change

When it comes to documenting a type 3 change, designers have varying preferences. In Figure 8-4, each attribute is designated as a surrogate key, as a natural key, or according to its slow change characteristic. The type 3 attribute pair is highlighted and labeled as type 3. As noted, you may prefer to designate the current member of the attribute pair as a type 1 attribute, since it behaves in exactly the same way as any other type 1 attribute.

Modeling tools often impose limitations on how you can document the slow change behavior associated with an attribute. Some dimensionally aware modeling tools allow you to note slow change characteristics, but most tools will not let you highlight a pair of type 3 attributes. Naming conventions and comments may be your only route to associating them.

Some modeling tools do not include the concept of a type 3 change, limiting your options to type 1 and type 2. Using these tools, you may be forced to label both members of the attribute pair as type 1. This will require some careful annotation to distinguish each attribute's purpose. You may convey the behavior of the attribute containing the previous value by noting its data source is the attribute that holds the current value.

Hybrid Slow Changes

Sometimes, conflicting business requirements arise in the handling of changed data. One set of users requires a type 1 response, while another set requires a type 2 response. In this situation, you can employ a hybrid response that provides both type 1 and type 2 functionality. A much less common hybrid combines types 1, 2, and 3.

Conflicting Requirements

Systems analysts develop a natural suspicion of situations where requirements seem cut and dried. When a user says, "We always do it this way," the requirement sounds too simple to be true. A seasoned analyst half expects the user to continue, "...except when we do it that way." Conflicting requirements like this can occur when trying to determine whether a source change should trigger a type 1 response or type 2. Sometimes, you get requirements for both.

Type 1 . . . *and* Type 2

Suppose you are designing a star to track orders. This time, the customers are corporate entities, not individuals. One of the attributes of the customer dimension will be company_name. Companies change their names from time to time. You need to determine how the dimension table should respond when a name changes.

You ask a user about how to handle changes in company names and receive the reply, "We always use the current name of the company for all our analysis." If the story stops there, the situation clearly calls for a type 1 response to name changes. When a company's name changes, overwrite the old value. This makes sense; companies tend to be known by their current names. You wouldn't want a change in name to get in the way of this year versus last comparisons.

As you reach for your pad to note this requirement, the user has an additional thought. "Oh, but sometimes we need to know the company name that was in effect at the time of an order. That's mainly for statutory reports." With this afterthought, the situation has become more complicated. A type 1 response won't associate a historically accurate company name with each order. That requires a type 2 response. Unfortunately, the type 2 response conflicts with the initial requirement to use the current name to study all history.

Type 3 Does Not Apply

When neither a type 1 response nor a type 2 response seems to meet all the requirements, your first reaction might be to consider a type 3 response. A type 3 response captures two versions of the attribute, which sounds promising. Recall, however, that *neither* version of the attribute can be used to segregate facts recorded before the change from facts recorded after the change. Either value can be used to study all facts, but there is no way to tell which version was in effect at the time of any individual transaction.

The Hybrid Response

When requirements call for changed data to result in both type 1 and type 2 behavior, the solution is disarmingly simple: provide for both. This cannot be achieved with a single attribute, but it can be achieved by providing a pair of attributes. Each attribute has the same source, but one will react to changes as a type 1 response and the other as type 2.

This solution is known as a *type 1/2 hybrid.* It's a good idea to name these attributes clearly, since each serves a different function. Use the suffix _current to identify the type 1 attribute, and _historic to identify the type 2 attribute. When the source for the pair of attributes changes, the ETL process must do two things:

- Update the _current value for all records that share the same natural key.
- Insert a new row, initializing both _current and _historic values to the new value.

When reporting on the data, developers choose which column to use based on the requirements for the report.

- Use the _current column to group all facts under the current values.
- Use the _historic column to group all facts under the historic values.

TIP A hybrid design allows for type 1 and type 2 treatment of the same source attribute by providing two separate dimension columns. One is designated as a type 1 attribute and can be used to group all facts under the latest value. The other is designated as a type 2 attribute and can be used to group facts with the historic values.

You may be a bit confused at this point. To understand better how a hybrid change works, look at the following specific example.

A Type 1/2 Hybrid Response in Action

A hybrid design for handling changes in company names is illustrated in Figure 8-6. The customer dimension in the figure records company names in two columns:

- **company_name_current** will capture the current name of the company. This attribute will exhibit type 1 behavior. When a company name changes, it will be updated.
- **company_name_historic** will capture the detailed history of company names. This attribute will exhibit type 2 behavior. When a company name changes, a new row will be created to capture the new value. The new row will be associated with any subsequent transactions added to a fact table.

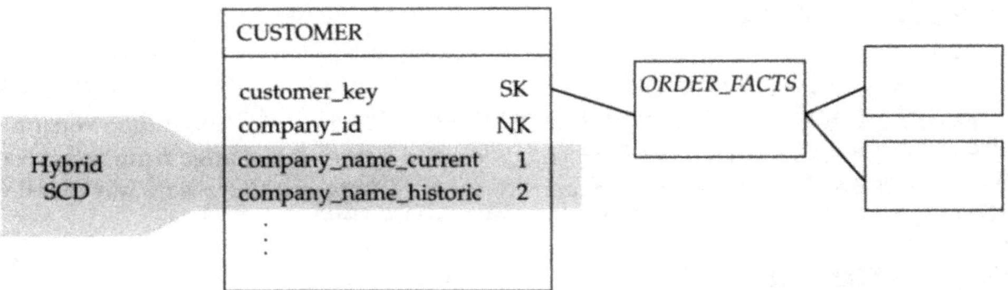

Figure 8-6 Hybrid treatment of changes to company name

Processing a Change Suppose one of the companies in the customer table is Apple Computer. You may recall that in 2007 the company changed its name from "Apple Computer, Inc." to "Apple Inc." Imagine that products have been ordered by Apple, both before and after the name change.

Figure 8-7 illustrates the two-step process that occurs when the name of the company changes. The top of the figure shows the row for Apple that was in place *prior* to the name change. The natural key for Apple is BB770. It has one row in the customer table, with a surrogate key value of 1011. The column company_name_current shows the name of the company as "Apple Computer, Inc." There have been no changes as of yet, so company_name_historic contains the same value.

The lower half of Figure 8-7 shows what happens when the name of the company changes:

1. The first row shows the previously existing record, with surrogate key value 1011. The company_name_current column is updated with the new company name "Apple Inc." This is the type 1 response. The company_name_historic value is untouched, since it is treated as type 2.
2. To process the type 2 change, a new row is added. It contains the new name "Apple Inc." in both the company_name_current and company_name_historic columns. This new row is assigned a new surrogate key, 2822, which will be used for new rows in associated fact tables.

This may appear convoluted, but it is no different from processing any table that contains both type 1 and type 2 attributes. The only difference is that both attributes happen to have the same source.

Using the Company Name Columns Facts can now be studied in two ways. When you want to be able to capture all orders under the new name (Apple Inc.), you can use the column company_name_current. This might be done to filter a query or to group aggregated facts. All activity with Apple is associated with the same name: Apple Inc. This is particularly useful for producing this year versus last year comparisons; all orders will have the same name, even if it recently changed.

When you want to group orders under historically accurate company names, you can use the company_name_historic. Transactions that took place before Apple's name change

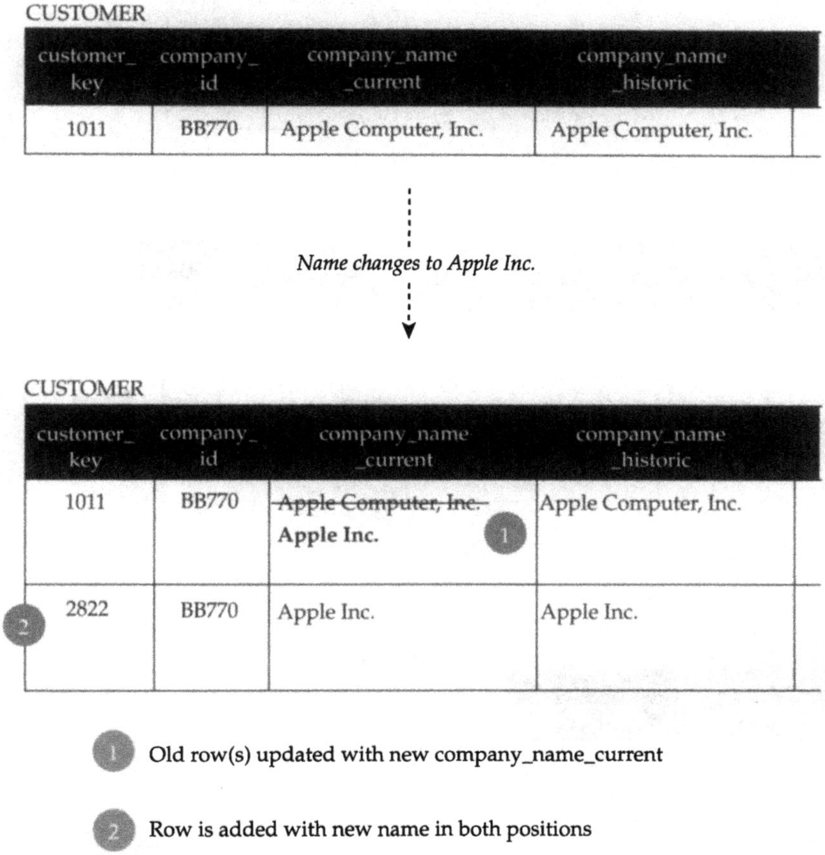

CUSTOMER

customer_key	company_id	company_name_current	company_name_historic
1011	BB770	Apple Computer, Inc.	Apple Computer, Inc.

Name changes to Apple Inc.

CUSTOMER

customer_key	company_id	company_name_current	company_name_historic
1011	BB770	~~Apple Computer, Inc.~~ **Apple Inc.** (1)	Apple Computer, Inc.
(2) 2822	BB770	Apple Inc.	Apple Inc.

1. Old row(s) updated with new company_name_current
2. Row is added with new name in both positions

Figure 8-7 A type 1/2 hybrid change in action

are grouped under "Apple Computer, Inc." Transactions that took place after the name change are grouped under "Apple Inc." This state of affairs is illustrated in Figure 8-8.

Repeatable Process The hybrid response is repeatable. Each time a company changes, the same two-step process is followed. First, all existing rows with the same natural key have their _current value updated. Second, a new row is added, with _current and _historic initialized to the new value.

Suppose that Apple decides to change its name again. The iPod and iPhone have been so successful they might rename the company "iApple Inc." Figure 8-9 shows how this change would be processed. First, the existing records in the dimension table for Apple, which is company BB770, are updated with the new company_name_current. This time around, there are two records to be updated: those identified by surrogate keys 1011 and 2822. That takes care of the type 1 processing.

Second, a new row is added to the table for iApple. This row records the new name, iApple Inc., in both the company_name_current and company_name_historic columns.

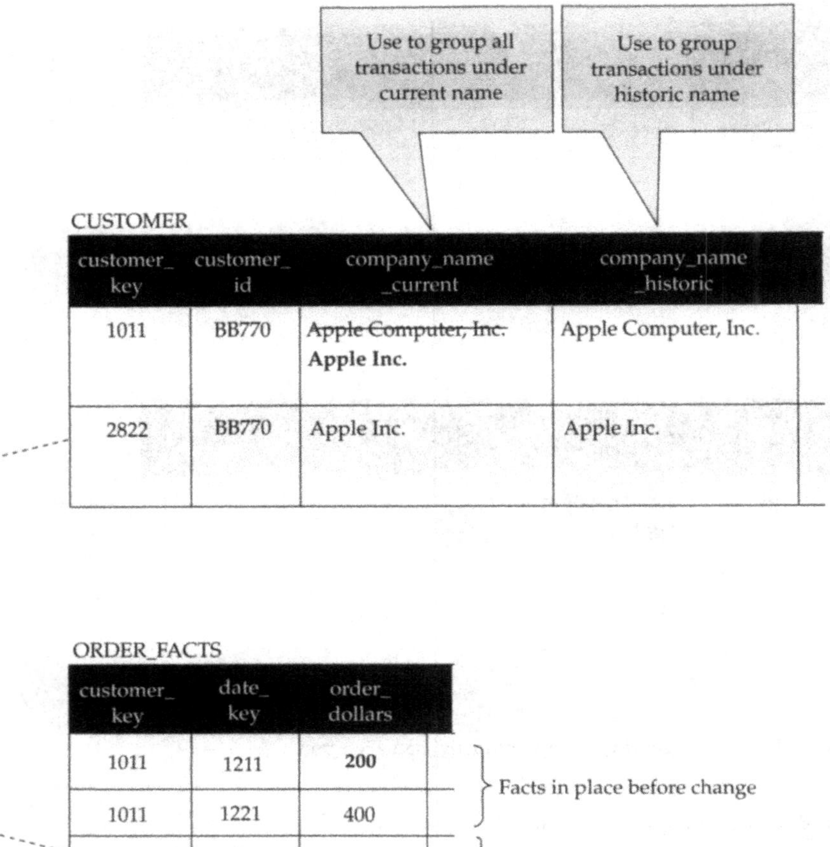

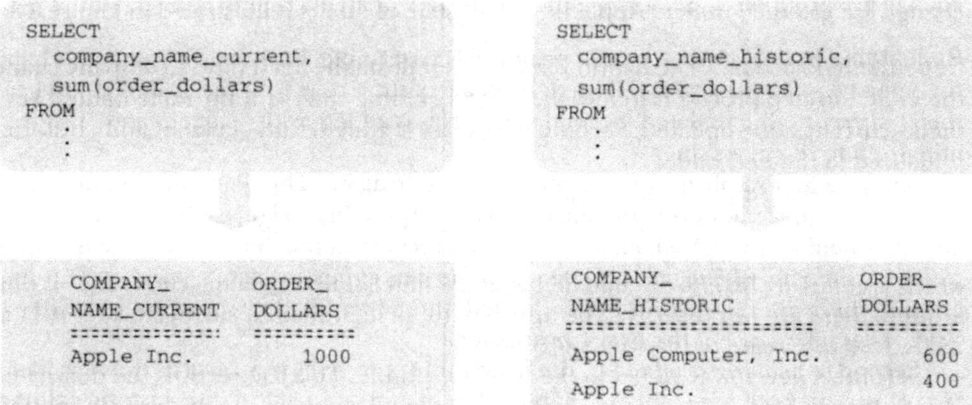

Figure 8-8 A hybrid response offers two analytic possibilities

CUSTOMER

customer_ key	company_ id	company_name _current	company_name _historic
1011	BB770	~~Apple Computer, Inc.~~ ~~Apple Inc.~~ **iApple Inc.**	Apple Computer, Inc.
2822	BB770	~~Apple Inc.~~ **iApple Inc.**	Apple Inc.
3100	BB770	iApple Inc.	iApple Inc.

ORDER_FACTS

customer_ key	date_ key	order_ dollars
1011	1211	200
1011	1221	400
2822	1344	400
3100	1411	1000

Figure 8-9 The company's name changes again

That takes care of the type 2 processing. This new row has surrogate key value 3100. Any new orders from iApple will use this key value in the fact table.

This process can be repeated as many times as the name of a given company changes. It will always be possible to use the current name of the company to study all facts by using company_name_current. It will always be possible to study all facts with historically accurate company names by using company_name_historic.

Evaluating and Extending the Hybrid Approach

The hybrid approach addresses conflicting slow change requirements at the expense of understandability. Hybrid solutions generate no end of confusion among end users and analysts, who are often uncertain about which column to use in a given report. When the wrong column is used for a situation, the results can be perplexing.

It is, therefore, important to use hybrid solutions judiciously. Evaluate the requirements carefully. In the case of the company name changes, for example, why do some people want access to the historically accurate name? If it is so they can reproduce a historic invoice, that purpose is better served by the operational system. On the other hand, if it is needed for certain forms of statutory reporting, the requirement may be valid.

TIP Only implement hybrid changes when there are real analytic requirements. Operational reporting can be left to the operational system.

When a hybrid approach is implemented, most analysis tends to focus on one of the columns. In the company example, the column of primary interest contains the current company name. To simplify the model exposed to end users, you can create a view of the customer dimension that hides the historic version. Developers trained in the complexities of the star can be provided with the full version of the table, for use in creating canned reports.

In extremely rare situations, you may find requirements that call for a type 1/2/3 hybrid. In this case, the attribute in question will be represented by three columns: the current value, the previous value, and the historic value. This situation will compound the confusion of users trying to choose which column to show in a report. Again, you will want to try to insulate end users from this complexity, exposing them only to the version required most often.

At this point, the reader may be thinking about other ways to combine these techniques. There is no need to describe a type 1/3 hybrid, because a type 3 change already includes a column that exhibits type 1 behavior. For the same reason, a type 2/3 hybrid is no different from the 1/2/3 hybrid described in the previous paragraph. It *is* possible to incorporate time stamps with any hybrid technique that involves a type 2 component. Remember that complexity increases the ETL workload and reduces usability; be sure that any solution is truly warranted by the requirements.

Frozen Attributes

Occasionally, there appear to be dimension attributes that defy classification using the standard 1/2/3 designations. Analytic requirements sometimes call for "freezing" an attribute value, most often to preserve its original state. It might be argued that this represents a fourth kind of slow change response, where the response is to do nothing at all. Careful study of these attributes reveals that they fit within the existing framework.

Most frozen attributes can be defined as type 1 attributes by carefully stating how they are computed. If a policy dimension includes a column that records the policy holder's age at the time the policy went into effect, you might say that age is "frozen" once the policy is signed. Careful definition of the attribute, however, reveals it is a type 1 attribute: the age at signing is the difference between the effective date of the policy and the birth date of the customer. This definition avoids making use of an age column in the source system. "Frozen" attributes like this often appear in conjunction with similar attributes designated for type 1 and type 2 response. Age_at_signing, for example, may be accompanied by current_age (type 1) and historic_age (type 2). The source of these attributes can be an age record in the source system.

Sometimes a frozen attribute is actually exhibiting a combination of type 1 and type 2 behaviors. This often occurs in situations where the dimensional model supports statutory reporting. In these cases, there may be attributes that can be updated until information is externally reported, after which they must not be updated. Subsequent changes must generate a new row. The "frozen" attribute is actually exhibiting both type 1 and type 2 behavior. A type 1 response occurs if the old value has not been externally reported; a type 2 response occurs if it has.

Summary

This chapter provided some advanced techniques for responding to changes in source data. Building on the basic type 1 and type 2 changes introduced in Chapter 3, this chapter added the time-stamped dimension, type 3 change, and hybrid change.

Time-stamped dimensions supplement the type 2 approach

- Type 2 changes preserve the historic context of facts but do not allow for point-in-time analysis within a dimension.
- A fact table can be used to log the change history of a dimension table, associating each version with the range of dates during which it was effective. This fact table will have the same number of rows as the dimension table.
- A time-stamped dimension does the same job without requiring an additional fact table. This is done by adding effective and expiration dates, and managing these columns so two rows for the same natural key do not overlap.
- A transaction history can be ordered by using the effective_date column. Effective_date and expiration_date can be used together to filter for records in effect at a particular point in time. A most_recent_row flag can be added to make it easy to select current records from the dimension.
- The time-stamped dimension is harder to load but makes it easier to load associated fact tables.
- A time-stamped dimension may contain attributes that behave as dimensions in some queries and facts in other queries.

Type 3 changes offer a different spin on history

- When users want to connect either the old or new value to all facts, regardless of when the change occurred, neither type 1 nor type 2 is sufficient.
- The type 3 solution involves maintaining the current value for the attribute, as with a type 1 change, and an additional column to capture the prior value.
- Analysis can use either value by selecting the appropriate column.
- Multiple versions are possible, but this can lead to situations that require table definition changes when adding new columns or hardcoding particular versions into reports.

Type 1/2 hybrid changes allow for both type 1 and type 2 responses

- When seemingly conflicting requirements call for an attribute to be treated as type 1 and type 2, design two attributes.
- One attribute will be treated as type 1. It will be updated whenever the source value changes and it can always be used to study all facts with the current value.
- The other attribute is treated as type 2: when a change occurs, a new row is added to the dimension table. This attribute can be used to group facts with the historically accurate value.
- End-user confusion can be avoided by careful naming, or by hiding the lesser-used attribute using a view. Analysts and report developers should be educated on the difference between the attributes, and when it is appropriate to use each of them.

Further Reading

The advanced slow change techniques presented in this chapter can be employed in a variety of situations. Consult the sources listed here for additional examples, including some interesting embellishments.

Time-Stamped Dimensions

- Ralph Kimball and Margy Ross provide a detailed example of a human resources solution that incorporates a time-stamped employee dimension in Chapter 8 of *The Data Warehouse Toolkit, Second Edition* (Wiley, 2002). They refer to the time-stamped dimension as a *transaction tracking dimension.*
- This chapter suggested that effective and expiration dates can be supplemented with effective and expiration *times,* if needed. For an example of this technique, see the Kimball and Ross example cited in the previous bullet.
- If a conformed rollup of a time-stamped dimension is also time-stamped, some unique issues will be faced in its maintenance. I discuss these issues in Chapter 8 of *Mastering Data Warehouse Aggregates* (Wiley, 2006).

Type 3 Changes

- In Chapter 4 of *The Data Warehouse Toolkit,* Kimball and Ross provide an example of a type 3 change in a product dimension. When the department associated with a product changes, there is a need to use the old and new values.
- This chapter suggested that the type 3 approach can be extended to carry multiple versions of the changed attribute. Kimball and Ross use a sales force realignment scenario to illustrate this technique, complete with four historic versions of the attribute. In Chapter 4 of *The Data Warehouse Toolkit,* they call this technique "predictable changes with multiple overlays."

Type 1/2 Hybrid Changes

- Kimball and Ross refer to the type 1/2 hybrid as "unpredictable changes with a single overlay." In Chapter 4 of *The Data Warehouse Toolkit,* they provide an example where department name changes can be handled using this approach. They suggest there is a similarity to type 3, but note that their example does not include tracking of the prior value.
- Kimball, Ross, Thornthwaite, Mundy, and Becker allude to an interesting spin on the type 1/2 hybrid in Chapter 6 of *The Data Warehouse Lifecycle Toolkit, Second Edition* (Wiley, 2008). They imagine a solution where the dimension table records type 2 changes. An outrigger table contains one row for each natural key, recording the current version of the attributes. This technique may be useful if there are several attributes in a table that demand the hybrid approach. Something similar can be achieved by joining a dimension table to an alias of itself using the natural key, and filtering the alias on a current_version flag.

CHAPTER

9 Multi-Valued Dimensions and Bridges

A crucial feature of every example in the first eight chapters of this book has gone unmentioned. Each and every dimension attribute has participated in a simple one-to-many relationship with every fact. This essential characteristic has allowed dimensions to be arranged around fact tables in the neat and powerful star configuration with which you are now familiar.

The real world, of course, is not always neat. Real-world complexity sometimes makes it *impossible* to model a process in this manner. This chapter explores two such challenges:

- **Multi-valued dimensions** occur when a fact table row may need to refer to more than one row in a dimension table.
- **Multi-valued attributes** occur when a dimension row needs to capture multiple values for a single attribute.

In both cases, a star configuration *simply will not support* the true complexities of the process.

The solution to both these challenges introduces a new kind of table, called a *bridge*. Think of a bridge table as a double-edged sword. It provides the ultimate power and flexibility, enabling a wide variety of analytic possibilities. This power comes with significant costs, and chief among these is *risk*. Put simply, the presence of a bridge increases the possibility that the schema can be *misused*, producing inaccurate results.

The specter of this risk is so great that many shops will refuse to consider using a bridge at all. This rejection, however, may severely cripple the analytic capabilities of a dimensional solution. Alternatives are available, but their analytic flexibility is limited. Before dismissing the bridge out of hand, you and your colleagues must understand it fully. Only then can you make an informed decision that balances the power and risk of the various options.

This discussion will begin by calling to the fore the previously implied one-to-many relationship of most dimension tables to the facts. The challenges of multi-valued dimension tables and multi-valued dimension attributes will then be studied in turn. You will learn the limitations of trying to address these challenges with a standard design, how a bridge can solve the problem, and the potential consequences. You will also be provided with techniques to mitigate such consequences, and challenged to think about slow-change processing in a new light.

Standard One-to-Many Relationships

Until now, each star schema you have seen in this book has been characterized by a distinctive and important feature. Every fact has been related to exactly one instance value of each dimension. In an order_facts table, for example, each order is related to exactly one product. Looking at these relationships from the opposite direction, it has also been true that each dimension value may be related to one or more fact table rows.

Putting these characteristics together, we say that dimensions and facts have a *one-to-many relationship.* A one-to-many relationship is sometimes called other names, such as master–detail or parent–child. The fact table is sometimes referred to as a dependent entity, since its definition depends on the primary keys of other tables. These terms all indicate the same thing: each fact is related to exactly one row in each dimension table.

Following the conventions of entity-relationship modeling, these standard relationships might be illustrated in a manner similar to the diagram in Figure 9-1. The crow's feet at the end of a line indicate the "many" side of the relationship. This style of diagramming is not normally used for dimensional modeling but will be useful for some of the issues explored in this chapter and the next. If you are familiar with IDEF modeling, you may be accustomed to a similar diagramming style in which solid circles replace the crow's feet.

In the example, a product may be related to zero or more order_facts, and each order_facts row must be related to exactly one product. (In the diagram, a solid line emanating from a table indicates a mandatory relationship, and a dotted line indicates an optional one, but we will not make further use of this convention.) The same holds true for each of the other dimension tables in the diagram. Diagrams in this chapter will not illustrate optionality (dotted lines) but some will indicate cardinality (crow's feet).

Because each fact table row relates to exactly one row in each dimension table, we can make a similar observation about the relationship between a fact table row and each dimension *column.* For example, if one of the columns of the product table is brand_name, then we can say that each row of order_facts is related to exactly one brand_name.

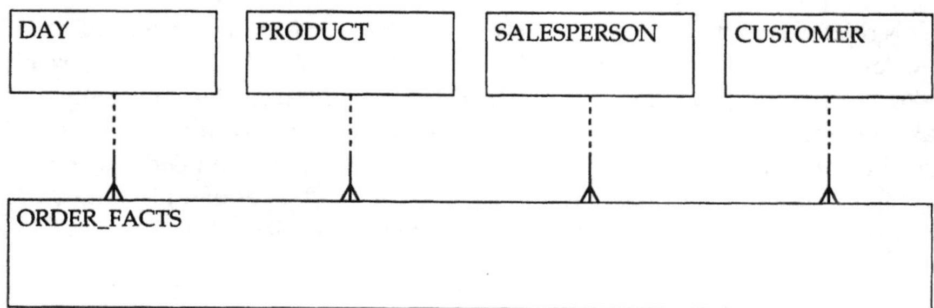

Figure 9-1 One-to-many relationships

The standard query pattern introduced early in this book relies heavily on the one-to-many relationship between facts and dimensions. Recall from Chapter 1 that a typical query will select one or more dimensions and use them to control the aggregation of facts. For example:

```
SELECT
  product.brand_name,
  sum (order_facts.order_dollars)
FROM
  product, order_facts
WHERE
  product.product_key = order_facts.product_key
GROUP BY
  product.brand_name
```

This technique works nicely, because each order is related to one and only one brand_name. Even in the case of an attribute hierarchy snowflake, as described in Chapter 7, this may hold true. The brand table in Figure 7-5, for example, participates in a parent–child relationship with product, which in turn participates in a parent–child relationship with the fact table. Some people like to call this a "grandparent–grandchild" relationship. For every fact, there is exactly one brand, and queries like the one earlier can accurately group the facts.

This configuration has permeated the first eight chapters of this book and has been quite handy in its simplicity. Unfortunately, the real world is not always that simple. What happens when a fact may be related to one or more instances of a dimension? Perhaps more than one salesperson can collaborate on an order, as depicted in Figure 9-2. This breaks with the conventions that have been implied to this point, because it means a given fact may have more than one associated salesperson. How does one design a dimensional model in such a situation? The fact table cannot hold a foreign key reference to the salesrep table, since there may be more than one salesperson. Similarly, the salesrep table cannot hold a foreign key reference to the fact table, since each salesperson may have booked more than one order.

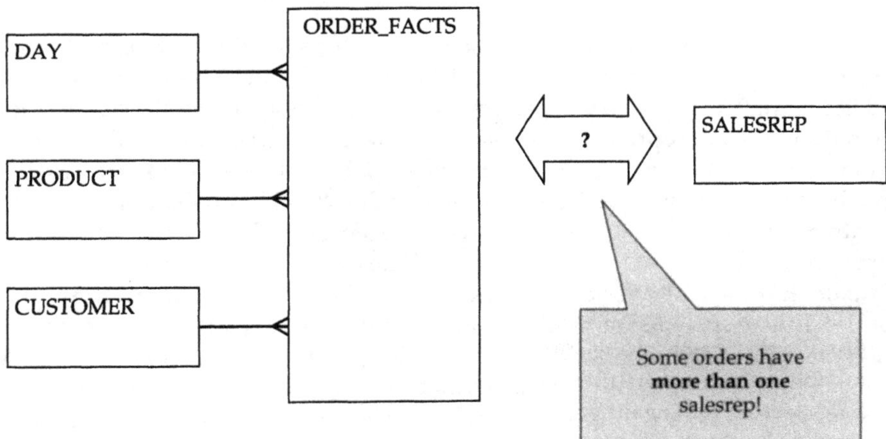

Figure 9-2 What happens when more than one salesperson may be involved?

As Chapter 7 hinted, the solution will involve a form of snowflaking. As you will see, it is possible to meet the requirements of the situation, but doing so will introduce new complications when it comes to ensuring accurate reporting. As with other design alternatives in this book, you will need to weigh your options carefully.

Multi-Valued Dimensions

For most stars, all the relationships between dimension tables and fact tables are of the one-to-many variety. Occasionally, though, you will encounter situations where a given fact may relate to one *or more* rows in a dimension table. The situation in Figure 9-2 is a clear example; each order may have more than one salesperson. Perhaps most orders have only one, but some have two, three, four, or any number of salespeople associated with them. The salesrep table is an example of a *multi-valued dimension.* With respect to a single fact, it can take on multiple values. A multi-valued dimension does not fit with the established primary key–foreign key relationship between dimension table and fact table.

One way to solve the problem of the multi-valued dimension is to place more than one key value in the fact table. This approach effectively flattens the complex relationship between fact and dimension but is somewhat limited. It renders certain forms of reporting difficult and only works for a set number of relationships.

An alternative is to bridge the relationship between fact table and dimension table with a special table, which is fittingly referred to as a *bridge* table. This approach is more flexible in terms of the information it can capture and the kinds of reports it can produce, but it offers its own set of problems. Most significantly, if such a table is not queried correctly, double-counting may result. Luckily, measures can be taken to avoid this outcome.

Simplifying the Relationship

The simplest way to deal with a multi-valued dimension is to decompose the many-to-many relationship into two or more one-to-many relationships. This solution makes use of roles, as covered in Chapter 6. The fact table will have not one relationship to the dimension table but two or more. For a given fact, each of the relationships will identify exactly one row in the dimension table.

In the case of collaboration among salespeople, order_facts can be designed with two salesrep_keys. One is designated as primary, the other as secondary. The resulting design is depicted in Figure 9-3. The figure depicts two aliases for the single salesrep table. Each is connected using the appropriate foreign key in the fact table. If only one salesperson is involved in a particular order, the secondary_salesrep_key will refer to a special row in the salesrep table for "not applicable," a technique also described in Chapter 6.

This design appears to solve the problem, but issues are lurking beneath the surface. First, there are certain forms of reporting that will now be much more complicated. Want to total up order_dollars for a particular salesperson? You'll have to filter your query twice, once for the primary salesperson and once for secondary, and link these filters with "or." Want to list all salespeople along with the total order_dollars in which they were involved? You'll probably need to query the fact table twice, once grouping order_dollars by the primary salesperson, and again grouping order_dollars by the secondary salesperson. Then, you can merge the result sets together. All this becomes more complicated if the fact table allows for three salespeople, or four, or more.

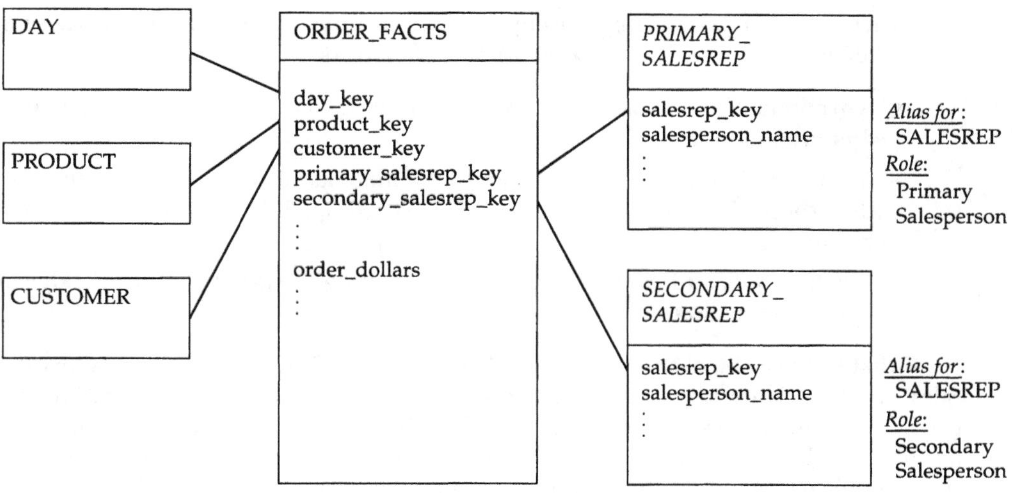

Figure 9-3 Allowing for two salespeople

The second problem is that the solution only allows for a fixed number of relationships. If there are two salesrep_keys in the fact table, for example, then nothing can be done when an order comes along with three salespeople. You might anticipate this and include enough keys for the highest number of collaborators ever encountered, but eventually a new record will be set.

TIP A multi-valued relationship between fact and dimension table can be resolved by breaking it down into two or more one-to-many relationships. However, this solution complicates reporting and supports only a finite number of relationships.

Although imperfect, this solution may be acceptable. If the frequency of collaboration is rare and can be limited to a fixed number of participants, it may be the right choice. Most reporting will focus on the primary salesperson, working in the standard way. Skilled analysts will be called on for the occasional report, which calls for factoring in collaboration. If this is not satisfactory, however, a bridge table will be required.

Using a Bridge for Multi-Valued Dimensions

In lieu of simplifying a many-to-many relationship, a multi-valued dimension can be accommodated through the design of a special table called a bridge. This approach is much more flexible but brings with it the danger of double-counting. It is not possible to eliminate the risk of double-counting, but it can be limited. If a bridged solution is chosen, special attention must be given to the behavior of slowly changing dimensions, and it may be necessary to add yet another table to satisfy the quirks of some software products.

Bridging the Relationship

The multi-valued dimension problem can be solved by developing a group table that sits between the fact table and the dimension table. Instead of directly referring to the dimension table, each fact will refer to a single group. The group table is called a bridge, because it links that fact table with the dimension table. Here's how it works:

- A group table contains a group_key and a foreign key column referring to the dimension in question.
- A row is added for each group member. If there are three members of the group, the group table will have three rows for that group. Each row shares the same group_key.
- The fact table and the bridge can be joined using the group_key; the bridge table is joined to the dimension in turn.

If that sounds a bit abstract, an example should help. Figure 9-4 shows a table called sales_group, which bridges the relationship between order_facts and salesrep. The table order_facts contains a sales_group_key, which indicates the set of salespeople involved in a particular order. The table sales_group has one row for each member of the group. Each row has only two columns: the group_key and the salesrep_key.

Suppose that two salespeople, Ann and Henry, work together to bring in an order. The salesrep table has rows for Ann and Henry, as you can see in the instance table in the lower right of the diagram. In order to load the order into the fact table, a group is created for Ann and Henry—assuming one does not already exist. The group is assigned a group_key. To make the example easy to read, a value of 1 is used, but the group_key has no intrinsic significance. There are two rows in the sales_group table for the collaboration between Ann and Henry. Each row contains the group identifier, 1, and salesrep_key of one of the participants: 222 for Ann and 333 for Henry. A row can now be loaded into the fact table for this group, holding the sales_group_key 1.

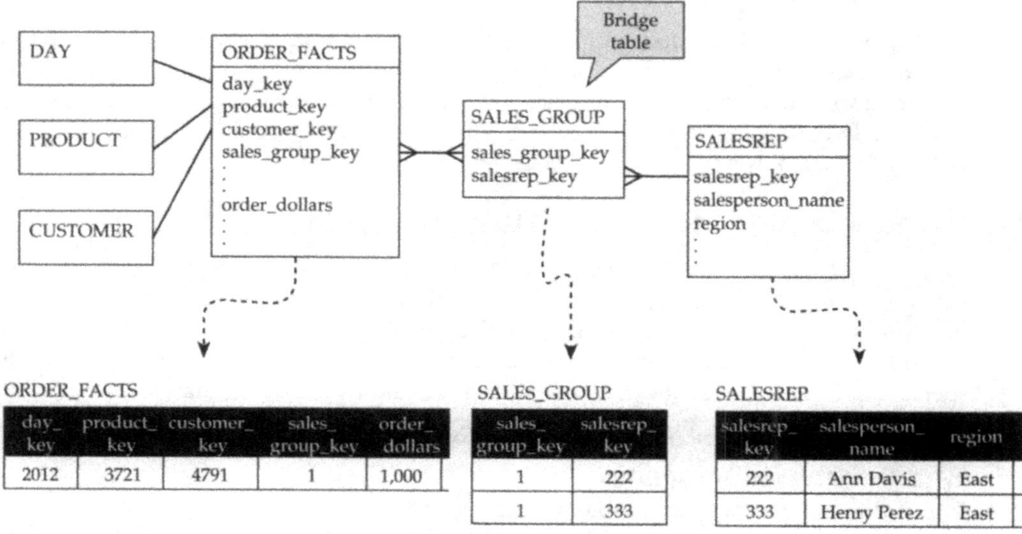

ORDER_FACTS

day_key	product_key	customer_key	sales_group_key	order_dollars
2012	3721	4791	1	1,000

SALES_GROUP

sales_group_key	salesrep_key
1	222
1	333

SALESREP

salesrep_key	salesperson_name	region
222	Ann Davis	East
333	Henry Perez	East

Figure 9-4 A bridge table associates any number of salespeople with an order

This design has obvious implications for the ETL process. As noted, the process must create and manage groupings. Each time a collaboration occurs, it will be necessary to come up with a group_key in order to load the fact. If the group has collaborated in the past, the same group_key can be used for the new fact. If it is a new collaboration, a group key must be assigned, and appropriate rows must be added to the sales_group table.

Unlike the simplification option, this approach can accommodate groups of any size. If three salespeople collaborate on an order, a group_key is created for the collaboration and three rows are added to the group—one for each member. If a group of 15 works together, a group is created and 15 rows are added. A group is also needed when a sale takes place involving only one salesperson. The group table will contain one row, associating the group_key with the single group member. Every fact will refer to a group.

This solution makes it easy to address some of the questions that posed challenges under the design that simplified the relationship. Computing total order dollars for a salesperson is easy; the salesrep table is constrained for the salesperson in question, and joined to the group table, which in turn joins to the fact table. Total sales for each salesperson can be accomplished in the same way, grouping data by salesperson_name.

TIP Compared to a solution that simplifies a many-to-many relationship, using a bridge table offers increased flexibility and simplifies reporting challenges.

You may have noticed that the relationship between the fact table and the bridge table in Figure 9-4 is many-to-many. That is not a mistake. If Ann and Henry collaborate again, the same group number can be used. Group number 1 will have multiple rows in the fact table, one for each order, and multiple rows in the group table, one for Ann and one for Henry. This works just fine most of the time but can confuse software tools which assume every join will leverage a primary key–foreign key association. We will look at what to do if your modeling, database, or reporting tool balks at this relationship shortly. First, though, it is necessary to address a more important issue.

Bridges and Double-Counting

While the bridge table offers increased flexibility and simplifies many reporting challenges, there is a downside (there's *always* a downside). By allowing a fact to refer to multiple rows in a dimension table, you open the door to the possibility of double-counting, triple-counting, or worse.

NOTE For the sake of simplicity, this book uses *double-counting* to describe any situation where a fact may be counted more than once. As you will see, in any particular situation, the error may be more severe.

In Figure 9-3, for example, the same order is associated with both Ann and Henry. If you query orders by region, the same order will be counted twice—once for Ann and once for Henry. If three salespeople had collaborated, the order would be triple-counted, and so forth. Countermeasures can be employed to reduce the possibility of double-counting, but sometimes it is precisely what is wanted.

When Double-Counting Is Wanted It may seem nonsensical at first, but sometimes this double-counting is actually a good thing. For example, it may be useful to have a report that shows order_dollars by salesperson. Such a report shows the sales volume associated with each salesperson. In this case, Ann and Henry's joint order should be counted in both their results.

This kind of report provides insight into the impact that a particular member of the dimension table has on the facts. Similar examples might include producing a report showing the total claim dollars by party, the total number of office visits per medical diagnosis, and so on. While the fact may be counted more than once, it is legitimately associated with each dimension instance.

On the other hand, it would be a serious error to take that information and produce a grand total. Ann and Henry may each have participated in $1,000 worth of orders, but this does not mean that total order dollars are $2,000. Unfortunately, it is all too easy with most reporting tools to request a grand total.

TIP When a bridge table is present, each fact may be associated with more than one dimension row. This makes double-counting a very real possibility. Sometimes this is intended, but it is easy to err in constructing a query or producing totals in a report.

Avoiding grand totals is not sufficient to stay out of trouble. It is necessary to group query results by *individual members* of the dimension table. This is sometimes referred to as the grain of the dimension table. Grouping results at any other level of summarization may result in double-counting. For example, Ann and Henry have the same region value in the salesrep table. The following query joins order_facts to salesrep via the bridge, and groups by region:

```
SELECT
  salesrep.region,
  sum (order_facts.order_dollars)
FROM
  salerep, sales_group, order_facts
WHERE
  order_facts.sales_group_key = sales_group.sales_group_key AND
  sales_group.salesrep_key = salesrep.salesrep_key
GROUP BY
  salesrep.region
```

When the RDBMS executes this query, it will find two rows in the salesrep for the single order booked by Ann and Henry. In order to join the rows, it will repeat the order, once for Ann and once for Henry. After that, the aggregation by region will be computed. This causes Ann and Henry's joint order to be counted twice within region "East."

TIP The only safe way to construct an impact report is to group by a column in the dimension that will have a unique value for each member of the group. Most often, this will be the natural key.

The specter of double-counting is enough to send many organizations retreating to the simplified relationship solution. Where the need is strong enough to warrant the bridge, however, measures can be taken to reduce the risk. Before looking at them, let's look at one adjustment that does *not* solve the problem.

One well-intentioned impulse is to eliminate the many-to-many relationship between fact table and bridge by asserting that each group will be used only once. If the same members collaborate again, a new group will be created. While this does reduce the many-to-many relationship to a one-to-many relationship, it is a one-to-many relationship *going in the wrong direction.* Even if we create a second group when Ann and Henry collaborate again, the order still refers to two salespeople, and it is still in danger of being double-counted. Worse, the bridge table is likely to grow very large, and it may even contain more rows than the fact table. Luckily, other techniques will provide limited success.

Adding an Allocation Factor Sometimes, it is possible to eliminate double-counting dangers by adding an allocation factor to the bridge table. The allocation factor indicates what percentage of the associated fact should be credited to each group member. The example in Figure 9-5 shows an allocation factor in the sales_group table. When Ann and Henry collaborate, 75 percent of the order_dollars are credited to Ann, and 25 percent to Henry.

The key to making allocations work lies in how the facts are accessed. It is essential that the allocation factor is applied to each granular transaction, prior to aggregation. The query in Figure 9-5, for example, selects the `sum (order_dollars * allocation)`,

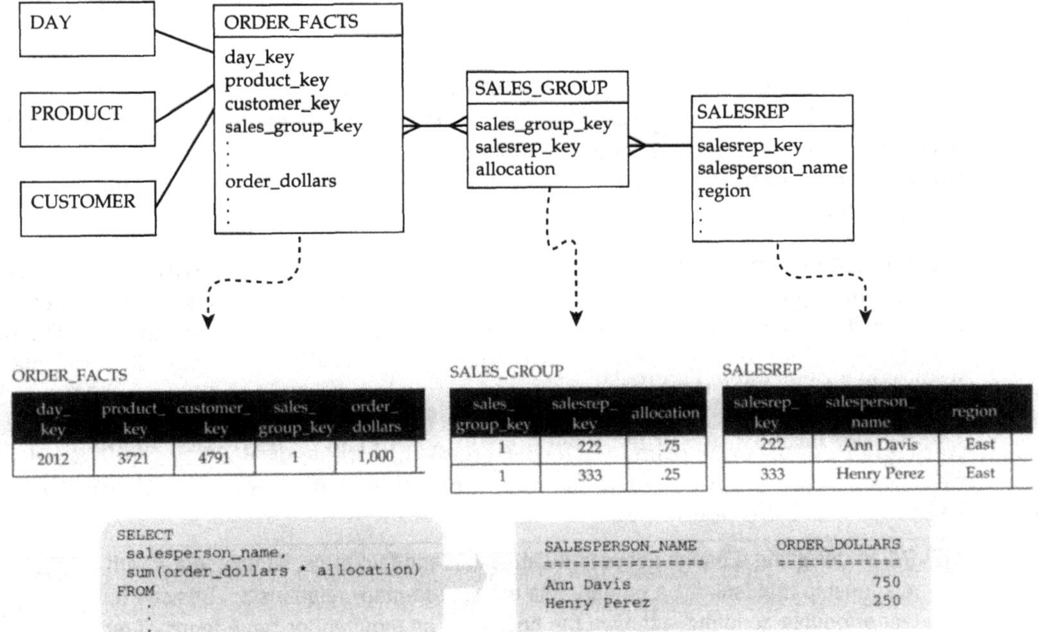

ORDER_FACTS

day_key	product_key	customer_key	sales_group_key	order_dollars
2012	3721	4791	1	1,000

SALES_GROUP

sales_group_key	salesrep_key	allocation
1	222	.75
1	333	.25

SALESREP

salesrep_key	salesperson_name	region
222	Ann Davis	East
333	Henry Perez	East

```
SELECT
 salesperson_name,
 sum(order_dollars * allocation)
FROM
 .
 .
```

```
SALESPERSON_NAME          ORDER_DOLLARS
================          =============
Ann Davis                           750
Henry Perez                         250
```

Figure 9-5 An allocation factor can help prevent double-counting

rather than trying to apply an allocation factor to `sum(order_dollars)`. As long as the allocation is computed correctly, this approach ensures that no order dollars are double-counted. This works, even if we create a grand total that adds together Ann and Henry's orders, or query for allocated order_dollars by region. The allocated amounts will always aggregate to the total order amount. We can even ensure that the facts are calculated this way by joining the bridge and the fact table within a view. For queries that do not involve the salesrep table, however, this view will only add unnecessary overhead.

Allocation looks like the perfect solution but is rarely a valid option. In most situations, an allocation rule simply does not exist. Determining an allocation factor in a sales situation may be possible, but what does one do if a healthcare charge has several associated diagnoses? It is tempting to try to define an allocation rule, but it must be based on real business logic, and must be approved by representatives of the business users. Many attempts at constructing allocation factors become bogged down in politics.

On the rare occasion that an allocation factor is available, it may make more sense to redefine the grain of the fact table rather than build a bridge. For example, in the case of salesperson collaboration, allocation may be factored in as part of the order entry system. A fully vetted allocation factor is not only available but is also presented to the ETL process by the operational source. Instead of designing a bridge with an allocation factor, as in Figure 9-5, it is possible to avoid bridging altogether. This is done by defining the grain of the fact table as "order lines allocated to salesreps."

TIP Double-counting can be avoided by adding an allocation to the bridge table and aggregating allocated facts. Ownership of allocation factors must rest with the business community, not the technical community. If a clean allocation factor exists, consider the possibility of changing the grain of the fact table instead.

Some facts cannot be meaningfully allocated. Suppose that Ann and Henry's $1,000 sale was a single item, perhaps a refrigerator. If the fact table had a column called quantity_ordered, it would contain the value 1. Allocating this fact produces fractional quantities; Ann will appear to have sold three quarters of a refrigerator. This may be confusing but is perhaps tolerable.

Supplementing the Bridge with a Primary Member Another way to avoid the danger of double-counting is to hide the bridge from inexperienced users. This is done by supplementing the bridged solution with a simplified solution recognizing only one dimension row. The bridge is hidden from everyone except carefully trained analysts. In the case of our sales example, such a solution is depicted in Figure 9-6.

Notice that a new foreign key has been added to the fact table: primary_salesrep_key. Every order has only one primary salesperson, so this can be used safely to join to salsrep to order_facts in the standard one-to-many configuration. The crow's feet are included on the diagram to drive this point home.

TIP When designing a bridge between a dimension and fact table, supplement it with a direct relationship that isolates a primary role in a one-to-many relationship. This can be used without fear of double-counting, although the bridge will be required for some forms of reporting.

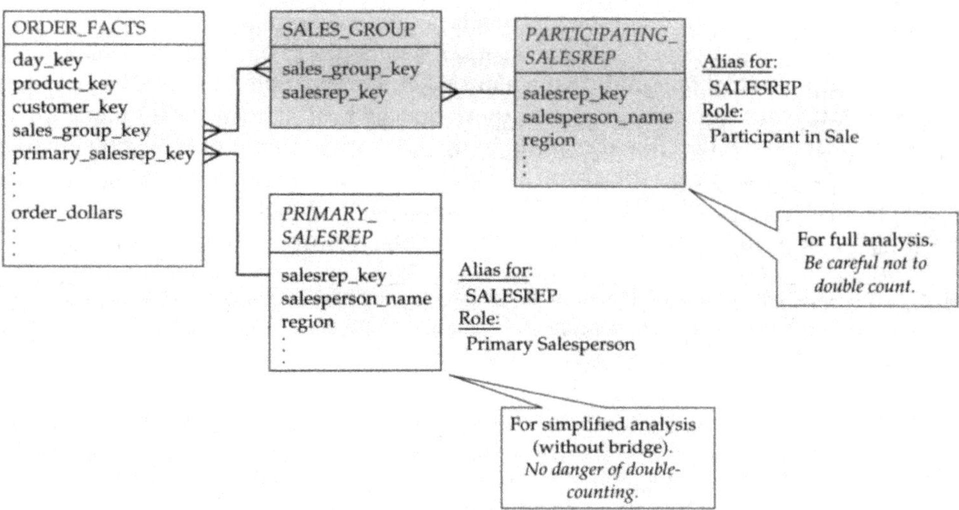

Figure 9-6 Primary group member can be used for simplified analysis

This solution combines the full flexibility of the bridge with a safe, simplified relationship. The shaded tables are hidden from end users, who are able to produce basic reports that only include the primary salesperson. Only trained analysts have access to the bridge table. When a report is required that factors in collaboration, they will be tapped to produce it.

Other Impacts of Bridging

If a bridged solution is chosen, special attention must be given to the behavior of slowly changing dimensions. It may also be necessary to add yet another table to the mix in order to satisfy the quirks of some software products.

Slow Changes As you learned at the end of Chapter 7, snowflake designs require that special attention be paid to the implications of slow changes. In the case of the dimension bridge, the implications are straightforward:

- If a bridged dimension row undergoes a type 1 change, it will remain associated with any existing groups. This behavior is desired.
- If a bridged dimension undergoes a type 2 change, a new group will be required the next time members collaborate.

In the example from Figure 9-4, if a type 1 attribute for Ann is updated, no further processing will be required. Ann will remain associated with group 1. On the other hand, if Ann undergoes a type 2 change, a new row will be created in the salesrep table with a new surrogate key. The next time Ann and Henry collaborate, it will be necessary to create a new group.

There may also be other situations to consider. If the groupings themselves are identifiable entities, it is possible to think about the groups themselves as undergoing slow changes—both to attributes of the group and to membership in the group. If the groups correspond to a well-defined entity in a source system, the group table may have one or more descriptive attributes and even a natural key. For example, Ann and Henry's group in Figure 9-4 may have a name, such as "Eastern Special Project Team." This name will repeat for the two rows that describe the group in the sales_group table. It is possible to allow for type 1 or type 2 changes to the group attribute. A type 1 change to the group name, for example, would overwrite both rows in the bridge table. A type 2 change would require creating a new group with two new rows in the table, one for each group member.

NOTE This situation, and any situation where groups are identifiable entities, would be better modeled by defining the group as a dimension table, and the members as multi-valued attributes. See the next section of this chapter for more details.

Changes in membership of closely tracked groups are slightly more complex. Suppose, for example, that Henry is dumped from the team, and two other salespeople are added. If the change in group membership is to be handled as a type 1 change, it is necessary to delete the row for Henry in the group table and add two new rows for the new team members. Like a type 1 change to a dimension row, this has the effect of associating previously recorded facts with the new information.

Handling the change in group membership as a type 2 change is slightly more involved. It will be necessary to establish a new group, and add rows to the bridge table for each member of the changed group. These changes to group membership may even be time-stamped, as discussed in Chapter 8, providing a history of point-in-time status of the group.

Resolving the Many-to-Many Relationship It has already been noted that a dimension bridge has a many-to-many relationship with the fact table. Although useful in a dimensional design, this form of relationship is strictly forbidden in the world of entity-relationship modeling. The principles of normalization call for such relationships to be "resolved."

Unfortunately, many software products have evolved to assume that this kind of relationship cannot exist. Database modeling tools, for example, may refuse to allow such a relationship in a design. SQL-generating business intelligence software may refuse to accept such relationships when being configured. Even the RDBMS itself may balk at the many-to-many join. Because these tools define relationships as primary key–foreign key relationships, they don't have a way to define a many-to-many relationship.

The bridge table from Figure 9-4 illustrates this conundrum. The relationship between order_facts and sales_group is many-to-many. Each order may refer to multiple rows in sales_group, as seen in the picture. If the group collaborates more than once, each group will refer to multiple orders. When a tool requires each foreign key to refer to the primary key of another table, there is no way to define this relationship. Although we want to join using the sales_group_key, it does not serve as a primary key in any table.

One solution is not to declare the relationship to the modeling tool or RDBMS. You can still issue SQL queries that make use of this relationship, but this may not be an option if you need to print a diagram showing the relationship, configure a SQL-generating ad hoc query tool, or configure the database to perform a star join.

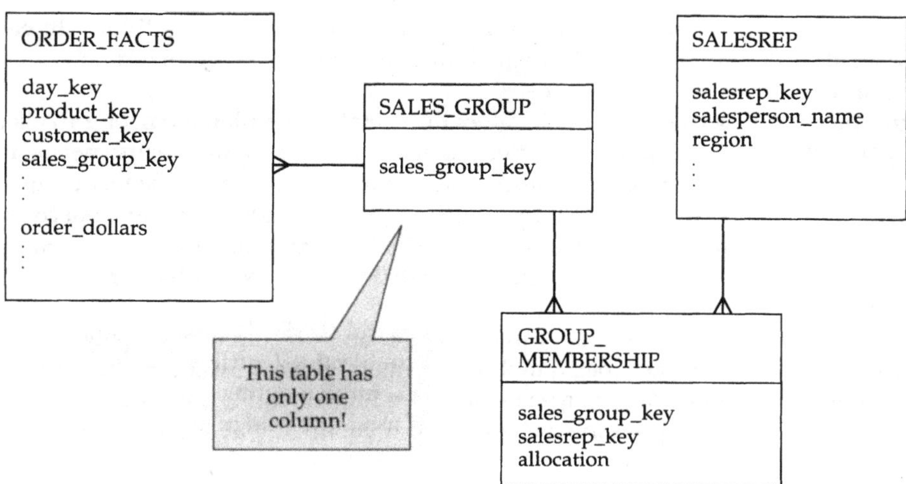

Figure 9-7 Resolving the many-to-many relationship

The solution to this problem is to do what an entity-relationship modeler would do: construct what they call an "intersect table." In the case of the dimensional model, this will have an amusing side effect: it requires you to maintain a group table with only one column, which is a key value. Figure 9-7 provides an example.

The many-to-many relationship between groups and salespeople is resolved by creating an intersect table called group_membership. The sales_group table is left with a single column, the group_key. If you issue the query `select * from sales_group`, the contents of this table would appear as a sequence of numbers. Although this may seem silly, this configuration should satisfy even the most particular of modeling tools. A primary key can be defined for the group table: sales_group_key. This allows the column to be used as a foreign key in the fact table.

TIP If you have a software product that will not allow a many-to-many relationship, you can create an intersect table to resolve it.

If the sales_group table in this revised solution seems extraneous, that's because it is. All the information is present in the group_membership table. The sales_group table is completely redundant. In fact, if you look closely, you will see that the group_membership table is identical to the original bridge! The necessity of this absurdity stems from software products that enforce entity-relationship modeling conventions on your dimensional design.

Multi-Valued Attributes

When a dimension attribute may take on more than one value for any given row in the table, we face a similar design challenge. How does one model an indefinite number of attribute values for a single row in the dimension? This situation is common. Customers have multiple phone numbers. Bank accounts have multiple account holders.

Students have multiple guardians. Patients have multiple medical conditions. In each case, a small subset of the dimension's attributes may take on more than one value for a single natural key value.

Attributes that may take on multiple values for a single dimension member are called *multi-valued attributes*. For example, in a dimension that captures business customers, it may be necessary to capture the company's industry. Each company has a single name, headquarters location, and chief executive. Most companies are in a single industry, as well, but some are in two, three, or any number of industries. Figure 9-8 illustrates this challenge. Company C operates in two industries, and it is possible that other companies may have three, four, or any number.

Like the multi-valued dimension, this challenge can be resolved by simplifying the problem or by using a bridge table. Simplifying a multi-valued attribute is often the best approach but sometimes limits analytic possibilities. Implementing a bridge provides increased analytic flexibility but introduces risk. If used, the bridge will be placed between the dimension and an outrigger.

As in the multi-valued dimension scenario, bridging a multi-valued attribute will introduce the risk of double-counting. Any given fact may link to more than one value for the bridged attribute, giving rise to the same set of problems encountered earlier. While the entire dimension table is not at risk this time, the repeating attributes are.

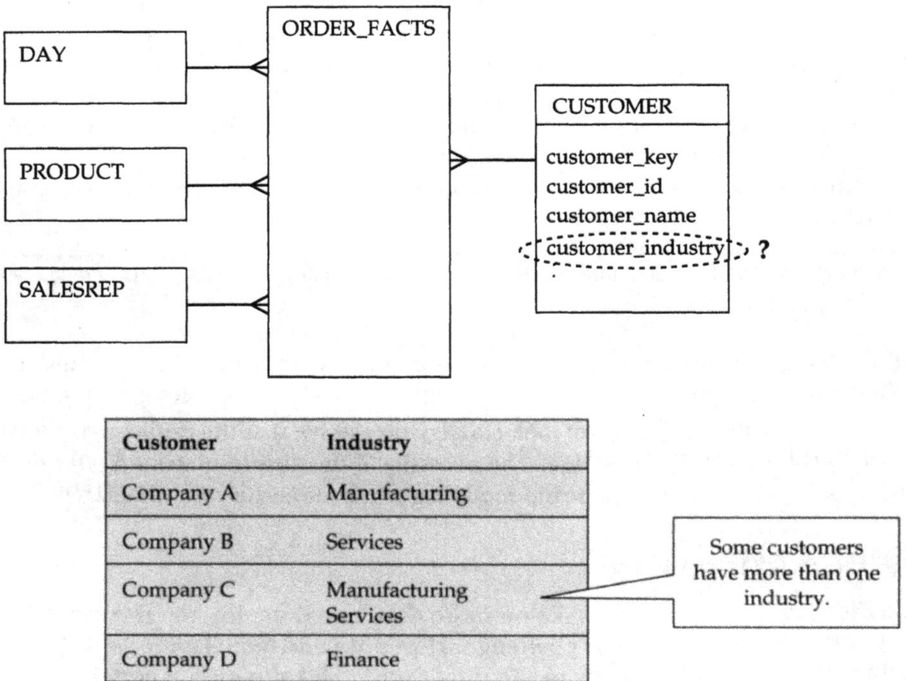

Customer	Industry
Company A	Manufacturing
Company B	Services
Company C	Manufacturing Services
Company D	Finance

Figure 9-8 A multi-valued attribute

Simplifying the Multi-Valued Attribute

When you are faced with multi-valued attributes, the first option to consider is simplification of the problem through a technique that is sometimes referred to as "flattening." Instead of designing a single column to capture the attribute, you can include two or more columns. For example, multiple phone numbers for a customer can be captured by designing separate columns for home phone number, office phone number, and mobile phone number. The multi-valued attribute is transposed into a repeating attribute.

This approach works best where a limited number of values is acceptable, where each version corresponds to an easily identifiable role, and where it will not be necessary to filter or group transactions in a fact table using values that may occur in any of the columns. In the case of phone numbers, these three conditions may be satisfied. The business is comfortable with carrying a maximum of three phone numbers in their analysis; each of the three numbers has a clearly identifiable role—home, office, mobile—and there will not be a need to search for or group transactions by a phone number that may appear in any of the three columns.

TIP When faced with a multi-valued attribute, evaluate the possibility of simplifying it into a fixed number of single-valued attributes. If the repeating attributes will not be used to filter or group query results, this is the simplest option.

In the example of company industries, simplifying the multi-valued attribute into a finite number of single-valued attributes is not viable. Illustrated in Figure 9-9, the dimension table is able to store three industry values for each customer. This solution has several shortcomings:

- The solution is limited to a specific number of values. Later, we may encounter a customer that requires more than three industries.
- Filtering a query for a particular industry will require defining multiple conditions, since the industry in question may appear in any one of the columns.
- Grouping facts by industry will be particularly challenging, since a given industry may appear in any of the three columns.

CUSTOMER
customer_key customer_id customer_name industry_1 industry_2 industry_3 ⋮

Simplified multi-valued attribute: industry_1, industry_2, industry_3

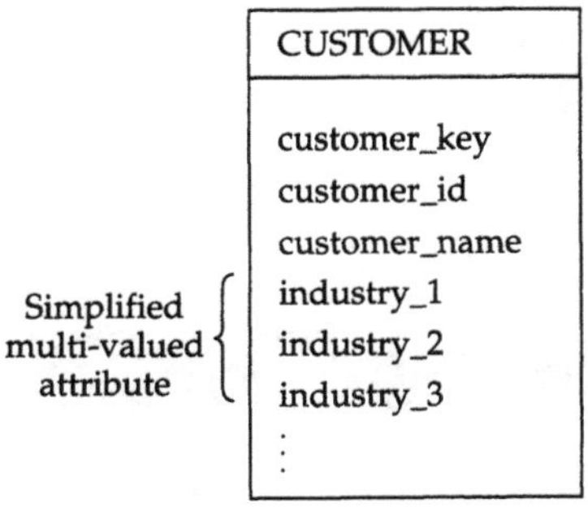

Figure 9-9 Simplifying a multi-valued industry attribute

The drawbacks to the simplification of a multi-valued attribute may seem familiar; they are similar to those identified when simplifying a many-to-many relationship between dimension table and fact table. The alternative is also similar: introduction of a bridge table.

Using an Attribute Bridge

An attribute bridge can be used to model multi-valued attributes in a dimension table. Technically speaking, these attributes will not be in the dimension table itself. Instead, they are placed in an outrigger. A bridge associates the values, providing a flexible and powerful solution. With this power comes risk; as with the dimension bridge, the possibility of double-counting exists.

Bridging the Relationship

A multi-valued attribute can be supported using an attribute bridge table, which works in much the same way as the dimension bridge in the previous section. This time, instead of placing the bridge between fact table and dimension table, the bridge will be placed between the dimension table and an outrigger. Here's how it works:

- The multi-valued attributes are not stored in the dimension table. Instead, they are placed in a separate table with its own surrogate key. This table will act as an outrigger.
- A bridge table is set up with two columns: a group_key and a second column referring to the outrigger.
- When a dimension row refers to a specific combination of values in the outrigger, a group is set up for those values in the bridge table.
- The dimension table and the bridge can be joined using the group_key; the bridge table is joined to the outrigger in turn.

Once again, this solution is best understood via an example. The design in Figure 9-10 uses a group table to capture multiple industries for each customer. Industry attributes are not stored in the customer dimension; instead, they are located in an outrigger table called industry. Customers and industries share a many-to-many relationship, so it is not possible to design a solution where these tables are joined directly. Instead, a group table is used to bridge the relationship between a given customer and its industry designations.

To understand the workings of this solution, look at the instance diagrams in the lower half of the figure. You may recall that Company C participates in two industries: manufacturing

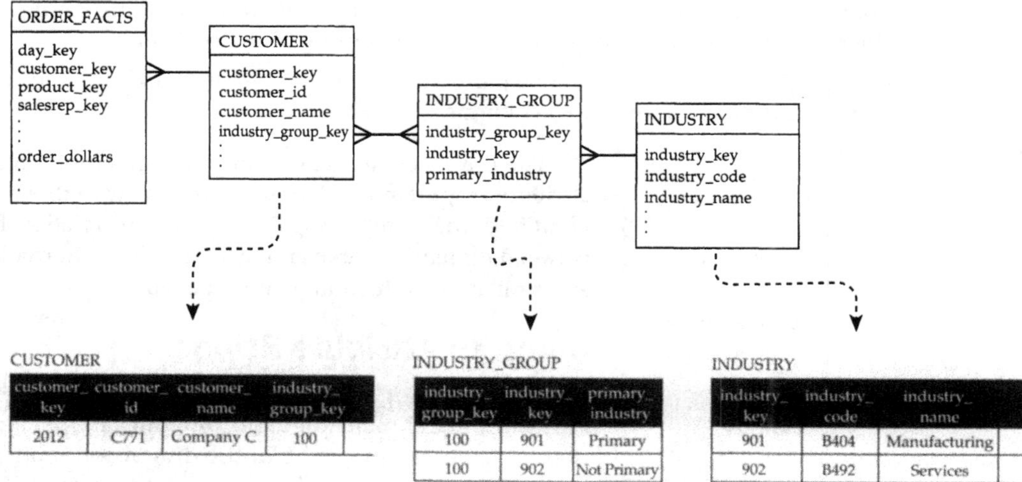

CUSTOMER

customer_key	customer_id	customer_name	industry_group_key
2012	C771	Company C	100

INDUSTRY_GROUP

industry_group_key	industry_key	primary_industry
100	901	Primary
100	902	Not Primary

INDUSTRY

industry_key	industry_code	industry_name
901	B404	Manufacturing
902	B492	Services

Figure 9-10 An attribute bridge table

and services. To represent this state of affairs, a group is set up in the industry_group table with an industry_group_key value of 100. The table for industry_group_key 100 has two rows; one has an industry_key value of 901, the other has an industry_key value of 902. These refer to manufacturing and services in the industry table. In the company table, the row for Company C simply references the group.

This approach provides maximum analytic flexibility. Unlike the flattened solution, it can accommodate groups of any size. In addition, it is easy to use an industry name to filter or group query results, simply by joining together the customer, industry_group, and industry tables. As before, the presence of the bridge will require additional work when loading the schema. The ETL process must detect and manage groupings. Groups with one member will be necessary for companies that have only one industry.

TIP Compared to a solution that simplifies multi-valued attributes, using a bridge table offers increased flexibility and simplifies reporting challenges.

Just as the benefits of the attribute bridge table mirror those of the dimension bridge table, so do the other impacts. It will be necessary to avoid double-counting and to consider the ramifications of changed data; it may also be necessary to work around the limitations of software products that will not tolerate a many-to-many relationship.

Double-Counting

When a query joins a dimension table to a bridged outrigger as well as a fact table, facts may be double-counted. This situation is sometimes called for but is also dangerous. Anyone who does not take care when aggregating the facts may produce erroneous results.

To understand this possibility, think about Company C once more. Through the bridge, it is linked to two rows in the industry table. You can see this quite clearly in Figure 9-10. If you were to join these tables together, the SQL would look like this:

```
SELECT
  customer.customer_name,
  industry.industry_name
FROM
  customer, industry_group, industry
WHERE
  customer.industry_group_key = industry_group.industry_group_key AND
  industry_group.industry_key = industry.industry_key;
```

When this query is executed, the result set will contain two rows for Company C:

```
CUSTOMER_NAME  INDUSTRY_NAME
=============  ==============
Company C      Manufacturing
Company C      Services

2 rows selected.
```

This occurs because the join conditions result in two industry matches for Company C; the RDBMS dutifully repeats company row once for each match.

Now consider what happens if a fact table is added to this query. Suppose Company C placed a $10,000 order that appears in the order_facts table. Adding the fact table to the query looks like this:

```
SELECT
  customer.customer_name,
  industry.industry_name,
  sum( order_dollars )
FROM
  order_facts, customer, industry_group, industry
WHERE
  order_facts.customer_key = customer.customer_key AND
  customer.industry_group_key = industry_group.industry_group_key AND
  industry_group.industry_key = industry.industry_key
GROUP BY
  customer_name, industry_name
```

In order to process this query, the RDBMS will repeat the $10,000 order for each related industry.

```
CUSTOMER_NAME  INDUSTRY_NAME  SUM(ORDER_DOLLARS)
=============  =============  ==================
Company C      Manufacturing              10,000
Company C      Services                   10,000

2 rows selected.
```

In some cases, this double-counting is just what is needed. For example, it is easy to produce a report that totals order dollars by industry. Once again, however, there is the danger that someone will misuse this information, constructing a grand total.

Primary Member and Hiding the Bridge

If it is possible to identify a single, primary member of each group, the bridge can be hidden from inexperienced users, while still providing limited access to the bridged attribute. This is achieved by adding a flag to the group table indicating the primary member of the group. A view or similar mechanism is used to hide all but the primary member from inexperienced users. Only trained developers will receive full access to the bridged solution.

The example from Figure 9-10 already bears the features necessary to implement such a scheme. Notice that the bridge table industry_group contains a column called primary_industry. For each group, only one row will have this flag set to the value "Primary." When the industry_group bridge is used to link the customer and industry tables, filtering for the value "Primary" will guarantee a single match. Every customer has exactly one primary industry. The same effect can be achieved by placing a primary_industry column in the customer table.

TIP When an attribute bridge is employed, any query involving the outrigger risks the possibility of double-counting. This risk can be minimized by using a flag to isolate a single member for each group; this can be used to constrain the view of the schema presented to inexperienced users.

When a report is required that factors in the variety of industries in which a company participates, trained developers will be called on to do the work. With unfettered access to the bridged solution, only they will be able to produce these impact reports. Measures may also be required to ensure that an end user who receives such a report will not have the ability to press a button for a grand total.

NOTE Business intelligence products that generate SQL queries can be hampered by designs in which there are more than one way to relate tables. Advice for handling this complication is provided in Chapter 16, "Design and Business Intelligence."

The Impact of Changes

As in any snowflaked situation, the presence of an attribute bridge will require careful attention to the impact of changes in source data. Type 2 changes in particular require careful scrutiny. Changes to the outrigger, the groupings, or the dimension itself may have ripple effects that impact other group members.

The Impact of Changes to the Outrigger As you learned in Chapter 7, snowflake designs require extra vigilance on the part of ETL developers. If an outrigger undergoes a type 2 slow change, it will most likely be appropriate for any associated dimension rows to do the same. In addition, it may be necessary to contemplate changes in group membership.

For example, a change to an industry classification may be handled by using the standard methods. A type 1 change causes little concern; the outrigger is simply updated. If, however, the change is handled as type 2, then every company referring to the changed industry is affected, as are the associated groups. For example, if "Services" is redesignated as the more descriptive "Financial Services," and this is handled as a type 2 change, a new row will be generated in the outrigger table. To associate this value with Company C for future facts, while leaving prior facts associated with the old value, it will be necessary to create a new version of Company C. This new version of Company C will be associated with a new set of rows in the group table for "financial services" and "manufacturing."

If a new version of Company C is not created in this manner, then the type 2 change to the industry will not be properly reflected when studying facts. For example, taking a shortcut by simply updating group 100 with the new key for the financial services industry effectively wipes out the old designation's association with previously recorded facts. Usually, if a type 2 change occurs in an outrigger, this is not the desired behavior.

TIP Type 2 changes in an outrigger will require type 2 changes in the dimension and new groups in the bridge table. These can also be supplemented with time stamps, if desired.

As with the dimension bridge, the story does not end here. Changes to group membership may also require attention. In this case, a simple change to one member may have a ripple effect that impacts multiple rows in the dimension table and the bridge.

The Impact of Changes to Group Membership Although they are represented through an outrigger and bridge, it is important to keep in mind that these structures are all used to accommodate the multi-valued attributes of the dimension table. The multi-valued attribute can be thought of as part of the dimension itself, even though it is implemented as a bridge and outrigger. If there is a change in the multi-valued attribute, it can be treated as type 1 or type 2. A type 1 change is a simple matter of updating a group key in the dimension table, but a type 2 change is more complicated. It will require a type 2 change in the dimension, along with the establishment of a new group in the bridge table.

For example, if Company C leaves the services industry and enters the insurance industry, it will be necessary to change its associations with the outrigger table. As a type 1 response, this may be handled by replacing the customer's industry_group_key with one that represents the new combination of industries.

A type 2 response to this change is more involved. The previously existing combination of industries must be preserved and linked to any previously recorded facts linked with Company C. In the dimension table, Company C must undergo a type 2 response; a new row will be inserted with the new group key. In documenting the dimension table, it is useful to flag the group_key as a type 2 attribute, in order to signal to developers that any change to a company's mix of industries will require a new row.

TIP In cases where the history of changes to group membership is to be maintained, any change to a group will require creating a row in the dimension table that refers to the revised grouping.

This concept is difficult for many practitioners to understand. If you have trouble with it, you can think of it this way: the group represented in the bridge and outrigger is itself a characteristic of the dimension. If the group undergoes a change, the thing represented by the dimension has changed.

Although some developers like to time-stamp the rows in the attribute bridge table, observe that a time stamp on the dimension table itself is sufficient. It captures the period of time during which the particular grouping was in effect for the dimension row. Placing time stamps in the bridge table does not add any information. Moreover, it now requires a separate group for each company that participates in the same set of industries. Time-stamping bridge table rows usually only makes sense for dimension bridge tables, as in the previous section.

The Impact of Changes to the Dimension Last, the dimension table itself may have to respond to changes in source data. In the case of a type 2 change, the new "version" will have a new surrogate key. If the multi-valued attributes have not changed, the new row can reuse the same group_key. For example, Company C may undergo a type 2 slow change to information unrelated to its industry. This causes a new row to be inserted in the customer table for Company C, with a new surrogate key. Company C is still in the same mix of industries, so the new row in the dimension table can refer to the same group of industries.

Other Impacts of the Attribute Bridge

Because they are usually described as "group" tables, bridge tables cause all kinds of confusion when the multi-valued attribute to be bridged is itself a group. Keep focused on the concept of bridging to work though this kind of design challenge. It may also be necessary to resolve the many-to-many relationship between dimension table and bridge if you have software products that will not acknowledge this kind of relationship.

When an Outrigger Represents Groups The word "group" has been used to describe the bridge table in these examples, because it is used to bundle a set of attributes into a group. Don't allow this terminology to confuse you. The bridge table is an association table, linking together the things on either side of it. This will help you through situations in which the multi-valued attribute is itself a group. For example, an employee dimension may be linked to an outrigger representing employee groups. These groups may represent committees, unions, or other associations. The groups are represented by an outrigger. The bridge associates each employee with the groups of which she is a member.

TIP When the outrigger is a group, try not to use the word "group" to describe the bridge. Doing so will lead to confusion.

The standard bridge table caveats apply when multi-valued attributes are real-world groups. Any employee may be a member of more than one group. If groups are brought into the query, the employee will be double-counted. This may or may not be desired, and controls will need to be put in place to mitigate the risk of double-counting. ETL developers will have their work cut out for them, and it will be necessary to plan how source changes will impact each component of the final design.

Folding the Outrigger into the Bridge If there are only one or two multi-valued attributes, the outrigger table may be deemed unnecessary. The attributes can be placed in the bridge table, simplifying the configuration. For example, the industry table in Figure 9-10 can be eliminated by placing the industry code and name directly into the industry_group table.

This approach will reduce the number of tables and joins in the solution. Industry names will be stored redundantly, but this is a common feature of dimension tables. It will be necessary to index the table appropriately, and also to take care that industry names appear identically each time they repeat.

Resolving the Many-to-Many Relationship An attribute bridge table usually shares a many-to-many relationship with the dimension table it supports. As mentioned earlier in this chapter, many tools cannot abide such relationships. Although it is possible to design, build, and use a design like this, the relationship may get in the way of optimal configuration of the database or business intelligence tool, and some modeling tools may not be able to represent it.

In these cases, the relationship can be resolved in two ways. The first option is to break the bridge table down into two tables: a table with one row for each group, and a membership table. The membership table serves as an intersect between the group and the outrigger, resolving the many-to-many relationship in the same way that the dimension bridge was resolved in Figure 9-7. The group table will have exactly one column, and its content will consist entirely of key values. An example appears in Figure 9-11.

Here, the many-to-many relationship between customer and industry grouping has been resolved by altering the group table. In this design, the table has one row for each group. Each row consists of a single column, identifying the group. The set of industries that associates with the group is now captured in group_membership, which looks exactly like the original bridge table.

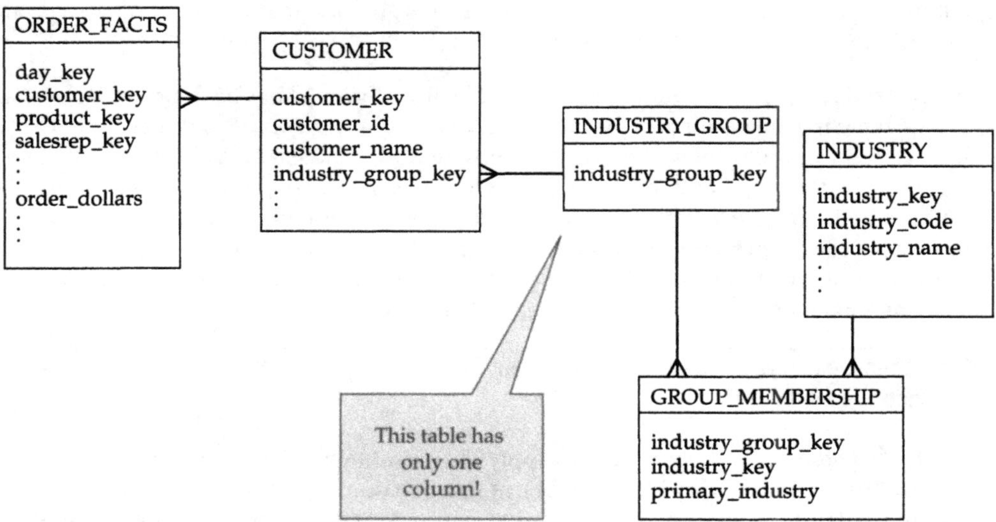

Figure 9-11 Resolving the many-to-many relationship

TIP If you have a software product that will not allow a many-to-many relationship, you can create an intersect table to resolve it. It looks silly, but it works.

The industry_group table in this example is entirely redundant. All information is present in the group_membership table. If you were to look at its content, it would be nothing more than a sequence of integers. Nevertheless, this design will satisfy tools that require a primary key–foreign key relationship to drive each join.

Another way to resolve the many-to-many relationship is to remove the group key from the dimension table and replace the bridge with a simple intersect table. Each row in the intersect table contains foreign keys that refer to a row in the dimension and a row in the outrigger. With industry groups, for example, the customer table and industry table are linked by an intersect table that contains a customer_key and industry_key. No group key is present in the customer table. The intersect table in this solution may grow larger than the one in Figure 9-11, since groupings cannot be not reused by more than one customer.

Bridge as Fact Table Because it consists primarily of foreign keys, a bridge table bears a strong resemblance to a fact table. Although it contains no facts, it serves the same purpose: capturing the relationship between attributes in the related tables. In Figure 9-10, industry_group resembles a fact table; it contains multiple key references to other tables. This resemblance is even stronger for the group_membership table in Figure 9-11, where the many-to-many relationship is resolved.

NOTE There *is* such a thing as a *factless fact table*, and the concept is fully explored in Chapter 12.

Many dimensionally aware software products will identify bridge tables as fact tables. If they contain allocation factors or flags, these may be identified as degenerate dimensions. It is possible to argue the pros and cons of referring to a bridge table as a fact table, but it would be an exercise in semantics only. Regardless of what you call it, the bridge table serves its purpose. There is, however, one significant consideration.

If you choose to call the bridge a fact table, or if your toolset makes that choice for you, you will need to relax a restriction that was introduced in Chapter 4. As you may recall, that chapter explored the consequences of joining two fact tables together. Because this kind of query can result in a Cartesian product, or double-counting, Chapter 4 cautioned not to do it, and instead recommended following drill-across procedures.

As you have seen in this chapter, a bridge table exploits this same Cartesian effect in a useful and powerful way. To call it a fact table, then, will require making an exception to the rule not to join fact tables. When one of the fact tables is a bridge, the join is essential and the Cartesian product is intended.

Summary

This chapter has provided tools to address real-life complexity that cannot fit within the traditional one-to-many relationship between dimension table and fact table. A quick recap of the primary lessons:

- When a fact must refer to more than one instance of a dimension, it may be possible to simplify the many-to-many relationship into multiple one-to-many relationships.
- This simplification may be less than satisfying, because it makes several types of reporting more difficult and only supports a fixed number of dimension values.
- A bridge table allows a fact table row to be associated with any number of dimension rows, and keeps the reporting simple.
- The bridge table makes it very easy to double count facts, so access and usage must be carefully controlled.
- A bridge may contain an allocation factor or be supplemented by a simplified relationship that isolates a single instance in a primary role.
- The many-to-many relationship introduced by the bridge can be resolved via an intersect table if required by your toolset.
- The presence of a bridge makes it necessary to think carefully about the implications of slow changes, not only to attributes but also to relationships.
- An attribute bridge works the same way as a dimension bridge but is placed between a dimension table and an outrigger.
- Some tools identify bridge tables as fact tables because they carry multiple foreign keys. This is fine, but be sure that the tool does not decide to drill across.
- Slow change considerations impact bridged solutions in interesting ways. A type 2 change can have a ripple effect that will impact multiple rows in multiple tables.

This is not the end of the story on the powerful but dangerous bridge table. The next chapter will show you how a hierarchy bridge can be used to represent a recursive relationship among dimension members, allowing facts to be rolled up or down to any level in a ragged hierarchy.

Further Reading

Bridge tables are complicated but powerful. If you are still struggling with any of the concepts in this chapter, it may help to see other examples. Here are some places you will find them:

Multi-Valued Dimensions

- In a health care example, Kimball and Ross describe the use of a bridge table to associate a billing fact table with multiple diagnoses. This allows the construction of an impact report illustrating total costs associated with any given diagnosis. This example also contains an allocation factor. See Chapter 13 of *The Data Warehouse Toolkit, Second Edition* (Wiley, 2002).
- The possibility of time-stamping changes to group membership in a dimension bridge table was suggested but not illustrated. For an example, see the earlier referenced health care scenario from Kimball and Ross. Although the time stamp is not pictured in the example, it is described in the text. It should be obvious that to maintain the time stamp it will be necessary to have a separate group for each patient who has the same set of diagnoses.
- Building aggregates to summarize within a bridged dimension can be risky. It is important to consider how to summarize the data appropriately, how double-counting will be eliminated, and what the resulting aggregate actually describes. I deal with this topic in Chapter 8 of *Mastering Data Warehouse Aggregates* (Wiley, 2006).

Multi-Valued Dimension Attributes

- In Chapter 8 of *The Data Warehouse Toolkit,* Kimball and Ross use a bridge to associate multiple skills with each employee in an employee dimension table.
- In the same example, Kimball and Ross explore an alternative not discussed in this book: the creation of a single attribute that concatenates the multiple values. This solution is effective when used with SQL substring functions to search for particular values but cannot be used to group results for an impact report.
- Kimball and Ross also show how an attribute bridge can be used to associate multiple account holders with an account dimension in Chapter 9 of *The Data Warehouse Toolkit.*

CHAPTER 10 Recursive Hierarchies and Bridges

Recursive hierarchies in real-world data pose one of the most perplexing challenges for dimensional designers. This chapter explores two ways to model this kind of hierarchy. One is simple and safe but is limited in its capabilities. The other is powerful and flexible but also easy to misuse and difficult to manage. Choosing between these options requires fully understanding the implications of both.

A recursive hierarchy is a set of relationships among instances of the same kind of object or entity. In a corporate organizational structure, one department may report to another department, which in turn reports to still another department. Systems of describing geographic regions can also be recursive, with regions falling within other regions.

These recursive hierarchies present a unique reporting challenge. When studying facts, people will want to choose a position in the hierarchy and report on all activity below it or above it. "Show me the total spending in departments beneath mine," is one example. If the hierarchy is to be used as a means for aggregating facts, it must be represented in the dimensional model.

The simple solution is to "flatten" the hierarchy, identifying a fixed number of levels that will be associated with each instance. For every department, for example, a flattened hierarchy might record the top-level and second-level departments to which it reports. As you will see, flattened hierarchies have the advantage of fitting nicely into the standard dimensional framework. Unfortunately, they are not always satisfying from an analytic perspective.

A far more powerful solution uses a hierarchy bridge table. Like the dimension bridge tables of Chapter 9, the hierarchy bridge table is a double-edged sword. The solution is able to address a much wider range of analytic questions than a flattened solution, and it does so with great flexibility. However, this analytic capability is accompanied by an increase in the complexity of the solution, danger of misuse, and significant new demands on the ETL process. These considerations are far more significant than those associated with the dimension bridges of Chapter 9, and often outweigh the analytic advantages.

The decision to use a hierarchy bridge, or not to use one, is important. It will have impacts in a variety of areas and requires evaluation by a group of team members representing different functions. To participate in such a decision, it is important to understand the options fully.

Recursive Hierarchies

In Chapter 7, you learned about attribute hierarchies. This term describes relationships between *columns* in a dimension table. The attributes of a typical product dimension table illustrate this concept: each product falls within a brand, each brand falls within a category. A dimensional design does not separate the levels of an attribute hierarchy into separate tables, but any level can easily be used to filter or group the facts.

Some hierarchies cannot be defined in this manner. When there is a relationship between particular *rows* of a dimension, rather than attributes, there is an *instance hierarchy*. This kind of hierarchy is said to be *recursive*, because each instance may refer to another. A recursive hierarchy is hard to represent in a single table without compromising the analytic possibilities. Contrary to popular opinion, this holds true whether the hierarchy has a fixed number of levels (balanced) or not (unbalanced).

Rows Referring to Other Rows

An instance hierarchy is a set of relationships among the individual rows of a table. The word *instance* refers to the data in a specific row. The simplest example of an instance hierarchy is a self-referring relationship. In an entity-relationship design, a self-referring relationship is one where each row of a table may directly refer to another row in the same table. Not all instance hierarchies involve direct self-reference, but this example will illustrate the key challenge.

An example of a self-referring relationship in an entity-relationship model appears in Figure 10-1. This diagram suggests that any given company may have a parent company. Unlike an attribute hierarchy, it is not possible to describe this relationship using the attributes of the entity in question—a company, in this case. With the product attribute hierarchy, we were able to say "products fall within brands; brands fall within categories." In the company instance hierarchy, we cannot use attributes to describe the hierarchy. All we can say is that "companies may be owned by other companies." One instance of a thing refers to another instance of the same kind of thing.

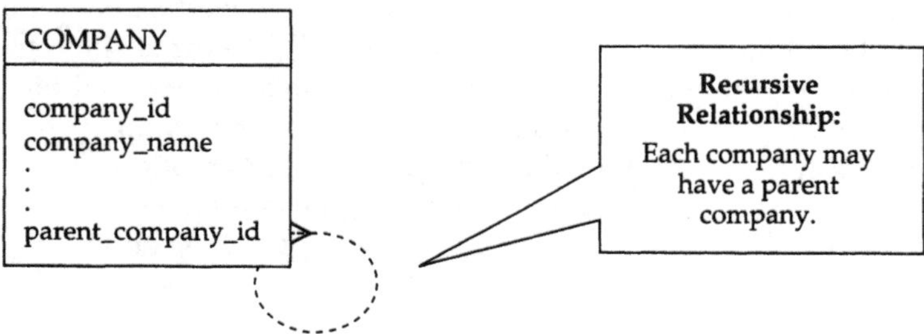

Figure 10-1 A self-referential relationship

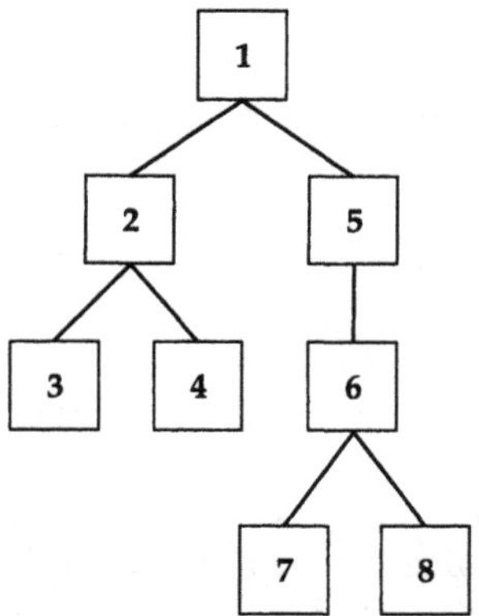

Figure 10-2 Companies under Company 1

At first glance, you might not recognize the illustration in Figure 10-1 as a hierarchy. It appears to be a single table. However, the "pig's ear" is a recursive relationship. This relationship can be read in two directions: each company may have a parent, and each company may have one or more children. When you trace through these nested relationships, a hierarchy emerges. One company may own several others, each of which in turn owns still others.

For example, Figure 10-2 shows a set of relationships among companies that can be traced back to one particular company, called Company 1. Notice that this hierarchy has an indefinite number of levels. Four levels are present in the example, with Company 1 at the top. There is no guarantee that all companies will participate in ownership structures with four levels. Other top-level companies may sit atop hierarchies that are shallower or deeper. Even beneath Company 1, not all branches of this hierarchy have the same number of levels.

A hierarchy like this one is variously referred to as an *unbalanced hierarchy* or a *variable-depth hierarchy*. Examples of other instance hierarchies that exhibit these characteristics include a parts breakdown structure (part assemblies composed of other part assemblies), departmental ownership (departments made up of other departments), reporting structures (employees reporting to other employees), and some geographical systems (regions falling within other regions).

Part III

Balanced vs. Unbalanced, Attribute-Based vs. Instance-Based

This book makes the distinction between attribute hierarchies and instance hierarchies. Attribute hierarchies are defined as a set of mandatory parent–child relationships among subsets of attributes. Instance hierarchies are defined as relationships between rows of the dimension. Instance hierarchies are recursive.

Another common way to understand hierarchies is to categorize them as balanced or unbalanced. A balanced hierarchy contains a fixed number of clearly defined levels, while an unbalanced hierarchy does not.

By definition, all attribute hierarchies are balanced. With a set of mandatory cascading parent–child relationships, the attribute hierarchy can always be described in terms of a fixed number of clearly defined levels. Every product has a brand; every brand has a category. Three levels always exist. If this were not the case, it would not meet the definition of an attribute hierarchy.

Instance hierarchies are usually unbalanced, but not always. In rare cases, instance hierarchies resolve into a fixed number of levels. For example, the departmental structure within a company may allow for a fixed number of levels. This possibility will be explored later in this chapter. It is somewhat rare, but when it occurs it does not always simplify the reporting challenges.

The Reporting Challenge

When users want to use a recursive instance hierarchy to summarize facts, a single dimension table solution provides some roadblocks. These roadblocks appear when users want to single out a particular member of the hierarchy and use it to group facts that are associated with members above or below it. These activities are referred to as "looking down" or "looking up."

The problem with studying facts by looking down or looking up is that the facts are associated with specific members of the dimension, with no regard for how the particular dimension row fits within a hierarchy. Looking up or down will require traversing the hierarchy, and it is here that usability and performance issues arise.

Suppose that a business sells products to other companies, among which are those that fall beneath Company 1 in Figure 10-2. A star schema that tracks orders might include a company table that embodies the recursive relationship. Figure 10-3 shows what the contents of this company dimension would look like. To keep this example simple, the key values correspond to the company names. In real life, of course, surrogate keys have no meaning.

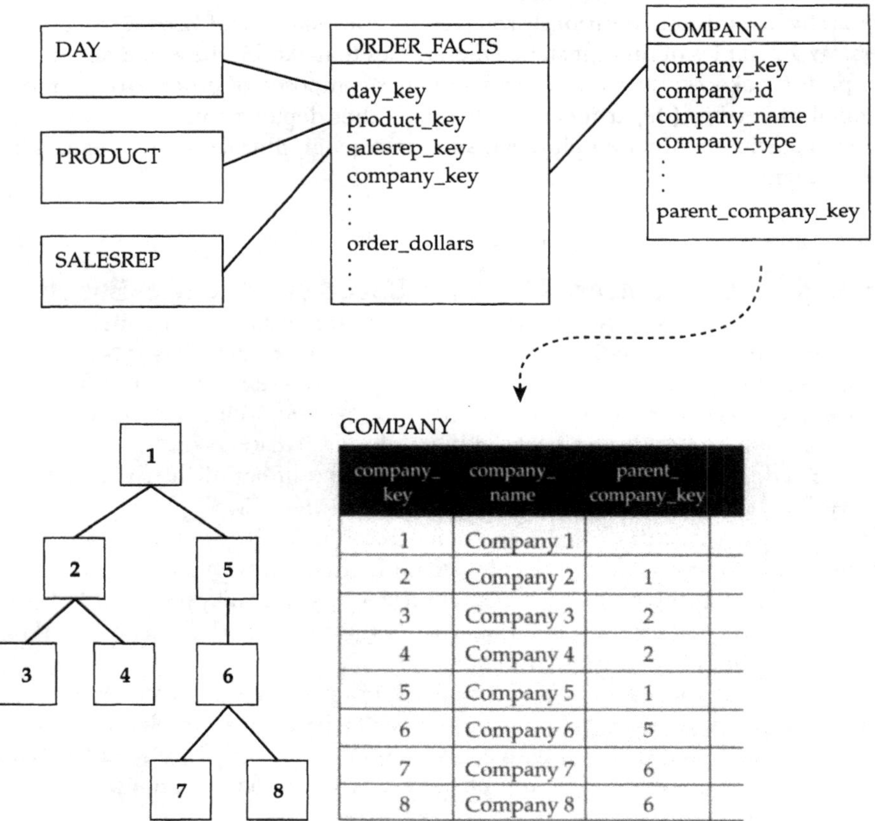

company_key	company_name	parent_company_key
1	Company 1	
2	Company 2	1
3	Company 3	2
4	Company 4	2
5	Company 5	1
6	Company 6	5
7	Company 7	6
8	Company 8	6

Figure 10-3 A recursive company dimension

> **Using Recursive SQL**
>
> It is possible to use *recursive SQL* to query a recursive relationship like the one in Figure 10-3. Unfortunately, most business intelligence tools cannot generate such queries. For this reason, most designers choose to implement one of the options presented in this chapter. There is nothing wrong, however, with designing a solution that will rely on recursive SQL. As long as the impact on the reporting process has been considered, a recursive relationship is acceptable. Be aware that many of the challenges in this chapter will still apply, including the need for multiple query configurations and the ripple effect of type 2 changes.

This star correctly reflects the fact that any company may place an order, regardless of its relationship to other companies. Each row in the fact table refers to a specific company: the company that placed the order. That company's relationships to other companies can be inferred by following the parent_company_key, which refers to the company_key of its owner.

Looking up or looking down occurs when users want to use this hierarchy to summarize facts. For example, if they want to see all orders that take place below a particular company, they want to study orders by looking down the hierarchy. They may also want to see all transactions that take place above a particular company, perhaps because they are considering a volume discount based on the orders of parent companies. In this case, they want to study the facts by looking up.

Neither looking down nor looking up is a simple process. For example:

- **All orders beneath Company 5** (Looking down.) This request requires finding all the companies that list Company 5 as its parent, then all the companies that list those companies as a parent, and so forth. Once the list is compiled, orders for this list of companies can be queried and aggregated.
- **All orders above Company 6** (Looking up.) This request requires using the parent_company_key of Company 6 to locate its parent, then its parent's parent, and so forth. Once the top is reached, orders for this list can be queried and aggregated.

A process known as *flattening* is sometimes called upon to mitigate this challenge. A flattened hierarchy may be easy to build and manage, but falls short of making our example queries easy to answer.

Flattening a Recursive Hierarchy

A recursive hierarchy can be flattened so it is not necessary to traverse a series of relationships at query time. The hierarchy is flattened by creating new attributes that represent a fixed number of levels. The flattened hierarchy looks and behaves like an attribute hierarchy. However, it does not really solve the problems of looking up or looking down. Flattening is most successful if the levels have consistent and distinguishable meanings.

A Flattened Hierarchy

An instance hierarchy can be flattened so it looks more like the attribute hierarchies you have seen before. Columns are added to the dimension to represent a fixed number of hierarchy levels. For each row in the table, the values assigned to these summary columns are computed by traversing the hierarchy ahead of time, during the ETL process. These new attributes "flatten" the hierarchy so it will not be necessary to traverse the recursive relationship at query time.

In the case of companies, for example, we can compute some extra information about each company and store it in new columns. For each company, we will identify the associated top-level company, second-level company, and so forth. These new attributes will become a part of each company's dimension record. Figure 10-4 provides an example. Ignore the shaded cells for the time being; they will be described shortly.

The company dimension in Figure 10-4 is flattened into four levels. As you can see from the instance chart, the various levels of ownership have been computed for each company. For example, the last row in the chart is Company 8. You can see that its level_1_company is Company 1, its level_2_company is Company 5, and so forth. The tree diagram to the left of the table can be used to verify the accuracy of this representation.

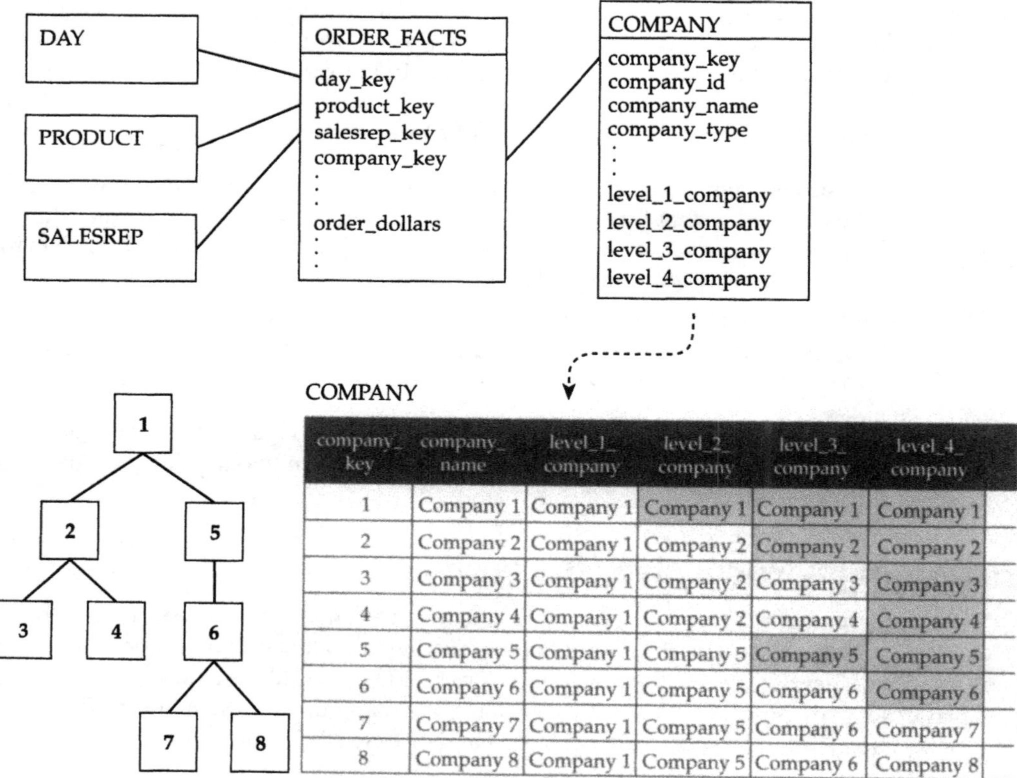

company_key	company_name	level_1_company	level_2_company	level_3_company	level_4_company
1	Company 1	Company 1	Company 1	Company 1	Company 1
2	Company 2	Company 1	Company 2	Company 2	Company 2
3	Company 3	Company 1	Company 2	Company 3	Company 3
4	Company 4	Company 1	Company 2	Company 4	Company 4
5	Company 5	Company 1	Company 5	Company 5	Company 5
6	Company 6	Company 1	Company 5	Company 6	Company 6
7	Company 7	Company 1	Company 5	Company 6	Company 7
8	Company 8	Company 1	Company 5	Company 6	Company 8

Figure 10-4 Flattening the company hierarchy

Each row still represents a single company, but it is no longer necessary to traverse a recursive relationship. Facts can be summarized at various levels in the hierarchy simply by grouping them according to the desired level. Rolling everything up to a top-level company, for example, is accomplished by grouping the facts by level_1_company. This is akin to rolling all products up to categories; the instance hierarchy is transformed into an attribute hierarchy.

Drawbacks of Flattening

Flattening an instance hierarchy poses a few problems. Though none are deal breakers, the utility of a flattened solution is limited. The importance of specific analytic requirements will determine whether flattening is sufficient.

Backfilling Is Necessary

The flattening of an instance hierarchy creates attributes to describe each row's place in a fixed number of levels. One problem with this is that not every row in the table represents the bottom of a hierarchy. For these rows, it will be necessary to decide what values to use for the lower levels. This phenomenon is clearly visible in the example. Not all companies are at the bottom of a four-level hierarchy. Company 1, for example, does not have a corresponding level_2_company, level_3_company, and so forth. So, what values will be used for these columns?

The usual solution for a member that is not at the bottom of the hierarchy is to "backfill" its own identity into the lower levels. In Figure 10-4, the shaded cells illustrate backfilled references. This allows a query to group data at any particular level, without losing transactions. So, for example, if we group all orders by level_2_company, we will not miss out on the transactions associated with Company 1. These will still be in our query results.

You may choose to use a text string such as "Higher Level Company" in lieu of backfilling. This makes some reports easier to read but loses the association of higher-level transactions with any specific companies.

Backfilling is necessary because flattening an instance hierarchy creates an artificial attribute hierarchy. Just as we could say "every product has a brand, every brand has a category," we need to be able to say "every company has a level 4 company, every company has a level 3 company," and so forth.

Looking Up and Down Is Still Difficult

The instance hierarchy makes it easy to respond to the instruction "show me all orders rolled up to level 2," but usually this is not what people want to do. The levels, after all, are an artificial construct that results from flattening. Most questions relating to an instance hierarchy will be geared toward using the hierarchy to summarize facts above or below a particular member.

Returning to the sample questions posed earlier, they are found to still be somewhat difficult to answer:

- **All orders beneath Company 5** (Looking down.) This request requires knowing that Company 5 is at level 2 in the hierarchy. If we know this, we can join the company table to the fact table, and apply the constraint `where level_2_company = "Company 5"`. As you can see in the illustration, this will result in transactions for Companies 5 through 8.

Part III

- **All orders above Company 6** (Looking up.) This request requires looking at the row for Company 6 to find the list of companies above it. A query can then be issued that joins order_facts to the company table, where the company name is in the list.

These queries are marginally easier to resolve than before, but it is probably not reasonable to expect an end user to be able to construct them, even with a state-of-the-art business intelligence tool.

Fixed Number of Levels Only

Last, a flattened solution limits the hierarchy depth to a fixed number of levels. If and when a case turns up that calls for an additional level, the table cannot accommodate it. For example, if Company 8 acquires another company, there are not enough attributes to accommodate a fifth level of ownership.

TIP Flattening an instance hierarchy may simplify reporting challenges but will not eliminate them. The solution will be limited to a fixed number of levels and will require backfilling. Studying facts by looking up and looking down will still be challenging, although it will be easier to report on specific numbered levels.

Variable Depth Is Not the Issue

Problems like these are often attributed to the unbalanced nature of the hierarchy. Notice, however, that only the last issue is related to variable depth. Even when an instance hierarchy has a consistent depth, the first two problems remain.

For example, suppose all company ownership relationships reach down exactly four levels. This is unrealistic, to be sure, but it will illustrate the point. Flattening still requires backfilling for the higher-level members of the hierarchy. When users wish to look up or down, the reporting challenges just noted will still exist. Only the issue of the appearance of a new level is avoided, and that is probably artificial.

When Flattening Works Best

Flattening a recursive instance hierarchy creates manufactured dimension attributes to represent levels. Flattening is usually not satisfactory because users are not actually interested in the manufactured elements. Normally, no one would ask to be able to summarize all transactions "to level 2." Rather, they desire to pick any particular point in the hierarchy and look "up" or "down."

NOTE If you *do* hear people asking to look at a "level 2 company" or the like, chances are the hierarchy has already been flattened in other systems. When you look at the operational system, you will likely find evidence of an instance hierarchy that was flattened. There will be attribute values that contain NULLs, read "N/A," or contain filler values. Other clues that a source system has flattened a hierarchy are columns that purport to hold one type of thing but actually contain another. For example, a column in a region table called "county" usually contains county names, but for some rows contains the name of a city. In this case, an attempt has been made to flatten a recursive relationship among regions, and one particular instance has not fit in cleanly. If the source system does not maintain the true unflattened hierarchy elsewhere, it may be impossible to recover it.

Sometimes, there is a set number of named levels that are easy to distinguish from one another, and these levels have a consistent relationship. When the hierarchy is flattened, users can use the vocabulary that already exists to reference each level, instead of using the "level number." While this will not do away with the need to backfill, it does make it much easier to look down from any particular location at the facts.

For example, suppose a retail chain uses a location dimension to identify where goods are received, stored, and sold. It has three clearly defined types of location, which always participate in standard parent–child relationships. Stores are supplied by warehouses, and warehouses are supplied by distribution centers. In a flattened location dimension, each row in the table will include a store name, warehouse name, and distribution center name, instead of level_1, level_2, and level_3. It will still be necessary to backfill. For example, a distribution center will have its own name filled in for the warehouse name and store.

Reporting will fare better than it did with the flattened company solution. Since people are accustomed to thinking about stores, warehouses, and distribution centers as different things, these attributes will be useful for looking down at the facts. For example, someone may want to see all shipments at or below Warehouse 57. They know it is a warehouse, so it is easy to choose the correct column to qualify in a flattened location dimension. It is still difficult to study the facts by looking up, but this may be of lesser importance.

TIP Flattening an instance hierarchy is most effective when the levels are consistent and have distinguishable meanings.

Unfortunately, this state of affairs is about as common as the balanced hierarchy—which is to say, it is extremely rare. In all likelihood, there will be exceptions that destroy the ideal. For example, a store near the distribution center may be supplied directly, bypassing the usual warehouse level. Some particularly large areas may have multiple levels of warehouses. The hierarchy is said to be *ragged*, because there are not a fixed number of levels with clearly defined meanings.

The Hierarchy Bridge

A bridge table provides the ability to study facts by looking up or down from within a recursive hierarchy, without limiting analysis to a preset number of levels or requiring awkward backfilling. This solution renders it simple to choose any point in the hierarchy for the aggregation of facts that occur either below it or above it. No procedural logic or correlated subqueries will be required.

With this power, however, come some drawbacks. Like the dimension bridge table from Chapter 9, the hierarchy bridge table can be used incorrectly, introducing the possibility of double-counting. Unlike with the dimension bridge, there is an additional complication: the way to join the bridge to other tables will depend on the purpose of the report.

Hierarchy Bridge Design

A hierarchy bridge table acts as a supplement to a standard dimension. A hierarchy bridge can, therefore, be added to an existing design. It is also possible to use the dimension without the bridge. Before studying exactly how the bridge table is used, we will look at its structure and its content.

Standard Star and Dimension Table

A hierarchy bridge table captures recursive instance relationships, so the dimension table will not need to. This means that a normal-looking dimension table can be used—one that does not include a pig's ear or flattened relationships. Stars for various processes can refer to this dimension table directly, in the standard way. In fact, it is possible to build and implement a standard star that completely ignores the recursive hierarchy, and add a bridge in a future project.

An example for the case of the company ownership hierarchy is shown in Figure 10-5. A standard company dimension appears in this design, with one row for each company. The shaded area of the diagram encloses a star schema for the orders process. The fact table in this star contains an order_dollars fact and refers to the company dimension directly via a company_key. This relationship captures the specific company with which an order transaction occurred, regardless of its place in any hierarchy. This star can be used to study orders by company in the usual way.

To the right of the orders star, the figure shows a hierarchy bridge table for the company dimension. The specifics of how this bridge table is designed and used will be dealt with

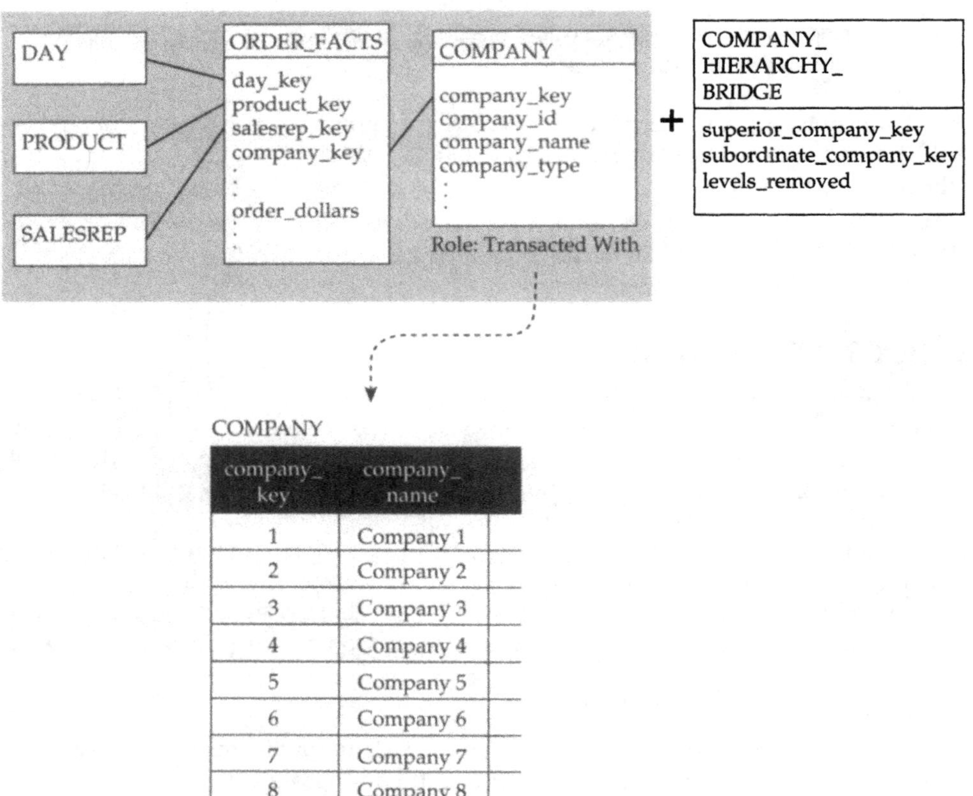

company_ key	company_ name
1	Company 1
2	Company 2
3	Company 3
4	Company 4
5	Company 5
6	Company 6
7	Company 7
8	Company 8

Figure 10-5 A star with a standard company dimension and a separate bridge

shortly. The important point here is that the star can be used without the bridge. If a user wants to group orders by the companies that placed them, the bridge is not needed. This means that the bridge table does not need to be built at the same time as the star; it can be added later. Without it, of course, there is no representation of the relationships between companies.

Structure and Content of a Hierarchy Bridge Table

The structure of a hierarchy bridge table is quite simple, but it is crucial to understand the nature of its contents. If you have dealt with a recursive relationship in an operational system, you may find the content of the bridge table to be familiar. Similar tables are often constructed to ease the process of operational reporting.

Structure of the Bridge Table Each row of a hierarchy bridge table captures a relationship between a pair of rows in the dimension table. In order to do this, the bridge table has two foreign key columns that refer to the dimension. One represents the higher-level entity in the relationship, and the other represents the lower-level entity. See the sidebar later in this chapter for tips on naming these columns.

The company_hierarchy_bridge table in Figure 10-5 captures relationships between companies. It has a pair of foreign keys that refer to the company dimension. The relationships themselves have not been drawn in the picture; that will be done soon enough. For now, note that the column representing the upper-level company in a given relationship is called superior_company_key; the column representing the lower-level company is called subordinate_company_key.

Unlike other tables you may have seen, a bridge table does not contain rows only for direct relationships. It also contains rows that represent indirect relationships, where the companies are more than one level apart from one another. In Figure 10-2, for example, Company 1 is two levels away from Company 3. A bridge table will capture indirect relationships like this one as well. An optional column in the bridge table describes how many hierarchy levels separate the two members. In Figure 10-5, this column is called levels_removed.

TIP A hierarchy bridge table contains two foreign keys which refer to related rows in the dimension table. Optionally, it may include an additional column to indicate how far apart the two dimension rows are from one another in the hierarchy.

This basic design can be supplemented with additional columns, which will be described later in the chapter. First, though, it is necessary to look at the content of the bridge table.

Content of the Bridge Table As previously noted, each row in a bridge table will represent a relationship between rows in the dimension table. These relationships are identified and populated during the ETL process by traversing the recursive relationships in the source data. This can be done in various ways, but it is easiest to describe the content of the table as follows.

For each row in the dimension table, the hierarchy bridge table will contain one or more rows:

- One row for each of its direct subordinates, if any. These are members that are one level away in the hierarchy.
- One row for each of its indirect subordinates, if any. These are members that are two or more levels away from it in the hierarchy.
- One row for itself (zero levels away).

If this last bullet puzzles you, hang on for a few moments. You will see why it is necessary when we look at how the bridge table is used. First, look at some examples.

Before studying the company hierarchy, consider a simpler example. For a three-member hierarchy where A is the parent of B and B is the parent of C, it will be necessary to record a total of six rows in the bridge table. For A, we will need the following rows:

- A's relationship to B (one level removed)
- A's relationship to C (two levels removed)
- A's relationship to A (zero levels removed)

For B, we will need to record the following relationships:

- B's relationship to C (one level removed)
- B's relationship to B (zero levels removed)

And for C, we will need to record just one row, since it has no subordinates:

- C's relationship to C (zero levels removed)

It should be obvious from this simple example that a hierarchy bridge table will contain more rows than the dimension table. Now let's return to the company example, which is a bit more involved.

The example in Figure 10-6 shows the content of the company hierarchy bridge table. So that you do not need to flip around while you study it, this figure repeats the hierarchy tree from Figure 10-2 and the bridge table design from Figure 10-5. Remember that in this example, company_keys correspond to company names. Choose any company in the hierarchy tree and look for the rows in the bridge table where that company's key is recorded in the first column, superior_company_key. You should find a row that relates the company you have chosen to itself (zero levels), a row that relates it to each subordinate (one level) and a row that relates it to each indirect subordinate (two or more levels). Trace through and make sure you can do this.

The number of rows you found depends on the company you chose. Bottom-level companies (3, 4, 7, and 8) have one row in the bridge table, since they have no subordinates. The top-level company (1) has numerous rows, since it is related to each company in the tree.

The mental exercise you just completed is an example of *looking down the hierarchy.* You chose a particular company in which you had an interest, and looked for its key value in superior_company_key. In the rows that you found, the subordinate_company_key represented companies *at or below* the company you chose.

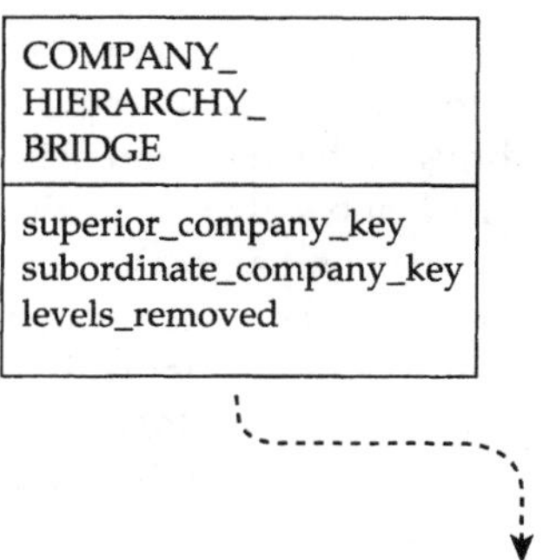

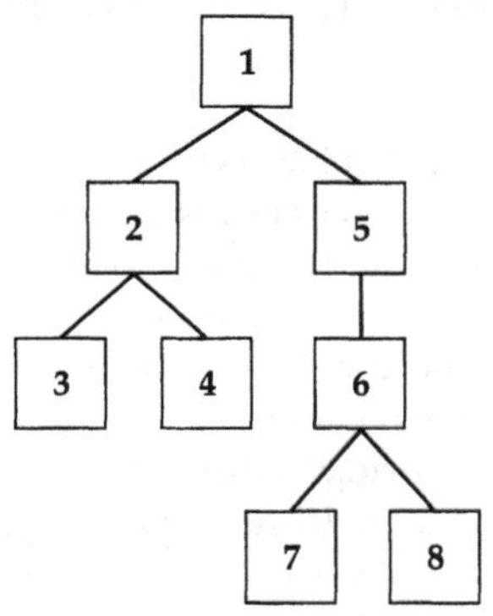

COMPANY_HIERARCHY_BRIDGE

superior_ company_ key	subordinate_ company_ key	levels_ removed
1	1	0
1	2	1
1	3	2
1	4	2
1	5	1
1	6	2
1	7	3
1	8	3
2	2	0
2	3	1
2	4	1
3	3	0
4	4	0
5	5	0
5	6	1
5	7	2
5	8	2
6	6	0
6	7	1
6	8	1
7	7	0
8	8	0

Figure 10-6 Contents of the company hierarchy bridge table

You can use the levels_removed column to refine this kind of search. If you want to find companies *below but not including* a particular company, look for rows where the superior_company_key is the company in question, and levels_removed is greater than 0. The resulting list of subordinate_company_key values will be the companies you want. Similarly, you can look for companies a specific number of levels below the company in question, again by using the levels_removed column to refine your search.

Although the content of the hierarchy bridge table has been defined from the perspective of looking downward from each dimension row, notice that it can also be used to look upward. You can use this table, for example, to find all the companies that are above Company 8. Scan the subordinate_company_key column for occurrences of Company 8's key. You will find one row that records a superior_company_key for each of the companies above it in the tree (Companies 6, 5, and 1) as well as one for Company 8 itself (at the very bottom of the table). Take a minute to look through the table and be sure you can find these four rows.

TIP For each row in a dimension table, the corresponding bridge table will contain one or more rows that contain the dimension row's key value in the superior key column. There will always be one row that carries the same key as a subordinate. If the dimension row has any subordinates in a hierarchy, there will be additional rows for each subordinate.

Keep in mind that Figure 10-6 shows only one group, or tree, of related companies—those that fall under Company 1. The company table will contain other companies as well. If any of these are involved in hierarchies, those trees will be represented in the bridge table as well. Any company that does not participate in a hierarchy will have a single row in the bridge table, with its own key for superior_company_key and subordinate_company_key.

If you have dealt with a recursive relationship in an operational system, you may have been able to read through the last few pages rather quickly. The bridge table is similar in structure and content to tables that are often built in operational environments to support reporting against a recursive relationship. Oracle users will recognize the bridge table as very similar to the output of a "connect by" statement, while users of DB2 or SQLServer will recognize the table as similar to one built to serve the same purpose. (Don't worry if you haven't had these experiences. While the last few pages may have been a bit more difficult for you, you have probably benefited from having less to "unlearn" in previous chapters.)

Now that you have a handle on the contents of the bridge table, you may also have an inkling as to how it will be used. As you will see, there is actually more than one way to take advantage of the bridge table.

Using the Bridge

There is more than one way to join a hierarchy bridge table to the other tables in a star schema. The way in which you link the tables together in a query will depend on the kind of analysis being performed. If the facts are to be analyzed by looking down the hierarchy, one configuration is used. If the facts are to be summarized by looking up the hierarchy, another configuration is used. Like the bridged solutions in Chapter 9, the use of a hierarchy bridge will involve a many-to-many relationship. If this confuses any of your software products, this relationship can be resolved by employing still more join configurations.

Looking Down

When facts are to be studied by looking down a hierarchy, the desire is to choose a member of the hierarchy and aggregate all transactions at its level and levels below it in the hierarchy.

Naming Key Columns in a Hierarchy Bridge Table

Schema designers often borrow a convention from the entity-relationship modeling world, naming the two key columns in a hierarchy bridge table the way they would appear in an ER model like the one in Figure 10-1: company_key and parent_company_key. In a dimensional design, this convention is inadvisable for two reasons.

First, note that the bridge table does not cover parent–child relationships exclusively. For a company at the bottom of the hierarchy, you will find a bridge row relating it to its parent but also to its grandparent, great-grandparent, and so forth. Therefore, parent_company_key is a misnomer; a better name might be ancestor_company_key.

Second, the ER naming approach implies a focus on a particular company, with the intent to look upward. Although it does not have to be used this way, this naming approach makes sense from an ER perspective where the columns are part of an entity. The column that represents the focus is simply called company_key. It is the primary key of the entity. The column used to find the parent, parent_company_key, is a foreign key. It gets a descriptive prefix in order to distinguish it.

The hierarchy bridge does not represent a company entity, and as you will see shortly, it can be used to look up *or down* the hierarchy, depending on how it is joined to other tables. (In ER parlance, one would say that the primary key of the bridge table is the pair of foreign keys.) It is, therefore, advisable to give *both* key columns a descriptive prefix, rather than just one. This helps ensure there is never any confusion about what each row represents.

The question, then, is what to name these columns. Although I am partial to the prefixes *superior_* and *subordinate_* as in the example, other prefixes are also possible. Upper_ and lower_ do the job just as nicely.

If you really like sticking to the parent–child analogy, use the column names ancestor_company_key and descendant_company_key. These names reflect the fact that not all rows are strict parent–child associations. You can even call the level indicator generations_apart. These names make more sense, although the language sounds a little weird when you are talking about ownership of companies. They work nicely for people, though.

Now that you are thinking about people in a parent–child relationship, it may have occurred to you that most children have not one parent but two. Children who have been adopted have three or more parents. We will deal with the multiple-parent issue later in this chapter.

In order to achieve this aggregation, the bridge table will be inserted in between the dimension table and the fact table. Since the intent is to aggregate transactions below the member in question, the lower- or subordinate-level key in the bridge will join to the fact table. The upper- or superior-level key will be used to join to the dimension table, where the query can be qualified for the member in question. This makes a lot more sense in the context of an example.

Part III

Figure 10-7 illustrates how the bridge table can be used to aggregate all transactions at or below Company 5. Once again, the tree picture and bridge table contents are repeated, so you will not need to flip between figures to understand how this works. The top of the diagram illustrates the tables needed and how they are joined to one another. We will work through this diagram step by step to be sure you understand what is going on.

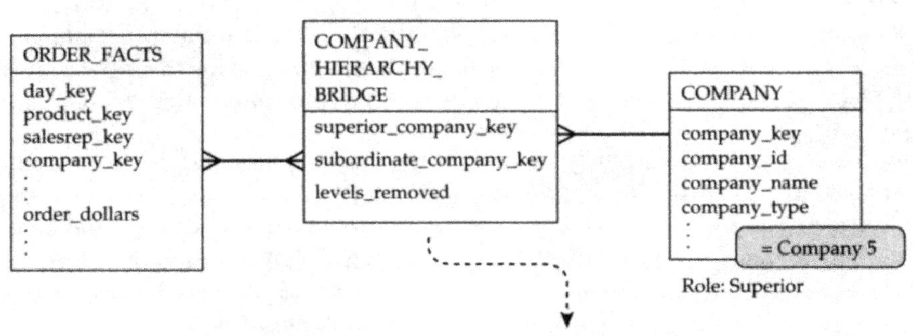

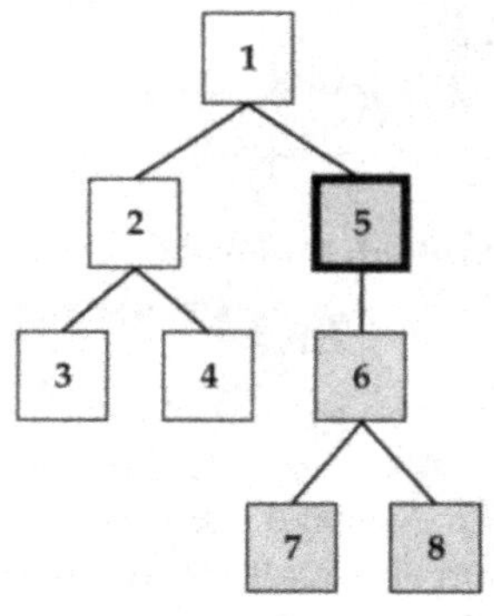

COMPANY_HIERARCHY_BRIDGE

superior_ company_ key	subordinate_ company_ key	levels_ removed
1	1	0
1	2	1
1	3	2
1	4	2
1	5	1
1	6	2
1	7	3
1	8	3
2	2	0
2	3	1
2	4	1
3	3	0
4	4	0
5	5	0
5	6	1
5	7	2
5	8	2
6	6	0
6	7	1
6	8	1
7	7	0
8	8	0

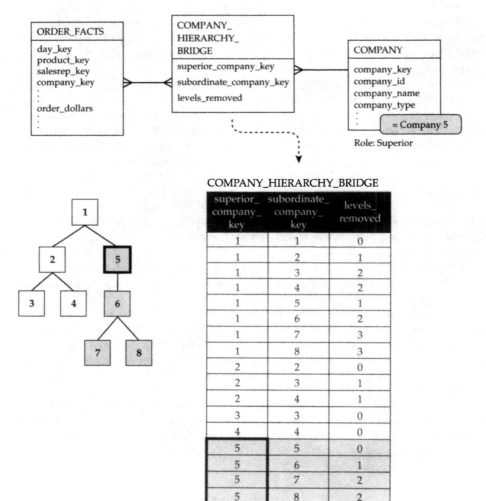

Figure 10-7 Looking down: orders booked with Company 5 and its subsidiaries

Starting at the right, observe that the company table is to be filtered for Company 5. This is the point in the hierarchy from which we want to look down when aggregating orders. This table is joined to the bridge table via the bridge's superior_company_key. If you look at the data grid beneath the table diagram, you will see that the constraint on Company 5 and this join will limit query results to the rows that are shaded.

The bridge table, in turn, is linked to order_facts via the subordinate_company_key. If you look at the key values in this column, you should be able to see that the subordinate_company_key values for rows where Company 5 is the superior company are just the ones we want: Companies 5, 6, 7, and 8. These correspond to the shaded companies in the tree. The query can select `SUM(order_facts.order_dollars)` to aggregate order dollars associated with these companies.

It should be clear at this point why a row is present in the bridge table linking each member to itself. Without such a row, a query like this would not include Company 5, only returning companies beneath it. This additional row, which often confuses dimensional designers, allows the query to capture transactions at Company 5 as well. If Company 5's transactions are not desired, you simply add the predicate `WHERE levels_removed > 0`.

Looking Up

A similar process with slightly different joins can be used to study the facts that occur at or *above* a particular member of the hierarchy. To look up in this manner, the fact table is joined to the upper- or superior-level key in the bridge, and the dimension is joined to the lower- or subordinate-level key.

Figure 10-8 illustrates the joins that would be needed to identify orders that occurred at or above Company 6. The configuration is similar to the previous one, except that the key columns in the bridge table that join to the fact table and dimension table have been reversed. Once again, study this diagram from right to left. At the far right is the company dimension table, upon which a filter is added to single out our focus: Company 6. Since this query will look upward from Company 6, company is joined to the subordinate_company_key in the bridge table. This has the effect of singling out the highlighted rows in the instance chart.

The bridge table, in turn, is linked to order_facts via the superior_company_key. If you look at the key values in this column, you should be able to see that the values for rows where Company 6 is the subordinate are just the ones we want: Companies 1, 5, and 6. The query can select `SUM(order_facts.order_dollars)` to aggregate order dollars associated with these companies.

Double-Counting

Whether you are using the bridge table to look upward or downward, there is the possibility of double-counting. The many-to-many relationship between the bridge and the fact table, which can be seen in both Figures 10-7 and 10-8, causes this potential danger. In the case of looking down, it is avoided by filtering for a particular top-level member, or grouping results by the top-level member. Similarly, care can be taken to avoid double-counting when looking up.

It is not reasonable to expect that novice users or developers will have the knowledge and skill needed to recognize and avoid this danger. To avoid potentially disastrous results, you can withhold access to the bridge table from these users. This will keep them out of

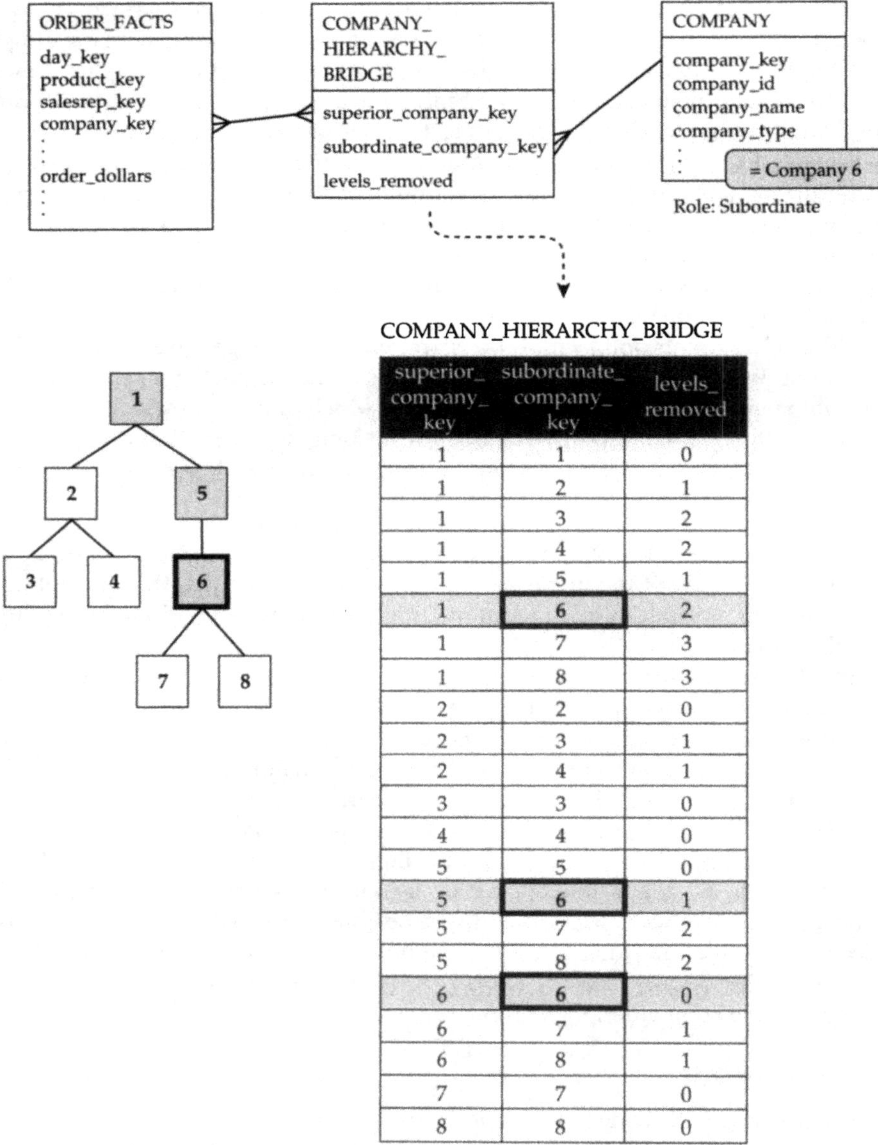

COMPANY_HIERARCHY_BRIDGE

superior_ company_ key	subordinate_ company_ key	levels_ removed
1	1	0
1	2	1
1	3	2
1	4	2
1	5	1
1	6	2
1	7	3
1	8	3
2	2	0
2	3	1
2	4	1
3	3	0
4	4	0
5	5	0
5	6	1
5	7	2
5	8	2
6	6	0
6	7	1
6	8	1
7	7	0
8	8	0

Figure 10-8 Orders booked with Company 6 and its superiors

trouble but will prevent them from being able to leverage the hierarchies in their reports. When this is necessary, a skilled developer should be entrusted with the job.

Avoiding Double-Counting

The possibility of counting a fact more than once is a real and present danger when a hierarchy bridge table is in use. In the case of looking down, this danger is avoided by selecting a single upper-level member of the hierarchy, or by grouping results by upper-level members. In the case of looking down, it is avoided by selecting a lower-level member or by grouping results by lower-level members. Double-counting can also be avoided by using the bridge in a subquery instead of joining it to the fact table.

To understand this danger and the solution, consider the content of the fact table. Suppose, for example, that Company 8 placed an order. The fact table will contain a row for this transaction, with the appropriate company_key for Company 8. If you look back at Figure 10-7, you will see that Company 8 is subordinate to several companies. To be specific, it lies beneath Companies 6, 5, and 1. There is also a row that links Company 8 to itself. That means that if we are not careful, Company 8's order may be counted as many as four times.

When the looking down configuration in Figure 10-7 was used to query the facts, a constraint was placed on the company table. This limited the results to those companies that could be found in the bridge that have Company 5 as a superior. As a result, Company 8 was counted only once. You can see this in the shaded area of the table. Although Company 8 is also linked to Companies 1, 6, and 8, these possibilities were eliminated when the query constrained on Company 5.

It is also possible to avoid trouble without establishing a filter if you take care to *group results* by a top-level member. Such reports are similar to the impact reports of the previous chapter. Facts may be counted in the groupings returned for each of the companies above them. For example, any orders by Company 8 will be included in totals for Companies 1, 5, 6, and 8. As long as these group totals are not subsequently added up to construct a grand total, the report is valid.

Filtering for a specific member of the hierarchy or grouping by specific members are the *only options* to avoid trouble. Using any attribute of the dimension may cause a severe miscalculation of the facts. For example, assume that the companies in Figure 10-7 are all in the finance industry. If the company constraint in Figure 10-7 is replaced by `company_type="Finance"`, a severe miscalculation will take place. Company 8, for example, appears under three companies in the finance industry (1, 5, and 6), so its orders will be counted more than once. It is only possible to avoid this by filtering for a specific company. Use of the natural key is the best route, since it is possible for company names or other attributes to be duplicated. Note that the slow change guidelines provided later in this chapter must be followed.

TIP When looking down a hierarchy, it is important to select a top-level member in order to avoid double-counting. When looking up a hierarchy, it is important to select a bottom-level member. Double-counting can also be avoided by grouping by a top- or bottom-level member. In the query, identification of the member should involve use of a natural key.

When looking up a hierarchy, a similar set of precautions prevents double-counting. In this case, it is necessary to establish a lower-level member from which the query looks upward. In Figure 10-8, this was achieved by filtering on the lower-level member Company 6. Instead of filtering for a single lower-level member, double-counting can also be avoided by grouping results by lower-level members. In this case, it is important to remember not to construct a grand total. Company 1's transactions, for example, will appear above Company 6's as well as above Company 5's.

If it is necessary to study all transactions above (or below) hierarchy members with a particular characteristic, it is not possible to qualify the query using a natural key. It will be necessary to make use of a subquery instead of joining the bridge to the fact table. The subquery will produce a distinct list of subordinates (or superiors) to members that have the characteristic in question. This list will be used to filter the main query. For example, a subquery can produce a distinct list of company_keys for companies that have superiors that are in the finance industry. This list of keys can then be used to qualify a query against the fact table to aggregate their transactions. See "Further Reading" for more information on this technique.

Hiding the Bridge from Novice Users

Even experienced designers and developers need to pause and check their work when writing a query that includes a bridge table. For a novice user, the likelihood that things will be joined and qualified correctly is quite low. To avoid the danger that things will be done incorrectly, you can withhold the bridge table from these users. This will keep them out of trouble but will prevent them from being able to leverage the hierarchies in their reports.

If you are keeping track, you may have noticed that this brings to three the number of possible ways to join the tables in a star when a bridge is available. The tables can be configured to support looking down at the facts from a member of the hierarchy, looking up at the facts from a member of the hierarchy, or studying facts in the context of direct transactions, with no regard for the hierarchy. Figure 10-9 depicts these three configurations.

The top configuration in Figure 10-9 does not involve the bridge. This configuration is used for reports in which the hierarchy is not of interest. Order facts can be selected or grouped based on the companies with which order transactions occurred. This configuration also happens to be safe; there is no many-to-many relationship that might result in double-counting. It is the only configuration that will be made available to novice users.

The other two parts of the illustration recap the configurations used to look down from a particular member in the hierarchy and to look up. These configurations risk double-counting if queries and reports are not constructed carefully. Only experienced developers will have access to the bridge table and these configurations, and it will be important to check and double-check their work.

TIP Only expose the bridge table to trained and experienced developers. End users building ad hoc reports cannot be expected to avoid the pitfalls of double-counting.

Because the bridge table will only be made available to elite developers, you may also choose to provide a flattened solution for end users. In this case, the company table will contain the flattened hierarchy attributes discussed earlier in the chapter; the bridge will be unchanged. This provides novice users with a limited ability to perform hierarchical summarization using the flattened version.

NOTE As you have just seen, the presence of a hierarchy bridge table means there will be at least three ways to join the tables in a star. Business intelligence products that generate SQL queries can be hampered by designs in which there is more than one way to relate tables. Advice for handling this complication is provided in Chapter 16, "Design and Business Intelligence."

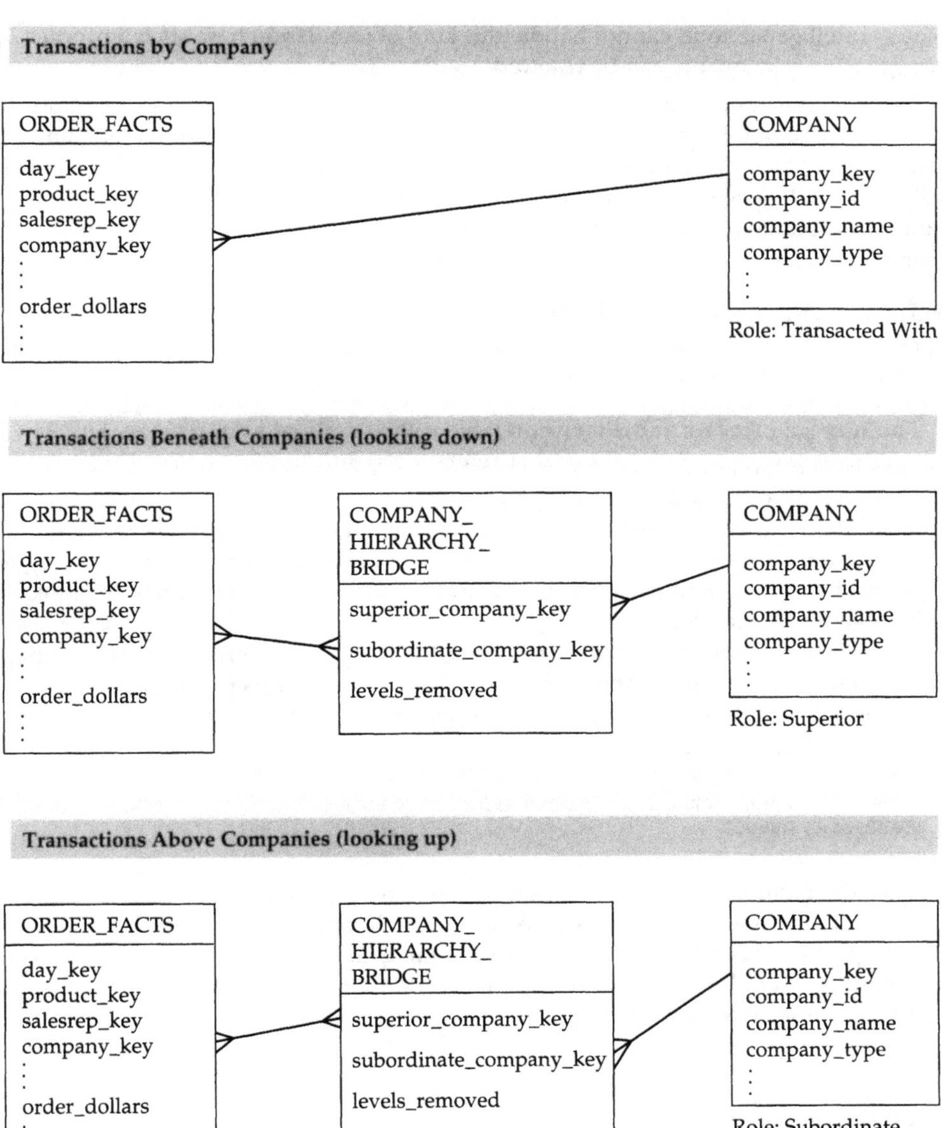

Figure 10-9 Three join configurations are possible

Resolving the Many-to-Many Relationship

When a hierarchy bridge is used to facilitate looking up or looking down, it is placed in a many-to-many relationship with the fact table. As long as you take the precautions described, this can be done safely. However, many software products will not accommodate such a relationship. As Chapter 9 pointed out, some modeling tools, database products, and business intelligence tools cannot handle this kind of join. If you have such a product, the many-to-many relationship can be resolved.

Resolving the many-to-many relationship between hierarchy bridge and fact table does not require developing a new table. For a modeling tool or RDBMS, primary key and foreign key relationships can be declared that avoid the many-to-many relationship. For a business intelligence tool, declaring query configuration without many-to-many relationships will require some aliasing. Although this will introduce some extra joins, it will also allow the upper- and lower-level members of a relationship to be identified in query results.

Declaring the Hierarchy Bridge to a Modeling Tool or RDBMS

In a modeling tool, relationships between tables are usually declared as primary key / foreign key relationships. For a fact table, dimension table, and bridge, it is possible to declare relationships without exposing the many-to-many relationship that will be exploited by queries.

The surrogate key for the dimension table will be defined as its primary key. The fact table will have a foreign key column that refers to the primary key in the dimension table. This is identical to the way a nonbridged dimension is related to a fact table. For the bridge table, the superior and subordinate columns are each defined as foreign key references to the dimension table. That is all that is needed to make your modeling tool happy, or to declare relationships to the RDBMS. Figure 10-10 shows what this looks like for the company example.

As the figure shows, the fact table has a single foreign key reference to the company dimension table. The bridge table has two foreign key references to company: one represents the superior-level company; the other represents the subordinate.

TIP The hierarchy bridge can be declared to a modeling tool or RDBMS as having two relationships to the dimension table. This avoids the need to declare the many-to-many relationship, which will be leveraged by queries.

While the relationships among the bridge, dimension, and fact table can be declared in this manner, they are not used this way. As you have already seen, leveraging the hierarchy bridge requires placing it *between* the dimension table and the fact table and isolating specific join columns depending on whether it will be used to look up or look down. This means the database administrator may still face a bit of a challenge when tuning the system for queries.

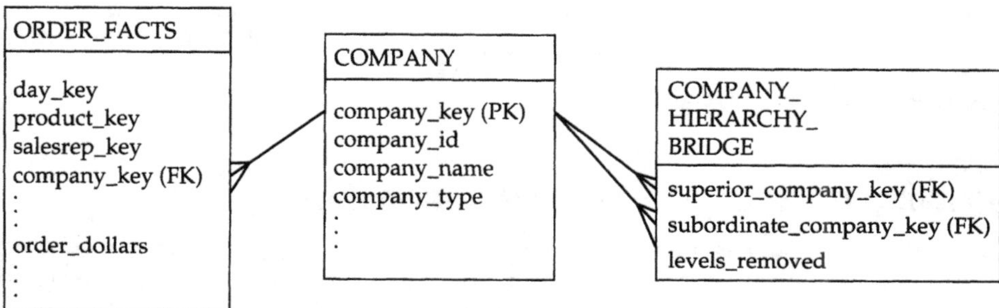

Figure 10-10 Declaring a hierarchy bridge table in a modeling tool or RDBMS

It also means that an alternative way to describe associations among tables will be needed for business intelligence tools that eschew many-to-many joins.

Declaring the Hierarchy Bridge to a Business Intelligence Tool

The illustration in Figure 10-10 captures essential relationships among tables. This is sufficient to design the tables in a modeling tool or declare them to an RDBMS. But this information is not sufficient for SQL-generating business intelligence tools. These tools need to know which joins to use in order to produce meaningful query results. As you have already seen, different join combinations are used when looking up or looking down. If the business intelligence tool balks at many-to-many relationships, the examples you have seen so far will not be acceptable.

Looking Down Without a Many-to-Many Relationship When configuring a query tool to looking down, the many-to-many relationship between fact table and bridge can be resolved by using aliases for the dimension table. One instance will represent the upper-level member of a relationship; the other will represent the lower-level member. Instead of joining the bridge directly to the fact table, one of the aliases will sit between them. Care is taken to use the appropriate join columns for looking down.

For example, when looking down from Company 5, the bridge table in Figure 10-7 was in a many-to-many relationship with the fact table. When declaring metadata to a business intelligence tool, the tool may complain about this relationship. It can be resolved by aliasing the company table twice. One alias will represent the superior company in a relationship; the other will represent the subordinate. Care must be taken to link the subordinate to the fact table and to the subordinate_company_key in the bridge table. The superior company alias is linked to the superior_company_key in the bridge. Figure 10-11 illustrates how this works.

The configuration in Figure 10-11 is similar to the one from Figure 10-7, except that two aliases appear for the company table. The role of each alias is indicated beneath it. The company alias on the far right of the diagram is the subject of the query and represents the point in the hierarchy from which we will look down. The other alias for the company table represents subordinate members. (Refer to Chapter 6 if you need a refresher on roles and aliases.) By defining your schema design as shown in Figure 10-11, your business intelligence tool is able to comprehend the model without having to worry about the many-to-many relationship. There is also an added bonus to this configuration. It is now possible to group query results by lower-level companies. For example, if you are looking at the transactions

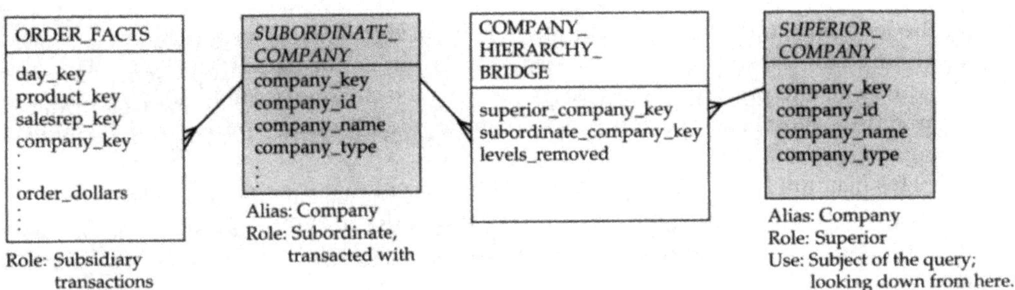

Figure 10-11 Resolving the many-to-many relationship when looking down

beneath Company 5, you can get a total for each subordinate, instead of one number. This is done by adding to the GROUP BY clause the company name or ID from the subordinate company table. In the case of companies beneath Company 5, this might look like:

```
SELECT
     superior_company.company_name AS "Superior Company",
     subordinate_company.company_name AS "Subordinate Company",
     SUM (order_facts.order_dollars)
   .
   .
   .
GROUP BY
     superior_company.company_name
     subordinate_company.company_name
```

The results of this query might look like the following:

```
Superior   Subordinate Sum( order_
Company    Company     facts)
========== =========== ===========
Company 5  Company 5         20000
Company 5  Company 6          1000
Company 5  Company 7         19900
Company 5  Company 8          2990
```

If the subordinate company is omitted from the SELECT and GROUP BY statements, all the transactions beneath Company 5 can be aggregated to a single number, as was possible in the original configuration from Figure 10-7. If this is what a query needs to do, the additional aliasing is not really necessary. The database will be processing an additional join to the subordinate company in order to resolve the query. If your tools are going to force this perspective, so be it.

Looking Up Without a Many-to-Many Relationship The many-to-many relationship in a looking-up configuration is resolved for a business intelligence tool in a similar way. Two aliases for the dimension table are brought into the query. One is inserted between the fact table and bridge, and represents the upper-level member of a relationship. It is joined to the fact table and to the superior_key in the bridge. The other represents the lower-level member. It is joined to the subordinate_key in the bridge. It represents the subject of the query, or the point in the hierarchy from which the query will be looking upward. Figure 10-12 illustrates how this would be done when looking up from a member of the company hierarchy.

This diagram looks similar to Figure 10-11, except that the roles of superior company and subordinate company have been reversed in order to support looking up. Two aliases of the company table are present, instead of the one instance in the looking-up configuration from Figure 10-8.

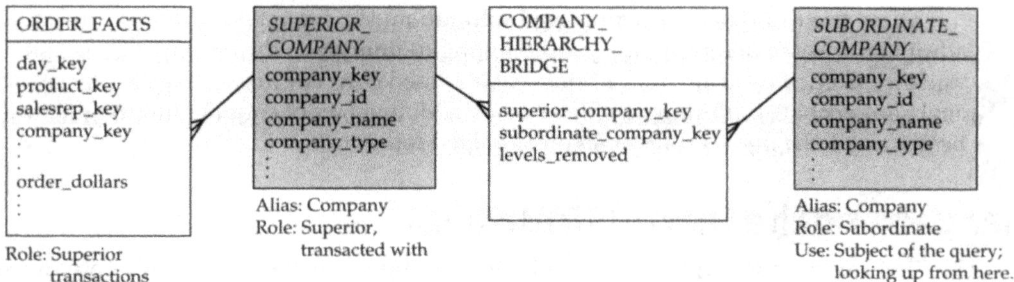

Figure 10-12 Resolving the many-to-many relationship when looking up

---

TIP In a query or business intelligence tool, the many-to-many relationship between the bridge and fact table can be resolved by aliasing the bridged dimension twice. One alias will represent the superior member of a pair; the other will represent the subordinate member. Appropriate joins are selected for looking up or looking down. This has the added benefit of being able to isolate both roles in query results.

In this configuration, the subordinate company is the focus of the query. The subordinate company is constrained for a particular value, such as Company 6. If the superior company is added to the query, from the shaded instance of the company table, this allows orders to be grouped by each of the companies at or above Company 6: Companies 6, 5, and 1.

Potential Misuse

If you have been keeping track of the ways in which a bridged dimension can factor into a query, you have noticed several exist. A quick recap:

- A nonbridged configuration, such as the shaded region of Figure 10-5
- A looking-down configuration, such as Figure 10-7
- A looking-up configuration, such as Figure 10-8
- A looking-down configuration that also includes the subordinate member, such as Figure 10-11
- A looking-up configuration that also includes the superior member, such as Figure 10-12
- A subquery that produces a distinct list of member keys, used in a main query to qualify a fact table, as described in "Avoiding Double-Counting," earlier in this chapter.

This collection of possibilities means anyone writing queries or reports must really understand what they are doing. It can also pose a challenge when configuring a business intelligence tool to generate SQL. These tools typically prefer having only one method to link a given set of tables together. Chapter 16 will discuss this issue and provide some workarounds.

You have also seen that in all configurations other than the first, it is of the utmost importance to qualify for or group by a single member to avoid double-counting. As already discussed, one way to avoid any issues is to make only the first configuration available to most users and developers. Only trained personnel will be able to use the bridge table.

These two drawbacks to the bridged solution must be weighed carefully against its advantages. Some organizations may be willing to undertake the additional work and vigilance needed to ensure that a bridge table is used correctly in exchange for the powerful analysis it enables. Unfortunately, there is one additional set of considerations that has yet to be discussed: the impact of changes on a bridged solution.

Changes and the Hierarchy Bridge

The final complication in the use of a hierarchy bridge table has to do with responding to changed data. It will be necessary to plan for slow changes that impact the dimension, as you are already used to doing. It will also be necessary to plan for changes that impact hierarchies themselves. Like other kinds of changes, hierarchy changes can be responded to in two ways: one that preserves the context of previously recorded facts, and one that does not. These are analogous to the type 2 and type 1 responses, respectively.

Responding to type 1 changes, either to the dimension or to its hierarchy, is relatively simple. In the case of type 2 changes, however, the presence of a bridge introduces some new challenges. A type 2 change to a row in the dimension has a ripple effect, requiring type 2 changes to other members of the hierarchy.

Type 1 Changes in the Dimension or Bridge

When changes involving a dimension with a hierarchy bridge do not require the preservation of the historic context of facts, processing is relatively simple. In the case of a dimension table, the processing of a type 1 change is identical to that presented in Chapter 3. In the case of a hierarchy change, it is a matter of updating the bridge to reflect the new relationships.

Type 1 Change to the Dimension

In a bridged solution, the mechanics of the type 1 change are identical to those you have already learned. A simple update to the dimension row is all that is required. The new state of affairs is now reflected in the star, with no evidence that things ever looked any other way.

After a type 1 change occurs, the bridge table can continue to be used to analyze facts by looking up or looking down from any member of the hierarchy. The same dimension rows are in place, although one has changed slightly. There is no impact on the bridge table itself, nor is there any impact on the various query techniques described earlier in this chapter.

Type 1 Change to the Hierarchy

If a hierarchy changes, rather than a member of the hierarchy, it is only necessary to adjust the bridge table. The dimension table is unaffected. The simplest method is to delete all rows in the bridge table relating to the changed ownership, and replace them with a new set of rows. It is also possible to update affected rows, if you prefer.

Referring back to Figure 10-8, suppose that Company 6 is to be sold off, but Companies 7 and 8 will be retained. In the bridge table, all rows relating to the hierarchy involving Companies 1 through 8 will be removed and replaced with a set of new rows representing the new state of affairs. If the company that purchased Company 6 is also a customer, it will also have an ownership hierarchy reflected in the bridge table. This tree, too, will require replacement.

Strictly speaking, it is not necessary to wipe out the entire hierarchy tree. It is possible to handle the change as a series of deletes, updates, and inserts as required. Many of the relationships between the companies under Company 1 remain unaltered after the sale of Company 6. These rows do not need to be replaced. All the rows relating to Company 6 will require deletion. Other rows can be updated—for example, after the sale, Company 8 is one level removed from Company 5 rather than two. This piecemeal approach is workable, but prone to error.

It is very rare that changes to a hierarchy are treated as type 1. If the hierarchy is significant enough to demand the extra ETL work and query complexity of a hierarchy bridge table, it is relatively certain that changes to the hierarchy will be deemed significant, calling for a more complicated type 2 response.

Type 2 Changes to the Dimension

When a dimension table has an associated hierarchy bridge, a type 2 response to source changes involves more than the addition of a new row. Because the entity that has changed also participates in a hierarchy, the bridge will require some new rows as well. This much may be readily apparent. Unfortunately, the story does not end here.

Remember that a standard type 2 response creates a version history of the changed dimension member. Queries can ignore this history by using the natural key. For example, a company undergoes a type 2 change when its headquarters moves. After the change, there will be two dimension rows for the company, each with the same natural key. One reflects the old location; the other reflects the new location. A report can ignore the fact that there are two versions of the company by using the natural key to group query results.

To preserve this capability in the presence of a hierarchy bridge table, a type 2 change requires a ripple effect that impacts all other members of the hierarchy. They will also require type 2 responses, even though their source data has not changed.

Before studying the reasons behind this complex response, the mechanics of the response itself will be presented. Once this is fully understood, the cause of this ripple effect will be fully explored and explained. You can skip the full explanation if you wish, but be sure you understand the mechanics of what must happen.

Mechanics of a Type 2 Response When a Hierarchy Bridge Is Present

When a dimension table has an associated hierarchy bridge, a type 2 response to changed source data will require several measures:

- The creation of a new row in the dimension table for the changed member
- The creation of new rows in the dimension table for all members that participate in a hierarchy with the changed member
- The creation of new rows in the bridge table to associate all these new dimension rows

This sounds complicated, but it is not. Although tedious, these steps can be executed in a routine fashion.

In order to illustrate this process, it will be necessary to drop the convention of using names like "Company 1" that correspond to key values. A type 2 change generates multiple

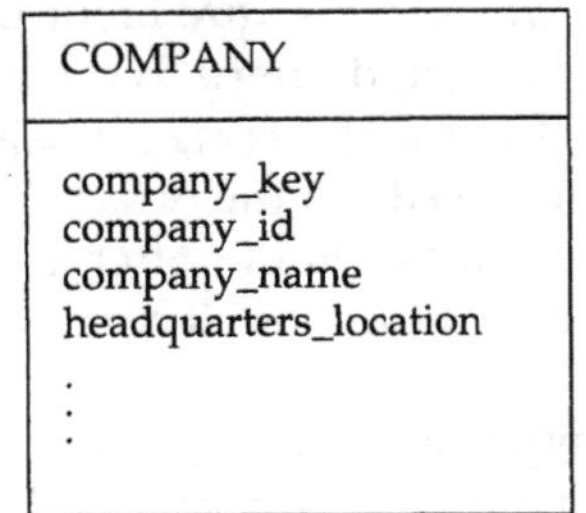

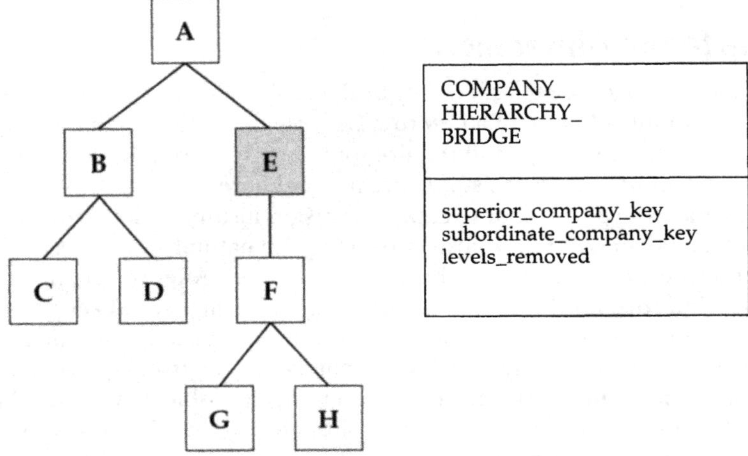

Figure 10-13 Company E is about to change

versions of a company, each with its own surrogate key. For this example, consider a set of companies identified as Company A through Company H. They participate in a hierarchy that is pictured in Figure 10-13. One of the companies in this hierarchy, Company E, is about to undergo a type 2 change.

The company dimension table includes a natural key called company_id, which uniquely identifies a company in the source data, as well as a surrogate key. Assume that the dimension table contains rows for Companies A through H. An associated order_facts table is tracking orders, and a hierarchy bridge has been implemented to allow facts to be studied by looking down or up from any point in the hierarchy.

In the source system, Company E undergoes a change. The company has moved, and its headquarters location has been updated. This change calls for a type 2 response. The response unfolds as follows:

1. In the dimension table, Company E receives a new row with a new surrogate key. The old version of Company E is left in place and remains associated with previously recorded facts. The new version of Company E, which we will call E-1, will be associated with any new facts.

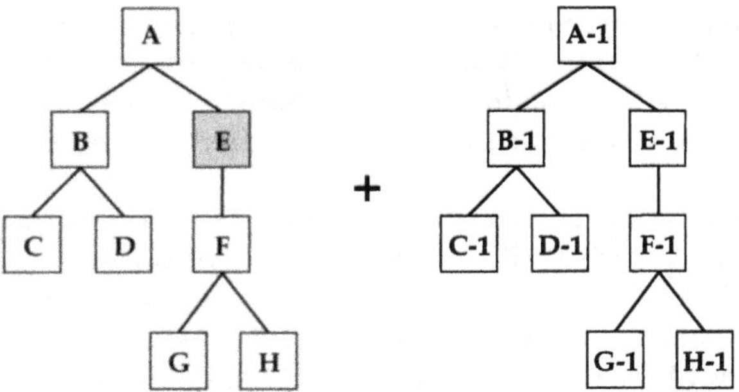

Figure 10-14 After Company E changes, the bridge reflects two hierarchies

2. Every company that participated in the hierarchy with Company E also receives a new row in the dimension table, with a new surrogate key. We will call these new rows A-1, B-1, and so forth.
3. New rows are added to the bridge table for the dimension rows A-1 through H-1.

Two versions of each of the Companies A–H now exist, even though only Company E has actually changed. A new set of rows has been added to the bridge table to reflect the relationships between these new versions of the companies. If you were to study the bridge table to reconstruct the hierarchies, you would now find there are two hierarchies for this set of companies. As pictured in Figure 10-14, one represents the relationships between the old version of Companies A through H, and the other represents the relationships between the new versions, A-1 through H-1.

The bridge can be used in all the configurations previously discussed. It can be completely omitted, with no danger of double-counting. It can be used in a looking-down configuration, providing the ability to aggregate all orders that occur at or below a particular company. Lastly, it can be used in a looking-up configuration, providing the ability to aggregate all orders that occur above a particular company.

The Reason for the Ripple Effect

Having read this far, you may be asking why it was necessary to create new versions of Companies A through H. Why not simply create a new version for Company E and add some rows to the bridge table to associate it with the hierarchy? Patching E-1 into the existing hierarchy results in a new hierarchy, shown in Figure 10-15.

This solution requires a few new rows to be placed into the bridge table. They will relate E-1 to the companies above and below it. For example, the bridge will need a row relating E-1 to F, a row relating E-1 to G, and so forth.

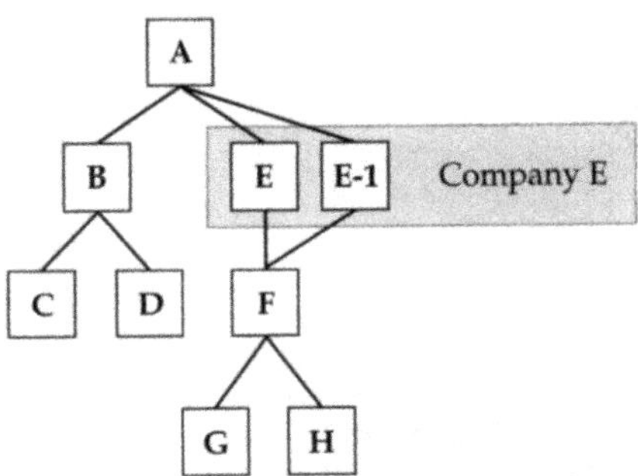

Figure 10-15 Patching into the hierarchy will cause problems

This solution appears appropriate, but remember that E and E-1 are the *same* company. This introduces the possibility of double-counting. If someone wants to look down from Company E, they may well double-count all transactions that occur with its subordinate companies. That's because Company E is represented twice in the hierarchy—once as E, and once as E-1.

If users want to aggregate all orders that occurred beneath Company E, both before and after its headquarters location changed, they will need to arrange the tables in a looking-down configuration. Figure 10-16 shows what this looks like. Instead of filtering for a single row in the superior company table, as was done in Figure 10-7, it is necessary to constrain for both versions of Company E: E and E-1. Presumably, this will be done by constraining on Company E's natural key.

With E-1 patched into the same hierarchy that originally involved E, notice that both instances are associated with Company F, below it. The bridge table will contain a row relating E to F, and another row relating E-1 to F. In this sample query, then, Company F's orders will be counted twice! The problems don't end there, either. The bridge table will also associate E with G and E-1 with G, so its orders will be double-counted as well. The same holds true for Company H.

The correct way to avoid this situation is to assign a new row in the dimension table for each member of the hierarchy, as visually depicted in Figure 10-14. When this is done, all old facts will fall under Company E, and all new facts will fall under Company E-1. Even when constraining for E or E-1 in a single query, the facts will not be double-counted.

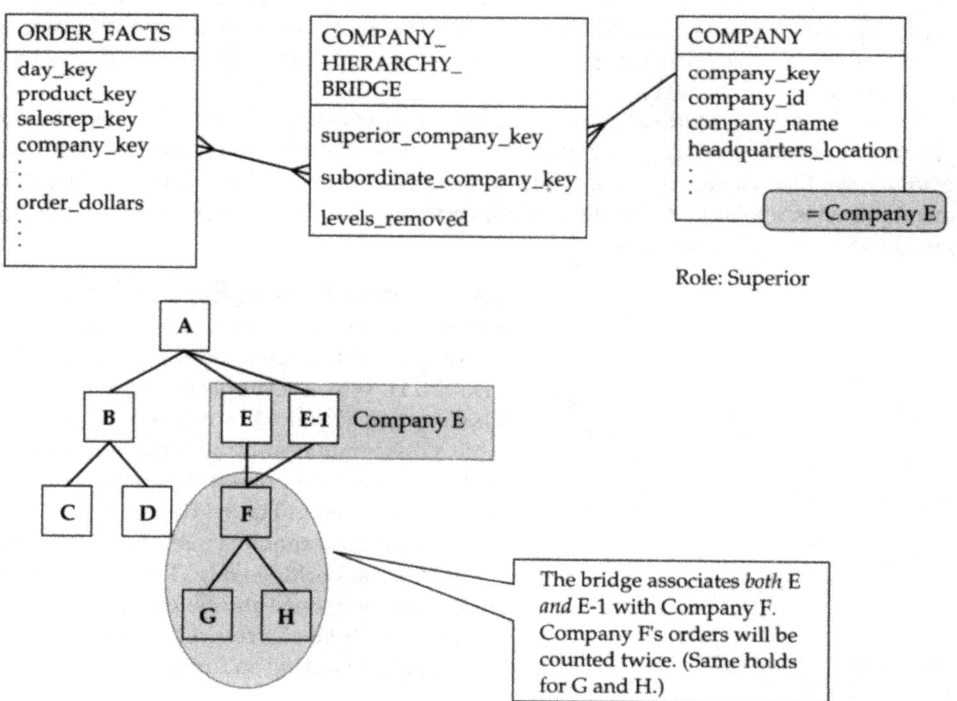

Figure 10-16 The danger of patching into the hierarchy

TIP When a member of a dimension table with a hierarchy bridge undergoes a type 2 slow change, all other members of the hierarchy must also undergo a type 2 change. Otherwise, it will not be possible to use the natural key of the changed member to look up or down.

Note that the required ripple effect does not solely extend upward and downward from the changed member; it extends to every member of the hierarchy. In the case of Company E, this meant new rows were needed for Companies B, C, and D as well. These were needed because a change to Company A resulted in an A-1. Since B, C, and D sit under company A, they must also undergo a change. Associating them directly with A-1 would have resulted in the same problem.

Do Not Resist the Ripple

Although steps can be taken to avoid the ripple effect, these are not worth the trouble. One approach simplifies the ETL process at the cost of adding query-time complexity; another severely hampers the analytic possibilities.

Designers may be tempted to avoid the ripple effect by stamping each bridge row with effective and expiration dates. Use of these stamps, however, would require correlation with the time dimension associated with the fact table. For each transaction, the bridge table would require a pair of constraints comparing the date of the transaction with the effective and expiration dates. This places undue stress on the query resolution process and opens the solution up to the possibility of error, all to save the ETL process from having to create a few additional rows. It is clearly not a viable alternative.

NOTE Though stamping bridge rows with effective and expiration dates is not an effective solution for reducing the ripple effect of a type 2 change, the technique does have value. As discussed later in this chapter, it can be used to support point-in-time analysis of the hierarchy itself, exclusive of facts.

A second way to avoid the ripple is to declare type 2 changes off limits. Unfortunately, this solution limits the analytic possibilities when the bridge is not being used. In our company example, changes to headquarters_location would require type 1 treatment. Without the type 2 change, it would be impossible to group orders by location in a manner that is historically accurate.

What may seem to be a third option is usually not plausible. You may have observed that the problem of double-counting in Figure 10-16 can be avoided if the query is qualified for a single version of Company E. Why not make this a simple requirement for analysis? Unfortunately, this is highly impractical. Selecting one version of Company E would be easy if you knew the surrogate key values that distinguish the two versions. Unfortunately, surrogate keys are meaningless sequence numbers. The only way to distinguish the versions would be to qualify on the natural key for Company E *and* every type 2 attribute, which is highly impractical. Unless the dimension is time-stamped, there is no easy way to qualify for a single version of Company E. If the dimension is time-stamped, date qualifications must be added to every query that involves the bridge. It is far safer to ripple the type 2 change.

Type 2 Changes to the Hierarchy

Having worked through the mechanics of a type 2 change to a dimension with a hierarchy bridge, the process of responding to a change in the hierarchy itself will not be surprising. It is virtually identical.

As before, a simple relationship change will require putting all members of the hierarchy through a type 2 change. This is necessary to properly isolate new facts from the member that has been removed, since users will be using natural keys to look up or down the hierarchy. Once again, you can skip the explanation if you want, but be sure you understand the mechanics first.

The Mechanics of Preserving History When a Hierarchy Changes

When the hierarchy itself changes, preservation of its history can be achieved by following the same steps used to carry out a type 2 change:

1. Create new rows in the dimension table for all members of the hierarchy that is changing.
2. Create new rows in the bridge table reflecting the new status of the hierarchy.

If a change involves a member leaving one hierarchy and entering another, both hierarchies will require this processing.

The Reason for the Ripple Effect

Once again, you might be tempted to avoid the ripple. Suppose, for example, that a company at the bottom of a hierarchy, Company H, is sold. It might appear that this company can be assigned a new key. Rows in the bridge table will still associate the old version of the company with the hierarchy but not the new version. Figure 10-17 illustrates this state of affairs graphically.

While all this is true, remember that looking down and looking up require being able to identify a point in the hierarchy to start from. Since this will be a natural key, the solution in Figure 10-17 is not sufficient. Looking up from Company H, for example, will identify two bottom-level rows: H and H-1. The bridge table still contains rows that associate H with F, E, and A, and these companies are still generating transactions in the fact table. These orders will be picked up by the query, *even if they took place after the change.* The same would happen in a looking-down configuration.

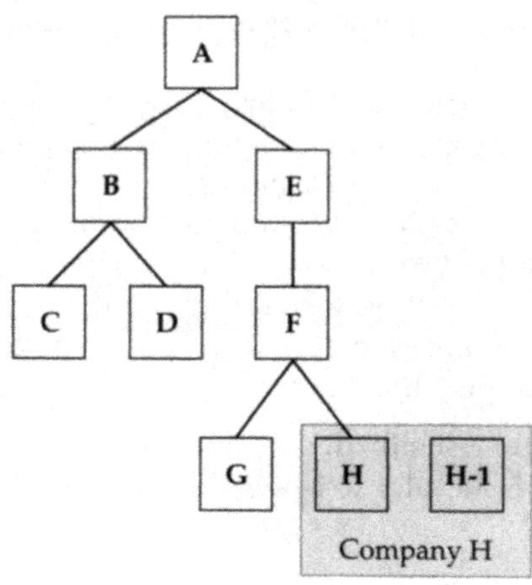

Figure 10-17 A relationship change with no ripple will cause problems

The user cannot be expected to specify a company by its surrogate key, avoiding H but selecting H-1, so an alternative solution is required. Future transactions with F, E, and A can be disassociated with any version of Company H by following the standard process of putting all members of the hierarchy through a type 2 change, as described earlier. New rows are added to the bridge table to reflect the post-change state of affairs. In this case, the bridge table will reflect three hierarchies, as shown in Figure 10-18. One is the original hierarchy, one is a new hierarchy that does not include any incarnation of Company H, and the last is the new hierarchy that Company H has joined.

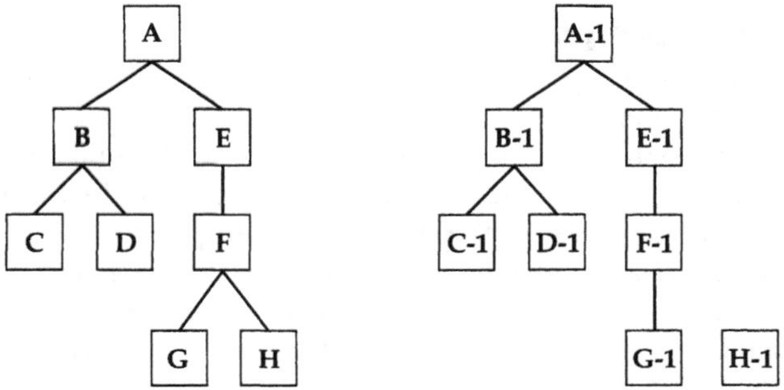

Figure 10-18 A relationship change generates type 2 changes for all members of the hierarchy

By processing a type 2 change for every member of the hierarchy, we avoid the problem encountered earlier. A user looking up from Company H will still use its natural key to constrain the query, and this will still pick up H and H-1. However, no new transactions will be added above H, since those companies have undergone type 2 changes as well. The only facts that will be counted are those that were in place above H before the change, or above H-1 after the change (none). Any new transactions with Companies F, E, or A will be associated with F-1, E-1, or A-1. These rows have no association with any version of Company H, so they will not be counted.

TIP When the relationships between members of a hierarchy change, process a type 2 change for each member and add the new relationships to the bridge table. Other solutions may lead to erroneous query results.

Time-stamped rows in the bridge table are an alternative, but will require that each query be carefully qualified in correlation with the granular facts. Even trained developers are likely to err when writing SQL to do this. In addition, business intelligence tools may not be able to generate the required SQL, and query performance may be degraded. Rippling the change is a far safer solution.

Variations on the Hierarchy Bridge

Further design options are possible for the hierarchy bridge. Embellishments to the basic design discussed in this chapter include the addition of effective and expiration dates and additional flags to signal the top or bottom of a hierarchy. It is also possible to construct a bridge that does not require each member to have only one parent, or to construct multiple bridges if there are multiple alternative hierarchies.

Embellishing the Bridge

Additional columns can be added to the hierarchy bridge to add to the analytic possibilities. It is extremely useful to add effective and expiration dates to each row, not to avoid the ripple effect, but to enable study of the hierarchy itself. Some designs also benefit from the addition of flags that indicate the top or bottom node of a hierarchy tree.

Effective and Expiration Date Stamps

Every hierarchy bridge table should include a pair of columns that indicate the effective and expiration dates for each row. Like the time-stamped dimensions described in Chapter 8, this permits point-in-time analysis of the hierarchy itself. Without these additional columns, it is impossible to know what the hierarchy looked like at a particular point in time, unless there happens to be a fact in a related fact table for the date in question.

As with a time-stamped dimension, when a row in the bridge table is superseded by a new row, the old row's expiration date should be set to the day prior to the new row's effective date. If the grain at which changes are tracked is finer than the day, these date stamps can be supplemented with a pair of time stamps.

The effective and expiration dates can be used together to qualify a query that produces a picture of the hierarchy at a particular point in time. The logic is much the same as it was for dimension tables. For example, if columns called effective_date and expiration_date were added to the table company_hierarchy_bridge, the state of affairs on December 23, 2008, could be determined by adding the following to the query predicate:

```
WHERE
    company_hierarchy_bridge.effective_date <= 1/23/2008 AND
    company_hierarchy_bridge.expiration_date >= 1/23/2008
```

These dates are added for the purpose of understanding the hierarchy itself over time, in the same way that time-stamped dimensions allow study of the dimension over time as explained in Chapter 8, "More Slow Change Techniques." Even if time stamps are added to the dimension table, it is advisable that type 2 slow changes to the dimension table or bridge be processed in accordance with the ripple effect described in this chapter. Use of time stamps to qualify bridge and dimension rows in a query involving a fact table is wide open to errors and may negatively impact performance.

TIP Add effective and expiration dates to the hierarchy bridge table. These will allow identification of the hierarchy at any point in time, regardless of the presence of facts. Do not rely on these dates to avoid the ripple effect of type 2 slow changes.

If it is not expected that anyone will analyze the hierarchy without involving a fact table, this extra information is still highly useful. It provides a way to track the accuracy of the ETL process, perform quality assurance checks on the state of the bridge table, and troubleshoot potential issues with the bridge table.

Adding Flags

Adding additional columns to the bridge table may further enhance the ability to explore or describe the hierarchy. It is sometimes useful to know that a particular member happens to be at the top or bottom of the hierarchy. This can be signaled by a pair of flags in the bridge table. Since each row in the bridge table actually references two members of the dimension, four flags are required. In the case of the company example, the additional flags indicate whether the superior company is at the top or bottom of the hierarchy, and whether the subordinate company is at the top or bottom of the hierarchy. This is shown in Figure 10-19.

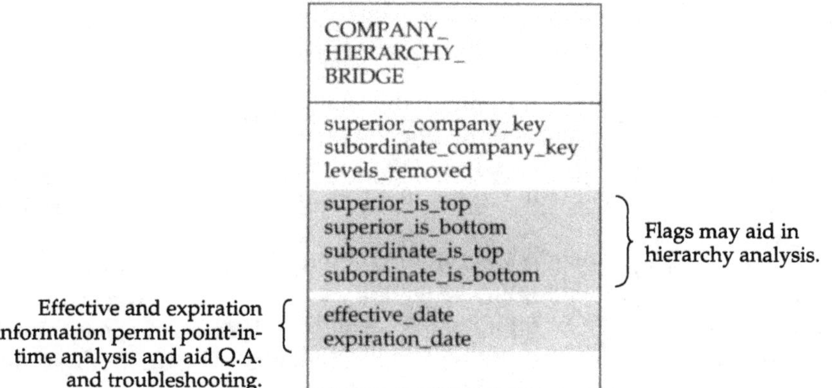

Figure 10-19 Embellishments to the hierarchy bridge

While it may sound absurd that the superior company can be at the bottom, or the subordinate at the top, remember that some companies may not participate in relationships with others. Such companies will have a single row in the bridge table, in which they appear as superior and subordinate. In the case of such a row, all four flags will be set to true values.

Multiple Parents

The examples provided in this chapter have assumed that each node in a hierarchy has a maximum of one parent. In rare cases, it may be necessary to model a situation in which a node may have more than one parent. Bridge tables can handle this kind of situation, but it will be necessary to eliminate the levels_removed column.

For example, suppose an effort is made to expand the company ownership example to accommodate shared ownership. Perhaps a pair of companies holds all the equity of a third. In this case, the third company has two parents. The bridge table can accommodate these relationships without any changes. Looking up and looking down can still be achieved by constraining on a single company, in the same ways that have already been described.

The multiple parent situations introduce one potential complication. If members of a hierarchy can have multiple parents, situations can occur in which there is more than one way to relate the same two members. In order to avoid double-counting, the bridge should only contain one row linking the companies in question. The levels_removed column should be removed from the design, since it may not be possible to specify a single value for a given pair of companies.

Multiple Hierarchies

In some situations, there may be more than one hierarchy that applies to the members of a dimension. Departments, for example, may participate in one hierarchy for budgetary purposes and another hierarchy describing the chain of command.

The best solution to this situation is to build multiple bridge tables: one for each hierarchy. For any given query or report, the appropriate bridge table is joined to the fact table and dimension tables as appropriate. This further increases the number of ways one might join the tables in a particular star; it is crucial to maintain clear documentation and to carefully educate developers of queries and reports to whom access to the bridge tables will be granted.

Multiple hierarchies put additional strain on the ETL process. A type 2 change to a dimension row, for example, now impacts not one but two hierarchies. A type 2 change to one of the hierarchies will affect the dimension table, and therefore the other hierarchy as well. This means both bridge tables will require new rows, even though only one reflects changed relationships.

It is possible, but not recommended, to capture multiple hierarchies with a single bridge table. This can be achieved by adding a column to identify the hierarchy to which a given row pertains. In the company example, there might be a hierarchy_name column that can take on the values "budgetary" and "chain-of-command." The disadvantage to this solution is that it will always be necessary to constrain this column for a single value. Omission of such a constraint will produce wildly inaccurate and nonsensical results.

Summary

The decision to include a hierarchy bridge is never an easy one. While it provides the most powerful and flexible analytic capability, the hierarchy bridge introduces room for error, makes the configuration of reporting software difficult, and severely complicates the ETL process. You should never make a design decision with these wide-ranging implications on your own, regardless of your role. The various points of view that should be represented in this and other design decisions are described in Chapter 18, "How to Design and Document a Dimensional Model."

When evaluating the option to implement a hierarchy bridge, you must fully understand the issues involved. Key points to remember include the following:

- An instance hierarchy is a recursive relationship within a dimension.
- An instance hierarchy can be flattened into a predetermined number of levels. This provides limited capability, but may be sufficient in some cases.
- When people want to use a point in the hierarchy as the context for studying facts, they will be looking up or looking down. Looking down aggregates facts associated with members at or below the point in question; looking up aggregates facts at or above the point in question.
- A hierarchy bridge table can be built to facilitate looking up or looking down.
- The bridge can be used in a variety of join configurations to achieve different analytic objectives.
- Use of a hierarchy bridge table poses a risk of double-counting when queries are not constructed properly. It is advisable to provide access to the bridge only to trained developers.
- The ETL process will be significantly impacted by the presence of a hierarchy bridge. Type 2 changes within the bridged dimension will have a ripple effect on other members of the hierarchy. Relationship changes will also require processing type 2 changes to hierarchy members.

- It is useful to add effective and expiration data to a hierarchy bridge table, both to support point-in-time analysis and to aid in quality assurance and/or troubleshooting.

While this chapter has covered the hierarchy bridge table in detail, there is still one aspect that is yet to be explored. Sometimes, the dimension in question has attributes that vary. As you will see in Chapter 13, "Type-Specific Stars," a bridge can be used in this situation only if the designers recognize these varying attributes as custom characteristics of a single dimension.

Further Reading

The hierarchy bridge is probably the most complex topic presented in this book. Great pains have been taken in this chapter to proceed in a slow, clear, and deliberate manner. Still, you may be left wanting more information. Here are some places to find it:

- The example in this chapter is very similar to one provided by Kimball and Ross in Chapter 6 of *The Data Warehouse Toolkit, Second Edition* (Wiley, 2002). When you read their treatment, keep a few important things in mind. First, the bridge table is presented as a solution to the variable-depth hierarchy, but may be of use even in a fixed-depth situation. This is relatively rare but worth noting. Second, the key columns in the bridge table bear the prefixes parent_ and subsidiary_. Keep in mind that the bridge table does not solely contain rows for companies and their parents but also their grandparents, great-grandparents, and so forth. Lastly, the top_flag and bottom_flag in their example pertain to the child company referenced by the row. To know whether the parent is at the top would require an additional column.
- It is possible to hide a hierarchy bridge table by creating a view that joins it to the fact table. Two views are possible, one for looking up and one for looking down. Examples of both possibilities are provided by Kimball and Ross in Chapter 6 of *The Data Warehouse Toolkit.*
- As mentioned in "Avoiding Double-Counting," you can look down or up from an attribute that is not a natural key (or a single member of the hierarchy) by making use of a subquery. Kimball and Ross provide an example in Chapter 6 of *The Data Warehouse Toolkit*, where a subquery aggregates all facts of customers with a superior in the city of San Francisco. A looking-up version of this kind of query is also possible. It is also possible to group results by multiple values.
- The presence of a bridge table must be considered carefully when developing aggregate tables. This topic is discussed in Chapter 8 of *Mastering Data Warehouse Aggregates* (Wiley, 2006) by Chris Adamson.
- For a short and fascinating tour of the ways in which a recursive hierarchy can be represented in an ER model, see Chapter 8 of Richard Barker's classic, *Case*Method: Entity Relationship Modeling* (Addison-Wesley, 1992).

PART IV

Fact Table Design

CHAPTER

11 Transactions, Snapshots, and Accumulating Snapshots

Each star schema in the preceding chapters features a fact table that measures activities. This kind of fact table is known as a *transaction fact table.* As you have seen, it supports a wide variety of analytic possibilities with great efficiency and can be used to capture detailed granular information about a process. Some facts, however, cannot be easily studied using this kind of design, and others cannot be accommodated at all.

This chapter introduces two additional kinds of fact table: the snapshot and the accumulating snapshot. It begins with a review of the transaction fact table design, highlighting some key characteristics covered in previous chapters. Snapshots and accumulating snapshots are then covered in detail. You will learn the kind of analytic challenge each design solves and the unique way each defines grain, and study the characteristics of each design that contrast with the others.

After reading this chapter, you will understand the purpose and characteristics of the three types of fact table:

- **The transaction fact table** tracks the individual *activities* that define a business process and supports several facts that describe these activities. It can provide rich analytic possibilities, and often serves as a granular repository of atomic data.
- **The snapshot fact table** periodically samples *status measurements* such as balances or levels. These measurements may be equivalent to the cumulative effect of a series of transactions but are not easy to study in that format. Some status measurements, such as temperature, cannot be modeled as transactions at all.
- **The accumulating snapshot** is used to track the progress of an individual item through a series of processing steps. It enables the study of *elapsed time* between major process milestones or events. This kind of fact table correlates several different activities in a single row.

In order to design the best dimensional model for a business process, you must master all of these design types. Some business processes may require only one kind of fact table, but others will require two or more. This chapter arms you with an understanding of the capabilities of each, so you can choose the right design for every situation.

Transaction Fact Tables

The fact tables presented in previous chapters share an important characteristic: they all track events. Events measured by these fact tables have included the booking of an order, the shipment of a product, and a payment on a policy. These examples all represent a type of fact table called the transaction-grained fact table, or simply *transaction fact table*. Other kinds of fact tables exist, and their properties differ from transaction fact tables in several ways. Before looking at these, it will be useful to review some notable properties of transaction fact tables.

Describing Events

Transaction fact tables capture details about events or activities. By storing facts and associated dimensional detail, they allow activities to be studied individually and in aggregate. The facts measure the activities: the margin on an order, the quantity shipped, or the dollar value of a payment. Each value recorded in the fact table describes the specific event represented by the row, and nothing else.

The word "transaction" has a formality to it and connotes the exchange of goods, services, or money. In fact, any kind of event can be considered a transaction. Examples you will encounter later in this book include tracking phone calls from customers and the logging of student attendance. Although no money passes hands, these activities can be considered transactions.

Properties of Transaction Fact Tables

You have already learned a great deal about fact tables, from the use of surrogate keys to the need to model separate fact tables for separate processes. Three important fact table characteristics are worth revisiting: grain, sparsity, and additivity. In these three areas, the properties of transaction fact tables contrast with those introduced later in this chapter.

Grain of Transaction Fact Tables

Declaration of grain is a crucial step in the design of every star. As you learned in Chapter 3, there are two ways to declare the grain of a transaction fact table. The grain may be defined by referencing an actual transaction identifier, such as an order line, or the grain may be specified in purely dimensional terms, as in "orders by day, customer, product, and salesperson." Both of these methods identify the level of detail represented by a fact table row.

Although the word "transaction" appears in its name, a transaction fact table's grain is not always the individual transaction. Many real-world transaction fact tables summarize activities, either because detail is available elsewhere or because the transaction volume is too large. The first fact table to appear in this book, in Figure 1-5, aggregated orders by day, salesperson, customer, and product. If the same salesperson booked two orders from the same customer for the same product on the same day, then both would have been combined in a single row in the fact table. Each row of the fact table describes specific events, though not individual events.

Transaction fact tables must have clearly defined grains, but this does not imply a mandatory relationship to all dimensions. For dimensions that do not participate in the grain of the fact table, an optional relationship is possible. In retail sales, for example, some transactions have a salesperson, but not all do. To avoid recording NULL-valued salesperson keys in the fact table, Chapter 6 advised creating a special row in the salesperson dimension to represent "the house" or "not applicable."

Transaction Fact Tables Are Sparse

Second, recall that transaction fact tables are sparse. As you learned in Chapter 1, this characteristic follows logically from the statement of grain. Rows are recorded only for activities that take place, not for every possible combination of dimension values.

For example, the simple orders star from Figure 1-5 did not record rows each day for every combination of salesperson, product, and customer. This would have led to excessive growth and cluttered up reports with numerous extraneous rows where all the facts had values of zero. Instead, rows were only recorded when orders took place.

Transaction Fact Tables Contain Additive Facts

Lastly, recall that transaction fact tables normally record additive facts. As you learned in Chapter 3, most nonadditive measurements, such as ratios, can and should be broken down into fully additive components. This allows the granular data in the fact table to be aggregated to any desired level of detail, after which the ratio or nonadditive fact can be computed. You want the ratio of the sums, not the sum of the ratios.

For example, if two products sell at a 10 percent margin, it is incorrect to say the total margin rate is 20 percent. Instead, the components of the margin rate—margin dollars and order dollars—are stored. When margin rate is needed, they are fetched and aggregated to whatever level of summarization is desired. Their ratio is computed only after any aggregation is performed. Storing fully additive facts provides the most flexible analytic solution.

Snapshot Fact Tables

Sometimes, measuring the *effect* of a series of transactions is as useful as measuring the transactions themselves. These effects are called *status measurements.* Common examples include account balances and inventory levels. Status can often be discerned by aggregating the transactions that contribute to it. You can figure out how many ballpoint pens are in the stockroom, for example, by adding up all the deliveries of ballpoint pens to the stockroom and deducting all the pens that were removed from the stockroom. This will give you the number of pens remaining, but it is a highly inefficient process.

Some status measurements cannot be described as the effect of a series of transactions. Examples include the water level in a reservoir, the air pressure inside a piece of industrial machinery, the oxygen level in the air, and the ambient temperature on a factory floor. These status measurements also describe levels, but it is not practical to describe them as a series of changes.

When the measurement of status is important, a transaction fact table is inefficient at best. The solution is an alternative design called a periodic snapshot fact table, or simply *snapshot fact table.* The snapshot fact table samples the measurement in question at a predetermined interval. This makes it easy to study the measurement in question, without the need to aggregate a long chain of transaction history.

The Challenge: Studying Status

A status measurement, such as an account balance, can often be constructed from transaction history. This is an inefficient way to monitor status, however, if the transaction history stretches very far into the past, or if it is necessary to compute the status of numerous things. If status is to be analyzed, it will be necessary to store it somewhere. One might be tempted to do so in the same fact table that records transactions, but this turns out to be a poor solution, and it will not work at all for status measurements that do not have corresponding transactions.

The Transaction Design Falls Short

Many status measurements represent the sum total of transactions up to a particular point in time. Your bank account, for example, can be fully described as a series of deposits, checks written, interest payments, fees, and so forth. Each transaction represents a change, or "delta," that affects a very important status measurement: your account balance. Imagine if determining your account balance at any point in time required consulting the entire history of transactions, starting with your initial deposit and accumulating them up to the current point in time. Worse, if a bank wanted to look at the total deposits of all customers, rather than just yours, it would have to do this for every current account. That could be quite a lot of transactions.

The transaction fact table in Figure 11-1 tracks the activity in bank accounts. Its grain is defined as one row per transaction per account. The day and time dimensions capture the time of the transaction; the account dimension captures the account affected by the transaction, and the degenerate dimension transaction_id identifies the transaction itself. Per the grain statement, a transfer between two accounts will generate two rows, one for each account affected. The type of transaction is captured in a transaction_type dimension, which includes rows for deposits, withdrawals, checks, fees, interest, and so forth.

NOTE The design in Figure 11-1 employs some of the advanced dimensional techniques covered in Part III of this book. The branch dimension is present in two roles: one indicates the branch at which the account is managed, and the other represents the branch at which the transaction took place. Since some transactions, such as online transfers, may not occur at a branch, the branch table will contain a special row for "not applicable," as described in Chapter 6. Similarly, there is a teller dimension which will not always apply. It too will have a special row for "not applicable." The account_holder dimension is present in the role of primary account holder. Accounts may have more than one account holder, and, though not shown, this might be dealt with by using an attribute bridge, as described in Chapter 9, to link the account dimension to an account_holder outrigger.

The account_ facts star provides for rich and varied analysis of transaction activity. It is possible to produce a list of transactions for a specific account, group aggregated transactions by branch, or study transactions of a particular type. All of these options may be quite useful. Missing, however, is an effective way to study account balances, which is a crucial metric. Account balances are used to compute interest payments or levy fees; total deposits at each branch are used to determine the amount of cash kept in the vault, and so forth.

While balances can be determined from transaction history, doing so for a single account requires aggregating all transactions starting from its inception. The sample data at the bottom of Figure 11-1 represents a series of transactions stored for a single account during the first two

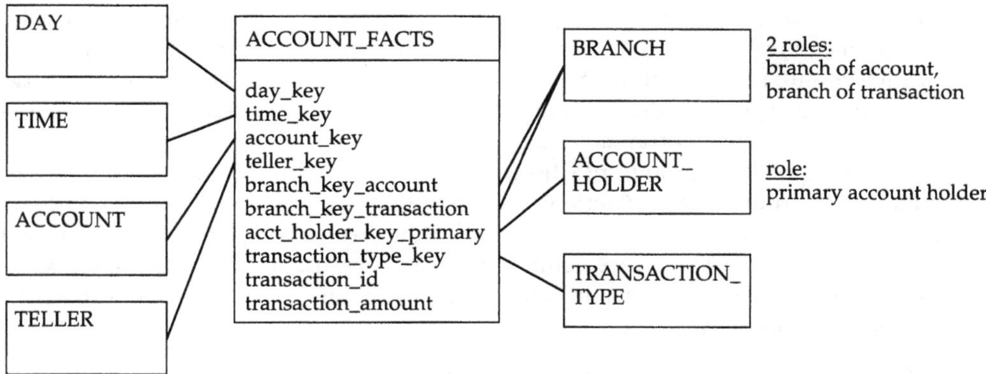

Account: 7922-3002
Period: 2/1/2009 – 2/14/2009

Granular transaction data stored in star:

Day	Transaction Type	Transaction Amount
2/1/2009	Initial Deposit	2000.00
2/2/2009	Withdrawal	(20.00)
2/3/2009	Check	(35.50)
2/3/2009	Check	(17.02)
2/6/2009	Check	(75.00)
2/6/2009	Deposit	75.00
2/7/2009	Check	(800.00)
2/10/2009	Check	(68.29)
2/14/2009	Withdrawal	(100.00)

Figure 11-1 A transaction fact table tracks account activity

weeks of February 2009. Each of these transactions is represented by a row in the fact table. To determine the balance of this account, it is necessary to aggregate all transactions up to the point in time in question. If the account was opened on 2/1/2009, this would be a simple matter of aggregating the transactions shown. If, however, the account has been active since the year 2002, computing the balance for February 12, 2009 might involve aggregating thousands of transactions. This is a simple process, but not effective for studying the combined balance of thousands of accounts.

Sometimes, Transaction Data Is Not Stored

Computing the balance from transactions becomes more problematic if the transactions reach further back into the past than is recorded in the data warehouse. The transaction detail for an account that has been active for 50 years, for example, might not be available.

In other cases, keeping transaction details online may be possible but not feasible. The sheer volume of transaction details may be deemed too large to warrant maintaining more than a few month's worth online. These two scenarios would require establishing a pseudo-transaction that represents the account balance as of the point in time at which the data warehouse begins tracking transactions.

Computing balance from transactions is impossible if transactions are not stored at all. Sometimes, the volume of transactions is so great that transactions are purged daily and may not be stored in the data warehouse at all. How then to compute the status? Last, there are some status-oriented measurements that do not correspond to transactions at all. Budgets, temperature readings, and reservoir levels are all examples of measurements that do not correspond to transactions.

Don't Store the Balance with Each Transaction

Designers faced with the challenge of tracking both transactions and their effects may be tempted to store the status measurement as an additional fact in the transaction fact table. You may be familiar with this approach if you have kept a handwritten log for your checkbook: each time you enter a transaction, you write down its amount and the new balance. This approach might make sense in an operational system, where the focus is always the individual transaction, but it does not work well in analytic environments.

There are two reasons why it does not make sense to record a status, level, or balance with each transaction. Perhaps the most obvious reason is that the transaction fact table is sparse. If there is no activity on a particular day, there is no row in which to record this important fact. In the case of the bank account shown in Figure 11-1, for example, there is no row for February 9, since there was no transaction on that day. If someone needed to know the total deposits at the branch as of the end of that day, it would be necessary to go through accounts one by one. Each would be checked for activity that day. If not found, the day before would be checked, and so forth, until a balance was found. This process would have to be repeated for each account.

A potential workaround would be to record a row each day for accounts with no activity. The transaction amount would be zero, but the account balance would be recorded. This ensures that a balance is present for each account for each day but will clutter up reports that are focused on transactions. Rows with the value zero will fill reports, a phenomenon that you learned in Chapter 4 leads to an ever-increasing series of workarounds. Even if accepted, there is still another issue to face when recording the balance with each transaction.

Less obvious, but equally problematic, is the fact that there will be some days where there are *more than one* transaction. If a balance is stored with each transaction, then it is likely it will be double-counted by queries. This can only be avoided by looking for cases where there are multiple rows for a given day, and filtering the query to consider only one row. Computing balance in this manner across a group of accounts, rather than just one, would require a correlated subquery. This might be mitigated with the addition of a flag to indicate the last transaction of the day, but the frog is starting to boil. (See Chapter 4 for more on boiling frogs.)

TIP Balances, levels, and similar status measurements often represent the cumulative effect of a series of transactions. If it is necessary to support the study of this kind of fact, *do not store it with the transactions*. Storing a transaction and its effect in the same row of a fact table is always problematic.

Of course, none of this will help in situations described earlier, in which transactions are not kept online or in which the status measurement does not correspond to any type of transaction. Clearly, an alternative solution is required to support the study of status measurements.

The Snapshot Model

As you have seen, a transaction fact table will not suffice for storing a measurement of status. The solution is to design a periodic snapshot fact table, or simply *snapshot fact table*. The snapshot fact table samples the measurement in question at a predetermined interval. This makes it easy to study the measurement in question, without the need to aggregate a long chain of transaction history.

A snapshot fact table design has several properties that distinguish it from a transaction fact table design. Whereas a transaction fact table's grain may be expressed in various ways, the grain of a snapshot fact table is usually declared in dimensional terms. While a transaction fact table is sparse, snapshots are dense. Last, while the facts in a transaction fact table are fully additive, a snapshot model will contain at least one fact that exhibits a property known as semi-additivity.

Sampling Status with a Snapshot

A snapshot fact table samples a status measurement at a predetermined interval. This interval, combined with one or more dimensions, will be used to define the grain of the snapshot fact table. Each row will contain a fact that records the status measurement in question.

The account snapshot fact table in Figure 11-2 records a balance each day for each account. This declaration of grain involves fewer dimensions than were used for the transaction fact table in Figure 11-1. The day dimension captures the interval at which measurements will be sampled, and the account dimension specifies what will be measured. Account branch and primary account holder are also present, but are not part of the grain. The sole fact, balance, records the status measurement: account balance.

With this design, it is now very easy to determine balances at any point in time, for individual accounts and across multiple accounts. Simply constrain the query for the day in question and aggregate the balance fact. This technique can be used to determine the combined balance for a customer across multiple accounts, study account balance by demographic characteristic, look at the balance across all accounts at each branch, and so forth.

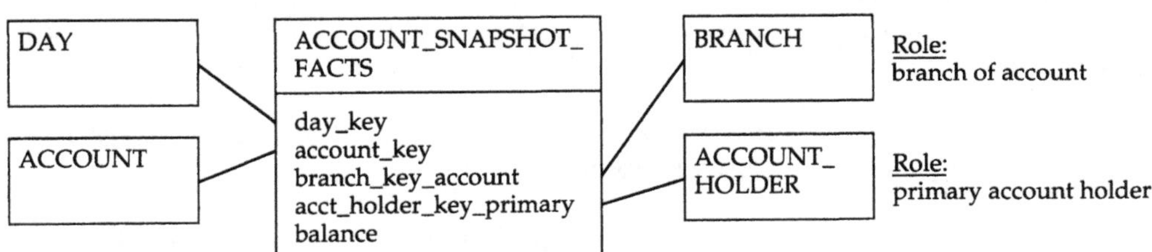

Figure 11-2 A snapshot fact table tracks account status

Snapshot Grain

Whereas the grain of a transaction fact table can be expressed by referring to a business artifact like an order_line or transaction_id, the grain of a snapshot is almost always declared dimensionally. There are two essential parts to the declaration of grain for a snapshot. The first identifies the snapshot period, and the second identifies one or more dimensions that will be sampled at the end of each period.

The account snapshot from Figure 11-2 was described as recording a balance each day for each account. The period in this grain statement is daily; this describes how often balances are sampled. The remaining dimension (account) specifies what will be sampled each period.

TIP The grain of a snapshot must include the periodicity at which status will be sampled, and a definition of what is being sampled. This is usually stated in dimensional terms.

Snapshots can be taken at periodicities other than day. A financial data mart, for example, might include a star that captures month-end snapshots for each G/L account. Snapshots may also require more than one dimension in their declaration of grain. A star that tracks store inventory, for example, might record daily stock levels for each product in each store. The period of this snapshot is daily; the inventory level is recorded for each combination of store and product. (More on this example will appear later in this chapter.)

Density vs. Sparsity

You have probably noticed another key difference between transaction and snapshot. While transaction fact tables are sparse, snapshots are *dense*. In a transaction fact table, a row is only recorded for a combination of dimension values if an activity links them. If there is no transaction on a particular day, no row is recorded. In a snapshot, however, rows are recorded regardless of activity. Failure to do so would render it useless.

The account snapshot in Figure 11-2 records a row for each account at the end of each snapshot period. Since the period is a day, each account will receive exactly one row per day in the fact table. Figure 11-3 shows how this differs from what is stored in the transaction fact table. The table on the left shows transactions for a particular account during a span of two weeks. Each of these transactions generates a single row in the account_facts table. The table on the right illustrates the balance of the account at the end of each day. Each of these periodic balances is represented by a single row in account_snapshot_facts. (Ignore the shaded regions. These will be discussed shortly.)

As you can see, the snapshot is dense; each account is represented for each day. Not so in the transaction fact table. If you examine the data closely, you will see there were a total of nine transactions in this account during these two weeks. In the snapshot, however, 14 rows are recorded for the account during the two-week span—one for each snapshot period.

TIP Snapshot fact tables are dense. Information is recorded each period in accordance with the grain statement, regardless of whether any activity took place.

This density is a crucial feature of the snapshot table. If a row is not recorded for each snapshot period, it becomes difficult to determine status. For example, no transactions

Account: 7922-3002
Period: 2/1/2009 – 2/14/2009

Granular transaction data stored in account_facts:

Day	Transaction Type	Transaction Amount
2/1/2009	Initial Deposit	2000.00
2/2/2009	Withdrawal	(20.00)
2/3/2009	Check	(35.50)
2/3/2009	Check	(17.02)
2/6/2009	Check	(75.00)
2/6/2009	Deposit	75.00
2/7/2009	Check	(800.00)
2/10/2009	Check	(68.29)
2/14/2009	Withdrawal	(100.00)

Periodic status data stored in account_snapshot_facts:

Day	Balance
2/1/2009	2000.00
2/2/2009	1980.00
2/3/2009	1927.48
2/4/2009	1927.48
2/5/2009	1927.48
2/6/2009	1927.48
2/7/2009	1127.48
2/8/2009	1127.48
2/9/2009	1127.48
2/10/2009	1059.19
2/11/2009	1059.19
2/12/2009	1059.19
2/13/2009	1059.19
2/14/2009	959.19

Two transactions occurred on this day
No transactions occurred on these days
Offsetting transactions occurred on this day

Figure 11-3 Account transactions vs. status for a two-week period

occurred on February 13, but a row will be recorded in the snapshot. Without this row, determining the balance for this date would require the following steps:

1. Check the date in question (February 13).
2. If no balance is found, check the previous date.
3. Repeat step 2 until a balance is found.

In this case, it would be necessary to go back to February 10 to find a balance. This is unacceptably onerous, particularly if a large number of accounts are being studied.

Note that this density does not necessarily imply that the snapshot will have more rows than the transaction fact table. Relative sizes will be determined by the snapshot's grain and transaction volume. If accounts average more than one transaction per day, the snapshot may actually be smaller.

In some cases, the density might not be quite so high. A star schema that tracks product inventory in stores would be likely to record rows only for products that are in stock. This avoids the pesky appearance of zero-valued rows making their way into inventory reports.

While a bank will likely want accounts with zero balance to show up on reports, the inventory managers may not want products with no inventory to show up. Products may be discontinued or stocked only at specific locations. The grain statement of the star should make it clear whether rows are to be recorded for zero-valued levels. For the inventory star, the grain can be stated as end-of-day snapshots of in-stock products by location.

Semi-Additivity

The status measurement collected in a snapshot fact table is usually semi-additive. Unlike the additive facts in a transaction fact table, the semi-additive fact cannot be summed meaningfully across the time dimension. This does not mean it cannot be aggregated across time; averages, minimums, and maximums may all be of use. Computation of an average, however, may require care.

The concept of semi-additivity is, sadly, familiar to anyone who owns a bank account. If there is $100 in your account at the end of each day of the week, that does not mean you have $700 at the end of the week. Unfortunately, your account balance is not additive across time. The balance is additive across other dimensions, however. On any given day, it makes perfect sense to add balances together from more than one account, such as your checking and savings accounts. A bank may add balances together for all accounts at a branch or for account holders with particular demographics. As long as the fact is not summed across multiple snapshot periods, it remains additive.

While it cannot be summed, a semi-additive fact may be meaningfully summarized across the problem dimension in other ways. Possibilities include computing the minimum, maximum, and average values. With a savings account, for example, the amount of interest paid each month is often computed using an average daily balance. Fees are often assessed based on the account balance falling below a minimum level during a particular period. Both these measurements summarize a balance across multiple snapshot periods.

TIP In a periodic snapshot, there is usually at least one semi-additive fact that cannot be summed across snapshot periods. This semi-additive fact can be summarized across periods in other ways, including the computation of minimum, maximum, and average values.

In every query and report, semi-additive facts must be used carefully. When summing the semi-additive fact, the query must be constrained by a unique row in the nonadditive dimension, or grouped by rows in the nonadditive dimension. Queries that sum account balances, for example, must either filter for a specific date or group the results by date. If the report contains subtotals or grand totals, the same rules must also be followed within the report itself—do not sum across the nonadditive dimension when creating a total.

The restrictions on the use of semi-additive facts can prove problematic for business intelligence software packages that facilitate *ad hoc* query construction. Generally, there is little that can be done to prevent users from summing the semi-additive fact over the problem dimension. Some tools provide the capability to force a constraint into each query, and this capability can be leveraged to force the user to constrain for a particular snapshot period. This technique has its drawbacks. Although safer, it limits the reports that can be produced to those focused on a single period. Experienced developers may be provided with a separate metadata layer that does not enforce this restriction, allowing them to build reports that group data by periods or construct averages across periods. These techniques are further discussed in Chapter 16.

The SQL AVG() Function

Special care must be taken when averaging values from a periodic snapshot. Sometimes, the SQL AVG() function will provide inaccurate results. The SQL average function works by summing a series of values and then dividing by the number of rows. In the case of the banking example, this allows the computation of a period average. The grain of the star guarantees that there will be one row for each snapshot period.

A snapshot design for store inventory, however, may record rows only for in-stock products. This technique avoids recording rows with zero quantity on hand, which would clutter up reports. If you are averaging the quantity on hand of a particular product during a particular month, it is necessary to sum the snapshot values and then divide by the number of days in the period, rather than rely on SQL's AVG() function.

Always consult the grain of the snapshot fact table before trusting in the SQL AVG() function to construct a period average.

You may have noticed that the last few paragraphs refer to "the nonadditive dimension" or "the problem dimension." For a balance or level in a periodic snapshot, the problem dimension is always the snapshot's period. There are cases, however, where a semi-additive fact's nonadditive dimension is something other than time. An example has already been encountered in this book. The sales_goal star from Figure 5-3 contained a fact called goal_dollars. This fact can be aggregated across months, to compute the total goal over time, or across territories, to compute goals across geographies, but it cannot be aggregated across versions of the sales plan. If two different plans set sales goals for July 2010, these two goal amounts cannot be meaningfully added. Similarly, in a financial system that supports budgeting, there are likely to be multiple versions of the budget. Amount budgeted cannot be aggregated across plan versions.

As already mentioned, some status measurements are not additive at all. Common examples include reservoir water levels, ambient temperature, or the internal pressure of a machine or device. These measurements may be valuable, however, if sampled on a periodic basis in a snapshot. While they cannot be added across any dimension, they can be studied in other ways that may provide valuable process insight, including the computation of minimums, maximums, or averages.

Snapshot Considerations

Despite the difficulties it presents in an *ad hoc* query environment, the snapshot fact table design can be a powerful tool. It may be useful to provide both transaction and snapshot representations of the same process; like two sides of the same coin, these models provide different and valuable perspectives of the same activities. The snapshot need not be limited to containing facts for balances or levels; these may be supplemented with other facts, most of which will be fully additive. Careful attention must be paid to the impact of slowly changing dimensions when it comes to snapshots. Schema designers and ETL developers must be cognizant of these impacts.

Pairing Transaction and Snapshot Designs

Transaction versus snapshot is not an either/or decision. The snapshot and transaction models reflect two aspects of the same process. The transaction model allows detailed analysis of the process activities, placing them in a rich dimensional context. The snapshot model sacrifices some detail, but allows flexible and powerful analysis of the effect of the transactions. Each provides a different but important form of analysis, and many implementations will include both.

In the case of the banking example, the transaction model from Figure 11-1 allows a close study of banking activities. Transactions can be studied by type, branch, teller, primary account holder, and so forth. Each of these dimensions includes a wide variety of attributes that can be used to further shed light on the activities that make up the account management process. The snapshot model in Figure 11-2 provides a different, but equally important, view of this process, allowing analysis of balances across a slightly smaller set of dimensions. Since the snapshot samples the day-end balance, dimensions associated with individual transactions are not included. These include the transaction type, teller, branch where the transaction took place, and degenerate dimension identifying a specific transaction.

When a design will include both a transaction fact table and a periodic snapshot, the snapshot can and should be designed to use the transaction fact table as its data source. This eliminates what would otherwise be duplicative ETL processing of the source data, both for the transactions as well as for the associated dimensions. It also ensures that dimensional data will be identified and loaded consistently.

TIP Transaction and snapshot models tend to complement each other nicely. If both are to be built, design the snapshot to use the transaction star as its data source.

Notice that it is not usually possible to do the reverse—construct transactions from snapshots. If you have any doubts about this assertion, refer back to Figure 11-3. You will see, for example, that there is a group of days during which a particular account has the same balance: February 3–6. It is not possible to tell from the snapshot whether there was

Is a Snapshot an Aggregate?

Students of dimensional design often ask if the snapshot model can be considered an aggregate of the transaction model. The answer is both yes and no. Clearly, a snapshot can be created using the transactional data as its source. For some periods, it may be necessary to factor in several transactions. In this sense, the snapshot is an aggregate.

The term *aggregate*, however, is reserved for a particular form of summarization—one that contains exactly the same facts as the original star. This concept will be explored in full detail in Chapter 15. In the case of a snapshot, the facts are decidedly different from the transaction star. In this sense, the snapshot is not a pure aggregate; it more closely fits the definition of a *derived table*, as described in Chapter 14.

From a purely pragmatic perspective, then, you may call a snapshot whatever you like. It certainly aggregates data, and you can think of it as a summary or aggregate if you like. If you do, be sure not to confuse its capabilities with those of the aggregate stars described in Chapter 15, which answer exactly the same questions as their source stars.

no activity between these snapshots, as is the case for February 4 and February 5, or whether there were offsetting transactions that netted out to a change in the balance of zero, as was the case on February 6.

As previously mentioned, cases exist where there is no transaction data associated with a periodic snapshot. Common examples include things like temperature levels, water levels, and other measurements that sample conditions. In other cases, transactions may contribute to the balance or level, but may be considered too numerous to maintain in any repository. In these cases, a snapshot model may be the only representation of a process and will be sourced directly from an operational system. The operational system itself may sample the status itself, rather than record individual transactions.

Additional Facts

The periodic snapshot need not be limited to storing facts that measure status. While this kind of fact is the *raison d'etre* of the periodic snapshot, additional facts may also prove useful. Facts that summarize the snapshot period can prevent the need to refer to the transaction star when working with the snapshot. In some cases, it is possible that a nonadditive fact, which cannot be reduced to fully additive components, may also be called for. The monthly snapshot in Figure 11-4 illustrates these enhancements.

When reporting on end-of-period status, we often want to know what the status was at the beginning of the period. By storing period-begin and period-end balances, we avoid the need to perform correlated subqueries or reporting tricks to provide this data in a single row. The fact table in Figure 11-4 provides both period-begin and period-end balances. Both facts are semi-additive. They are also redundant; each period-begin balance will be the same as the period-end balance recorded for the account in the snapshot of the prior period.

It can also be useful to provide summary-level information on the activities that occurred during the period. These may include counts of different kinds of transactions, as well as their total magnitudes. In Figure 11-4, additional facts have been added to indicate the number of credit and debit transactions during the snapshot period, as well as the total dollar amount

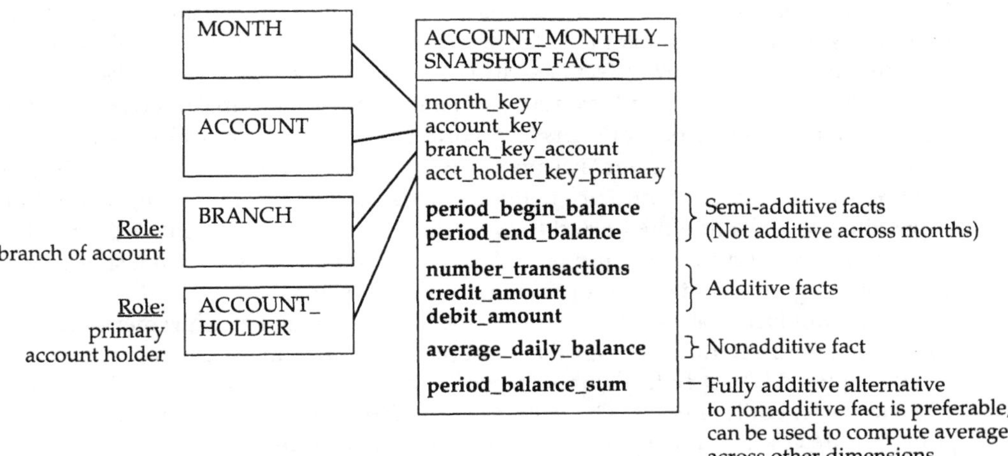

Figure 11-4 Additional facts for a periodic snapshot

of each kind of transaction. Notice that these four facts are fully additive; they can be meaningfully aggregated across any and all dimensions, including the snapshot period.

There may also be interest in recording one or more nonadditive facts with the snapshot. For example, the bank may be interested in the average daily balance of an account over the snapshot period. The average daily balance is nonadditive; it makes no sense to add together averages across accounts, time periods, or any other dimension. If the average daily balance was to be included in each snapshot record, it would only be useful when studying individual accounts. The average daily balance can be decomposed into fully additive components: number of days and a sum of account balances. This latter measurement can be stored in the fact table. Although it has no intrinsic meaning, the sum of the day-end balances of multiple accounts can be divided by the number of days in a period. An average daily balance can be computed for an aggregate of accounts or a range of periods. The star in Figure 11-4 includes facts for both approaches.

TIP A snapshot design can be embellished with additional facts to simplify the query and reporting process. Period-begin and period-end balances are redundant but make many reports much easier to build. Fully additive facts may summarize the quantity and magnitude of transactions of various types during the period; these facts are fully additive. Average balance information may also be useful but is nonadditive. A sum of daily balances for the period makes little sense on its own but is useful in computing averages across various dimensions. Period-to-date metrics may also find a home in the snapshot table.

None of these embellishments is meant to take the place of the transaction fact table. Even with the additional transaction counts and dollar amounts, the periodic snapshot still lacks the transaction-level detail of the original star in Figure 11-1. The transaction model remains of immense utility, though in many cases it may be unmanageably large.

Period-to-Date Measurements

Businesses often track a variety of period-to-date measurements. Examples include month-to-date orders by customer, along with quarter-to-date, year-to-date, and lifetime-to-date versions. These measurements are similar to balance measurements in several ways. Like a balance, they measure the cumulative effect of activities, rather than activities themselves. Also, like a balance, these facts are not additive across the time dimension. It makes no sense to add together lifetime-to-date order dollars for a customer across two successive days.

Period-to-date measurements are not usually stored in transaction fact tables, for the same reason that balance measurements are not stored with transactions. It would be impossible to determine the period-to-date status at a particular point in time unless there happens to be a transaction, and if there are two transactions on a single day, both will have the period-to-date value, risking double-counting.

A snapshot fact table is the logical home for period-to-date measurements. It is sampled on a regular basis, in the same way that a useful period-to-date measurement is sampled, and it is defined by a specific combination of dimensions, in the same way the period-to-date measurement is defined. The period component of the grain statement describes the point in time at which the measurement is collected; the other dimensions describe the entity being measured. For example, the fact table in Figure 11-4 contains one row per account sampled at the end of each month. Several period-to-date facts could be stored, including year-, quarter-, and month-to-date deposits, fees, and withdrawals.

Do not confuse the period component of the snapshot definition with the period being summarized by a period-to-date measurement. The period component of the snapshot grain describes the frequency at which the measurements are sampled. A monthly snapshot can sample quarter-to-date, year-to-date, or lifetime-to date measurements. It should be the case, however, that the remaining dimensions that define the snapshot grain also define the period-to-date measurements. In the case of an account snapshot, stored period-to-date measurements should also describe accounts. This ensures that the period-to-date measurement will remain additive across dimensions other than time. A period-to-date measurement at a higher level of summarization, such as branch, would not be additive since it would repeat for multiple accounts held at the same branch.

Designation of the Period Dimension

The monthly snapshot of account balance may raise a question. Instead of recording the snapshot period with a month dimension, why not simply record the date on which the snapshot was taken? In the case of the monthly snapshot, this date would be the last day of the month—the date on which the balance is sampled.

This approach is valid and used by many schema designers. It may simplify the configuration of some query and reporting tools, particularly those that are not well equipped to handle conformed dimensions such as month and day. However, associating a date with a monthly snapshot also has some drawbacks. Most importantly, there will be many days in this dimension table—roughly 29 out of every 30—for which there is no snapshot data. This can lead to tremendous confusion on the part of users or developers attempting to assemble queries. The use of a period-end date also associates some characteristics of a day dimension, such as day of week and holiday flag, with a row of data that is meant to summarize a period. This is somewhat nonsensical, but you may find it acceptable.

A more semantically consistent approach is to use a conformed version of the time dimension that represents the period being summarized. In the case of the monthly account snapshot in Figure 11-4, this is the month dimension table.

TIP For period snapshots, consider using a time dimension that represents the period being summarized, rather than a day dimension that represents the period-end date.

ETL developers may find utility in an *additional* dimension table representing the last day of the period. This extra piece of information can be useful in constructing snapshots for the current period. During the month of February, for example, the February snapshot for each account can be recomputed and updated. Having a day dimension can help ETL developers maintain this leading edge of the snapshot. If a more summarized period dimension, such as month, is part of the design, this extra day dimension can be hidden from end users.

Snapshots and Slow Changes

As you have seen, dimensions are typically used to define the grain of a periodic snapshot. You have encountered three examples; each includes a time dimension, representing the period, and one or more additional dimensions, representing what is to be sampled. They are restated here, with references to dimensions in bold type:

- **Daily** snapshot of balance for each **account**
- **Daily** snapshot of in-stock product levels by **product** and **location**
- **Monthly** snapshot of balance by **account**

In each of these grain statements, the dimensional references describe the circumstances in which a row will be recorded in the fact table. These references describe unique natural key values. When these dimensions undergo type 2 slow changes, any given natural key may have more than one row in the dimension table. The snapshot, however, must record a row for only one row of each natural key. To record more than one would introduce the very real possibility of double-counting.

Consider the month-end snapshot of account balances from Figure 11-4. Suppose a particular account, perhaps your own, has undergone a type 2 change as a result of a change of address. This means your account will be represented by two rows in the account dimension: one with your old address and the other with your new address. When the month-end snapshot is recorded, the fact table should contain only one row for your account, using whichever version was current at the time.

Were the snapshot to record more than one row for your account, your balance would probably be double-counted in many queries. While you might like what this does to your net worth, it is of course inaccurate. The inventory example, which involves two dimensions in addition to the snapshot period in its grain statement, will record one row for each product/store combination. Products and stores may undergo type 2 changes, but each snapshot row will only refer to what was current at the end of the snapshot period.

TIP A periodic snapshot records only one row for each combination of natural keys in the dimensions that define its grain.

Understanding this requirement is essential for all members of the warehouse team. Although the impact on the ETL process is most obvious, it is important that all team members be made aware of this requirement and that documentation of the star reflects this state of affairs. If an account had multiple versions that were current during different parts of the period, report developers should not assume that all are present in the snapshot. Such an assumption could lead to serious consequences.

Accumulating Snapshot Fact Tables

A transaction fact table records one row for each significant event in a business process. When the focus of analysis is the elapsed time between events, this form of organization is not optimal. Queries will be complex and perform poorly. When it is easy to identify the individual things being processed, an *accumulating snapshot* can streamline this kind of analysis.

Challenge: Studying Elapsed Time Between Events

Many business processes can be described as a series of stages, steps, or statuses through which something must pass. In made-to-order manufacturing, an individual item is ordered, manufactured, quality assured, packaged, and shipped. In banking, a mortgage application is submitted, reviewed by a loan officer, prepared for underwriting, evaluated by an underwriter, and eventually consummated at settlement. In technical support, a problem ticket is logged, assigned, diagnosed, and closed.

The efficiency of a process is often measured as the amount of time it takes to complete one or more steps. The manufacturer may like to know the average number of days between order and shipment, or between manufacturing and packaging. The bank may want to understand the average amount of time it takes to process an application from beginning to end, or group that information by product type or mortgage officer.

These studies of elapsed time require correlating multiple statuses. In a transaction model, each status change is logged in a separate fact table row. This approach works nicely for studying particular status events over time, but it is not useful when these events must be correlated with one another. If correlated analysis of elapsed time will be conducted on a regular basis, something more will be required.

Tracking Process Steps in a Transaction Fact Table

When the item that undergoes a process is readily identifiable (an individual item being manufactured, a specific mortgage application, a trouble ticket), and the processing steps or milestones are well defined (the manufacturing process stages, the mortgage processing stages, the support process), a transaction fact table may be used to track status. Such a fact table records one row for each status change or milestone achieved. This kind of fact table may be tremendously useful in studying processing volume or workload at various steps, and for recording the history of individual items.

When it comes to studying the time spent at each step, however, a transaction table falls short. Although it contains the essential information to study these elapsed timings, its organization renders analysis difficult. The best way to understand this shortcoming is to look at an example. The star in Figure 11-5 tracks the status history of a mortgage application. The fact table receives one row for each status change to an application.

The contents of the status dimension reveal the major processing steps. When someone submits a mortgage application, it is assigned a status of "Submitted." A row is inserted into the fact table, referring to the application, the date of the status assignment, and the name of the status. Each time the status changes, an additional row will be added. In this example, submitted applications are subjected to a review by a mortgage officer, who assesses the application and discusses it with the customer. Once the review is complete, the officer assigns the status "Reviewed." An additional row is added to the fact table for the application, capturing this status change. Applications that have been reviewed are assigned to an administrator who gathers information that will be necessary to underwrite the mortgage—information such as the applicant's most recent tax returns, pay stubs, and so forth. Once this is complete, the application is assigned the status "Processed" and is forwarded to an underwriter to assess the risk. After the work of the underwriter is completed, it is assigned the status of "Underwritten" and the applicant may now schedule a settlement date for the home purchase. On this date, the status becomes "Settled" and the process is over. The mortgage amount may be changed at each step of the way until it is finalized at settlement.

This fact table is useful in studying how many applications achieve particular milestones over time or for studying workload at any particular stage. For example, a business question asked might be, "How many applications were submitted, reviewed, processed, underwritten,

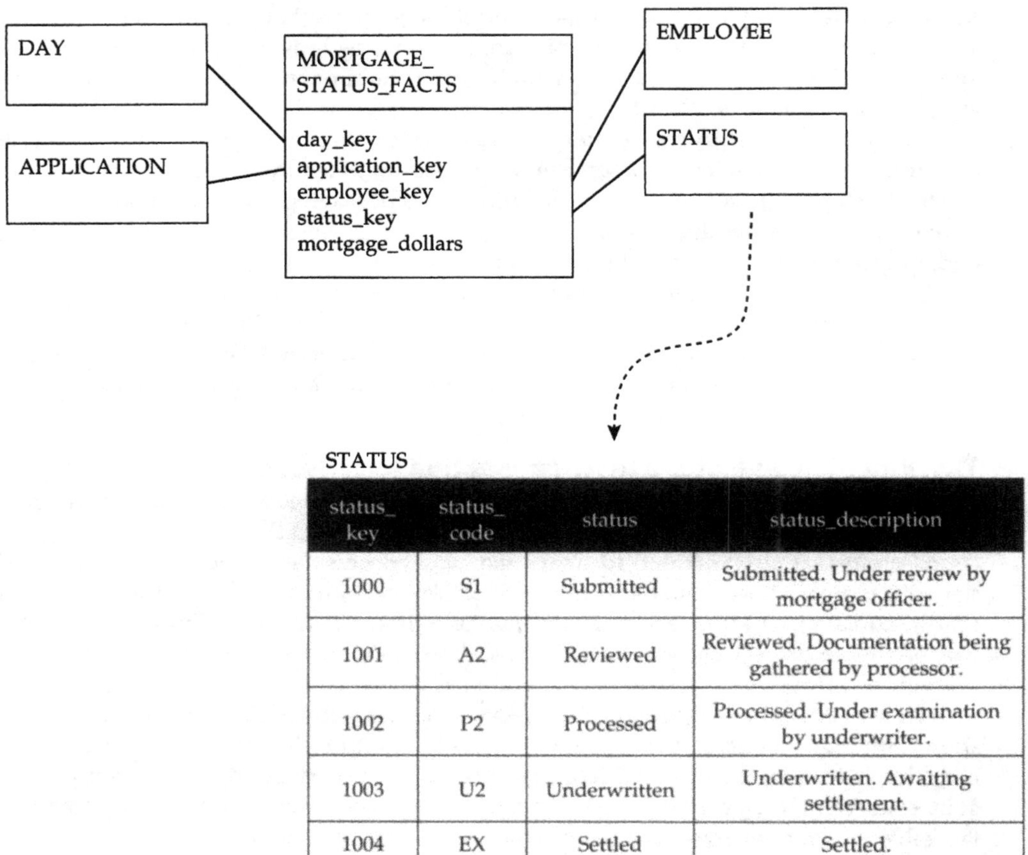

status_key	status_code	status	status_description
1000	S1	Submitted	Submitted. Under review by mortgage officer.
1001	A2	Reviewed	Reviewed. Documentation being gathered by processor.
1002	P2	Processed	Processed. Under examination by underwriter.
1003	U2	Underwritten	Underwritten. Awaiting settlement.
1004	EX	Settled	Settled.

Figure 11-5 A transaction fact table captures status changes

and closed this month?" This question can be answered by grouping row counts by status for the month in question. The question can be made easier to answer by introducing facts that correspond to each milestone. Each will contain the value zero or one. For example, a number_submitted fact will be set to the value 1 in the fact table row for the application that captures its submission, and 0 in all other rows for the application. Similar facts can be added for number_reviewed, number_processed, number_underwritten, and number_settled. These facts make aggregating milestone counts even easier.

TIP A dimension attribute can be transformed into a set of facts, each of which contains the values 0 or 1. This is useful when it is necessary to count the number of transactions that represent the achievement of various status milestones.

Processing volumes are easily analyzed using a transaction fact table like this one. However, it is much more difficult to study processing efficiency. How long did an application spend at each step in the process? This kind of question can be answered, but sometimes with great difficulty.

Where the Transaction Model Falls Short

A key measurement of process efficiency is the amount of time spent at each step in a process. What is the average number of days spent during the review stage for a mortgage application? Does this vary by officer? What about the total time spent processing and underwriting? Does this take longer for particular types of applications?

These questions deal with elapsed time at specific stages. To answer them, it is necessary to correlate rows that represent the status changes. To figure out how long it took to review an application, for example, requires computing the elapsed days between its submission date and its approval date. These statuses are captured in separate rows. To compute this for a group of applications, say those processed by a particular officer, a correlated subquery will be required. For each approved application, the correlated subquery finds the submission date. This kind of query is neither easy to write nor likely to perform very well.

Begin and End Dates Are Not the Answer

For some questions, a correlated subquery can be avoided by using a *pair* of day keys for each status. One represents when the status became effective, the other represents when it expired. In this manner, the amount of time spent at a particular status is represented by the difference between the associated dates. It can be determined by examining a single fact table row, without the need for a correlated subquery. How long was an application at the review stage? Find the row for "Submitted" and look at its begin and end dates.

Unfortunately, this approach has a few shortcomings. First, it typically introduces a problem of vocabulary. Most operational systems that report on status do so in terms of completed milestones. It is more likely that end users will be familiar with statuses of "Submitted," "Reviewed," and "Processed" rather than time-bounded designations such as "Under Review" and "Processing." This may easily be overcome through education and the careful naming of columns, but other shortcomings are not so easily dismissed.

Second, this approach does not help when there is not a linear progression between stages. If an application can be sent back to the review stage after an error is detected during processing, for example, then there will be multiple rows for a particular stage. Information about elapsed time at a particular stage is no longer self-contained in a single row. Depending on how a query is constrained, correlation may still be required in order to find all rows associated with a particular stage, or to determine whether the stage has really completed.

Last, and most importantly, this approach does not eliminate the correlated subquery when looking at the time spent *across multiple stages*. For example, someone might want to know the elapsed time between submission and settlement. Here, the inclusion of begin and end dates for each stage does not help. Submission and settlement are not consecutive milestones; various stages exist between them. For each application, the submission and completion dates will be found in separate fact table rows. This question places us squarely back in the land of the correlated subquery.

TIP A transaction model that describes process steps falls short when studying the time expended at various stages or the time between various milestones.

These shortcomings do not render the transaction model useless. It serves as a useful and reliable source of step-specific analytics. Each row captures all the salient details about the entity in question as it achieves each step in the process. Rather than throw this model away, it may prove useful to supplement it with a fact table of a different design.

The Accumulating Snapshot

Tracking time elapsed at one or more steps of a business process can be supported with a third kind of fact table, called an accumulating snapshot. This kind of design contrasts sharply with transaction and snapshot designs in that fact table rows will be updated, and on a regular basis. The grain of an accumulating snapshot, however, allows it to be used in correlating the dates that various status milestones are achieved and the time spent at each processing stage.

Tracking Process with an Accumulating Snapshot

The grain of an accumulating snapshot design is framed in terms of an identifiable entity that passes through the business process. The fact table will have exactly one row for each instance of the entity. Multiple relationships to the day dimension represent the achievement of each significant milestone or status. Corresponding facts capture the number of elapsed days at each processing stage.

Grain To design an accumulating snapshot, it must be possible to identify unique instances of an entity that is being processed or tracked. The grain will be defined as one row per instance of the entity in question. For mortgage processing, the entity is an application. An accumulating snapshot for mortgage processing will contain exactly one row for each application. That simple statement describes the grain of the fact table, mortgage_processing_facts, in Figure 11-6.

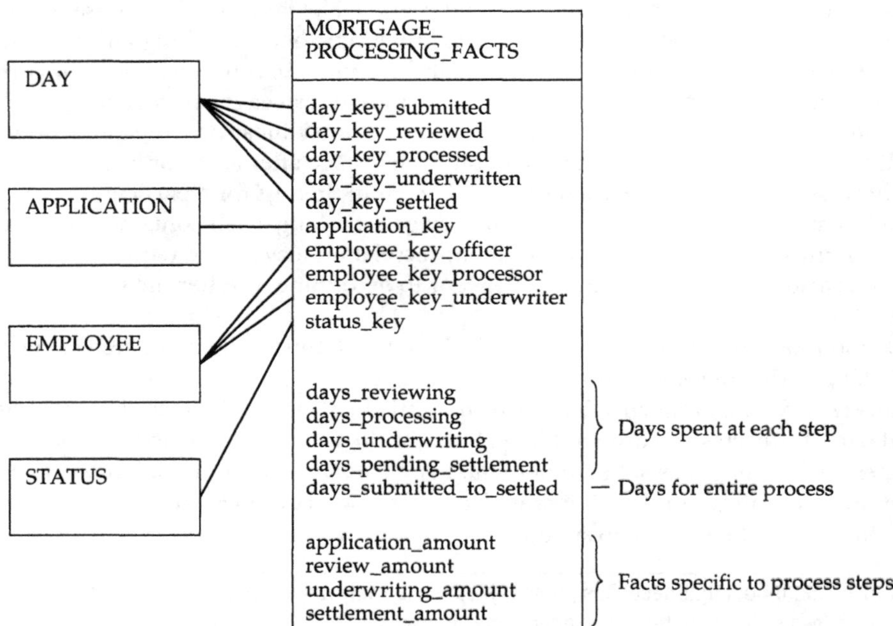

Figure 11-6 An accumulating snapshot with one row per application

This statement of grain contrasts with the grain of a transaction fact table, which typically records one row *per event*, or the grain of a periodic snapshot, which records a row for something *for each period*. Also unlike these designs, the rows in the accumulating snapshot will be regularly updated after they have been inserted. An example of this progression will be studied shortly.

Completion Dates for Milestones The snapshot records the date each monitored processing stage was completed. These dates are represented by a set of day_keys in the fact table. In the case of mortgage_processing_facts, these various dates are named after the milestones. Day_key_submitted, for example, represents the date that the application was submitted by the applicant. At this point, the application is assigned to an officer to be reviewed. Day_key_reviewed represents the date the review was completed and the application was passed along to the processing stage. One date is present for each of the processing stages to be studied.

In this example, there are also three relationships to an employee table. These three relationships represent the officer who reviewed the application, the processor who gathered the supporting materials, and the underwriter who assessed its risk.

NOTE There is no need to build multiple versions of the employee or day dimensions; each role can be isolated using a view, or through the aliasing capability of SQL. (If you need a refresher on the use of a single dimension table in multiple roles, see Chapter 6.)

Facts for Elapsed Time at Each Stage Each row in the accumulating snapshot contains a group of facts that measure the number of days spent at each stage. When an application has "Submitted" status, it is in the reviewing stage. The amount of time an officer spends reviewing an application after it is submitted is captured by days_reviewing. Once it has achieved "Reviewed" status, it is in the processing stage. The time spent by the processor processing the application is captured by days_processing. An additional fact, called days_submitted_to_settled, tracks the time spent from the beginning of the process to the end. This fact is redundant; its value is equal to the sum of the other counts. It can be omitted, if desired.

These facts are sometimes referred to as "lags" because they represent the elapsed time between the dates associated with successive status milestones. An alternative way to name them is to describe the two milestones that demarcate each stage. The days_reviewing fact, for example, can also be thought of as the lag time between the submission of the application and the completion of the review. It could be called lag_submitted_reviewed. Naming the fact after the processing stage, however, is a more flexible approach. As you will see, it allows the fact to remain useful in situations where a particular application may reenter a given stage.

Note that some other facts are also present in this fact table. The amount of the mortgage may be changed at the end of each stage; separate facts capture its value at the end of each stage. The exception here is the processing stage. During this stage, documents are gathered, but the application itself is not altered.

Life Cycle of a Row

Unlike transaction and snapshot fact tables, accumulating snapshot fact tables will have their rows updated on a regular basis. Facts for elapsed time will be incremented as days go by, and milestone dates will be set whenever a new status is achieved. Mortgage_processing_facts, for example, will be updated nightly. During each load, the time an application has spent at its current stage will be incremented. If an application reaches a new stage, the appropriate day_key will be set, and the mortgage amount for the completed stage will be recorded.

Figure 11-7 illustrates this process. It shows the evolution of a *single row* in the fact table over time. The row in the example represents a mortgage application that has a surrogate key value 1011. The state of this row is shown at various points in time; the shaded areas show what has changed. Keep in mind that this diagram represents *the same row* at various points in time, not a series of different rows.

The top of the diagram shows the row placed in the fact table on the day that this mortgage application is submitted. The row contains the application's surrogate key. It is populated with a day_key_submitted for the current date. This is the date the application entered the review stage. Since the application has not yet reached the other stages, the associated day_keys are populated with key value 0, which refers to a special row in the day table for events that have not yet occurred. (Chapter 6 describes this kind of special-case row in more detail.) The requested mortgage amount of $100,000 is recorded in the column application_amount. The remaining amount columns are initialized to the value 0.

The next day, the status of the application has not changed. It is still at the review stage. The days_reviewing fact is incremented, showing that the application has spent one day at that stage. No other changes have occurred.

No status changes occur on days 3–9. Although not shown, the days_reviewing fact for application 1011 is incremented at the end of each of these days.

On Day 1 (Submitted; under review by officer):

application_key	day_key_submitted	day_key_reviewed	day_key_processed	day_key_underwritten	day_key_closing	application_amount	review_amount	underwriting_amount	days_reviewing	days_processing	...
1011	1021	0000	0000	0000	0000	100,000	0	0	0	0	

Day 2 (No status change):

application_key	day_key_submitted	day_key_reviewed	day_key_processed	day_key_underwritten	day_key_closing	application_amount	review_amount	underwriting_amount	days_reviewing	days_processing	...
1011	1021	0000	0000	0000	0000	100,000	0	0	1	0	

Days 3–9 (not shown)...

Day 10 (Reviewed; documents being gathered by processor):

application_key	day_key_submitted	day_key_reviewed	day_key_processed	day_key_underwritten	day_key_closing	application_amount	review_amount	underwriting_amount	days_reviewing	days_processing	...
1011	1021	1031	0000	0000	0000	100,000	90,000	0	9	0	

Day 11 (No status change):

application_key	day_key_submitted	day_key_reviewed	day_key_processed	day_key_underwritten	day_key_closing	application_amount	review_amount	underwriting_amount	days_reviewing	days_processing	...
1011	1021	1031	0000	0000	0000	100,000	90,000	0	9	1	

Remaining steps...

Figure 11-7 Evolution of a row in an accumulating snapshot

On day 10, the officer finishes reviewing the application and passes it along to the processor. Days_reviewing is incremented one last time. The day_key for the current date is used to populate the day_key_reviewed, indicating that the review is complete. The officer has changed the mortgage amount to $90,000, and this is recorded in the review_amount column.

On day 11, the application remains at the processing stage. The days_processing fact is incremented. This will continue daily until the next status is achieved, at which point the appropriate date will be filled in and the next elapsed days fact will begin accumulating.

NOTE It is not always possible to engineer a solution where every row of an accumulating snapshot is updated daily. In the mortgage example, there may be less than 100,000 active applications at any given time. An ETL process can efficiently update each row in the fact table for this volume of applications. When the number of items being tracked is too large for this kind of processing, the ETL process can be designed to update fact table rows only for items that have undergone a status change. This saves on ETL processing, but makes it more difficult to use the accumulating snapshot. Reports that aggregate time spent at various stages will require extra work if they are to include items that have yet to complete the stage.

Using the Accumulating Snapshot

Constructed in this manner, the accumulating snapshot is a useful and powerful tool for studying time spent at any processing stage or any combination of stages. Elapsed days can be studied in terms of their minimums, maximums, or averages across any relevant dimensions, simply by aggregating the appropriate facts as required. No correlated subquery is necessary.

For example, the average processing time for applications that were processed in January 2009 can be determined with a simple SQL statement:

```
SELECT
   AVG( days_processing )
FROM
   mortgage_processing_facts,
   day
WHERE
   mortgage_processing_facts.day_key_processed = day.day_key AND
   day.month = "January" AND
   day.year = 2009
```

Similarly, the average time spent reviewing and processing an application is easily computed:

```
SELECT
   AVG( days_reviewing + days_processing )
FROM
   mortgage_processing_facts,
   day AS day_processed
WHERE
   mortgage_processing_facts.day_key_processed = day_processed.day_key AND
   day_processed.month = "January" AND
   day_processed.year = 2009
```

Part IV

Queries like these can be further embellished, for example by grouping results by a particular processor, customer characteristic, or application characteristic. In all cases, a correlated subquery is not required.

TIP An accumulating snapshot design can measure time spent at various processing stages. One row is recorded for each instance of the entity on which the process operates. This row will have multiple day keys that refer to the date of entry into each status, and facts that will accumulate the number of days spent in each status. These facts can be aggregated or averaged across various dimensions to study the efficiency of the various processing stages.

Averages are not the only option. Queries may look for minimum or maximum values, using the SQL `MIN()` and `MAX()` functions. Some reports may list the number of applications that spend more than a certain amount of time at a stage, making use of the `COUNT()` function in conjunction with a `WHERE` clause, as in `COUNT(*) WHERE days_processing > 5`.

The accumulating snapshot is an effective vessel for recording facts that describe elapsed time at various processing stages and enabling powerful reporting capabilities. Of course, the story does not end here. A variety of additional considerations should be reviewed when building an accumulating snapshot.

Accumulating Snapshot Considerations

As with the periodic snapshot, the accumulating snapshot is not a replacement for the transaction model. In many cases, the two will complement each other nicely. Sometimes, the major milestones of interest when measuring elapsed time do not correspond directly to individual statuses, but instead summarize them. In other cases, the operational process may not be a standard linear progression. In still other cases, separate operational systems may track different elements of status. These complications can all be overcome but will increase the ETL complexity. Finally, it is important to consider the impact of slowly changing dimensions on the accumulating snapshot design.

Pairing Transaction and Accumulating Snapshot Designs

The accumulating snapshot is a useful tool for studying the elapsed time spent at one or more processing steps. Keep in mind, though, that this is not the only way to study a process. Other forms of analysis are better suited to a transaction model like the one in Figure 11-5. Common examples include the reporting of numbers of items processed at various stages, studying workloads, and the analysis of process patterns.

When the design for a business process includes both a transaction star and an accumulating snapshot, the accumulating snapshot should use the transaction star as its source. This step ensures consistency across the two stars, both in terms of the activities they represent and in terms of the representation of dimensional detail. As an alternative to sourcing both stars to an operational system (or enterprise data warehouse in a Corporate Information Factory architecture), this approach also simplifies the ETL processing and eliminates some redundancy.

TIP Transaction and accumulating snapshot models complement each other nicely. The accumulating snapshot allows the study of elapsed time at processing stages, while the transaction model allows analysis of the steps themselves. If both are built, design the accumulating snapshot to use the transaction star as its source.

In some cases, it may be possible to do the reverse: construct a transaction star using an accumulating snapshot as the source. This approach tends to be additional work, however, since most operational data is collected in a format that is closer to the status model. Some variations on the accumulating snapshot design may render this impossible. As you are about to learn, an accumulating snapshot may not include every processing step, instead limiting those measured to major milestones.

Focus on Key Status Milestones

In the mortgage processing example, the accumulating snapshot captured the dates and elapsed time at five processing stages. Sometimes the number of possible statuses is far larger. It is not uncommon for an operational system to support a complex process with dozens of possible status values. An accumulating snapshot becomes highly impractical as the number of statuses recorded grows this large.

When there is a very large number of status values, an accumulating snapshot can be designed to provide a simplified view of the process. Rather than track each individual status, you can design the snapshot to track the major milestones of a process. Schema designers work with business managers to identify the key milestones, each of which is mapped to one or more status values. These milestones become the subject of the accumulating snapshot.

For example, suppose that the mortgage approval process is tracked by an operational system that has far more than five statuses. The status codes in Figure 11-8 illustrate a much more detailed view of the processing activities. The total number of status codes in this case may be closer to 75. Clearly, this is too many statuses to record in an accumulating snapshot.

Status Codes from Operational System

status_code	category	status	
S1	Submitted	Submitted	Review activity
S2	Submitted	Under review by officer	
S3	Submitted	Awaiting customer response	
R1	Reviewed	Under review by processor	Processing activity
R2	Reviewed	Taxes requested	
R3	Reviewed	Paystubs requested	
R4	Reviewed	Credit fee requested	
R5	Reviewed	Taxes received	
R6	Reviewed	Paystubs received	
R7	Reviewed	Credit fee received	
R8	Reviewed	Credit report ordered	
U1	Processed	Forwarded to underwriter	Underwriting activity

Figure 11-8 A larger set of operational status codes can be mapped to a small number of milestones

Part IV

Although the list of status codes is long, the key metrics of interest to the business are short. Managers want to study the amount of time applications spend between the major milestones of submission, review, and so forth. These milestones imply a series of stages, and the individual status codes can be mapped to these stages, as illustrated to the right of the sample table. Time spent in any of the first three statuses, for example, is counted as part of the review process; time spent in any of the next set of eight statuses is counted as part of the processing stage; and so forth.

With statuses mapped to major milestones in this manner, it is possible to build an accumulating snapshot that focuses on the milestones and the time elapsed between them. The resulting star will be no different from the one presented in Figure 11-6, but the ETL process will be more complex.

TIP An accumulating snapshot does not have to track every status change recorded in the operational system. It can be designed to track key milestones, or summary-level statuses, that are tracked by the business.

Sophisticated status tracking systems may record a good deal of information with each status change, noting a completed milestone as well as the current activity with each status code. They may also provide categories or groupings. Sometimes, categories are exactly what the business wants to study. The status categories in Figure 11-8, for example, happen to map nicely into the major milestones. These groupings do not have to exist in order to summarize a set of statuses, but they may help.

Multi-source Process Information

In some cases, information about a business process is not gathered in a single place. This does not prevent the development of an accumulating snapshot, but may provide additional challenges for the schema designers and ETL developers.

Suppose that the mortgage processing is handled in separate systems. One supports customers and mortgage officers early in the process; the other supports the processing and underwriting stages. These systems may collect different kinds of information about processing steps. The underwriting system, for example, may collect information on associated documents and various measurements of assessed risk. An application identifier is the unifying link between these systems.

When more than one operational system tracks the same process, the systems can serve as the basis for a single accumulating snapshot. The schema designers must think through the process that will be used to match data from the two systems, determine what to do if both systems record a status for the same item, and develop rules to use when the systems are in disagreement.

For example, once the initial phases of the application are completed by the mortgage officer, the early-stage operational application may continue to track the application at a very high summary level. The underwriting system, in parallel, begins tracking more detailed status information. In designing a consolidated accumulating snapshot, it will be necessary to determine which status is used at each stage, and what to do in situations where the status designations do not agree.

In a Corporate Information Factory, this consolidation may take place at the enterprise data warehouse, prior to the construction of a data mart. In this case, a single source will be available. However, it may also be the case that the enterprise data warehouse tracks the subprocesses differently, since each subprocess has a different set of attendant detail. In this case, the dimensional designers of the data marts will be required to integrate the data. In other architectures, it will always fall to the dimensional design team to plan for this integration. It may be done as part of the process of developing a single integrated transaction star of all status changes, or separate transaction fact tables may be designed for each subprocess, with integration taking place at the accumulating snapshot.

Nonlinear Processes

Many business processes are not linear or predictable. Rather than proceeding through a standard rigid set of milestones, the process may involve optional, alternative, or repeating steps. These situations do not preclude the use of an accumulating snapshot, but they will require some additional due diligence during the schema design process.

The mortgage process modeled earlier went through a predictable and consistent set of steps. Each application went through the following statuses, in order:

Submitted → Reviewed → Processed → Underwritten → Settled

The process may not be this cut and dried. Applications may skip steps in special cases or be returned to a prior stage for various reasons. Suppose, for example, that after the processor receives an application, it is discovered that the applicant's signature is missing. In this case, the application is sent back to the officer, its status reverting from "Reviewed" to "Submitted." For this particular application, the series of statuses looks like this:

Submitted → Reviewed → **Submitted** → ...

When the process is nonlinear, it is still possible to accumulate accurate time spent at each stage. Recall that as each milestone is achieved, the fact associated with the next milestone begins incrementing. For example, when an application is submitted, the days_reviewing fact is incremented daily until the next status is achieved. Once the application has been reviewed, the days_processing fact starts incrementing. If the application is then returned to an earlier status, the ETL process can simply resume incrementing the appropriate fact. In this case, a return to the submitted status will require resumption of daily increments to the days_reviewing fact.

A potentially thornier issue is what date to use for the various status milestone dates in the fact table. If an application is returned to the "Submitted" stage and is then approved again, what date values should be referred to by day_key_submitted and day_key_approved? If the milestones are significant, chances are good that the business already has a rule. For example, the bank may consider the submission date to be the earliest day that an application is assigned that status, while the official approval date is the latest date on which an approval status has been assigned.

TIP A process that does not proceed through a fixed series of predictable milestones can still be tracked by an accumulating snapshot. This will require careful definition of rules defining which fact should be incremented at any given time. It will also require determination of which date to use if a particular status is achieved more than once. These choices should be made by business users, not designers or developers.

When working with a nonlinear process, it is essential to work with business users to make determinations about which facts to increment at any given time and which dates to use when a milestone is reached. Remember that the star is meant to represent a business process and that these decisions reflect how the business measures the process. Although a schema designer or ETL developer may be able to conceive of one or more options, it must be left to the business to determine the one that reflects how the process is evaluated.

Slow Changes

One final consideration for the design of accumulating snapshots has to do with type 2 changes. The accumulating snapshot should contain only one row per natural key value found in the dimension that defines its grain. When the dimension undergoes a type 2 change, the surrogate key in the fact table should be updated with the most current value. Use of the natural key in the fact table is not advisable; such an approach can easily lead to double-counting.

As you have learned, the grain of the accumulating snapshot is one row per "thing," or instance of an entity, that moves through the process. This thing will be represented by a row in a dimension table. The subject of intense scrutiny, this thing will probably be closely monitored for changes, too. When a type 2 change occurs, the thing that is being processed has *more than one row* in the dimension table. A mortgage application that has undergone a type 2 change, for example, has two rows in the application dimension. Each has its own surrogate key, but they share the same natural key.

Though the dimension table may carry more than one for a given natural key, *the accumulating snapshot should contain only one.* The fact table grain calls for one row per instance of the entity being tracked, not more than one. Mortgage_processing_facts, for example, must have one row per mortgage application. Carrying two or more rows would either cause double-counting or defeat the purpose of avoiding the correlated subquery.

Whenever the defining dimension of an accumulating snapshot undergoes a type 2 change, the corresponding row in the fact table should be updated with the most recent surrogate key. When a type 2 change is logged against a mortgage application, for example, the row in the accumulating snapshot for that application is updated to contain the surrogate key for the new version. This is not as onerous as its sounds, since the ETL process must revisit each row of the accumulating snapshot on a regular basis anyway. By using the most recent surrogate key, you associate the entire history of the process with the current view of the thing being processed.

Since the fact table will have only one row per natural key, you might be tempted to use the natural key in the fact table instead of a surrogate key. Although this may seem logical at first, a closer look reveals that this approach can only lead to disaster. If that natural key of the mortgage application were to be used as a foreign key in the fact table, and that application has undergone a type 2 change, the single fact table row would have *two* corresponding rows in the dimension table. This would cause the application to be counted twice in many queries, unless specific predicates were added to the query to eliminate duplicates.

TIP When something represented by the defining dimension of an accumulating snapshot undergoes a type 2 change, there will be two rows for it in the dimension table. The surrogate key of the most recent row should be used in the fact table. Do not use the natural key since this will result in double-counting.

One side effect of this requirement generates a notable contrast with other types of fact tables: the dimension table is likely to have more rows than the fact table itself. This should not be viewed as an error; it is in keeping with the analytic requirements. It can pose a tuning challenge for database administrators, who may find that star-join optimization is not the most efficient way to resolve a query involving an accumulating snapshot.

Finally, note that an accumulating snapshot does not associate a historically accurate version of the thing being processed with each milestone achieved. It refers to the entity once, and that reference is the most up-to-date version. If the historic context of each processing step is required, this information can be obtained by consulting a transaction-based star, such as the one depicted in Figure 11-5. Together, the two designs can be used to answer a wide variety of business questions. If a transaction design is not required for other purposes, the accumulating snapshot can be supplemented to carry multiple references to the dimension—one for each milestone.

Summary

This chapter introduced two new forms of fact table design: the periodic snapshot and accumulating snapshot. Each was motivated by a particular analytic challenge that is not well served by a transaction fact table design, and each has unique characteristics.

- A transaction fact table tracks events. Its grain usually corresponds to an individual transaction or a summary of transactions.
- Facts that describe a level, balance, or similar status can sometimes be computed from the transactions that contribute to their value, but not always. When they can be computed, the process is not usually very efficient.
- A snapshot fact table samples a balance, level, or status measurement at a predefined interval across specified dimensions. Unlike a transaction fact table, a snapshot tends to be very dense.
- Balance or level measurements in a periodic snapshot are usually semi-additive; it does not make sense to sum them across snapshot periods. In some cases, they may be nonadditive.
- A snapshot can be embellished with period-begin and -end balances, as well as fully additive facts that summarize the period. They may also include a sum that can be used to compute the average balance or level.
- A business process that represents a series of steps or statuses may be tracked using a transaction fact table. This model is useful for studying and quantifying the various activities but is notoriously difficult to use when studying the elapsed time spent at one or more stages.
- If the items being processed can be readily identified, an accumulating snapshot can be designed. It will have one row for each instance of the item undergoing the business process. This row is repeatedly updated as the process unfolds.
- The accumulating snapshot includes multiple day_keys, each representing the achievement of an important milestone. Facts record the elapsed time associated with each stage. Additional facts may be present that track significant values at the time of each milestone.

Remember that it is not necessary to make either/or decisions between transaction stars and periodic or accumulating snapshots. Analytic requirements for a particular process may call for a pair of fact tables. In this case, the transaction model should be used as the source for the snapshot or accumulating snapshot.

Further Reading

The snapshot and accumulating snapshot are common dimensional design techniques, and many additional examples can be found. Whether you are seeking more information or just looking for additional examples, here are some places you will find what you are looking for.

Snapshot Fact Tables

- The examples in this chapter have been chosen to illustrate key design concepts. Although they are set in the financial services industry, these designs should not be interpreted as a complete treatment of the subject area. For a deeper discussion of financial services, consult Chapter 9 of *The Data Warehouse Toolkit, Second Edition* (Wiley, 2002) by Ralph Kimball and Margy Ross. The chapter includes an account snapshot model similar to the one presented here, and incorporates other techniques such as mini-dimensions, householding, multi-valued attributes, and stars for separate account types.
- This chapter mentions the snapshot model's applicability when studying inventory. For a detailed example, see Chapter 3 of *The Data Warehouse Toolkit.*
- A snapshot can also be used to study capacity and utilization. An example from the hotel industry appears in Chapter 6 of *Data Warehouse Design Solutions* (Wiley, 1998) by Chris Adamson and Mike Venerable. (The chapter also includes an inventory snapshot design.)
- Kimball and Ross show how transaction and snapshot can complement each other in an accounting subject area. In Chapter 7 of *The Data Warehouse Toolkit,* they pair a transaction star with a snapshot to model activity in G/L accounts.
- Snapshots that track the status of other financial processes, such as budgeting and spending, can be found in Chapter 8 of *Data Warehouse Design Solutions.*
- Kimball and Ross also use a snapshot model to track the status of insurance policy premium payments. You can find it in Chapter 15 of *The Data Warehouse Toolkit.*

Accumulating Snapshots

- This chapter described pairings of a transaction star with either a periodic snapshot or an accumulating snapshot. Kimball and Ross provide a scenario that calls for all three: inventory. As already mentioned, this example can be found in Chapter 3 of *The Data Warehouse Toolkit.*
- An accumulating snapshot used to track order fulfillment is presented by Kimball and Ross in Chapter 5 of *The Data Warehouse Toolkit.* A similar example appears in Chapter 6 of *The Data Warehouse Lifecycle Toolkit, Second Edition* (Wiley, 2008) by Ralph Kimball, Margy Ross, Warren Thornthwaite, Joy Mundy, and Bob Becker.

- Accumulating snapshots may also track promised versus actual time that is spent processing an item. Chapter 4 of *Data Warehouse Design Solutions* presents a fulfillment model that does this for a flower delivery business.
- An accumulating snapshot that tracks the college admissions process can be found in Chapter 12 of *The Data Warehouse Toolkit.*
- The complex billing life cycle associated with health care services is given the accumulating snapshot treatment by Kimball and Ross in Chapter 13 of *The Data Warehouse Toolkit.*
- An accumulating snapshot for the claims process in the insurance industry appears in Chapter 15 of *The Data Warehouse Toolkit.*

Aggregate Design

- Snapshots and accumulating snapshots must be evaluated carefully when they are to serve as the source of a summary table or aggregate. These issues are fully explored in Chapter 8 of *Mastering Data Warehouse Aggregates* (Wiley, 2006) by Chris Adamson.

CHAPTER

12 Factless Fact Tables

In a dimensional design, the fact table is the locus for process measurement. It is the place where measurements are stored. The measurements are called facts, which is where the fact table gets its name. Paradoxically, a fact table does not always require facts to measure a process.

A fact table that contains no facts is called a *factless fact table.* This oxymoron aptly describes the design technique discussed in this chapter. Although no facts are explicitly recorded in a factless fact table, it does support measurement. A factless fact table is useful in two kinds of situations:

- **Factless fact tables for events** record the occurrence of activities. Although no facts are stored explicitly, these events can be counted, producing meaningful process measurements. Examples include the number of documents processed or approved, the number of calls to a customer support center, or the number of impressions of an advertisement.
- **Factless fact tables for conditions** are used to capture significant information that is not part of a business activity. Conditions associate various dimensions at a point in time. When compared with activities, they provide valuable insight. Examples of conditions include eligibility of people for programs, the assignment of salesreps to customers, active marketing programs for a product, or special weather conditions in effect.

This chapter teaches the ins and outs of factless fact table design in each of these situations. You will learn when factless fact tables are necessary, how to design them, and how they are used.

Events with No Facts

Sometimes, there appear to be no facts to describe an important business activity. You may be able to define the process, identify fact table grain, and specify numerous dimensions, but find yourself unable to identify any facts.

This should not stop you from designing a star schema to track the process. In this situation, you can design a *factless fact table*. Although it contains no facts, it measures the business activity. Analysis is conducted by counting rows in the fact table. Adding a fact that is always populated with the value 1 can simplify query writing but is not required. Sometimes, if you look closely enough, you may find a fact after all, but a factless design is perfectly acceptable.

Nothing to Measure?

For many business processes, the only measurement is the occurrence of events or activities. There are no dollar amounts to be aggregated, no quantities to be summed, no balances to be averaged. Activities *are* taking place, however—sometimes at a breakneck pace.

Businesses measure this kind of process simply by counting the activities. Examples of this kind of activity abound. For example:

- The processing of documents (like contracts or applications) is measured by counting how many are handled by day across a variety of dimensions, including activity (received, reviewed, rejected, etc.), customer, and person doing the processing.
- Customer support is measured by counting the number of service requests opened, closed, or otherwise processed by representative, customer, product, and problem ticket.
- Advertisers count the number of impressions, or exposures to an advertisement, across a variety of dimensions.
- Web site usage is measured by counting page views or interface clicks.
- Schools and businesses track attendance or absence.

You may hear dimensional modelers say no measurements exist for these processes. This is not entirely true: counts *are* legitimate and important measurements. It just so happens it is not necessary to *store* a fact to support counting. The fact table may be factless, but the process *is* measured.

The Factless Fact Table

When the only thing measured is the occurrence of events, it is possible to design a factless fact table. Like any other fact table, it has a grain. The grain is defined such that each row represents an individual activity. Every row contains foreign keys that refer to the dimensional context of the activity, and perhaps one or more degenerate dimensions. Although no facts are explicitly recorded, the mere existence of a row in this table constitutes a measurement: one activity occurred.

TIP Activities with no associated facts can be tracked in a factless fact table. Each row is a set of foreign keys that describes the dimensionality of the event. The presence of a row constitutes a measurement.

Customer contact can be measured in this manner. Suppose that a business wants to measure the amount of contact that takes place with customers. Understanding this may help it fine-tune various activities, avoiding situations where customers are contacted too frequently or too infrequently. In this example, assume there are two channels for customer contact: e-mail and telephone. A given contact may be initiated by the customer (inbound) or by the business (outbound). Some outbound contacts may be automated, such as an e-mail newsletter, while others are not. This activity is measured by the factless fact table in Figure 12-1.

The fact table contact_facts measures customer contact activities. Its grain is defined as one row for each contact event with a customer. Each row includes foreign keys that refer to dimension tables, and nothing else. The dimensions include the date and time of the contact, the customer contacted, and the type of contact. Examples of contact types are illustrated beneath the schema diagram.

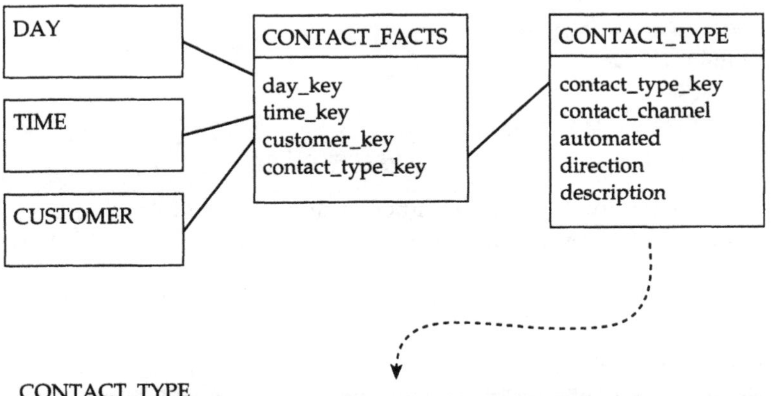

CONTACT_TYPE

contact_ type_key	contact_ channel	automated	direction	description
100	E-Mail	Automated	Outbound	Weekly Coupons
101	E-Mail	Automated	Outbound	eNews Mailing
102	E-Mail	Not Automated	Inbound	Tech Support
103	E-Mail	Not Automated	Outbound	Tech Support
104	Telephone	Not Automated	Outbound	Promotional Offer
105	Telephone	Not Automated	Inbound	Tech Support
106	Telephone	Not Automated	Outbound	Tech Support

Figure 12-1 A factless fact table

Using a Factless Fact Table

Although no facts are stored in a factless fact table, it does support measurement of the business process. It can be used to answer a wide variety of analytic questions, simply by counting rows in the fact table. Dimensions can be used to filter or group the counts in a variety of useful ways.

Using the contact_facts star, it is possible to measure how often a customer is contacted by counting rows in the fact tale. This is done by choosing an arbitrary column in the fact table to count. The number of times John Smith was contacted during the month of January 2009 can be measured by the following query:

```
SELECT
   COUNT( contact_facts.contact_type_key )  /* Count an arbitrary
                                               fact table column */
FROM
   day,
   customer,
   contact_facts
WHERE
   customer.name = 'John Smith' AND
   day.month = 'January' AND
   day.year = 2009 AND
   day.day_key = contact_facts.day_key AND
   customer.customer_key = contact_facts.customer_key
```

The query returns a single number—the number of contacts with John Smith during the month. It can be embellished by grouping results by channel from the contact_type dimension table:

```
SELECT
   contact_type.contact_channel,
   COUNT( contact_facts.contact_type_key )
   .
   .
   .
GROUP BY
   contact_type.contact_channel
```

This version provides the number of contacts for channels such as "E-mail" and for "Telephone." Adding the direction attribute would further group results by "Inbound" and "Outbound."

The variations on this theme are limited only by the availability of dimension attributes. Dimension values can be used to constrain the query, sort data, group facts, and so forth. As always, a rich set of dimensions enables a wide range of analytics.

TIP The events in a factless fact table can be aggregated by counting rows. Any column in the fact table can serve as the basis of the count.

Earlier in this book, you encountered another example of a factless fact table. The star in Figure 8-2 was used to track the history of changes to an insurance policy dimension. The grain of the fact table was defined as one row per change to a policy. Foreign keys referred to the policy dimension, the effective date, and the expiration date. Like contact_facts, the fact table contained no facts but could be used for various kinds of analysis. While the policy_change_facts design was easily converted into a time-stamped dimension, this is not an option for contact_facts.

Adding a Fact

When a factless fact table tracks events, it is possible to make it resemble a standard fact table by adding a special fact. This fact will always contain the value 1. Although superfluous, the addition of this column makes it easier to read and write the SQL to analyze the process. In the case of contact_facts, this is achieved by adding a fact called "contact," as depicted in Figure 12-2. The new fact, contact, will always contain the value 1, as shown in the instance grid beneath the schema diagram.

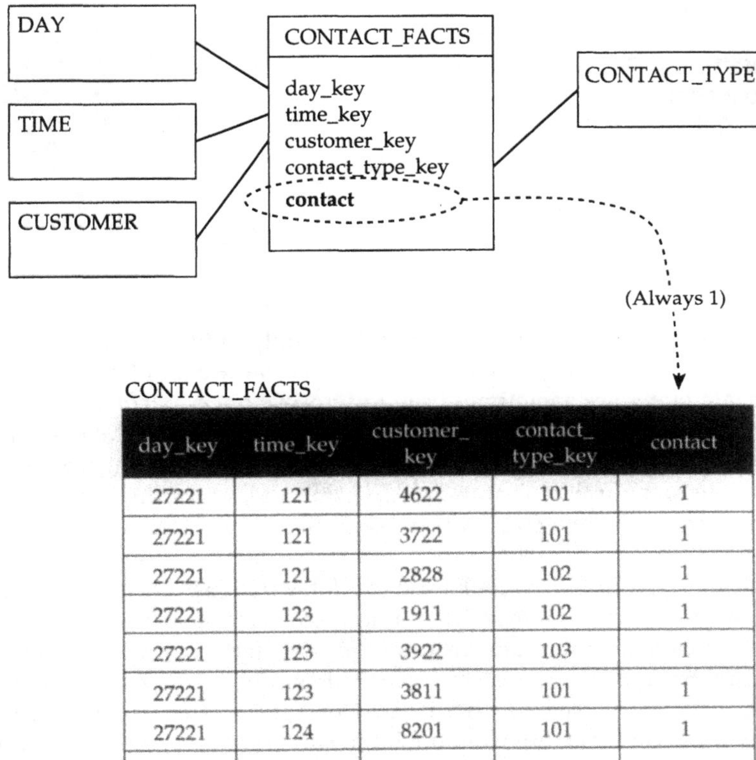

day_key	time_key	customer_key	contact_type_key	contact
27221	121	4622	101	1
27221	121	3722	101	1
27221	121	2828	102	1
27221	123	1911	102	1
27221	123	3922	103	1
27221	123	3811	101	1
27221	124	8201	101	1

Figure 12-2 Adding a fact to the factless fact table

With this fact in place, the fact table is no longer factless. It is not necessary to count an arbitrary column when querying this table. Instead, the new contact fact can be summed. This works in exactly the same way that any other fully additive fact is summed. A query that determines how many times each customer was contacted, for example, would begin as follows:

```
SELECT
   customer_name,
   SUM( contact_facts.contact )
FROM
   .
   .
   .
```

The presence of a column containing a single constant value may look like a kludge or a workaround. From a dimensional perspective, however, this column is a legitimate fact. It represents a quantity. While it will always contain the value 1 at a granular level, it will take on other values when aggregated to other levels. The results of the preceding query, for example, might look like this:

```
CUSTOMER_      SUM
NAME           (CONTACT)
============   =========
Smith, M.E.            4
Burns, K              10
Smith, B               6
Rogers, S              1
Scanlon, C            12
```

Here, it is clear the number of contacts is a meaningful and fully additive fact.

Aggregation does not occur solely at query time. As you will learn in Chapter 15, "Aggregates," aggregate tables are sometimes used to improve query performance. An aggregate table partially summarizes data from the original fact table. In the case of contact_facts, an aggregate might summarize contacts by month. In this aggregate, the contact fact will take on a variety of values. In the same way, a monthly contacts cube constructed using data from contact_facts will also contain values other than 1 for the contact fact.

It is often possible to find a fact if you look for it carefully. Designs that start out factless often become the home for measurements of duration or cost. A factless fact table that tracks phone calls, for example, might track the duration of each call. Cost-oriented facts may also emerge from other business areas. The finance department may have a standard "average cost" metric that can be assigned to each call. Don't try to make up a measurement like this on your own; make sure it comes from the business. Also, don't go out of your way to accommodate a fact if it doesn't quite fit. In the contacts example, e-mail messages do not have a "duration." That fact is only relevant for telephone contacts.

Count() vs. Sum()

Adding a fact that always contains the value 1 makes SQL readable, allowing queries to use the SQL function `SUM()` rather than `COUNT()`. As your database administrator may point out, this technique may have an unwanted side effect: it can generate unnecessary database activity at query time.

To understand this effect, it is necessary to think about how a relational database actually assembles query results. Every SQL query is evaluated by the database optimizer, which parses the request and determines the best plan for fetching the results. When responding to a query that calls for counting contacts that occurred in January 2009, for example, the optimizer will need to decide how to access the various tables, apply the query predicates, carry out joins, and compute the count. It may begin by identifying the day_keys that correspond to January 2009 and then use a fact table index to identify corresponding fact table rows. Here is the important part: since all that is needed is a count, it is not actually necessary for the RDBMS to *read* these rows; it simply counts the number of "hits" in the index.

If, on the other hand, the database is asked to `SUM()` a fact table column called contact, it has no way of knowing that this column always contains the value 1. After determining which fact table rows apply to January 2009, *it must read these rows* from disk to get the contact values, and then add up the values. This means extra disk I/O will be required, and that may take some extra time. The `SUM()` will take longer than the `COUNT()`, particularly if the rows for January 2009 are not clustered together on the disk.

This may seem like an isolated example, but remember that many RDBMS products have star-join optimizers that apply dimensional constraints first and access the fact table last. This query execution scheme can be applied even when the query selects one or more dimension values or when constraints are applied in more than one dimension table. Not all database optimizers work this way, and those that do may offer additional mechanisms to tune or change behavior based on expected usage. So, while the addition of a constant-valued fact is very useful, it pays to talk it over with your database administrator.

The good news is you can have it both ways. Adding the additional fact does not stop anyone from writing a query that counts rows. `COUNT()` and `SUM()` are both available options.

Conditions, Coverage, or Eligibility

Factless fact tables can also be used in situations that do not clearly correspond to events or activities. Some common examples include:

- Tracking the salesperson assigned to each customer
- Logging the eligibility of individuals for programs or benefits
- Recording when severe weather alerts are in effect
- Capturing the marketing campaigns that are active at a given time

These examples all describe conditions, coverage, or eligibility. They are usually not thought of in terms of transactions or activities. Despite this, they can be modeled in the same way as an activity: using a fact table. Fact tables that describe conditions are usually factless.

Factless fact tables that describe conditions differ from those that describe activities in how they are used. In most cases, the information captured by these stars will rarely be studied on its own. Factless fact tables that describe conditions, coverage, or eligibility almost always serve as a basis for *comparison* with other business processes.

Why Model Conditions?

Fact tables capture relationships between dimensions. They are massive intersect tables, each row associating instances of various dimension tables in a specific context. Normally, that context is a transaction or activity.

Conditions at a point in time *also* link dimensions in a particular context. The environment at a point in time may link a salesperson with a customer, a product with a promotion, or an individual with an eligible benefit. These conditions can play an important part in understanding activities like orders, sales, or benefit participation.

To understand how conditions might inform the analysis of a process, consider a star schema that tracks orders, once again. The star in Figure 12-3 is activity-based. The grain of the fact table order_facts is the order line. The order line is represented by a pair of degenerate dimensions: order_id and order_line. Each row in this table associates a customer, product, and salesperson on a particular day. The context of this association is the placement of an order. If Russell Wilkinson (a salesperson) books an order from Company XYZ (a customer) on January 31, 2009 (a day), for a single product, a row in the fact table will associate these dimension instances.

This fact table does not contain rows for every possible combination of dimension rows. It only contains rows that represent the activity being tracked, as defined by its grain statement. Russell Wilkinson and Company XYZ are associated in order_facts because of an order placed.

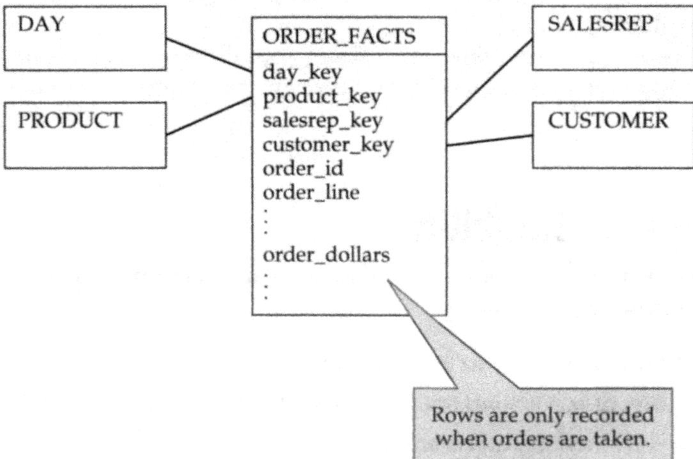

Figure 12-3 Customer and salesperson are related via order_facts

As you learned in Chapter 3, fact tables that track activities are sparse. If Bruce Calderwood (a salesperson) *does not book an order* from Company QRS (a customer), there will be *no* fact table row linking them in the fact table.

Suppose that, at any given time, each customer is assigned to a specific salesperson. This happens a lot in businesses that sell enterprise software to other businesses. Information about customer assignments may be important when analyzing orders, but it cannot be gleaned from order_facts. If a salesperson does not sell to a customer, there is no row to link them. Worse, the existence of a sale may not be a reliable indicator. A salesperson may sell to someone who is not their customer.

The assignment of a customer to a salesperson is an example of a "condition" that is in effect for a period of time. Conditions like this do not correspond to order transactions, nor to any other transaction fact tables associated with the sales process. Yet they are significant; the business may wish to compare conditions to sales activities.

The Venn diagram in Figure 12-4 illustrates several ways that sales assignments may inform the study of orders. Each circle represents a set of salesperson/customer pairings. The circle on the left represents salespeople and their assigned customers; the circle on the right represents salespeople and the customers from whom they have taken orders.

Each of the regions of this diagram may be a useful object of analysis. The lightly shaded region where the two sets intersect is the area in which order activity should be taking place. This area captures salespeople who have taken orders from assigned customers. The business might want to limit analysis to this area, for example, when computing salesperson compensation. The dark shaded area on the right represents salespeople who have sold to unassigned customers. Hopefully, this region of the diagram is very small, as it is likely to be the source of controversy among the sales staff. The region on the left indicates relationships between salespeople and the assigned customers that do not have any corresponding orders.

TIP Conditions represent relationships between dimensions that are not captured by business activities. The study of an activity can be colored by factoring in conditions.

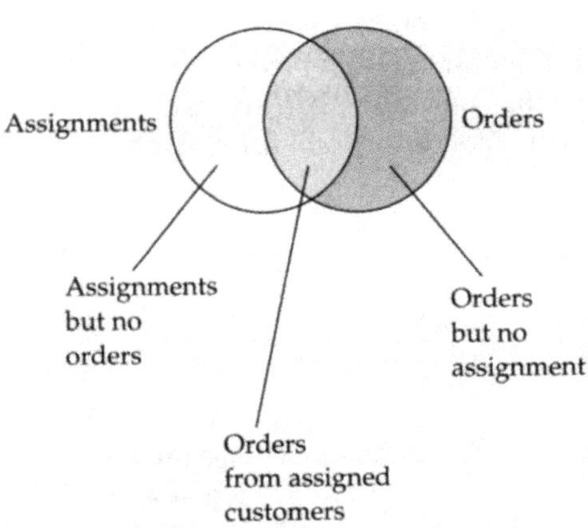

Figure 12-4 Customer/salesperson relationships

Similar examples can be identified in other situations. On a particular day, for example, a product may be actively promoted on the radio and in the newspaper. These conditions can be compared to sales of the product to assess the effectiveness of the marketing program. An employee may be eligible for a particular benefit program. This condition can be compared to benefit participation to assess popularity or value. On a particular day, there may have been snowfall and a severe storm warning. These conditions can be compared to movie ticket sales to determine the impact of the weather. In each case, the star capturing the activities is not suitable to record the conditions.

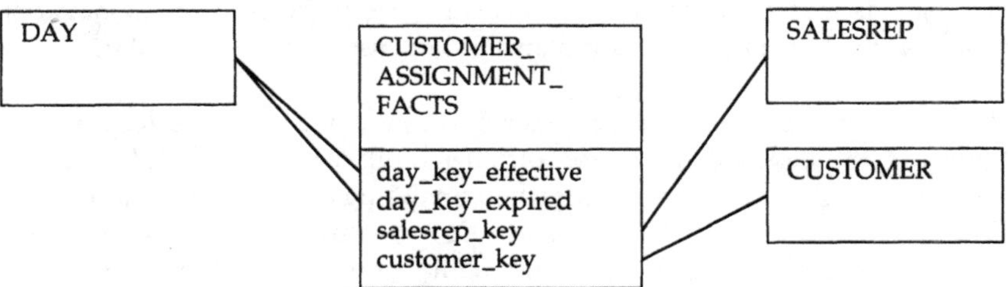

Figure 12-5 Customer assignments

Factless Fact Tables for Conditions

Conditions are modeled using a factless fact table. The star associates dimensions with one another to represent conditions at a particular point in time, or for a period of time. A factless fact table for customer assignments is shown in Figure 12-5.

The customer_assignment_facts fact table contains one row for each assignment of a salesperson to a customer. These two dimensions are represented by the salesrep_key and the customer_key. The fact table also had two day_keys. One represents the day on which the assignment became effective; the other represents the day on which it expired. The day dimension will include a special row for unexpired assignments. For current assignments, the day_key_expired will refer to this special row. It will contain the largest date value supported by the DBMS, rather than a NULL or blank. (For more on special rows in dimension tables, see Chapter 6, "More on Dimension Tables.")

TIP Conditions, coverage, and eligibility should be modeled as factless fact tables.

To some readers, customer_assignment_facts *does* describe a business activity: the activity of assigning salespeople to customers. Each assignment can be thought of as a transaction. Viewed in this light, the design characteristics of the customer_assignment_facts are not much different from contact_facts. Each captures information about events—one about the assignment of customers and the other about the contact with customers.

Whether you choose to make a semantic distinction between factless fact tables that describe events and factless fact tables that describe conditions, you are likely to notice a difference in their usage. A fact table that describes conditions will primarily be used to compare those conditions with other activities.

Snapshots of Conditions

Factless fact tables are not the only way to model conditions. Chapter 11, for example, suggested that a snapshot could be used to sample temperature at a point in time. Periodic snapshots can be construed as representing conditions during the snapshot period.

It is also possible to construct a factless snapshot. Rather than associate dimensions at a specific time, a factless snapshot associates them for a period, such as a month, quarter, or year. For example, a factless snapshot of customer assignments may contain one row per customer assignment per month. This is much less granular than the customer_assignment_facts star, but may simplify some SQL.

Comparing Activities and Conditions

Most of the time, a star that captures conditions is not very interesting on its own. Conditions are likely to be accessible elsewhere or to be the subject of operational reporting. Customer_assignment_facts, for example, can be used to identify the salesperson to whom a customer is assigned at any point in time, but presumably that is something that sales management is already able to do with operational data.

Conditions are most interesting when they are incorporated into the study of events. The diagram in Figure 12-4, for example, illustrated how conditions (salesperson/customer assignments) can be combined with activities (salesperson/customer transactions) in useful ways. We might want to compare customer assignments with orders to produce a list of customer assignments with no corresponding orders during the first quarter of 2009. This corresponds to the white region in Figure 12-4.

The stars in Figures 12-3 and 12-5 can be used to answer this question. A comparison like this might be carried out in at least three ways. Two involve the use of specific SQL capabilities; the third involves construction of an additional star or cube.

Using Set Operations

One way to compare conditions and activities is to make use of SQL's ability to perform set operations. In looking for customer assignments with no corresponding orders, the SQL `MINUS` operator will come in handy. It can be used to combine two queries, one identifying customer/salesrep assignments for Q1 2009, and the other representing customer/salesrep orders for Q1 2009. The query looks like this:

```
SELECT
   --
   -- Creates set of Salesrep/Customer pairs for assignments
   --
   salesperson_name,
   customer_name
FROM
   salesrep,
   customer,
   day ALIAS effective_day,
   day ALIAS expiration_day,
   customer_assignment_facts
WHERE
   effective_day.date <= 3/31/2009 AND
   expiration_day.date >= 1/1/2009 AND
   salesrep.salesrep_key = customer_assignment_facts.salesrep_key AND
   customer.customer_key = customer_assignment_facts.customer_key AND
   effective_day.day_key = customer_assignment_facts.day_key_effective AND
   expiration_day.day_key = customer_assignment_facts.day_key_expired

MINUS
```

Part IV

```
SELECT
   --
   -- Create set of Salesrep/Customer pairs for orders
   --
   salesperson_name,
   customer_name
FROM
   salesrep,
   customer,
   day,
   order_facts
WHERE
   day.date >= 1/1/2009 AND
   day.date <= 3/31/2009 AND
   salesrep.salesrep_key = order_facts.salesrep_key AND
   customer.customer_key = order_facts.customer_key AND
   day.day_key = order_facts.day_key
```

In this SQL statement, each `SELECT` statement corresponds to one of the sets in Figure 12-4. The `MINUS` operation is used to select the members of the first set that are not present in the second set. The result is exactly the region we are interested in. The two `SELECT` statements can be reversed to identify salespeople taking orders from customers that have not been assigned to them.

Numbering Sequential Time Periods

You may have been confused by the date conditions in the first `SELECT` statement of the `MINUS` query in this section. These conditions are needed to identify customer assignments that were in effect for any portion of the period.

Because conditions like these can easily be botched, many designers choose to create an attribute that identifies quarters as a series of integers, assigning the column a name like quarter_number. The first quarter recorded in the database is assigned the value 1, the second the value 2, the tenth the value 10, and so forth.

When you are looking for date ranges that overlap with a particular quarter, this trick enables simplification of the necessary constraints. For example, if Q1 2009 is quarter_number 15, the date constraints in the first half of the `MINUS` query can be replaced with:

```
effective_day.quarter_num <= 15 AND
expiration_day.quarter_num >= 15
```

The same technique can be used to numerically identify calendar months. The downside to this technique, of course, is that you must know that Q1 2009 is the 15th quarter.

Another way to simplify this kind of query is to construct a factless snapshot to model customer assignment, as described earlier in the boxed text titled "Snapshots of Conditions."

Correlated Subqueries

Another way to identify customer assignments without orders is to use a correlated subquery. In looking for customer assignments with no corresponding orders, this might work as follows. A standard query is used to identify customer/salesrep assignments. In the `WHERE` clause, the keywords `AND NOT EXISTS` are used to introduce a subquery that looks for order facts for the salesperson/customer pair. The essential structure looks like this:

```
--
-- The main query identifies sales assignments
--
SELECT
   assigned_rep.salesperson_name,
   assigned_customer.customer_name
FROM
   salesrep ALIAS assigned_rep,
   customer ALIAS assigned_customer,
   day ALIAS effective_day,
   day ALIAS expiration_day,
   customer_assignment_facts
WHERE
   effective_day.date <= 3/31/2009 AND
   expiration_day.date >= 1/1/2009 AND
   ...joins...
   AND NOT EXISTS
     --
     -- Here begins the subquery, used to exclude assignments with orders
     --
    ( SELECT *
      FROM
          salesrep ALIAS order_rep,
          customer ALIAS order_customer,
          day ALIAS order_day,
          order_facts
       WHERE
          order_day.date >= 1/1/2009 AND
          order_day.date <= 3/31/2009 AND
          ...joins...
          AND
          order_customer.customer_id = assigned_customer.customer_id AND
          order_rep.salesrep_id = assigned_rep.salesrep_id
    )
```

The final lines of this query, which appear here in bold print, correlate the subquery with the main query. For each salesperson/customer assignment in the main query, the subquery looks for orders. If none is found, the pair is part of the final result set. This gives us the group we are interested in: assignments without sales. Note that the correlation should make use of *natural keys*, rather than surrogate keys. This precaution is necessary in case both entities happen to have gone through a type 2 change during the period.

This approach, though not as easy to read or write, may be useful if the final output will contain information that is only present in one of the stars. For example, if you want to study order_dollars only for orders that are taken from assigned customers, the main query can fetch and aggregate order dollars, with a correlated subquery that limits the results to legitimate assignments. The subquery would be introduced by `AND EXISTS` rather than `AND NOT EXISTS`.

Precompute the Results

It is not reasonable to expect anyone but a seasoned developer to make use of SQL's set operations or to write a correlated subquery. Even query and reporting tools that generate SQL may not be able to put these statements together. Depending on the size of the data sets, performance may also become an issue. If any of these factors is a concern, a third path is available: compute the results in advance.

In the case of sales assignments with no orders, it is possible to build an additional star that holds the required information. Its dimensions include the period summarized, the salesperson, and the customer. This simple star is very easy to query. The hard work is eliminated for query writers, but it is now handled at load time. The ETL process that creates this star can use whatever technique is most efficient, even leveraging procedural logic.

The new star is an example of a *derived schema*, a topic that is fully explored in Chapter 14, "Derived Schemas." As you will see, conditions and events can be used to produce a variety of derived stars, each serving a particular analytic purpose. Each of the regions in Figure 12-4 may be represented by a derived star, as can various combinations of regions.

Slowly Changing Dimensions and Conditions

When there are type 2 changes to the dimensions in a star that represents conditions, these changes will necessitate new fact table rows. Suppose that a salesperson named Lawrence Falconi is assigned the customer ABC Holdings. A row in the factless fact table associates them. Later, a change to ABC Holdings occurs in the source system, triggering a type 2 response in the customer dimension. This new version of ABC Holdings must be associated with the salesperson as well, requiring a new row in the factless fact table.

TIP When a star measures conditions, type 2 slow changes in its dimensions will require the addition of new fact table rows.

As already noted, the possibility of type 2 changes complicates the development queries that compare conditions with activities. The most reliable comparisons will leverage natural keys, as in the correlated subquery illustrated earlier. Notice that the `MINUS` query presented at the beginning of this section relies on the names of the salesperson and customer. If these names are the subject of a type 2 change, an assignment using the old name will not match a sale using the new name. This can be overcome by replacing the names with natural keys in each `SELECT` statement.

Summary

Factless fact tables are essential in many business situations. The techniques outlined in this chapter will help you model a process with no apparent facts, or to capture the conditions that can be used to study activities.

- Some processes are measured only by counting events or activities.
- These processes can be modeled as a fact table whose grain is a single activity. No facts are required.
- Useful analysis is conducted by counting fact table rows. Dimensions are used to constrain the query, group or sort counts, and drive subtotals.
- A fact with a constant value of 1 can be added to the design to make SQL easier to read and write.
- Some important relationships between dimensions do not clearly correspond to a process or activity. Examples include conditions, coverage, and eligibility.
- Conditions and processes can be combined for useful analysis.
- Conditions are modeled using a factless fact table.
- Activities and conditions can be combined in various ways using set operations, correlated subqueries, or derived schemas.
- Type 2 slow changes will generate new rows in related fact tables that describe conditions.

Further Reading

The techniques in this chapter have applicability in a wide variety of industries and across many subject areas. If you want to refine your knowledge, you can learn more about factless fact tables by studying more examples. The following are some places to start.

Factless Fact Tables for Activities

- A factless fact table can be used to capture information about attendance. An example can be found in Chapter 6 of *The Data Warehouse Lifecycle Toolkit, Second Edition* (Wiley, 2008) by Ralph Kimball, Margy Ross, Warren Thornthwaite, Joy Mundy, and Bob Becker.
- Kimball and Ross update the attendance model to incorporate absences in Chapter 12 of *The Data Warehouse Toolkit, Second Edition* (Wiley, 2002). In this case, the fact table is no longer factless; it includes a fact that contains the values 0 or 1 (absent or present). This can also be achieved with a pair of facts—one used to count absences and one used to count attendance. In the same chapter, the authors provide a factless design to track student course registrations.
- In the insurance industry, a factless fact table can be used to track accident events. Kimball and Ross describe this in Chapter 15 of *The Data Warehouse Toolkit.*

- When factless fact tables for events are summarized, the resulting aggregates are not factless. This phenomenon is explained in Chapter 8 of *Mastering Data Warehouse Aggregates* (Wiley, 2006) by Chris Adamson.

Factless Fact Tables for Conditions

- A factless fact table used to track marketing promotions supplements a retail sales star in Chapter 12 of *The Data Warehouse Toolkit.* Note that Kimball and Ross refer to factless fact tables that describe conditions, coverage, or eligibility as *coverage tables.*
- Another condition that can be tracked by a factless fact table is the availability of a resource. Kimball and Ross make use of one to study utilization of facilities in Chapter 12 of *The Data Warehouse Toolkit.*
- It is generally not useful to aggregate a fact table that describes conditions, because doing so destroys the meaning of the original data. This phenomenon is explored in Chapter 8 of *Mastering Data Warehouse Aggregates.*

CHAPTER 13

Type-Specific Stars

The things represented by a dimension table can often be subdivided into categories or types. Sometimes, the attributes you would like to record in the dimension table vary by type. A department store, for example, describes clothing items with a very different set of attributes from electronic items, yet all of them are products. Similarly, businesses often collect very different information about direct customers and corporate customers, or track different kinds of information for different kinds of facilities or locations.

Specialization by type may also extend to the fact table. The facts surrounding an order, for example, may vary depending on whether the order was for merchandise or for a subscription. Tests, inspections, and citations may also have one or more facts that vary by type.

In these situations, the dimensional modeler is faced with a dilemma. On one hand, there is a desire to study a business process across all types. On the other hand, there is a desire to study each particular type, using the type-specific attributes. This chapter shows you three ways to accommodate heterogeneous attributes, both within dimensions and within fact tables.

- A **single star** solution calls for one star that contains all possible attributes. This is the simplest approach but is not viable if the number of type-specific attributes is very large.
- The **core and custom** approach provides multiple stars. A core star contains all common attributes; one custom star for each type contains any type-specific attributes. This is the most flexible approach and may be accomplished using a variety of implementation techniques.
- The use of **generic attributes** creates multipurpose columns, the contents of which are determined by type. This technique is only viable when all interaction with the star will take place through a customized application.

None of these approaches is right or wrong; the best design option depends on the situation. If you are faced with heterogeneous attributes, study the implications of each option before making your design decision.

Type-Specific Attributes

The need to support heterogeneous attributes within a dimensional design becomes evident when gathering requirements for the data warehouse. You may notice that managers of different parts of the business have different ways of describing and measuring their processes, while senior management likes to lump them together. Book sales and subscription sales, for example, may be processed by different groups and measured in different ways, while senior management likes to lump these together into a single view of sales. These different views may be reflected in operational systems, or they may not. Regardless of the structure of the operational data, however, it will be necessary to support both kinds of views in the data warehouse.

Operational Systems

Operational systems usually support a type-specific view of the data. In some cases, this may be immediately obvious simply by studying the documentation of the operational systems. More often than not, however, the commonality across types is not clearly recorded.

In the world of entity-relationship modeling, type-specific attributes can be represented using a concept called subtyping. This technique can be easily identified in a logical-level ER diagram. One diagramming standard, for example, represents subtypes as boxes within entities. The outer box, or *supertype*, contains attributes that are common across all types. Each inner box, or *subtype*, contains the appropriate type-specific attributes. Alternate diagram notations represent relationships between supertypes and subtypes in different ways, such as relationship lines that incorporate special symbols.

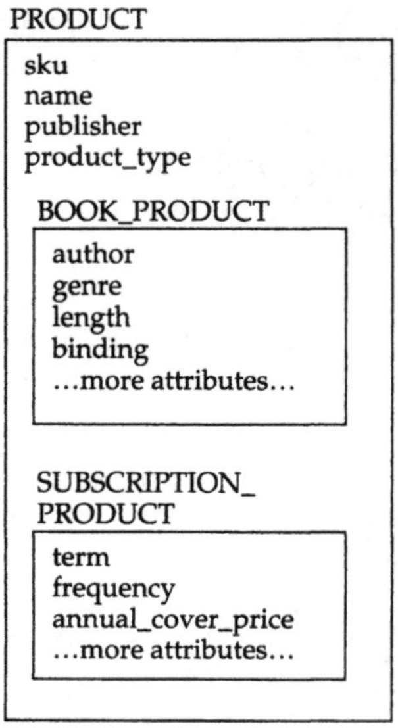

PRODUCT
sku
name
publisher
product_type

BOOK_PRODUCT
author
genre
length
binding
...more attributes...

SUBSCRIPTION_PRODUCT
term
frequency
annual_cover_price
...more attributes...

Figure 13-1 Subtypes in an entity-relationship model

An example of an ER diagram containing subtypes appears in Figure 13-1. The product entity in this diagram represents the products sold by a seller of books and magazines. A single product entity contains subtypes for books and subscriptions. All the products have certain core attributes, such as the SKU (an internal identifier), the product name, and the publisher. Each subtype has some additional attributes. Other entities may be related to the supertype (products) or to one of the subtypes (books or subscriptions).

More often than not, heterogeneous attributes within an important entity will not be clearly laid out. Operational systems are focused on the minutia of process execution and may not provide for a consolidated point of view. Subscription and book orders, for example, might be handled in entirely different systems, with no acknowledgment that subscriptions and books are examples of a single thing called a product. This may reflect the way the business is organized, result from a history of mergers and acquisitions, or be the result of an organic evolution of internal systems.

Analytic Systems

The data warehouse must reflect all the ways in which a process is analyzed and measured. If limited to a single analytic perspective, its overall utility is greatly reduced. Management may want to study orders across all products—books and subscriptions—using shared facts and dimensions. They may also call for a more detailed representation when focusing on a particular product type, using facts and dimensions unique to the particular type. Failure to deliver one or the other of these capabilities destroys the value of the overall solution.

The Single-Star Approach

The simplest way to deal with heterogeneous attributes in a dimensional model is to build a single star containing all possible attributes. For a seller of books and magazines, a single product dimension would contain all possible product attributes, including those specific to books or magazines. For any particular row in this table, many of these attributes will be blank (or will contain a NULL alternative such as N/A, as described in Chapter 6). Similarly, if different facts are collected for book orders and magazine orders, all potential facts are included in the fact table. For each order, only the relevant facts are recorded.

This approach is fully valid. It permits the business to conduct analysis across types or to perform type-specific analysis. The attributes included in each query or report determine its focus. A report that contains attributes common to books and magazines, for example, describes the overall orders process. The details of subscription orders can be studied by limiting analysis to subscription products and using attributes from the product table that apply only to subscriptions.

Drawbacks to the Single-Star Approach

Sometimes a star that consolidates all possible attributes is not practical. The obstacles may be technical or semantic. On the technical side, extreme variability in a dimension may result in more attributes than can be managed in a single row. Department stores, for example, may have scores of different product types, each with 50 to 100 attributes. Consolidating all of these into a single table might require over a thousand attributes, of which only a small percentage are populated for any given row. Clearly this approach will be untenable.

Semantic objections to the single-table approach are also possible. A star that consolidates all possible attributes may give rise to nonsensical reports. This is likely to occur when there are type-specific dimensions *and* facts. Combining a dimension specific to one product type with a fact specific to another is a distinct possibility. For example, the seller of books and magazines may record the value at cover price as a fact associated with each subscription order. This fact has no relationship to books. In a single-star design, however, nothing would stop a user from combining it with book-specific attributes such as author or number_of_pages. This semantic objection may or may not be deemed significant.

TIP When subtypes require type-specific dimensions or facts, a single star may incorporate all possible attributes. This may not be practical if the variation in the dimension is extreme or if the combination of incompatible type-specific dimensions and facts is a concern.

In cases where either of these obstacles is present, an alternative approach to the handling of heterogeneous attributes is required. The alternative involves creating separate logical stars for each point of view. These may be implemented as separate sets of tables or simply simulated using views.

Part IV

Core and Custom Stars

A dimensional design can handle heterogeneous attributes by incorporating multiple stars. A *core* star includes all common attributes and supports analysis across all types. Type-specific *custom* stars include all the core attributes, plus any type-specific attributes. Each custom star contains data for a single type. Custom stars are used when analysis is limited to a single subtype.

Successful implementation of a core/custom design requires conformance of common attributes between the core dimension and each of the type-specific custom dimensions. Sometimes there are custom dimension attributes but no custom facts. Even in this situation, custom fact tables are recommended to avoid analytic mishaps. Physical implementation may take the form of separate and distinct core and custom tables or be accomplished using database views.

Core and Custom Dimension Tables

When the attributes of a dimension vary by type, and it is impractical or undesirable to build a single table with all possible attributes, the alternative is to build multiple versions of the dimension table. One version will contain only the attributes shared by all subtypes and contain a row for each instance, regardless of type. This table is known as the *core* dimension table. The remaining versions each correspond to a single type. They contain the core attributes, plus any type-specific attributes. These are known as *custom* dimension tables.

Figure 13-2 illustrates core and custom product dimension tables for a seller of books, music, and magazine subscriptions. The core dimension table contains attributes common to

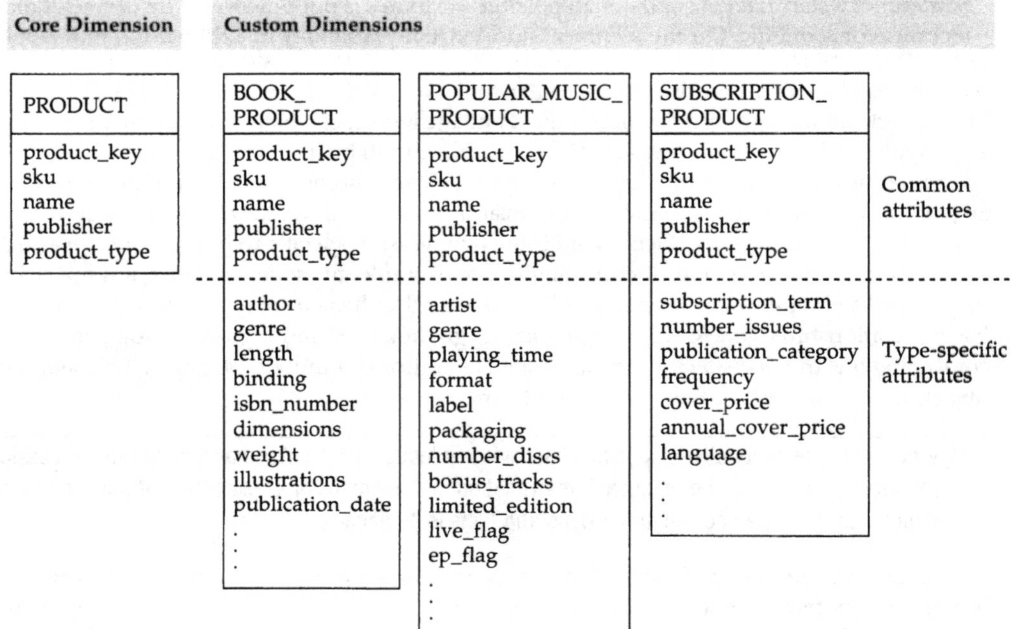

Figure 13-2 Core product dimension and type-specific custom dimensions

all products sold. These include SKU (an internal identifier or natural key), the product name, the publisher, and product type. Custom dimension tables for each product type include these same attributes, *plus* any additional attributes that are specific to the type of product.

These variants of the product dimension will be used to service the diverse analytic demands placed on the data warehouse. The core product dimension will be called on when the analytic questions look across all product types. Joined to the appropriate fact table, it will be able to provide information like the order_dollars by publisher or product type. The custom product dimensions will be used to service analytic requests focused on a single product type. Within their respective types, they can provide deeper insight, such as the ability to break out subscription orders by subscription term.

TIP Heterogeneous dimension attributes may be handled by designing multiple dimension tables. A core dimension includes all common attributes; custom dimensions include core attributes plus type-specific attributes.

The presence of the core attributes in each of the custom dimensions allows access to those attributes when studying a particular type. Analysis of music products, for example, may include the product name or publisher. Because these attributes are present in the custom dimension tables, additional joins will not be necessary when bringing them into a query.

Conforming Attributes

The common attributes of core and custom dimensions should *conform.* This means they must be the same in terms of their *structure* and *content,* as you learned in Chapter 5. For the core and custom product tables in Figure 13-2, this means the columns SKU, name, publisher, and product_type must have the same names and data type definitions in each table. It also means that the content of these columns must be expressed in a consistent manner. A book called *The Contrarian Pathway* should have exactly the same product name in the core product table and in the custom book_product table. This conformance is illustrated in the table instance diagrams of Figure 13-3.

The core attributes of the book_product table conform with those in the product table. They have the same type definitions and names, and their content is expressed identically. The highlighted rows show conforming rows for product A220022. Core attributes are expressed identically. This figure also illustrates the scope of the core and custom dimension tables. The core table, product, contains rows for all product types; the custom table book_product contains rows only for products of type "Book."

Common Surrogate Keys

Conformed core and custom dimensions differ from the conformed dimensions of Chapter 5 in one important respect. They share one additional element in common: the surrogate key. Looking back to Figure 13-2, for example, you will see that the product-specific custom dimensions use the same product_key values as the core dimension table. Core and custom dimension tables share a common key domain.

The use of a common set of surrogate keys allows the appropriate version of the dimension table to be joined to a fact table interchangeably. For example, the highlighted product in Figure 13-3 has the same key value in both versions of the product dimension. This means that either version can be joined to a fact table for meaningful analysis. If you are studying all products, the core dimension may be joined to the fact table; if you are focusing on book products, the custom dimension may be joined to the fact table.

PRODUCT

product_ key	sku	name	product_ type
100	B221101	Summer in New York	Book
101	N22911	Music Criticism Journal	Subscription
102	B33921	Gadget Review Weekly	Subscription
103	A220022	The Contrarian Pathway	Book
104	Q27822	Cooking and Decorating	Subscription
105	C770077	Havana, 3AM	Book

Same attribute content
Same key values

BOOK_PRODUCT

product_ key	sku	name	product_ type	author	genre	cover_ type
100	B221101	Summer in New York	Book	Michael Jones	Travel	Paperback
103	A220022	The Contrarian Pathway	Book	John Mellor	Lifestyle	Paperback
105	C770077	Havana, 3AM	Book	P. Gustave Simonon	Fiction	Hardcover

Figure 13-3 Core and custom dimensions conform

TIP The common attributes of core and custom dimensions must conform and share a common key domain.

Since core and custom dimensions contain conforming attributes and share a common key domain, the core dimension can be thought of as representing a union of the common attributes of each custom dimension table. In fact, many ETL developers build them in this manner. Bear in mind that, in rare situations, it may be possible for a single item to appear in more than one custom dimension. An example of this phenomenon will be explored shortly. For the SQL-literate reader, this implies the use of `UNION` rather than `UNION ALL`.

Slowly Changing Dimensions

Type 2 slow changes can produce a notable side effect with core/custom designs. As you learned in Chapter 3, the type 2 response to a change in source data calls for the insertion of a new row into the dimension table, complete with a new surrogate key value. When the dimension design includes core and custom tables, the change must be applied both to the core dimension table and to any custom dimension tables. This will preserve their interchangeability when joined to a fact table.

A curious side effect occurs when the changed values happen to be in custom columns. In the custom table, the old and new rows for the changed item will be visibly different. In the core table, however, the only difference between old and new rows will be the surrogate key value. In all other respects, the old and new versions will appear identical. Figure 13-4 illustrates this effect.

PRODUCT

product_key	sku	name	product_type
100	B221101	Summer in New York	Book
101	N22911	Music Criticism Journal	Subscription
102	B33921	Gadget Review Weekly	Subscription
103	A220022	The Contrarian Pathway	Book
104	Q27822	Cooking and Decorating	Subscription
105	C770077	Havana, 3AM	Book
201	C770077	Havana, 3AM	Book

These rows are identical in the core dimension table, save for their surrogate keys.

They were precipitated by a type 2 change to the product's genre.

BOOK_PRODUCT

product_key	sku	name	product_type	author	genre	cover_type
100	B221101	Summer in New York	Book	Michael Jones	Travel	Paperback
103	A220022	The Contrarian Pathway	Book	John Mellor	Lifestyle	Paperback
105	C770077	Havana, 3AM	Book	P. Gustave Simonon	Fiction	Hardcover
201	C770077	Havana, 3AM	Book	P. Gustave Simonon	Classics	Hardcover

Figure 13-4 Core and custom dimensions conform

In the illustration, the book identified by SKU C770077 has undergone a change in genre, from "Fiction" to "Classics." This change was handled with a type 2 response. A new surrogate key value of 201 was assigned, and new rows were inserted in the core and custom tables. In both tables, the old and new versions of the product are highlighted. In the core table, the old and new rows appear identical, save for their surrogate keys. This occurs because the changed attribute, genre, appears only in the custom table book_product.

Core and Custom Fact Tables

Core and custom dimension tables can be joined interchangeably to fact tables as required by the analytic situation. Nevertheless, it is highly recommended that corresponding custom fact tables be designed in order to avoid possible analytic confusion. These need not be physical tables; views or similar alternatives will suffice.

If there are custom facts that correspond to specific types, then custom fact tables for each type *will* be necessary. Each custom fact table will contain any core facts, along with type-specific facts. It will contain rows only for the specific type represented.

The Same Facts for All Types

If the same facts are recorded for all types, you have seen that core or custom versions of the dimension can be joined to the fact table as required by the analytic situation. The core version is used when studying across all types; analysis will be limited to common dimension attributes. A custom version is used when studying a specific type; analysis can include type-specific attributes. This interchangeability is facilitated by the common key domain.

In the case of the core and custom product dimension tables from Figure 13-2, for example, if all orders involve the same facts, a single order_facts table is possible. It will contain a row for each order line; one of the associated dimensions will be product. When conducting analysis across all product types, the core product dimension can be joined to the fact table; analysis focused on subscription products can be accomplished by joining the subscription_product dimension table to the fact table.

While this meets all the analytic requirements, there is a potential drawback. Any query that joins to a custom dimension *implicitly constrains the fact table for a specific type.* For example, suppose that a user studying subscription orders builds a report that groups order_dollars by publication_category. This report requires that order_facts be joined to the custom subscription_product dimension table. Although the query has no filter in its `WHERE` clause, results are effectively constrained as if the following filter had been added to the SQL:

```
WHERE product_type = 'Subscription'
```

This is not a problem in and of itself, but can lead to confusion as analysis continues. If the report designer subsequently decides to remove the publication_category from the report, the join to the subscription_product table is no longer needed and may be removed from the query. This also removes the implicit filter on product_type, opening the report up to all product types, rather than simply subscriptions. The result is a huge jump in the value of facts on the report, such as order_dollars.

This problem can easily be solved by building custom replicas of the order_facts table, each of which only contains the rows for a particular product type. The result is a set of core and custom stars, as depicted in Figure 13-5. The core star contains the core product

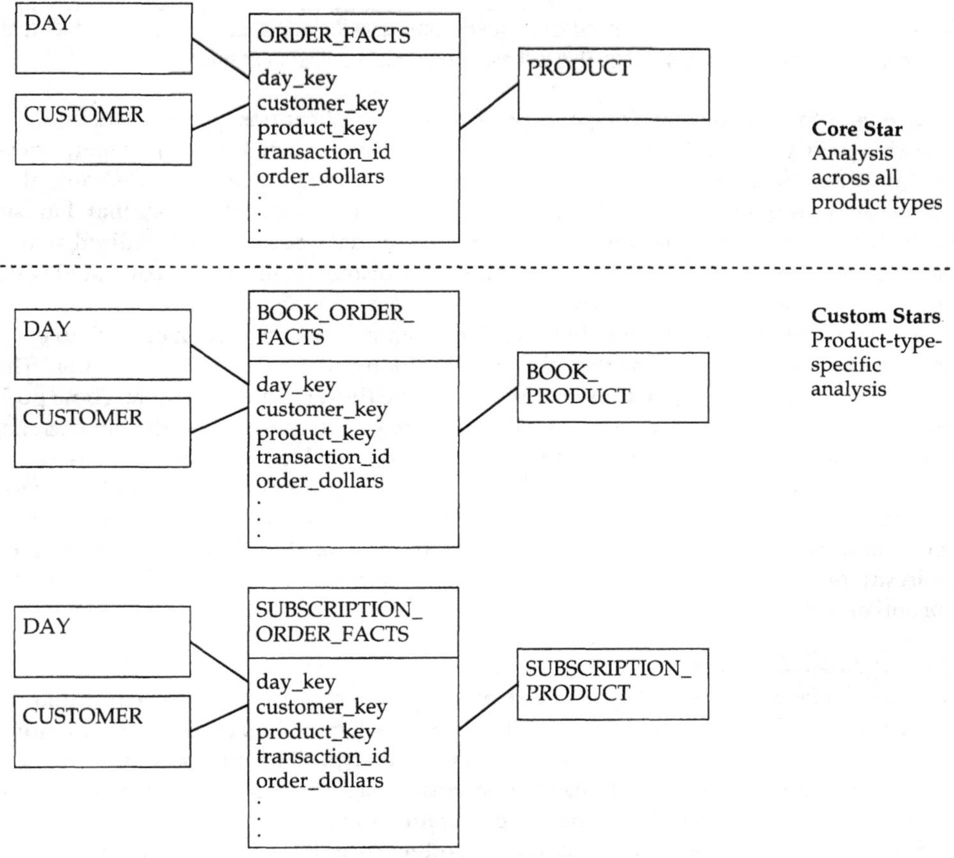

Figure 13-5 Core and custom stars for orders

dimension, and a fact table that contains rows for all orders. Each custom star contains a custom product dimension, and a fact table that contains rows only for the corresponding product type.

Analysis focused on a particular type takes place by working with the appropriate custom star. The user can build, execute, and refine queries, maintaining a focus on the particular type regardless of which attributes are included in the query.

This approach does not require the development of physical replicas of the order_facts table; each type-specific copy can be created using a view, like this:

```
CREATE VIEW subscription_order_facts AS
  SELECT day_key, customer_key, product_key, transaction_id, order_dollars
  FROM order_facts, book_product
  WHERE order_facts.product_key = book_product.product_key
```

This simple view will only include rows from the order_facts table that refer to book products.

TIP When a design involves core and custom dimensions, also include custom versions of fact tables, *even if there are no custom facts.* This will avoid potential confusion at query time.

The use of views may have negative performance implications. Queries will be written as if the view were a fact table. They will join it to dimensions such as day, customer, or even book_product. Because the view itself contains a join, the database may not choose the optimal plan for query execution. Depending on the behavior of the relational database, it may be more appropriate to build a separate table or make use of a materialized view, materialized query table, or the like. Database administrators should be consulted when choosing an implementation approach.

If separate fact tables are not built for each custom star, you may find it difficult to get your data modeling software to define the relationships among all the tables of the solution. The database administrator, too, may find it difficult to tune the database effectively. These problems stem from the fact that any fact table containing a foreign key reference to the dimension in question must be defined as referring to the *core* dimension table. The modeling tool or RDBMS will likely not acknowledge that the fact table foreign key can alternatively refer to one or more *custom* dimension tables. In the case of the modeling tool, this shortcoming may be overcome via text-based documentation addenda. In the case of the RDBMS, the database administrator may use hints or additional indices, or simply create a custom fact table with the appropriate foreign key definition.

Type-Specific Facts

When special facts are associated with particular types, custom fact tables become mandatory. The core fact table will contain rows for all types and will contain facts that are common across all types. Custom fact tables will be built for each type. These contain the core facts, plus any type-specific custom facts. As with dimension tables, conformance is the order of the day; the common facts must share the same structure and content.

Suppose, for example, that the types of product from Figure 13-2 happen to have some facts of their own. A subscription includes the length of the subscription term in issues and the value of the subscription at cover price. A book order, on the other hand, includes quantity, extended cost dollars, and various other facts. The core and custom stars in Figure 13-6 add these custom facts. Notice that all stars have the core fact order_dollars.

As before, analysis is conducted by first choosing the appropriate star. Analysis across all types is performed using the core star; it will be limited to core facts and dimensions. Analysis that will require facts or dimensions that are specific to a particular type is performed using the appropriate custom star; it will be limited to transactions of the particular type.

Other Considerations

Some variations on the custom star technique should be noted. First, it may be possible for a particular item to appear in more than one custom dimension table. This occurs when multiple levels of types exist, resulting in overlapping sets of custom attributes. Second, some designers prefer not to replicate core attributes, opting for a snowflake-like alternative. Last, the core and custom technique can be combined with an attribute hierarchy for powerful effect.

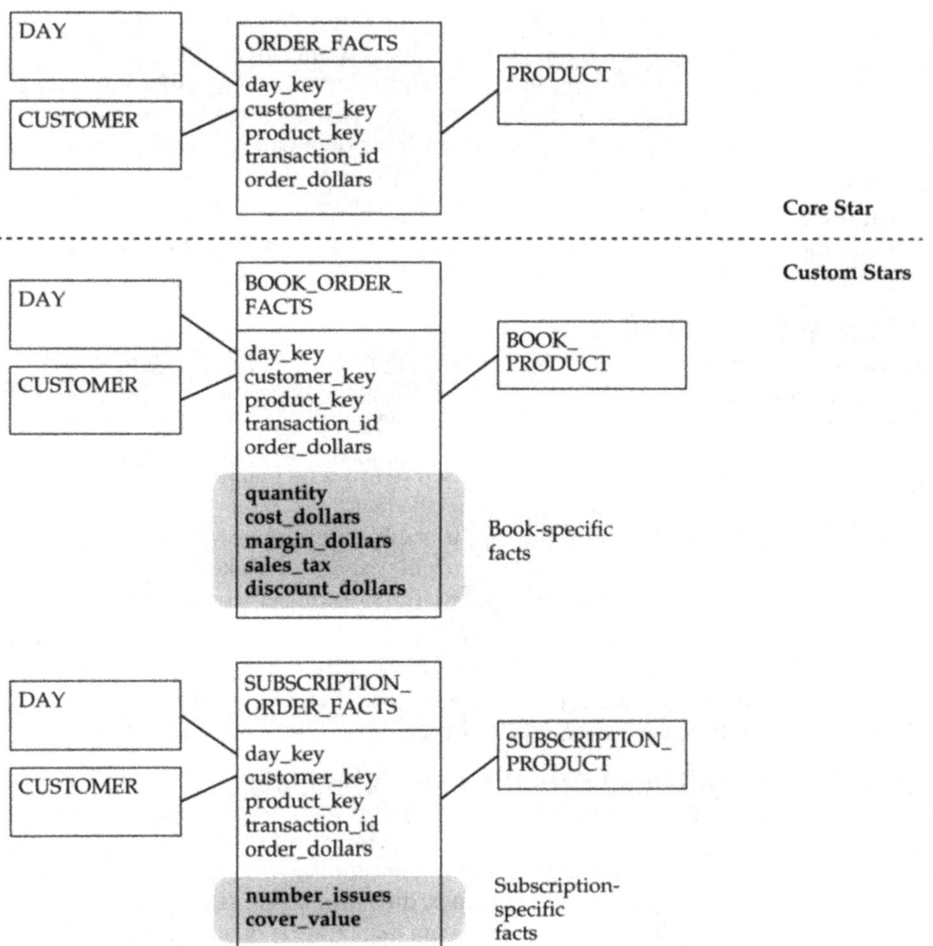

Figure 13-6 Custom stars with type-specific facts

Overlapping Custom Dimensions

Core and custom stars correspond to generalized and detailed views of an item, respectively. Sometimes there is more than one level of type within a dimension. When there are types within types, it is possible to design multiple levels of custom stars. A core star contains attributes common across all types; first-level custom stars contain the core attributes plus attributes specific to first-level types; a second set of custom stars adds attributes common to second-level types. In cases like this, a single item will appear in the core star, a type-specific star, and a second-level type-specific star.

For example, products sold by a retailer may have some attributes that are common across all products, some that are category-specific, and some that are product-type–specific. A shirt, for example, has a product name and SKU, as does every other product sold. It also has a set of attributes that are specific to the product category called "Clothing," including its color, size, and material. Last, it has attributes that are specific to the product type "Shirts," indicating whether it is long sleeved or short sleeved and whether it has buttons.

In this case, there may be two sets of custom stars. One set includes a star for each product category; a second contains a star for each product type. A single product, such as a shirt, will be present in the core star, a custom star for clothing, and a custom star for shirts. In situations like this, the redundancy involved in creating custom fact tables can become overwhelming. A view-based solution may be chosen to avoid the need for redundant fact tables, and even for redundant dimension tables.

The Outrigger Alternative

A variant on the core/custom theme seeks to eliminate the redundancy caused by the repetition of core attributes in custom tables. Under this variant, the custom tables include the surrogate keys and custom attributes and omit the core attributes. They are joined to the core dimension as an outrigger. Fact tables may also make use of an outrigger-like concept for custom facts. A transaction identifier may be used to link a fact table row containing the core facts to a custom extension containing type-specific facts.

This approach may save some space, but it is subject to the potential drawbacks of snowflaking, as discussed in Chapter 7, "Hierarchies and Snowflakes." If considering this approach, be sure you understand how your RDBMS optimizer works, and that snowflakes will not hamper star-join or similar optimizations. Also bear in mind that use of custom outriggers may generate confusion in the same manner discussed earlier: when someone performing type-specific analysis removes a constraint on an outrigger, the query may suddenly return results for all types. Views or a similar solution may again be useful.

Using a Hierarchy Bridge with the Core Dimension

A common modeling dilemma involves situations where a set of entities appears to participate in some sort of hierarchy, but the levels of the hierarchy are difficult or impossible to nail down. This commonly occurs with regional or organizational structures. For example, a corporation may be viewed as a set of companies, divisions, business units, and departments. People like to use these entities to summarize data like budgets or spending, noting that, for the most part, there is an organization principle:

Company → Division → Business Unit → Department

Unfortunately, this rule has a handful of exceptions. Some departments fall directly beneath a company, some divisions have no business units, and so forth. This can wreak havoc on any effort to use these dimensions to support summarization of activities.

The apparent complexity of this situation stems from the fact that companies, divisions, business units, and departments are being treated as different things. If viewed as a single thing, say an organization, the rule is simple: each organization may fall under another organization. In this context, a hierarchy bridge table, like the one described in Chapter 10, can be used easily to summarize data.

The key to solving this problem lies in recognizing that a group of things that have distinct attributes—companies, divisions, business units, and so forth—can also be viewed as instances of the same thing—an organizational unit. While no source systems represent them as examples of the same thing, and no business representatives describe them that way, their commonality is evident when you discover that they are all used to summarize activity. What are initially viewed as a group of distinct dimensions are actually custom versions of an undiscovered core dimension.

Late Discovery of Core Dimensions

Sometimes, two or more dimensions are placed in production before it is recognized that they share some core attributes. This is a common dilemma faced when subject areas are developed without an enterprise focus. Resolving the situation will require significant rework; the alternative is to ignore the problem and reconcile data through a complex reporting process.

This situation might occur, for example, if the seller of books and magazines allowed data mart development to take place on a departmental level. The department responsible for processing book orders develops a star schema for orders, with a dimension called book. Likewise, the subscription department has its own data mart, with a dimension called magazine.

Later, finance wants to add a data mart that allows for profitability analysis. They would like to correlate cost data, which is available by product, with orders. What were initially modeled as separate dimension tables—books and magazines—are now discovered to be custom versions of a core product dimension. It turns out that many other organizations in the business have a concept of product as well, including shipping, warehousing, and so forth.

The difficulty in this situation is that the custom dimensions have already been built. Their common attributes do not have consistent names or data types, and they do not share a common key domain. Building a core dimension after the fact will require some restructuring of the original tables, adjustment of their content, and reassignment of key values. This, in turn, will have a ripple effect on related fact tables, in which foreign key references will be updated. Existing reports, too, will require SQL to be rewritten.

Using Generic Attributes

A dimensional design can accommodate heterogeneous attributes through the use of generic columns. For a given row, what is held in each column is determined by its type. Auxiliary tables can be used to map the purpose of each column to each type.

This approach is very flexible for *storing* information but less nimble when it comes to *querying* the information. This may seem contrary to the purpose of a dimensional design, but it can be powerful when all interaction will take place through a custom-developed front-end application. Though not a common feature of a dimensional design, it may be worth considering in rare situations.

Generic Attributes

The use of generic attributes seeks to capture the diversity of various types using a single set of columns. In a dimension table, a set of columns describing core attributes is supplemented by a set of multipurpose columns, the purpose of which will vary by type.

For example, a business might choose to handle location data in this manner. There may be several types of facilities—factories, warehouses, stores, and offices. Each has a

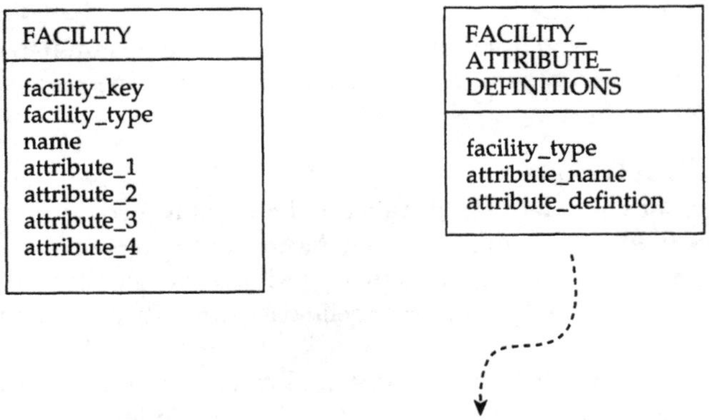

FACILITY
facility_key facility_type name attribute_1 attribute_2 attribute_3 attribute_4

FACILITY_ ATTRIBUTE_ DEFINITIONS
facility_type attribute_name attribute_defintion

FACILITY_ATTRIBUTE_DEFINITIONS

facility_ type	attribute_ name	attribute_definition
Warehouse	attribute_1	Warehouse Manager
Warehouse	attribute_2	Distribution Region
Warehouse	attribute_3	Facilities for Perishables
Warehouse	attribute_4	Number of Loading Docks
Factory	attribute_1	Foreman
Factory	attribute_2	Factory Type
Factory	attribute_3	Clean Room
Factory	attribute_4	Entrances

Figure 13-7 A dimension table with generic attributes

name, an attribute that identifies the individual in charge, and several type-specific characteristics. Figure 13-7 illustrates a facility dimension table that abstracts these type-specific attributes into a set of generic attributes.

For any given row in the facility table, the meaning of each generic column is determined by the facility type. The generic column names are mapped to type-specific definitions in an auxiliary table called facility_attribute_definitions. Consulting this table, you can identify what each column indicates on a type-by-type basis. For the facility type "Warehouse," for example, attribute_3 indicates whether the facility has the capability to stock perishable goods. For factories, this same column indicates whether the facility has a clean room.

This design is very flexible when it comes to storing information, permitting the storage of customized attributes for a large number of types, all within a single table. Some types may make use of all of the generic attributes, while others make use of some of them. As long as there are enough generic columns of the appropriate data types, it is possible to accommodate any type. A similar technique can be used to capture variation within a fact table.

Using a Generic Design

Though very flexible for storing information, a generic design is less flexible when it comes to *retrieving* information. Because column names are generically defined, the construction of queries requires referring to information on column content. Query results, as well, will need to be repackaged with decoded attribute labels. These activities are not directly supported by standard query and reporting software.

For example, suppose the dimension table in Figure 13-7 is part of a star describing inventory levels. A report is needed that provides inventory levels for warehouses that have facilities for perishable goods, and the results will be grouped by region. Construction of a query to fetch this information will require using reference data to identify which column indicates whether the warehouse has the capability to store perishables. This turns out to be attribute_3, which can be used to constrain the query, as in:

```
WHERE facility.attribute_3 = 'Has Perishable Storage Facilities'
```

Grouping the results by region also requires identification of the appropriate attribute. In this case, attribute_2 contains the needed information:

```
GROUP BY facility.attribute_2
```

Packaged query and reporting software does not normally perform this value-based translation of attribute names. Whether intended for developer use or end-user use, most tools are based on a paradigm where each attribute in a schema has a single name or business definition.

Development of a custom application that is aware of the supplemental information, however, can lead to some very compelling analytic applications. A custom-built application can leverage the attribute definition information to adapt column headers or field names dynamically, based on attribute type. Some OLAP products also have the capability to do this.

Such an application can guide users or developers through the process of constructing queries, adapting attribute definitions as specific types are selected. This kind of application may also perform attribute translation on query result sets, even when more than one type is included. For example, an application can be coded to accept result sets for warehouses and factories, each of which contains attribute_1 through attribute_4, and place them in separate report sections with the appropriate labels. Such a tool might also support dynamic attribute labeling as a user drills into data.

TIP The use of generic attributes is usually undesirable because they render the data less accessible. However, in combination with a custom-developed application, they can contribute to a compelling analytic experience.

A hybrid approach enables this kind of application, while at the same time making the data accessible to more traditional query and reporting software. Core and custom fact tables are designed for standard queries and reports. In addition, generic attributes are added to the core tables. These will be used by specialized reports or applications that have been developed to be aware of the abstraction layer. These columns will only be used by this application; they are hidden from standard query and reporting software.

Summary

Type-specific facts and dimension attributes complicate schema designs. Three primary mechanisms exist for coping with these heterogeneous attributes.

- A single dimension table can be designed to include all possible type-specific attributes. The same can be done in the fact table for type-specific facts.
- This approach may leave a lot of columns empty and can lead to nonsensical reports, but it is relatively simple to design and build. It may not be feasible if the number of possible attributes is very large.
- A core and custom approach creates a single dimension table for all common attributes, and additional type-specific dimension tables for each type. The same can be done in the fact table for type-specific facts.
- The custom tables also include core attributes, in order to simplify analysis. The common attributes of the core and custom tables must conform in structure and content.
- Type-specific attributes can be captured in generic, multipurpose columns. This makes the data more difficult to report on and is most effective when used with a specially designed front-end application.

Further Reading

Heterogeneous type-specific attributes are a common occurrence. You can probably visualize several examples on your own. If you would like to read more about them, here are some places to look.

- Ralph Kimball and Margy Ross describe the use of core and custom tables in the financial industry. Their example deals with the different dimensions and facts associated with different account types, such as checking accounts, savings accounts, and mortgage accounts. It appears in Chapter 9 of *The Data Warehouse Toolkit, Second Edition* (Wiley, 2002).
- In that same chapter, Kimball and Ross describe another situation in which this technique may be useful: sales of products and services. They also point out that heterogeneous attributes are often present in the insurance industry; see Chapter 15 of *The Data Warehouse Toolkit.*
- This chapter mentioned an implementation alternative involving the placement of custom attributes into outriggers. This technique avoided the duplication of core attributes, but risks defeating advanced DBMS query optimizers. Kimball and Ross call these *context-dependent dimension outriggers.* For an illustration, see Chapter 9 of *The Data Warehouse Toolkit.*
- The process of designing and building aggregate tables must be carefully thought out when there are core and custom stars. Aggregates can focus on core attributes, but there may also be room for type-specific aggregates. These possibilities are discussed in Chapter 8 of *Mastering Data Warehouse Aggregates* by Chris Adamson (Wiley, 2006).

PART V

Performance

CHAPTER

14 Derived Schemas

Performance is a guiding principle of dimensional design, as you learned in Chapter 1. It is also one of the foundational principles of data warehousing in general. By restructuring data at load time, rather than query time, answering analytic questions about business processes is faster and easier.

Sometimes, however, faster is not enough. While a well-designed schema can deliver answers to most queries with reasonable rapidity, some queries will require more complex processing. As data sets grow large, even simple queries may exhibit degraded performance.

Luckily, there are solutions to these problems. In this chapter, you will learn how *derived tables* take information from an existing dimensional schema and restructure it for special purposes. In Chapter 15, you will learn how *aggregate tables* are used to pre-summarize information in large data sets. Both techniques can dramatically boost the performance of a dimensional design, without requiring investment in proprietary hardware or software solutions.

Derived schemas store copies of existing dimensional data that has been restructured. These data structures can improve query performance and reduce report development complexity, at the cost of additional work loading and managing them. This chapter highlights some derived structures that have already been encountered, and illustrates four more:

- **Merged fact tables** precompute drill-across results, making it easier and faster to compare facts from different fact tables.
- **Pivoted fact tables** transpose row-wise data into column-wise data, or vice versa, simplifying the construction process for some kinds of reports.
- **Sliced fact tables** contain a subset of rows of the original fact table. They are useful for distributed, departmental, and mobile applications, and may also be used to enforce role-based security.
- **Set operation fact tables** store results from comparing two stars with union, intersect, or minus operations, dramatically improving the performance and complexity of reports that require these comparisons.

These techniques are especially well suited to the design of cubes, as well as stars. In keeping with the approach of this book, most of the principles and examples in this chapter will make use of relational terminology—referring to stars, fact tables, and dimension tables. Keep in mind that you can substitute cubes for stars in any of these situations, with powerful results.

Restructuring Dimensional Data

For most of the dimensional designs you have seen this far, it has been assumed that data comes from a nondimensional source. In an Inmon-style architecture, data comes from the enterprise data warehouse—an integrated repository of atomic data that is not designed dimensionally. In a Kimball-style architecture, or in a stand-alone data mart, data comes directly from operational systems.

Derived schemas provide a second layer to the dimensional architecture. They piggyback on existing dimensional structures, rather than drawing data from the original sources. By definition, derived schemas are redundant. Redundancy, however, is not a bad thing in the dimensional world.

Derived schemas offer some distinct advantages that are in keeping with the overall purpose of the data warehouse. Of course, this redundancy does have costs as well, requiring the loading and maintenance of new data structures. You have already encountered several forms of derived schemas, including snapshots, accumulating snapshots, and core fact tables.

Uses for Derived Schemas

The advantages of derived schemas are relatively easy to intuit. Even without formal training, many uses will be patently obvious. Derived schemas can improve query performance and reduce report complexity.

Less obvious, but equally important, a derived schema can be used to produce a replica of the base schema that is limited in scope. This helps control the size of data sets in distributed, departmental, or mobile applications, and allows for the application of role-based security for sensitive data.

Lastly, derived schema designs are very handy when deploying OLAP cubes for analytic purposes. Targeted at particular analytic needs, derived designs can produce compact cubes that optimize performance and minimize complexity for specific classes of business questions.

Query Performance

A well-designed database schema can usually answer a large percentage of business questions in a reasonable response time. For the remaining minority of questions, however, it may perform poorly. This is true of any kind of design, dimensional or otherwise. It is an example of the famous "80/20 rule" at work: any design will meet 80 percent of the needs smoothly; the remaining 20 percent will be more difficult. Although numbers may not always be the same, the principle applies.

Derived schemas can address performance issues of the minority queries—those for which the original dimensional design is not optimal. Data is reorganized into a format that is better suited to answer the question. For example, it can be costly to perform a subquery or set operations when comparing information from more than one fact table. By precomputing the operation and storing the result in a new fact table, performance is enhanced.

The techniques in this chapter provide performance benefits for specific classes of query. Merged fact tables eliminate the need to use the multi-step drill-across process when comparing business processes. Pivoted fact tables eliminate the need to transpose rows and columns when reports require it. Set operation fact tables eliminate the need to perform subqueries or leverage SQL set operators. In each case, the derived star is specifically adapted to a specific kind of query.

Report Complexity

Performance is not the only area in which business questions are not created equal. As IT managers are well aware, *reports* vary in terms of development cost as well. One schema design may deliver sufficient performance for all queries but render a subset of reports very difficult to produce.

This complexity can become a concern for two reasons. First, it will be difficult or impossible for end users or analysts to develop these problem reports. They will have to be handled by trained developers or allowed to go unanswered. The former will introduce a lag between question and answer and introduces backlog; the latter will cast the pall of failure over the data warehouse as a whole.

Second, complex reports can cost significantly more to develop. While performance may be acceptable, the necessary work involved in producing the report takes longer, leverages advanced or obscure features of the reporting tools, requires additional skill, and is harder to test and modify. For example, a particular business question might require the development of a report that takes query results, parses them into a set of variables, applies layers of conditional logic, and transposes data. Even if it performs well, this kind of report requires more time and skill to produce, test, and maintain.

When a large number of important questions are rendered complicated to answer, a derived schema may alleviate these problems. By restructuring data, a derived schema makes answers accessible to users of less skill, and may also reduce report development costs.

Schema Scope

The information in a dimensional schema may serve a variety of groups and purposes. In many cases, analytic requirements will not call for access to all information contained in the schema. When only a subset of the data is called for, a derived schema may be useful. This is most helpful in distributed, departmental, or mobile solutions, where limiting data set size is an advantage.

For example, sales data being replicated to regional offices need not include the entire contents of a star. The amount of data propagated to each region can be limited to the region's own transactions. The size of the data set is reduced without sacrificing detail.

The same principle can be used to enforce a role-based security requirement. Derived schemas can be produced that are limited to what particular groups are permitted to access. For example, a sliced fact table, as presented later in this chapter, may be used to provide order data for a particular region only.

Use of Cubes

While this book uses star schema examples to illustrate dimensional design techniques, any dimensional model can also be implemented as a multidimensional cube. Cubes can be incorporated into a dimensional architecture in two ways, as you learned in Chapter 3, "Stars and Cubes." One approach calls for the cube as a primary storage mechanism of dimensional data; the other uses cubes as high-performance supplements derived from stars.

When a cube serves as the primary storage mechanism for dimensional information, the derivation techniques in this chapter provide the same benefits. Derived cubes are deployed in lieu of derived stars. Like their relational counterparts, derived cubes may be used to improve the performance of queries, reduce the complexity of report development, or limit the scope of the schema.

Sometimes cubes are not used for the primary storage of dimensional data because relational structures do a better job storing large volumes of data. Instead, cubes are used as high-performance *supplements* to the relational data. In this case, the cubes are derived by definition, and may mirror any of the derived schema designs in this chapter. The underlying star schema is relied upon as a data source for a variety of derived cubes, each of which is a compact high-performance data structure, targeted for a specific category of business question.

Derived Schemas Already Covered

If you are reading this book cover to cover, you have already encountered several examples of derived schemas. Each offers benefits over the original dimensional schema for specific kinds of analysis. These examples included the snapshot, accumulating snapshot, and core fact tables.

Snapshots

Snapshot fact tables are sometimes derived from transaction fact tables, as discussed in Chapter 11. A snapshot fact table samples a measurement of status, such as an account balance or inventory level, at a predefined interval. While status can be determined by aggregating individual transactions, doing so can be very inefficient. The snapshot fact table makes this kind of analysis easy.

Figuring out your bank account balance on a particular day, for example, should not require aggregating the entire history of transactions dating back to the day you opened it. This is possible but is highly inefficient. If it were necessary to do this for hundreds of accounts at a time, report performance would be very poor. Instead, a daily snapshot of account balances makes short work of figuring out this information. It is constructed from data in the transaction fact table during the load process. There is no need to aggregate years' worth of historic transactions during the query process.

Snapshot-grained fact tables are not always derived. As noted in Chapter 11, some snapshots capture measurements that do not represent the cumulative effect of transactions. Examples include ambient temperature, internal air pressure, and reservoir levels. These measurements can only be captured by sampling real-world conditions at the predetermined interval. In other cases, snapshots may be employed because transactions are too voluminous to keep in the data warehouse. In these cases, the snapshot is not considered a derived schema; instead, it serves as the primary storage mechanism for dimensional data.

Accumulating Snapshots

An accumulating snapshot is another example of a derived schema. As you learned in Chapter 11, it is often useful to study the time between significant events. This may require correlating activities across multiple stars, such as orders, shipments, and payments, or across multiple rows in a single star, such as the submission, approval, and settlement on mortgage applications. In either case, understanding the average time at each stage may require aggregating a very large number of correlations. This can be an extremely intensive and poorly performing process.

The accumulating snapshot represents various process steps in a single fact table row. By correlating activities in advance, it eliminates the need for complex correlations at query time. This makes the accumulating snapshot particularly well suited to the study of time spent at various processing stages.

The accumulating snapshot is almost always derived from one or more stars. The original stars remain useful in supporting analytic activities that are focused on individual tasks. The accumulating snapshot is called on in situations that require aggregating correlated activities. Its design is specifically adapted to these particular questions.

Core Fact Tables

Chapter 13 described the use of core and custom stars as a means for coping with heterogeneous attributes. When there is type-specific variation in the facts and dimensions associated with a process, custom stars permit detailed analysis of each type, while core stars permit analysis across all types.

For example, the dimension attributes and facts associated with an orders process may vary with the kind of thing being ordered. Product types might include books, compact discs, and subscriptions. Certain dimension attributes are common, such as the product category and name, and at least one common fact—order dollars. Other attributes, such as the publication format or record label, are specific to particular types.

As Chapter 13 pointed out, the custom fact tables are often built first. The core fact table, then, becomes a "union all" of the common facts. This approach is very helpful when the various custom types correspond to different sources, allowing the ETL routines that load each fact table to focus on a single source. The core fact table is then derived from the custom, or type-specific, fact tables.

As with any other form of derived schema, this arrangement allows different structures to serve different analytic purposes. Analysis that is confined to a particular type may focus on a custom star, with full access to the unique dimension attributes or facts associated with the particular type. Analysis across all types focuses on the core star, with integrated access to all common attributes.

The Cost of Derived Schemas

It is important to recognize that a derived schema does not achieve these benefits at no cost. Benefits are achieved by moving work out of the query and reporting process and into the ETL process. This is in keeping with the overall objectives of data warehousing but must be factored into design decisions.

The presence of derived schemas has another impact as well. Developers of queries and reports are now faced with multiple representations of the same process and must choose the appropriate dimensional structure for each business question. This potentially limits the understandability of the solution.

ETL Processing

Data warehouses are designed and built to answer questions about business processes. The data warehouse assembles a repository of data that is drawn from throughout the business, integrates it, and organizes it for analytics. By doing this "heavy lifting" in advance, the questions are easier to answer.

The same principle applies to the development of derived schemas. The benefits they achieve do not come for free. Additional "heavy lifting" is added to the ETL process. Each derived schema must be loaded and maintained by ETL developers and tuned by database administrators. This additional work at load time buys improved performance or reduced complexity at query time.

It is important not to lose sight of the additional work that will be required by derived tables. More tables must be designed, loaded, and maintained. More ETL routines must be developed, tested, and deployed. More dependencies will be added to a load window that may already be fully utilized. More processing resources may be required to crunch the data during load time.

These impacts must be balanced with the benefits of the derived schema. While additional load-time activity is consistent with the fundamental principles of data warehousing, there must be sufficient business benefit to justify it. As you will learn in Chapter 18, "How to Design and Document a Dimensional Model," the best way to make this kind of design decision involves representatives of a variety of points of view, including report developers, ETL developers, database administrators, end users, and IT management.

Multiple Stars to Choose From

The derived schema also has an impact on usability. Anyone setting out to develop a query or report must choose the appropriate star for the task. With derived schemas in place, a single business process is represented by multiple stars, such as snapshot and transaction, core and custom, process-specific and merged, and so forth.

As the number of analytic options increases, so too does the number of choices one must make when commencing development of a report. While it may be a relatively minor issue, some basic techniques can help. The easiest technique is to make the derived schemas available only to select power users. The original schema will satisfy the bulk of the analytic requirements and can be made generally available. Business questions that require the derived schemas are handled by power users or trained developers. An alternative is to provide multiple queries and reporting environments, each of which is carefully named and well documented. This allows people developing reports to choose the appropriate star before they begin, without realizing a choice has been made. There will be more on this in Chapter 16, "Design and Business Intelligence."

The Merged Fact Table

The merged fact table is the most common form of derived schema. It consolidates facts from one or more stars in a single fact table. The resulting star can be used to compare processes in lieu of drilling across. This can be a lifesaver if your business intelligence tools do not support this activity. It also makes queries much easier to read and write, and may provide a valuable performance boost.

Precomputed Drill-Across Results

The merged fact table combines facts from one or more stars, storing them at their lowest level of compatibility. The resulting star can be used to perform cross-process analysis, without the need to perform the multi-step drill-across process described in Chapter 4. For this reason, the merged fact table may also be referred to as a *drill-across fact table* or *consolidated fact table.*

A common use of the merged fact table supports the comparison of plans or goals to actual performance. Plans and actual results are normally recorded in separate stars; comparing them requires drilling across. Rather than perform this operation at runtime, you can have them done ahead of time. The precomputed results are stored in a merged fact table.

Figure 14-1 depicts an example. In the top of the diagram, first-level stars capture information about order targets (sales_goal_facts) and actuals (order_facts). Sales goals are established for each territory and month, and may be revised or restated in one or more plan versions. Orders are captured by day, product, customer, and salesperson. The stars conform at the month level (a conformed rollup of day) and territory level (a conformed rollup of salesrep).

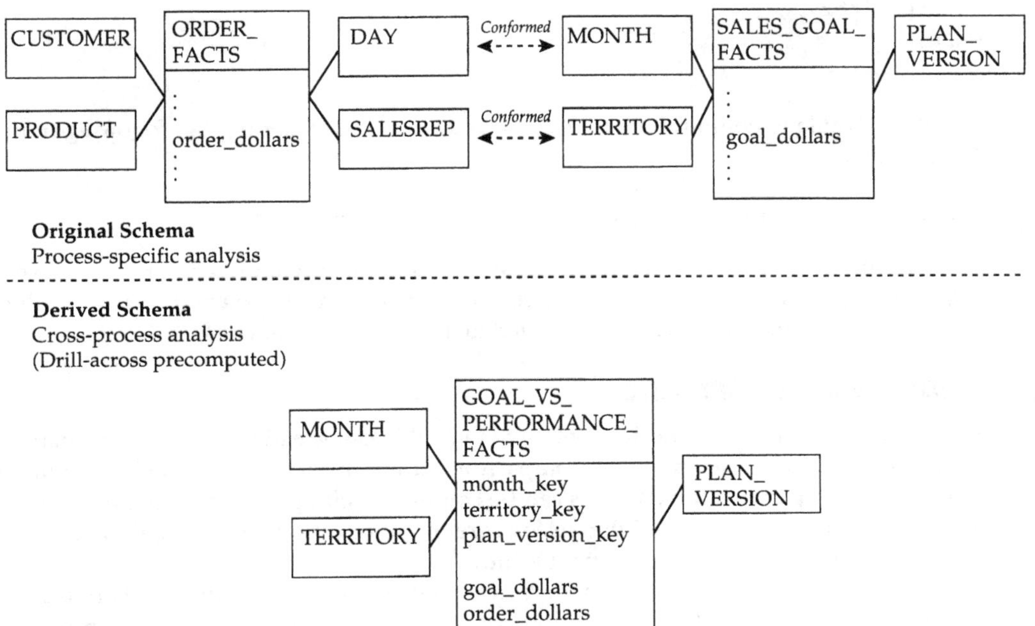

Figure 14-1 A merged fact table compares plans to actuals

Without a merged fact table, comparing goal dollars and order dollars would require drilling across the conformed dimensions. The two-step process for drilling across these two stars was illustrated in Figure 5-4. First, each star is queried, aggregating the fact to a common level of dimensional detail. Second, the result sets from the two queries are merged together through a full outer join.

The merged fact table goal_vs_performance_facts precomputes the drill-across comparison. Shown in the bottom of Figure 14-1, it summarizes order_dollars and goal_dollars at a common level of dimensional detail: month and territory. Notice it contains one additional dimension: plan_version. Its presence will be explained shortly.

Simplified Process Comparison

With the merged fact table in place, it is no longer necessary to drill across. Since goal_dollars and order_dollars are recorded in the same fact table, comparison can be achieved using a simple query:

```
SELECT
    territory,
    sum( goal_dollars ),
    sum( order_dollars )
FROM
    goal_vs_performance_facts,
    territory
WHERE
  ...
```

It is also possible to compute the percent of goal achieved by adding the following to the SELECT clause:

```
sum(order_dollars) / sum(goal_dollars) as percent_of_goal
```

This simplified SQL is much easier to write and understand, reducing the skill level required to perform process comparisons. This may be a "nice to have" feature, but there are other factors that may make the merged fact table a "must have."

Improved Performance

In addition to simplifying queries, a merged fact table can greatly improve performance. In the case of the goal versus actual comparison for the orders process, the benefit may be minimal. Drilling across two data sets can be completed with great efficiency, particularly when a small number of shared dimensions are in the result set, and those dimensions take on a relatively small number of distinct values.

The performance advantage of a merged fact table is more pronounced when data sets are larger, or when comparing a large number of processes. In Chapter 4, for example, a sales report was described that pulled together data from four fact tables. Sales calls, proposals, orders, and revenue were combined into a single report, organized by quarter and region, as shown in Figure 4-13. In this case, performance may be significantly improved by a merged fact table.

Profitability analysis is another common example where a merged fact table can provide significant performance improvements. Studying profitability requires the comparison of revenue and costs, which are generated by separate processes represented by separate stars. A manufacturer of consumer products, for example, may have stars that capture sales, shipments, returns, commission payments, marketing promotions, manufacturing costs, and other overhead activities. Profitability analysis brings these disparate processes together over a set of common dimensions such as time or product. Bringing together more components can create a finer picture of profitability but also impacts performance. A merged fact table for profitability analysis removes this bottleneck.

Supporting Tools that Cannot Drill Across

Many packaged query and reporting tools can be configured to recognize situations that require drilling across and then automate the process. Using some tools, it is also possible to assemble a drill-across report manually. Three methods of drilling across were illustrated in Figure 4-14. As noted in Chapter 4, some business intelligence tools cannot be used in any of these manners. Others present configuration challenges that prevent such use.

When the data warehouse architecture does not include tools that can be used to drill across, the merged fact table becomes an essential part of the dimensional design. Merged fact tables must be designed and implemented to support all cross-process reporting. The drill-across activity is performed during the ETL process; the resulting merged fact tables support cross-process analysis without requiring the use of multiple stars.

TIP A merged fact table consolidates facts from multiple fact tables by precomputing the drill-across activity. This makes cross-process analysis queries easier to write and can improve performance. If the available reporting tools do not support drilling across, a merged fact table will enable comparisons that would otherwise be impossible.

Single-Process Analysis

The drill-across fact table should not be thought of as a replacement for the first-level stars on which it is based. When studying a single process, you should direct queries to the appropriate process-specific star—not the merged star. There are two reasons for this guideline.

The most obvious reason the process-specific star is still required is that the merged star does not always contain the most granular data possible. In the case of orders, for example, the merged goal_vs_peformance star does not include product or customer detail. It also lacks day and salesperson-level detail, summarizing them by month and territory. When you are studying orders, use of the original order_facts star will allow access to the most granular detail possible.

There is another reason not to use the merged fact table when studying a single process. Since the merged fact table contains information from more than one process, it may record zero-valued facts. For example, suppose there is a sales goal for the Eastern territory for the month of March but no orders. The merged fact table goal_vs_performance_facts will contain a row for the Eastern territory for March. The order_dollars for this particular row will contain the value 0. If this table was used to produce a report showing orders by territory, the Eastern territory would be included in the result set despite the fact that there are no orders. This is akin to the problem of zero-valued rows resulting from the recording of orders and shipments in the same fact table, as discussed in Chapter 4. As in that example, the proper solution for single-process analysis is the use of a process-specific fact table.

TIP A merged schema should be used only when comparing processes. Single-process analysis should be conducted using the original first-level dimensional structures.

In some cases, it may be useful to include each territory, even if there are no sales, but notice that the merged fact table does not necessarily facilitate this. A zero is recorded for the Eastern territory because there is a goal. If there is another territory for which there is *no* goal, that territory will *not* appear on the report. The occurrence of zero-valued rows will appear to be random. An alternative technique should be used if an orders report should include all territories. This may be supported by features of the reporting tool or handled with SQL.

Including a Nonshared Dimension

When comparing facts from two or more stars, it is often necessary to filter one of the stars using a dimension that is not shared. When designing a merged fact table to support such comparisons, it is necessary to determine how this dimension will be incorporated. It may be omitted from the merged star, which will limit analytic possibilities, or it may be included in the merged star, which will require that every query constrain on the dimension in question.

The sales_goal_facts star at the top of Figure 14-1 tracks several versions of a sales plan. For a given year, there may be a proposed plan, an approved plan, and a revised plan. The plan_version table captures this information. For any given month and territory, there may be three rows recorded in the fact table: one for each version of the sales plan.

When you are comparing goals to performance, sales_goal_facts must be constrained to select a single version of the plan. This is done during the first stage of drilling across, as sales_goal_facts is being queried. Failure to do so will cause goal_dollars to be double- or triple-counted. By constraining for a single version of the plan, you can retrieve a single goal_dollars value for each month and territory. These amounts can be safely compared to order_dollars by month and territory in the second stage of the drill-across operation.

When building a merged fact table to support the comparison of goals to orders, it will be necessary to decide how to handle plan_version. This dimension is not shared with order_facts. The merged fact table can be designed to select only the most recent plan_version during the ETL process. The resulting star, however, would only be able to support analysis of performance versus goal for the most recent sales plan.

The alternative, as depicted in Figure 14-1, is to include the nonshared plan_version dimension in the merged fact table. Although this dimension does not strictly relate to order_dollars, its inclusion allows the merged fact table to track more than one sales plan. For a given month and territory, there may be two or more rows in the merged fact table—one for each plan. During the ETL process, it will be necessary to *repeat* the order_dollars value for each of these rows.

This approach permits goal versus performance analysis using any version of the sales plan. In order to make proper use of this table, it is necessary to select a specific plan_version in *every* query. Failure to do so can potentially double-count goal_dollars across multiple plans, and will also double-count the order_dollars.

TIP A merged star may contain a nonshared dimension. Queries against the merged fact table must always qualify this dimension for a single value, lest double-counting occur.

When a merged fact table contains a nonshared dimension, proper training will be required for anyone who will be developing queries or reports. This requirement should be well documented. Report developers can be taught to constrain the dimension in question every time they build a query, but end users conducting ad hoc analysis may not be counted on to do the right thing. One way to solve this dilemma is to provide end users with a view that constrains the merged fact table in advance. They will have less analytic flexibility but will not produce inaccurate results. Some business intelligence software can be configured to prompt for a constraint automatically whenever the fact table in question is queried.

The Pivoted Fact Table

The pivoted fact table lies at the center of another kind of derived schema. In this case, data from the original fact table is transposed from a row-wise to column-wise orientation, or vice versa. This kind of derived fact table is sometimes desirable because it simplifies certain forms of reporting. Performance is generally only marginally improved, so the pivoted fact table is generally saved for report-heavy applications, where it can save a significant amount of report development time.

The Need to Pivot Data

The schema in Figure 14-2 illustrates a financial data mart in which a pivoted fact table may be of use. The original schema in the top of the diagram is used to analyze data from an

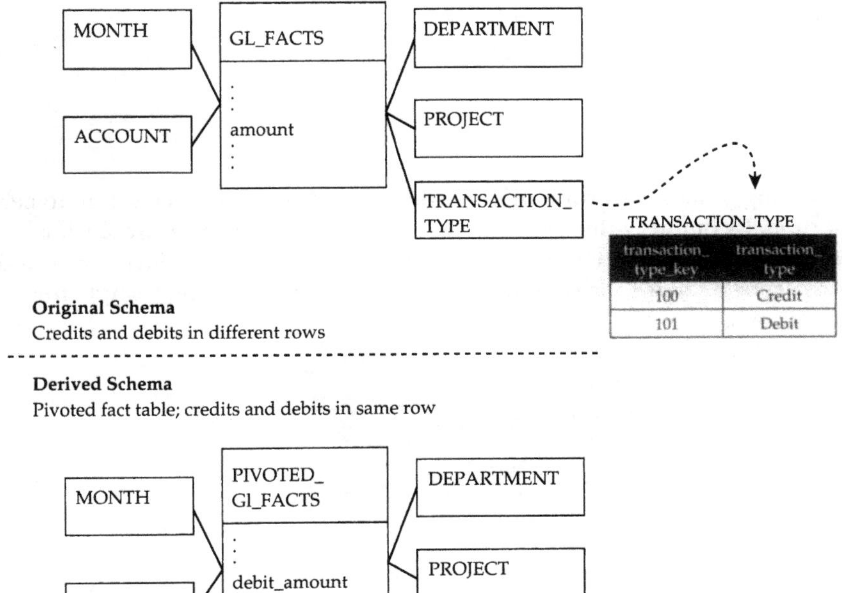

Figure 14-2 A pivoted fact table

Part V

accounting system. It captures monthly totals by transaction type and account. There is one fact: amount. This simple example also has two transaction types: debits and credits.

In the original schema, when the transaction type is used to group results, debits and credits will appear in different rows of the result set. For example:

```
SELECT
    account,
    transaction_type,
    sum(amount)
FROM
  .
  .
  .
GROUP BY
    account,
    transaction_type
```

This query yields results in the form:

```
ACCOUNT    TRANSACTION_TYPE  SUM(AMOUNT)
========   ================  ===========
01-2211    Credits             20,301.00
01-2211    Debits            - 17,691.30
07-4499    Credits              1,221.23
07-4499    Debits            -  2,220.01
   .
   .
   .
```

There is nothing inherently wrong with this design, and it may be well suited to certain forms of reporting. By omitting the transaction_type from a query, for example, it is possible to aggregate a net value for all transactions against an account during a period. However, many reports call for the presentation of credits and debits on a single row, rather than in different rows:

```
ACCOUNT        DEBITS     CREDITS
========   ==========  ==========
01-2211     17,691.30   20,301.00
07-4499      2,220.01    1,221.23
   .
   .
   .
```

It may be somewhat trivial to transpose the original result set into a format like this by using SQL wizardry or by making use of report variables or other such features. However, if a large number of reports will require this restructuring, it may prove useful to provide a derived star that precomputes the transformation of row-wise data into column-wise data. Benefits will also be more obvious in situations where a larger number of columns must be transposed.

The Pivoted Advantage

The schema in the lower portion of Figure 14-2 pivots information from the original schema so it is in the desired format. Rather than holding a single fact and a transition type, it contains multiple facts—one for each transaction type. Reports that require credits and debits to appear on a single row can be constructed using this star, rather than the original star. Fancy SQL will not be required, nor will the use of advanced report development features. It is possible to implement this particular pivoted fact table using a view. In other cases, it may be better implemented as a physical table and loaded by an ETL process.

TIP A pivoted schema transposes row-wise data to column-wise data or vice versa. This effort can reduce the complexity of the query and reporting process.

Notice that either star in the example can be used to construct the other. It would have been equally possible to derive the top star from the bottom star, transposing each fact table row into rows for each of the transaction types. This is not always possible with pivoted schemas. Sometimes the derivation can only take place in one direction. If the original star had a transaction-level grain, for example, then the derived star would have summarized data across numerous transactions. In this case, it would not be possible to derive the top star from the bottom star.

Drawbacks to Pivoting

While a pivoted fact table may simplify the construction of certain forms of reports, it is not without its drawbacks. As with any form of derived schema, it behooves the user to choose the appropriate data structure to use for any given report. To avoid potential confusion, pivoted schemas are sometimes made available only to trained developers.

In many cases, the additional effort required to develop and maintain a pivoted schema is not justifiable. In the example in Figure 14-2, the benefits of the transposed schema may seem trivial. The original schema is highly summarized, and there is only a need to transpose two transaction types. The relatively small effort required to do so within a report may not justify the additional burden of loading and maintaining an additional star. The value of a pivoted schema increases as the number of rows to be transposed into columns increases. If, for example, there were several dozen transaction types to be transposed, the value proposition changes significantly.

The Sliced Fact Table

A sliced fact table is exactly the same as the original star but only contains a subset of rows. Sliced fact tables are typically defined using a specific dimension attribute and may be useful in providing distributed applications, enforcing role-based security, or in reducing schema scope for use in an OLAP tool.

Creating Slices of a Star

A sliced fact table is derived from a star by selecting all rows that refer to a common dimension value. The resulting star has the same attributes as the original but may be significantly smaller. Additional slices may be created for each possible value of the dimension attribute.

For example, the familiar star at the top of Figure 14-3 tracks orders by day, product, salesperson, and region. One of the attributes of the salesperson dimension table is region. This dimension takes on values such as "East," "West," and so forth. Order_facts contains orders for all regions.

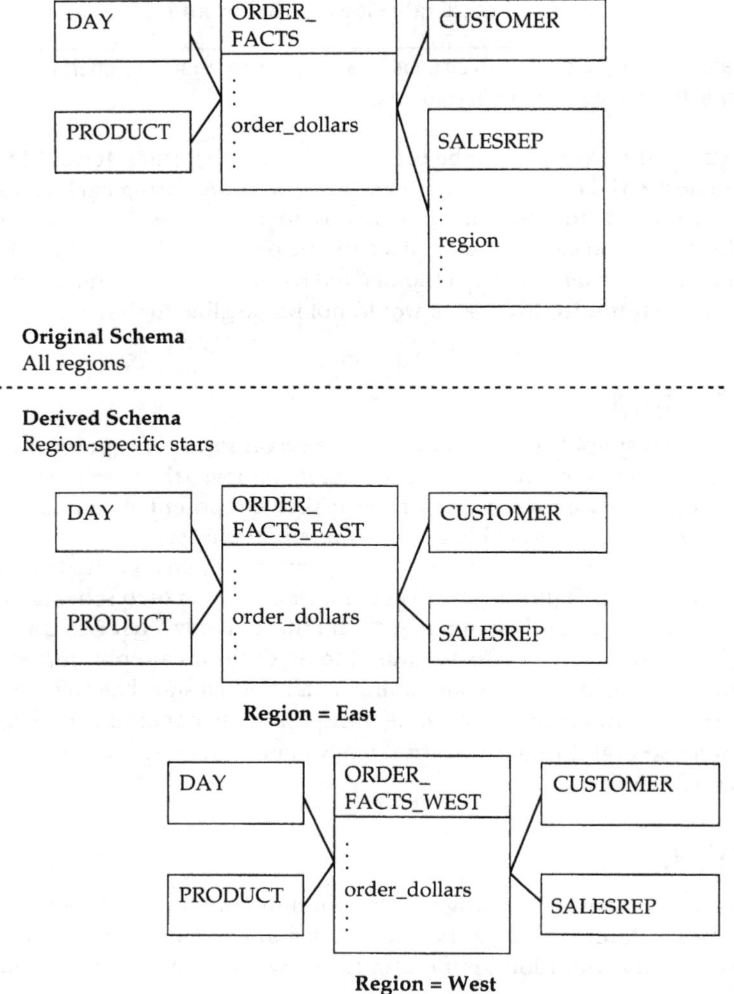

Figure 14-3 Sliced fact tables

Regionally focused fact tables can be derived from order_facts. Each regionally focused star will contain all rows from the original fact table that are associated with a particular region. The lower part of Figure 14-3 shows sliced fact tables for the East and West regions. Although the diagram repeats each of the dimensions, it is not necessary to replicate these tables, unless the slicing is performed to support regionally distributed data. One set of unaltered dimension tables can be joined to the original order_facts table as well as each regional slice.

Uses for Sliced Fact Tables

Sliced fact tables serve handily in a variety of situations. The most common involves a regional or departmental focus, as in the example. Slices limit the size and scope of the data set without sacrificing detail. This makes them easier to distribute across physical locations, enables deployment in mobile applications, helps enforce security requirements, and permits generation of cubes of manageable size.

Distributed solutions require replication of data to different platforms or locations. Where distributed systems have a regional focus, a sliced fact table reduces the amount of information that must be replicated, without sacrificing detail. By deploying sliced fact tables or cubes, you replicate all dimensions at each location, along with only the relevant subset of facts.

Mobile solutions may be more severely limited by the size of the data set that can be carried offline. Sliced fact tables may be a convenient way to reduce the overall data set size, without sacrificing analytic detail. Another useful data structure for mobile solutions is the aggregate table, discussed in Chapter 15, "Aggregates."

Sliced fact tables offer a convenient mechanism for the enforcement of security requirements. Access to slices is granted to users based on their needs, ensuring that individuals only have access to the appropriate subsets of the data as called for by their job function. Table-level access is typically easier to configure and administer than row-based security schemes for the original schema.

As previously noted, cubes do not always scale as well as relational data structures. Defining cubes as slices of the original data set is an effective way to limit their overall size, as are all of the other derivation techniques in this chapter, as well as the aggregation techniques in Chapter 15.

NOTE The slicing technique is often referred to as "horizontal partitioning" of the fact table; the result contains all of the columns of the original fact table but only a subset of the original rows. Each partition, or slice, is defined by a dimension value. Related to the concept of horizontal partitioning is that of vertical partitioning. A vertical partition takes some subset of the attributes of the original data set, as opposed to a subset of rows. This may give rise to an aggregate table, as discussed in Chapter 15.

Slices First

Sliced fact tables are not always derived from the whole. It is possible to construct the whole as a union-all from the slices, but extreme care must be taken in handling the dimensions. This may occur in situations where regional fact tables are constructed in parallel, then combined into a whole at the end of the processing window. Effective derivation of the whole from slices requires a consistent data architecture and a carefully coordinated ETL process. There must be no overlap in the slices. More importantly, each of the slices must share the same common set of dimensions. This implies a load process that handles the following steps sequentially:

1. Process common dimension tables.
2. Process fact table slices, in parallel if desired.
3. Derive combined fact table from slices.

Failure to process a common set of dimension tables *prior* to loading slices generates issues. Problems may include nonconformance, overlapping key values, or inconsistent representation of slow changes. For the solution in Figure 14-3, if the whole were to be derived from the slices, all regions should be working with the same product table, customer table, and so forth. By establishing a unified set of dimensions first, it is possible to load facts from various subsets of data in parallel, while guaranteeing that the resultant slices can be unioned into a single fact table.

Set Operation Fact Tables

The last form of derived fact table takes two stars as an input and produces an output based on the application of set operations or the use of a subquery or correlated subquery. The resulting star provides performance advantages over the original schema, avoiding the use of set operators at query time.

Comparing Two Sets of Data

As discussed in Chapter 3, transaction-grained fact tables are sparse. Rather than record a row for every possible combination of dimension values, they record rows only where an activity or transaction occurs. Order facts, for example, are recorded only when orders take place.

Tracking the conditions that may or may not influence activities is done in a factless fact table, as described in Chapter 12. For example, the assignment of customers to salespeople can be captured in a coverage star. The fact table contains rows relating customers to salespeople, regardless of whether any orders are placed.

Identification of sales assignments that are nonproductive involves comparing order facts with sales assignments. One way to perform this comparison leverages set operations. The set of salesperson/customer assignments for a period, *minus* the set of salesperson/customer orders for the period, yields nonproductive assignments. As shown in Chapter 12, this can be a beastly query to write and may not perform very well. Set operations are not always used for this kind of query, as Chapter 12 also noted. Subqueries can also be employed, in conjunction with the `EXISTS` or `NOT EXISTS` qualifiers. The end result is no less complex, nor is it likely to exhibit significantly improved performance.

Rather than perform this query at runtime, it can be computed during the ETL process, with the result sets stored in a new fact table. Queries and reports no longer need to compute the difference between the sets, as represented by the original fact tables. Instead, they access a derived fact table, using simple straightforward SQL.

Several Possible Comparisons

Given any two fact tables that share common dimensions, a variety of set operations can be precomputed. Candidates include union, intersect, and multiple minus operations. Not every set will have a use, or even a useful meaning, but if any will be required on a regular basis, a derived fact table may save considerable reporting effort and execution time.

TIP Set operation fact tables precompute the comparison of two data sets using set operations or subqueries, storing the result in a new fact table. This greatly simplifies the processing required within queries or reports.

The possible set operations involving a pair of fact tables that relate customers and salespeople are depicted in Figure 14-4. Each of the circles represents customer/salesrep

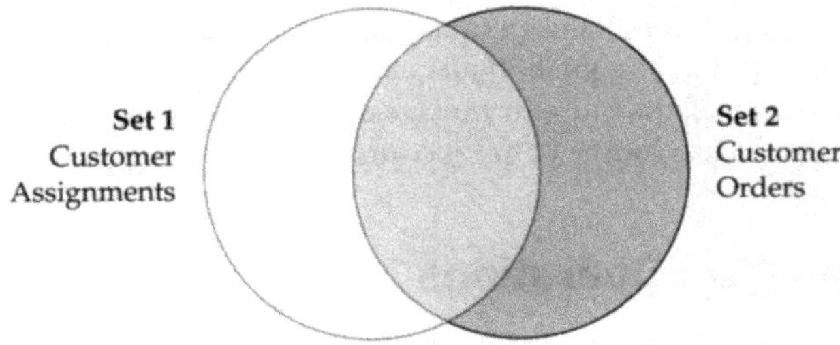

Possible Derived Schemas		
1 Minus 2		Customer assignments with no orders
1 Intersect 2		Orders taken from assigned customers
2 Minus 1		Orders taken from unassigned customers
1 Union 2		Assignments and/or orders

Figure 14-4 Set operations on stars

relationships. The circle on the left corresponds to customer assignments; the circle on the right corresponds to orders. Each is represented by its own star. The table beneath the Venn diagram illustrates the different ways these sets can be compared.

The first example represents a set in which sales management may be particularly useful: salespeople who did not sell to assigned customers. This set is defined by the SQL `MINUS` operation, as in the query from Chapter 12. Precomputed results can be stored in a factless fact table, with dimensions for the period, salesperson, and customer. The derived table can also be computed by adding a `NOT EXISTS` predicate to a query for customer assignments; these SQL keywords will introduce a correlated subquery that looks for orders. See Chapter 12 for the full story.

Additional set operations are also possible. The intersection of the two sets represents sales to assigned customers. This set may be computed and stored in a fact table that includes the same facts as order_facts. If salespeople are only compensated for sales to their assigned customers, this fact table will be useful for commission reporting.

The sets can also be compared to identify sales to unassigned customers. This set result may include facts from the original order_facts table. If all customers are assigned to specific salespeople, then this set of orders represents those in which salesreps have taken orders from *someone else's* customer. This behavior is the source of great controversy in sales organizations with named customer assignments!

Choosing to Precompute Set Operations

The application of set operations does not always have a useful result. If it cannot be clearly defined using business terms, the set is not likely to support relevant analysis and, therefore, is not useful from a business perspective.

For example, it is possible to create a union of all salesperson/customer relationships for a period—those that represent a customer assignment and those that result from orders being taken. This set has no real semantic significance or use to the business. In other applications, however, a `UNION` operation may be useful.

Precomputing the results of set operations is most often useful with intersect and minus operations and almost always involves a coverage table. Other examples include identifying products that did or did not sell while under promotion, the effect of weather on sales, and the participation of eligible parties in a benefits program. Each of these examples compares the content of a factless fact table that describes conditions or coverage with a transaction fact table that describes events.

Examination of reports sometimes reveals the potential for precomputation of set operations. When these comparisons are not computed in advance, reports that do the work grow excessively complex. Intricate procedural logic or calculations are the result. Precomputation can dramatically simplify reports, making them significantly easier to develop and maintain.

As with any other form of derived table, appropriate use of derived fact tables for the results of set operations requires balancing the cost savings in terms of report development or execution time with the increased burden on the ETL process. Set operations can be expensive. If they will be required infrequently, it may make more sense to compute them within an occasional report. On the other hand, if 20 percent of reports will focus on a subset, it may be highly advantageous to precompute it, either as a derived star or as a cube.

Summary

This chapter covered the use of derived schemas to enhance query performance or reduce the complexity of report creation. Key lessons included the following:

- A single schema design can rarely meet 100 percent of the reporting needs with maximum efficiency. For a minority of business questions, an alternative format may be optimal.
- A derived schema takes data from the original dimensional schema and restructures it for specific kinds of use.
- A derived schema may be implemented as a star or as a cube. Supplementing a star containing granular data with cubes derived for reporting purposes is a powerful combination.
- *Snapshots* may be derived from transactions, although they are not always. When derived, they greatly simplify the process of determining the cumulative effects of individual transactions on status measurements like levels or balances.
- *Accumulating snapshots* are usually derived from one or more stars. Each row correlates multiple activities, greatly simplifying the otherwise complex process of studying the time spent at various process stages.
- *Core fact tables* are often derived from type-specific custom fact tables. The core fact table makes it possible to conduct analysis across all types, without the need to perform unions.
- *Merged fact tables* precompute the results of drilling across two or more fact tables. This makes cross-process comparison easier and faster, and is especially helpful when existing tools cannot be used to drill across.
- *Pivoted fact tables* transpose facts organized row-wise into multiple facts in a single row, or vice versa. There may not be a large performance benefit, but there may be value in the reduced complexity of report development.
- *Sliced fact tables* take subsets of the original star, normally defined based on a single attribute value. These tables have a smaller size and scope but do not sacrifice detail. They may be useful in departmental, distributed, or mobile applications, or as the basis of a role-based security architecture.
- *Set operation fact tables* precompute the results of comparing two fact tables using subqueries or union, intersect, or minus operations. They can be significant timesavers, and dramatically simplify the necessary report SQL.

Remember that derived tables do not achieve their advantages for free. The cost is an increased burden for the loading and management of warehouse data structures. "Do the heavy lifting up front" is an admirable mantra but must be balanced with the business benefit of derived structures. This balancing act will be discussed in Chapter 18, "How to Design and Document a Dimensional Model."

Further Reading

Relatively little is written about derived schemas in dimensional modeling, other than snapshots and accumulating snapshots. Perhaps this is so because derived schemas are easy to intuit when the situation calls for them.

In situations that call for derived schemas, Kimball and Ross refer to the original dimension structure as a *first-level data mart*, and the derived structure as a *consolidated data mart*. This terminology has been avoided here, since this book reserves the term "data mart" for a subject area, rather than a single star. Recognizing what Kimball and Ross mean by these terms, however, will help you interpret some of the following references:

- Kimball and Ross allude to the use of derived tables for profitability by precomputing the results of drilling across several stars representing costs and revenue. This is described in Chapter 3 of *The Data Warehouse Toolkit, Second Edition* (Wiley, 2002).
- That same chapter suggests that some consolidated data marts may represent a simple union of first-level data marts. As you read it, think of deriving a core fact table from custom ones, or deriving a whole from slices.
- Kimball and Ross describe a merged fact table that can be used to study budget variances in Chapter 7 of *The Data Warehouse Toolkit*. This is similar to the goal versus performance example from this chapter.
- Kimball et al. describe a merged fact table used to compare forecast to actual data in Chapter 6 of *The Data Warehouse Lifecycle Toolkit, Second Edition* (Wiley, 2008) by Ralph Kimball, Margy Ross, Warren Thornthwaite, Joy Mundy, and Bob Becker.
- Like any other dimensional schema, a derived table may serve as the basis for a pre-summarized aggregate. In Chapter 9 of *Mastering Data Warehouse Aggregates* (Wiley, 2006), I discuss the construction of aggregates to supplement merged, pivoted, and sliced fact tables.

CHAPTER

15 Aggregates

Optimization of data warehouse performance is a never-ending process. As technology vendors have improved the capabilities of computer hardware and software, warehouse developers have responded by storing and analyzing larger and more granular sets of data.

In this ongoing quest for performance, the most powerful and effective tool at your disposal is the aggregate. Planned and integrated carefully, aggregates can have an extraordinary impact on the performance of your data warehouse. Their benefits can be realized without significant investment in specialized hardware and software, using tools that are already present in the data warehouse. Additional tools may help create and manage aggregates, but they are not required.

Like a derived schema, an aggregate is a supplemental data structure that helps make things go faster. Derived schemas, which you learned about in the previous chapter, improve performance by *restructuring* data in a manner suited to a particular class of query. Aggregate schemas achieve a performance benefit by *summarizing* data.

In this chapter, you will learn how to design and use aggregates. The principle of conformance, introduced in Chapter 5, will be put to use again, resulting in aggregates which provide query results that are consistent with the original schema. It also makes writing queries that leverage aggregates as simple as possible. Dimensional aggregation is also a very useful way to think about cube design in an environment that mixes star schemas and OLAP cubes.

The benefits of aggregates are not free. Putting them to work requires selecting the correct aggregate to use for each query. It also requires that aggregates be populated with data and kept in sync with the base schema. The latter requirement can be particularly tricky when type 1 changes occur. Luckily, it is possible to minimize the impact of these requirements.

The ideal aggregate would be invisible to users of the data warehouse, silently providing its benefit whenever possible. Although not mandatory, an aggregate navigation capability can help achieve this objective, and potentially provides a raft of additional benefits. The ideal aggregate would also be maintenance free, automatically generated and maintained without intervention by ETL developers. A variety of tools can be employed to fill this need as well.

As you have already learned, aggregates are not the only way to summarize data. Other forms of summarization may be useful as well. Any summarization that transforms the organization of a data structure is better classified as a derived schema, like those from the previous chapter. There is one summarization technique, however, that should be avoided—storing the summary in the same table as the detail.

Fundamentals of Aggregates

An aggregate can reduce the amount of work a database must perform in responding to a query. This simple principle can have a dramatic effect on individual queries. Applying principles of conformance presented in Chapter 5 makes it as easy as possible to write a query that leverages an aggregate, and ensures that the aggregate will provide results consistent with the original schema.

In exchange for the performance benefit of an aggregate, it will be necessary to load and maintain it. This can present a unique challenge for the ETL process. A type 1 change can wreak havoc on attempts to maintain aggregates incrementally.

Because a cube is a high-performance data structure to begin with, it rarely makes sense to construct an aggregate that summarizes a cube. This may be useful, however, if the original cube is tuned for maximum capacity rather than maximum performance. When the original data is stored in a star, a cube makes an excellent counterpart for high-performance analysis. In this scenario, each cube represents a dimensional aggregate. Many OLAP products are designed to work hand-in-hand with a star schema.

Summarizing Base Data

Dimensional aggregates improve the performance of queries by summarizing granular data in advance. The level of detail provided by an aggregate star is specified in the same way as for any other star: as a statement of grain. The facts and dimensions of the aggregate conform to those of the base star. This guarantees consistent results from the base star and aggregate, and makes it as easy as possible to write queries that take advantage of the aggregate.

Storage of Granular Data in the Base Schema

The grain of a fact table is usually defined at the lowest possible level of detail. This guideline is sometimes relaxed for data marts in an architecture based on Inmon's Corporate Information Factory, since a separate component of that architecture stores atomic data. Even in this architecture, however, fact tables may contain very granular data. Kimball's dimensional data warehouse calls for the star schema to be used as the repository of granular data, and stand-alone data marts are usually designed to capture detailed information as well.

While the data in a fact table is usually stored in a granular format, many reports do not require presentation of the individual details. As you saw in Chapter 1, a typical query will aggregate facts to a specified level of dimensional detail. This level of detail is usually controlled in a query by indicating dimensions that will be used to group results. Although the individual atomic measurements do not appear in the final result set, the database must access them in order to compute their sum.

Suppose, for example, that an orders star captures order_dollars by order line. Assume that the fact table, shown at the top of Figure 15-1, stores approximately 300,000 rows per month. A simple query that summarizes order_dollars by product, for January 2009, will require the DBMS to access 300,000 rows from the fact table. This will be necessary *regardless of how many products were sold* during the period. Even if there were only 200 products sold, the database must use the detailed data to compute their totals.

Storage of Pre-summarized Data in an Aggregate

Dimensional aggregates store information that has been summarized in advance. They improve query performance by reducing the amount of data that must be accessed and processed by the DBMS. When possible, using the aggregate table instead of the base schema allows the DBMS to spend less time reading data from disks, sorting it, joining rows together, computing sums, and so forth. These reductions in work allow query results to return faster. This also improves overall throughput. Since fewer resources are consumed, they are available to process other queries.

Suppose an aggregate fact table is built that includes the same facts about orders as the original schema but at a coarser grain. Depicted in Figure 15-1, order_facts_aggregate summarizes order_dollars by month, product, and salesrep. The original fact table contained roughly 300,000 rows per month; the summary contains roughly 1,000 rows per month.

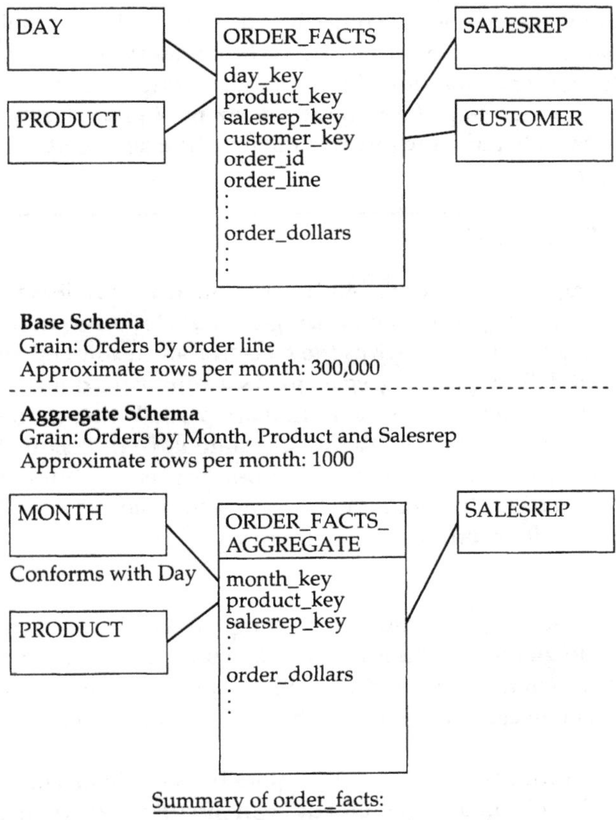

Figure 15-1 An aggregate star pre-summarizes order data

Using this aggregate fact table, determining order_dollars by product for a particular month requires accessing roughly 1/300th the number of rows that must be accessed when using the base fact table. This translates into significantly less work for the database—work that includes reading information from disks, joining fact table rows to dimension table rows, grouping data by product, and adding together the individual transactions. The improvement in response time is not necessarily 300× but will be significant.

TIP An aggregate table improves response time by reducing the number of rows that must be accessed by the DBMS when responding to a query.

Like the derived schemas from Chapter 14, the aggregate star does not provide this performance benefit for free. The aggregate tables must be loaded and maintained, resulting in additional work for ETL developers and database administrators. Software tools are available that help automate part or all of this additional work, but even these tools will require configuration, testing, and maintenance.

Describing the Aggregate: Grain

The easiest way to describe an aggregate schema is to describe the grain of the fact table, as opposed to trying to describe what is being summarized. This is best understood by looking back at the example. Order_facts_aggregate was described as summarizing facts about the orders process by month, product, and salesrep. This simple statement of grain describes the aggregate fact table concisely, by indicating the dimensionality of the aggregate schema: month, product, and salesrep.

TIP Define an aggregate schema by stating its grain.

Trying to describe order_facts_aggregate in terms of what it summarizes can leave you tongue-tied. One might speak of the aggregate as summarizing the facts "across customers" and "across order lines," or by stating that it summarizes the facts "for all customers" and "for all order lines." This manner of defining the aggregate works within these dimensions but will leave you tongue-tied when it comes to dimensions that are partially summarized. Order_facts_aggregate includes a month dimension—a partially summarized version of the day dimension. Stating that the aggregate summarizes facts "across days" is true but not very specific; a quarterly summary would also fit that definition. Saying it summarizes data "for all days" is not quite right either, since it groups days into months.

Conformance

An aggregate table must provide the same query results as the original schema. From a design perspective, the easiest way to guarantee this is to require that the aggregate star *conform* to the base star. This ensures semantic consistency across any common attributes, and equivalent content. It will also be necessary to enforce this conformance as part of the ETL process.

In an aggregate schema, the conformance requirement applies both to dimension attributes and to facts. Dimensional conformance has already been discussed. As you learned in Chapter 5, two dimension tables conform if they are the same in structure and content, or if the attributes of one are a subset of the other and share common structure and content.

By guaranteeing the same structure and content of common dimension attributes, the principle of conformance ensures that each replica represents the same thing.

Like dimensions, facts can conform. As with conformed dimensions, conformed facts share a common structure and content. Structural equivalence requires that the facts should have the same name, business meaning, and data type. Content equivalence requires that they return the same information when aggregated to the same level of detail. The facts in an aggregate schema conform with those of the base schema. This ensures that the aggregate facts can be used interchangeably with the original facts, while guaranteeing consistent results.

TIP The facts and dimensions of an aggregate schema conform to those of the base schema. This guarantees consistent results.

Following these guidelines, the dimension tables associated with order_facts_aggregate in Figure 15-1 must conform with those in the base star. Salesperson and product will be the same tables, or identical replicas. The month table will be a conformed rollup of day, as depicted in Figure 5-5. This guarantees that dimensions from the base and aggregate star can be used interchangeably.

The facts in order_facts_aggregate must also conform to the base star. Only one fact is shown: order_dollars. It must have the same name and meaning as it does in the base star. It should share the same data type, although it may require greater scale, since it is likely to hold larger numbers. Content must also be the same. Query results that include this fact should return the same results as those from the base fact table. Order dollars by month, for example, should produce exactly the same results from each star.

Structural conformance can be controlled at design time, but the conformance of content must be enforced at load time. One way to ensure consistent representation of data in the base and aggregate schema is to use the base star as the source for the aggregate data. This option will be explored later in this chapter.

Delivering Benefit

To deliver a performance benefit, an aggregate schema need not have a grain that exactly matches the grain of the query to be optimized. This may be obvious, but is worth noting. As long as the aggregate contains the dimensionality necessary to formulate the query, it can be used to answer the question. Data within the aggregate may be *further summarized* at query time. The query will still benefit from the pre-summarization performed when the aggregate was created.

For example, the aggregate schema in Figure 15-1 stores order_dollars by month, product, and salesrep. It can be used for any query that requires this level of detail *or less*. A report that lists order dollars by product for January 2009 can leverage the aggregate star, even though it does not require information about the salesperson. The DBMS will have to do some aggregation, but it will be far less work than would be required if it were using the original order_facts star.

Obviously, a single aggregate cannot provide a performance benefit for every query. Multiple aggregates can summarize the same base schema in different ways. Rather than represent successive levels of summarization, each aggregate pre-summarizes data across a different set of dimensions. This maximizes the number of queries that can be supported by aggregate tables.

There will always be queries that cannot be optimized through the use of aggregates. Any query that requires access to the granular data must be directed at the original star. For example, limiting query results to order lines with a dollar amount over $500 cannot be done without the granular data. In this case, an aggregate star will not help. If performance is an issue here, the report may be run during a batch window, or a derived table may be designed to store precomputed results. Also note the presence of aggregates to support *other* queries may make more system resources available to answer this one, even if it must make use of the base schema.

Using Aggregates

To reap the benefit of an aggregate table, it is necessary to rewrite a query to access it. When a summary conforms with the original schema, this is a relatively simple process—at least for technical personnel. For any given query, optimal performance will depend on choosing the most summarized schema capable of responding.

Writing (or Rewriting) Queries

Conformance of the aggregate star to the base star makes it relatively simple to write queries to take advantage of the aggregate. Because the two stars have a very similar structure and content, a query against the aggregate is structured in the same way it would be against the base star. The result sets are identical.

It is also quite simple to rewrite a preexisting query to make use of an aggregate. Facts and dimension attributes share the same names in both stars; all that is necessary is to replace table names from the base schema with those from the aggregate. If any conformed rollup dimensions are present, it will be necessary to replace surrogate keys in the SQL statement as well.

For example, using the base star in Figure 15-1, determining order dollars by product for January 2009 would require the following SQL statement:

```
SELECT
    product,
    SUM(order_dollars)
FROM
    day,
    product,
    order_facts
WHERE
   day.month='January' AND
   day.year = 2009 AND
   product.product_key = order_facts.product_key AND
   day.day_key = order_facts.day_key
GROUP BY
   product
```

Rewriting the query to take advantage of the aggregate requires no changes to the facts or dimensions in this SQL statement; all that is necessary is to replace the table names with those from the aggregate star. Within the time dimension, it will also be necessary to substitute month_key for day_key. The resulting query looks like this:

```
SELECT
    product,
    SUM(order_dollars)
FROM
    month,
    product,
    order_facts_aggregate
WHERE
   month.month='January' AND
   month.year = 2009 AND
   product.product_key = order_facts_aggregate.product_key AND
   month.month_key = order_facts_aggregate.month_key
GROUP BY
   product
```

Changes from the original query are highlighted in bold. No facts or dimension attributes have changed; only the names of tables and, in the case of month, the name of the surrogate key.

TIP The facts and dimension attributes in an aggregate star conform to those in the base star. Rewriting a query to take advantage of the aggregate involves replacing table names and key columns.

Determining Which Star to Query

When aggregates are available, formulating a query requires choosing between the base star and the aggregate star. If there are multiple aggregates, there are still more options from which to choose. This may be an easy decision for a seasoned report developer to make, but it can be bewildering for a less experienced analyst or business user.

Faced with a portfolio of aggregates, determination of the most appropriate schema for a query requires understanding what information is needed, identifying which stars can supply that information, and narrowing the pool down to the star with the smallest fact table.

For example, Figure 15-2 illustrates a portfolio of aggregates that summarize the base order_facts star. A report is needed that shows sales by customer for the first quarter of 2009. Three stars can be used to answer this question: the base star, the month/salesperson/customer aggregate, and the quarter/salesperson/customer aggregate. The latter is likely to have the least rows in its fact table and is, therefore, the best choice for this query.

This selection process may be easy for developers who have been provided with basic schema documentation and some information about relative table sizes. For an end user, however, it may be difficult to choose.

The situation is more complicated for *ad hoc* users, who may want to modify their query after seeing its results. Adding or removing dimensions from a query may change which star is able to answer most effectively, and may also alter which stars are able to answer at all. For example, the user may decide to take the Q1 2009 report of sales by product and break the

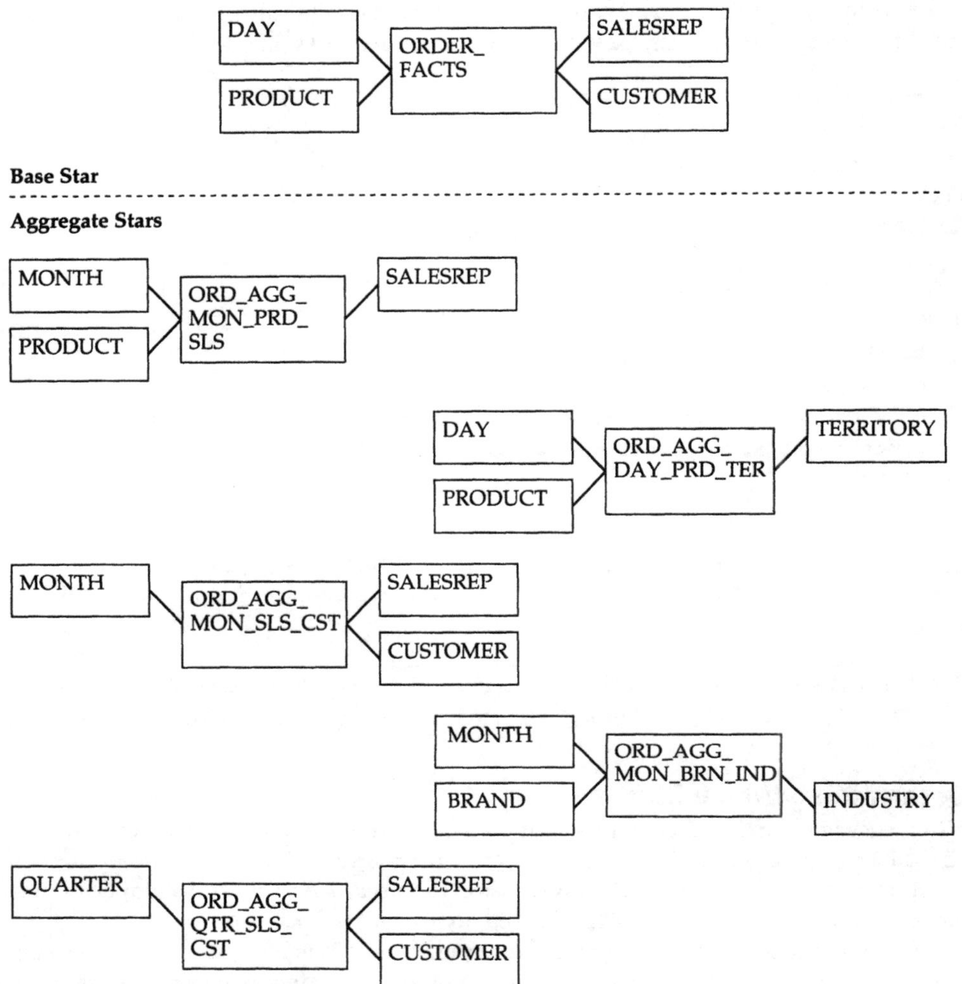

Figure 15-2 A base star and several aggregates

results down by month. The quarter/salesperson/customer aggregate is no longer able to respond; the query must be rewritten to use a different star.

TIP When you are choosing which aggregate star to use for a given query, optimum performance is delivered by the one with the fewest rows in its fact table that is able to answer the question.

One way to avoid end-user frustration is to limit aggregate access to experienced developers. End users and novice developers are provided access to the base star and nothing more. They will not attain any of the performance benefits offered by the aggregates, but they will not face the confusing task of choosing which star to use. As they add and remove dimensions to and from their analysis, they will not need to rewrite queries accordingly. The base star is able to

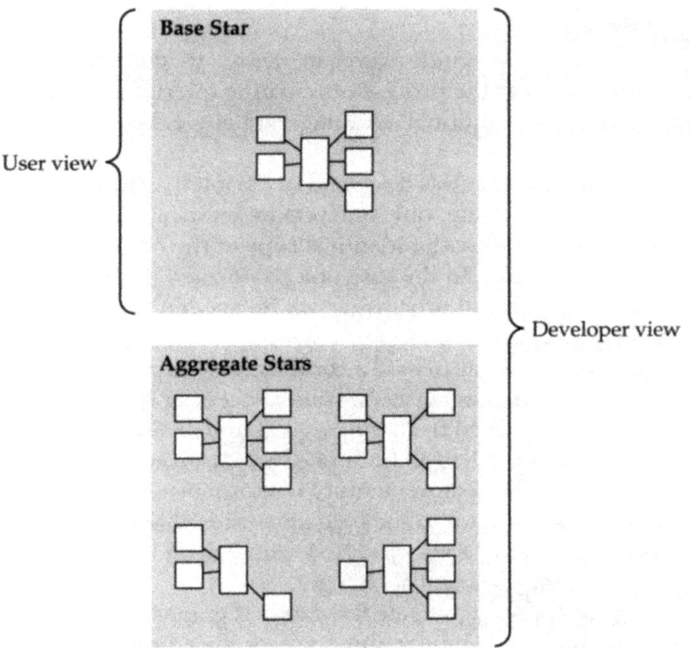

Figure 15-3 Reducing complexity for users

answer all questions, although not with optimum performance. Developers, on the other hand, can be trained to select from among the base star and corresponding aggregates. They are exposed to the entire portfolio of aggregates, as depicted in Figure 15-3.

Even this situation is not optimal. The reports written by end users do not achieve any of the performance advantages offered by the aggregates. Any reports written by developers are "hard-coded" to use a particular aggregate. If a new aggregate is added that would offer better performance for a particular report, it must be rewritten to take advantage of this possibility. Conversely, if an aggregate is removed, then any reports that were written to take advantage of it will be broken. They will not work until they are rewritten to make use of one of the remaining stars.

As you will see later in this chapter, many software products offer features that seek to address these shortcomings. These tools can be configured to redirect queries automatically based on available aggregates. A variety of different approaches to this task have evolved; the function is referred to generically as *aggregate navigation.* In some cases, these tools may also offer assistance in the creation and maintenance of the aggregate tables.

Loading Aggregates

Before an aggregate can be used, it must be built. As with the derived tables of Chapter 14, this is the price we must pay for increased performance. Designed around the principle of performance, it makes sense to source aggregate tables from the original star. The occurrence of a type 1 change can make it quite difficult to maintain aggregates incrementally, leading many developers to adopt a "drop-and-rebuild" approach.

The Source of an Aggregate

By allowing the concept of conformance to guide aggregate design, we guarantee consistent results from the summary, while keeping the process of rewriting queries as simple as possible. This same guideline has one additional advantage: it helps keep the ETL process simple as well.

Construction of conformed dimensions was discussed in Chapter 5. If a dimension table is shared by the base star and aggregate, only one version exists; no additional work is required at ETL time. If the aggregate uses an identical copy of the original dimension, this can be handled via simple replication. In the case of a conformed rollup, such as the month table in Figure 15-1, some additional processing will be needed. The rollup will summarize attributes of the base dimension table, but it has its own surrogate key.

As you learned in Chapter 5, the best way to load a conformed rollup is to use the base dimension table as its source. This eliminates any redundant processing that would be required if the rollup dimension were loaded from the original source. More importantly, it eliminates the possibility that processing rules will be applied inconsistently. This guarantees consistent structure and content, the twin requirements of conformance. The process can be streamlined by adding housekeeping columns to the base dimension that indicate the date the row was created and the date the row was last modified. These dates can be used by the process that loads the conformed rollup to identify changes.

The development of ETL routines for aggregate fact tables is guided by the same principle. Sourcing the aggregate from the base star guarantees the conformance that is required, both in terms of structure and in terms of content.

TIP Source aggregate tables from the base schema to guarantee consistent structure and content.

Following these guidelines, the overall dependency of table load routines during the ETL process might look like this:

1. Load base dimensions
2. Load conformed rollups
3. Load base fact table
4. Load aggregate fact table

Actual dependencies are slightly more relaxed than this. For example, after base dimensions have been loaded, it is possible to load the base fact table. Unfortunately, there is a complication.

Type 1 Changes

One potential roadblock stands in the way of this simple workflow: the type 1 change. When base data and aggregates are loaded sequentially, the occurrence of a type 1 change can force the need to reload the aggregate completely, rather than update it incrementally.

To understand why this happens, consider a very simple example. Suppose an aggregate of order_facts contains rows that summarize orders by product manager, which is a type 1 attribute. This aggregate will call for a simple conformed rollup of the product dimension, which includes only the column product_manager.

The product dimension has hundreds of products. Each is managed by one of three people: Richard Meyers, David Yu, and Robert Jones. The product_manager table has one row for each of these people. Orders for all the products are recorded in order_facts, and the aggregate fact table summarizes orders by product_manager.

Subsequently, one of the products that Richard Meyers managed is reassigned to David Yu. If we try to follow the process flow outlined earlier, this type 1 change gets us into trouble. Step by step, here is what happens:

1. **Load base dimensions**—The type 1 change calls for the product in question to be updated; its new manager is David Yu.
2. **Load conformed rollups**—If there is a date_updated on the base dimension table, it tells us the product has changed. The manager on the changed record is David Yu. A record already exists for David Yu in the product_manager table since he managed other products as well, so nothing needs to happen here.
3. **Load base fact table**—Any new orders are added to the base fact table.
4. **Load aggregate fact table**—The new orders are added to the aggregate fact table, associated with the correct manager.

The problem here is that *we are not finished.* Because of the change in product manager, some previous order summaries that are already in the aggregate fact table must be adjusted. Some orders previously attributed to Richard Meyers are now attributed to David Yu. If we have followed this four-step process, we might not have been aware of this by the time we reached step four, especially if the aggregates were to be sourced from the base tables.

One way to avoid this breakdown is to note that a change occurred during step one. Then, when loading the aggregate, we can fix things. In this case, we might note that product A11 had its manager changed to David Yu. When we get to step four, we can go back and look for orders of product A11 and add their totals to the summary row for David Yu.

We are still not done. We *also* need to deduct these orders from whoever managed the product before David did. This happens to be Richard Meyers, but we cannot tell that from looking at the base dimension table, since it was updated in step one!

The moral of this story is simple: when an aggregate contains type 1 attributes, a type 1 change forces processing that requires access to the before and after values, and access to the granular data.

This is enough additional work that many ETL developers opt for a simpler brute-force approach: after updating the base schema, drop and re-create the aggregate. Often, this proves to be less processing-intensive than the alternative. Some tools that automate the creation of aggregate tables or cubes operate in this manner; if the aggregate contains a type 1 attribute, the cube is destroyed and rebuilt each time a change occurs.

TIP Type 1 changes can significantly complicate aggregate processing. If an aggregate star includes a type 1 attribute, it may be best to drop and rebuild the aggregate fact table.

Another way to avoid this situation is to exclude type 1 attributes from aggregate designs. Type 2 changes don't pose the same problem, since they don't restate the context of previously recorded facts.

Developers can sometimes minimize the impact of a type 1 change if the rollup dimension also includes a type 2 attribute that the type 1 attribute describes. In this case, the type 1 change may be applied only to the appropriate row, and aggregate facts will not require an update. Designers sometimes borrow language from entity-relationship modelers to describe this case: the type 1 attribute in the aggregate dimension is "fully dependent" on the type 2 attribute. This approach, however, provides new challenges for the ETL process. See "Type 1 Complications" in Chapter 3 for more details.

Cubes as Aggregates

While this book uses relational designs to illustrate most concepts, Chapter 3 pointed out that this is simply a convenience. Most of the principles of dimensional modeling apply equally well, whether implemented in a star schema or a cube. The benefit of summarization, however, differs when it comes to cubes.

Cubes Summarizing Cubes

The multidimensional cube is intended as a high-performance data structure. Generally, cubes achieve near-instantaneous performance by precomputing the value of facts across the various members of each dimension. This permits the interactive analysis style for which OLAP is famous. This also means there may be little performance benefit in creating one cube that summarizes another.

TIP When a cube is used as primary storage for a dimensional design, the data set is already optimized for high performance. A summary cube is not necessary.

Of course, there is an exception to every rule. Vendor innovations that are intended to improve the scalability of the cube are also bringing back the value of summarizing it. As noted in Chapter 3, the cube has traditionally been less scalable than a star schema. Because of the need to precompute facts across each member, cubes grow exponentially larger as more and more dimensions are added. To cope with this drawback, some products now allow an administrator to control the degree of pre-summarization within a cube. This allows the cube to contain more data but also reduces its performance.

In this case, additional cubes may be useful as high-performance summaries of the base cube. The two stars in Figure 15-1 might easily be replaced with cubes. The base cube, which contains orders by order line, may be configured to maximize storage efficiency of the facts. The aggregate cube, which contains orders by month, product, and salerep, can be configured to maximize performance.

Cubes Summarizing Stars

Many architectures incorporate *both* the star schema *and* the cube. As noted in Chapter 3, the star scales well, while the cube performs well. The best of both worlds is achieved by relying on the star to store granular, detailed data, with cubes containing high-performance extracts.

In this scenario, one or more cubes summarize data stored in a base star. Queries and reports are designed to make use of the cubes, to afford optimum performance. In Figure 15-3, for example, cubes might replace one or all of the aggregate stars.

This arrangement is the foundation for many highly successful data warehouse implementations. Since they are both dimensional, cubes and stars have a natural affinity. Many multidimensional products have been specifically built to support the design and creation of cubes based on an underlying star. This will be further explored later in this chapter.

Making Aggregates Invisible

An aggregate schema is similar to a database index. Like an index, it takes up some extra space, and it makes queries go faster. Once it is defined, however, an index becomes invisible. Someone writing a query does not need to specify that it should be used, and no one needs to update the index as data changes. These things happen automatically.

Aggregates do not necessarily share this invisibility. As you have seen, aggregates require attention on two fronts:

- It is necessary to write (or rewrite) queries to take advantage of the aggregate.
- It is necessary to load and maintain the aggregate, keeping it in sync with the original schema.

Ideally, you shouldn't have to worry about these things. A truly invisible aggregate would automatically be exploited whenever appropriate and automatically updated as the original schema changes.

Many software products strive to make this a reality. Some tools can rewrite queries automatically; some can generate and maintain aggregates; some can do parts of both. Software features that help achieve this invisibility may be found in reporting tools, ETL tools, and database management systems.

Implementations vary widely, and none are perfect. Some basic principles will help you understand how to evaluate and leverage the capabilities of available tools. The two aspects of invisibility are aggregate navigation and aggregate generation. For some tools, these are separate concepts; for others, they are closely linked together.

Aggregate Navigation

An aggregate navigation capability eliminates the need for someone who is writing a query to choose between the base star and one or more aggregates. Tools provide this capability in different ways, and in different parts of the architecture. Aggregate navigators can open a host of additional benefits as well.

The Aggregate Navigator

As you learned earlier in this chapter, the presence of aggregates requires that a decision be made each time a query is written: which star to use. This can be confusing for end users. Some data warehouse teams choose not to make aggregates accessible to end users, as depicted in Figure 15-3. However, this means that users who create their own reports will not obtain any performance advantage from the aggregates.

Aggregate navigation is a generic term that describes the process of choosing from among the base star and one or more aggregates. Software products or features that perform this service are often called *aggregate navigators,* although product-specific terminology is sometimes used as well.

An aggregate navigation function may be embedded in one of several components of the architecture, including the reporting tool, the database, or some intermediary element. Implementations vary, but the basic principle is the same: aggregate navigators automatically redirect queries to aggregates when appropriate. Someone writing a query does not need to know that aggregates exist, and does not need to check whether an aggregate is suitable for their query.

The concept of aggregate navigation is illustrated in Figure 15-4. Two logical views of the data warehouse schema are depicted. One, known to end users and applications, consists only of the base order_facts star. The other, known only to the aggregate navigator, includes additional information about the aggregates.

In the diagram, a query is written to retrieve order_dollars by product for January 2009. Unaware of the presence of aggregates, the user has written an SQL statement to fetch data from the order_facts star. This SQL is labeled "base SQL." The aggregate navigator, fully aware of the available aggregates, rewrites this query to take advantage of an aggregate table. The resulting "aggregate-aware" SQL is used to fetch the data, which is returned to the user.

TIP An aggregate navigation function makes aggregates invisible to front-end applications. Queries and reports can be developed without any awareness of underlying aggregates, yet still receive a performance benefit.

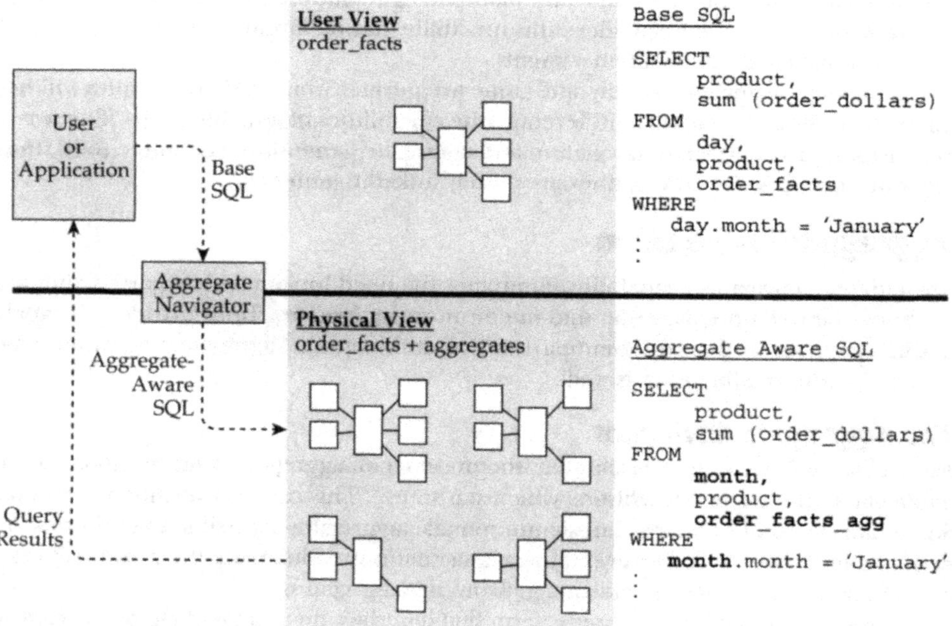

Figure 15-4 Aggregate navigator

In order to rewrite a query to take advantage of an aggregate, some information is necessary. First, there must be information about which aggregates correspond to the base star and what level of detail they contain. This allows the aggregate navigator to identify which aggregates, if any, can respond to the query. Second, there must be information about how many rows each fact table contains. This information will be used to choose the smallest possible star that can respond to the question. Using this information, the query can be rewritten. Notice that the practice of conforming the aggregate to the base star makes this process as simple as possible.

Keep in mind that the diagram in Figure 15-4 is conceptual. The actual creation of aggregate-aware SQL may be handled in a variety of ways and in a variety of places. It may be done by the reporting tool, by the database, or by some intermediate product that intercepts and rewrites SQL. When handled by a DBMS, the aggregate navigation function is sometimes referred to as *query rewrite*. However, this term does not fit in other situations. Some business intelligence products generate aggregate-aware SQL directly, rather than creating base-level SQL and then rewriting it.

Other Potential Benefits

The most obvious benefit of the aggregate navigator is that it simplifies the user or developer's view of the database, eliminating the need to choose between a base star and one or more aggregates. Other benefits are possible as well, though not every tool delivers them.

Changing Aggregates at Will Without an aggregate navigator, queries must be explicitly written to take advantage of an aggregate. When a new aggregate is added to the database, existing queries and reports must be rewritten to take advantage of it. When an aggregate is removed, any report that used it will be broken. It will fail to return any results until it is rewritten to use tables present in the database.

An aggregate navigator opens up the possibility to add and remove aggregates over time, without the need to revisit existing reports. As aggregates are added to or removed from the database, the aggregate navigator is made aware of the changes. This may be automatic, or it may require a developer to declare the changes to the tool. When queries are executed, the aggregate navigator uses this up-to-date information to determine whether and how they should be redirected.

To attain this benefit, it is necessary for aggregate navigation to occur when a query is *executed*, not when it is *written*. Some products rewrite SQL to leverage aggregates as part of the report design or generation process. Although the person creating the report need not be aware of or understand aggregates, these reports are hard-coded to use specific tables once they are saved. If a new aggregate is added, they will need to be regenerated or recompiled to take advantage of it. If an aggregate is removed, any report that used it will become broken.

Placing Aggregates Online and Offline Runtime aggregate navigators can provide another similar advantage. They may offer the capability to take aggregates offline as needed. This is useful when it is necessary to rebuild or refresh an aggregate. While a particular aggregate is offline, the aggregate navigator stops directing queries to it. Performance will be slower since the aggregate is not used, but nothing will stop working. Once the aggregate is back online, the aggregate navigator will resume redirecting queries to it.

Once again, this capability requires runtime aggregate navigation. Information about which aggregates are available is not known when a report is being written or compiled. This information is only useful if queries are written when they are executed. It is also necessary for the tool to provide a mechanism to identify when tables are being taken on- or offline, which may introduce a maintenance requirement for the database administrator.

Heterogeneous Databases An aggregate navigator may do more than simply rewrite SQL. It may also direct it to a different physical database, a database from a different vendor, or even translate SQL into another language. These possibilities greatly expand the potential flexibility of a solution, allowing specialized tools to respond to queries, regardless of location, time, or access technology.

Some of these capabilities, like the ability to redirect to a different physical database, have been possible for over a decade. Others, such as the ability to redirect an SQL query to a multidimensional cube, have started to emerge relatively recently. Separation of the data storage technology from the data access language is an exciting development, which should lead to a new dynamic breed of data warehouse that can be configured in real time to respond to users regardless of their request, location, or access language.

Heterogeneous Front Ends Last, it is also possible for an aggregate navigation function to provide benefit to a variety of different front-end tools. An ideal aggregate navigator rewrites any query, whether submitted by a business intelligence tool, a reporting tool, or a command-line SQL utility.

Aggregate navigators built into front-end tools typically cannot provide their services to other front-end tools, and may miss out on this possibility. This does not mean you should not make use of such a capability, but it does limit its benefit. Inefficiencies may also be observed if there is more than one front-end tool and each requires configuration of its own aggregate navigator. This is as much a consequence of having multiple front-end tools as it is of their design.

Aggregate Generation

The other half of the invisibility equation deals with the automatic generation and maintenance of aggregates. For some tools, aggregate navigation and generation capabilities are closely bound together, while others separate them or only offer one or the other.

Generating and Maintaining Aggregates

Tools that generate aggregate stars or cubes provide a user interface that allows a developer to specify the characteristics of the desired aggregates. Such tools range from a command-line utility to a graphical user interface, and allow the developer to identify the level of summarization for each aggregate. Based on information provided by the designer, the tool then generates an aggregate table or a cube.

Relational database products provide this kind of capability in a number of ways. Many such tools support the definition of materialized views or materialized query tables, which can be used in the service of aggregation. Some databases and OLAP products work in a similar way but generate multidimensional cubes.

Tools that generate aggregates or cubes are built around a native understanding of the star schema and dimensional data. These products understand such concepts as facts, dimensions, surrogate keys, natural keys, and slow changes. When sufficient information about a dimensional schema is provided, they can walk the developer through a set of questions and create a cube or aggregate that is automatically maintained by the DBMS.

Allowing the DBMS to maintain an aggregate structure sometimes requires surrendering complete control over how the aggregate is maintained or kept up to date. Some warehouse teams decide to forgo this automation in favor of finer or more efficient control, instead opting to build and maintain aggregates as part of the overall ETL process.

Hierarchies and Aggregates

As described in Chapter 7, an attribute hierarchy represents a known set of master–detail relationships among attributes in a dimension table. Just as parent–child hierarchies among attributes are not *required* to drill into data, they are also not required to define a level of summarization. However, many tools that generate aggregate tables or cubes are designed to work with hierarchies. In these cases, there may be value in defining and documenting aggregates around these relationships.

Suppose, for example, that natural hierarchies exist among the attributes in the dimension tables of the order_facts star in Figure 15-1. Each product falls within a brand, and each brand falls within a category. Similar hierarchies exist for the attributes of day, salesrep, and customer. The resulting hierarchies are depicted in Figure 15-5. Notice that the diagram also incorporates the degenerate dimension order_line, which contributes to the grain of order_facts.

When dimensional hierarchies are expressed in this explicit manner, an aggregate can be defined simply by drawing a circle around the portions of the hierarchies that will be included. As drawn in Figure 15-5, the outlined region represents the grain of the order_facts_aggregate table from Figure 15-1: orders by month, product, and salesrep.

Tools that can generate cubes based on the existence of attribute hierarchies often require some additional information. They require the developer to identify which attributes appear at each level of the hierarchy and optionally require identification of a subset of attributes that will guarantee an instance of the level. For example, brand_code, brand_name, and brand_manager are present at the brand level. A code and name are sufficient to identify a brand; brand_manager is a type 1 attribute that will be overwritten.

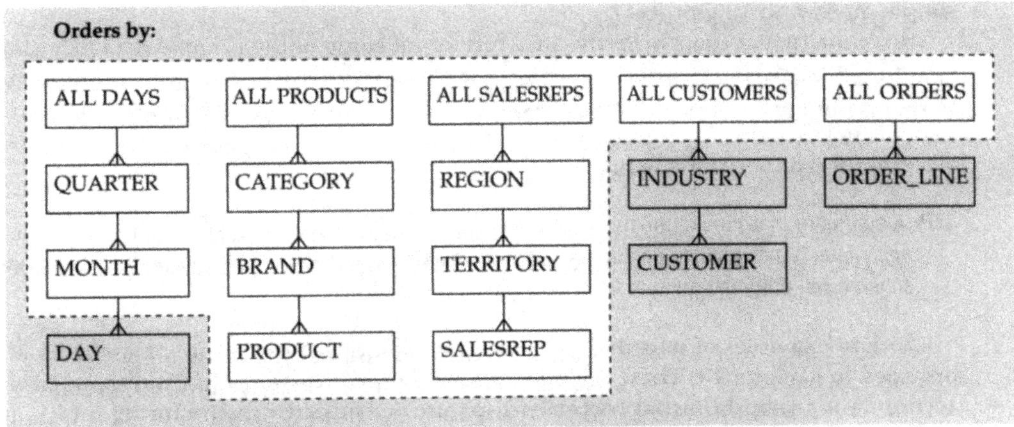

Figure 15-5 Designing aggregates around attribute hierarchies

Armed with this metadata, the tool is able to determine what can be included in a brand-level attribute and maintain the aggregate structure accordingly.

TIP Summarizing dimensional data does not require an attribute hierarchy, but some tools rely on this kind of relationship to define and generate aggregates.

The existence of hierarchies like these may help define an aggregate, but they are not necessary. Brands, for example, might not fall neatly into categories the way Figure 15-5 depicts. This would not prevent either brand or category from being used to define an aggregate of order_facts. Indeed, even a "product-level" attribute, such as the product's color, might be used to define a summary table. Don't let tools that focus on attribute hierarchies cause you to lose sight of possibilities like this. It may still be possible to generate the aggregate, even if it requires working around a hierarchy-based view of dimensions.

Alternative Summary Designs

A dimensional aggregate schema that conforms to the base schema is but one way to organize the storage of summary data. Derived tables, as described in the previous chapter, may provide a useful alternative. A single-table design, on the other hand, is likely to lead to trouble.

Transformative Summaries May Also Be Useful

As defined in this chapter, an aggregate schema is a very specific form of summarization: one that conforms to the original, base schema. Data can be summarized in other ways that do not preserve the organizational structure of the base data. These too are valid summaries. Since they transform the structure of the base data they summarize, they are examples of derived schemas, as discussed in Chapter 14.

As you have learned, the tables in an aggregate schema conform to those in the base schema it summarizes. The aggregate facts have the same name, meaning, and content as those in the base fact table; dimension tables are the same as those in the base star, or are conformed rollups whose attributes share the name, meaning, and content of those in the base star. This conformance ensures semantic consistency across stars and facilitates a simple query-rewriting process.

A summary that transforms the structure or meaning of the original data may also be of value. Its content, by definition, does not conform to the original schema. It may contain a fact that is not present in the original star, exclude certain data, or require a different query structure. Summaries that transform the original dimensional structure in any of these ways are examples of derived schemas.

TIP A summary that transforms the structure of the base star is a derived schema rather than an aggregate. It may provide useful performance benefits. A query that takes advantage of a derived schema will differ in structure from one against the base schema.

Several examples of stars that transform the dimensional structure of a schema were provided in Chapter 14. These included snapshots that were derived from transactions, and accumulating snapshots that correlate disparate activities. By restructuring information in advance, these stars made certain forms of reporting much easier. Although they may summarize the original table, they require that queries be written differently. For this reason, they are not classified as aggregates.

Additional examples of derived stars in Chapter 14 merged data from multiple fact tables, transposed row-wise and column-wise fact storage, took slices of fact tables, or precomputed comparisons using set operations or subqueries. Each in some way transforms the structure of the base schema, requires queries to be written differently, and alters the nature of the query results. While some of these derived tables summarize the original data sets, they are not considered to be aggregate schemas in the sense defined in this chapter. They may, however, be valuable additions to the dimensional model.

Earlier in this chapter, an example was provided that could not be aided by a dimensional aggregate. Filtering a query so it only includes order lines with a dollar amount that is greater than $500 requires access to the granular detail, even if results are highly summarized. An aggregate will not include the necessary detail to perform this filtering. However, it is still possible to compute this information and store the result in a derived schema. In the derived schema, a fact similar to the original order_dollars will be recorded. Because it represents the dollar amount only for high-value orders, the summary fact will return different results. It does not conform to the original fact and should be given a new and unique name, such as high_value_order_dollars.

Single Table Designs Should Be Avoided

One alternative manner of storing summary information is less likely to prove an asset to the dimensional model. When a single fact table is called on to store both detailed and summarized data, the result may appear compact and neat, but a potential problem arises. It becomes possible, and in fact likely, that the aggregate will be misused, producing inaccurate results.

A single fact table design seeks to simplify the storage of aggregates by storing summarized data together with the detail, rather than in separate tables. For example, an orders star might be called upon to house both daily order information and monthly summaries. In order to make this work, it will be necessary to construct a time dimension table that can represent either a month or a day. Figure 15-6 provides an example.

Each row in the day table represents *either* a day *or* a month. A column called "level" is used to indicate what each row represents. It takes on the values "Month" or "Day." Not all the attributes of the table apply to months; those that do not default to a preselected value such as "N/A" for textual data. The shaded row shows what this looks like for the row that represents January 2009. Some designers prefer to use NULL values for nonapplicable columns, although these can lead to problems at query time, as you learned in Chapter 6.

This multipurpose dimension table makes it possible to store monthly summaries in the same fact table that records daily data. The fact table includes a day_key. For rows that contain daily data, this key will refer to a dimension row that represents a day. For rows that contain monthly data, it will refer to a dimension row that represents a month. In this scenario, a query can make use of the monthly aggregates by adding a constraint like this one:

```
WHERE day.level = "Month"
```

A query that focuses on the daily detail includes a constraint like this one:

```
WHERE day.level = "Day"
```

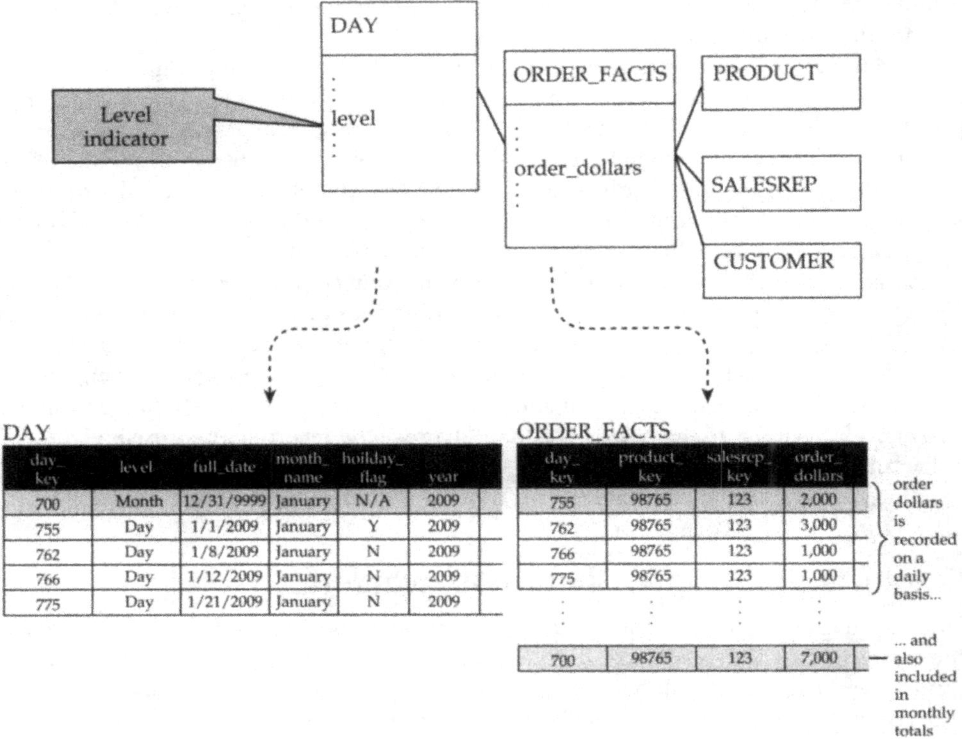

DAY

day_key	level	full_date	month_name	hoilday_flag	year
700	Month	12/31/9999	January	N/A	2009
755	Day	1/1/2009	January	Y	2009
762	Day	1/8/2009	January	N	2009
766	Day	1/12/2009	January	N	2009
775	Day	1/21/2009	January	N	2009

ORDER_FACTS

day_key	product_key	salesrep_key	order_dollars
755	98765	123	2,000
762	98765	123	3,000
766	98765	123	1,000
775	98765	123	1,000
⋮	⋮	⋮	⋮
700	98765	123	7,000

Figure 15-6 Single table design with level indicators

The drawback to this approach lies in the fact that the fact table records every transaction twice: once as the daily detail and once as part of the monthly summary. For example, the fact table in the illustration records order dollars for a particular product and salesrep for four different days in January of 2009. It also records these transactions in a summary row. If a user fails to constrain on the level column, these transactions may be double-counted. For example:

```
SELECT
   SUM(order_dollars)
FROM
   day,
   order_facts
WHERE
   day.year = 2009 AND
   day.month = "January" AND
   order_facts.day_key = day.day_key
```

This query will pick up all January 2009 orders twice: once for the daily totals and once from the monthly summary.

TIP Do not store different levels of aggregation in the same table. This can easily lead to double-counting or worse.

Avoiding this problem requires constraining the level column in *every* query. If it is necessary to store an aggregate that summarizes more than one dimension, the level column will be required in other dimensions as well. A month/brand/salesrep aggregate, for example, would require a level column in the day dimension to identify months, one in the product dimension to identify brand, and one in the customer dimension to distinguish between a specific customer and all customers. Each of these level columns must be constrained to avoid double-counting, even if the dimension in question is not part of the query.

Summary

Aggregates are the primary tool for boosting the performance of a dimensional model. As you have learned in this chapter, following some simple principles helps ensure they provide accurate results.

- Aggregates must provide the same query results as the original schema. Using the principle of conformance in their design helps guarantee this.
- Queries must be written to take advantage of an aggregate. The principle of conformance makes this as simple as possible.
- Aggregates may be hidden from end users so they do not have to choose which schema to use. Without an aggregate navigation function, however, they will not receive a performance benefit.
- Aggregates must be kept in sync with the base schema. While it is useful to process only changed data, a type 1 change in an aggregate dimension can make this very difficult.
- Cubes make excellent aggregates. They summarize data in a base schema in exactly the same way as an aggregate star.

Aggregates can be implemented without adding any special tools to the data warehouse architecture. However, many software products have features that make them easier to create and use:

- An aggregate navigation function automatically formulates SQL to access aggregates. Tools offer this capability in a variety of ways. The best make it possible to leverage a new aggregate without having to rewrite a query or recompile a report. Some also offer the capability to take aggregates online and offline, in real time.
- Aggregates may be constructed using features of database products or specialized tools. To achieve the maximum benefit, these tools usually need to know a lot about the base schema. In return, they are able to generate performance structures automatically, and may also provide aggregate navigation services.

Other ways to summarize data that do not meet this chapter's definition of an aggregate include the following:

- Derived tables, as described in the previous chapter, may provide a useful alternative.
- A single-table design, on the other hand, is likely to lead to trouble.

Further Reading

The basic principles of aggregates are simple and intuitive. As a result, most discussions of dimensional design devote very little time, if any, to the discussion of aggregates.

- Although relatively simple in concept, incorporating aggregates into your architecture has many implications. Several nuances have only been touched on here. For a complete treatment of aggregation, see *Mastering Data Warehouse Aggregates* (Wiley, 2006) by Chris Adamson.
- Kimball and Ross provide a brief description of the principles of aggregation in the context of a clickstream data warehouse in Chapter 14 of *The Data Warehouse Toolkit, Second Edition* (Wiley, 2002).
- Aggregation strategy is briefly discussed in Chapter 16 of *The Data Warehouse Toolkit.*
- Some architectures use aggregated data as the basis for a data mart application. In a dimensional data warehouse, aggregates are more akin to an index, summarizing granular data solely for performance reasons. The authors make this important distinction in Chapter 4 of *The Data Warehouse Lifecycle Toolkit, Second Edition* (Wiley, 2008), by Ralph Kimball, Margy Ross, Warren Thornthwaite, Joy Mundy, and Bob Becker.
- The effect of a type 1 change on an aggregate can be very frustrating, but it is not a shortcoming of the dimensional approach. As Kimball et al. describe in Chapter 8 of *The Data Warehouse Lifecycle Toolkit,* this problem is encountered when using stars, snowflakes, cubes, and even normalized designs.
- Storing summary and detail data in the same star by leveraging a "level" column is discussed in further detail in Chapter 13 of the first edition *of The Data Warehouse Toolkit* by Ralph Kimball (Wiley, 1996). Although out of print, this edition may be available in libraries or used bookstores. The topic is also discussed in Chapter 3 of *Mastering Data Warehouse Aggregates.*
- The additional tables in a snowflake design can provide some reduction in complexity when it comes to aggregates. If the dimension already contains outriggers, then it may not be necessary to construct conformed rollups. An example of an aggregate in a snowflake design is discussed in Chapter 8 of *Mastering Data Warehouse Aggregates.*

PART VI

Tools and Documentation

CHAPTER

16 Design and Business Intelligence

A good dimensional design maximizes the potential value of your data warehouse. If it is not easy to access the information, however, even the best dimensional schema becomes a black hole. Luckily, there are a wide variety of software products available that can help make sure this does not happen.

Tools that are used to provide information to end users range in functionality from simple report writers to sophisticated business intelligence software products. They can provide information in a numerous formats (charts, tables, dashboard widgets), over a variety of channels (computers, mobile devices, telephones), and according to varied access paradigms (on demand, scheduled, exception alerts). For the sake of simplicity, these tools will be referred to collectively as *business intelligence tools*. The individual information products they provide to end users will be referred to as *reports*.

As the face of the data warehouse, these tools determine how information can, *and cannot*, be made available to the people who can use it. Tool features are product-specific, and beyond the scope of this book. However, most of these tools share one thing in common: *they do not require the person developing a report to write a query*. When configured appropriately, business intelligence tools generate SQL queries for the report developer. The SQL generation capabilities of these products can be a limiting factor for how dimensional data is accessed.

Another class of business intelligence tools supports OLAP applications. These tools work with multidimensional cubes rather than relational stars. Like their SQL-based cousins, most of these tools also do not require hand-coding of queries. The capabilities of an OLAP solution stem directly from the depth and breadth of cubes that are made available in the analytic environment.

This chapter explores the impact of business intelligence tools on your dimensional designs. You cannot control the query generation capabilities of business intelligence tools in your architecture, but understanding their workings gives you important insight into what kinds of reports can and cannot be produced. Some shortcomings can be addressed with standard dimensional techniques, such as derived tables. Other limitations may be addressed by controlling who has the ability to build certain kinds of queries, and planning for report development resources accordingly.

Business Intelligence and SQL Generation

While report developers are usually capable of writing SQL queries, most reporting tools for relational data do not require them to do so. These tools allow a user to specify what information is desired, and then generate SQL accordingly. They can be tremendously valuable parts of the data warehouse architecture, opening the report creation process to technical and nontechnical users alike, while ensuring proper and consistent use of the dimensional model. Leveraging SQL generation capability requires some degree of advance configuration. It is important to recognize that no SQL generator will be able to produce the same range of queries as a skilled developer.

SQL Generators

Many commercial products allow developers to design reports, charts, or dashboard widgets that present information from a relational database. Most of these tools are capable of generating queries for the developer. They vary in sophistication from a simple schema-based framework to a more sophisticated semantic layer. What these tools share in common is an ability to take predefined information about the database schema and use it to auto-generate SQL.

Schema-Driven SQL Generators

The most basic example of a query-generating tool works by allowing a developer to graphically specify the tables in a query, and the joins that relate them. This framework can then be used as the basis of a report. Columns are dragged from the graphical depiction of the schema onto a layout canvas. As the developer does this, the tool automatically constructs the appropriate SQL.

Figure 16-1 depicts an example of how this works. This illustration captures common components of a simple reporting tool's interface:

1. The report developer uses the top portion of the window to identify the tables and joins that will be used.
2. The developer can drag specific column names from this framework onto a canvas that is used to lay out a report.
3. Based on what the developer has added to the canvas, and the information about the tables and joins, the tool generates an SQL query.

This is the essence of how a reporting tool generates SQL. Specific tools, of course, have their own interface formats and processes, but the underlying concept remains the same.

Query Generators and Semantic Layers

Some business intelligence tools take this process a step further, adding a business view of information on top of the technical view. The business view is a representation of "things available to report on." It is the *only* view made available to users or report developers for

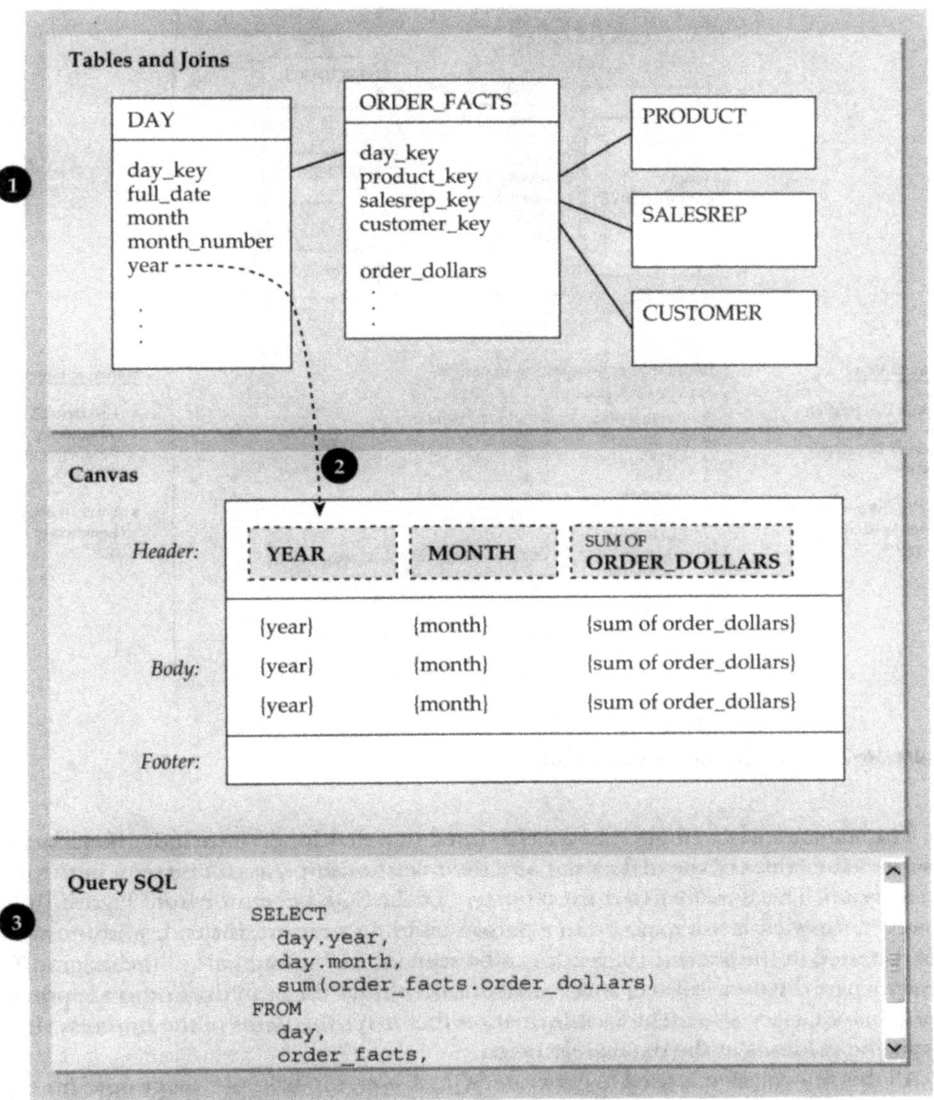

Figure 16-1 A reporting tool generates SQL

dragging elements onto a canvas. Behind the scenes, an architect has tied the business view of information to the database schema, and identified the tables and joins.

The concept of a business view that is mapped to physical structures is called a *semantic layer*. It allows a user or developer to build a report without any knowledge of the underlying database. Pioneered and patented by Business Objects (now a part of SAP AG), this concept is now employed by numerous commercial products. Figure 16-2 depicts an example of a semantic layer. This is not a picture of a particular product or tool, but rather a generalization of the essential elements involved.

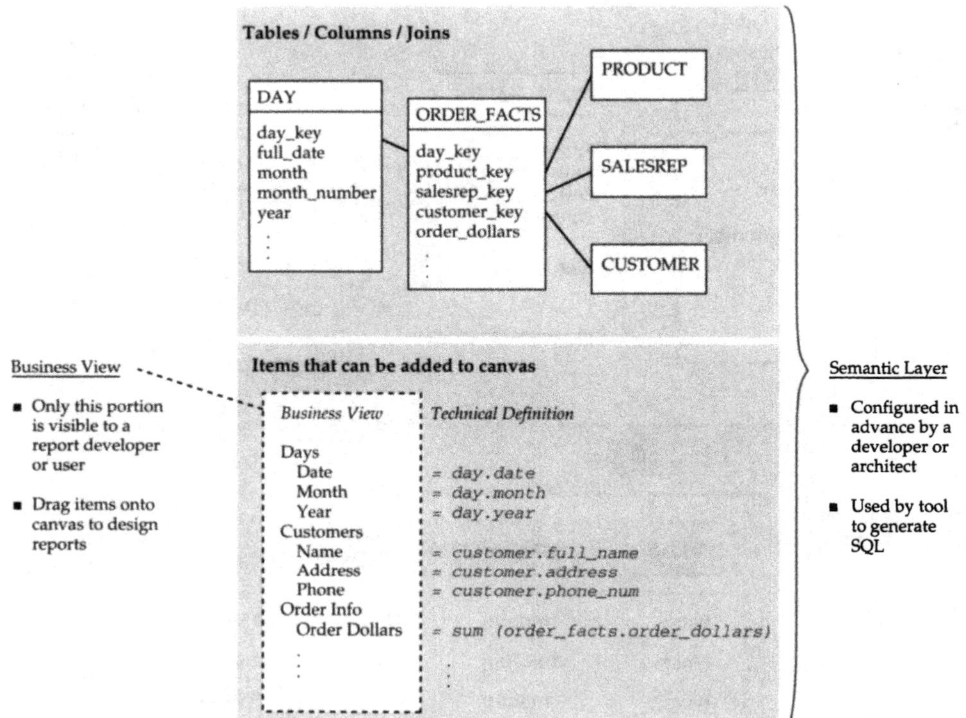

Figure 16-2 A reporting tool generates SQL

The semantic layer in Figure 16-2 is defined by a developer. It includes metadata that describes the tables of the orders star and their relationships, as can be seen in the top of the diagram. This is similar to the top portion of the SQL generator from Figure 16-1. However, this view is not exposed to a person building a report. Instead, a business view is incorporated in the semantic layer. It can be seen in the bottom part of the diagram. This is the only part the user will see, and it contains the things they can drag onto a report canvas. The semantic layer also includes information that maps the items in the business view back to specific columns in the database schema.

All this information is used to generate SQL. A user, for example, drags onto his or her canvas something called "Name" and something called "Order Dollars." The query generator uses the information in the semantic layer to determine how to fetch this information. It identifies these elements as corresponding to the column called full_name in the customer table, and the sum of the column called order_dollars in the order_facts table. The table relationships are consulted to determine how these tables are joined together, and then an SQL statement can be constructed. Of course, the specific mechanics vary widely by product implementation.

Business intelligence products can be used to produce sophisticated semantic layers. Most allow an element in the business view that maps back to a combination of columns; have associated help text or data definitions; are capable of generating complex SQL, including subqueries; are capable of expressing complex query predicates; and can enforce security access rules.

All these functions mean that business intelligence tools can be extremely powerful components of the data warehouse architecture. At a minimum, they simplify work for report developers and may enable end users to build their own "self-serve" reports. Business intelligence tools also add value in additional ways, incorporating an infrastructure for the development, automation, and sharing of reports, charts, widgets, messages, and alerts and for collaboration among users.

Configuring SQL Generators

Any tool that generates queries must be configured to do so. This configuration activity is typically carried out by a developer. A basic tool may require the developer to specify tables and joins as part of the report definition, as in Figure 16-1. Tools that incorporate a business view of information, as in Figure 16-2, require that this information be configured as a separate task, prior to the creation of any reports.

Regardless of the level of sophistication, all these tools require that someone, somewhere, has provided some information about the database schema, and perhaps set up configuration options that control how SQL is generated. For simplicity's sake, this chapter will refer to all this information as the *semantic layer,* even though the software industry tends to reserve that term for solutions that include a separate business view of information. This configuration information is often described as "metadata" because it describes, at least in part, the physical storage structures.

The Limitations of SQL Generators

Query generators are not intelligent. They do not understand the information contained in the database, or what a user wants to see. When called on to generate SQL, they apply a set of heuristics to the user request and available schema information to generate a query. Hopefully, this results in an SQL query that is exactly what the user wants.

Generated SQL always follows some standard formats, or templates. The range of possibilities is a function of the product in question. Breadth and accuracy of generated SQL are also influenced by the *configuration* of the semantic layer. Users will only be able to combine elements from the database into a query or report in ways that are enabled by the semantic layer, as set up by a developer.

Taken together, these factors—the query generation capabilities of a business intelligence product and its configuration—determine what kind of queries can be formulated. For users who rely on the tool to create reports, this effectively limits the ways in which the dimensional model can be utilized. Understanding these limitations is crucial in completing any dimensional design. The limitations of SQL generators fall into two major categories: the inability to generate a desired query and the ability to generate an undesired query.

Inability to Generate Desirable Queries

No tool is capable of generating an appropriate query for every situation. Standard features of dimensional models sometimes pose particular difficulties for query generators. Some tools are unable to automate the drill-across process, comparing orders to shipments, for example. If other tools are available, it may be possible to overlook this shortcoming.

However, comparing facts from multiple stars is the basis for many important and powerful reports.

This kind of limitation may be overcome by enhancing the schema design. A derived star, or cube, may be added that performs the activity the query generator cannot. The inability to drill across, for example, can be addressed by adding a merged fact table, as discussed later in this chapter. The burden is essentially shifted from the business intelligence tool to the ETL process.

Developers are frequently cautioned not to modify a database design based on the capabilities of a particular tool. The capabilities of the front-end tools, however, are usually beyond the control of the schema designers. Failure to adapt may result in the loss of important functionality. Dogmatic adherence to theoretical principles can severely reduce the value of the data warehouse. In the case of a derived table, however, this is a moot point.

The addition of a derived schema in no way compromises a dimensional design. It is completely within the realm of best practices, as discussed in Chapter 14. A properly designed derived schema is consistent with and conforms to the original dimensional data structures. It may be added to the model for a variety of reasons, including the capability of tools to generate queries, the performance of the original schema, and the ease of use. Some of these factors may come into play even if the front-end tool is capable of formulating desired queries.

Ability to Generate Undesirable Queries

SQL generators can also pose a second kind of problem: often, they *are* able to generate queries that are *not* desired because the result is inaccurate. For example, most business intelligence tools will happily generate a query that aggregates a semi-additive fact, such as a bank account balance, across an inappropriate dimension, such as days. This may not be a concern if well-trained developers are using the tool but can have devastating effects if the tool is made available to novices.

In cases like these, derived schemas may again come to the rescue. By making use of standard dimensional design techniques, it is often possible to provide a derived schema that avoids some of the potential dangers inherent in dimensional designs. In the case of the semi-additive account balance, for example, a sliced fact table can be created that provides access only to the current period's balance. Novice users can be limited to this view of data. While less flexible, it keeps them out of trouble. Power users and developers can be provided access to the original fact table, and trusted not to sum the account balance across days.

Note that this particular solution may be achieved without actually building the derived star. It can be implemented by creating database views, or even through the use of features of the business intelligence tool itself. Regardless of its physical implementation, however, it establishes a derived star at the logical level.

Solutions like this often require that the data warehouse team recalibrate their expectations of the business intelligence tool. It may be necessary to create *multiple* semantic layers—one for the novices, who can view current account status, and one for the experts, who can view daily account status. This runs counter to the expectation that a single semantic layer should be created, providing a "single view" of the truth. Establishment of multiple views of data, however, is consistent with this principle, as long as they are fully compatible with one another. Conformed facts and dimensions guarantee a single view of the truth, even if they are available in more than one place.

Making Use of SQL Generators

If you are going to rely on a product that generates SQL for any of your data warehouse reporting, understanding how the tool influences the range of possible queries will help you to ensure that the full analytic possibilities of the schema are realized, while minimizing the possibility of inaccurate results. There are several standard features of dimensional designs that may fall into either of these categories. Before exploring them in detail, however, it is useful to learn some basic "do's and don'ts" surrounding the use of your business intelligence tool.

Guidelines for the Semantic Layer

Business intelligence tools offer a tremendous variety of capabilities, all aimed at achieving a rich and valuable range of analytic options. Some of the things you can do with these tools, however, may be better done as part of the ETL process. These features may be useful in making up for shortcomings of existing designs, but when it comes to new dimensional designs, they are best avoided. There are also capabilities that should always be exploited when the opportunity affords it.

Features to Avoid

Business intelligence tools allow you to hide the technicalities of the database design from people building reports. As you have seen, configuring a semantic layer replaces a technical with a business view. Some of the features offered may be useful and powerful, but it does not always make sense to use them.

Dimensional designs should be rich and understandable. Heavy reliance on the semantic layer to achieve these goals indicates shortcomings in the underlying design. Many BI features that transform a technical view to a business view are best saved for legacy stars. For new designs, your objective should be to require a minimal semantic layer.

Renaming Attributes

Business intelligence tools allow the items in the business view to bear different names from those of the underlying database columns. A cryptic column name like cust_addr_line_1 may be translated into something that is more easily understood, such as "Address." This allows a more understandable view than what is provided by the physical schema.

In the case of a dimensional design, however, most attributes should *already* be understandable. As you learned in Chapter 1, a dimensional model is a representation of the way in which a business views and evaluates a business process. With the exception of surrogate keys and other housekeeping columns, every attribute is either a fact or dimension carrying business significance. In a good design, the names and contents of every attribute will be familiar and understood by business users.

A schema designer should not operate on the assumption that cryptic naming schemes can be "cleaned up" in the business intelligence tool. It is useful to transform column names into neat, mixed-case items without any underscores or the like. Any further transformation in the semantic layer represents a missed opportunity to name the column well as part of the design.

TIP When designing a dimensional model, choose attribute names that are recognizable and understandable. Do not rely on a business intelligence tool to provide user-friendly translations.

This is not to say that this capability of a business intelligence tool should never be used. If an existing schema design falls short in the understandability department, then the capabilities of a business intelligence tool can be used to make up for this fact. It may also be useful to name things differently for different groups of users. When designing a star, however, your goal should be to choose column names that will make obvious sense.

Creating Virtual Attributes

Like a view in a relational database, a business intelligence tool can be used to combine existing columns to create new items. For example, if a table contains columns for first name and last name, you might use a business intelligence tool to create something called "full name." This item simply concatenates the first name, a space, and the last name, perhaps by injecting the following SQL into a generated query:

```
concat( first_name, ' ', last_name )
```

A new dimension has been constructed using two existing dimensions.

This construct is a *virtual* attribute. Like a column in a view that does the same thing, it can be used in a query even though it is not actually stored in the database. When a user drags "full name" onto the canvas and runs the report, the necessary concatenation will occur at query execution time, in the SQL statement that fetches data.

This capability may seem useful, since it saves a little space in the dimension table. Remember, though, that a dimension like "full name" can do more than simply appear on reports. It may also be used to constrain queries, control how facts are aggregated, sort data, or even serve as the basis for drilling across. When used in any of these ways, computing the value as part of the query will hamper performance—often seriously.

When developing a dimensional design, your goal should be to anticipate useful permutations of data elements and incorporate them directly into the schema design. Including an element like "full name" in the dimension table, rather than computing it at query time, will vastly improve performance. The burden of computing it is shifted from the DBMS to the ETL process, and it will be possible for database administrators to index it for optimal performance. Incorporating the dimension attribute directly into the schema design also makes it available to other tools in your architecture that may be used to develop reports, guaranteeing that it is computed consistently.

TIP Do not rely on a semantic layer to save space. The dimensional design should include any useful combinations of data elements, even if they are redundant.

This guideline extends beyond simple concatenations. As you learned in Chapter 3, the dimensional design should include useful combinations of attributes, include text values that correspond to standard codes, express flags in readable terms rather than Boolean "Yes/No" values, and so forth. You can use a business intelligence tool to cause these transformations of data to take place at query time, but doing so will hamper performance. Furthermore, these will only make these items available to users of the tool itself; anyone writing SQL or using a different tool will not benefit.

Dimensions are not the only area where this capability may prove tempting. Facts, too, often contain some degree of redundancy. For an orders model, you might be tempted to design a fact table that contains order_quantity, and use the semantic layer to multiply the value by standard price and cost data to produce fully additive facts like order dollars. Once again, though, this generates a runtime burden for the RDBMS, which must compute extended amounts on the fly. Further, it provides no such benefits to people using a different tool.

Relying on Subqueries

Many business intelligence tools are capable of producing subqueries, which can be very powerful in qualifying analysis. For example, the business may categorize customers based on spending behavior—high-volume, average volume, and low-volume customers. This categorization is based on analysis of previous spending, as recorded in a fact table somewhere. A user might want to use this categorization to filter query results.

A business intelligence tool may provide the capability to define this computation so that it can easily be added to a report as a filter. When invoked by the user, it generates the necessary subquery to segment customers. However, this capability is often difficult to make use of. More importantly, it is likely to hamper response time.

If it is to be commonly used, this kind of classification is better incorporated directly into the dimensional design as a behavioral dimension. As you learned in Chapter 6, behavioral dimensions precompute categorizations based on existing facts as part of the ETL process, dramatically improving performance at query time. Implemented in this manner, they will also be accessible to all users of the schema, ensuring a consistent definition is used for concepts like "high-volume customer."

TIP If users will use past behavior to qualify a query, don't rely on a business intelligence tool to generate subqueries. Instead, incorporate a behavioral dimension into the design.

Once again, this does not mean you should completely avoid use of such features. Adding this ability within a business intelligence environment may allow for speedier deployment, since it does not impact the design of an existing schema or the alteration of an existing ETL process. In addition, computing this kind of information at query time, rather than when the schema is loaded, may make sense if it is not frequently used.

Features to Use

While some business intelligence capabilities should not be used when it is possible to achieve the same thing in the schema design, there are other situations where the opportunities offered by a semantic layer are highly useful.

Compute Nonadditive Facts

Many important facts are not additive. For example, margin rate is usually expressed as the percentage of an order that represents margin. Ratios like this are not additive; selling two items at 10 percent margin does not result in 20 percent margin. As you learned in Chapter 3, nonadditive facts should be broken down into fully additive components. These can be stored at a detailed level and rolled up as needed. The ratio is computed in queries or reports as a final step, after the data has been aggregated. The nonadditive fact is not stored explicitly, since it would not be possible to aggregate it.

If the business intelligence tool allows it, the semantic layer is an ideal place to define a nonadditive fact. For margin rate, it might be defined as follows:

```
sum( margin_dollars ) / sum( order_dollars )
```

By defining this computation centrally, you ensure that reports will compute it correctly and consistently as the ratio of two sums. For this to work, the SQL generator must dynamically construct the appropriate `GROUP BY` clause when this item is added to a query.

TIP Use business intelligence tools to define nonadditive facts that can be computed from fully additive components.

This is one of the most valuable contributions that a semantic layer can make to the dimensional design. Other contributions, such as concatenated columns or decoded values, can be duplicated by creating a view. A nonadditive fact cannot be expressed in a view, because the scope of aggregation varies with each query. The `GROUP BY` clause must contain whatever dimension attributes have also been requested. A query generator can handle this dynamic aspect with grace.

Isolate Dimension Roles

Many fact tables include multiple relationships to a single dimension table. As you learned in Chapter 6, these various relationships represent different roles for the dimension. A fact table tracking mortgage applications, for example, contained three references to an employee dimension: one for a mortgage officer, one for a clerical processor, and one for an underwriter.

Isolating a particular role in a query involves aliasing the dimension table and joining it to the appropriate foreign key column in the fact table. This may be achieved using SQL aliasing or views. Quite often, it can also be done within a business intelligence tool's semantic layer. Leveraging this ability makes good sense, because it reduces the need to maintain external views and guarantees that the correct joins are used to isolate individual roles.

TIP Make use of the built-in aliasing capability in the semantic layer to support dimension roles.

As you will see, aliasing may provide additional advantages as well. Careful application of aliasing techniques may be useful in separating parts of the database schema so that a query generator does not attempt to link them together.

Simplify Presentation

Business intelligence tools do not present information to end users in table/column format. Instead, they typically offer some alternative organizing principle, such as a folder-based metaphor or a hierarchical tree that can be expanded and collapsed. Items can be placed in whatever arrangement makes sense.

This kind of presentation metaphor can be used to make the model more understandable to a user. For example, the semantic layer can be used to relocate degenerate dimensions, grouping their presentation to end users with other dimension attributes, rather than co-locating them with facts. Attributes from very large dimensions may be subdivided into groups, or vice versa. All these techniques can aid in making the available facts and dimensions more comprehensible to end users.

TIP Make use of a semantic layer's capability to organize the available facts and dimensions in a manner that will make sense to end users.

It is also useful to note that the semantic layer does not need to expose every aspect of the dimensional schema. There is no need, for example, to expose surrogate keys to end users. These attributes carry absolutely no business meaning, serving only as a means to uniquely identify rows of data. Other housekeeping columns that support maintenance of ETL processes may also be hidden from users.

Working with SQL-Generating BI Tools

Getting a handle on how the business intelligence tools of the target architecture generate queries is essential to ensuring attainment of the full breadth of analytic possibility afforded by a dimensional model. Capabilities of the BI tool may necessitate the addition of derived schemas or views. Balancing the need to guard against inaccurate results with the need for analytic flexibility may require setting up different semantic layers for novice users and expert developers. Some dimensional constructs will also call for different join configurations based on the question being asked.

In each of these cases, standard features of dimensional designs may require adjustment in order to work well with the BI tool. Common examples include the presence of multiple stars, multi-table browses, semi-additive facts, and bridges. The way each of these is handled by the SQL-generating BI tool will influence the configuration of the BI tool as well as the schema itself.

Multiple Stars

Learning to work with a business intelligence tool often takes place in the context of a schema that contains a single star. This is unfortunate, because many of the challenges for query generators stem from the presence of multiple stars. It is important to understand whether and how the tool will handle drill-across reports, queries that do not involve facts, and conformed dimensions. In addition, it is important to realize that most tools will not be able to generate queries when there is more than one way to compare two processes.

Drilling Across

When a report requires combining information from more than one fact table, it is called a drill-across report. As you learned in Chapter 4, drilling across is a two-step process:

1. Aggregate facts from each star *separately*, grouping each result set by the same dimensions.
2. Merge the result sets together based on the common dimensions, using full outer join logic.

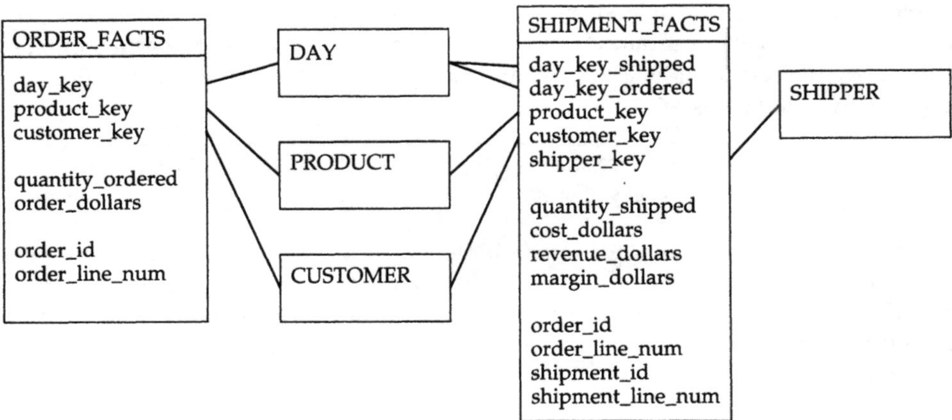

Figure 16-3 Two stars share conformed dimensions

These two steps may take place inside a single SQL statement or be executed as separate processes. Failure to subdivide the task in this manner risks double-counting a fact.

The orders and shipments stars in Figure 16-3, for example, may be used to compare the quantity ordered with the quantity shipped by product. Doing this in a single SQL `SELECT` statement is likely to result in some double-counting. If there is one order and more than one shipment for a product, the DBMS will create a Cartesian product. The order will be double-counted. This effect was fully explored in Chapter 4.

Many business intelligence tools can be configured to recognize and avoid this pitfall by drilling across. Query generators may carry out the two-step drill-across operation in various ways. Chapter 4 described three common approaches:

- Issue multiple queries, then merge result sets in the reporting environment.
- Issue multiple queries that create temporary tables, then issue an additional query that joins the temporary tables.
- Issue a single SQL statement that performs a full outer join on subordinate queries from each star.

Products have a variety of different names for this capability, including multi-pass queries, cross-stitching, multi-SQL, and the like. Some configuration is usually required so that the tool will invoke the mechanism automatically.

If the business intelligence tool is *unable* to drill across, it will not be possible to generate reports that compare two or more business processes. As you learned in Chapter 4, these are often high-value reports; the inability to produce them would be a serious blow to the analytic environment. As already mentioned, there is a solution, and it can be incorporated directly into the schema design without compromising any of the best practices you have learned in this book.

When faced with a tool that cannot drill across, add a merged fact table to the dimensional design, as depicted in the bottom of Figure 16-4. The merged fact table stores the precomputed results of drilling across. This shifts the burden from the

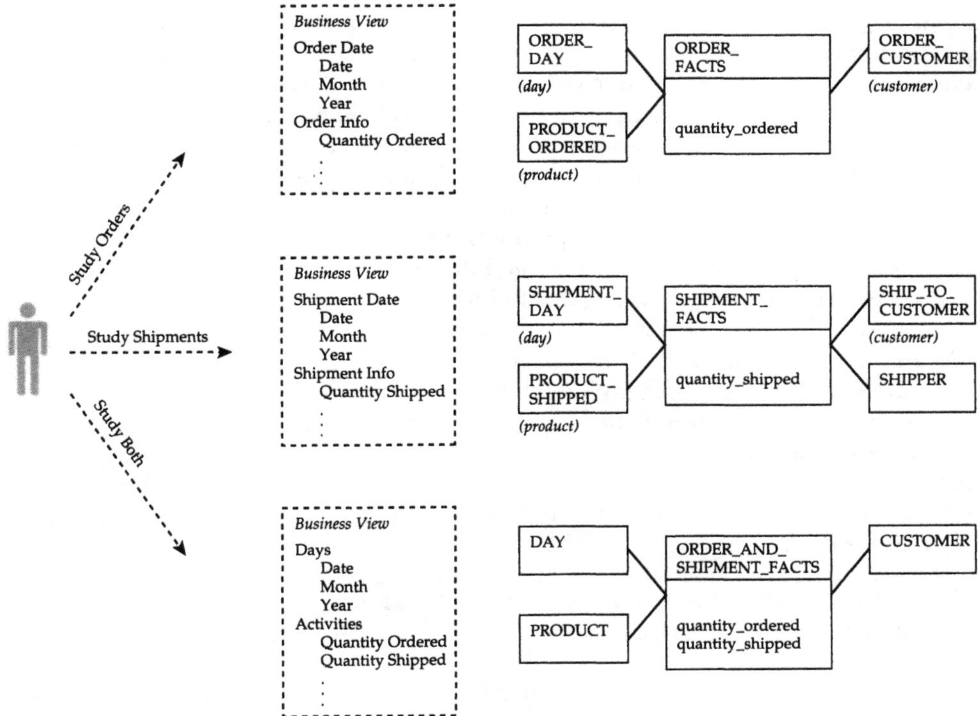

Figure 16-4 Add a merged fact table when tools cannot drill across

reporting process to the ETL process. Queries that compare facts from multiple stars are simplified, since all necessary information now resides in a single star schema.

Notice that this solution requires the user to select which star to use for each report. This potentially confusing matter can be simplified by constructing multiple semantic layers—one for the study of orders, one for the study of shipments, and one for comparing the processes. The user's choice of star is thereby made before he or she even begins bringing items onto a reporting canvas.

TIP A merged fact table can be used to make up for reporting tools that cannot drill across.

The addition of a merged fact table may be appealing even when the business intelligence tool *is* capable of drilling across. Because the work of comparing processes is shifted to the ETL process, the merged fact table is likely to be a better performer. This is particularly true when stars for the individual processes reside in different physical locations or in heterogeneous products. The solution may also be easier for users to understand and work with.

Queries with No Facts

Even if your tool can generate drill-across queries, you are not out of the woods. The presence of multiple fact tables may introduce some additional concerns. The first has to do with reports that include two or more dimension tables but involve no facts. This kind of query is sometimes called a *cross-browse.* Unlike a standard browse query, a cross-browse requires going through a fact table to link the requested dimensions.

The difficulty is that when there are multiple stars, there may be more than one way to relate two dimensions. Query generators don't do well in this situation, since a list of data elements requested by the user is not enough to choose a join path.

In Figure 16-3, for example, products and days can be related in the context of orders or shipments. If a user wants a list of products that were ordered on January 8, choosing date and product does not provide enough information for the SQL generator. It must be able to determine whether to relate day and product via order_facts or via shipment_facts. A query like this cannot be formulated unless the tool has some mechanism for asking users how they want to relate products and days. Some tools have an option that can be configured to ask the user in a situation like this.

This obstacle can be overcome by creating a separate semantic layer for each star—one for orders and one for shipments. In essence, choosing which star to work with answers the question even before the report is formulated: "I am working with orders. I want to see a list of products by day." Since each star is now isolated, a merged fact table will once again be required for drilling across.

TIP When multiple stars share two or more dimensions, cross-browse queries can trip up SQL generators. If these queries are common, separate semantic layers for each star may be necessary.

The same effect can be achieved by making heavy use of views or aliasing within a single semantic layer. For example, creating separate views of the product, day, and customer table for use with orders and with shipments allows each star to have its own virtual replica of the shared dimensions. This may make for a cluttered semantic layer, since it will have to distinguish between the versions of each dimension attribute—for example, ordered_product_name vs. shipped_product_name.

When the model includes a factless fact table, there are likely to be *numerous* queries that do not specify a fact. For example, the orders star may be supplemented with another that specifies products that are on promotion. When a user selects product and day, it is not sufficient to assume that the factless fact table be used. To do so will provide products that are on promotion for the day in question, but the user may be looking to see what products were sold on the day in question. Without the ability to prompt the user or default to a particular path, the SQL generator can only guess as to what is intended. Even if a tool is able to prompt users, the result may be confusing.

The alternative, once again, is to provide distinct options through separate semantic layers: one for promotions and one for orders. Many warehouse teams prefer this kind of arrangement because it eliminates any ambiguity for users or novice report developers.
A derived fact table can be created for any process that will benefit from comparison of the promotions and orders. This is particularly useful with factless fact tables that describe conditions, since comparing them to other fact tables normally involves set operations or subqueries, as described in Chapter 12. These queries are hard to specify or generate, and may run slowly. A derived table is the ideal solution.

More Than One Way to Compare Processes

Another potential complication occurs when there is more than one way that people might want to compare the same two processes. As with the factless query, a given set of attributes can be related in multiple ways. Even a tool that can drill across cannot be expected to infer what a user wants. Separate merged fact tables can be built for each flavor or comparison, or multiple semantic layers can be constructed for the different forms of comparison.

In Figure 16-3, there are two dates associated with each shipment: the date of the shipment, and the date of the order being fulfilled. Either may be used to compare shipments with orders. One option compares orders by order date with shipments by shipment date. This gives an overview of all activities that occurred on each day. The other option compares orders by order date with shipments by *order date* (rather than shipment date). This gives an overview of the fulfillment status of orders placed each day.

The queries to answer these questions involve exactly the same columns of the dimensional schema, but they are constructed in different ways:

- In the former case, drilling across requires querying quantity_ordered by order date and quantity_shipped by *shipment date.* These intermediate result sets are then merged based on dates.
- In the latter case, drilling across requires querying quantity_ordered by order date and quantity_shipped by *order date.* These intermediate result sets are then merged based on dates.

If the user brings date, quantity_ordered, and quantity_shipped to the canvas, a business intelligence tool does not have enough information to choose among these options.

This problem may be solved by producing two merged fact tables: one that drills across on order date and one that drills across on order date for orders and shipment date for shipments. Alternatively, two semantic layers can be set up, with the appropriate business views, aliases, and joins to support the two viewpoints.

TIP When there are multiple ways to compare two processes, a query generator cannot infer what users want based on the data elements they have requested. Build multiple merged fact tables for each possibility, construct different semantic layers for each possibility, or leave drilling across in the hands of expert developers.

Conformed Dimensions

Multiple stars may bring yet another challenge. It is necessary to understand whether and how your reporting tool supports conformed dimensions. When two distinct dimension tables conform, a *single* logical attribute can be found in *multiple* physical locations. This occurs when conformed replicas are stored in different databases, or when one dimension is a conformed rollup of another. In the semantic layer, it is generally preferable to have a single logical dimension attribute. Some reporting tools are unable to comprehend situations like this.

In Figure 16-5, for example, dimension attributes such as month, quarter, and year can be found in multiple places. In the orders star, they are found in the day table. In the sales goals star, they are found in the month table. It might be desirable to provide a single set of date attributes in the semantic layer. They can be combined with the goal facts to study

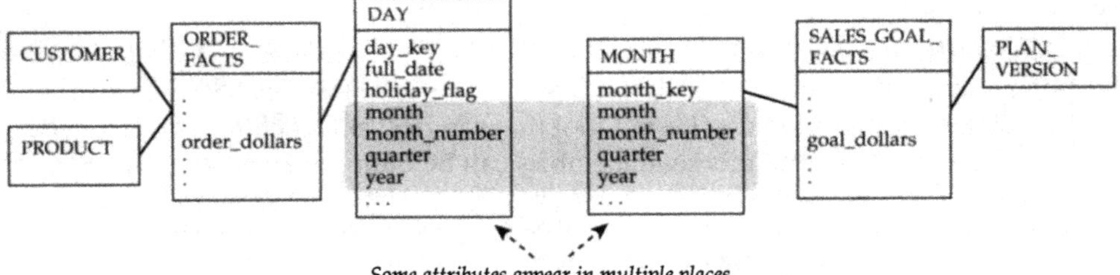

Figure 16-5 Conformed rollups pose another problem for SQL-generating tools

plans, order facts to study actuals, or both to drill across. Unfortunately, many tools are unable to comprehend the possibility that there are multiple possible places to find month (or quarter, or year.)

When a business intelligence tool is unable to identify cases where conformed attributes, such as month, can appear in multiple tables, it will not be able to drill across automatically. In this case, drilling across may once again be left to developers who manually construct queries. Alternatively, a separate merged fact table can be provided, eliminating the need to drill across.

TIP Conformed dimensions may result in a single logical attribute appearing in multiple physical locations. Some reporting tools can understand this, and generate SQL that fetches the attribute from the appropriate location. If a tool does not have this ability, drilling across will be a manual process. A merged fact table can be added to obviate the need for manual drill-across reports.

Reporting tools that cannot identify conformed dimensions may be able to automatically drill across in this situation if the schema is designed as a snowflake, rather than a star. This approach, depicted in Figure 16-6, ensures that each attribute is stored in a single location.

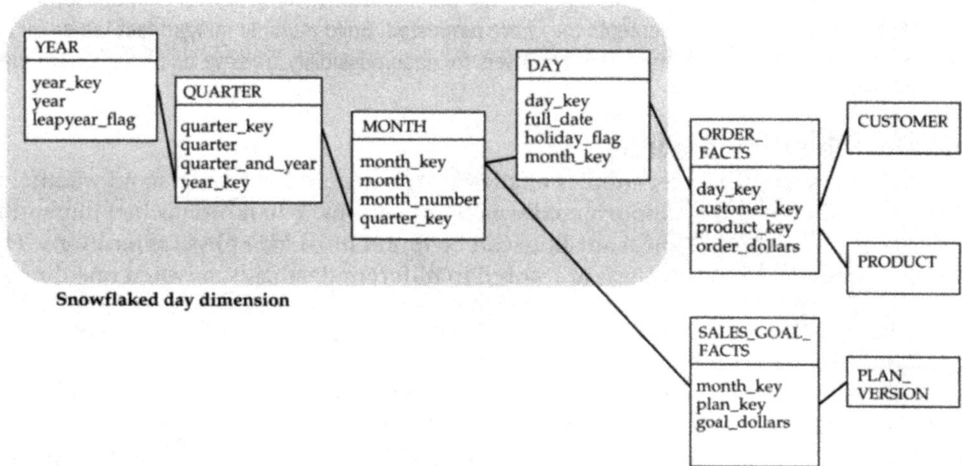

Figure 16-6 Snowflaking for the benefit of the reporting tool

An SQL generator that cannot comprehend conformed rollups like day and month may be able to drill across in this scenario.

If the primary reporting tool in a particular environment cannot drill across conformed rollups, as in Figure 16-5, but can with a snowflake, as in Figure 16-6, then the warehouse team might seriously consider relaxing the general guideline against snowflaking. Blind adherence to a principle simply limits the value of the solution. In this limited case, the drill-across benefit may outweigh the disadvantages of snowflakes as discussed in Chapter 7. If there are no other options, this may be a very good reason to snowflake.

This decision should be made carefully. Once the solution is built, it will be hard to reverse. If the reporting tool is ever replaced, significant rework will be required to convert to a star configuration. You may wind up living with drawbacks of snowflakes indefinitely, including potential impact on query performance, defeat of a star-join optimizer, the need for additional key management, and the ripple effect of slow changes through the snowflaked dimension.

Semi-Additivity

Semi-additive facts pose a different kind of challenge for business intelligence deployments. It is usually impossible to prevent a query generator from aggregating them across the non-additive dimension, producing incorrect results. For tools that *can* prevent this, another problem emerges: the rare case where this behavior is desired will also be prevented.

The best solution to this problem calls for limiting full access to trained developers and power users. A less functional but safe version of the star can be made available to novice users. They will be able to accomplish less, but at least they will not be making mistakes that could have serious consequences.

Using Semi-additive Facts

Semi-additive facts can be safely summed across some but not all dimensions. As you learned in Chapter 11, fact tables that are periodic snapshots usually have at least one semi-additive fact, which cannot be summed across snapshot periods. The bank account example from Figure 11-2 depicts a daily snapshot of account balances. Its dimensions include day, account holder, branch, and account. The account balance fact is semi-additive. It may be summed across account holders, branches, or accounts in a meaningful manner. However, it is not appropriate to sum it across days. The balance in your bank account on Friday is not the sum of balances from Sunday through Thursday. It is also important to recognize that for some semi-additive facts, dimensions other than time are the problem. A star that tracks sales goals, as in Figure 16-5, contains facts that are not additive across versions of the sales plan.

When using a semi-additive fact, it is important to do one of two things:

- Constrain the query for a specific instance of the non-additive dimension, or
- Group the query results by instances of the non-additive dimension

An example of the former is to select the sum of account_balance for a specific date. An example of the latter is to sum account_balance and group the results by day. In this case, it will also be important not to create totals within the report.

Many query-generating tools do not comprehend the concept of semi-additivity and are, therefore, unable to see to it that one of these steps is taken whenever a semi-additive fact is summed. For these tools, a fact is a fact. If it is present in a query, it will be aggregated and grouped by whatever dimensions are included.

If it is likely that inexperienced users will be putting together reports, it is quite possible that they will inadvertently sum the semi-additive fact across the problem dimension. While they are likely to understand that this does not make business sense, it is easy to forget that the query must either be filtered or grouped by the dimension in question. The result is a disastrous misstatement of the facts.

When Tools Do Not Prevent Misuse of Semi-additive Facts

The misuse of the semi-additive fact can be avoided by constructing a derived table that limits the user to a single instance of the problem dimension—a single day in the case of the account snapshot, or a single plan version in the case of sales goals. Usually, this sliced fact table is defined by taking the most recent period or version. In this derived schema, the problem facts are fully additive, and it is possible for the user to sum them in any manner without fear of inaccurate results.

A derived schema may be implemented as a physical table, simulated via a view, or constructed using view-like features within the business intelligence tool. It serves as a sandbox—an area in which inexperienced users can play safely. However, this solution also limits flexibility. It is not possible, for example, to access any day other than the current day, nor is it possible to group balance data by day for a range of dates. For novice users, this may be a valuable trade-off, with the potential for misuse outweighing the need for analytic flexibility.

TIP If the business intelligence tool is unable to prevent generation of a query that sums a semi-additive fact incorrectly, create a derived schema that is limited to one instance of the problem dimension. Novice users can work with this star without producing incorrect results, although they will not be able to produce some key reports.

Expert users, on the other hand, can be trusted not to ask the tool do something that is incorrect, such as sum account balances across days. These users can be exposed to the original star, made available either as a separate semantic layer, or by leveraging of role-based security features of the business intelligence tools. This group will be able to produce reports for prior dates, group totals by day, or compute period averages, minimums, and maximums.

NOTE There may be other solutions to this problem. Some tools, may be able to force a prompt every time a user requests the semi-additive fact, asking the person to choose a date, for example. Other tools may be able to force the problem dimension into the query when the user requests the semi-additive fact. In this latter case, it will be important to make sure that the user cannot violate the semi-additive properties by creating a total in the report. The Holy Grail, of course, is a query BI tool that is dimensionally aware. It must allow a developer to define a semi-additive fact, and the dimension across which it cannot be summed. It must then enforce these rules, *both* when it generates queries *and* when users work with the results.

When Tools Do Prevent Misuse of Semi-additive Facts

If your business intelligence tool is able to block misuse of a semi-additive fact, you will face a different problem. There will be situations where you actually *want* to sum the fact in question across the problem dimension. This does not occur often, but when it does the tool will most likely prevent the activity.

This kind of activity occurs when the report will use the result to compute a period average. For example, assume you have a fact table that is a periodic snapshot of inventory levels by day. You wish to find the average daily inventory level of a product for January. To do this, you must first sum the daily inventory levels for the month. After the query returns this result, you will divide by the number of days in the period. (As you may recall from Chapter 11, you must do this yourself; the SQL `average()` function computes the sum of daily inventory levels and divides by the number of rows, rather than the number of days in the period.)

If your BI tool is configured to prevent novices from summing the semi-additive fact across days, this will not be possible. The first step in producing the period average will be blocked. The alternative, once again, is to provide multiple semantic layers: one for general users, which enforces a ban on summing the semi-additive fact across the forbidden dimension, and one for power-users who know what they are doing.

Alternatively, those reports that require the special calculation can be coded by hand. In some cases, it may be possible to make use of the business intelligence tool to compute period averages. This often requires some SQL trickery, since different periods tend to include a different number of days, but it can sometimes be accomplished.

Browse Queries

Most people need to spend some time exploring dimension content before formulating a query. This allows them to choose which attributes should appear on a report and which should be used as filters. As you learned in Chapter 1, the act of exploring a dimension table is called browsing. Unfortunately, this is an alien concept to most business intelligence tools, which treat the browse as they would any other query.

Although most lack a browser interface, business intelligence tools work just fine when building reports that include data from a single dimension table. This is a reasonable stand-in for the browse, particularly if the user interface allows the user to interactively explore the results. However, there are still some design features that may lead to trouble. Mini-dimensions and split dimensions both pose problems when users wish to browse them.

Mini-Dimensions and Browsing

When a dimension table is likely to experience a high rate of type 2 changes, designers can mitigate excessive growth by splitting some attributes off into a separate table, called a mini-dimension. As you learned in Chapter 6, the mini-dimension will contain a subset of attributes, each of which has a finite set of possible values. The table is constructed with a Cartesian product of all possible combinations, and never requires further updating. Because these attributes have been removed from the main dimension, the number of new rows generated by type 2 changes is dramatically reduced.

The drawback to a mini-dimension is that it is no longer possible to browse the attributes together with the main dimension. They are now in a separate table and only related via facts.

In Figure 6-5, for example, coverage attributes were separated from a policy dimension. Once separated, the attributes of these two tables are only linked via the fact table. Developers sometimes add a shortcut key in the main dimension that refers to the current corresponding row in the mini-dimension. This is depicted in Figure 16-7.

While the intentions are good, this design feature tends to trip up query generators. Policy and policy_coverage can be related in two ways: directly or through the fact table. We would like the join between policy and policy_coverage to be exploited only when browsing. When a fact table is involved, it should be omitted. This is very important, since the coverage data for an old fact may be different from what is current. As you should now be able to recognize, query generators do not respond well when there are multiple possible ways to relate tables.

If your business intelligence tool does not have some features that can help work around this situation, the best strategy is to create a separate logical view of the schema, which merges policy with the current coverage characteristics. This can be done by using a view, or from within the semantic layer of the business intelligence tool. A second alias of the coverage table will be connected to the fact table. The result is depicted in Figure 16-8.

The user will have different versions of coverage attributes to choose from when creating reports: one set that represents current coverage characteristics of policies, and the other which represents those that were in effect for each fact. For example, family_size in the view represents the current family size. It can be "browsed" with attributes of policy, even though it is technically a separate table. Family_size also appears in historic_coverage,

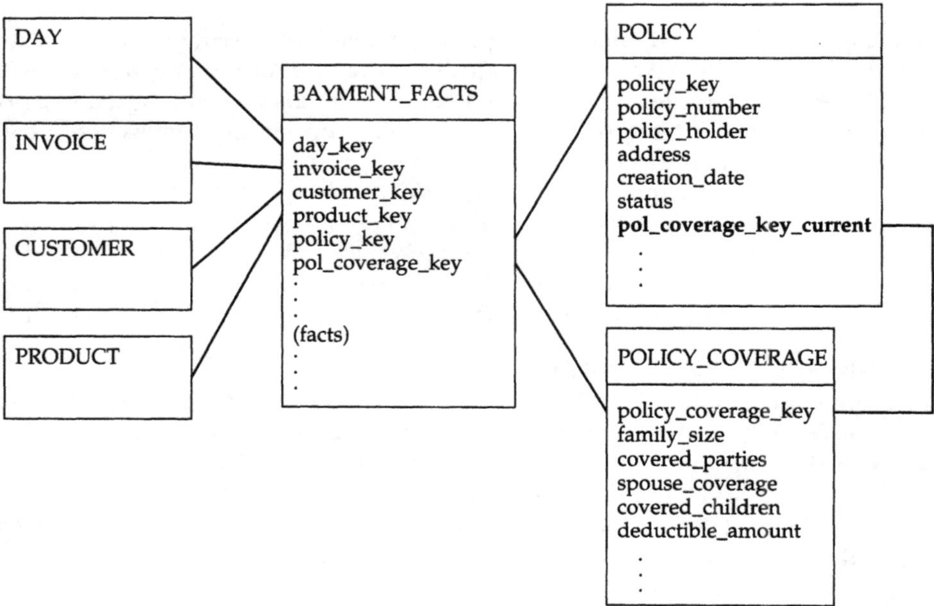

Figure 16-7 A shortcut join between main dimension and mini-dimension can confound query generators

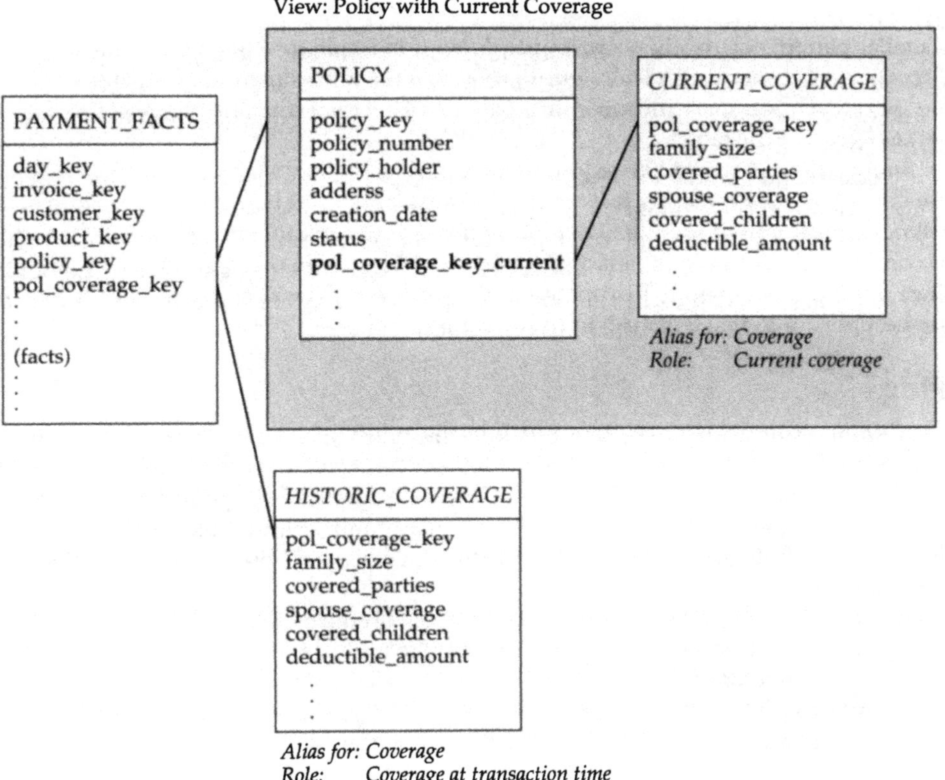

Figure 16-8 Aliasing two roles for the mini-dimension eliminates confusion

where it represents the status at the time of each transaction recorded in the fact table. When added to the query, it will be joined to the fact table, not back to the policy table.

TIP When there is a shortcut relationship between a mini-dimension and the main dimension, it is important that it not be brought into queries involving the fact table. To avoid this problem, create separate aliases for the mini-dimension. One will be joined to the main dimension; the other will be joined to the fact table.

To make the two versions of each attribute in the mini-dimension easily distinguishable, the views (or semantic layer) should name them appropriately. For example, the version of family_size that appears in the view that joins to the policy table can be named current_family_size; the other can be named historic_family_size.

Notice that it is only possible to cross-browse the policy table with current coverage attributes. This is a consequence of the mini-dimension, not the business intelligence tool. As discussed in Chapter 6, mini-dimensions disrupt the ability to study historic correlations between the main dimension and the mini-dimension, unless a factless fact table is added to the schema to track the history.

Split Dimensions

A similar pattern occurs when a very wide dimension is split into two tables arbitrarily. Also discussed in Chapter 6, this technique differs from the mini-dimension in that both "halves" of the split dimension share the same surrogate key. There is a true one-to-one correspondence between rows of the tables.

In this case, we would like to join the two tables together when browsing, but join each to the fact table when querying facts. The join between the two halves of the split dimension will not compromise the results, but it may disrupt performance. The best alternative here is to configure the lesser-used half of the split dimension as an outrigger. This is also not ideal, since it has the potential to disrupt a star-join optimizer. The database administrator may be the best person to make the call in this situation.

Bridge Tables

The last dimensional feature upon which business intelligence tools may have an impact is the bridge table. As you learned in Chapters 9 and 10, bridge tables allow a single fact to refer to more than one instance of a dimension. A bridge table exploits the Cartesian product that is created when the dimension is placed in a many-to-many relationship with the fact table. Although this provides powerful analytic possibilities, it also introduces the potential for misuse.

The potential for double-counting when using a bridge table can be compensated for by creating an alternative view of the schema for novice users. Like many of the other techniques in this chapter, that may be accomplished using views, or by taking advantage of features that are built into your business intelligence product. This "safe" configuration for the novice must be accompanied by a more flexible, albeit dangerous, solution for the experts.

Dimension Bridge Tables

A dimension bridge table allows a fact table to be associated with more than one row in a dimension table. This allows modeling of a multi-valued dimension—one that can take on more than one value for a given fact. The technique is very flexible, allowing an indefinite number of dimension instances to be associated with each fact. This permits the development of impact reports, which associate the same fact with each member of the dimension.

The bridge table sales_goup, at the top of Figure 16-9, permits any number of salesreps to be associated with each order. A group_key is assigned for each collaboration, and rows are added to the sales_group table for each salesrep who contributed. This allows the fact table to carry a single group_key, regardless of the number of salespeople involved. When the sum of order_dollars is grouped by salesperson_name, the value will be repeated for each salesrep who participated in the sale. This kind of report illustrates the involvement of each salesrep in the orders process. It is known as an impact report, since it would not be accurate to create a grand total from the results.

Proper use of the bridge table avoids aggregating the fact across members of the group. There are three ways to avoid doing so:

1. Group results by dimension rows (generally with the natural key)
2. Constrain the query for a single member of the dimension (again using a natural key)
3. Constrain the query to isolate a single member of each group

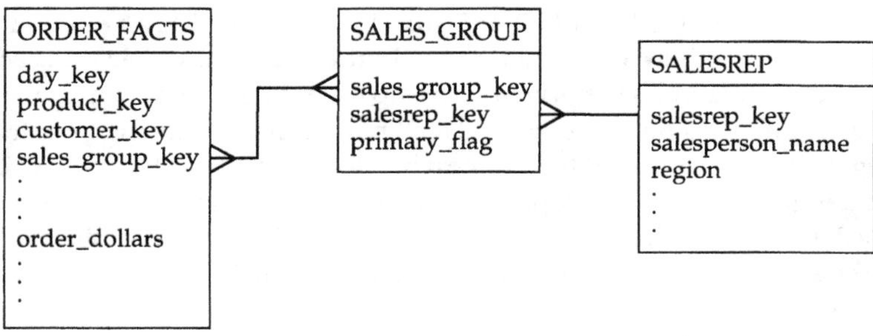

Expert Configuration
Able to produce an impact report
Double-counting is possible

Novice Configuration
Limited to single salesrep per order
Avoids possibility of double-counting

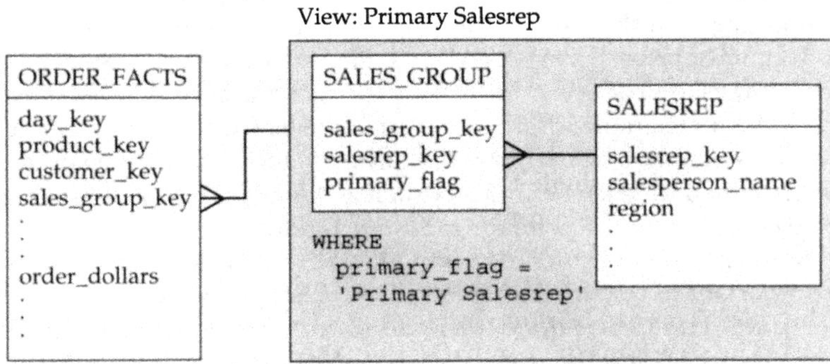

Figure 16-9 Two ways to leverage a dimension bridge table

In the case of multiple salesreps, the first option can be achieved by grouping the result by salesperson_name. Care must also be taken not to create a grand total with the results, since this would result in a double-count. The second option can be achieved by filtering the query for a *single* salesrep. The natural key is the best way to accomplish this, but it is also possible to use the salesperson's name. It is not sufficient to constrain on other attributes of salesrep, such as department, since this will select more than one individual. The last option filters the group table for rows where primary_flag contains the value "Primary Salesrep." For this to work, every group must have exactly one salesrep flagged as the primary salesrep.

This handful of rules may be easy for an experienced developer to follow, but is very likely to be unintelligible to a novice developer, let alone an end user. If steps such as these are not taken, the result can be disastrous. In the example, it can mean a dramatic overstatement of order_dollars. Configuring a business intelligence tool will require preventing users from making such a mistake.

The solution, as depicted in the lower half of Figure 16-9, is to provide an option for end users that associates only one salesrep with each order. In the illustration, a view is used to achieve this effect. The view identifies the primary salesrep for each group by joining the bridge to the salesrep table, and filtering on the primary_flag. It may be possible to accomplish the same thing by using the native features of the business intelligence tool in place of the view.

An alternative design approach was depicted in Chapter 9. The schema in Figure 9-6 stored a primary_salesrep key in the fact table, rather than a primary_flag in the bridge. The end result is the same; novice users are presented with an environment that associates only one salesrep with each order.

Expert developers can be provided with a different semantic layer, one that does not contain any such restrictions. Only these users will be able to make use of the bridge to create impact reports. They must be sure to use one of the previously listed techniques, thus ensuring that queries generated by the business intelligence tool do not perform any double-counting.

Attribute Bridge Tables

Like a dimension bridge, an attribute bridge allows a single fact row to be associated with more than one value of a dimension attribute. In this case, the bridge table lies between the dimension and an outrigger, but the effect is the same. The multi-valued attribute, in conjunction with a fact, must be used to group results, filtered for a single instance value, or constrained in such a way as to produce a single value for each instance of the dimension.

Figure 16-10 provides an example where each company may participate in numerous industries; one industry will always be designated as primary. Industry must be used to group results, be constrained for a single industry such as "Finance," or be limited to one value per company by filtering on the primary_industry column.

Since this is a complicated set of rules to expect anyone but an experienced developer to follow, it will be important to construct a semantic layer that prevents the generation of SQL that breaks the rules. This can be done by creating a view of company that includes the primary industry. The view joins the company table, the bridge, and the industry outrigger, constraining on primary_industry. This can be safely joined to the fact table without any concern for double-counting, as shown in the bottom of Figure 16-10.

TIP Misuse of a dimension bridge or attribute bridge results in double-counting. If novice users will be using the business intelligence tool, provide a semantic layer that prevents generation of such queries. Experienced users can be given a less restrictive semantic layer that allows use of the bridge to create impact reports. This version will not enforce restrictions; expert users must take steps to ensure that they do not generate inaccurate query results.

The dimension bridge and attribute bridge both set up a many-to-many relationship between the bridge and another table. This kind of relationship is often hard for modeling tools to represent, or may make it difficult for a database administrator to declare table relationships. To cope with these situations, bridged designs can be extended to resolve the many-to-many relationship. This is done by establishing a single-column table that has one row for each group, as described in Chapter 9. This variation on a bridged design does not eliminate the possibility of double-counting. It will still be necessary to set up a safe query environment for novice users in which generated queries will not double count.

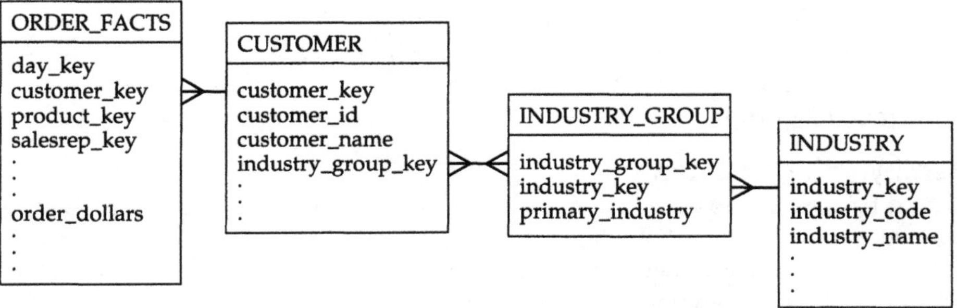

Expert Configuration
Able to produce an impact report
Double-counting is possible since some companies have multiple industries

Novice Configuration
Limited to single industry per company
Avoids possibility of double-counting

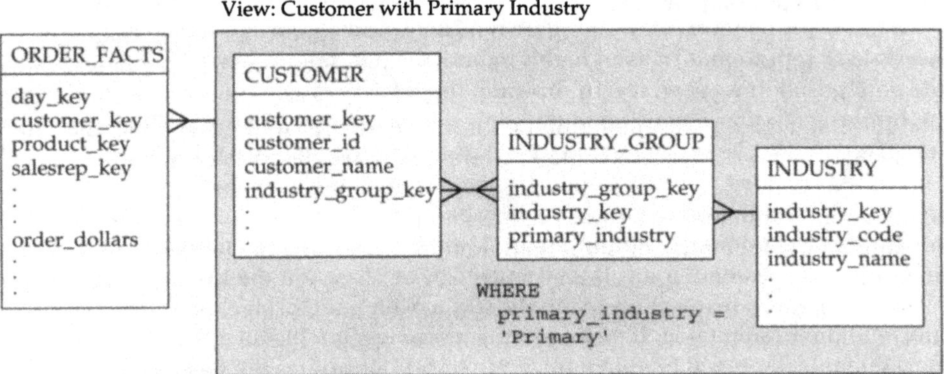

Figure 16-10 Two ways to leverage an attribute bridge table

NOTE A schema design can also avoid the many-to-many relationship by using each group exactly once. If the same salespeople collaborate on a second order, a second group will be created; if two companies have the same combination of industries, two groups will be created. This technique tends to generate overly large group tables and should, therefore, be avoided. Keep in mind, however, that it does *not* resolve the potential for double-counting. A single fact may still be associated with more than one instance of a dimension table or attribute. The many-to-many relationship has been resolved, but there is still a one-to-many that runs in the "wrong" direction. It will still be necessary to safeguard against double-counting.

Business intelligence products that are dimensionally aware can be confused by bridge tables. Some tools identify fact tables by looking for tables that contain multiple foreign key columns. Since a bridge table fits this description, it may be classified as a fact table. This is acceptable, and may even be considered correct. In essence, a bridge table is a kind of factless fact table, associating each member with a group. If your business intelligence tool identifies it as such, you will want to be sure that it does not cause drill-across tactics to be invoked. In the case of a bridge, the potential Cartesian product is exactly what is wanted; drilling across will disrupt this behavior.

Hierarchy Bridge Tables

A hierarchy bridge can be used to aggregate facts up or down a recursive hierarchy. Companies, for example, may be composed of other companies. If a fact table records transactions with each company, a hierarchy bridge can be used to roll them up to any level, regardless of how deep the hierarchy is. As described in Chapter 10, this is a common requirement, often found in organizational structures, geographic designations, and parts-breakdown arrangements.

Since a hierarchy bridge table allows a single fact to be associated with any number of dimension attributes, it is once again necessary to take precautions when using it. If facts are to be aggregated up the hierarchy, the developer must constrain for a single top-level node. Alternatively, results may be grouped by top-level node, as long as grand totals are not created inside the report. In the case of companies, this means that using the hierarchy bridge to roll up orders requires selecting a single company to which they will be rolled up, or group results by company. Once again, this is an example of an impact report.

It will likely be difficult to configure a business intelligence tool to generate SQL that meets these requirements. Even highly experienced developers may err, so once again a safe configuration is called for. In this case, the safe query environment does not involve the bridge at all; the dimension in question is linked directly to the fact table. Experienced developers can make use of a separate environment that exposes the bridge.

For the star involving a hierarchy bridge, the story does not end here. There is at least one other configuration of tables that may be useful: one that allows facts to be summarized by looking up the hierarchy, rather than down. For example, it might be useful to choose a company and see whether any sales occurred at or *above* it in the hierarchy. As you learned in Chapter 10, this involves reversing the way in which the bridge table is joined to the fact table and dimension table. If you are using a business intelligence tool, this means that a third semantic layer will be called for. Figure 16-11 illustrates the possibilities.

TIP A hierarchy bridge table, used incorrectly, leads to double-counting. For novice users, prevent business intelligence software from generating inaccurate queries by omitting the bridge. They will not be able to leverage the hierarchy but will be prevented from producing inaccurate reports. Expert developers will require two additional configurations, one used for looking down the hierarchy, the other for looking up.

In addition to these three basic configurations, there are other possibilities. The many-to-many relationship in either expert configuration can be resolved by inserting an additional alias for the bridged table. In the case of looking down from a company, this additional instance of the company table would represent the subordinate, or child company. In the case of looking upward from a subordinate, it would represent the superior company, or parent. These configurations were illustrated in Figures 10-11 and 10-12, and represent the potential for still more semantic layers.

A developer may also desire to produce a report looking for transactions above or below a *group of companies*, rather than a single company. This kind of question, which was

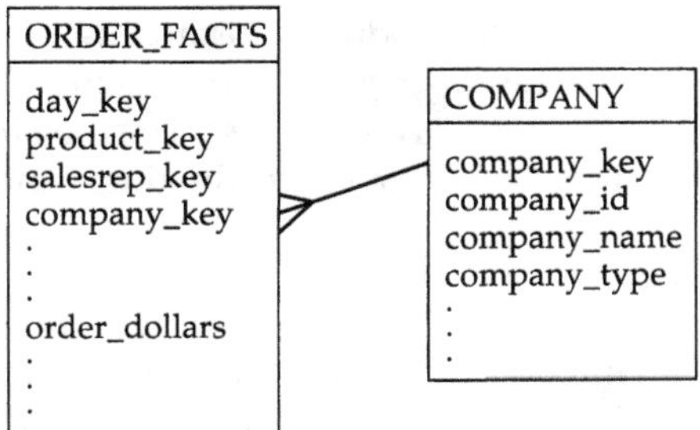

Novice Configuration
Study only the company that placed the order
Avoids double-counting

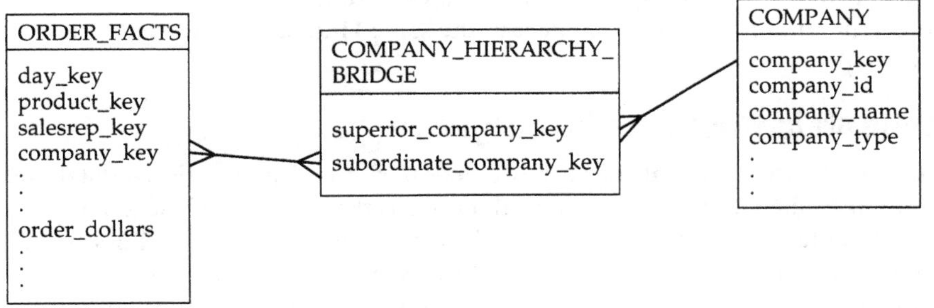

Expert Configuration 1: Looking Down from a Company
Groups transactions that occur at or below each company
Double-counting is possible

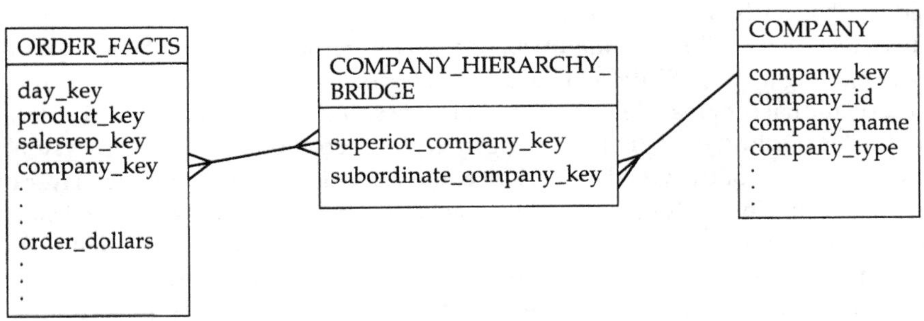

Expert Configuration 2: Looking Up from a Company
Groups all transactions that occur at or above each company
Double-counting is possible

Figure 16-11 Two ways to leverage an attribute bridge table

also discussed in Chapter 10, requires use of a subquery to produce a distinct list of companies below (or above) the group in question. This distinct list is then used to filter the main query. It is not likely that this kind of query will be generated successfully by a business intelligence tool; such reports will likely require that SQL be edited by hand.

Working with Cube-Based BI

Many business intelligence solutions are based on multidimensional cubes, rather than relational stars. These are generally referred to as Online Analytical Processing (OLAP) tools. Because the derived schema is already a central concept in cube-centric implementations, many of the solutions and workarounds from the SQL-generating world are a natural fit in the OLAP world.

In environments where cubes are created based on relational star schemas, the business intelligence product may be capable of automatically generating cubes. When this is the case, auto-generated cubes will be subject to the same kind of careful scrutiny as auto-generated SQL.

Cube-Centric Business Intelligence

Business intelligence tools that support interaction with multidimensional databases center on cubes, rather than a semantic layer. With cubes as the top level of the analytic taxonomy, these implementations lend themselves nicely to solutions that provide different views of the data for different purposes. Whereas multiple semantic layers may seem confusing in the relational world, multiple cubes are natural in the multidimensional world.

Focus on the Cube

Business intelligence tools geared for multidimensional databases provide a user experience that is very different from those provided by tools geared for relational databases. As discussed in Chapter 3, these applications take advantage of the cube's ability to precompute the value of facts across different members of each dimension. This results in instantaneous response, enabling a level of interactivity that contrasts sharply with the query/response cycle for a relational schema. This characteristic is responsible for the first two letters in the acronym OLAP (Online Analytic Processing). "Online" connotes real-time interactivity.

As the focal point of the OLAP experience, the cube replaces the semantic layer of an SQL generator. Specific tools may provide a mechanism to provide an abstracted view of a cube, but the presentation of available data elements is intrinsically dimensional and usually does not require the creation of "virtual" dimension elements. To compute these on the fly would eliminate the performance advantage of OLAP. OLAP tools often do, however, support calculated facts.

When working with an OLAP tool, the user starts by choosing a cube with which to work. Because of this, OLAP tools are ideally positioned to provide alternative perspectives on data. Want to study orders? Access the orders cube. Want to study shipments? Access the shipments cube. Want to compare the process? Access the orders and shipments cube. Sophisticated OLAP tools may provide the ability to link two or more cubes, but the affinity remains. It is expected that different cubes will be provided for different purposes, or for users of different skill sets.

Online performance comes at a cost; as the number or cardinality of attributes grows, cubes can become extremely large. This has led to the cube being tagged as "less scalable" than relational storage in a star schema. Vendors have countered by providing the ability to optimize cubes for large data sets, but this requires sacrificing some of the performance benefit. Many data warehouse architectures manage the trade-off between relational scalability and OLAP performance by using the star schema to store granular dimensional data from which cubes are created for OLAP applications. This paradigm was discussed in Chapter 3. Cubes built in this architecture summarize or transform the structure of the underlying dimensional data held in the star. This provides a wealth of opportunities to design cubes for specific purposes. Cubes can take the form of any of the numerous derived schema designs from Chapter 14 or aggregate designs from Chapter 15.

Multiple Cubes

Because multiple cubes are expected and accepted in an OLAP environment, none of the hand-wringing caused by the need to deploy multiple semantic layers in SQL-generating environments will be encountered. Drilling across, dealing with multiple fact tables, and providing multiple configurations for bridged solutions are handled with grace, simply by producing multiple cubes and controlling who can access them.

Cubes for Each Process, Cubes for Comparing Processes Although many OLAP tools are capable of drilling into multiple cubes simultaneously, the ability to do so is less of a concern for the OLAP BI tool. The addition of a merged cube that compares two processes fits naturally into this environment, although it may seem a kludge for SQL generators.

Because each cube can be selected individually, there is also far less concern about how to deal with factless queries. The path for linking dimensions together is determined when a cube is selected as the focus of analysis. Scenarios that are factless also present no problem; the simple process of selecting the cube determines the scope of analysis.

If there are multiple ways one may wish to compare data from two processes, as you saw with orders and shipments earlier in this chapter, the creation of a separate merged cube for each style of comparison eliminates any potential confusion or misuse of the data. Cube-oriented business intelligence incorporates these viewpoints naturally.

The benefits of cube-oriented business intelligence are further evident as you look back at some of the other issues described earlier in this chapter. Anything that can be solved by producing a derived schema or view can also be solved by creating a new cube. Solutions that require different viewpoints for safety vs. flexibility are therefore a clean fit. For an OLAP tool that does not enforce semi-additivity, for example, the solution is obvious: produce a safe but limited cube for novices, and a flexible but more dangerous cube for experts.

When cubes are created from star schemas, the various ways of dealing with a bridge can be incorporated into separate cubes. With a multi-valued dimension, it is possible to create one cube that isolates a single dimension member for each fact, and another that captures impact. In the case of collaborating salespeople, the first cube contains only the primary salesrep. This cube is safe but incapable of producing an impact report. Another cube is created that repeats an order for each salesrep. This cube can produce impact reports, but care must be taken not to double count.

A New Concern: Cube Proliferation Because they are less scalable, cubes are usually more targeted. In addition to providing cubes for various processes, it may be necessary to produce multiple cubes for each process, leveraging the principles of derivation and aggregation from Chapters 14 and 15 in order to maintain a performance standard. Thus, the possibility of overproliferation of cubes becomes the primary concern in the OLAP world, replacing the need to deploy multiple semantic layers in the SQL-generation world.

Careful selection of the appropriate mix of cubes necessitates evaluating the various analytic requirements for required dimensionality and grain. The one-cube-per-report approach must be avoided at all costs. Each additional cube requires resources to design, build, and maintain. Unchecked, this can lead to an unmanageable environment. Each cube should be designed to support a mix of reporting needs; each new report should attempt to make use of existing cubes.

Auto-Generation of Cubes

Many multidimensional architectures provide the ability to generate and maintain cubes automatically based on information that comes from a relational schema. Cube-generating tools work especially well when the relational source is a star schema, since both technologies are used to store information based on a dimensional model. Cube generation is much like SQL generation in that it requires a watchful eye to ensure that information in the star schema is not misused. Additional attention may be required when it comes to defining hierarchies.

Generation vs. Manual Control

Use of a business intelligence tool that generates multidimensional storage structures requires careful configuration and oversight. It is possible for a cube-generator to produce inaccurate results, just as it is with an SQL generator. Similarly, cube-generating tools cannot generate every possible cube, just as SQL-generating BI tools cannot generate every possible query.

Cubes that are most likely to be generated effectively and accurately from star schemas are those that summarize the base data without transforming its dimensional structure. This kind of cube represents an aggregate of the data in the star, as described in Chapter 15. The similar dimensional structure of the aggregate to the original schema renders such cubes easy to generate. Also simple to generate are cubes that represent a sliced version of the original star, as described in Chapter 14. These cubes limit scope by focusing on a subset of the original members, such as a single department or region.

Other forms of cubes may be more difficult to generate in an automated manner. A merged cube, for example, must be constructed according to the standard drill-across process, lest it result in double-counting. Many cube-generating tools can handle this requirement; for those that do not, it may be necessary to build the cube manually. This may involve use of tools provided by the vendor to define cube-processing routines. It may also be achieved by building a merged fact table, then using it as the basis to auto-generate the merged cube. Other kinds of derived cubes also require one of these techniques. Examples include building snapshot cubes from a transaction star, accumulating snapshots from transactions, cubes that juxtapose coverage with a process, and so forth.

Developers may choose to forgo automatic generation of cubes so that they can retain control of when and how cube processing takes place. Some products require the developer to relinquish control of cube maintenance, save for some configuration options, in order to generate cubes. This can make it difficult to integrate the maintenance of cubes into a complex, dependency-laden architecture. In order to retain control of the refresh cycle for all analytic data, it is often useful to assume manual control—even where automatic control is possible.

Attribute Hierarchies

Multidimensional products often rely on the declaration of attribute hierarchies in the source star schema. These hierarchies may be used to define the level of detail to be included in a generated cube. They may also be used to support drilling within a generated cube. Attribute hierarchies, however, represent a narrow view of the potential ways in which data may be summarized, as you learned in Chapter 7. More importantly, there may be more than one possible attribute hierarchy within a dimension.

Hierarchies' Influence on Cube Generation or Drilling An attribute hierarchy represents a dimension as a series of levels in a successive master-detail relationships, placing each dimension attribute within one of the levels. The attributes of a product dimension table, for example, might be grouped into three levels of successive detail: categories, brands, and products. One additional level, representing all products, is typically added to this representation. The hierarchy might be represented as follows:

All Products → Categories → Brands → Products

Similar attribute hierarchies may be defined for other dimensions:

All Salesreps → Regions → Territories → Salesreps
All Customers → Industries → Customers
All Dates → Years → Quarters → Months → Days

Defining attribute hierarchies in this manner makes it possible to define a cube's level of summarization simply by choosing the appropriate level from each dimension. Figure 15-5 depicted this act diagrammatically: a summary of order facts was defined that included month, product, saleserep, and all customers. Some tools that generate cubes work on this paradigm. The relational source is described in terms of attribute hierarchies, which are then used to define the level of aggregation for each cube. If brand is included in a cube, for example, the generator will include all category and brand-level attributes in the generated data structure.

Similarly, subdivision of dimension attributes into levels facilitates the "drilling" feature of many OLAP tools. Once a cube is constructed, the attribute hierarchy is used to determine what happens when a user requests to drill into a data element. If he or she drills into a category, for example, the attribute hierarchy determines that the next level is brand.

For products that make use of attribute hierarchies, either to define cubes or to facilitate drilling, it will be necessary to document the attribute relationships as part of the dimensional design. Figure 7-3 provided one way to do this. This diagram illustrated the included attributes at each level. Some tools may require additional information, such as the declaration of a unique identifier for each level.

Competing Hierarchies For OLAP tools based on attribute hierarchy paradigms, problems arise when it is necessary to support more than one hierarchy within a dimension. A day dimension, for example, may possess two hierarchies: one for calendar years and one for fiscal years. A product dimension, too, may be subject to alternative hierarchies: one that segments products based on how they are produced and one that segments them based on how they are marketed.

Some OLAP tools that work with attribute hierarchies do not accommodate competing hierarchies. Using these tools to generate cubes will require aliasing a source star twice, so that each can be defined with a different hierarchy. This makes it possible to define each desired cube. If calendar and fiscal views of order facts are required, for example, it will be necessary to present two logical versions of the orders star to the OLAP tool. For one version, a fiscal hierarchy is defined in the time dimension; for the other, a calendar hierarchy is defined. These two versions of the star are required at the logical level only. Their physical implementation may be achieved by using views or aliases. They can then be used to define and generate the necessary cubes.

When used to guide drilling processes, attribute hierarchies may also necessitate the creation of multiple cubes. For example, one cube may be used to study orders using marketing's product hierarchy; another may be used to study orders using manufacturing's product hierarchy. Although these cubes contain the same attributes, they differ in what the OLAP front-end application will do if someone drills into the product dimension.

Other Kinds of Hierarchy An attribute hierarchy is one of many ways that the information in a dimension may be organized to describe a progression from summary to detail. As you learned in Chapter 7, the same set of data may be explored in many different ways, some of which do not hinge on this kind of representation. A product, for example, has a color. In an attribute hierarchy, color would be included at the product level. However, color may be a particularly low cardinality attribute. It may be useful to summarize products by color in a cube, or to drill from color to product.

When this kind of summarization is useful, either to define a cube or to support a drill-down process, it will be necessary to work around the attribute-hierarchy focus of some OLAP tools. Following the same approach used for competing hierarchies, an alternative view of the schema is declared for which the product hierarchy is specified as:

All Products → Product Color → Product

This alternate view of the source star is used as the basis of cubes that will aggregate based on color, or for cubes that will support drilling along this path.

Type 1 Changes

Where cubes are automatically generated and maintained, the type 1 change can pose a unique challenge. It is often difficult or impossible to apply incremental updates to a cube that contains a type 1 attribute. This is exactly the same dilemma that is faced when trying to maintain an aggregate star that contains a type 1 attribute, as described in Chapter 15. Tools that automatically generate cubes will discard and rebuild them when there is a change to a type 1 attribute.

The difficulty posed by the type 1 attribute was described in detail in Chapter 15. When a type 1 attribute changes, it may be necessary to restate some of the facts in the cube using the new value. Knowing how to do this requires access to the original detail, including before and after values. This information is generally lost once the source star is updated, so that it is subsequently impossible to update the cube accordingly. Unless cube updates are handled simultaneously with updates to the base data, the type 1 change will require the cube to be discarded and rebuilt. This can be an unwelcome and time-consuming process.

For many designers, this is reason enough to avoid the type 1 change altogether, or at least bar type 1 attributes from appearing in cubes. While this resolves the technical challenge, it limits analytic flexibility. In many business situations, a type 1 change is the appropriate way to handle a change to source data. Such an approach will be impossible if type 1 attributes are barred from the design. The alternative is to accept the type 1 attribute as part of the design and to plan for complete rebuilds of necessary cubes each time data is refreshed.

Summary

To get the most out of a dimensional design, it is essential to understand your business intelligence tools. Their capabilities may influence schema design or suggest the need to provide different levels of access for users with different skill sets.

When working with SQL generators

- SQL-generating tools provide a semantic layer that maps a business view to a physical view.
- For new designs, don't plan to make use of features that are better handled in the model itself. Save those only for legacy models. Do make use of features like adding non-additive facts to the semantic layer and hiding surrogate keys.
- Multiple semantic layers are acceptable in providing different perspectives on a model, supporting alternative ways to link the same tables, or providing a separate and safe view for novice users and a flexible view for expert users.

Some dimensional features pose problems for SQL generators

- Some SQL-generating tools cannot generate a drill-across query. Supplying a merged fact table provides a workaround for this limitation.
- SQL generators may be unable to create cross-browse queries when there are multiple fact tables; in this case, separate semantic layers may be required.
- Some tools may function better if snowflakes are used rather than conformed dimensions. If the tool is central to the architecture, this argues for a snowflake design, but fully explore the other impacts.
- Dimension browse queries can trip up SQL generators if they link a mini-dimension to the main dimension. Views may be of some limited use here, at the cost of complicating the semantic layer.
- It is often impossible to prevent a user from summing a semi-additive fact across its non-additive dimension. If novice users must access the data directly, it may be useful to build a derived schema that is limited to a single value of the dimension in question. Expert users can access the full schema.

- Bridge tables can cause double-counting if misused. For novice users, provide a view of the schema that eliminates this possibility. For expert users, provide full access to the bridge.
- Hierarchy bridge tables introduce the possibility of joining the tables of a star in at least three different configurations; each will likely require a separate semantic layer.

When working with OLAP tools

- Multiple cubes are the norm and are to be expected.
- Make use of multiple cubes to support different perspectives, to support alternative ways to link the same underlying data elements, or to segregate novice from expert users.
- Work toward a solution where each cube supports a range of analytics or reports; avoid the one-cube-per-report paradigm.
- It may be necessary to work around OLAP tools that use attribute hierarchies to generate cubes. For competing hierarchies, supply different views of the same underlying star.
- Some tools also use attribute hierarchies to control the drilling process. For these tools, competing hierarchies will require separate cubes.
- A type 1 change to a cube attribute may require the entire cube be rebuilt. If this is undesirable, limit the use of type 1 attributes in cubes.

Further Reading

Because the features of business intelligence and reporting tools are so diverse, you may be best served by reviewing documentation of the products in your architecture. You can learn more about how these tools fit into a data warehouse in the following books:

- Many organizations build their own front-end tool for creating reports from dimensional data. Careful thought must be given to the process of retrieving and assembling information. This is discussed in detail in Chapter 13 of *Data Warehouse Design Solutions* (Wiley, 1998) by Chris Adamson and Mike Venerable.
- Business intelligence and reporting tools are an important part of the technical architecture. They may factor into product selection processes, budgets, and resource management plans. Their configuration and use are integrated into design, build, test, and deployment phases of project plans. These aspects and more are covered in *The Data Warehouse Lifecycle Toolkit, Second Edition* (Wiley, 2008), by Ralph Kimball, Margy Ross, Warren Thornthwaite, Joy Mundy, and Bob Becker.

CHAPTER

17 Design and ETL

One of the most difficult tasks in data warehousing is ETL development. The process that loads a star schema varies significantly from implementation to implementation. It is influenced by the software tools used, the latency profile of the solution, and the data architecture of the data warehouse. Despite these variations, every load process must perform certain fundamental activities. This chapter explores how design adjustments can aid these activities.

The process of loading a dimension table is made complex by the need to handle slowly changing dimensions. It will be necessary to identify new and changed data and process it accordingly. This is more difficult than it may seem, since what constitutes a "change" may be very different in the source and the star. Natural keys play a central role in this processing, participating in a series of comparisons that will determine how source data should be handled.

Loading a fact table presents its own fundamental processing challenges. The most significant of these involves foreign keys. As supplied by a source system, transactions will be accompanied by natural keys. The load process must replace these with surrogate keys. Here, too, the phenomenon of slowly changing dimensions can complicate matters, since a single natural key value may be present in multiple rows of a dimension table.

The load process is always under time pressure; it must be fast and efficient. Optimization methods are largely implementation-dependent, but, once again, some fundamental techniques can benefit just about any solution. One such technique is to perform the identification of new and changed data at the source before information is extracted for processing. This can dramatically reduce the amount of information that must be processed, but it may have impacts on the operational system. Identification of type 1 and type 2 changes may also be optimized by simplifying the necessary comparisons using hash functions. This requires some minor adjustments to dimension tables.

The load process must also deal with poor source data and is often called upon to clean it up. Many data cleansing tasks can be sensibly automated as part of the load process, while others are best left for cleanup at the operational source. Data cleansing can be represented by rules and in some cases through mapping tables. In many cases, operational transactions will refer to dimensional data that cannot be validated. Special techniques can be employed to incorporate this data into the star, even if appropriate dimensional detail is missing.

Last, this chapter will recap the various forms of housekeeping columns that have been encountered throughout the book. These special columns streamline the reporting process, ETL development, or the quality assurance process. Some additional columns can be added to assist in the development of derived and aggregate tables, and to provide a record of the activities that last touched each row.

The ETL Process

This book uses the term ETL to describe any process that moves data from one system or data structure to another. A variety of other terms are used to describe this activity, including data movement, data integration, and data presentation. The term ETL is used for convenience; it is not meant to imply a particular data warehouse architecture or a particular kind of software product.

The ETL process is complex, and its development is a significant challenge. The way this process is organized varies tremendously. It is influenced both by the specific tools used to develop it, as well as the data warehouse architecture in which it functions. Though the details differ widely, every solution that populates a star schema with information must address some fundamental requirements.

A Complex Task

Development of an ETL process is one of the most challenging tasks in data warehousing. It is hard to overstate its complexity. It often consumes the lion's share of project resources and is a primary source of project risk.

The magnitude of the ETL task accounts for its complexity. The ETL process must work with a variety of different source systems, based on heterogeneous technologies, to create a single integrated view of information. It must do this with data that is often of dubious quality. It must function within tightly prescribed processing windows and have minimal impact on operational systems. It must be fully automated, able to process exceptions, and able to recover from errors.

A heavy emphasis on the load process is consistent with basic principles of data warehousing in general, and star schema design in particular. By doing the hard work of restructuring operational data in advance, it is easier to analyze it at query time.

Tools Used by the ETL Process

The ETL process is a coordinated effort between numerous tools and utilities that are configured and assembled to load the star schema as required by its design documentation. Packaged software products known as ETL tools are often leveraged to accomplish some or all of this process. When used, these tools are likely to be supplemented by other utilities as well. Some organizations opt not to leverage these specialized tools, instead incorporating "hand-coded" programs written using general-purpose tools. Regardless of the underlying technologies, the entire process is referred to here as "ETL."

Architecture and the ETL Process

Different data warehouse architectures organize the task of data movement in different ways. As you learned in Chapter 2, Ralph Kimball's dimensional data warehouse calls for a logical repository of atomic data, drawn and integrated from operational data sources. This information is dimensional in structure and may be queried directly. Optional second-line data marts, composed of derived and aggregate tables, may supplement this information. Both are populated by ETL processes.

W.H. Inmon's Corporate Information Factory architecture also calls for the establishment of an integrated repository of atomic data. This repository is called the enterprise data warehouse. Unlike Kimball's repository, it is not dimensional, nor is it queried directly. Instead, this repository serves as the data source for star schema data marts. All layers are populated by ETL processes. (Note that Inmon reserves this term for the first stage only; the second is referred to as data presentation.)

Stand-alone data marts do not involve an integrated repository of enterprise data. They are developed without an enterprise context, focused instead on a single subject area. An ETL process draws data directly from operational sources to populate the data mart.

Although these three architectures are organized differently, all require that information from source systems eventually make its way into a star schema. A developer charged with populating a star schema in a Corporate Information Factory may have an easier job: there is a single source of data, which has already been integrated and standardized. In all cases, however, the same fundamental processing requirements must be met.

Loading a Star

The process of loading a star schema involves two major categories of activity: processing data for dimension tables, and processing data for fact tables. Loading a dimension table is an incremental process; it is made complex by the need to process slowly changing dimensions. The load must identify new and changed data, manage surrogate keys, and insert or update dimension records as appropriate. Loading a transaction-grained fact table is comparatively simple, at least at a high level. The major challenge for this process involves replacing the natural keys that describe business transactions with surrogate keys that refer to the dimension tables.

A Top-Level Dependency

Understanding how a star schema is loaded begins with recognizing a fundamental dependency: each fact table row contains foreign key references to dimension table rows. This implies that before a row can be inserted into a fact table, the appropriate dimension rows must be ready. This high-level dependency is depicted in Figure 17-1.

With this high-level dependency in mind, the discussion that follows will consider dimension processing first and then look at fact table processing. Dimension processing, represented by step 1, will be decomposed into a series of activities that must be executed for each of the dimension tables in a given star. In most situations, there are no dependencies among the dimensions themselves. This means, for example, that processes for loading product, customer, and salesperson may take place simultaneously. After considering dimension processing, we will break step 2 down into a series of activities that must be executed to load the fact table.

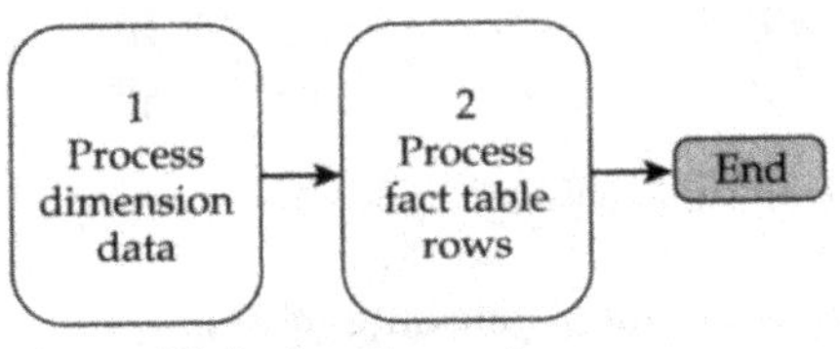

Figure 17-1 Loading a star

Bear in mind that the actual load process may or may not execute these tasks separately. Load processing is usually broken up into one module or program for each warehouse table. When this is the case, execution of these modules is organized to reflect the dependencies among the tables; dimensions are loaded first, then fact tables. It is possible, however, to develop a single module that loads the tables of a star simultaneously. For example, a system that loads a schema in real time may process transactions individually, as they occur. It is possible to define a single SQL transaction that inserts a row into the fact table and simultaneously applies necessary changes to the dimensions. Such a module must still ensure the referential integrity between fact tables and dimension tables.

Loading a Dimension Table

Loading a dimension table is an incremental process, not a one-time-only affair. It is necessary to inspect the data sources of dimension tables for new and changed information on a regular basis, and insert or update records as appropriate. These basic requirements have significant implications on the ETL process.

What a Dimension Load Must Achieve

The process of loading a dimension table must incorporate the following major requirements:

- Extract source data from source(s)
- Assemble the dimensional attributes
- Identify new and changed dimension records
- Manage surrogate keys
- Process new records
- Process type 1 changes
- Process type 2 changes

These activities will not necessarily occur in the order listed, but every load incorporates them in some way. While the list appears relatively simple, complexity is lurking just beneath the surface. Processing new and changed records, for example, requires identifying what records have changed. As you have learned, what constitutes a change may be quite different in a source system versus a star. Natural keys will play a central role in sorting this out.

In order to study the complexities of the dimension load, it is helpful to break it down into a series of steps that can be discussed individually. The process flow in Figure 17-2 will guide the discussion. This diagram decomposes the processing of a dimension table into a series of activities. This entire set of activities must be executed for *each* dimension table in a star.

These fundamental activities are part of every ETL architecture, although they may be organized and sequenced in radically different ways. For example, implementation of a changed data identification system allows the identification of new records to occur prior to extraction. Likewise, the capabilities of a packaged ETL tool may enable processing of various types of slow changes within a single step.

This process will be discussed in the context of a nightly batch load. These same activities are necessary, however, even when processing data in real time. The organization of the activities may be different, but the same fundamental processing takes place.

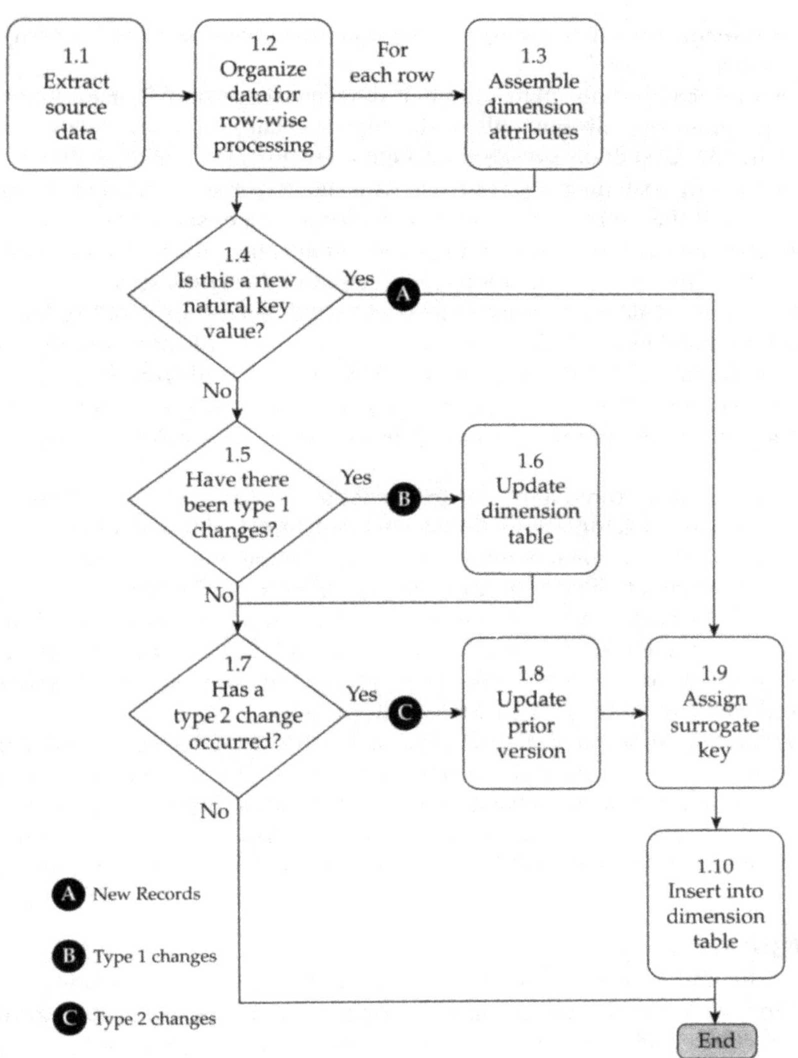

Figure 17-2 Loading a dimension table

Preparing Records for Processing

In order to process dimensional data, it must be obtained from the source and assembled into a dimensional format as required by the target table's design. These activities are represented by the first three steps in Figure 17-2.

Step 1.1 calls for the acquisition of the source data needed to load the dimension. In a Corporate Information Factory, most dimension tables will have a single source: the enterprise data warehouse. In other architectures, it is possible for a dimension table to have multiple sources. A dimension table with multiple sources may require multiple extraction processes, with additional processing to consolidate the information extracted into a single pool of records for processing. Or, separate load processes may be designed for each of the sources.

Source data may be acquired through a number of means. For example, mainframe data may be extracted programmatically into a file or through specialized utilities. Relational data may be extracted directly via SQL or provided through an export file. Real-time data may arrive through a messaging system or a web service. External data may be supplied online or through batch extracts. If the source data is relational, distinct values should be queried to avoid unnecessary processing. If it is nonrelational, developers may choose to bulk-load it into a relational staging area so SQL operations can be used in this initial step.

Once extracted, source data often needs to be reorganized so it can be processed one row at a time. This is represented by step 1.2. Source data may need to be pivoted or transposed, so that all the elements that constitute a dimension record are in a single row. In many cases, little work needs to be done, but in other cases this step may call for intensive processing. Hierarchical data structures may require flattening, denormalized data structures may require pivoting, and so forth.

Once the source data is captured and restructured as a series of rows, step 1.3 takes each row of source data and assembles the dimensional attributes. This is a matter of applying transformation rules as spelled out in the design documentation. Codes may be decoded into descriptive values. Fields with multi-part attributes may be split into a series of attributes. Sets of fields may be concatenated. NULL field values may be replaced with more understandable text such as "unavailable" or "unknown." The case and format of attributes may be adjusted, and so forth. This task might also be broken down to include data cleansing tasks, such as name and address standardization.

In simple cases, it may be possible to execute tasks 1.1 through 1.3 with a single SQL statement; other cases may be significantly more complex. Once these first three tasks are completed, one or more potential dimension records are ready for further processing. The next several tasks will determine how each record is handled. New records, type 1 changes, and type 2 changes must all be processed. Some records may include both type 1 and type 2 changes.

Processing New Records

New records are those that have a natural key that has not been previously encountered in the star. When a new record is identified, it must be assigned a surrogate key and inserted into the dimension table. In Figure 17-2, these records are identified and processed in steps 1.4, 1.9, and 1.10.

To determine whether an incoming record is new, step 1.4 searches for its natural key in the dimension table. This check is often referred to as a *lookup.* If the natural key value is not found in the existing table, the record is new. Step 1.9 assigns the next available surrogate key to the record, and step 1.10 loads it into the dimension table. If, on the other hand, a record is found during step 1.4, then the natural key is already present in the dimension. The record must be further examined to determine if it has undergone type 1 or type 2 changes.

As previously mentioned, a changed data identification system may obviate the need to look for new records after extracting data. These solutions monitor the source directly, identifying new and changed data prior to extraction. The same requirements must be met, however: it is necessary to extract the source data and process the new records.

TIP New dimension records have a natural key value that has not previously been encountered. They can be identified by looking up the natural key value of a source record in the existing dimension table. If a match does not exist, a new record has been identified.

The sample data in Figure 17-3 contains an example of a new source record that must be added to an existing product dimension table. The top part of the figure shows the design of the product dimension. It contains a surrogate key called product_key—a single

Design of PRODUCT dimension table:

PRODUCT	
product_key	SK
sku	NK
product_name	1
brand_code	2
brand_manager	2
⋮	
current_version	HK

<u>Legend:</u>

SK Surrogate Key
NK Natural Key
1 Type 1 Change (Overwrite)
2 Type 2 Change (Insert new record)
HK Housekeeping Column (Internal use)

Existing content of PRODUCT Dimension Table:

SK	NK	1	2	2	HK
product_key	sku	product_name	brand_code	brand_manager	current_version
22	A-0033	Flat Box 12"	110	Lei, Michelle	Current
344	A-1011	Packing Tape	221	Jones, Paul	Current
1001	B-3691	Twine Spool	501	Smith, Dei	Not Current
1201	B-3691	Twine Spool	501	Klein, Pete	Not Current
2700	B-3691	Twine Spool	702	Jones, Fay	Current
2711	Z-3320	Envelope A5	109	Harvey, Ned	Current

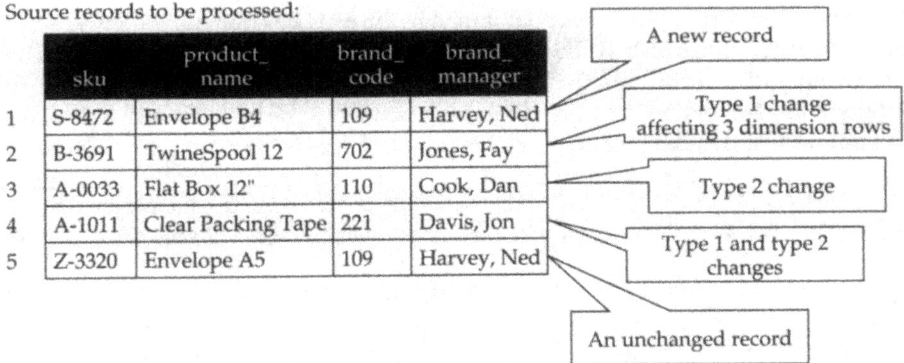

Source records to be processed:

	sku	product_name	brand_code	brand_manager
1	S-8472	Envelope B4	109	Harvey, Ned
2	B-3691	TwineSpool 12	702	Jones, Fay
3	A-0033	Flat Box 12"	110	Cook, Dan
4	A-1011	Clear Packing Tape	221	Davis, Jon
5	Z-3320	Envelope A5	109	Harvey, Ned

Figure 17-3 Processing the product dimension

attribute that uniquely identifies a row in the dimension table. The natural key SKU (an acronym for "stock keeping unit") uniquely identifies a product in the source system. The designation of the remaining attributes indicates how to respond if a change occurs on the source—type 1 changes will result in overwrites; type 2 changes will trigger the insertion of a new row. Because type 2 changes are possible, a single product may have multiple rows in the dimension. The housekeeping column current_version indicates which is current.

Beneath the table diagram, an instance grid shows the current content of the product table. Each time the load is executed, this table must be modified with new and changed data. Right now, it contains several rows of data. If you look closely, you will see that these five rows correspond to four products in the source system: SKUs A-0033, A-1011, B-3691, and Z-3320. The Twine Spool (B-3691) appears three times, presumably because it has already undergone some slow changes. One of these versions is flagged as "Current."

The bottom of the diagram shows some source records that are being processed as part of a nightly load. These records have already passed through the first three steps in the flow, which fetched the source data and assembled what is shown. The first record in this group bears the SKU S-8472. Step 1.4 in the dimension load process calls for searching the existing dimension table for this natural key value. For S-8472, the lookup does not find a match; the record is new. The warehouse has never encountered this SKU before. It will be assigned a surrogate key (step 1.9) and be added to the product dimension table (step 1.10).

Each of the remaining SKUs in the example is already represented in the product dimension table. They must now be examined to determine whether they contain type 1 or type 2 changes.

Processing Type 1 Changes

Every record that is not new may contain type 1 changes. When a type 1 attribute changes on the source side, it is overwritten in the data warehouse. To identify a type 1 change, an incoming record is matched to the current record in the warehouse for the natural key value. The type 1 attributes are compared. If they do not match, a type 1 change has been identified. In Figure 17-2, this comparison is performed in step 1.5.

In the example data from Figure 17-3, each record with a natural key that is present in the dimension table must be checked for type 1 changes. This requires finding the current record for the natural key value and comparing the type 1 attributes. This can be accomplished via a lookup as well. If the type 1 attributes do not match, the SKU has undergone a type 1 change. The second source record, SKU B-3691, has a type 1 attribute value that does not match the current corresponding record in the product table. The product_name has changed from "Twine Spool" to "TwineSpool 12." The dimension table must be updated with this change; processing flows through the branch of the diagram labeled "B."

TIP Type 1 changes can be identified by comparing the source record to the current dimension record for the natural key value. If any type 1 attributes do not match, a type 1 change has occurred.

Type 1 changes must be applied to *all* corresponding warehouse records with the same natural key. There may be more than one dimension row corresponding to the source record that has changed, because it may already have undergone type 2 changes. In step 1.6

of Figure 17-2, type 1 changes are applied to all existing dimension table records that share the natural key value—not the current version only.

In the case of SKU B-3691, the dimension table contains *three* corresponding records. Past changes to the SKU's brand_manager, a type 2 attribute, have resulted in numerous versions of this product. For all three versions of B-3691, the product_name must be updated. Updating only the current version would be a serious error, since all versions may be connected to facts in the fact table.

TIP It is necessary to apply a type 1 change to *every row* in the dimension table that shares the same natural key. Applying it only to the current version results in inconsistent facts.

Once the type 1 change has been applied, processing for the source record is not complete. It must also be checked to see whether any type 2 changes have occurred. Likewise, any records that did not contain a type 1 change must also be checked for type 2 changes. Both branches out of step 1.5 in Figure 17-2 therefore lead into step 1.7.

This example conveys the basic principle behind type 1 processing, but reality can be far more complex. As noted in Chapter 3, a type 1 change to an attribute that is not completely dependent on the natural key will require more complex processing. See the sidebar "Type 1 Complexity" for more information.

Type 1 Complexity

When a dimension table contains a type 1 attribute that is not fully dependent on the natural key, simple comparison to the existing dimension record is not sufficient to determine if an update is needed.

For example, suppose the table in Figure 17-3 also contains a brand_name column. Brand_name is determined by brand_code. It is therefore only partially dependent on the product's natural key. Suppose that brand_name is designated as a type 1 attribute. If the brand_name of an existing product changes, this may *or may not* call for an overwrite. It is necessary to determine if the brand_code, a type 2 attribute, has also changed. If so, the product has been assigned a new brand, and a new row is required. There has been no type 1 change. If the brand_code has not changed, however, the new brand_name is indicative of a type 1 change.

It is important that dimensional designers be cognizant of the increased ETL complexity that will be necessitated by attributes like this. In order to avoid this situation, designers may choose to forgo the use of type 1 attributes that do not correspond to the grain of the dimension. As noted in Chapters 3 and 15, type 1 attributes can also increase the complexity involved in maintaining aggregates or cubes.

If the use of such an attribute *is* necessary, design documentation must carefully spell out the dependency of the attribute so that ETL developers can process it correctly. Notice that in a snowflake design, the ETL challenge is slightly mitigated because the attributes of brand will be in a separate table.

Processing Type 2 Changes

After type 1 changes have been identified and applied, the source record must be checked for type 2 changes. In Figure 17-2, this takes place in step 1.7. This task can be accomplished by a third lookup, using the combination of the natural key and all type 2 attributes. If a match is found in the dimension table, the incoming record is properly represented and processing is complete. If it is not found, a type 2 change has occurred. The prior record is no longer current, so step 1.8 is used to update its current_version to "Not Current." The new version is assigned a surrogate key (step 1.9) and is loaded into the warehouse table (step 1.10).

TIP Type 2 changes can be identified by comparing a source record to dimension records that have the same natural key. If there is no corresponding record with the same values for all type 2 attributes, a type 2 change has occurred.

Look at the sample data in the bottom of Figure 17-3. The third row of source data contains the SKU A-0033. This SKU is represented in the product table, but its brand_manager has been changed. This requires the insertion of a new row into the product dimension table.

A single record can contain both type 1 and type 2 changes. In Figure 17-3, the fourth SKU to be processed, number A-1011, has undergone changes in product_name and brand_manager. The product_name change is handled via a type 1 response, calling for the existing dimension row to be updated. The new brand_manager is a type 2 change, which requires a new record to be inserted for the SKU. This explains why step 1.6 is connected to step 1.7, and not to the end of the process flow.

TIP A source record can contain both type 1 and type 2 changes. It is a grave error to consider this an either/or proposition.

Source records that do not contain any changes may pass all the way through this process without any impact on the dimension table. The last record to be processed in Figure 17-3, SKU Z-3320, is already present in the dimension table (step 1.4), the corresponding record has the same values for the type 1 attributes (step 1.5), and also has the same values for all type 2 attributes (step 1.7). As you will see, performing changed data identification at the source can prevent having to perform these checks.

Loading the Fact Table

The fact table load process takes transactions from the source system, calculates facts, identifies the appropriate foreign keys, and inserts records into the star. The most complex part of this process involves identification of the appropriate foreign key values. Source systems supply only a natural key, but the fact table must use foreign keys to refer to the dimensions. For each fact in a source system, the natural keys that identify dimensional context must be replaced by surrogate keys that identify rows in dimension tables. Because type 2 changes are possible, there may be multiple rows in the dimension table for a particular value. Figuring out which surrogate key to use is an important task and may be assisted by some schema design tweaks.

What a Fact Table Load Must Achieve

Much of the difficult work of loading a star schema is done in the dimension loads, where slow change processing is performed. Relative to the dimension load, the fact table load may seem simple. The fact table load is governed by the following requirements:

- Extract data from the source systems
- Compute the facts
- Aggregate facts to match the grain of the fact table
- Obtain surrogate keys for each of the dimensions
- Load fact table records into the warehouse

A process flow supporting these requirements is depicted in Figure 17-4. Once again, this is a logical breakdown, meant to guide the discussion of the load process. The specific tasks and techniques used will vary based on source and target systems and design, the capabilities of the ETL tool being used, and developer preferences.

Preparing Records for Processing

The first step is the extraction of the source data, step 2.1 in Figure 17-4. As in the dimension table load process, acquisition of source data may take place in a number of different ways, depending on the systems and tools available. The information needed to load a transaction into the fact table includes the data elements that will be used to create the facts and the natural keys that will be used to identify associated dimensions. This information should be enumerated as part of the design documentation for the warehouse schema, as described in Chapter 18.

After source data has been acquired, it may be necessary to restructure the data so it can be processed one row at a time. This is represented by step 2.2 in Figure 17-4. For example, some facts may be stored in a series of repeating groups that represent different dimensional qualifications of the same fact. This data must be transposed into a format that represents the structure required in the data warehouse. In the top portion of Figure 17-5, product orders appear in separate columns for each salesperson. Each record must be transformed into a set of records for individual salespeople.

In another common situation, source systems provide each fact in a separate record. The records must be combined into a single row that contains each of the facts for a given

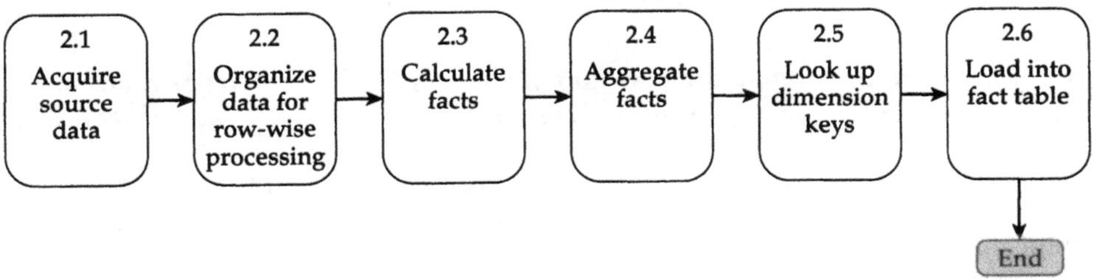

Figure 17-4 Loading a fact table

date	sku	adams	benson	chiu	roberson
1/8/2009	A-1011	744.00	1,222.00	3,011.11	0
1/8/2009	Z-3320	100.00	0	600.00	200.00

date	sku	salesperson	order_dollars
1/8/2009	A-1011	Adams	744.00
1/8/2009	Z-3320	Adams	100.00
1/8/2009	A-1011	Benson	1,222.00
1/8/2009	A-1011	Chiu	3,011.11
1/8/2009	Z-3320	Chiu	600.00
1/8/2009	Z-3320	Roberson	200.00

---

date	order_line	sku	type	value
1/8/2009	Q1977-001	A-0033	Sales Dollars	10,000.00
1/8/2009	Q1977-001	A-0033	Margin Dollars	2,000.00
1/8/2009	Q1977-001	A-0033	Quantity Ordered	100
1/8/2009	Q1977-002	B-3691	Sales Dollars	14,000.00
1/8/2009	Q1977-002	B-3691	Margin Dollars	700.00
1/8/2009	Q1977-002	B-3691	Quantity Ordered	70

date	order_line	sku	sales_dollars	margin_dollars	quantity_ordered
1/8/2009	Q1977-001	A-0033	10,000.00	2,000.00	100
1/8/2009	Q1977-002	B-3691	14,000.00	700.00	70

Figure 17-5 Organizing source data for row-by-row processing

event or transaction. In the bottom portion of Figure 17-5, source data provides sales_dollars, margin_dollars, and quantity_ordered in separate rows. For each order line, these records must be consolidated into a single row.

After data is extracted and transposed, facts must be calculated from the data provided by the source system. The additive fact order_dollars, for example, may be constructed by multiplying the source attributes unit_price and quantity. This activity is represented by step 2.3 in Figure 17-4. Calculation of facts can be more complex, and should be documented as part of the schema design.

If the source data is provided at a finer grain than is required by the fact table, it must also be aggregated. For each distinct set of natural key values, the individual source transactions are summarized. Care must be taken not to aggregate semi-additive facts improperly; it is assumed nonadditive facts have been broken down into fully additive components in the schema design. In Figure 17-4, aggregation is performed by step 2.4.

TIP Fact processing begins by acquiring the source data, transposing it as necessary, computing facts, and aggregating them if needed.

Where there are multiple source systems, this process may be repeated for each. Alternatively, the initial extractions may be performed separately, with extracted data consolidated into a single staging area. Subsequent tasks are then performed using this consolidated data set.

When there is a single source that is relational, these first four steps may be carried out in a single query. The query selects the relevant natural keys and then aggregates and calculates facts. The next step will be to assign surrogate keys.

Identification of Surrogate Keys

Each transaction from the source system is extracted with natural key values that describe its context. In fact tables, the foreign keys that refer to dimension tables do not contain natural key values. The source values must be replaced by surrogate key values in order to load the record into the fact table. This process is represented by step 2.5 in Figure 17-4. It must be done once for each dimension referred to by the fact table.

Identification of the surrogate key values is carried out as a lookup process. The dimension table is searched for a row that contains the natural key value provided by the source system. Once the appropriate dimension record is found, its surrogate key is obtained. Unfortunately, this activity is a bit more complicated than it sounds.

For example, suppose you are loading facts into an orders star. One of the dimensions in the star is product. The top portion of Figure 17-6 shows some orders that are being processed to load into the fact table. For each order, you must use the product's natural key to figure out what product_key goes in the fact table. You'll need to do something similar to choose a day_key and customer_key as well.

In the source system, each product is identified by its SKU. This natural key was extracted with the transaction data during the first step of the load process. In Figure 17-6, the first record to be processed bears SKU S-8472. In the dimension table, the SKU column is searched for this value. This is represented by arrow "A." The value S-8472 is found; the corresponding row is shaded. This row contains product_key 2799. This key is added to the fact record, as represented by arrow "B." The same kind of lookup must be performed to obtain a date_key, customer_key, and salesrep_key.

This process is complicated by the presence of type 2 slowly changing dimensions. If type 2 changes have occurred in the dimension table, more than one row may be found during the lookup. In the example from Figure 17-6, this happens with the second order transaction to be processed. It bears SKU B-3691, which appears in the product dimension table three times. It will be necessary to figure out which of these three is the correct version for the order in question.

Orders being processed for FACT load:

	date	order_ dollars	margin_ dollars	customer_ id	salesrep_ id	sku	product_ key
1	3/12/2010	1,700.22	643.06	2201	1197	S-8472	2799
2	3/12/2010	984.31	201.64	3832	1197	B-3691	

A B

PRODUCT Dimension Table:

SK	NK	1	2	2	HK
product_ key	sku	product_ name	brand_ code	brand_ manager	current_ version
22	A-0033	Flat Box 12"	110	Lei, Michelle	Not Current
1192	A-0033	Flat Box 12"	110	Cook, Dan	Current
344	A-1011	Clear Packing Tape	221	Jones, Paul	Not Current
2828	A-1011	Clear Packing Tape	221	Davis, Jon	Current
1001	B-3691	TwineSpool 12	501	Smith, Dei	Not Current
1201	B-3691	TwineSpool 12	501	Klein, Pete	Not Current
2700	B-3691	TwineSpool 12	702	Jones, Fay	Current
2799	**S-8472**	Envelope B4	109	Harvey, Ned	Current
3001	Z-3320	Envelope A5	109	Harvey, Ned	Current

Figure 17-6 Looking up surrogate keys

To guarantee the correct dimension key, the lookup must be refined in one of several ways:

- If the dimension design includes a current_record column, this can be used to identify the correct version.
- If the dimension design includes effective and expiration dates, the transaction date can be compared with these dates to identify the correct version.
- If neither of these design features is available, all type 2 attributes must be extracted with source transactions along with natural keys, and they will be used in the lookup process.

In the case of SKU B-3691, the first method can be used. The dimension table has three records for this SKU, but only one is labeled "Current." Assuming this status is updated on the same schedule as transactions are processed, this is the version we need. It has the product_key value 2700.

If a source record can undergo multiple significant type 2 changes between loads, or if it will be necessary to load past history into the fact table, this procedure will be ineffective. Knowing which version of a product is current at the end of the day is not enough to determine which should be assigned to a transaction. It will be necessary to replace the current_flag in the dimension design with an effective date and time and expiration date and time. These values can be used to pinpoint the precise version of the product record that was in effect at the time of each transaction.

If the dimension design allows for type 2 changes and does not include a current_version or time stamps, the lookup will be much more complicated. It will be necessary to include all the type 2 attributes in the lookup. In this example, it would necessitate knowing the brand_code and brand_name associated with each transaction. These attribute values would be included in the product lookup.

TIP Before transactions can be inserted into a fact table, they must be assigned the appropriate foreign key values. For each dimension, the natural key value associated with the transaction is used as an index into the dimension table, and the corresponding surrogate key is retrieved.

If type 2 changes are allowed, a natural key value may appear in the dimension more than once. The lookup must be supplemented to identify the correct version. Dimension design can aid this process:

- Adding a current_version column to the dimension makes it easy to identify the most recent version for a natural key value.
- Adding effective and expiration dates makes it easy to identify the correct version for a natural key value at any point in time.

If neither of these mechanisms is available, it will be necessary to fetch all type 2 attributes with source transactions and include all of them in the lookup process.

Optimizing the Load

Developers are almost always under pressure to develop a load process that is fast and efficient. For loads that operate in a batch, the available time window is likely to be shared with processes that construct derived and aggregate tables, build cubes, rebuild indexes, execute scheduled reports, and cache their results. For a real-time load, the continuous flow of new transactions results in a similar requirement for processing efficiency.

Various kinds of bottlenecks are possible when loading a star schema, but some are fundamental. These result from the need to perform slow change processing. In the worst-case scenario, it is necessary to inspect each source record for new and changed dimensions. Doing so may require as many as three different comparisons to data in the dimension table, as Figure 17-2 illustrated. For example, each time the product dimension is updated, it may be necessary to review all products in the source system for new records (step 1.4), type 1 changes (step 1.5), and type 2 changes (step 1.7). Some of these comparisons, in turn, may be resource-intensive. Finding type 2 changes to a customer record, for example, may require comparing dozens of type 2 attributes.

The fundamental bottlenecks of slow change processing can be addressed in two ways: reduce the amount of data to be processed, and simplify the necessary processing. Many packaged ETL solutions offer features that work on these principles, and hand-coded solutions can be developed as well. Other kinds of optimization, such as parallelization, do not address these bottlenecks directly, but they can multiply the benefits of solutions that do.

Changed Data Identification

One way to improve load performance is to reduce the amount of data that must be processed. Usually, only a small percentage of source records contain new or changed data. To find those that do, it is necessary to process all of them. If new and changed records can be identified ahead of time, the volume of data that must be processed can be dramatically reduced.

For example, suppose a customer dimension table is updated on a nightly basis. The source system contains a customer file with 200,000 records. This file must be processed every night, even though less than 1 percent of the customers are new or changed. If this handful of records can be identified in advance, the number that must be processed is reduced from 200,000 to less than 2,000.

New and changed data can be detected in many ways. Some source systems do so automatically, logging and time-stamping changes to key entities. Loading a corresponding dimension is greatly simplified by leveraging these time stamps. For relational systems that do not do this, it may be possible to make use of triggers or stored procedures to generate a change log for key entities. This requires some development effort, and may intrude on the performance of the source system. Some databases offer native logging capabilities that can be exploited for the same effect. ETL developers may also choose to maintain a staging area, where the data extract for each load iteration is compared to that of the previous iteration. With sorted data sets, this comparison can take place very quickly.

The benefits of changed data identification must be balanced with the costs of developing and maintaining the solution, as well as any impact it has on the source system itself. In some cases, the added benefit may not be justified over processing the entire dimension. In others it may be worthwhile to invest time and resources into logging new and changed data.

TIP Identification of new and changed source data can increase load efficiency by reducing the number of source records to be processed. The magnitude of this benefit must be balanced with its impact on the source system, the size of the load window, and the cost to develop and maintain the solution.

In a data warehouse based on Inmon's Corporate Information Factory architecture, the source data for dimensional data marts is the enterprise data warehouse. This atomic repository of data has already been extracted from source systems and integrated, and changed records are usually logged and time-stamped. This takes a significant burden off the shoulders of the developers charged with loading star schema data marts, providing a single source of source data with logged changes. This benefit does not come free of charge. The work of identifying the changes still takes place—it is part of the process that maintains the enterprise data warehouse. In addition, there may be less time available in the processing window to update the dimensional schema.

Real-time load processing can also benefit from the identification of new and changed data. When changes to the sources of dimensions are propagated to a load process in real time, extraneous dimensional processing is avoided. It would otherwise be necessary to check associated dimensional data each time a transaction occurs, producing a drag on the process that inserts new facts into the star.

Simplifying Processing

Another way to optimize slow change processing is to simplify it. As Figure 17-2 illustrated, as many as three different lookups or comparisons may be necessary for each source record: looking for new records (step 1.4), looking for type 1 changes (step 1.5), and looking for type 2 changes (step 1.7). Each of these lookups requires comparing one or more columns of a source record to corresponding records in the dimension table.

Eliminating Lookups

Developers may be able to squeeze performance out of the process by eliminating one or more of these lookups. For example, new records are handled in much the same way as type 2 changes: by inserting data into the table. It is possible to forgo the first lookup, allowing new records to be processed through the same steps that identify type 2 changes. Similarly, developers may be able to save time by assuming that all source records contain type 1 changes, skipping the comparison. Issuing an update for each source record may save time if a large number of type 1 changes are expected, or if the database has an "upsert" capability that can combine this with processing new records.

Caching Lookups

Most lookups cannot be eliminated, but they can be optimized. One way to optimize a lookup is to load the entire dimension into primary memory while the ETL process is running, or to load the columns involved in comparisons. This technique is variously called *pinning* or *caching*. It ensures that lookups will take place quickly. This benefit is offset by the amount of time it takes to load the data into primary memory. The time it takes depends both on the number of rows that must be cached, as well as the number of columns. In addition, dimension processing may result in new or changed rows; these must be maintained in the cache as well.

Simplifying Lookups with Hash Functions

The efficiency of a lookup can also be enhanced by reducing the number of columns that must be compared. This can be achieved by using a hash function.

Determining whether a type 2 change has occurred normally requires comparing the type 2 attributes of a source record with the corresponding attributes in the dimension table. If a customer dimension table has 75 type 2 attributes, all 75 of them must be checked. This may require undue processing resources or make caching impractical. A hash function can reduce the number of columns compared to one.

A hash function, when applied to a string of data, produces a comparatively compact string or number. This value is referred to as a hash value or checksum. The same hash function will always provide the same hash value when applied to the same string of data. This principle can be used to simplify lookup processing. The 75 type 2 attributes of each customer, for example, can be concatenated to a single string, to which a hash function is applied. The resulting hash values are stored with each customer row in the dimension table. An example involving 12 attributes is illustrated in Figure 17-7.

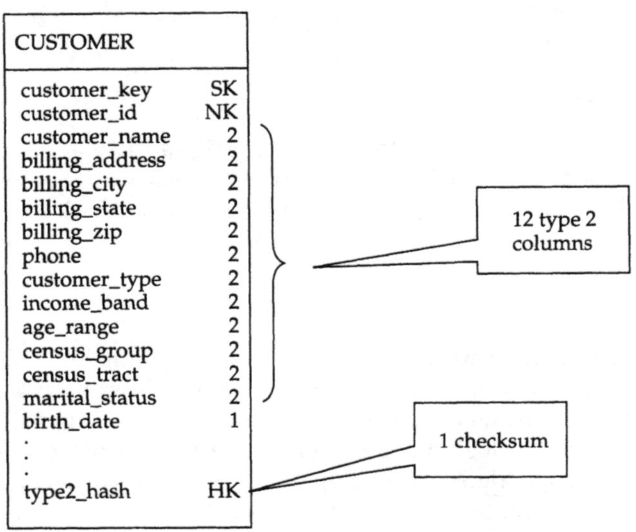

Figure 17-7 A checksum for 12 type 2 attributes

With this solution in place, source records can be tested for changes without comparing all the type 2 attributes to content in the dimension table. Instead, the hash function is applied to the source record. The resulting hash value is compared to the one stored in the dimension table. This greatly simplifies the lookup process, requiring the comparison of a single value rather than all the type 2 attributes. This also facilitates caching when the number of type 2 columns would have rendered it impractical. It is not necessary to cache the entire dimension table; all that is needed are the natural key, hash value, and surrogate key. An additional hash value may be computed on the type 1 attributes.

TIP Lookups involving large numbers of columns may be simplified using hash functions. A hash value is computed and stored for each dimension record. The same function can be applied to source data, so that lookups only involve the hash value.

This benefit, of course, is not free. In exchange for forgoing comparison of a large number of attributes, it will be necessary to compute hash values for each dimension record, and for each source record being processed. In addition, there is the risk of collisions—situations in which a hash function returns the same value for two different strings of data. A hash algorithm must be selected that renders this possibility sufficiently small.

Cleansing Data

The load process is often called upon to clean up source data. Many data cleansing tasks can be sensibly automated as part of the load process. Some, however, are best left for cleanup at the operational source. Some basic principles help distinguish the former from the latter.

When data is to be cleansed, it is necessary to have a set of rules that describe what must occur. In some cases, it is possible to define simple data-driven requirements in tabular format. These may be instantiated as physical tables, allowing the rules to be maintained separately from ETL code. However, this separation may also hamper processing efficiency.

Frequently, the ETL process will encounter a fact for which it cannot identify valid dimensional detail. Failure to load this data may result in inconsistencies between the star schema and the operational systems. Special techniques can be employed that allow it to be loaded in the absence of critical dimensional detail, so that the two systems are reconciled. This will require taking measures that allow the facts to be adjusted once the required detail is available.

What Should Be Cleaned Up

Data can be changed, or cleaned up, in a variety of ways. Some kinds of cleansing are best done as part of the process that loads the data warehouse, while some are not. It is reasonable, for example, to standardize the formatting of phone numbers while loading a star schema. On the other hand, it is definitely not a good idea to reassign an order transaction from one salesperson to another. These are black and white extremes, but in between lies a gray area. What should one do, for example, if a salesperson was entered inconsistently? How does one sort out the kind of cleansing that is reasonable from that which is not? The answer lies in the fundamentals of data warehousing.

The purpose of a data warehouse system is to provide operational data that has been restructured for analysis. It provides facts that are consistent with what is represented in operational. Changing the meaning of facts or creating new facts as part of the load process goes beyond this simple mission, providing a view of the business that is inconsistent with that provided by operational systems. This situation calls into question the validity of the data warehouse and erodes user confidence.

TIP Creating data is not the province of the data warehouse. All information should be drawn from operational and reference sources. If the data warehouse provides facts that are inconsistent with operational systems, users will lack confidence in its accuracy.

This simple guideline can be used to evaluate which kinds of information should be cleaned up as part of the load process, and which types should not. When evaluating any cleansing activity, ask yourself: "Will this action result in a fact that is consistent with operational data?" If so, the proposed cleansing activity is probably reasonable. If not, it should probably be avoided.

Consider, for example, the activities that are usually involved in constructing a rich set of dimension attributes. Examples include concatenation of source values, reformatting of phone numbers and addresses, supplementing codes with associated reference text, or transforming Boolean flags into descriptive text. These best practices produce a rich and descriptive set of dimension attributes, as described in Chapter 3. They do not change the meaning of facts; the end result presents facts that are consistent with operational systems. This kind of activity is a sensible and useful part of the load process.

Now consider processing an order that was assigned to the incorrect salesperson. If you know of this error, does it make sense to correct it as part of the ETL process? This time, the answer is no. Such an action would result in a fact that is inconsistent with the operational data. The source system would show order dollars associated with one salesperson, while the star would show order dollars associated with a different person. If, on the other hand, the reassignment of the order is also captured somewhere in a source system, then the data warehouse would provide a representation that is consistent.

Ralph Kimball and Margy Ross make this important point using a vivid metaphor. They describe the process of loading the data warehouse as one of *publishing* information, as opposed to operational systems that create information. You can use this metaphor to guide decisions about data cleansing, even if you have not implemented Kimball and Ross's recommended data warehouse architecture. Even in a Corporate Information Factory or stand-alone data mart, your goal should be to publish data, not manufacture it.

Staying out of the business of manufacturing data will help ensure user confidence in the data warehouse. As an added bonus, the star schema will shine a light on issues with source data, serving as an impetus for efforts to correct these problems. These activities will range from the simple correction of invalid data to system enhancements that alter the way information is collected. The star schema becomes a tool for managing the cleanup of operational data and a means to view the progress of such efforts.

Cleaning Up Dimensional Data

A change to data that does not produce an inconsistent view of the facts is a valid candidate for automation. To automate changes, it must be possible to express them using a set of rules. These rules can be incorporated into the schema design documentation and automated by the ETL process. Examples of schema documentation that capture transformation rules can be found in Chapter 18.

In many cases, it is possible to define data-driven transformation rules. These may be expressed as tables that link expected values with corresponding translations. Figure 17-8, for example, illustrates a table that documents the standardization of data elements from disparate systems. Systems 001 and 002, both capture brand codes, but they use different representations. This table maps source-specific brand numbers to standardized corporate codes. Performing this translation of values does not change the meaning of any associated transactions, as long as the rules accurately reflect how the various brand codes are mapped to the standard corporate list.

source_ system	source_ element_name	source_ element_value	warehouse_ element_name	warehouse_ element_value
001	brand_id	100	brand_code	100
002	brand_num	B-100-09	brand_code	100
001	brand_id	200	brand_code	200
002	brand_num	B-200-12	brand_code	200

Figure 17-8 A table maps the disparate representation of brand codes

When data transformation rules can be expressed in this manner, it may be attractive to build a database table that the ETL tool can use as part of the transformation process. This has the advantage of removing processing rules from the actual ETL code. A change in the way a source system records a brand code would not require reworking the ETL process—all that is necessary is to update a row in the table. As you have already learned, however, lookups into database tables can be expensive in terms of processing. Hard-coding these rules directly into the ETL process may be necessary to ensure maximum performance. The table still serves as useful documentation. It is a valuable reference for ETL developers and quality assurance analysts.

Facts with Invalid Details

The load process often collects transactions from one operational system, while attendant detail comes from another. An order entry system, for example, may be the source for the fact table in the orders star, while the product dimension is loaded from a master product file. In situations like this, it is possible that the ETL process may receive a transaction with invalid reference data. An order arrives, for example, with a product_code that cannot be validated. This may occur because the order entry system propagates new products to the orders file on a delayed schedule, or simply because the warehouse processed the information out of sequence.

The order in question may be rejected from the star and saved in an exception log, where it will remain until it can be validated. However, failure to load the transaction will result in an inconsistent representation of orders. Total order dollars in the star will be different from what is reflected in the source system. Exclusion of the order also means that *valid* characteristics of the transaction, such as the salesperson associated with the order, are excluded from the star as well, even though they are known.

The solution to this dilemma requires three elements. First, a special row is added to the dimension. It will be referred to by facts that cannot be validated. Second, a transaction identifier must be stored somewhere in the star. This will allow the fact to be corrected later, once the value is validated. Last, a means must be in place to associate the transaction with the data value that could not be validated. This can be used to automate the update of the fact once the value has been incorporated into the dimension.

In the case of the invalid product, a solution is depicted in Figure 17-9. First, a special row is placed in the product table to designate invalid products. This technique was introduced in Chapter 6. In the example, this row has the product_key value 0, and each of its attributes contains a value indicating "invalid." When a transaction is encountered that cannot be validated against the product table, this product key can be used to load it into the fact table. This allows the fact table to represent total orders, orders by date, orders by salesrep, and so forth, even if the product is not known.

The fact table itself includes the order_line_id, which identifies the transaction. This will allow the order to be identified and corrected once a product has been added to the dimension for the failed product code. An exception table is not strictly required, but it will help in automating this correction process. It contains the value that failed validation, and the transaction identifier that can be used to find the fact table row.

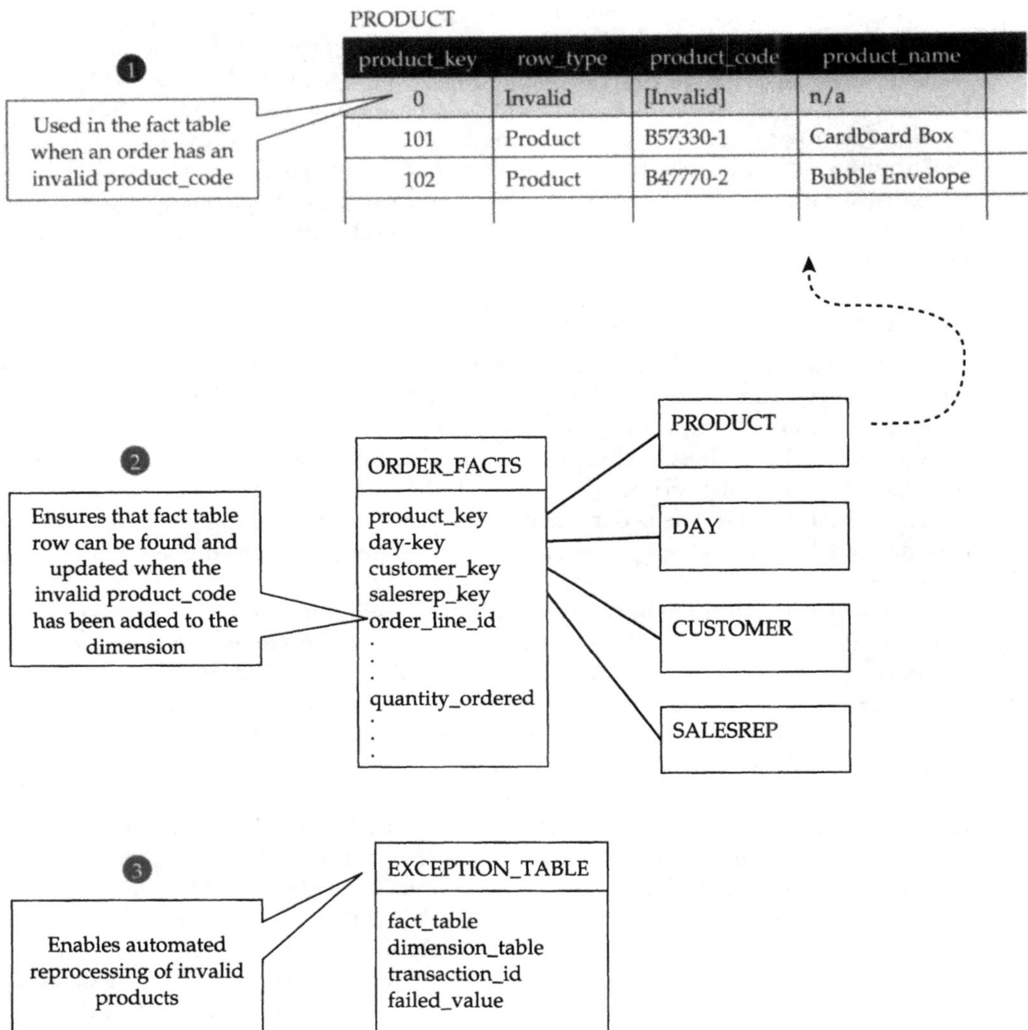

Figure 17-9 Dealing with invalid product codes

TIP Special case dimension rows for invalid data are useful when transactions may be presented to the load process without valid dimensional context. The transaction can be loaded into the fact table and linked to the special case row in the dimension. A transaction identifier must be present in the star so the value can be adjusted once the data element becomes known and validated.

A variation on this approach stores the failed value directly in the dimension table, as part of a row that is flagged as row_type = "Invalid." This may simplify aspects of the processing, and eliminates the need for an exception table. It may also result in a large number of invalid rows appearing in dimension tables; the design team will need to evaluate the pros and cons.

Delayed processing of slow changes introduces a similar challenge. In this case, what appears to be the correct dimension record when the fact is loaded is later displaced by a change that arrives after the fact. This situation can be accommodated by making use of time-stamped dimensions, as discussed in Chapter 6. Whenever new "versions" of a record are added to the dimension, they are stamped with an effective date. Existing facts for the natural key value are scanned; any with transaction times that occurred after the updated version became effective are updated.

Housekeeping Columns

A discussion on the relationship of dimensional design and the ETL process would not be complete without touching on the various kinds of housekeeping columns that may prove useful in a dimensional design. Mentioned throughout this book, housekeeping columns in a dimension table are generally not intended for end-user consumption. Rather, they are added to aid specific ETL or reporting activities. Similar housekeeping information can be attached to each row of a fact table as well.

CUSTOMER	
customer_key	SK
customer_id	NK
customer_name	2
billing_address	2
billing_city	2
billing_state	2
billing_zip	2
phone	2
customer_type	2
income_band	2
age_range	2
census_group	2
census_tract	2
marital_status	2
birth_date	1
. . .	
current_version	HK
effective_date	HK
expiration_date	HK
type2_hash	HK
type1_hash	HK
creation_date	HK
update_date	HK
update_process	HK

(Housekeeping Columns: current_version through update_process)

Figure 17-10 Housekeeping columns in a dimension table

Housekeeping Columns in Dimension Tables

Each column in a dimension table is a surrogate key, a natural key, or a dimension attribute. As you learned in Chapter 3, dimension attributes are normally classified as type 1 and type 2, although it is possible that a single attribute can be treated in either way if the source system logs the reason for a change. In Chapter 6, you also learned that a type 3 attribute is possible; it stores the prior value associated with a type 1 attribute.

Housekeeping columns are added to this system of categorization to designate columns not normally intended for end-user consumption but that serve a useful purpose for the load process or ETL process. Figure 17-10 provides various examples.

The first few housekeeping columns in Figure 17-10 have been encountered already. These columns aid ETL and reporting processes in specific ways:

- current_version can be used to filter the dimension table for current versions of records only. This may be useful for browse queries if type 2 changes have occurred. It may also be possible to use this column when loading facts to identify the appropriate surrogate key for a transaction.

- `effective_date` and `expiration_date` may be useful when point-in-time analysis of the dimension must be supported. As discussed in Chapter 6, time-stamping the dimension allows this analysis, while avoiding the need to build a separate fact table to track change history. These dates may also be used when loading facts to identify the appropriate surrogate key for each transaction.
- `type1_hash` and `type2_hash`, as discussed earlier in this chapter, can be used to streamline the identification of type 1 and type 2 changes during the ETL process.

Figure 17-10 also provides some additional housekeeping columns.

- `creation_date` contains the date and time that each row was inserted into the table.
- `update_date` contains the date and time of the last time the row was altered.
- `update_process` indicates the name of the process that last touched the row.

This trio of columns may prove useful in three different ways. First, analysts responsible for developing a quality assurance process will use these columns to construct and automate counts of records that were created or updated by the ETL routines. These may be compared with source data as part of a quality assurance process.

Second, these columns may prove useful to a database administrator or analyst who is charged with investigating a questionable data element. This information provides insight into the process that last touched the row, and it may be useful in unraveling any controversies. If it turns out to be necessary to hand-correct a row using SQL, the update_process can be set to the name of the individual who made the adjustment.

Finally, maintaining information about when each row was created and last adjusted is useful to ETL developers who are building derived or aggregate tables. These dates serve an analogous purpose to changed data identification in a source system, allowing incremental loads to process only those records that are new or changed.

TIP Housekeeping columns are added to a dimension table to support reporting, ETL functions, and quality assurance. These columns are not ordinarily intended for end-user consumption, although some may offer analytic value.

Variations on this theme are possible, but many introduce complexity disproportionate to the added value. An additional column can be added to flag exactly which columns have changed, for example, perhaps making use of a bitmap. This, however, would require significant additional processing by the ETL process. Similarly, logging each type 1 change would require an additional table, since a single row might undergo any number of changes over time. This again produces an additional ETL burden of dubious value.

Housekeeping and Fact Tables

While it may be useful to maintain similar information about when and how each fact table row was created and last updated, these columns add a significant number of bytes to each row. Since fact tables tend to accumulate rows far more quickly than dimension tables do, this is not desirable.

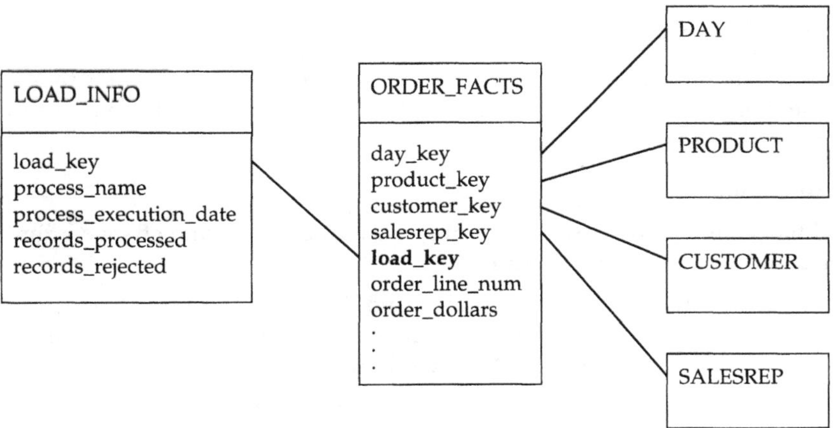

Figure 17-11 Housekeeping dimension for a fact table

The solution is to add a housekeeping dimension table that can keep track of updates to the fact table. This table maintains some of the same information that can be stored directly in dimension tables: the date the record was created or updated, and the name of the process or user who did so. This same table is a natural place to maintain other statistics about the ETL process execution itself.

Figure 17-11 illustrates how this technique is used to add housekeeping data to a fact table. The load_info dimension contains the housekeeping data; each fact table row contains a load_key value that refers to the appropriate row. If a fact table row is altered, this key value can be replaced.

Developers are cautioned not to get carried away with housekeeping data. While it can be useful, it is easy to extend the solution unnecessarily. One might be tempted to generalize this solution, for example, to log changes to any table—fact or dimension. This may seem elegant, but it introduces undue complexity to a solution that is intended primarily for the support of ETL processing, quality assurance, or data forensics. Similarly, the addition of metrics to these tables likely duplicates information that is already present in log files maintained by the ETL tools. Too much time spent developing stars that describe the load processes may result in your being admonished for neglecting the load process itself!

Summary

It is useful for everyone on the data warehouse team to have a basic understanding of the ETL process. It illustrates the influence of the schema design on processing complexity. Conversely, it also illustrates the potential influence that the ETL process may have on the design, suggesting potential adjustments that make things easier to process. A high-level understanding of the load process also affords ETL developers an opportunity to review key concepts and avoid common mistakes.

Here is a quick review of the basic principles covered in this chapter.

- Fact tables are dependent on dimension tables. Loading a fact requires that associated dimension rows have been previously loaded or have been prepared for loading in the same transaction.

Loading Dimensions

- The dimension load process must identify and process new and changed dimension records and handle them accordingly.
- New records contain a natural key that has not been previously loaded into the dimension table. A source record can be identified as new by looking up its natural key in the dimension table. If not found, it is new.
- A source record can be inspected for type 1 changes by assembling its type 1 dimension attribute values and comparing them to those of a record in the dimension table that shares the same natural key value. If they do not match, a type 1 change has occurred.
- Type 1 changes must be applied to all rows in the dimension table that share the same natural key value (rather than only to one that is flagged as current).
- A source record that contains type 1 changes may also contain type 2 changes.
- A source record can be inspected for type 2 changes by assembling its type 2 attribute values and comparing them to those of the current record in the dimension table with the same natural key. If they do not match, a type 2 change has occurred.

Loading Facts

- Loading a fact table row requires identification of the foreign key values that will refer to dimension tables. Source systems provide transactions with natural keys; these must be translated into surrogate keys.
- For each transaction, surrogate keys can be determined by looking up the natural key value in the dimension table. There may be multiple matches; the lookup must be supplemented in some way to determine the correct version.
- Adding a current_version flag to the dimension table allows surrogate keys to quickly identify the latest dimension entry for a natural key; adding effective and expiration flags allows identification of the version in effect at any point in time.

Optimizing the Load

- Limit the amount of data that must be processed by implementing a mechanism that identifies new and changed data in advance.
- Reduce the complexity of processing by simplifying lookups.

Cleansing Data

- The data warehouse should not transform or manufacture data if it will result in a different version of the facts from that provided by the operational systems.

- Data cleansing rules can be described using rules or by mapping data elements to one another.
- Transactions may arrive with natural keys that cannot be validated against dimension tables. These should not be excluded from the fact table since they will alter the magnitude of facts. Accommodate these facts with special case dimension rows and transaction identifiers that will permit their correction later.

Housekeeping Columns

- Housekeeping columns are added to the star schema to support reporting, ETL, or quality assurance.

Further Reading

ETL is a deep and complex process. This discussion has only touched the surface. Once you are familiar with the basic concepts presented here, you may be interested in digging deeper. If you are using a packaged ETL solution, you will want to read the documentation to learn the specifics of your product. For further general discussion, consult the following resources:

- Ralph Kimball *et al.* break down the ETL process into 34 subsystems, and describe how to plan and execute their development. See Chapters 9 and 10 of the *Data Warehouse Lifecycle Toolkit, Second Edition* (Wiley, 2008), by Ralph Kimball, Margy Ross, Warren Thornthwaite, Joy Mundy, and Bob Becker.
- Ralph Kimball and Joe Caserta also provide an expanded book-length treatment of this topic in *The Data Warehouse ETL Toolkit: Practical Techniques for Extracting, Cleaning, Conforming, and Delivering Data* (Wiley, 2004).
- This chapter mentioned Kimball and Ross's publishing metaphor for data warehousing. You can find it in Chapter 1 of *The Data Warehouse Toolkit, Second Edition* (Wiley, 2002), by Ralph Kimball and Margy Ross.
- Integration of aggregate processing into the ETL process is described in Chapters 5 and 6 of *Mastering Data Warehouse Aggregates* (Wiley, 2006) by Chris Adamson.

CHAPTER

18 How to Design and Document a Dimensional Model

There is great diversity in the ways organizations leverage the potential strategic value of dimensional design. Equally diverse are the development methodologies that IT organizations use to structure their work. Despite all these differences, the development of a dimensional design always calls for some common activities, and the deliverables share some common features.

This chapter will guide you through the process of designing and developing a dimensional model. It is not geared to any single architecture or any single methodology. Instead, it looks at the common tasks required in *any* design effort, whether conducted as part of an upfront enterprise strategy project or embedded within a subject-area implementation.

Dimensional design activity can be grouped into four major tasks: planning the activity, conducting interviews, developing the design, and documenting it. In some cases, an additional prioritization activity is added. These major stages can be applied on different scales, as dictated by the data warehouse architecture. This chapter provides detailed advice on how to break down each task—from how to plan the project, to some simple steps for development of the dimensional design itself.

Documentation of a dimensional design should always include some essential elements, regardless of its format. This chapter divides design documentation into three major levels, and spells out detailed requirements for each. The first level is a functional declaration of business capability, or *requirements.* Next, a top-level design includes rigorous definitions of the stars and conformed dimensions that support these requirements. Last, detailed attribute-level documentation identifies the data type and definition of each attribute, as well as its data sources and transformation rules. Checklists are provided for essential information to include in each part of the final documentation.

Dimensional Design and the Data Warehouse Life Cycle

The strategic importance attached to dimensional design varies according to data warehouse architecture. A dimensional data warehouse exploits the strategic benefits of dimensional design on a large scale; a Corporate Information Factory can do so optionally; a stand-alone data mart leverages its benefits only within a subject area.

Regardless of the level of emphasis, however, dimensional design must always precede the design of ETL programs and reports. This means it is usually conducted *prior* to the typical design stage of an implementation project, although exactly when and how can vary greatly.

The Strategic Importance of Dimensional Design

Fundamentally, a dimensional model deals with the measurement of business processes. It describes how a business process is evaluated, and it can be used to frame questions about the process. In this respect, it speaks clearly to the *business users* of the data warehouse.

A dimensional model also has technical implications. Its definition determines the data sources that must be integrated, how information must be cleansed or standardized, and what queries or reports can be built. In this respect, it speaks clearly to the *developers* of the data warehouse.

These business and technical characteristics of the dimensional model make it an ideal focal point for managing data warehouse strategy. A dimensional model can serve as the basis for a *shared* understanding of project priorities, scope, and progress. From a business perspective, it imparts a clear understanding of functional capability; from an IT perspective, it supports a clear understanding of the level of effort required for implementation.

Data warehouse architectures place varying emphasis on the strategic value of dimensional design. It is most strongly emphasized in Kimball's dimensional data warehouse architecture, which uses conformed dimensions as a central organizing feature. In Inmon's Corporate Information Factory architecture, this emphasis is often reduced, though similar benefits can be leveraged. A stand-alone data mart places the least amount of strategic emphasis on the dimensional design.

Kimball's Dimensional Data Warehouse

Kimball's dimensional data warehouse architecture, also known as the bus architecture, places a strong strategic emphasis on the principles of dimensional design. This emphasis stretches far beyond the design of database tables. As a framework for understanding process measurement, the dimensional model is used to capture analytic requirements from across the enterprise; as the basis for project scope, it is used to establish development priorities and resource requirements.

Most importantly, the development of an enterprise dimensional model enables the incremental implementation of subject-area applications, while avoiding the risk of incompatibilities, or *stove pipes*. This benefit is made possible by planning implementations around a set of conformed dimensions. As you learned in Chapter 5, conformed dimensions serve as the basis for comparing data from different subject areas, through a process called drilling across.

In the dimensional data warehouse architecture, dimensional design is the basis for an logical repository of atomic data that has been drawn from throughout the enterprise. As you learned in Chapter 2, a subject area within this repository is called a data mart. It may be queried directly, or serve as the basis for a second level of dimensional structures focused on the needs of particular departments or groups.

In the best of all possible worlds, the dimensional data warehouse life cycle begins with the development of a dimensional model of enterprise scope. This strategic effort gathers requirements for process measurement from across the enterprise and translates them into a series of fact tables for each subject area that are linked together by a set of conformed dimensions. These designs are mapped to source systems, and all necessary transformation logic is identified.

This dimensional model is then subdivided into subject areas, or data marts, which are prioritized for implementation. The dimensional design is used to define project scope, communicating both functional capability and technical requirements. Implementations proceed with subject area focus; each implementation works together with those that came before it as well as those that come after it.

Sometimes there is not sufficient organizational support for upfront strategic activity that does not culminate in a new analytic system. Many organizations therefore opt to follow the same process on a smaller scale, focusing on a particular line of business or group of departments at a time. Within this more narrowly defined area, the same benefits can be achieved. Expanding to new subject areas, however, may reveal incompatibilities that must be addressed. This approach is fully valid, as long as it is an informed decision made by top-level representatives of the business processes and IT.

Similarly, the modification of an existing data warehouse may proceed in an opportunistic fashion, one subject area at a time. As new development is funded, projects are organized to bring subject areas into conformance with one another, one piece at a time. Any inefficiency stems not from the principles of dimensional design but rather from the management of the overall life cycle.

Inmon's Corporate Information Factory

The dimensional model can provide similar benefits in a Corporate Information Factory, although it does not play the same central architectural role. As you learned in Chapter 2, the Corporate Information Factory also contains an integrated repository of atomic data, drawn from throughout the enterprise. Unlike the dimensional data warehouse, this repository is not dimensional and is not queried directly. Instead, it serves as the data source for departmental data marts, which are dimensional.

Although the dimensional model is not the foundation of the Corporate Information Factory, it can be used in many of the same ways. For example, enterprise-level requirements can be expressed in terms of process measurement. These requirements guide the development of a normalized enterprise data warehouse repository. Although not dimensional itself, this repository is dimensionally ready, having integrated disparate data sources and identified new and changed data. It serves as the source for dimensional data marts.

In a Corporate Information Factory, data mart development projects can be planned across multiple subject areas, based on a framework of conformed dimensions. This allows the data marts to work together as they are implemented incrementally. While not required, this helps avoid incompatibilities across subject areas, eliminating the need for future rework or development of more data marts for cross-process analysis.

The dimensional design is also a useful tool for managing the scope of individual data mart implementation projects. It communicates both the business capability and the technical complexity of the project. Conformed dimensions ensure that the stars within a data mart can be used together, albeit on a smaller scale.

Stand-alone Data Marts

Of the three major architecture paradigms, the stand-alone data mart places the lowest emphasis on the strategic value of dimensional design. A stand-alone data mart is developed without any enterprise context, as explained in Chapter 2. By definition, then, it does not exploit the strategic benefits of dimensional design.

Within a stand-alone data mart, however, the best practices of dimensional design can be used on a smaller scale. Dimensional design principles can be used to define requirements and stars for each subprocess in order to establish a conformance framework that ties them together. If necessary, this design can be used as the planning basis for phased implementation. The entire process mirrors that of the dimensional data warehouse but on a smaller scale.

When to Do Dimensional Design

In addition to being influenced by architecture, the data warehouse life cycle is also shaped by development methodology. Organizations follow diverse methods for the definition, prioritization, and execution of technical projects. Methodologies may be formal or informal, but each has its own way of subdividing projects into major stages. One familiar classification breaks work down into six phases: strategy, analysis, design, build, test, deploy. Others omit or add stages, provide for iterative processes, and so forth.

Regardless of data warehouse architecture or project development methodology, all dimensional implementations are characterized by a common dependency: the work to design an ETL process, a query, or a report is dependent on the dimensional design. To develop a design for a load process, for example, developers must have the target dimensional schema. To design a report, pivot table, or chart, developers must have access to the dimensional design.

Dimensional design, therefore, is not a design-stage activity. It must be completed before the work of designing load process and reports can take place. Where exactly it fits into the life cycle varies based on the strategic emphasis it is given. It may be central to defining an overall data warehouse strategy, in which case it is performed upfront as part of a special strategy project that incorporates all subject areas. It may serve a lesser role, in which case it will be folded into individual subject-area implementation projects. No matter when or how it takes place, all dimensional design efforts incorporate some common activities.

Design Activities

The development of a dimensional design incorporates some fundamental activities, regardless of project scope, methodology, or architecture. At a high level, these activities can be grouped into four categories or stages: planning, conducting interviews, doing the actual design work, and documenting it. When dimensional design is used to drive implementation strategy, there will also be a prioritization stage. This set of activities is illustrated in Figure 18-1.

You may prefer to think of these activities as "analysis activities." They are typically conducted *prior* to the design stage of a project, and their outputs include a dimensional representation of system *requirements*. Some organizations subdivide the activities and deliverables into *two* categories: *requirements analysis* and *design*.

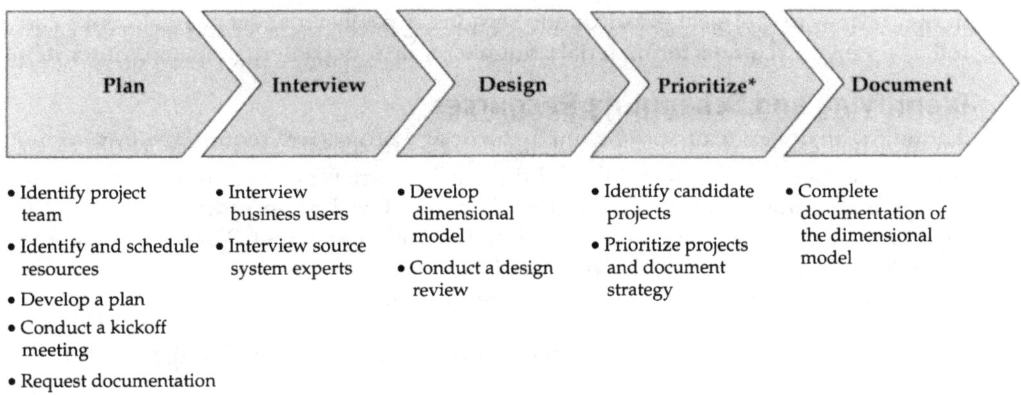

Figure 18-1 Dimensional design activities

Regardless of what you call them, these activities may be organized into a single project or incorporated into the plan for a larger project. They do not always occur in a linear sequence as depicted. For example, design work normally begins after the first interview has been completed; it will be revised and refined throughout the process.

Planning the Design Effort

Even for a narrowly defined subject area, some planning is essential in order to ensure the dimensional design is completed in a timely manner. Orderly development of the dimensional model requires a clear understanding of roles and responsibilities of team members. It will also require the availability of a diverse set of resources external to the project team, from business analysts and end users to the developers of source systems.

Identifying the Project Team Members

The project team consists of dimensional designers, project sponsors, and, optionally, a project manager. The dimensional designers form the core of the team. Their efforts are best led by an experienced dimensional modeler, in partnership with one or more business or technical analysts with domain expertise. Keep this group small. Others will be given the opportunity to participate in major design decisions as part of a design review task.

This core design team should have direct access to sponsors with decision-making authority in two major areas: within IT and within relevant business units. These people will be called upon to make resources available, review progress, and settle questions of scope. They will be instrumental in determining who the team will be interviewing, both on the business side and on the technical side. They will also be the primary participants in any prioritization activities.

The addition of a project manager to the team can be very helpful. This individual can assume responsibility for monitoring progress and reporting it to sponsors. The project manager will handle scheduling interviews, rescheduling after cancellations, and organizing design reviews and project prioritization sessions. A project manager can also take care of following up on requests for materials, sample reports, documentation, and other items.

Identifying and Scheduling Resources

Although the design team may be small, the design project will require the involvement of a number of additional resources. Many of these people are very busy. Project sponsors will be essential in securing their attention and involvement. It will be necessary to provide these people with an understanding of the required level of involvement. Their involvement must be scheduled in accordance with a project plan.

These participants can be grouped into several roles:

- **Business users and analysts** who will provide information about the business processes. These people will be asked to prepare for, and participate in, at least one interview and be available for follow-up questions.
- **Source system developers** will provide information about the source systems, available data, its quality, and operational profiles. These people will be asked to provide information, participate in extended interviews, and work with the project team to map a dimensional design to source systems.
- **Design reviewers** will participate in extended briefings on the dimensional model and be asked to participate in major design decisions. In addition to including the core team, this group should include people who can provide the perspective of database administrators, report developers, ETL developers, and the data warehouse architects.
- **Project planners** will work with the team to develop the high-level assessment of implementation efforts.
- **Decision makers** will assign priorities to projects and establish a high-level implementation strategy. This may be done by project sponsors, or it may include a larger group of decision makers.

Additional resources may also be involved, as required by the overall project plan. Modification of an existing design, for example, will require more direct involvement from data architects, ETL developers, and report developers. If dimensional design represents a new direction for your organization, the project may also involve interviews with the existing warehouse team and the incorporation of planned changes to the technical architecture into the prioritization process.

Developing a Plan

Although many modelers would prefer to "wing it," the various people who must be involved argue in favor of developing a formal plan. If design is part of a larger project, design activity should be incorporated into that project's plan. The plan need not be onerous; a few pages of text and a timetable may be sufficient. It can be far more extensive if desired.

The plan for the project should include the following elements:

- A statement of scope
- Responsible sponsors
- Team members

- People to be interviewed
- Design review participants
- Project planners
- Strategic decision makers
- Timetable
- Key deliverables

Many warehouse teams like to document these items in presentation format and schedule a formal kickoff meeting. This is a useful way to let participants know the extent of their involvement and the importance attached to their participation by senior management, and to set expectations. Setting expectations is essential when design is conducted as a stand-alone project; participants must be made aware that the project will not produce a solution but rather a blueprint and timetable.

Requesting Documentation

The last of the planning activities involves requesting documentation of the source systems that fall within the project's scope. Data dictionaries, ER diagrams, file format specifications, and the like should all be requested in advance so these materials are available to the team during the interview process. The individuals providing these materials are likely to be interviewed as part of the project; thus, it is essential to convey to them that supplying documentation is not the full extent of their involvement.

Conducting Interviews

The interview process has two primary objectives. The first objective is to identify individual business processes and determine how they are measured. These interviews require a concerted effort to listen carefully and seek feedback, particularly when you already possess a working knowledge of the business process.

The second objective is to determine what source data is available to support process measurement. These interviews often require coaxing a high-level overview out of individuals who are accustomed to working among the details. It will also be necessary to develop an understanding of the flow and quality of available data.

Conducting Business Interviews

It is generally best to interview people individually, or in very small groups. The most senior of those to be interviewed in a given area are likely to provide useful advice as to how to choose and group interviewees, based on the processes and personalities involved. The lead data modeler should be present for all interviews, if possible. Only one or two members of the project team should be present for each interview; of those present, one should be designated to lead the interview.

When conducting an interview, your primary job is to learn. Surprisingly, this can be difficult if you already think you know something about the process. You may be tempted to impress interviewees with your knowledge of the business or activities. This is always counterproductive. Exhibiting any business knowledge will cause the subject to omit essential details he or she assumes you know. Similarly, if you withhold basic questions, there will be crucial gaps in what you learn. Worst of all, attempts to impress interviewees with knowledge of their job can cause offense. Imagine if the roles were reversed: as an IT professional, how would you feel if a business user told you how your job was done?

TIP When conducting interviews, forget what you think you know about the business. It will only get in the way of learning. Your job is not to impress the people you are interviewing. Let them speak and do not be afraid to ask questions.

A typical interview should not last more than two to three hours. Occasionally, an intricate business process may require an extended follow-up. Divide each interview into two parts. Devote the first part to learning about the interviewee's job activities and how they fit within a larger picture.

It is usually not hard to get people talking about what they do. After providing a brief overview of the project, invite them to describe their role in the business process, and how they or their managers measure it. This is usually all it takes to get the ball rolling. Listen to what they have to say, and ask questions.

Presume you are proceeding from a blank slate. As you learn about a subject's involvement in the business, repeat it back in your own words and ask, "is that right?" If the subject says "yes," that's good, and he or she will likely provide more detail. If the subject says "no," that's good too; you've uncovered a misunderstanding that might have gone unnoticed. The interviewee will be able to set things straight.

This simple technique is a surprisingly powerful way to handle interviews. It places interviewees at ease while you correct errors and uncover detail. Don't be embarrassed if you sound like the television detective Colombo from 1970s police drama of the same name. Although he seemed dim-witted or slow at times, he exposed detail by repeating things back and probing deeper. Methodical plodding always helped him get his man.

TIP Listen to interviewees and repeat what they tell you in your own words. Don't be afraid you will get it wrong.

In the second part of the session, shift the focus to the specifics of measurement. Recapping your understanding of the interviewee's activities is a perfect way to make this shift, allowing you to link the processes to information. Find out how each process is measured and at what level of detail. For each process, a single interviewee may be able to provide as many as four measurement perspectives. Look to understand what information interviewees use from others, what information they produce or work with, what information they provide to others, and what information they report to their managers.

Do not be afraid to use words like "measurement" and "dimension." The impulse to avoid technical terminology is valuable when interfacing with users, but these are not technical terms. They have business meaning, and most people will understand them. It is perfectly reasonable, for example, to say something like, "From what you have told me, to plan commission payments, you need access to information at the individual order line level of detail, including product, date, salesperson, and any promotions in effect. Did I miss any dimensions here?" Similarly, you can ask about how they themselves are measured. "When you are done, what detail must you provide to managers? It sounds like you need to produce commission payment dollars by salesperson on orders that were closed during the month, grouped by the type of customer."

Close every interview by thanking the participants. If they've offered to provide additional materials, remind them. Let them know what the next project steps are and when final results are expected. Most importantly, leave the door open to come back with follow-up questions as the project proceeds.

It is valuable to reserve some debriefing time after each interview. Compare notes with the others who were present and brief team members who were not. Summarize what you have learned by identifying individual processes, specifying both measurements and the level of detail for each. This information will serve as the basis for dimensional design. For some projects, these summaries can be consolidated into statements of requirements by subject area, as you will see later in this chapter. Sketch out sample dimensional designs. These will no doubt change and evolve, but they provide a useful framework for understanding what has been learned. These efforts will also provide insight into the major design choices that will have to be made, such as how to group dimensions into tables, or whether it will be necessary to provide derived schemas to supplement transaction data.

Analytic Applications: A Different Approach to Design

The process described here heavily emphasizes the interview process, which serves as the source for requirements for the design. While this is a valuable and useful approach, other processes are also possible. For example, projects that are focused on a narrow subject area often make heavy use of domain experts. These projects may require little or no interview activity at all; requirements and data sources flow from the knowledge of these subject matter experts. A design review is still warranted.

Another approach places a strong emphasis on exactly how the solution will look and operate from the end-user perspective. Called *analytic applications,* these solutions are designed in a similar manner to operational systems. They place as much emphasis on the design of individual reports and screens as they do on the database design. Detailed specifications document what each user will see when logging on, as determined by his or her role and preferences, the time of year, or particular conditions detected in the data. The design of these information views includes detailed information on what occurs when the user wishes to drill up or down from a particular part of the display, and how reports are connected to one another. This targeted, guided analysis can be a powerful unifying framework.

In the development of an analytic application, dimensional design sometimes takes a back seat to the development of design for the front-end application itself. The interview process is used to identify roles and requirements that are documented as mock-ups for screens and use cases. These specifications, in turn, serve as the basis for dimensional design. The end result can be extremely compelling, and it is likely to be heavily used by target users. However, the dimensional design may miss details that become important in the future and may fail to capture conformance requirements that relate to other subject areas.

Conducting Source System Interviews

Learning about a source system is most useful when there has already been some exposure to the business process it supports. Source system interviews are best interspersed among the business interviews, rather than left for the end, since they can provide important insight into what is possible, the condition of the data, and current business issues.

In Corporate Information Factory architecture, dimensional data marts get their information from the enterprise data warehouse. This simplifies matters, since much of the work of integrating data from operational systems has already been performed. It may be necessary to track down some information that is not present in the warehouse, but hopefully most of the needed data will already be centralized and well documented. Few interviews will be necessary, and a structured overview will likely already be available. In dimensional data warehouse architecture, it will probably be necessary to gather information about a variety of source systems. To a lesser extent, the same holds true for a stand-alone data mart.

Source system interviews can involve the entire design team and, typically, take much longer than business interviews. Team members will be using what is learned here to map dimensional designs directly to source data elements and specify any necessary processing rules or transformation logic. This requires digging deeply, working through individual tables or files, and understanding what they contain.

Like a business interview, a technical interview can be organized into two phases. During the first phase, the interviewee is asked to provide an overview of the system, describe the process flow it supports, and walk you through the data model. Developers who "live the details" often have trouble providing a high-level overview, so it may be necessary to coax one out. Looking at actual screens can sometimes be useful. After this overview, the focus should be shifted to identifying the system's ability to provide the specific measurements you have learned about in the business interviews, and the specific data entities that will map to dimensions of analysis. This phase is likely to consume most of the time.

When the session is completed, it is once again important to thank the interviewees and inform them of the next steps. Follow-up questions are a certainty, so be sure they are aware they will be consulted again. If the project plan calls for it, let them know they will be enlisted to assist in the task of mapping the dimensional design back to source system data elements. They will also be called upon to help estimate data volumes.

Designing the Dimensional Model

Although this overview describes "design" as a discrete step, design work usually begins as soon as the first interview is completed. As the interview process proceeds, the design team will begin to develop an understanding of the key business processes and dimensions that fall within the project scope. Design ideas will begin to gel and evolve.

Once all interviews are completed, informal back-of-the-napkin sketches and impromptu white board scribbling must be consolidated into a formal design for review by a larger group. Whether sketching initial ideas or formally recording a proposed dimensional model for a design review, the design team should capture several key elements.

After a proposed dimensional design is formulated, it is essential to conduct a design review. This critical project step allows interested parties who are not part of the core design team to provide their own input and participate in key design decisions. It is a grave mistake to accept the draft design of a dimensional modeling expert without such a review.

Developing the Dimensional Model

Experienced dimensional modelers tend to think in terms of facts and dimensions, processes and grain, additivity, and conformance. For these people, the development of a draft design is a natural and intuitive process. For the rest of us, it can be useful to follow some basic steps.

Sketching a Star Kimball and Ross recommend a simple four-step method for sketching out a dimensional design. These steps are a useful way to get started, regardless of whether you subscribe to their recommended architecture. Following these steps takes care of some of the basics. Later in this chapter, you will learn exactly how to document them.

As you learned in Chapter 4, each star usually corresponds to a discrete process or activity. Review your interview notes, and try to identify individual processes. Pick one, and sketch out a star by following these steps:

1. Describe the process.
2. Set the grain of the fact table.
3. List the facts.
4. Identify the dimensions.

These four steps will get you started, and also force you to consider some essential characteristics of every design.

Suppose, for example, that you are doing design work for a sales data mart. Through the course of interviews, you have spoken with a variety of individuals. Reviewing your notes, you are able to list a series of subprocesses that fall under the umbrella of sales:

- Making sales calls
- Issuing proposals to customers
- Booking orders
- Shipping products
- Processing returns
- Paying commissions to salespeople

Each of these processes is a candidate for a fact table. Some may or may not be required, and some may turn out to break down into more than one subprocess, but this is a good place to start.

Taking one of these processes, you can apply Kimball and Ross's four steps. The specific things you should document are described in more detail later in this chapter. For now, think about each step and what kinds of things to look for. The first step is to name the process. Do this in business terms, if possible: "Recording orders from customers."

The second step is to establish the grain. As you learned in Chapter 3, grain is usually set at the lowest level of detail possible. For orders, you might state it as "Order Information at the individual order_line level of detail." As part of this declaration, note the type of fact table implied. In this case, it is a transaction fact table. As you learned in Chapter 11, the other kinds of fact tables are snapshots and accumulating snapshots.

Next, you can enumerate some facts. Remember that you should look for additive facts and not be afraid if some are redundant. Try to define each one and note its additivity characteristics. For orders, you might come up with several facts: quantity ordered, the dollar amount of the order line, and the extended cost associated with the order line (not the unit cost!). The design should also include margin dollars, even though it can be computed as order dollars minus extended cost.

Don't be disheartened if you have trouble finding facts. As you learned in Chapter 12, some fact tables do not contain any. You will usually be clued into this possibility when you hear people saying they want to count things. Number of applications approved, number of phone calls made, number of sales calls—these counts may not manifest themselves as explicit facts, but are implied by factless fact tables with appropriate grain. Note them as part of your design.

At this point, you should also be thinking about nonadditive facts that can be computed based on the design. As you will see later in this chapter, it is useful to write them down. If you have already sketched out a design for another star, you may also see some opportunities to drill across, or compare processes. "Close rate," for example, might be the ratio of facts in two fact tables: proposals and orders. Write these kinds of facts down, too, because they will be useful. Semi-additive facts are a common feature of snapshot designs, as you learned in Chapter 11. If you find any of these, be sure to note the dimension across which they should not be added.

The fourth step is to enumerate the dimensions. Do not limit yourself to those that guarantee uniqueness of a fact table row. An order line, for example, is enough to define a fact table row. It may make a fine degenerate dimension, but what other dimensions are implied? There is almost always one occurrence of a time dimension, which captures when the activity took place. In this case, it is the order date. Time is sometimes available in other contexts as well. If orders result from proposals, then each order may also have an associated proposal date. Other key dimensions will have revealed themselves as part of the interview process. In this example, they include customer, salesrep, and product.

Candidate dimensions will shift and change as you work through and revise a dimensional model. As you learned in Chapter 5, dimensions play a central role in ensuring that multiple stars can work together. Moving on to other stars, you will find other processes that share some characteristics with dimensions you have already sketched out. Be on the lookout for dimensions that offer more or less detail than ones you have already laid out. These are likely candidates for conformance. You may also have trouble deciding what elements to include in a single dimension table and what should be split into multiple tables. Review the guidelines in Chapter 6 for some help with this.

Beyond Individual Stars The four steps focus on individual stars. After sketching out some stars, step back and look across processes. Three additional steps can guide your next efforts:

1. Work out a conformance framework.
2. Identify the slow change characteristics of dimension tables.
3. Consider alternative models for each process.

A conformance framework is the centerpiece of a dimensional design. This holds true whether you are designing a dimensional data warehouse in the style advocated by Ralph Kimball, departmental data marts in the style advocated by W.H. Inmon, or stand-alone data marts. As recommended later in this chapter, it is essential to document how dimensions conform, and create a matrix that links fact tables to the key dimension tables in the design.

The details of slow change processing will be addressed in depth later, when you produce a detailed design. At this point, however, it is useful to consider some key requirements that are likely to affect the capabilities of the solution and the complexity of the ETL process. It is safest to proceed from the assumption that most changes will be type 2, but where is that not the case? Are there changes that are not significant? Are there cases that call for a type 3 change, or a hybrid change? These will have a significant impact on the ETL process; write them down.

Last, remember that, in many cases, a single process will require more than one fact table. The most common examples are transaction and snapshot pairs, or transaction and accumulating snapshot pairs, as described in Chapter 11. If you find you have modeled any of these designs, ask yourself if a complementary fact table would be useful. Review your interview notes to find out. Other forms of derived tables, as described in Chapter 14, may be useful for specific kinds of reporting.

If You Get Stuck Sometimes, efforts to follow the first four steps stall from the start: identifying the process. As noted in Chapter 4, processes can usually be decomposed into subprocesses, so it is hard to know where to begin. The preceding example took one process, "Sales," and broke it down into six processes, for proposals, orders, returns, and so forth. This breakdown may not be evident. If the four steps are not working for you, you may want to try another approach.

Review your interview notes, making a list of candidate dimension tables. Don't worry about getting these exactly right; you will be able to revise them later. Next, make a list of candidate facts (individual facts, not fact tables), and cross-reference them with the candidate dimension tables. This can be done in a matrix, as in Figure 18-2. The rows of the matrix represent facts that have been identified from interview notes. The columns represent candidate dimensions. The checkmarks indicate the level of dimensional detail at which each fact is available.

Once you have made a cross-reference of facts and dimension tables, look for facts that share identical dimensionality. You can re-sort your matrix so that they appear together. In Figure 18-2, these groupings are shaded in gray and white bands. The facts in each group may belong together in a single fact table. Ask yourself if they share the same level of dimensional detail and if they are available at the same time. As you learned in Chapter 4, the answer to these two questions will help you determine if they belong together in a single fact table.

Once you have identified these natural affinities, you have a group of candidate processes. They can be used as the basis for individual fact table designs. Each one can now be taken through the four steps described earlier.

	day visited	day proposed	day ordered	day shipped	day returned	product	salesrep	customer	warehouse	proposal	order line	shipment line ID	return ID	return reason
Number of sales calls	✓							✓						
Quantity proposed		✓				✓	✓	✓		✓				
Proposal dollars		✓				✓	✓	✓		✓				
Quantity ordered			✓			✓	✓	✓			✓			
Order dollars			✓			✓	✓	✓			✓			
Cost dollars			✓			✓	✓	✓			✓			
Margin dollars			✓			✓	✓	✓			✓			
Revenue dollars			✓	✓		✓	✓	✓	✓		✓	✓		
Quantity shipped			✓	✓		✓	✓	✓	✓		✓	✓		
Quantity returned			✓	✓	✓	✓	✓	✓	✓		✓	✓	✓	✓
Return dollars			✓	✓	✓	✓	✓	✓	✓		✓	✓	✓	✓

Figure 18-2 Affinities among facts provide process clues

Conducting a Design Review

As the high-level dimensional design is being worked out, it should be documented, as described later in this chapter. Once this is complete, it is essential to conduct a design review. This review allows a variety of other interested parties to contribute in a positive manner.

Impacts of Design Decisions The principles of dimensional design do not dictate a single "correct" design solution for a given process. Even if you follow all the best practices laid out in this book, it will be necessary to make some choices. You have seen several examples of decisions made during the design process:

- How to break up related things into dimension tables (Chapter 6)
- Whether use of an outrigger is justified (Chapter 7)
- When the extra effort of a hybrid slow change is necessary (Chapter 8)
- Choosing to develop a bridge table versus keeping things safe for end users (Chapters 9 and 10)
- Deciding if an accumulating snapshot is warranted versus computing correlations in queries (Chapter 11)
- Opting to design core and custom stars as opposed to placing all attributes in a single star (Chapter 13)
- Determining if derived tables are justified for simplifying certain reports (Chapter 14)

In addition, a conscious decision may have been made to deviate from best practices. For example:

- Not setting fact table grain at the lowest level possible (Chapter 3)
- Not attempting to bring into conformance incompatible views of what might otherwise constitute a conformed dimension (Chapter 5)
- Developing a snowflake to facilitate the use of a particular reporting tool (Chapter 7)

While these decisions may contradict best practices, pragmatic considerations sometimes drive choices like these.

Design decisions should not be made by a data architect alone. They impact a number of important areas, and a number of important functions. The various perspectives that factor into design decisions are illustrated in Figure 18-3. This diagram shows several key roles and illustrates how each is affected by a design decision. Conspicuously absent from this group is the data architect!

Perhaps the most important impact of a design decision is how it affects analytic capability. This is the primary concern represented by the user role in Figure 18-3. Someone in this role considers what business questions can be answered by a design option and what questions cannot be answered. Forgoing a bridge table, for example, may make it difficult to summarize activity across a hierarchy.

The report developer considers how the design option impacts the development of queries and reports. The complexity of these tasks is directly affected by schema design choices. Some reports may be particularly difficult to develop without an accumulating

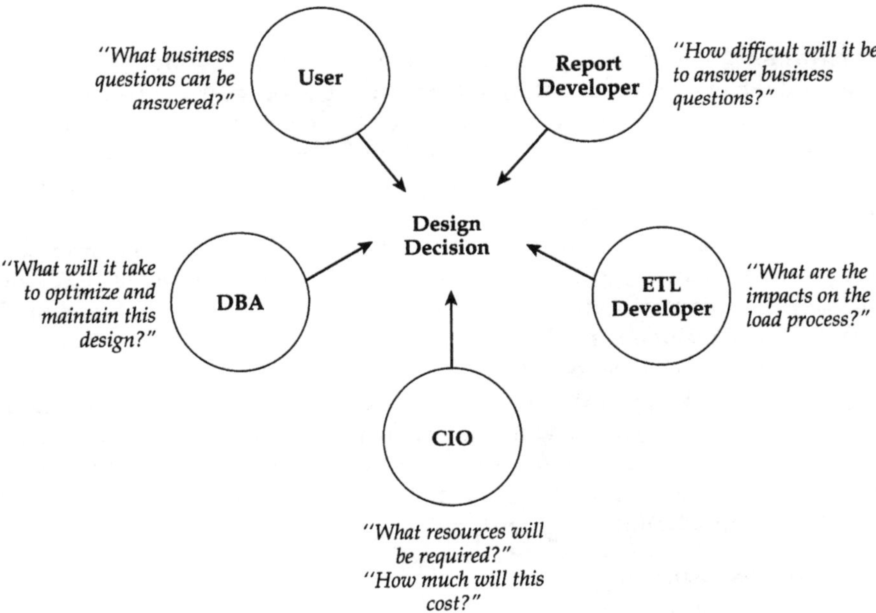

Figure 18-3 Different perspectives on a design choice

snapshot, for example. Others may be complicated by limitations of the particular tools that will be used. Still others may be greatly streamlined through the use of derived tables.

The ETL developer's perspective is crucial in determining how each option impacts the development of the load process. The impact on ETL developers is often inversely proportional to the impact on the report developer. Adding an accumulating snapshot, for example, requires development of processes to load and maintain an additional star. The ETL developer may also be impacted by choices that benefit analytic capability; a hybrid slow change, for example, satisfies more users but requires additional work.

The database administrator's perspective takes into account the process of maintaining the database tables and optimizing them for performance. The database administrator will be charged with implementing features like parallelism, developing an indexing scheme, and tuning SQL. Outriggers, bridge tables, and other considerations may directly impact how the database is configured, and whether certain DBMS features will be applicable. The use of materialized views, materialized query tables, and like features will similarly impact the work of the DBA.

Last, the CIO's perspective takes into account the cost of every design decision. These costs can be evaluated in terms of human resources and in terms of dollars. There may be short-term and long-term implications of each choice, as well as business and technical perspectives.

This diagram does not include a data architect or design expert. Although they should not make design decisions on their own, these people do play an important role in the decision-making process. They facilitate discussion among the participants. The data architect can present the options and provide advantages and disadvantages of each. In the end, however, the final decision should balance the considerations of the groups shown in Figure 18-3.

The Design Review The primary purpose of a design review is to bring these diverse perspectives into the design process. During the planning process, participants are selected to represent each role. Each role may be represented by one individual or several. Some individuals may represent more than one perspective. Together, this group can validate or revise the design as needed. The two sponsors, one representing the business and one representing IT interests, have final authority to resolve any issues.

In addition to requiring the groups depicted in Figure 18-3, the plan may also call for bringing in people with an expert understanding of specific tools that will be used, such as BI products or ETL products. If the organization has a data administration function, this perspective should be included as well, ensuring conformance to standards for representation of key data elements.

A design review will take anywhere from a few hours to over a day, depending on the scope of the project, the size of the model, and the number of people involved. It should be facilitated by the lead dimensional designer and proceed in a structured format. A recommended sequence maps closely to the organization of high-level design documentation, as described later in this chapter. Specifically:

1. Review project scope and roles.
2. Perform a high-level review of the model, cross-referencing fact tables by dimension tables.

3. Perform a detailed walkthrough of the dimension design.
4. Perform a detailed walkthrough of fact table design.

This review is usually best performed in presentation format. It also helps if all participants have hard copies of the materials. The elements to be discussed in each of these areas are discussed in the "Top-Level Design Documentation" section later in this chapter. For some participants, the review may represent their first encounter with dimensional design; allow for some education along the way.

In addition to establishing buy-in from all quarters, the review process tests the model for completeness and helps the team identify relative complexity of the various components. This last piece will aid in the process of prioritizing implementation plans.

Prioritizing Plans

While it makes sense to conduct dimensional modeling efforts with enterprise-wide scope, *implementation* works best when done incrementally. The prioritization tasks produce an implementation strategy or roadmap. This effort requires subdividing the dimensional model into candidate projects, estimating their complexity, and establishing priorities. It is strategic in nature and requires the involvement of decision makers with the authority to establish strategy and the leadership to ensure implementation.

The prioritization stage is noted as optional in Figure 18-1, in deference to the variety of architectures and project methodologies. Notice, however, that prioritization activities are not limited to projects of enterprise scope. A large subject area may also be broken up for incremental implementation. When the design effort is part of a smaller project that is focused on a specific implementation, these activities may not be omitted.

Identifying Candidate Projects

The dimensional design serves as the basis for defining project scope. Projects are defined according to the stars that will be implemented. This communicates scope in two key dimensions: business capabilities and implementation complexity. Each of these perspectives is essential in prioritizing projects.

Business objectives often dictate the scope of implementation projects. These objectives can be mapped to the areas of the dimensional model that support them, establishing the scope of implementation projects. When business priorities are not clear, the project team can subdivide the model in accordance with major business processes. The team may take into account available implementation resources to further subdivide implementation plans within a subject area.

The implementation complexity of each project is influenced by a variety of factors. These include:

- The number of new dimension tables that must be built
- The number of new fact tables that must be built
- The number of source systems involved
- Expected data volumes

These high-level indicators of complexity can be further decomposed. For a dimension table, complexity is further influenced by:

- The need to reconcile information from multiple sources
- The complexity of processing rules
- The degree of slow change processing required
- The need to implement core and custom versions
- The number of conformed replicas and rollups
- The presence of behavioral attributes
- The use of snowflaking or outriggers
- The presence of bridge tables
- The availability of changed data identification mechanisms

Similar factors contribute to fact table complexity:

- The number of source systems that provide facts to the fact table
- The need to construct snapshots from transaction data
- The complexity of logic required to construct accumulating snapshots, and the number of stars from which they are derived
- The quantity and nature of derived and aggregate tables

These and other factors of complexity are visible as part of the dimensional design documentation, which is described in detail later in this chapter. The high-level design brings these factors to the fore; the detailed design provides more specific information.

Factors like these may be further influenced by analytic solutions already in place. Development of core and custom product dimensions, for example, may be complicated by the presence of an existing product table that focuses on only one category. Changing the way an existing table handles slowly changing dimensions may influence existing stars and reports. Bringing two incompatible dimensions into conformance may require the reassignment of keys. These examples may all have ripple effects on previously existing stars and reports, making these modifications akin to replacing a bridge while traffic is driving across it.

Using this information, the project team works with the designated project planners to develop a high-level assessment of project durations and resource requirements. This group may include project managers, IT management, lead architects, and developers with expert skills in the target implementation toolset. Your organization may opt for very broad-brush assessments or choose to provide a more detailed assessment through the development of individual project plans. The output of this estimation task will be used by decision makers to set priorities.

Prioritizing Implementation Projects

Prioritization of implementation plans is established by senior executives representing the subject areas supported and the IT function. The smaller this group is, the easier it will be to come to agreement. It is necessary, however, that all areas receive representation. The strategy is usually set through one or more sessions.

During the strategy sessions, the project team presents a high-level overview of the design and reviews the recommended sequence and scope of implementation projects. These projects are discussed in terms of the capability they provide, the interested parties within the business, and the technical complexity required for implementation.

Decision makers may suggest reorganization of the proposed implementation plans with respect to sequence or project scope. These directives may require that the team work with project planners to adjust project definitions and resource assessments. These revisions are presented to decision makers in a follow-up session, for final acceptance of the strategy.

Documenting the Results

Almost the moment the team begins interviews, the team will begin working on the dimensional design. The design will change and evolve throughout the process. Once interviews are complete, the high-level design becomes fairly stable. It may be adjusted as part of the design review, or tweaked when developing project definitions and the implementation strategy, but its overall organization will remain consistent.

Once this stage has been reached, it is advisable to begin detailing the dimensional design. As described later in this chapter, the detailed design includes column-by-column information describing things like data types, detailed attribute definitions, sample values, data sources, and transformation rules. It will also include information about transaction volumes, security requirements, and archive strategy, as applicable. This legwork need not be complete to conduct design reviews and strategy sessions, but it must be finished by the end of the project.

Much of this work will be performed by the lead designer and the design team. Portions of the job may be farmed out to other parties if possible. For example, database administrators may help in establishing naming standards and data types; analysts may assist in developing attribute definitions; source system experts may develop the bulk of the data source definitions.

Some organizations prefer to use specialized tools for these activities, which are capable of producing model documentation as well as generating scripts to set up the required database tables. While useful, these tools are not necessary to establish a dimensional design.

Documenting a Dimensional Model

Dimensional designers use a wide variety of formats and tools to document their models. The descriptions in this chapter capture the essentials; these elements should be incorporated into all design documents. They make no assumptions about the tools used to produce the design. In fact, this documentation can be compiled using nothing more than a word processor, drawing tool, and spreadsheet program.

The dimensional design documentation should be grouped into three major sections, which start at a high level and become progressively more detailed. Requirements documentation captures measurement requirements by process in each major subject area. Top-level design documentation describes the stars for each process and the associated conformed dimensions. Detailed design documentation includes column-by-column specifications for each table.

Requirements Documentation

When the dimensional model will be used as a basis for data warehouse strategy, documentation should begin with a functional description of the capabilities in each subject area. While you will recognize that these descriptions map very closely to stars, facts, and dimensions, these technical underpinnings are not necessary to convey functional capability. Tables, columns, and joins will be introduced later as part of the high-level design documentation and fleshed out in the detailed design.

When focused on an individual subject area, this part of the dimensional documentation may be omitted. If included, however, it will provide high-level insight into how the subject area is broken down into processes, and how each process is measured.

Enumerating Business Requirements

Subject area requirements can usually be defined with characteristic simplicity. Recommended documentation is outlined in Table 18-1.

For a given subject area, documenting this information can usually be accomplished in one to two pages of very brief tables. Figure 18-4 provides an example for a Sales subject area. The subject area is defined clearly, mapped to various departmental interests, and described in terms of measurement detail.

Although simple, this framework for stating requirements is very powerful in its ability to communicate business capabilities. Nontechnical users can cultivate a clear understanding of what kind of analysis is supported by each subject area, even if they do not delve into the high-level design documentation.

Enumerating Cross-Subject-Area Requirements

Not every analytic requirement fits nicely into a single subject area. As you have learned, many powerful forms of analysis require comparing facts from one or more subject areas. This kind of requirement must also be documented. It can be done in a similar manner to the subject-area-specific requirements, depicted previously. After the list of requirements by subject area, list additional requirements that cross subject areas.

Item	Description	Notes
Subject Area Description	Defines the subject area and maps it to familiar business processes	This can usually be accomplished in one or two sentences.
Roles	States the interest each department or user group has in the subject area	This helps prevent subject areas from being confused with departments. Single phrases or short sentences should do the job.
Analytic Requirements	Statements describing the kinds of measurements and level of details	These statements will strike you as similar to grain statements for fact tables, but here they express very specific business requirements.
Process Measurement	Specific breakdown of measurements, broken into groups by process along with associated dimensional context	These statements detail the facts associated with each analytic requirement, as well as the major dimensions of analysis.

Table 18-1 Enumerating Requirements by Subject Area

Sales Subject Area

Description:

Engagement of prospects and customers for the purpose of securing new orders

Roles:

Sales	Direct sales activities, including sales calls, proposal creation, and order taking
Sales Management	Monitoring activities of salespeople
Marketing	Correlation of orders with marketing activity
Fulfillment	Use of sales data for demand forecasting and inventory management
Finance	Computation of salesperson commission payments

Analytic Requirements:

1. Tracking **sales calls** by **date, salesperson,** and **customer**
2. **Proposal information** by **proposal line, date, salesperson, customer,** and **product**
3. **Order Information** by **order date, order line, salesperson, customer,** and **product**
4. **Shipments** by **shipment date, shipment line, salesperson, customer, product, order line,** and **order date**
5. **Returns** by **date, reason, product, customer, order line,** and **salesrep**

Process Measurement:

Process	Measurements	Measurement Context
Sales calls	Number of sales calls	Date/Time Salesperson Customer Call Type
Proposal	Proposal Quantity Proposal Dollars	Proposal Line ID Salesperson Customer Product Proposal Type
Orders	Order Quantity Order Dollars Order Cost Dollars Margin Dollars	Order Line Order Date Salesperson Customer Product
Shipments	Shipment Quantity Revenue Dollars	Shipment Date Shipment Line ID Shipper Product Customer Salesperson Order Line Order Date
Returns	Quantity Returned Return Dollars Return Cost Dollars Return Margin Dollars	Return Date Order Line Order Date Salesperson Customer Product Return Reason

Figure 18-4 Documenting requirements for a subject area

Requirements documentation should also include a high-level indication of compatibility across subject areas. A simple matrix can communicate the necessary information, cross-referencing each measurement group with the major dimensions of the business. This effectively communicates if and how two subject areas can be compared. An example appears in Figure 18-5.

As with the other artifacts of requirements documentation, you will notice that this matrix bears a strong resemblance to a more detailed item: a conformance matrix that cross-references fact tables with dimension tables. Framed for a business audience, this matrix communicates the same information from a business perspective. It does not contain all dimensions; rather, it only shows major dimensions that will link subject areas.

It is possible to scan this matrix to understand which processes can be compared and how. For example, it is possible to determine that orders and shipments can be compared based on order_line but that commission payments are not allocated to the order_line or even the customer. This viewpoint also fosters a business user's understanding of the importance of developing a common representation for major dimensions of analysis; departmental users come to realize that "their" data is important in other parts of the business as well.

Top-Level Design Documentation

Documentation of the dimensional design itself should be broken into two levels of detail. Top-level documentation provides a technical and functional description of each star. Detailed documentation adds column-by-column details, definitions, and data sources.

The top-level documentation is likely to be the focal point of the design review sessions. Like the requirements documentation, it can be produced in presentation or document format. Top-level design documentation should include at least three major sections: definitions for each star, definitions for each dimension, and a conformance matrix.

		day		*product*		*salesrep*					
		day	*quarter*	*product*	*category*	*salesrep*	*territory*	*region*	*customer*	*warehouse*	*order_line*
Sales	Sales Calls	✓	✓			✓	✓	✓	✓		
	Proposals	✓	✓	✓	✓	✓	✓	✓	✓		
	Orders	✓	✓	✓	✓	✓	✓	✓	✓		✓
	Shipments	✓	✓	✓	✓	✓	✓	✓	✓	✓	✓
	Returns	✓	✓	✓	✓	✓	✓	✓	✓	✓	✓
Inventory	Inventory	✓	✓	✓	✓					✓	
	Demand Forecast		✓		✓			✓		✓	
Finance	Recievables	✓	✓						✓		✓
	Sales Goals		✓				✓	✓			
	Commission Payments	✓	✓			✓	✓	✓			

Figure 18-5 Requirements cross-reference

Stars

Top-level documentation of each star should include all the salient characteristics of the design, stopping short of column-by-column definitions. For each star, salient detail should be provided that, in conjunction with a diagram, provides sufficient material for the design review. The elements that should be captured for each star are enumerated in Table 18-2.

This information should be accompanied by a high-level diagram of the star. This diagram should include all columns of the fact table. It need not include every column of each dimension table; their content should be limited to surrogate and natural keys, along with selected attributes of significance. The illustration in Figure 18-6 combines a diagram for the orders process with top-level documentation for the star.

Item	Description	Notes
Process	A brief description of the process the star measures	Particularly important when grain is specified dimensionally (see below).
Type	Type of fact table: transaction, periodic snapshot, or accumulating snapshot	Also note if the fact table is factless, or if it is an aggregate or derived table (see Chapters 11, 12, 15, and 16).
Grain	States the exact level of detail represented by each row in the fact table	Grain is best stated in business terms, but may also be specified dimensionally (see Chapter 3).
Facts	Lists facts stored in the fact table	Highlight any semi-additive facts (see Chapter 11) and factless facts (see Chapter 12).
Nonadditive Facts	Lists nonadditive facts that are *not* stored in the fact table as well as those that *are* stored	For nonstored nonadditive facts, list the fully additive components available in the fact table.
Dimension Tables	Lists all dimension tables that are part of the star	If a dimension is referenced more than once, also specify roles (see Chapter 6). Also list any degenerate dimensions (see Chapter 3).
Load Frequency	Indicates how often the fact table is updated	Examples include daily, weekly, or real time.
Drilling Across	Lists important drill-across measurements in which the fact table participates	List only those that link to requirements in the previous section. (The full list of drill-across possibilities is documented by the conformance matrix, following.)
Usage Notes	Identify special characteristics of the star, especially those that offer alternative ways to join tables	Call out the use of core/custom dimensions (Chapter 13), mini-dimensions that can be joined to the main dimension for browse (Chapter 6), and bridges that can be used in multiple configurations (Chapters 9, 10).
Project	Identifies project during which the star will be created	This section may link to a project roadmap or strategy document.

Table 18-2 Top-Level Design Documentation for Stars

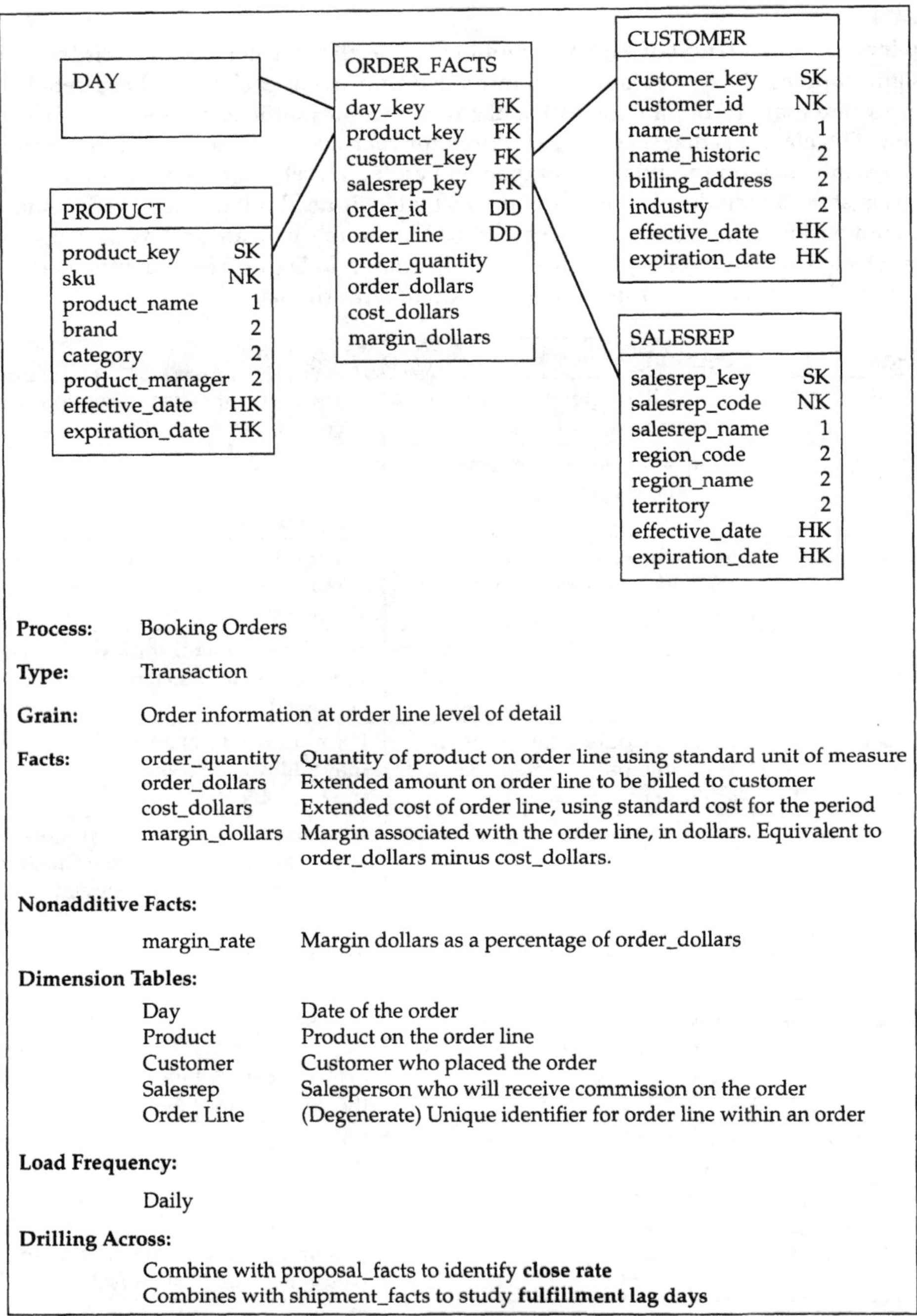

Process: Booking Orders

Type: Transaction

Grain: Order information at order line level of detail

Facts:

order_quantity	Quantity of product on order line using standard unit of measure
order_dollars	Extended amount on order line to be billed to customer
cost_dollars	Extended cost of order line, using standard cost for the period
margin_dollars	Margin associated with the order line, in dollars. Equivalent to order_dollars minus cost_dollars.

Nonadditive Facts:

margin_rate	Margin dollars as a percentage of order_dollars

Dimension Tables:

Day	Date of the order
Product	Product on the order line
Customer	Customer who placed the order
Salesrep	Salesperson who will receive commission on the order
Order Line	(Degenerate) Unique identifier for order line within an order

Load Frequency:

Daily

Drilling Across:

Combine with proposal_facts to identify **close rate**
Combines with shipment_facts to study **fulfillment lag days**

Figure 18-6 Top-level documentation for the orders star

Top-level documentation of each star need not require more than two pages in document format. This same information can also be provided in presentation format, which can be useful for design review sessions. This information does not complete the top-level documentation; it is also necessary to provide top-level documentation for dimension tables, as well as a conformance matrix.

Dimensions

Top-level documentation must also include detailed information about dimension table design. Sufficient information should be included to communicate the scope and use of the dimension table, and to facilitate review of important design considerations.

Required elements for top-level documentation of dimension tables are enumerated in Table 18-3. The detailed design, covered later in this chapter, will supplement this top-level documentation with column-by-column definitions, data types, sources, transformation logic, and the like.

This information should be accompanied by diagrams that illustrate key features of the dimension, such as conformance with other dimensions, participation in significant hierarchies, or core/custom relationships. These diagrams need not capture all columns; detailed column definitions will appear in the detailed documentation. The illustration in Figure 18-7 combines top-level documentation for a salesrep dimension with depictions of conformed rollups and a major hierarchy.

Item	Description	Notes
Definition	Brief description of the dimension table	Use business terms whenever possible.
Natural Key	Lists the column or columns that constitute the natural key in the source system(s)	This is essential information for the development of a load process and also informs slow change behavior.
Conformed Dimensions	Lists any dimensions that conform with the table	Each conformed dimension should also be documented separately.
Significant Hierarchies	Lists any hierarchies of importance	List hierarchies that will be used to drive reporting, guide analysis, configure reporting tools, or drive auto-generation of derived tables (see Chapters 7 and 15).
Usage Notes	Special characteristics of the dimension, especially those that offer alternative ways to join tables	Highlight junk dimensions (Chapter 3), mini-dimensions (Chapter 6), potential use as an outrigger (Chapter 7), use of special case rows (Chapter 6), any relationships to bridge tables (Chapters 9, 10) and core/custom versions (Chapter 13).
Project	Identifies project during which the dimension will be created	This section may link to a project roadmap or strategy document.

Table 18-3 Top-Level Design Documentation for Dimension Tables

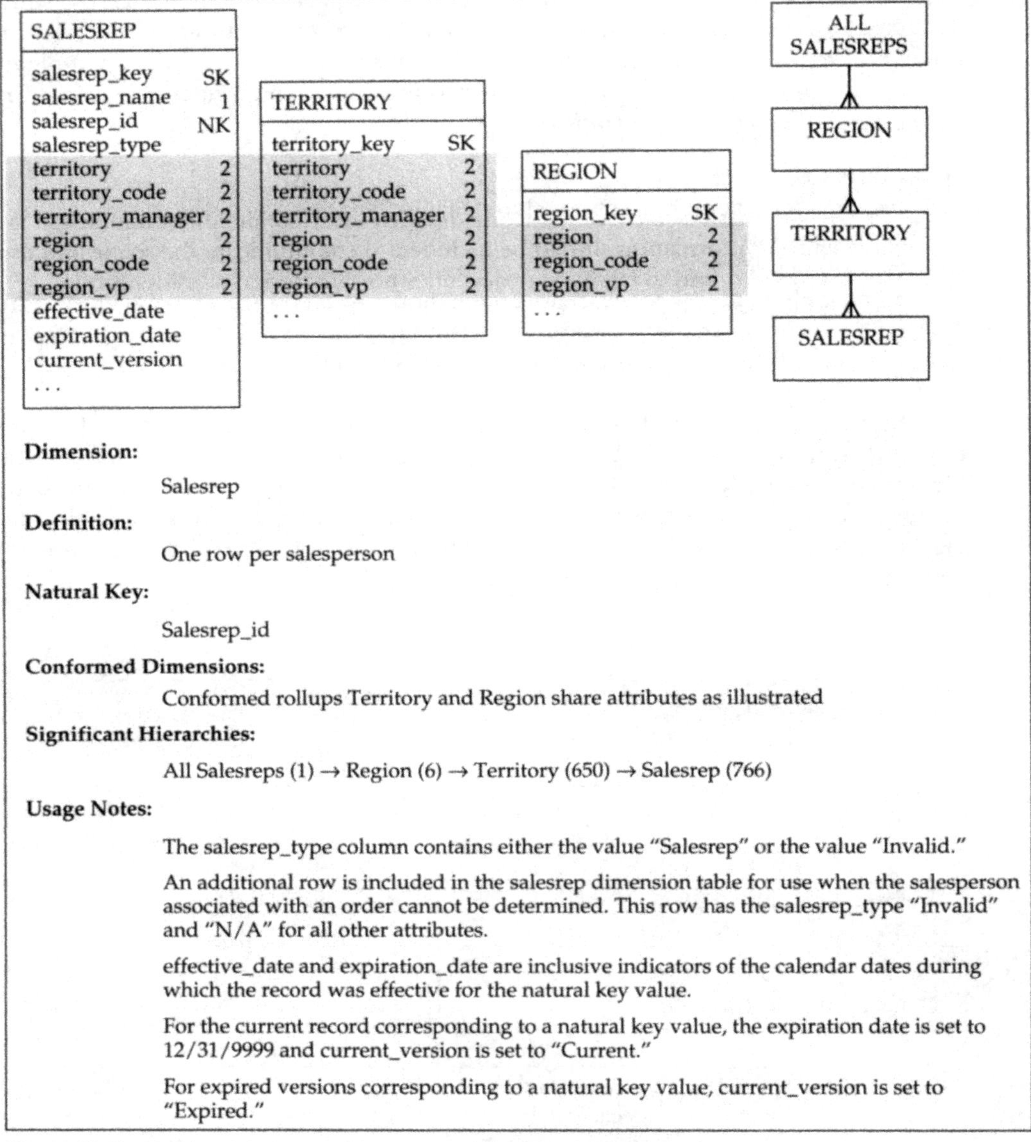

Figure 18-7 Top-level documentation for the Salesrep dimension

Other key information that may be included in top-level documentation for dimension tables includes:

- Type 3 and hybrid slow change characteristics, which may be illustrated as depicted in Figures 8-4 and 8-6
- Implementation of a mini-dimension, and optional relationship to the main dimension, as depicted in Figure 6-6 or Figure 16-8

- Use of outriggers, as depicted in the top portion of Figure 7-9
- Core and custom versions, as depicted in Figure 13-2
- Configurations for bridge tables, as illustrated in Figures 16-9, 16-10, and 16-11

As with the stars, top-level dimension documentation may be provided in document or presentation format. This material will be the primary focus of design reviews. Detailed documentation will add column specifications, definitions, sources, and transformation rules.

Matrix

The most important part of a dimensional design is the framework of conformed dimensions. As you have learned, conformed dimensions are the key to linking data from more than one fact table, whether within a single subject area or across subject areas. The process of linking this information together within a report is referred to as drilling across, as discussed in Chapter 5.

Use of a table diagram to depict conformed dimensions is usually impractical. When more than three fact tables are displayed, it becomes difficult or impossible to lay out a diagram in a readable format. A better way to depict conformed dimensions is to make use of matrix diagrams. Each row of the matrix corresponds to a fact table; each column corresponds to a dimension table. Conformed dimensions are grouped in shaded bands for readability. Degenerate dimensions are included as well. For each fact table, checkmarks are placed beneath all dimensions for which information is available. An example is depicted in Figure 18-8.

		day		*product*		*salesrep*					
		day	*quarter*	*product*	*category*	*salesrep*	*territory*	*region*	*customer*	*warehouse*	*order_line*
Sales	sales_call_facts	✓	✓			✓	✓	✓	✓		
	proposal_facts	✓	✓	✓	✓	✓	✓	✓	✓		
	order_facts	✓	✓	✓	✓	✓	✓	✓	✓		✓
	shipment_facts	✓	✓	✓	✓	✓	✓	✓	✓	✓	✓
	return_facts	✓	✓	✓	✓	✓	✓	✓	✓	✓	✓
Inventory	inventory_status_facts	✓	✓	✓	✓					✓	
	demand_forecast_facts		✓		✓			✓		✓	
Finance	receivable_facts	✓	✓						✓		✓
	sales_goal_facts		✓				✓	✓			
	commission_payments_facts	✓	✓			✓	✓	✓			

Figure 18-8 Documenting conformance

Notice that this diagram is made easier to use by placing checks beneath all applicable headers. For example, order_facts includes full details on salesrep. Rather than simply placing a checkmark under salesrep, the diagram also places checks under conformed rollups region and territory. This practice allows instant identification of compatible fact tables. If two fact tables have checkmarks in the same column, that dimension can be used to compare them. The region dimension, for example, is a conformed rollup of salesrep. It can be used to compare demand_forecast_facts with order_facts.

The conformance matrix in Figure 18-8 only contains major dimensions of significance to the enterprise. This kind of conformance matrix may also be supplemented with a second conformance matrix, which includes all dimension tables that are part of the solution. Such a matrix will be significantly wider.

Detailed Design Documentation

Top-level documentation of stars and dimension tables must be backed up with detailed column-level and table-level specifications. The detailed specifications define each column, its data type, its data source and transformation rules, and other salient characteristics. This information is normally presented in a tabular format. It can be produced using a spreadsheet tool. Some data modeling tools may also be able to produce this information. Detailed design specifications should be divided into two major sections: one for dimension tables and one for fact tables.

Dimension Detail

The detailed design specifications for each dimension table are made up of two parts. The first part is a spreadsheet-style table with one row for each attribute in the table. Columns provide the documentation elements described in Table 18-4. The second part depicts table-level characteristics described in Table 18-5.

For dimensions that include multiple sources, it will be necessary to expand on this format. In the case of discrete sources that each provide separate subsets of the dimension, the source element and transformation rules can be repeated, once for each data source. In situations where the data sources must be cross-referenced and mediated for each row in the dimension table, this processing may be described using pseudo-code as part of table-level information.

Table-level specifications provide information pertaining to the table itself. This includes information about the relationships between the various source systems, any pseudo-code necessary to indicate how to filter the source data, and other processing logic that cannot be expressed at the column level as described previously.

Normally, this table-level detail is provided after the column-level detail. For particularly complex load processes, it may be necessary to reverse the order, in which case table-level information and high-level pseudo-code describe the overall processing approach and are followed by the column-level documentation.

A complex load process may be aided by the creation and management of one or more staging tables. These tables do not fall within the domain of the dimensional model and will not be accessed by users or reports. They may be designed and documented by the ETL developers. Such intermediate tables need not be included in the dimensional design documentation, unless they are necessary to provide a logical overview of processing rules.

Item	Description	Notes
Column	Name of the column	Follow standards for the naming of keys, flags, codes, and short vs. long versions of descriptions.
Data Type	Data type of column	Include precision/scale for numeric data.
Size	Column size in bytes	Used for row size estimation and planning growth.
Column Type	Type of column	Use standard abbreviations: SK (surrogate key), NK (natural key), 1 or 2 (type 1/type 2 dimension), HK (housekeeping column). Also note type 3 pairs and hybrid pairs.
Definition	Business description of the column	May serve as source for help text or data dictionary.
Example Data	One or more example values	Clarifies the content of the attribute: especially useful with flags, codes vs. descriptions, and so on.
Source Element(s)	Source table/column or file/field	Source element and transformation rule may be repeated for some multi-source dimensions (once for each source).
Transformation Rule	Indicates rules used to construct the dimension value	The rule operates on the source element. Pseudo-code or SQL fragments are used. If processing is complex, requires special lookups, or otherwise requires additional information. Refer to the following table-level processing rules.

Table 18-4 Detailed Documentation: Dimension Tables, Column-Level

Item	Description	Notes
Sources	Lists source systems	Sources may be assigned standard abbreviations and will have appeared in the source element field of column-level documentation.
Relationships	Relationships among source tables or systems	For relational sources, describes how source tables are joined together; for other sources, describes the necessary sort/merge/filter processing.
Processing Rules	Load requirements for the table that could not be defined at the column level	For some dimensions, it may be necessary to identify a load strategy. Describe special pre- or post-processing, conditional rules, or complex logic. Use pseudo-code if necessary.
Security Requirements	Lists any significant security considerations for the table	This includes a description of who is allowed to see data in the column, and also highlights any data subject to mandated confidentiality.
Load Interval	Indicates how often the fact table is updated	Examples include daily, weekly, or real time.
Initial Rows	Number of rows expected upon implementation	Used for capacity planning.
Annual Growth	Estimated number of new rows each year	Used for capacity planning.

Table 18-5 Detailed Documentation: Dimension Tables, Table-Level

If intermediate tables are included in the documentation, process flow diagrams depicting phases of the load may also be useful.

Fact Table Detail

Like the dimension tables, the detailed design specifications for each fact table are made up of two parts. The first part is a spreadsheet-style table with one row for each attribute in the table. Columns provide the documentation elements described in Table 18-6. The second part depicts table-level characteristics described in Table 18-7.

When transactions come from multiple sources, it will be necessary to expand on this format. The source element and transformation rules can be repeated, once for each data source. For fact tables such as periodic snapshots and accumulating snapshots, processing logic may be complex. For example, when an accumulating snapshot includes milestones that may be achieved more than once, the logic required to choose which date to use may require multiple passes through the data set. Information like this, which cannot be succinctly conveyed on a row-by-row basis, may be described at the table level using pseudo-code.

Table-level specifications provide information that does not pertain to a specific column. This includes information about the relationships between the various source systems, any pseudo-code necessary to indicate how to filter the source data, and other processing logic that cannot be expressed at the column level.

Item	Description	Notes
Column	Name of the column	Choose descriptive names and follow standards.
Data Type	Data type of column	Include precision/scale for numeric data.
Size	Column size in bytes	Used for row size estimation and planning growth.
Column Type	Type of column	Use standard abbreviations such as: FK (foreign key reference to dimension table), Fact, DD (degenerate dimension), and HK (housekeeping column).
Definition	Business description of the column	May serve as source for help text or data dictionary.
Example Data	One or more example values	Clarifies the content of the attribute, especially useful with degenerate dimensions.
Source Element(s)	Source table/column or file/field	Source element and transformation rule may be repeated for some multi-source dimensions (once for each source).
Transformation Rules	Indicates the rules used to construct the dimension value	The rule operates on the source element. For foreign key columns, this includes reference to the natural keys that accompany source data.

Table 18-6 Detailed Documentation: Fact Tables, Column-Level

Item	Description	Notes
Sources	Lists source systems	Sources may be assigned standard abbreviations and will have appeared in the source element field of column-level documentation.
Relationships	Relationships among source tables or systems	For relational sources, describes how source tables are joined together; for other sources, describes the necessary sort/merge/filter processing.
Processing Rules	Load requirements for the table that could not be defined at the column level	Load requirements for the table that could not be concisely defined under the Transformation Rules heading for an attribute will appear here. Examples include the logic required to construct an accumulating snapshot. Use pseudo-code as necessary.
Security Requirements	Lists any significant security considerations for the table	This includes a description of who is allowed to see data in the column, and also highlights any data subject to mandated confidentiality.
Load Interval	Indicates how often the table is updated	Examples include daily, weekly, or real time.
Initial Rows	Number of rows expected upon implementation	Used for capacity planning.
Annual Growth	Estimated number of new rows each year	Used for capacity planning.

Table 18-7 Detailed Documentation: Fact Tables, Table-Level

Logical vs. Physical

The design documentation described in this section can be considered a record of the logical design or of the physical design, depending on project scope and organizational objectives. As presented, this information is primarily a logical design; physical implementation may make use of alternative data structures, such as materialized views, index-organized tables, and the like. The physical design will also include an indexing scheme, table partitioning plans, and so forth. If desired, the dimensional design effort can be extended to include such physical-level considerations. This will add additional time to the design process but eliminates the need to perform this work later.

Taken together, all this information provides a useful basis for several aspects of data warehouse implementation. These include the definition of scope for implementation projects from functional and technical perspectives, the design and development of a process to load the database (the ETL process), the development of specifications for reports and other information delivery vehicles, the development and execution of quality assurance testing processes for the loading and reporting processes, and the foundation for educational courses, data dictionaries, or other system documentation for end users.

Summary

Putting together a dimensional design can be a fulfilling task, regardless of project scope or architecture. This chapter has provided you with the essential tasks of a design effort and detailed requirements for the deliverables.

Emphasis on Dimensional Design

- A dimensional design communicates business functionality and technical complexity. It can be used to represent requirements, develop a strategy, and guide the scope of implementation.
- Architectures emphasize these capabilities to different degrees.
- In all cases, dimensional design is a critical path activity that must precede design of ETL programs and reports.

Developing the Design

- Development of a dimensional design normally includes stages for planning, interviewing, designing, and prioritizing.
- The planning stage includes identifying team members and other participants, planning the activities, requesting documentation, and conducting a kickoff.
- The interviewing stage includes sessions with business users, which will define requirements, and with developers who maintain source systems.
- Design activities will take place throughout the project. Stars can be worked up using a simple four-step process, augmented with some additional steps that look across stars. A design review is essential.
- Developing an implementation strategy requires grouping the design into candidate projects and prioritizing them.

Documenting the Design

- Specialized tools are not necessary to document a dimensional design, though they may be helpful. The dimensional design can be documented using a word processor and spreadsheet.
- The design should include three levels of detail. The first captures measurement requirements by process, measurement requirements that span processes, and cross-references processes with major dimensions. This information conveys the business capabilities of the design.
- Top-level design includes detailed information on stars, dimension tables, and a conformance matrix. This information is supplemented with design illustrations and will be the primary focus of design reviews.
- Detailed design enumerates specifications for each table and column of the model, including data types, definitions, data sources, and transformation logic. This information is typically provided in tabular format. The detailed design will serve as an important reference for developers building the ETL process or reports.

Further Reading

This chapter has presented core essentials for the development and documentation of dimensional designs. For additional information on the design process, model documentation, or the larger systems' development life cycle, consult the materials listed here.

- The process described here expands on treatments in my previous books, and generalizes them to address diverse architectures. See Chapter 7 of *Mastering Data Warehouse Aggregates* (Wiley, 2006) by Chris Adamson, as well as Chapter 14 of *Data Warehouse Design Solutions* (Wiley, 1998) by Chris Adamson and Mike Venerable.
- Kimball and Ross describe their "four steps" in Chapter 2 of *The Data Warehouse Toolkit, Second Edition* (Wiley, 2002).
- Kimball *et al.* provide an extended, book-length treatment of their process, complete with detailed tasks and deliverables, in *The Data Warehouse Lifecycle Toolkit, Second Edition* (Wiley, 2008), by Ralph Kimball, Margy Ross, Warren Thornthwaite, Joy Mundy, and Bob Becker.
- For an alternative treatment of the design process that is focused on the Corporate Information Factory architecture, see *Mastering Data Warehouse Design* (Wiley, 2003) by Claudia Imhoff, Nicholas Galemmo, and Jonathan G. Geiger.
- For information on incorporating aggregates into the design process and design documentation, see Chapter 7 of *Mastering Data Warehouse Aggregates* (Wiley, 2006) by Chris Adamson.
- Over ten years ago, I wrote a detailed chapter on how to plan and conduct interviews. To this day, I find it useful to direct novice analysts to this treatment, which contains what is perhaps my favorite section heading I ever wrote: "You Don't Know Anything." See Chapter 15 of *Data Warehouse Design Solutions.*

Index

A

B

C

D

E

F

G

N

O

S